THE 1967 IMPOSSIBLE DREAM RED SOX: PANDEMONIUM ON THE FIELD

Edited by Bill Nowlin and Dan Desrochers

Library of Congress Cataloging-in-Publication Data

Edited by Bill Nowlin and Dan Desrochers. Foreword by Jim Lonborg and Tom Werner. Introduction by Richard A. Johnson and Peter Gammons.
Title entry: '67
Originally published: Rounder Books, 2007.
Includes bibliographical references.
Contents:
ISBN 1-57940-127-9 (pbk.)
1. Boston Red Sox (baseball team). 2. 1967 baseball season. 3. Biography. I. Nowlin, Bill. II. Desrochers, Dan.
796357'092

2006940364

ISBN-13: 978-1-5794-0141-2
ISBN-10: 1-5794-0141-4

Edited by Bill Nowlin and Dan Desrochers.
The 1967 Impossible Dream Red Sox: Pandemonium on the Field

1. Boston Red Sox (baseball team).
2. 1967 baseball season.
3. Biography. I. Nowlin, Bill. II. Desrochers, Dan.

First edition
2006940364
796.357'092
ISBN-13: 978-1-5794-0141-2
ISBN-10: 1-5794-0141-4

Published by Rounder Books

an imprint of
Rounder Records Corp.
One Rounder Way
Burlington, MA 01803

Graphic Design by Jay Walsh

Cover Design by Steve Jurgensmeyer

Insert design by Sarah Radawich

CONTENTS

CONTENTS

CONTENTS

CONTENTS

We dedicate this book to the members of the 1967 Red Sox team who are no longer with us: Jerry Adair, Ken Brett, Tony Conigliaro, Joe Foy, Elston Howard, Al Lakeman, Sal Maglie, Don McMahon, Eddie Popowski, Bob Tillman, John Wyatt.

We also dedicate this book to Ken Coleman, Neil Mahoney, Ned Martin, Dick O'Connell, Haywood Sullivan, Tom Yawkey, and other Red Sox-related personnel who served in 1967.

Lastly, we wish to honor the many fans now departed who rooted for the Red Sox during this year of the Impossible Dream.

The Impossible Dream Realized

"The pitch...is looped toward shortstop. Petrocelli's back. He's got it! The Red Sox win! ..."

–Ned Martin, October 1, 1967 radio broadcast of the final regular season game.

"As the ball came down in Rico Petrocelli's glove for the last-and-final out, the town went up in the air like a beautiful balloon." –**Bud Collins**

"It wasn't hit that high," he says. "But it seemed like it was a thousand feet in the air. It didn't hit me at first, but then I put my hands in the air, and Dalton came over and said, 'We won.'" –**Dan Shaughnessy**

After pitching a complete game to win the 1967 pennant, winning pitcher Jim Lonborg was mobbed by delirious fans who made off with various items of clothing before he reached the safety of the clubhouse.

FOREWORD

1967

by Jim Lonborg

The year before, in 1966, the Red Sox started off the season with five losses. By the All-Star break, we were in last place. By the end of the season, we were in ninth place, but we won more games in the second half than any other team in the American League except Baltimore. Even with those wins, we still wound up in ninth place. That shows you how badly entrenched we were.

But it's always great to leave a season with positive thoughts, whether you're a young player or a veteran player. I think a lot of the ballplayers on that particular team went into the offseason from '66 to '67 with a great feeling about what we had accomplished from the All-Star break on. When you take those thoughts and nurture them in your mind, it allows you to have a lot of confidence going into the following season.

I myself went down to Venezuela to pitch. I was having trouble getting the curveball over when the count was 3 and 1, or 2 and 1, so the ball club arranged for me to go down there and pitch in Venezuela. I pitched for Maracay and developed a breaking ball I had confidence in, so when it came time for spring training to start, I got off the ski slopes and...

Seriously, I left Heavenly Valley, California for Winter Haven in the best shape of my life. For all the bad things said about my skiing, one of the reasons that I had a great year in 1967 was that I had never been in greater physical shape in my life.

All those good things that built up during the latter half of 1966 carried into the spring of 1967.

Dick Williams challenged us all to develop a frame of mind that allowed us to think outside of our individual efforts—to become more concerned about playing consistent baseball, playing fundamental baseball every single day. If you made a mistake in spring training, he would caution you in the way that Dick Williams would caution people—and you didn't make that mistake very often after that.

We started playing very decent baseball early in the season. We came off that road trip after winning 10 games in a row believing in ourselves, and not only did we believe in ourselves but we were met by several thousand fans at Logan Airport who welcomed us back off of the trip. I think that was probably the moment that we decided that we had a chance.

I was 0-3 against the Twins going into the final game that year. I'm not really superstitious but for some reason that particular summer, I had won more games on the road than I had at home. We were in the clubhouse after we beat the Twins on Saturday, and Ken Harrelson, who had replaced Tony C in right field, knew that I lived in a bachelor apartment at Charles River Park. And he knew the guys that I

was living with—Neil McNerny and Dennis Bennett. Neil owned a couple of bars and there was a lot of traffic in the apartment. Ken thought that I probably needed a good night's sleep so he offered his room at the Sheraton Hotel. I pretended that it was a road trip and so I stayed at the Sheraton. I went to Fenway Park to find I had really good stuff that day. It didn't look good for the first five innings but we finally got to Dean Chance and we went on to win the ballgame.

I think that any kid who plays Little League baseball wants to have that experience of being on the ball field when you win a ball game and 35,000 of your closest, favorite, loyal friends come down and celebrate the victory. To share that moment with the fans of New England was really a special thing and, yes, it got a little scary but some of Boston's finest came and helped me. It truly was pandemonium on the field. What happened after that game could never happen again. There are too many big horses out there these days. But it was such a joy to be there with your teammates and because of all the years it had taken for something good like that to happen at Fenway.

–Jim Lonborg, November 2006

"...And there's pandemonium on the field!"
–Ned Martin

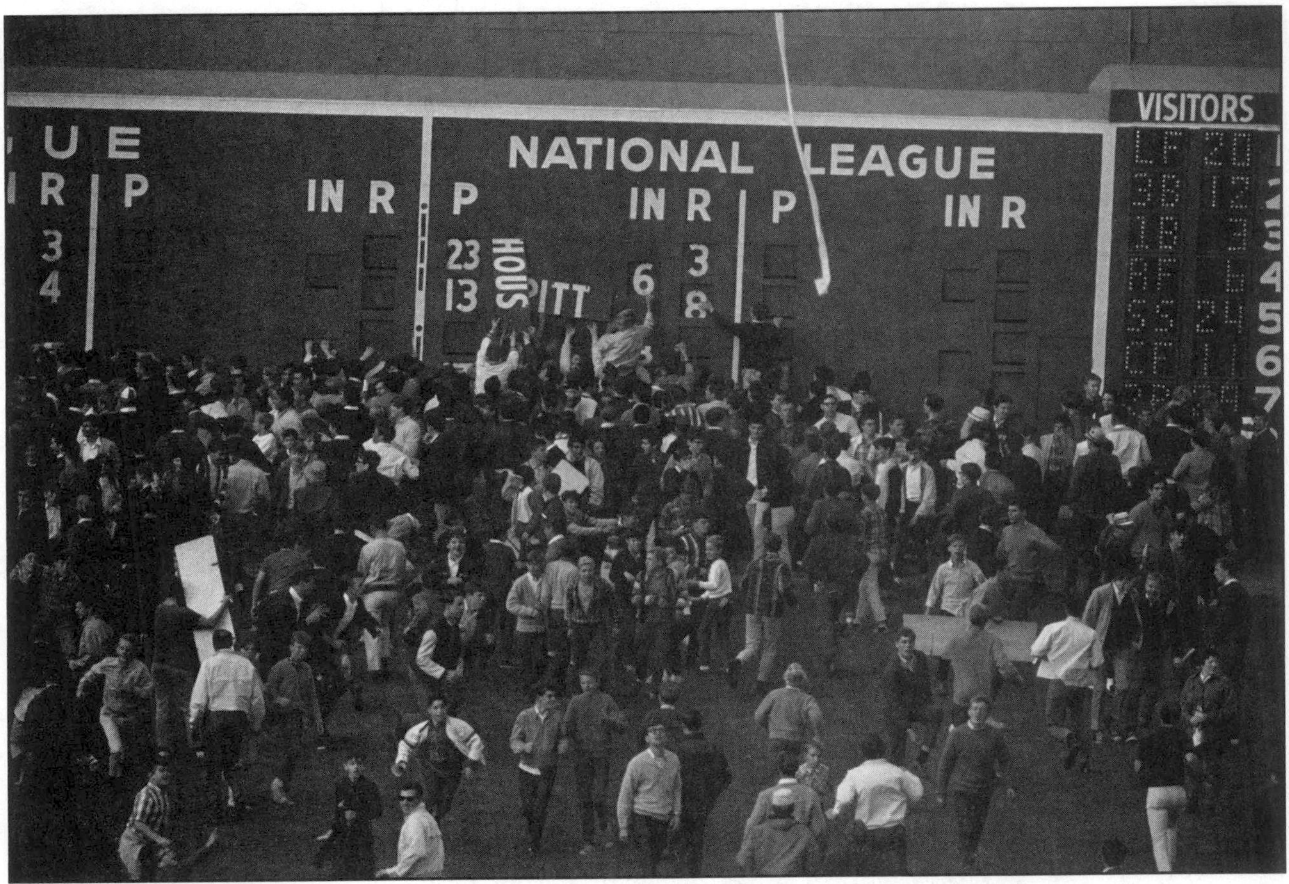

Talk about pandemonium! The fans on the field after first place was clinched did a lot of damage to Fenway in their desire to take home mementos. October 1, 1967. "Growing more fervent, the crowd split into platoons. One attacked the scoreboard, ripping down signs and everything else that could be lifted for souvenirs." —**Bud Collins**

Just prior to Game One of the World Series, starting pitcher José Santiago views the field through a movie camera.

Harvard student Tom Werner first became a Sox fan in '67 and would later bring his own film camera to Fenway to document Opening Day. Werner became one of television's most successful producers and currently serves as Chairman of the Boston Red Sox.

FOREWORD

1967

by Tom Werner

Two important events changed my life in 1967, when I was a teenager: I was accepted into Harvard College that April and I fell in love with the Red Sox that same summer.

I started following the Red Sox shortly after I had received my acceptance letter. At the start of the year, the team was a 100-to-1 underdog to win the pennant, but, as the summer progressed, they were clearly competitive in a remarkable five-team race. Furthermore, Carl Yastrzemski was in the middle of a historic season, and—much like David Ortiz in the last couple of years—Carl was winning game after game in clutch fashion. But he was not the only impact player that year: I remember the heroics of Tony C. and the brilliant pitching of Jim Lonborg.

I still remember reading about the time the team came back to Boston after a brilliant road trip. There were 10,000 fans waiting for the Sox at the airport. Like so many others in this "Impossible Dream" season, I was swept up in the excitement.

When September finally came around, I made my way to that cathedral we call Fenway Park. I still remember seeing the Green Monster for the first time, a memory I can easily recall to this day. How beautiful was the grass; how unusual were the asymmetrical lines of the outfield, how small was the footprint of the park as compared to the Polo Grounds, Shea Stadium, and Yankee Stadium. I had seen games from Fenway on my black and white TV, but this was simply breathtaking in color!

I still recall listening on the radio to the last couple of games of the year. The Red Sox trailed the Twins by one game going into the last weekend series, but they prevailed in the last two contests and met the Cardinals in the 1967 World Series. I figured out a way to get into the ballpark for the World Series and saw Jim Lonborg pitch a brilliant one-hitter in Game Two.

So started my love affair with the Red Sox. A couple of years later I convinced a professor in my Visual Studies class to allow me to make a short film about Opening Day at Fenway. I was given permission to enter the park a few days early and filmed the grounds crew and such getting the place ready for the start of the season. I can't believe America's Most Beloved Ballpark will be having a 100th birthday celebration in just a few years.

Some 20 or so fans decided to climb the screen behind home plate, which was suspended from immediately below the broadcasters' booth, though the screen was never intended as weight-bearing and could have tumbled them to the seats and concrete below at any moment.

INTRODUCTION

SAVIORS

Richard A. Johnson

Was there a better time to be a Boston sports fan than the spring of 1967? Bill Russell and company boasted an unfathomable string of eight straight basketball world titles while the Bruins, led by a rookie named Bobby Orr, emerged from the NHL basement. And, just as both tenants of the Boston Garden seemed destined for greater glory, the Patriots played the role of lovable underdogs in the underdog AFL while the Red Sox, occupants of Boston sport's proverbial "mansion on a hill," worked feverishly on an edifice that had fallen into total disrepair.

At the start of the '67 season, the Bosox made banner headlines when newly hired skipper Dick Williams laid down the law on several fronts. His first salvo was directed at team captain Carl Yastrzemski. Williams told his players, "This club has become a cruise ship overrun with captains and players thinking they are captain. The cruise is over and you don't need a captain anymore. You have a new boss now—Me. Eliminating the club captaincy is my way of letting you know that things will be done one way. My Way."

Shortly thereafter, team vice president and God-In-Residence Ted Williams stormed out of spring training as the result of a tiff he'd had with that-other-guy-named-Williams over the wisdom of pitchers playing volleyball for conditioning. This seemingly silly, and hitherto unimaginable, event marked a change of the guard. The new manager looked and acted nothing like the old bosses who preceded him on the poopdeck of the "S.S. Crony Island."

At first, the other Mr. Williams made for good copy, but soon inspired Boston's legion of writers to search their dictionaries for adjectives to describe a turnaround they could scarcely believe.

Dick Williams invoking help from above.

By the end of the magical 1967 season chronicled within these pages, Williams's tough love inspired nothing less than the rebirth of Red Sox. This rebirth was complete and encompassed competitive, economic, social, and spiritual dimensions. For those of us old enough to have witnessed them, the names of players such as Yastrzemski, Tartabull, Foy, Andrews, Lonborg, Conigliaro, and Rohr—among

others—provoke an immediate and visceral reaction. To this day, I cannot hear the name Petrocelli and not hear the soft drawl of Mel Parnell's play-by-play call of the soft popup that ended the last great pennant race in major league history and the single most compelling season in franchise history.

In the scrapbook I started at age 11, there is a faded news clipping from the *Worcester Telegram* that contains a photograph I feel best captures the essence of that unforgettable season. It immediately encompasses the full spectrum of what endears them to Sox fans to this day. It shows Reggie Smith, Carl Yastrzemski, George Scott, and Mike Ryan stripped to the waist in the visitors' clubhouse at Comiskey Park, holding up teammate Joy Foy's number "1" jersey to proclaim the Red Sox perch atop the American League.

This one image contains nothing less than the DNA of a winner. For here is a picture that depicts the soul of a team that seemed to change for the better before our eyes. In an era before political correctness skewed and distorted our perspectives of social norms, the '67 Red Sox embraced integration in the spirit of winning. The team, which in earlier years rejected Jackie Robinson and Willie Mays, now featured a lineup as diverse as any in baseball. Winning for these men broke down barriers and helped make the team a role model whose shining example continues to inspire.

Without the Possible Dream of 1967 there'd be no Red Sox Nation, no NESN, no Yawkey Way, no Rem-Dawg, no Monster seats, no fawning celebrity posse of George Mitchell, Stephen King, Doris Kearns Goodwin, et al., no $45 grandstand tickets, no Fenway Park—and possibly no Red Sox.

To truly appreciate the stunning achievement of Dick Williams and Company, one must recall the dire circumstances from which they rescued the franchise.

On the final day of the 1965 season the Red Sox lost their hundredth game before a crowd of 487 as Whitey Ford won an 11-5 decision over Arnie Earley. Such was the conclusion of the worst season for the team under the ownership of Tom Yawkey and the nadir of an era known to most as "The Country Club."

Within 730 days the stands were full and the franchise has never looked back.

The saga of this team includes countless serendipitous events created by a cadre of role players whose character and grace under pressure will amaze you once more in the prose of the writers assembled within these pages. Play Ball.

Reggie Smith, Carl Yastrzemski, George Scott, and Mike Ryan exult after the big August 26 win in Chicago landed the Red Sox in first place.

'67: WHEN THE DREAM BEGAN

Peter Gammons

We are in the 25th year since the galvanization of a franchise that, in effect, has seen no equal since*. The Red Sox were always New England's team, yes, but it took the Impossible Dream of 1967 to coalesce the romanticized mystique that keeps the fans coming by the millions.

Sixty-seven began on Sept. 16, 1965. Dave Morehead no-hit the Indians that day, the last no-hitter thrown by a Red Sox pitcher. There weren't 500 people in the Fenway stands that afternoon. This was the low in the Yawkey history of the club.

They were on their way to a 62-100 season, finishing 40 games behind Sam Mele's Twins. "A lot of players thought it was funny," recalls Jerry Stephenson, now the assistant to Dodger general manger Fred Claire, then 21-year-old rookie pitcher. "And to guys like Dennis Bennett, it was funny." To the fans, however, it was as funny as BCCI. They sold 652,203 tickets; far fewer showed up. Some columnists called for Tom Yawkey to sell the team, others called for a new ballpark. There was speculation that indeed, Yawkey might sell, and he speculated about a modern, man-sized ballpark.

The manager was Billy Herman, and one day he went to take Jim Lonborg out of a rout and had to apologize to the rookie lefthander because of the pitiable defense of the Eddie Bressouds of the world, but then, those were such dark and silent days that Lenny Green was the Opening Day center fielder. Of course, Herman was so much in control of the club that Carl Yastrzemski recounted his giving stern spring training clubhouse talk because of some of his rogues' night habits, and as he spoke, a gold ball fell out of his back pocket. "He practiced his golf swing in the dugout during games," Yastrzemski once said.

Dark days preceded the dawn

The color and power that Yawkey had put together, first by purchasing big-name players like Joe Cronin, Jimmie Foxx, and Lefty Grove, then by letting Eddie Collins build a strong organization, had crumbled like the last day of a Latin American patriarch. Yawkey had surrounded himself with drunkards, cronies and thieves, and by the late '50s, all they had built in the '30s and '40s was rotting. They drew between 1.4 million and 1.6 million from 1946 through '49, and even in the '50s—when only once, by the grace of Billy Klaus, were they in contention until Labor Day—they drew a million all but two years. But after The Hub bid The Kid adieu, the painful reality was that the people didn't care about Don Buddin, Gene Conley, Bob Heffner and Roman Mejias. From 1961 through '65, they averaged fewer than 800,000 and

Demand for tickets was light early in the season, with some 25,000 empty seats even on Opening Day.

Midsummer game day fans line up for admission.

Ticket line stretches onto Van Ness Street.

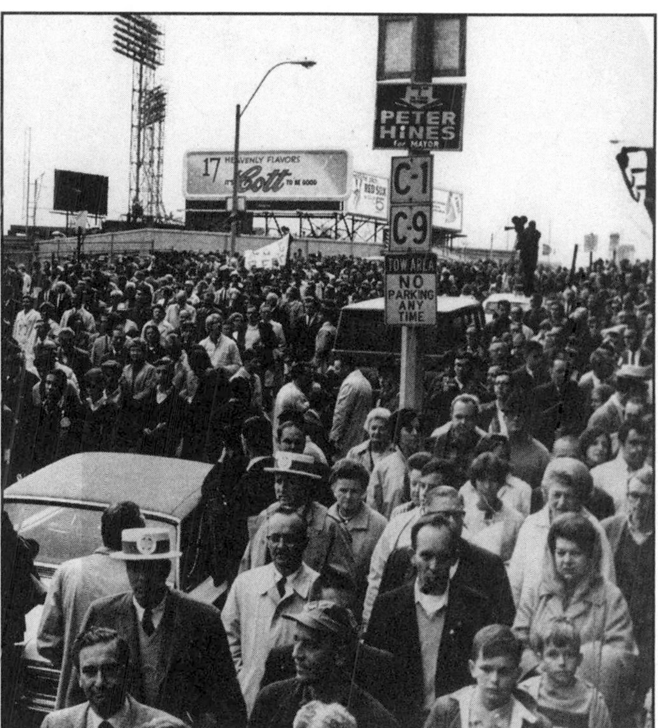

The crowd on Brookline Avenue leaving Fenway Park after Game Seven. The Sox went from some 8,300 Opening Day fans to 35,188 for the final game of 1967.

finished an average of 30 games out of first place.

By Sept. 16, 1965, the vultures had begun pecking through the screens of the Fenway palace. Morehead was in the seventh inning of his no-hitter when Bud Collins scurried through Kenmore Square to get to Fenway to see history concluded. Collins passed Mike Higgins, going away from Fenway toward the Kenmore Hotel. Higgins, the hard-drinking Texan who once called writer Larry Claflin a "nigger lover" because he asked why Pumpsie Green was sent to the minors, a man who made Earl Long look like Bill Bradley, had been fired as general manager.

Yawkey had had enough of recreating the first 100 pages of "The Sound and the Fury." He put Dick O'Connell in charge, and Red Sox history was forever altered. Yawkey also brought in the bright, brash manager of the Kansas City Athletics—Haywood Sullivan—who had been a big part of that club's blossoming talent, and whose reputation in helping non-white players deal with the segregated Southern League had brought him industry-wide acclaim.

O'Connell and Sullivan began the reconstruction, helped by a fabulous group: Reggie Smiths, George Scotts, Rico Petrocellis, et al., that Neil Mahoney's farm system was uncovering. They backed up the truck, and while some deals worked—Sullivan stole José Santiago—Bill Monbouquette for two guys named George—they cleared out all stench of the Higgins era. In the second half of 1966, with Lonborg rising, José Tartabull hustling, and rookies like Scott and Joe Foy, they actually had a winning record. They missed finishing in last place by half a game, but O'Connell and Sullivan knew Herman wasn't the right guy, and that Dick Williams was.

It was near-last-to-near-first before Steve Avery was even born. This was Four Roses to Forever Fenway. And never again could we walk the tracks to the Ayer train station. Take the Boston & Maine to North Station and sit wherever we wanted. They finally beat John Buzhardt Opening Day, '67, and finally, we could see clearly, the rain had gone.

Ticket Office, Boston Red Sox
Fenway Park
Boston, Mass. 02215

Date____________________

Please send me the following number of tickets for the games of____________________

(Order now for any home game on the 1967 schedule)

______ Roof Boxes @ $3.75 each

______ Box Seats @ $3.00 each

______ Res. Seats @ $2.25 each
(Indicate number of each)

IMPORTANT
To insure prompt attention to this order, please enclose a large self-addressed envelope along with your check or money order. Orders will be filled from best available seats.

Check or Money Order in the amount of $__________ is enclosed.

Name____________________
(Please Print)

Street____________________

City__________ State__________ Zip__________

I prefer: 1st base________ Home________ 3rd base________

Check Here________ if you are interested in learning about a special Red Sox season ticket plan.

Little did anyone know that 25 years later, they'd be going at 2.5 million, September dates would be sold out in January, Roger Clemens would have a larger recognition factor than the governor, and Mike Greenwell would be three days of front-page tabloid news for driving around a racetrack oval slower than cabbies go through Copley Square.

Sure, we all got caught up with the Braves last year, and, once they hit the stage, the Twins. But each was different from '67. As great as it was in Minneapolis last October, it wasn't quite the same as in '87, because, well, you can't be a virgin twice. Atlanta was wild, wooly, wacky, wonderful, but it was a kind of revelation. Sixty-seven was in New Englander's hearts and dreams, but we'd become too jaded to sit down next to our father's desk and figure out another trade that would bring McCovey and Kirkland to Boston for Mad Dog Thomas and Ach Duliba. The Braves were the Beatles; '67 was the crumbling of the Berlin Wall.

Here it is 25 years later, and every one of us gray enough to remember knows exactly where we were when the Red Sox beat John Buzhardt—the symbol of White Sox torture—on Opening Day. Or whom we called the day Billy Rohr nearly threw the perfect game in Yankee Stadium (not to mention how many times we've put Ken Coleman's historic call of Yastrzemski's catch on our answering machine); I called my brother Ned, who'd suffered far longer than I and who, in fact, had moved to New Jersey and Delaware and had actually started to give up on the Smirnoff Sox. But the real night when dark turned to light was June 15, when the White Sox scored at the top of the 11th to go up 1-0, then Tony Conigliaro hit a two-out, 3-and-2, two-run homer off Buzhardt for a 2-1 win. A week later, when Thad Tillotson hit Joe Foy in Yankee Stadium and Lonborg promptly drilled Tillotson and Dick Howser, the Red Sox punched everyone in sight. I was at the University of North Carolina at the time and, listening to the game with some roommates in our apartment in Chapel Hill, I was somewhat surprised when a Yankee fan named Sandy Treadwell said to me, "Even I may jump on the Red Sox bandwagon."

There was the 10-game winning streak, and back then, no one ever thought about fans waiting at the airport. Well, Logan was jammed. We all were sickened when the long-simmering Red Sox-Angels beanball wars claimed Tony C, but two days later they overcame an 8-0 deficit and Jerry Adair homered off Minnie Rojas for the 9-8 lead, my sister-in-law Gretchen was so excited she leaped and stuck an architect's compass into the ceiling. The next weekend, Stephenson beat the White Sox to put them in first place on a Saturday; in those days the *New York Times* had several headlines leading its sports section, and this day it combined baseball with the winner of a horse race named What a Pleasure, so when we cut out the headlines and clipped it, it read:

Red Sox beat Chicago 6-2 to take first place;
What a Pleasure.

Two days later, José Tartabull threw Ken Berry out at the plate. "I'm reminded of that hundreds of times a year," says Tartabull. And Berry says, "Every time I meet someone in New England, he says, 'I remember Tartabull threw you out.' " We killed a car battery the night Yaz homered off Fred Lasher, which was followed by Dalton Jones' homer off Mike Marshall.

Two years later, the Mets had their miracle, and 24 years later came the Braves and the Twins. But '67 had no bottom line, no television ratings, no exaggerations.

It was better because we were more naïve, we knew too little to argue, to judge or to call talk shows because they got swept by Jim King and the Senators. It was the end of innocence. In '68 and '69, we expected them to win but it was the beginning of one of the phenomena of the Red Sox. For a decade, they were not good enough to be cursed by the Bambino, much less Merlin Nippert.

MAKING BELIEVERS

After Ted Williams retired in 1960, the Red Sox were mired in their dark ages, below .500 on the field and under 1 million in home attendance. But starting with that memorable '67 campaign, they became winners -- on the field and in the stands. Indeed, after '67 they were never to go below one million fans a season, and went over 2 million beginning in '86. Here's a look at the six years before and after 1967.

Year	Record	Fin.	Attendance
1961	76-86	6th	850,589
1962	76-84	8th	733,080
1963	76-85	7th	942,642
1964	72-90	8th	883,276
1965	62-100	9th	652,201
1966	72-90	9th	811,172
1967	**92-70**	**1st**	**1,727,832**
1968	86-76	4th	1,940,788
1969	87-75	3rd	1,833,246
1970	87-75	3rd	1,595,278
1971	85-77	3rd	1,678,732
1972	85-70	2nd	1,441,718
1973	89-73	2nd	1,481,002

Fenway became the place to be

As the impossible season wore along, we watched Don Gillis do a special on the Pittsfield pitching staff, which included Ken Brett. We never had that sort of thing before. In August, Yawkey was accosting official scorer Clif Keane because he felt Mike Andrews shouldn't have been given an error, and the junior senator from Massachusetts, Ted Kennedy, sent the team a telegram. By the final day, Lonborg vs. Dean Chance, there were 35,770 in Fenway, including Lee Remick and Dale Robertson, and star/ball/chic was officially born, days before Jackie and John-John showed up for the World Series. The top radio man in town was Jess Cain, and his "Carl Yastrzemski" song was more popular than Jimi Hendrix' "Hey, Joe." *Time* magazine that fall was building The Boston Sound as "the next San Francisco," and one hot band was Earth Opera, whose first cut on the first album was "The Red Sox are Winning," 20-something years before Huey Lewis was doing anthems. The Bosox Club was formed in the summer of '67. At the end of the summer, Yaz became one of the first autobiographical heroes; the phenomenon of the season review record (*The Impossible Dream*, with Ned Martin's immortal, "and there's pandemonium on the field") was not only first, but the forerunner to the video madness.

They better than doubled their '66 attendance to 1,727,832, and they outdrew that in '68. Higgins and the early '60s had killed all hope. Since '67, the Red Sox have hoped every January. They slid in the early '70s, but '75 revived dreams of another dynasty, and in Don Zimmer's salad days, they set records of 2.1 million to 2.4 million in 1977-79. When Fred Lynn, Carlton Fisk, and Rick Burleson were about to leave, the interest died down again, but beginning with Roger Clemens' arrival in 1984, the attendance has risen every year. Clemens is a big part of the increase to 2.56 million: It isn't unreasonable to believe that if the Red Sox can win the division, Clemens will win two games in the playoffs, three in the World Series, and The Curse will be ended.

Bob Stanley used to say that he wished Fenway were empty when he pitched, but he—and most players—have never understood what it is to be part of the Red Sox. It was easier to play in '65. They're not paying Clemens for '65 feelings, either.

We look out now and see lines around Yawkey Way two days before tickets go on sale. We know they have no season ticket cancellations between first and third bases, that the 600 Club keeps growing, that there's a waiting list for the luxury boxes, that Clemens gets more for a card show than Lonborg made in '67.

But it was a rotting franchise in '65. So when they have the Old-timers' Day this season, it might not be a bad idea for some current players to thank Lonborg for drilling Tillotson, tell Billy Rohr what he means, or tell Dalton Jones they wouldn't have won without that homer off Mike Marshall, shake Lee Stange's hand for the near-perfect game, remind Rico Petrocelli how great he was, or remember Ken Poulsen.

It was not always the way it is now, and might never have been but '67.

*This article first appeared in the April 3, 1992 *Boston Globe*. Reprinted here courtesy of Peter Gammons.

Dick Williams both managing and making a point.

JERRY ADAIR

by Royse Parr

	G	AB	R	H	2B	3B	HR	RBI	BB	SO	BA	OBP	SLG	SB	CS	GDP	HBP
1967 RED SOX	89	316	41	92	13	1	3	26	13	35	.291	.321	.367	1	4	10	2

Kenneth Jerry Adair was born to Kinnie and Ola Adair on December 17, 1936, at Lake Station, an unincorporated area named for a station on a trolley car line between the northeastern Oklahoma cities of Sand Springs and Tulsa. Jerry claimed Sand Springs as his hometown. He was a fair-skinned, blond-haired descendant of mixed-blood Cherokee tribal leaders who once were the warlords of the southern Appalachians. The strong "will to win" of Cherokee warriors was exemplified in the life of Jerry Adair, who was an exceptional multi-sport competitor.

A notable Adair who lived with the Cherokee tribe in the eighteenth century was an Irish trader, James Adair. He wrote a lengthy book about his belief that the unique, dignified Cherokees were one of the biblical lost tribes of Judah. In 1838, a majority of the Cherokees under the terms of an onerous treaty with the United States government were forcibly removed on the Trail of Tears to Indian Territory. Thousands of Cherokees died along the way. In 1907, Indian Territory and Oklahoma Territory were combined to form the state of Oklahoma.

Bordering on the state of Arkansas in the flint hills of northeastern Oklahoma, Adair County is named for one of Jerry Adair's Cherokee family members of the Civil War era, Judge William Penn Adair. Jerry's grandfather George Starr Adair was enrolled in a tribal census as a 28-year-old member of the Cherokee Nation in 1900 in what became Adair County, Oklahoma. His son, Kinnie Adair, spoke Cherokee when he visited with friends and relatives from Adair County. Today, heavy concentrations of the inhabitants of the county are descendants of the original Cherokee settlers.

Jerry Adair's life was described by the *Tulsa World*'s sports editor Bill Connors as "an experience of two lifetimes." Connors' obituary after Jerry's death in 1987 surmised, "The first half was exaltation. The second half was tragedy." Connors described Jerry as "the best athlete to come out of the Tulsa area in his lifetime." He would not have stretched the truth if he had stated that no athlete from Oklahoma had a more storied pre-professional career than Adair, not even Mickey Mantle, who was five years older. Mantle had close relatives who were Cherokee; his grandmother was born in Indian Territory, but he was not a mixed-blood American Indian.

Jerry's father played sandlot baseball on his employer's teams in the Sand Springs area. Like Mantle's father, Kinnie Adair always had time after work to play ball with his son. A tool grinder by trade, Kinnie also coached Jerry's Little League teams. Jerry told Ray Fitzgerald, a *Boston Globe* sports columnist, about his Little League days when he "did a lot of pitching. Anybody who could throw a curveball was a pitcher, and I was a pretty good one."

Kinnie Adair died in 1986, one year and three days before Jerry's death. He had remarried after Jerry's mother died in 1952 and had a son, Dennis, who died in 2005. Jerry's only sister, Joyce, who was born in Adair County, still lives in Sand Springs.

Jerry's high school coach, Cecil Hankins, was a legendary football and basketball player at Oklahoma A&M College, now Oklahoma State University (OSU), in Stillwater, Oklahoma. Hankins regarded Jerry as the greatest all-around athlete he ever coached. Jerry earned nine letters at Sand Springs High School, three each in football, basketball, and baseball. During his high school years, he earned the nickname "Iceman" because of his cool demeanor. He is particularly remembered for his coolness during the football game against Ponca City during his senior year. Ponca City grabbed a 20-0 lead in the first quarter. Playing quarterback, Jerry scored just before halftime and kicked the extra point to cut the deficit to 20-7. In the third quarter, Jerry engineered a scoring drive and kicked another extra point for a 20-14 score. Late in the fourth quarter, Jerry scored a touchdown and kicked the extra point to win the game 21-20 for Sand Springs. Bill Connors once wrote, "Adair demonstrated All-American possibilities as a high school quarterback at Sand Springs."

After football season in the fall of 1954, *Daily Oklahoman* sports writer Ray Soldan telephoned coach Hankins to tell him that he had selected Jerry for the all-state football team. For many years Soldan made Oklahoma's all-state team selections. Only seniors were eligible and a player could be selected for only one sport. Coach Hankins spoke with Jerry, who said he did not want to make all-state in football; he wanted to make it in basketball. Soldan said he would give no assurance that Jerry would be selected for basketball,

but Jerry said he would take the chance. Another player was named to replace Jerry on the all-state football team. After basketball season, Jerry was selected on the all-state basketball team. Playing in the state all-star game in the summer of 1955, Jerry was selected as the most outstanding player in the game.

Jerry also played Ban Johnson League baseball during the summer of 1955. He was scouted by Toby Greene, the longtime head baseball coach at OSU. Jerry's team was leading 1-0 in the bottom of the ninth inning, but the opponent had loaded the bases with no outs. Greene watched as the manager motioned for Jerry to pitch. Jerry nodded and walked to the mound from his third base position with a big cud of tobacco in his mouth. He threw two balls to the catcher and announced he was ready. Greene thought this was the cockiest player he had ever seen. Jerry struck out the three batters he faced. Greene later declared to Coach Hankins, "I'll take him, he can play anywhere." Jerry Adair was one of Coach Greene's seven All-Americans at OSU.

Jerry entered OSU in the fall of 1955 on an athletic scholarship to play basketball and baseball. Freshmen were not then eligible for varsity competition and played only limited schedules in all sports. Jerry's first varsity competition was during the 1956-1957 basketball season under Hall of Fame coach Henry Iba, the "Iron Duke." A rare sophomore starter at OSU, the 6-foot, 175-pound Adair was the team's playmaking guard and second leading scorer on the nation's top defensive team. During his junior year, he was again the team's second leading scorer. Bill Connors once wrote, "Long time Iba watchers say Adair was one of the few players who was not yelled at by Iba. 'There was no need to yell at Jerry,' Iba said at the time. 'He does everything right.'"

To this day, what is referred to as "The Game" at Gallagher Hall (now Gallagher-Iba Arena and Eddie Sutton Court) at OSU is the February 21, 1957, rematch between OSU and the Kansas Jayhawks, led by their phenomenal sophomore center Wilt "The Stilt" Chamberlain. Earlier in the season, Iba's team was said to have played one of their best games of the season when they held the Jayhawks to a ten point margin on their home court at Lawrence, Kansas.

Chamberlain did not disappoint the fans as he scored an arena record of 32 points. But OSU came from far behind to win the game, 56-54. The high OSU scorer with 18 points was forward Eddie Sutton, who would return to his alma mater as head coach in 1990. Although he scored only six points, Jerry Adair, according to Bill Connors, "played brilliantly on the floor." Jerry had no fouls and one field goal, and was four-for-four from the free-throw line.

The highlight game of Jerry's junior year and his last basketball season at OSU was a 61-57 verdict over the Cincinnati Bearcats. Their future Hall of Fame player, Oscar Robertson, scored 29 points. Jerry was OSU's second leading scorer, and made two free throws and a field goal down the stretch to preserve the victory. The 1957-1958 OSU team finished 21-8 and won two games in post-season NCAA play. They were eliminated by Kansas State in the western regional to finish fifth in the nation.

Baseball was a much lower profile sport than basketball at OSU in the 1950s as well as today. OSU won the NCAA basketball championships in 1945 and 1946. Henry Iba had been the OSU basketball and baseball coach from 1934 to 1941. When he was also the athletic director in 1942, he passed the baseball coaching reins to Toby Greene, who was Jerry Adair's head baseball coach during the 1957 and 1958 seasons.

The 1957 OSU baseball season was essentially "called on account of rain." Nine games were cancelled because of rain or unplayable fields. The year's record for OSU was 12 won and three lost. When three consecutive days of rain prevented the Missouri Valley conference championship series from being played, Bradley University was given the NCAA tournament bid because of its better conference record.

Regarded as a "converted basketballer," sophomore Jerry Adair was the starting shortstop on the experienced 1957 OSU baseball team. Two of his senior teammates signed professional contracts at season's end. Center fielder Mel Wright, who was the other starting basketball guard with Adair during the 1956-1957 season, signed with the Kansas City Athletics. He had four undistinguished seasons in the minor leagues. Pitcher Merlin Nippert signed with the Boston Red Sox, with whom he had a cup of coffee in 1962 before finishing his career in the Pacific Coast League.

Competing in the Big Eight conference in 1958 for the first time, OSU was rained out of its last two games of the year with champion Missouri, which thus backed into the NCAA tournament bid. OSU's record for the year was 17-6. Junior shortstop Jerry Adair was the team's leading hitter with a .438 batting average. He was the first player from OSU named to the All-Big Eight team. He was also named to the All-American second team by the American Baseball Coaches Association. One of three excellent OSU pitchers was future Chicago White Sox ace Joel Horlen, who would lead the Adair-less 1959 team to OSU's first and only NCAA baseball championship.

On August 24, 1957, Jerry married his high school

sweetheart, Kay Morris. They had met in an English class at Sand Springs High School. While he was playing semipro baseball during the summer of 1958 for Williston, North Dakota, in the Western Canada Baseball League (WCBL), Kay gave birth in Tulsa to Kathy, their first of four children.

Adair won the batting title with a .409 average, with the runner-up trailing at .371. He tied for the lead in home runs and finished close behind the RBI leader. Jerry was the league's top fielding shortstop. He was the starting pitcher in three games and was credited with the victory in each. He batted .444 in 14 playoff games and led his team to the league title on August 30, 1958.

After being signed by Baltimore Orioles scout Eddie Robinson for a reported $40,000, Jerry made his major league debut defensively at shortstop for the O's on September 2, 1958, in a 4-3 loss to the Senators in Washington. (The Red Sox had offered Jerry a larger signing bonus than Baltimore, but he figured he would move up the ladder more quickly with the Orioles.) Playing right field for the Orioles that day was former Yankee Gene Woodling whose steadying influence and advice helped Jerry adjust to major league life. At third base for the Orioles was future major league manager Dick Williams who would be Jerry's future ticket to participating in three World Series.

The news that Adair had signed a professional baseball contract came as a complete surprise to OSU's athletic director and basketball coach, Henry Iba. He had understood that Jerry would return to OSU to confer with him before making a definite commitment to a major league club. Iba had once counseled OSU's baseball and football star, Allie Reynolds, to take a baseball contract offered by the Cleveland Indians instead of one offered by the New York Giants in Allie's then favorite sport, football. As to Adair, Iba was quoted in the *Tulsa World* as saying "He has an excellent chance in baseball, I believe, for he is a fine baseball player and a boy with a great competitive spirit." With his playmaking guard not in the lineup for the 1958-1959 season, Iba was to suffer through his first losing basketball season (11-14) since his arrival at OSU in 1934.

After playing only as a late-inning substitute in 11 games with the Orioles in 1958, with just 19 at-bats, Jerry was shipped in the spring of 1959 to the Amarillo Gold Sox, the Orioles' farm team in the Double-A Texas League. His Amarillo manager, George Staller, was quoted in the *Tulsa World* as saying that Jerry was a surefire major leaguer but that he needed a season of Triple-A experience. At the beginning of the season in Amarillo, Jerry batted around .275 and failed to

Jerry Adair sets his sights on helping the Sox.

cover much ground. Suddenly he caught fire, both at bat and in the field. Staller credited Adair with being instrumental in Amarillo's surge from 17 games below .500 to four over that mark. Recalled Adair in a *Tulsa World* article, "My fielding improved when my hitting got better and I learned to play the batters. That's the big difference. When you're hitting everything seems to go well. Knowing the hitters is the key. That's why I didn't do so well with Baltimore."

In 146 games, mostly at shortstop, for Amarillo in 1959, Jerry batted .309. Called up at season's end by Baltimore, he batted .314 in 12 games, playing second base or shortstop, mostly as the starter. After playing in an instructional league in the fall of 1959, he batted .266 in 1960 playing for the Miami Marlins of the Triple-A International League. He was named the league's All-Star shortstop. During the season, he played three games at second base for the Orioles at the very end of the year.

Jerry had an excellent 1961 spring training with the Orioles to make the club, but by Opening Day was unable to dislodge veterans Ron Hansen from shortstop or Marv Breeding from second base. But as the season progressed, he replaced Breeding as the regular second baseman and substituted occasionally for Hansen at shortstop. Batting .264 for the season, he outhit both Hansen and Breeding and played 107 games at second base, 27 games at shortstop, and two at third base. Jerry hit nine home runs and drove in 37 runs. From 1961-1965, Adair was recognized as one of the premier-fielding infielders in the American League. He batted .258 during these five seasons, substantially above the league average for middle infielders. However, he was overshadowed by the Orioles' spectacular third baseman and future Hall of Famer, Brooks Robinson.

Adair is particularly remembered for setting a major league record for second basemen. In 89 games from July 22, 1964, to May 6, 1965, he handled 458 chances without an error. In 1964 and 1965, he led all American League second basemen in fielding percentage. He shares an American League record with Bobby Grich and Roberto Alomar for the fewest errors in a season by a second baseman (five in 1964). For his career he had a better fielding percentage (.985) than all three Hall of Fame second basemen of his era: Nellie Fox, Bill Mazeroski, and Nellie Fox.

Although Jerry was known primarily for his glove, he told the *Boston Globe*'s Ray Fitzgerald in August of 1967 that his biggest moment in the major leagues came in late August 1962 in a five-game Orioles-Yankees series. Jerry recalled that the Orioles won all five games and that he had 13 hits in the series. His best day came in a twi-night doubleheader that opened the series when he was 3-for-4 in the first game and 5-for-6 (with a double and a triple) in the second game.

When Orioles manager Hank Bauer gave the second base job to rookie Dave Johnson, Jerry demanded a trade—more than once—and was finally dealt to the White Sox for Eddie Fisher on June 13, 1966. The trade cost him the opportunity to be a member of the Orioles when they defeated the Dodgers in the 1966 World Series and also cost him about $12,000 World Series money.

After hitting .243 for the White Sox in 1966, he shared second base with Wayne Causey early in the 1967 season. After having missed out on a pennant in 1966, things balanced out when on June 2, 1967, the White Sox traded him to the Red Sox. Dick Williams was glad to get him; the two had been teammates for several years in Baltimore and author Bill Reynolds said that Williams viewed him as "the ultimate professional." Adair's toughness appealed to Williams. Reynolds recounted a 1964 doubleheader when Jerry was hit in the mouth by a throw in the first game, received 11 stitches, then played in the second game. He described Adair as having "a face right out of the *Grapes of Wrath*." Jerry was hitting only .204 with the White Sox when the trade was executed, but would hit .291 in 89 games while playing three infield positions for the Red Sox. The Red Sox were 22-21 before he joined them but were 70-49 afterward.

Adair filled in for the injured Rico Petrocelli at short for a solid month, playing errorless defense. Adair played pivotal roles on offense in several games, too, but his biggest single day was likely the Sunday doubleheader at Fenway Park on August 20. Jerry was 3-for-3 in the first game, a 12-2 rout of the Angels. In the second game, California got off to an 8-0 lead after just three innings. The Sox crept back, and Adair's single in the bottom of the sixth tied the game, 8-8. In the bottom of the eighth, his leadoff home run gave the Red Sox the lead and the 9-8 win. As Herb Crehan wrote in *Lightning in a Bottle*, "Role players like Adair seldom get their moment in the sun. But in the summer of '67 every Red Sox fan thought of Jerry as a hero."

In the final game of the season, Adair was 2-for-4 at the plate. He singled and scored the tying run in the bottom of the sixth, but his big play of the day came in the top of the eighth as Jim Lonborg was working with a 5-2 lead. Pinch hitter Rich Reese singled to lead off the inning, but Cesar Tovar grounded to second. Adair charged the ball, sweeping it up with his glove, tagging the oncoming Reese, and firing accurately to George Scott at first, though he was spiked so severely he had to leave the game and receive several stitches. Red Sox broadcaster Ken Coleman called Jerry Adair "Mr. Clutch" and wrote that if there had been a "Tenth Player Award" in 1967, he would have deserved it.

After the wild clubhouse celebration when the Red Sox clinched the American League pennant on the last day of the season, Jerry telephoned his sister to say that manager Dick Williams had just kissed him and other Red Sox players. In the World Series that was won by the pitching heroics of Bob Gibson for the St. Louis Cardinals, Adair appeared in five games, starting the first four (all against right-handers), but had only two hits in 16 at-bats. He did have Boston's only stolen base of the series and one RBI. Williams started Mike Andrews in Game Five against lefty Steve Carlton, then stuck with Andrews in Games Six and Seven.

Neil Singelais, a sports writer with the *Boston Globe* later quoted 1967 Red Sox catcher Russ Gibson

Adair's clutch hit knocks in the tying run in the September 30 game against the Twins.

as saying, "No one could pivot as well as Jerry on a double play ball. He could play anywhere and he was a tough guy to get out." Jim Lonborg, the 1967 ace of the Red Sox pitching staff, added that the trade that brought Adair to Boston "was like adding a gem to a beautiful necklace. He did such a magnificent job for us. He was a quiet guy around the clubhouse. He was so invaluable, older and more experienced."

In 1968, Jerry had a poor year at the plate for the Red Sox, batting only .216 in 74 games while filling a journeyman's role and playing four infield positions. In the 1968-1969 offseason, he was selected by the Kansas City Royals in the American League expansion draft. He was the regular second baseman for the Royals in 1969 and batted .250 for the season. On April 8, in the first game the Royals ever played, Adair hit second and knocked in their first-ever run—Lou Piniella had led off with a double, and Jerry singled him home.

In 1970, the Royals awarded the second base position to Luis Alcaraz, and Adair played sparingly. In May, the Royals abruptly released Adair as he was boarding an airplane. He had spent most of the spring with his daughter, Tammy, who died of cancer shortly after his release. Jerry resented the Royals not taking his family problems into consideration at the time of the release. Later that season, Adair played near his hometown with the Tulsa Oilers of the Triple-A American Association, the top Cardinals farm club.

In 1971, Adair joined the Hankyu Braves in Japan and batted .300 for the season. The Braves won the pennant in the Pacific League, but were defeated by the perennial champion Yomiuri Giants of the Central League in the Japan Series. In 1972 and 1973, Jerry earned World Series rings as a coach under his friend Dick Williams, manager of the Oakland Athletics. Williams quit the A's after the 1973 World Series. Jerry stayed on and earned another World Series ring in 1974 under new manager Alvin Dark. In 1975 and 1976, Jerry was reunited with Dick Williams when Williams managed the California Angels, but the major league coaching doors were closed to Jerry after the Angels fired Williams during the 1976 season.

Jerry's wife, Kay, died of cancer in June 1981. Personal and financial problems forced Jerry, always an introvert, into a shell. A cancerous mole was removed from his arm in 1986. Prior to gall bladder surgery, it was discovered that the cancer had spread to his liver. As the former OSU basketball players were making plans to have a Saturday night banquet in Stillwater, Oklahoma, honoring Henry Iba, Jerry was out of the hospital and optimistic for a new treatment for his disease. Friday night he was readmitted to the hospital. At the very hour of the event that Iba called the happiest of his life, Adair's condition worsened. He died Sunday morning, May 31, 1987. Jerry was survived by his sister, Joyce; his half-brother, Dennis; and three children, Kathy, Judy, and Michael. Graveside funeral services were held at Woodlawn Cemetery in Sand Springs.

Sand Springs friend Ron Dobbs helped perpetuate Jerry's memory by displaying Jerry's sports memorabilia at his pizza restaurant in Sand Springs. Many of the items were still on display years after Dobbs sold the restaurant. Jerry's fierce competitive nature was evident early on, according to Dobbs. Like the Dodgers' Pee Wee Reese, Jerry was regarded by his friends as a world class marbles shooter in grade school. He was said to have more marbles at his house than any other kid in Lake Station. Dobbs and one of Jerry's former Sand Springs teammates, Oklahoma State Representative David Riggs, helped get the Sand Springs Little League complex named in his honor. In 1992, Jerry was inducted into the Sand Springs Sandite Hall of Fame. In 2001, he was inducted into the OSU Baseball Hall of Fame.

Mike Andrews

by Saul Wisnia

	G	AB	R	H	2B	3B	HR	RBI	BB	SO	BA	OBP	SLG	SB	CS	GDP	HBP
1967 RED SOX	142	494	79	130	20	0	8	40	62	72	.263	.346	.352	7	7	9	2

From his key contributions as a rookie on the pennant-winning Red Sox of 1967 to his final games spent entangled in one of the most controversial incidents in World Series history, Mike Andrews packed plenty of memorable moments into seven-plus big-league seasons. And while his baseball career may not have lasted as long—or ended—as he envisioned, it led directly to a second vocation that the former All-Star second baseman considers even more rewarding than playing on two AL championship teams.

As chairman of the Jimmy Fund of the Dana-Farber Cancer Institute, located less than a mile up Brookline Avenue from Fenway Park, Andrews has spent more than 25 years helping to raise hundreds of millions for research and treatment into childhood and adult cancers. Rather than spin tales of his athletic feats during his many public appearances, he speaks of the dedicated scientists, caregivers, and patients engaged in the cancer fight at Dana-Farber—"true heroes" whom he first encountered as a rookie.

Andrews is the perfect man for the job. The Jimmy Fund has long been a favorite charity of the Red Sox, and Mike is accustomed to quietly turning in clutch performances that help others shine. All Sox fans worth their weight in Big Yaz Bread know who led the club in hitting down the stretch of the 1967 American League race, but it's a forgotten footnote that rookie Andrews was second to Carl Yastrzemski among regulars with a .342 batting average during the most pressure-packed September in team history.

"Just today, I had an electrician at my winter house in Florida, and when he found out who I was, he named the entire starting lineup from '67," Andrews recalled recently. "That happens all the time. It was just a magical team; 2004 was great, but I'm not sure everybody will remember all the individuals the same way because players move around so much now. Plus the Red Sox are always contending, whereas the team had been bad for years before we came along—and the excitement kept building each month. That season brought baseball back in New England."

He's been here so long that many assume Andrews is a New England native himself, but he's in fact a Southern California boy. Born on July 9, 1943 in Los Angeles, he grew up in nearby Torrance rooting for the Pacific Coast League's LA Angels and Hollywood Stars.

Andrews got his early big-league fix from television's "Game of the Week," and after the Dodgers fled Brooklyn for the West Coast during his teenage years, he followed the exploits of their pitching aces, Sandy Koufax and Don Drysdale. His athletic genes came from his father, Lloyd, who had played football and basketball at the University of Montana and owned and operated Callahan's Bar in nearby Hermosa Beach. Mike starred in football, baseball, and basketball at South Torrance High.

The 6-foot-3, 195-pounder initially chose the gridiron—accepting a full scholarship to UCLA that required his attendance at one year of junior college to complete the necessary foreign language requirement. Andrews earned JC All-American honors as a split end at El Camino College, but then came a life-altering decision for the 18-year-old.

The Pirates and Red Sox had scouted him, and he wanted to marry his high school sweetheart, Marilyn Flynn, and start a family. Several more years of college football without a paycheck seemed like forever, and Boston scout Joe Stephenson was offering him a cash bonus of $12,000 plus $4,000 more if he made the big-league roster. Andrews accepted the deal in December 1961, got engaged early the next spring, and shortly thereafter reported to Boston's Class A club in Olean, New York. (Interestingly, Stephenson's son, Jerry, would later be one of Mike's teammates on the Red Sox.)

Up the ladder

Like many young prospects, Mike's first taste of professional baseball was humbling. All around him on the '62 Olean squad were other former high school hot shots, and as he later recalled for the *Boston Globe*: "I didn't think much of my chances. So all I could do was give it everything I had." Perhaps this self-deprecating attitude took the pressure off at the plate, as Andrews hit .299 with 12 homers and 89 runs scored in 114 games as the club's starting shortstop.

Moved up the chain to Winston-Salem for 1963, he hit just .255 there, but .323 after a midseason switch to Single-A Waterloo. He cut his combined error total at short by nearly 50 percent, and Sox brass boosted him

again to Reading the next year. Mike batted .295, raised his fielding percentage again, and in 1965—while still just 21 years old—earned an invitation to Red Sox spring training in Scottsdale from new manager Billy Herman.

Farmed out for the regular season to Triple-A Toronto, the top of Boston's minor-league ladder, he had a disappointing (.246, 4 homers) year toiling for a fiery young manager named Dick Williams. It was Williams who played a part in Andrews' winter-league switch to second base (Rico Petrocelli already held the starting shortstop slot in Boston), and Mike excelled when he returned to Toronto for a second season in 1966. He played solid defensively at his new position, boosted both his batting average (to .267) and home run output (to 14) considerably, and led the International League in runs scored with 97.

The performance earned Andrews a September call-up to the ninth-place Red Sox, where he started five games in the waning days of the season. He batted seventh in his first major league contest, against his hometown Angels at Fenway Park on September 18, and went 0-for-4 with a run scored. His next action came a week later at New York, and on September 24 he notched his first big-league hit with a single off Fritz Peterson at Yankee Stadium in a 1-0 Sox loss.

"Mickey Mantle was one of my idols," Andrews recalls of the event. "When he said, 'Nice job, Mike,' that was terrific." Overall Andrews was 3-for-18 in the trial, with his other two safeties coming in the season finale at Chicago.

After Herman was fired and Williams named Red Sox manager for 1967, the new skipper announced before spring training that the starting second base job was "Andrews' to lose." Mike had hurt his lower back lifting weights in the offseason, however, and the lingering injury affected his defensive range in exhibition play. The tough-talking Williams was not sympathetic.

"We can't wait any longer," the manager stated flatly after two Andrews errors on March 26. "He has a bad back and he can't bend. If he can't bend, he can't play." Even though Mike had notched a five-hit game and was batting close to .400 in Winter Haven, Williams announced that day that he was moving fellow Southern Californian rookie Reggie Smith from outfield to second base and putting Andrews on the bench.

This was still the arrangement when the regular season started two weeks later, but it didn't last much longer. Smith had his own defensive troubles at second, while the center-field platoon of José Tartabull and George Thomas that replaced him was batting under .200. On April 19, with Andrews' back improving, Williams reinstated Smith in center and Mike at second. With very few exceptions, Mike Andrews would be their starting second baseman for the next four years.

"I really wasn't worried about losing my job, because I knew that with his super arm and speed, Reggie was destined to be a great outfielder," Andrews remembers of early 1967. "I had played for Dick a couple years, and had a very good spring. It was just one of those unfortunate things. My back went bad on me, and the start of the season was so cold, I just took it easy. I'm glad I did as it worked out, because I almost played every game after that."

Key contributor

Once he got his chance, Andrews made the most of it. He hit .321 during the rest of April, and settled in with Petrocelli to provide strong middle-infield defense for the surprising Red Sox. On April 25 he hit his first major league home run, a three-run shot off the Senators' Pete Richert in a 9-3 Boston victory at DC Stadium. Later in the same contest, he had his first big-league stolen base and scored on a Carl Yastrzemski double.

A solid May (.281, including an 11-for-18 stretch)

Mike Andrews works to make key contributions at the plate.

followed for Mike and featured the team's first trip to his home state for a series with the Angels. A huge contingent of 90 family members and friends made the 45-minute drive to Anaheim on two buses originating from his dad's bar, and Andrews received rousing applause from the sign-waving group even when he drew a walk in one of the games—thus earning him several weeks of ribbing from his teammates. A home run followed the next day, however, and Mike would go on to enjoy several more clutch performances in front of his biggest fans over the years (including another homer at Anaheim later in the season). Briefly in May, the rookie was among the American League's top 10 in hitting.

His batting average dropped off in the months to come, but even while dipping below .250 from June through August, Andrews was consistently in the thick of things as the Red Sox and their fans enjoyed Boston's first true pennant race in more than a decade. Most often used as a leadoff man in front of the likes of Tony Conligliaro, Yastrzemksi, and George Scott, he also hit quite often in the second, seventh, and eighth slots—and was effective in each position.

July offered a prime example of Mike's value; he batted just .236, but scored 18 runs in as many games to help the team to a 15-3 stretch. He was a key man in a 10-game winning streak from July 14-23 that many signal as the turning point of the season, with two hits (including a three-run homer) in a 6-4 win at Baltimore July 19 and three more safeties (with another homer) in a 4-0 shutout at Cleveland on July 22 that drew Boston within half a game of first-place Chicago. Happy with Andrews' contributions, owner Tom Yawkey quietly gave him a midseason salary boost from $11,000 to $15,000.

Making Mike's performance all the more impressive were two factors—he was a 24-year-old rookie playing 3,000 miles from home, and (unbeknownst to all but his teammate and close friend Russ Gibson), he was the subject of a death threat late in the season. A Chicago fan who had apparently wagered a bundle on the White Sox winning the pennant sent Andrews and fellow AL second basemen Rod Carew and Dick McAuliffe (all from contending teams) menacing letters threatening their lives.

"Dick Williams called me into his office," Andrews recalls, "and Dick O'Connell and an FBI guy were in there. The FBI guy says, 'We don't think it's a valid threat, but there have been one or two correspondences, so we want to watch it closely.' I believed that there probably wasn't anything to worry about, so I didn't even tell my wife right away. But I remember looking around the stands at Fenway when I first ran on the field for the next game."

By August, with a four-team scramble under way for the AL lead, every game was a huge one—and Andrews continued to deliver. On August 1-3 he went a combined 7-for-12 with two homers, five RBIs and five runs scored over three contests (the Red Sox won two), and all told had eight multi-hit games during the month. This was just a warm-up for September, when he hit a phenomenal .342 (25-for-73) and along with Yastrzemski and Dalton Jones kept the team in the hunt while others slumped. Mike was actually well over .400 for the month until an 0-for-9 skein prompted Williams to sit him in favor of veteran Jerry Adair for several games down the stretch.

Then, with the Sox needing to sweep Minnesota in two games on the season's final weekend for a chance at the pennant, Andrews came through again. On Saturday he was 2-for-3 in the leadoff slot with a key infield single ahead of Yaz's game-breaking three-run homer, and after starting on the bench in Sunday's finale, he played a significant defensive role subbing for Adair after Jerry suffered a spike wound to his leg while turning an eighth-inning double play. Two straight Minnesota hits immediately brought the tying run to the plate in a 5-2 game, and Bob Allison hit a hard liner off Jim Lonborg into the left-field corner for what looked like a double and two RBIs. The shot did score one run, but it also became the inning's third out when Yastrzemksi threw a bullet to Andrews just in time for a sweeping tag on the sliding Allison.

Now down 5-3, the Twins got the leadoff man on in the ninth, but Mike turned a clutch "tag 'em out, throw 'em out" double-play on a Rod Carew grounder to set the stage for Petrocelli's catch of Rich Rollins' popup and the bedlam that followed. Andrews and Scott were the first to reach pitching hero Lonborg, and managed to hoist him to their shoulders for a few moments before thousands of charging fans turned the team's celebration into the city's.

All told, Mike finished the regular season with a .263 average, 8 homers, and 40 RBIs in 142 games after his late start. He also led the league with 18 sacrifice hits, and was runner-up to Rookie of the Year Carew among second basemen in voting by major-league players, managers, and coaches for the Topps All-Star Rookie Team. As the Red Sox readied for the World Series, the *Boston Record American* featured a huge front-page photo of Marilyn Andrews and the couple's two-year-old son, Michael, in the window of their Peabody home,

waving a "GOOD LUCK RED SOX" banner.

It's unclear if Dick Williams saw the picture, but he again benched Andrews in favor of Adair during the first four games against the St. Louis Cardinals. Adair went 2-for-16, however, and after two pinch-hitting appearances (and one hit) Mike was back in the starting lineup for Game Five—where he remained the rest of the series. He wound up batting .308, but the Sox and a weary Lonborg lost to Cards ace Bob Gibson in the seventh game. "The script was there, but it just wasn't meant to be," Andrews says of the setback. "It was like, 'You guys have had your fun, now welcome back to the world. Here's reality.'"

Shining on field and off

Reality hit hard in 1968, as the team fell to a distant fourth place and the offensive output for many Boston hitters dropped off markedly. Andrews was an exception. In the "Year of the Pitcher," during which Yastrzemski was the only everyday AL player to hit .300 for the season, Mike battled for the league batting lead up until Labor Day before finishing at .271 (12th in the circuit) with 7 homers and 45 RBIs. He also topped his rookie totals with 22 doubles and 145 hits. His tiny dip from 79 runs scored to 77 was more a factor of Tony Conigliaro's yearlong absence due to his horrific '67 beaning and George Scott's anemic .171 average than any sophomore slump on Andrews' part. After a few crucial errors early in the season, he was steady on defense and developing into a team leader. Boston sportswriters named him the club's "Unsung Hero" for the season.

None of this was lost on Red Sox coach Bobby Doerr, the top second baseman in team history, who told *New York Times* columnist Arthur Daley of Andrews: "This kid will be around for a long while. What I like best about him is that he's a natural athlete who won't fall apart when he has a bad day. He has the ideal throwing arm for a second baseman, whipping it across his body. He's capable of .285 with 20 homers once he gets settled." Daley was similarly impressed, stating that, "The Bostonians have been searching for a second baseman of Doerr's superlative skills ever since Bobby retired in 1951. It could be that Mike will become that long-sought successor."

Off the field, Andrews was shining as well. During his rookie year, he had become aware of the Jimmy Fund's status as the team's official charity—its billboard in right field was the only one allowed at Fenway Park by owner Tom Yawkey for years—and along with his teammates voted a full 1967 World Series share to the charity. Like other players, he also periodically met with young cancer patients brought to Fenway by then-Jimmy Fund Executive Director Bill Koster. One day such a visit gave him a reality check of a different kind.

"I was busy warming up, but I spent a few minutes with the kid, who was a Little League star looking forward to playing the next year after his treatment was done," recalls Andrews. "I wished him luck. Bill came up to me afterwards and said, 'Thanks, Mike. That meant a lot. There isn't much we can do for that boy. We're sending him home.' That made me realize that an 0-for-4 day at the plate really doesn't mean too much in the scheme of things."

Andrews became a Jimmy Fund regular and in 1968 was named "Man of the Year" by the Bosox Club (the team's official fan club) for "contributions to the success of the Red Sox and for cooperation in community endeavors." He didn't know it at the time, but the seeds of his future career had been planted.

Mike made Doerr and Daley look prophetic in '69. Now batting second in Boston's lineup more often than leadoff, he firmly established himself as one of the most productive second basemen in the majors when healthy. He had a .293 average (10th in the league), 15 homers, and 59 RBIs despite missing nearly 40 games in midseason after being hit in the hand by Minnesota pitcher Dave Boswell and suffering a blood clot that required extensive treatment. When a bad back kept Baltimore's Davey Johnson from going to the All-Star Game, Mike took his place and backed up starting second baseman Rod Carew. (Andrews played the last four innings for the American League and grounded out facing Jerry Koosman in his only plate appearance.) Unfortunately, the Red Sox were again unable to recapture the magic of two years earlier, and with a third-place finish assured, Dick Williams was fired in the waning days of the season.

A change of Sox

The young lineup that was expected to lead the Red Sox to several pennants was still quite potent—Boston's 203 home runs in 1970 led all big-league clubs—but without the pitching to compete with the Baltimore Orioles, it was not enough. Back atop the batting order exclusively, Andrews reached new offensive heights himself that summer. He had 28 doubles, 17 homers, and 65 RBIs, and led off four games with homers—giving him eight leadoff clouts in his career (still third on the team's all-time list). He also topped AL second basemen with 19 errors, but even if management had big changes in store after a second straight third-place

Mike Andrews greets Maine's Governor Kenneth Curtis in a pre-game ceremony. Mike later became Executive Director of the Jimmy Fund, and a Fenway fixture at such presentations.

finish, Mike's spot with the club seemed safe.

On December 1, however, one day after Dick O'Connell was quoted saying "Andrews is not available for trade," Mike and backup shortstop Luis Alvarado were sent to the woeful Chicago White Sox for Luis Aparicio, a future Hall of Famer. Aparicio would be slated to play short alongside newly acquired second baseman Doug Griffin in Boston, with Petrocelli moving to third. "The way I understood it, O'Connell was looking either for a shortstop or a third baseman," says Andrews. "If they got a third baseman, they'd leave Rico at short and me at second. But Aparicio became available, so they went that route."

He would later joke in his self-deprecating style that "at least I was traded for a Hall-of-Famer, even if he was 55 at the time" (Aparicio was actually 36), but the move "crushed" Mike—who had a wife and three young kids happily settled in the Peabody house where he and Marilyn would live until 2004. The majority of fans interviewed were also upset, both because of Andrews' reputation as a heady, tough athlete and Aparicio's age.

Like Fred Lynn and Mo Vaughn in later years, Mike was a popular ballplayer whose career and luck never seemed the same after he left the Red Sox. He made headlines in Chicago by holding out during his first spring training with the White Sox (who had averaged 98 losses the previous three seasons), but won Comiskey Park fans over with his grittiness. He homered in his first series back at Fenway Park as a visiting player, but suffered from arm, shoulder, back, and wrist injuries at various points during 1971.

When he inexplicably developed problems with his throws to first base as well, he tried playing through the struggles; after that didn't work, he moved to first himself. "I never figured out what caused it," Andrews says today. "It was identical to what Chuck Knoblauch and Steve Sax later went through, and I just couldn't work my way out of it." Despite these travails, Mike's hitting was better than ever during a late August spree in which he tallied four homers in a seven-game stretch. But then he suffered a fractured left wrist in a collision at first with Harmon Killebrew on September 1, the fifth time that year he had been knocked from a game by injury. Out for the season, he finished with a .282 average, 12 homers and 47 RBIs in 109 games to help the team improve from 56-106 to 79-83.

Things looked promising for Andrews and the White Sox the following spring training. Manager Chuck Tanner gave Mike back his second base job when the club picked up slugging first baseman Dick Allen, and Andrews said he felt better than ever after dropping some weight and giving his body time to heal. The White Sox shot out to a fantastic start and suddenly found themselves fighting with the Oakland A's for the AL West crown. It was a baseball revival on Chicago's South Side much like that experienced at Fenway Park five years before, with Comiskey attendance reaching its highest levels in 20 years amidst the excitement of Allen's MVP season and a 24-win performance from knuckleballer Wilbur Wood.

Andrews, unfortunately, could not match his team's resurgence. He batted just .200 in April, and after rebounding in May (.291) never hit higher than .245 in any other month. He was part of some big moments, most including Allen, but his final average of .220 (with 7 homers and 50 RBIs) was the worst of his career. In the field he was vastly improved, but still led AL second baseman in errors for the third straight year. Of some consolation to Mike was that the White Sox wound up with a fine 87-67 record, just five-and-one-half games behind World Series champion Oakland.

Oakland odyssey

Still just 29 years old going into the 1973 season, Andrews looked for a bounce-back year at a position new both to him and to baseball: designated hitter. The first DH in White Sox history, he seemed to thrive in the role with a fantastic .417 start (15-for-36) through 10 games. A dreadful slump followed, however, and by July 4, Mike's average had fallen below .200.

On top of this, Andrews was engaged in a heated dispute with general manager Stu Holcomb. The GM had wanted to cut his $60,000 salary a full 20 percent before the season, and Mike was still playing without a contract when on July 10 he asked to be released. Holcomb complied, and later that same month he himself resigned amidst controversy over this and other player squabbles.

Here Dick Williams—by then manager of the A's—resurfaced into Andrews' life. Williams had reportedly attempted to trade for his former rookie standout upon first taking the Oakland job back in 1970. Now, with his defending champs trying for another pennant, he picked Mike up as a free agent on July 31. Andrews hit just .190 in 18 games, but the A's won the West and Williams saw fit to leave the veteran on his club's playoff roster.

Mike was hitless in two pinch-hit appearances against Baltimore in the AL Championship Series, and then was given the same task in the eighth inning of Game Two of the World Series against the New York Mets at Oakland-Alameda County Coliseum on October 14. Grounding out for Ted Kubiak, he stayed in the game at second base. Then the nuttiness began.

The score was 6-6 in the top of the 12th when the Mets scored four runs, due largely to two straight errors by Andrews—the first on a bad-hop grounder by John Milner, the second (one batter later) on a low throw that appeared to cause first baseman Gene Tenace to pull his foot off the bag. Replays indicated the umpire missed the second call, and Dick Williams thought Tenace deserved an error, but the damage was done. A rally in the bottom of the inning fell short, and New York won, 10-7.

Even before the game was over, meddling A's owner Charlie Finley was on the phone with team physician, Dr. Harry Walker, and behind closed doors in the locker room after the contest Andrews received an impromptu medical exam from Walker. Mike was then asked to sign a document stating that he had a "chronic" shoulder injury and was going on the disabled list. Feeling pressured, he signed it.

Andrews flew home to Boston as Finley schemed to add rookie Manny Trillo to the roster, but teammates who had seen Finley meeting with Mike rightfully suspected something was up. The story made national headlines, and prompted A's players to affix Andrews' No. 17 to their uniforms with athletic tape as a sign of solidarity. Within a few days Mike explained in a press conference that he had been forced into signing the document.

"Finley told me, 'If you want to help this team, the best thing you can do is step aside and let us put Manny [Trillo] in there,'" Andrews recalls. "He kept beating me down, and finally I just signed it." Commissioner Bowie Kuhn ordered that Mike be reinstated for Game Four, and he earned a standing ovation at Shea Stadium when he came up as a pinch-hitter in the eighth. After grounding out to third, he received another one.

Now pitching for Jimmy

That would be his last at-bat in the major leagues. Andrews didn't expect the A's to keep him after the '73 season, and once Dick Williams quit following Oakland's World Series victory Mike's fate was likely sealed. Released on October 26, he cleared waivers a few days later and failed to catch on with another club. He spent that year working around his Peabody

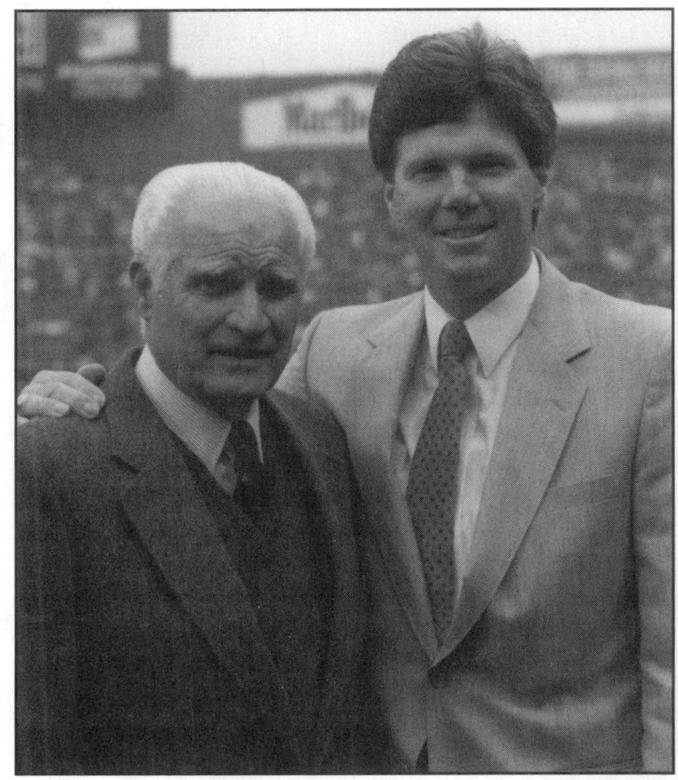

Shown here with Bobby Doerr, Mike Andrews now serves as the Executive Director of the Jimmy Fund.

home and then took a big-money offer to play in Japan during 1975 with the Kintetsu Buffaloes. "I was one of two gaijin [non-Japanese] players on the team, along with our top slugger, Clarence Jones. Even though we were both starters and playing well, they cut us before the playoffs with no explanation."

At this point, Andrews quit pro ball for good. Still popular in New England, he took a position as an agent with the Mass Mutual Insurance Company and followed the big-league exploits of his brother Rob, a second baseman with the Astros and Giants from 1975 to 1979. Then he received a surprising phone call from Ken Coleman, the former Red Sox broadcaster who had come back to Boston from the Cincinnati Reds to resume his duties as the team's radio voice and take over as executive director of the Jimmy Fund.

"Mike had always been helpful to the Jimmy Fund during his days with the Red Sox, and he was the type of intelligent and personable individual whom I thought could be a great asset as we attempted to grow our fundraising program," Coleman recalled shortly before his death in 2003. "We needed more people, and he was at the top of my list."

Signing on as Coleman's assistant director part-time in 1979, Andrews needed just a few months to realize "this is what I wanted to do" and give up insurance altogether. He succeeded Coleman as the charity's director in 1984.

Today Mike can still often be seen at Fenway Park for Jimmy Fund events and check presentations. He participated in both the Ted Williams memorial in 2002 (which benefited Dana-Farber) and the World Series ring ceremony on Opening Day of 2005, and delights in showing his own 2004 championship ring to young Jimmy Fund Clinic patients. The 18-hour WEEI/NESN Jimmy Fund Radio-Telethon has become a staple of New England's summer fundraising calendar, and in 2006 raised nearly $3 million during its 18-plus hours on the air live from Fenway. His popularity as the public face of the charity led to *Boston Sports Review* magazine naming Andrews one of the city's most powerful sports figures.

Mike and Marilyn sold their Peabody home a few years back, but still live in the Boston area. His boyish good looks and California smile remain intact, with only a full head of white hair hinting that this grandfather many times over couldn't be just a decade or so removed from the majors. When Andrews starts talking about the rapidly improving survival rates for various children's and adult's cancers, he seems younger still.

Forty years after his rookie exploits, Mike Andrews is still helping make Impossible Dreams come true.

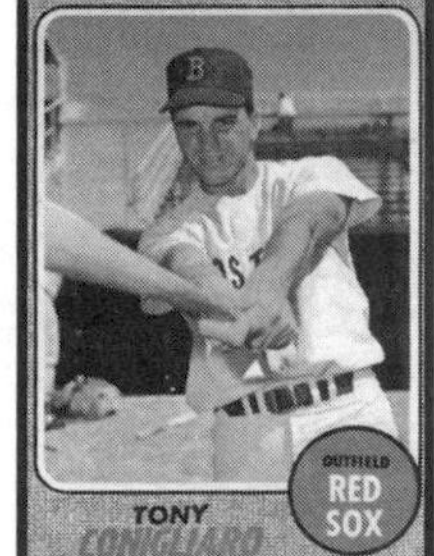

Tony Conigliaro

by Bill Nowlin

	G	AB	R	H	2B	3B	HR	RBI	BB	SO	BA	OBP	SLG	SB	CS	GDP	HBP
1967 RED SOX	95	349	59	100	11	5	20	67	27	58	.287	.341	.519	4	6	3	5

No matter how you measure it, Tony Conigliaro's career got off to a terrific start, but tragedy repeatedly intervened and the great promise of his early years remained unfulfilled. A local boy made good, Tony was born and raised in the Boston area, signed with the hometown team, and made his major league debut in 1964 soon after he turned 19 years old. In his very first at-bat at Fenway Park, Tony turned on the very first pitch he saw, and pounded it out of the park for a home run. By hitting 24 home runs in his rookie season, he set a record for the most home runs ever hit by a teenager. When he led the league in homers with 32 the following year, he became the youngest player ever to take the home run crown. When he hit home run #100, during the first game of a doubleheader on July 23, 1967, he was only 22—the youngest American League player to reach the 100-homer plateau. He hit #101 in the day's second game.

As if that wasn't enough, Tony Conigliaro was a bona fide celebrity and singer with a couple of regional hit records to his credit.

Tony C was born on January 7, 1945 in Revere, Massachusetts, and grew up both there and in East Boston, where he first played Little League ball at age nine. Tony and his younger brother Billy (b. 1947) were obsessed with baseball, playing it at every possible opportunity, usually with the support and guidance of their uncle Vinnie Martelli. "He used to pitch batting practice to me for hours, till my hands bled," wrote Conigliaro in his autobiography *Seeing It Through*. In his first at-bat for the Orient Park Sparks Little League team, Tony hit a home run over the center-field fence. He credits coach Ben Campbell for giving him tremendous encouragement in youth baseball.

At a very early age, Tony confessed, "I discovered how much I hated to lose." His teams didn't lose often. By the time he was 13 and in Pony League, they were traveling out of state in tournament play. Tony went to high school at St. Mary's in Lynn, where his father Sal worked at Triangle Tool and Dye. Sal and Tony's mother Teresa were very supportive of Tony's athletic endeavors and were a fixture at Tony's various ballgames.

Playing shortstop and pitching during high school, Tony came to the attention of scouts like Lennie Merullo and Milt Bolling, and by the time he graduated claimed to have had as many as 14 scouts tracking him. In his final couple of years, he recalled batting over .600 and having won 16 games as well as his team winning the Catholic Conference Championship. He played American Legion ball in the summer, with the same .600 batting average. The Red Sox asked him to come to a 1962 workout at Fenway Park, and both he and Tony Horton showed their stuff. When the Legion season ended and Tony's father courted bids, Boston's Milt Bolling and Red Sox farm director Neil Mahoney made the best one at $20,000 and Tony signed with the Red Sox.[1] He was sent to Bradenton for the Florida Instructional League.

It was his first time far from home, and he didn't stand out at winter ball. In the spring of 1963, he was invited to the Red Sox minor league camp at Ocala. He did well there, and was assigned to Wellsville in the New York-Penn League. Before he reported, he went home to see his girlfriend, got in a fight with a local boy, and broke his thumb. He wasn't able to report to Wellsville until the end of May. That was the end of his pitching career, but the scouts were looking at his hitting more than his pitching in any event. Tony did well at Wellsville, batting .363, hitting 24 homers, and winning the league's Rookie of the Year and MVP awards. He played winter ball in Sarasota and was added to the Red Sox 40-man roster. The next spring,

Armed and ready.

1964, he was brought to the big league spring training headquarters in Scottsdale, Arizona.

Boston's manager was Johnny Pesky who, as it happened, lived on the same street in Swampscott to which the Conigliaro family had recently moved: Parsons Street. Pesky saw the fire in Tony Conigliaro and played him that spring; Tony hit a monster home run off Cleveland's Gary Bell on March 22, the first day his parents came to visit him in Scottsdale. Ted Williams admired Conigliaro's style and told him, whatever he did, "Don't change that solid stance of yours, no matter what you're told." Ted told reporters, though, "He's just a kid; he's two years away."

Johnny Pesky thought otherwise. Tony C was 19, only in his second year in organized ball, but he made the big league club as the center fielder for the Red Sox. Pesky was taking a chance on a relatively-untested player, but the 1964 Sox, frankly, didn't have a great deal of talent.

Conigliaro's first major league game was in Yankee Stadium on April 16. In his first major league at-bat, he stepped into the box with men on first and second, and grounded into a double play. His third time up, he singled, finishing the day 1-for-5. The next day, April 17, was Opening Day at Fenway Park. Tony was batting seventh in the order, facing Joe Horlen of the White Sox. He swung at Horlen's first pitch and hit it over the Green Monster in left field, and even over the net that hung above the Wall. Tony Conigliaro, wearing #25, took his first home run trot. Tony told writers afterward that he always swung at the first good pitch he saw. "I don't like to give the pitcher any kind of edge," he said.

In that same spirit, Conigliaro crowded the plate. And pitchers, quite naturally, tried to brush him back. He was often hit by pitches, and suffered his first injury on May 24 when Moe Drabowsky hit him in the left wrist, causing a hairline fracture. Fortunately, Tony missed only four games.

Back in the lineup, back pounding out homers, Tony hit #20 in the first game of the July 26 doubleheader against Cleveland. In the second game, he got hit for the fifth time in the season, by Pedro Ramos. It broke his arm. This time he missed a month, out until September 4. Conigliaro finished the season with 24 homers and a .290 average.

In 1965, under manager Billy Herman, Tony played in 138 games and hit 32 more homers, enough to lead the league, though his average dipped to .269. During the June free-agent draft, there was more good news in the Conigliaro family: the Red Sox used their first pick to select Tony's younger brother Billy. Tony was struck by another ball on July 28, when a Wes Stock pitch broke his left wrist. It was the third broken bone Tony had suffered in just over 14 months. He simply refused to back off the plate. Orioles executive Frank Lane intimated that Red Sox pitchers could defend Tony a bit better by retaliating.

Suffering no serious injuries in 1966, Tony got in a very full season, seeing action in 150 games. He banged out 28 homers and drove in 93 runs, leading the league in sacrifice flies with seven. His average was .265 and the Boston writers voted him Red Sox MVP. The Red Sox as a team, though, played poorly in those years. In 1966, they were spared the ignominy of last place only because the Yankees played worse. Boston ended the year in ninth place, 26 games behind the first place Orioles, and the Yankees ended in tenth, 26 1/2 games back. In his first three years in the majors, the highest that one of Tony's teams finished was eighth in 1964.

Tony C's brilliant play shone all the more because of the colorless team around him. The local boy made good was a teenage heartthrob and the 6'3" handsome star attracted a lot of attention from local girls, and girls on the road. Assigning older players as roommates to provide a stabilizing presence didn't do the trick. Dick Williams wrote in his autobiography, "I never saw him. Not late at night, not first thing in the morning, never. I was providing veteran influence to a suitcase." In the early part of 1965, Tony Conigliaro the pop star released his first recording.

Billy Conigliaro joined his brother as the two traveled together to spring training in 1967. Tony got hit by a fastball in early workouts and he hurt his back as well. (Billy was sent out for more seasoning; he wouldn't make the big league club until two years later.) Tony got off to a slow start that season, batting well enough but without much power. He didn't hit his third home run until June 11. And he still crowded the plate. Johnny Pesky told author David Cataneo, "He was fearless of the ball. He would just move his head, like Williams did. A ball up and in, Tony would just move his head. He thought the ball would never hit him."

The Red Sox surprised everyone with their play in 1967. Tony contributed as well. One game that stood out was an extra-inning affair at Fenway. Boston was hosting the White Sox and the game was scoreless for 10 full innings. Chicago took a 1-0 lead in the top of the 11th, but Joe Foy singled and Conigliaro hit a two-run homer off John Buzhardt for a walkoff win. The win moved the Red Sox up by percentage points to take third place, just four games out of first, and the next day's *Boston Globe* referred to the "Impossible Dream"

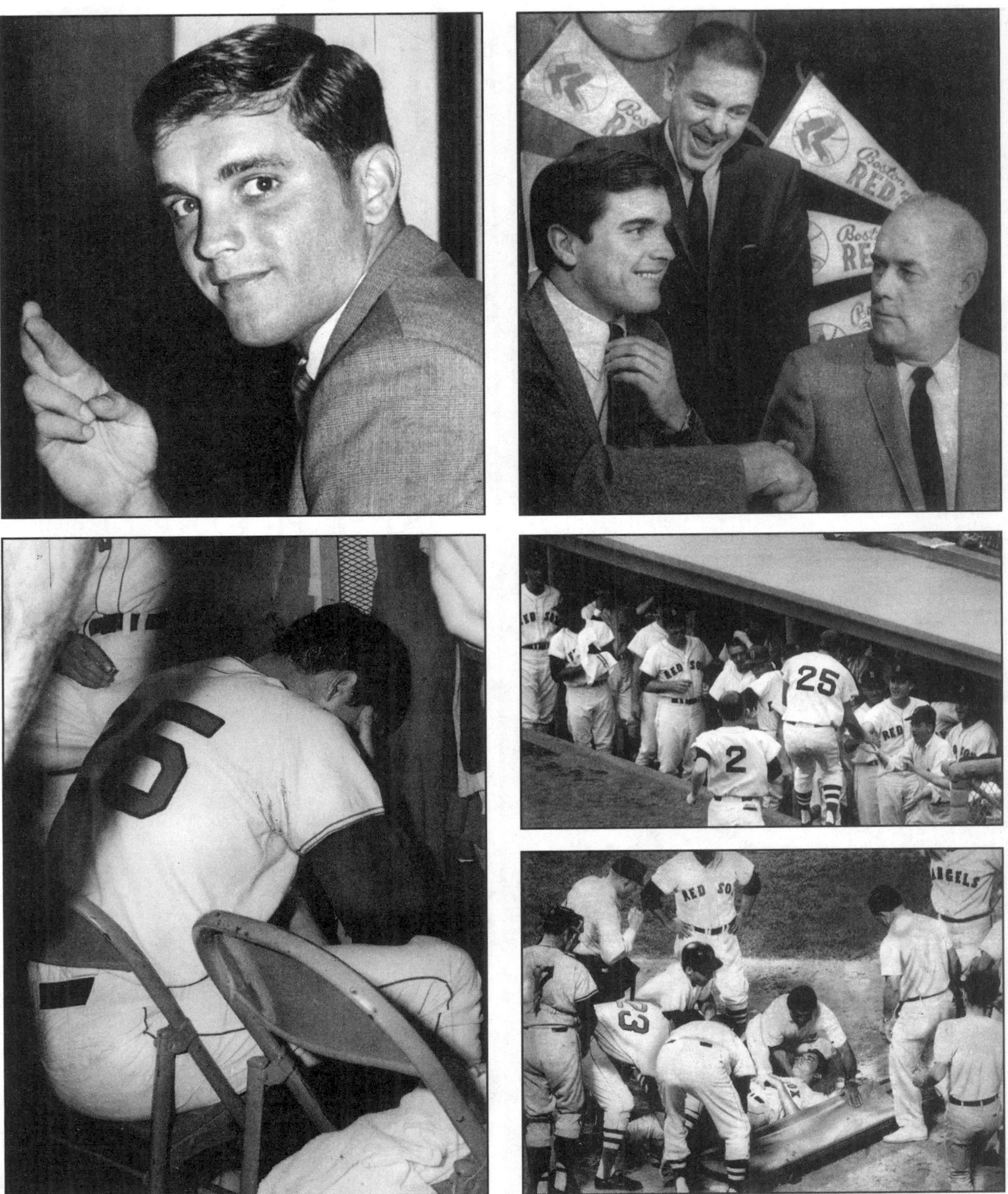

Clockwise from top left: ***Hope:*** *In this April photo, Tony Conigliaro looks forward to the 1967 season.* ***Recognition:*** *Tony signs a new contract January 24, 1967, with Dick Williams and Dick O'Connell.* ***Triumph:*** *Tony enters the jubilant Red Sox dugout after smashing his 14th homer in an 11-5 victory over Baltimore on July 14 that started the 10-game win streak.* ***Tragedy:*** *Teammates gather around the seriously-injured Tony C.* ***Despondency:*** *The morning after the season's final game, the* Record American *ran this photograph with the caption, "Tony Conigliaro, Out With Injury Weeps From Tension at Locker After Yesterday's Big One."*

season the Red Sox team was having for itself.

It was on July 23 that Tony hit the 100th and 101st home runs of his major league career. The Red Sox were just one-half game out of first place. It was a tight race, with the Red Sox hanging just out of first, but never quite making it on top. As late as August 14, the Red Sox were in fifth place—but only three games out.

On the 17th, Tony's partner in the music business, Ed Penney, was visiting his sons at the Ted Williams Baseball Camp in Lakeville, MA. Ted warned Penney, "Tony is crowding the plate. He's much too close. Tell him to back off. It's serious time now. The pitchers are going to get serious." As Penney was leaving the camp later that evening, Williams shouted to Penney, "Tell Tony what I said. Don't forget to tell Tony what I told you." Penney did tell him, before the game the very next night. Tony was in a slump at the time, and told brother Billy he couldn't back off the plate or pitchers wouldn't take him seriously. If anything, he was going to dig in a little closer.

The Red Sox were facing the California Angels the next day—August 18—and Jack Hamilton's fourth-inning fastball came in and struck Tony in the face, just missing his temple but hitting him in the left eye and cheekbone. Tony later wrote that he jerked his head back "so hard that my helmet flipped off just before impact." He never lost consciousness, but as he lay on the ground, David Cataneo wrote, Tony prayed, "God, please, please don't let me die right here in the dirt at home plate at Fenway Park." Tony was fortunate to escape with his life, but his season—and quite possibly his career—was over. Conigliaro had been very badly injured.

The 1967 Red Sox made it to Game Seven of the World Series before the bubble burst. It had nonetheless been a tremendous year for the team, and reignited the passion for the Sox in the city of Boston. Since 1967, tickets for Fenway Park have been hard to come by. Tony, however, felt he'd let the team down. He was down on himself and downplayed his contribution in the drive to the pennant. His teammates were the first to reassure him that they never would have reached the postseason had it not been for his contributions early on. There is little doubt, though, that Conigliaro was missed in the World Series itself. George Scott was unambiguous in his assessment: "I've said it a million times, if Tony had been in the lineup, we would have won. He was one of those guys. Reggie Jackson was a big-game player. Tony was that kind of player."

There was concern he might lose the sight in his left eye. He tried to come back in spring training, but there was just no way. His vision was inadequate, and his doctor told him, "I don't want to be cruel, and there's no way of telling you this in a nice way, but it's not safe for you to play ball anymore." Tony C wouldn't quit, though, and against all odds, his vision slowly began to improve. By late May, he was told he could begin to work out again. Tony also learned new ways to see the ball. When he looked straight at the pitcher, he couldn't see the ball, but he learned to use his peripheral vision to pick up the ball and was able to see well enough by looking a couple of inches to the left. Tony wanted badly to get back into baseball, and he spent a good amount of time in the late summer of 1968 trying to learn to become a pitcher, and started several games in the Winter Instructional League for the Sarasota Red Sox, but he rolled up a record of 0-3, giving up 15 runs in one game, and developed a sore arm as well. He played in the outfield on the days he wasn't pitching and he began to connect for a few solid hits. He gave up the idea of pitching, emboldened to try to come back as a hitter in spring training 1969.

Tony returns with a smile. Opening Day 1969.

Not only did Tony make the team in 1969, but he broke back in with a bang, hitting a two-run homer in the top of the 10th during Opening Day in Baltimore on April 8. The O's re-tied the game, but Tony led off in the 12th and worked a walk, eventually coming home

to score on Dalton Jones' sacrifice fly to right. Tony had the game-winning hit in the fourth inning of the home opener at Fenway Park on April 14, though admittedly it wasn't much of a hit. Tony came up with the bases loaded and wanted to break the game open. Instead, he sent a 15-foot dribbler toward Brooks Robinson at third, and beat it out as Ray Culp scored from third. Tony C was back. It was never easy, and the various books on Conig's struggle document how hard he had to work at what once seemed so effortless, but Tony played in 141 games, hit 20 home runs, and drove in 82 runs. Tony won the Comeback Player of the Year Award. There wasn't any question who would win it.

1970 was Tony's best year at the plate, with a full 36 homers and 116 RBIs. He also scored a career-high 89 runs. Brother Billy had made the Red Sox, too, in 1969, getting himself 80 at-bats and acquitting himself well. Billy became a regular in 1970, appearing in 114 games and batting .271. Add his 18 homers to Tony's 36, and the resulting total of 54 set a record for the most home runs by two brothers on the same major league club. On July 4 and September 19, they homered in the same game.

In October, the Red Sox traded Tony Conigliaro. Stats aside, they knew that Conigliaro was playing on guts and native talent, but may have sensed that his vision was still questionable. His trade value was as high as it would likely ever be. Not even waiting for Baltimore and Cincinnati to finish the World Series, they packaged Conigliaro with Ray Jarvis and Jerry Moses and swapped him to the California Angels for Ken Tatum, Jarvis Tatum, and Doug Griffin. Even years later, Red Sox executives neither explained nor took credit (or responsibility) for the trade. The news stunned the baseball world—and Red Sox fans in particular. As author Herb Crehan wrote in *Red Sox Heroes of Yesteryear*, naming Boston's current mayor, "it was as if Mayor Menino were to trade the *USS Constitution* to Baltimore for the *USS Constellation*." Ken Tatum may have been the key to the trade; the Sox were after a strong reliever and he'd done very well for California.

A family affair. *The Conigliaro family visits Tony at Fenway.*

Tony was crushed, and as Crehan noted, he "never adjusted to life as a California Angel." David Cataneo writes, "Tony C and southern California just didn't happen." Conigliaro batted just .222 in 1971, with only four homers and 15 RBIs just before the All-Star break. Tony had headaches coming back. He wasn't feeling well. Cataneo mentions a string of ailments, from a bad leg to a pinched nerve. He even put himself in traction for an hour before every game. Some of the Angels lost patience with him and began to mock him. Finally, fed up, he packed his bags and left the team after the July 9 game, announcing his retirement. He also told reporters that he simply couldn't see well enough, but took the Red Sox off the hook for having dealt tarnished goods. "My eyesight never came back to normal... I pick up the spin on the ball late, by looking away to the side. I don't know how I do it. I kept it away from the Red Sox... I had a lot of headaches because of the strain to see... my search for that damn baseball."

When he heard the news that Tony had left the Angels, Bill Conigliaro exploded in the Red Sox clubhouse, telling reporters that the reason for the trade to California in the first place had been Carl Yastrzemski, that Yaz had all the influence on the ballclub. "Tony was traded because of one guy—over there," he charged, indicating Yastrzemski. Yaz "got rid of Pesky, Ken Harrelson, and Tony. I know I'm next. Yaz and Reggie [Smith] are being babied, and the club better do something about it."

Billy was part of a major 10-player trade with Milwaukee, but the trade was not made until October. Billy never rejoined the Red Sox—but Tony did. It took a while.

An eye exam Tony underwent after returning to Boston showed that the blind spot in his vision had grown considerably; his vision was deteriorating once more. Tony hadn't given up yet and in October 1973 talked about wanting to mount another comeback with the Angels in 1974. It appears that the Angels wanted him to play for their Salt Lake City affiliate, to see how he worked out, but Tony was past wanting to play for a minor league team and so seems to have stayed on the voluntarily retired list. Late in 1974, he wrote to

the Red Sox asking for another shot at a comeback and GM Dick O'Connell said he could come to spring training, but not at financial cost to the Red Sox. If he was willing to pay his own way, he was welcome to give it a try. The Angels graciously granted him his outright release in November 1974. The Red Sox offered him a contract with the Pawtucket Red Sox, which he signed on March 5, 1975.

Tony took up the challenge, and he had an exceptional spring. On April 4, he got word that he had made the big league team. Opening Day 1975 was four days later, at Fenway Park on April 8, and Tony was the designated hitter, batting cleanup. With two outs and Yaz on first, Tony singled and Yaz took third. The crowd gave Tony C a three-minute standing ovation. Perhaps Milwaukee pitcher Jim Slaton and his batterymate Darrell Porter were a little offguard; the Red Sox scored a run when Tony and Yaz pulled off a double steal.

Tony's first home run came three days later, off Mike Cuellar in Baltimore. With a first-inning single the following day, he drove in another run, but his .200 average after the April 12 game was the highest he posted for the rest of the season. Tony appeared only in 21 games, for 57 at-bats, and was batting just .123 after the game on June 12. He was hampered by a couple of injuries; it just wasn't working out. The Red Sox needed to make room on the 25-man roster for infielder Denny Doyle and they asked Tony to go to Pawtucket. After thinking it over for a week, he agreed to and reported, traveling with the Pawsox, but not getting playing time. Manager Joe Morgan said, "He had lost those real good reflexes," and teammate Buddy Hunter told David Cataneo, "Any guy who threw real hard, he had trouble with." Hunter added, "He was dropping easy fly balls in the outfield." In August, Tony Conigliaro finally called it a day, and retired once again, this time for good. "My body is falling apart," he explained.

Before too long, Tony found work as a broadcaster, first in Providence and then in the San Francisco area. He lost a nice gig in the Bay Area in early 1980, but filled in with other stations. In a life full of setbacks, even the health food store Tony owned in California was lost to mudslides in December 1981.

In early 1982, though, Tony learned that Ken Harrelson was leaving his job as color commentator with Channel 38 in Boston, the Red Sox station. Now there was a job with appeal! He interviewed for the position on the day he turned 37, January 7, 1982. The audition went very well, and he was told he'd gotten the job. Tony had a couple of other stops to make, then planned to return to the Bay Area to pack up his gear for the move back to Boston.

Just two days later, on January 9, 1982, Billy Conigliaro was driving Tony to Logan Airport when Tony suffered a heart attack in the car. Though rushed to the hospital, Tony suffered irreversible brain damage and was hospitalized for two months before being discharged into the care of Billy and the Conigliaro family. He lived another eight years before succumbing at age 45 on February 24, 1990.

Thanks to Wayne McElreavy for considerable assistance with this profile.

Notes:

1. Conigliaro with Zanger, pp. 145, 146. Some contemporary press reports put the figure at $25,000.

Don Demeter

Jonathan Arnold

	G	AB	R	H	2B	3B	HR	RBI	BB	SO	BA	OBP	SLG	SB	CS	GDP	HBP
1967 RED SOX	20	43	7	12	5	0	1	4	3	11	.279	.326	465	0	0	0	0

Tall, rangy, 6'4" Don Demeter played major league baseball for 11 seasons, mostly patrolling the outfield grass, while also spending time at the infield corners. A man of deep abiding faith, he was a member of the Fellowship of Christian Athletes and is currently a pastor in his hometown, Oklahoma City. A very highly regarded player during his career, he is largely a forgotten man now. While a member of the 1967 team for only a few months, he was part of the trade that brought over Gary Bell, a key member of the Impossible Dream.

Donald Lee Demeter was born on June 25, 1935, in Oklahoma City, Oklahoma. Don's father was a painting contractor and his mother a housewife. When he was about 10, the family moved to Denver. A little over a year later, his parents broke up and he was sent to live with his grandparents back in Oklahoma City. His mother then married a man from Keene, New Hampshire and Don spent a winter there but soon returned to Oklahoma City where he went on through high school. During his high school years, he lived with a foster family, who instilled in him the faith that carries him to this day. His foster father, George Stevens, was a Sunday School superintendent and chairman of the deacons at a local Baptist church. "I saw their family life," Don recalls, "That's what I wanted for my family. He was a real witness and testimony for me."

Don had an older brother, who became a dentist, as well as both an older and a younger sister. His own interest in baseball began around fifth grade—the first time school had offered organized ball teams. "I was always able to run faster than most of the kids. All the kids had an interest in baseball. There wasn't any television to watch. That's just what we did—we went from baseball to basketball to football." Baseball was his best sport, and from an early age he knew that was what he wanted to do. "It never dawned on me that I wouldn't play in the major leagues. If I'd known the odds...."

That self-confidence served him well. He had an uncle, Leland Enochs, who was very supportive. His mother's brother worked at a local meatpacking company but enjoyed taking in ballgames and often took Don along, later coming to see him play while he was on the Capitol Hill High School team in Oklahoma City. There was a Double A baseball team in Oklahoma City and Don played Y League ball locally. Team members received passes to see the Texas League pro team play, so Don and uncle Leland hit all the games—seeing visiting teams from cities like Fort Worth, Dallas, and Houston. "I became real interested at that point," he says. "I got to watch a guy play that I roomed with in the major leagues. He played for Fort Worth. Don Hoak." When they were both on the Philadelphia Phillies as roommates, the subject came up. "Don didn't believe me but I showed him some old scrapbooks and, sure enough, I'd gotten his autograph when he was playing for Fort Worth and I was in the kids league."

Don was a center fielder, and he had quite a high school team. The team won the state championship both his junior and senior years. A full 11 boys from the school signed pro contracts—nine of them signed with the Brooklyn Dodgers and two with the Yankees. This was during the era that most major league clubs had extensive farm systems and hundreds of kids in the pipeline. Of the 11 Capitol High players who signed, Don Demeter was the only one to make the major leagues.

It helped that the high school coach, John Pryor, was a birddog scout for the Dodgers, but the man who signed Don was Bert Wells. Ironically, Don was the only boy on the starting high school team who didn't make Oklahoma City's All-City team. "Everyone but the center fielder," he laughs.

Bert Wells of the Brooklyn Dodgers signed him in 1953 for an $800 bonus, and Don began his professional baseball career at the Class D Sooner State League, playing for the Shawnee Hawks. A mediocre batting average of .223 did not hold the center fielder back, as he moved up to the Class C Bakersfield Indians in 1954, where he had an excellent season, hitting .267 and swatting 26 home runs.

Demeter continued his quick ascension through the deep Dodgers system. In 1955, a strong two months for Pueblo, Texas, of the Class A Western League (.262 in 39 games) earned a promotion to Double A Mobile of the Southern Association, where he clubbed 11 home runs and hit .251 over the second half of the season. Don also played winter ball in Venezuela for two

years, following both the 1954 and 1955 seasons. He remembers it as good competition and a privilege to be selected, offering a chance to advance in the Dodgers organization.

In 1956, he was at Fort Worth (Texas League), where his 41 home runs, 128 RBIs, and .287 average proved his was ready for the final step. Don was 21 when the Dodgers called him up to the big leagues that September.

Demeter made his major league debut for the Dodgers at Ebbets Field on September 18, 1956. He struck out in a pinch-hit appearance that day. "I didn't even take a swing. The next night I got to pinch hit again and the first swing I took, I hit a home run. They put me in the Ebbets Hall of Fame because I have a .500 average in Ebbets Field. I had an at-bat in Pittsburgh. I think I grounded out." Don finished the season going one for three. The Brooklyn Dodgers went on to capture their second consecutive National League crown.

He was re-introduced to a former high school classmate, Betty Madole, that summer of 1956, and married her a few months later. They were to have two boys, Russ, born in 1959 and Todd, born in 1962, and a daughter Jill, born during the family's stay in Boston.

He spent the entire 1957 season playing for the St. Paul Saints of the American Association, where he hit 28 home runs and sported a solid .309 batting average. It was then that Don's father first saw him play baseball, when St. Paul paid a visit to Denver.

Don was one of 13 players who were to have been called up by the Dodgers after the minor league playoffs were over, but when St. Paul was eliminated on September 21, Brooklyn had just five games to play. Demeter never appeared on the parent club during the 1957 season. "I just wasn't ready," he says. He also fit in a stint in the Army between seasons.

In the off-season, his Dodgers relocated from Brooklyn to Los Angeles. Demeter was a "highly regarded power-hitting outfielder" in the spring of 1958, and began play for the new Los Angeles Dodgers after his Army hitch, on April 24, getting his first major league start a week later on May 1 against the Pirates. He also got involved in team functions, like helping out at the Los Angeles Food Brokers Club luncheon and at various youth clinics sponsored by the team. Don remembers the move: "The guys who had been in Brooklyn—Duke Snider and Carl Erskine and Clem Labine and those guys—really, really hated to move. It was their home away from home, I guess. But they acclimated. They treated us really nice in L.A. People out there welcomed us so much."

However, he was sent back to St. Paul on May 13, just before the Dodgers' first transcontinental trip, so he could get more work in the outfield. He continued to display his versatility by playing left and center field, as well as a little first and third base. He was batting .283 with 14 home runs and 48 RBIs when he was recalled to Los Angeles for good on July 30, 1958, as both Carl Furillo and Duke Snider were ailing. Said his manager, the legendary Walter Alston, of the promising youngster, "Don can give you the long ball and he can also pull pretty good. As for his outfield play, there's nothing I could fault him on. He can play all three spots out there." He made his re-appearance on August 5 against the Cardinals, and played regularly for the Dodgers the rest of the year, although he struggled at the plate, hitting only .189, with five home runs.

Demeter really started getting noticed in 1959, when the press began calling him "Dangerous" and "Dazzling" Don Demeter, as well as "Big D." This was especially true after he smacked three two-run home runs, including an inside-the-park home run, in a single game, on April 21, to help beat the Giants 9-7. One Los Angeles paper even had a contest to give him a nickname. The winning name? "Spee-Demeter." He led the Dodgers in RBIs through July, although his inconsistency led to spotty playing time as the year wore on. He did finish the year with a very respectable .256 batting average, 18 home runs, and 70 RBIs.

He helped the Dodgers win the National League pennant that year, when they beat the Milwaukee Braves in a two-game playoff. He started the first game of the playoffs, going one for four, and appeared as a pinch hitter in the second game. The Dodgers went on to capture the World Series title against the Chicago White Sox, with Demeter appearing in all six games, starting three, and going 3-for-12 (.250), while scoring two runs. He later called this his greatest thrill in baseball.

The winter of 1959 had Demeter prominently mentioned in trade talks, especially with Calvin Griffith of the Minnesota Twins. One report had Griffith backing off from a deal when it was rumored that Demeter was going to quit baseball and join the ministry. As it was, Demeter began the 1960 season with the Dodgers, but he fractured his wrist in a collision with Maury Wills on July 3, effectively ending his season. Originally thought to be only a sprain, as early X-rays failed to disclose the fracture, he wasn't called out for the season until the end of August as the injury took longer to heal than expected. He hit .274, with 9 home runs in 168 at-bats for the year.

He also became an excellent golfer, even playing one-handed while his wrist was injured in 1960.

Demeter was once again a central figure in trade rumors over the winter, with the Milwaukee Braves, along with the Detroit Tigers and New York Yankees, mentioned as possible landing spots. He opened the 1961 campaign still a Dodger, with high hopes for a successful and healthy season. After struggling at the plate, the Dodgers finally traded him along with third baseman Charley Smith to the Phillies for hard throwing reliever Dick "Turk" Farrell and light-hitting infielder Joe Koppe. One columnist said the Dodgers had "shucked him off as an inadequate third baseman." He was hitting only .172 at the time, with one home run, but he rebounded nicely once with the Phillies, finishing the year at .251 and smacking 20 more home runs. He had the second three-homer game of his career, when he cracked solo, two- and three-run jobs on September 12, driving in a total of seven runs, as the Phillies beat his old team, the Dodgers, and future Hall of Famer Sandy Koufax, 19-10.

He went on to have his finest season as a professional for the 1962 Phillies, hitting .307, with 29 home runs, and knocking in 107 runs while scoring 85. He finished 12th in the MVP voting that year, leading the NL in sacrifice flies, and ranking sixth with a slugging percentage of .520.

He also began an errorless game streak as an outfielder of 266 games in September of 1962. He wasn't to make another error until July 1965, and it ended in a bizarre fashion during a game in Kansas City. These were the years when owner Charlie Finley kept some mules at the ballpark. Another Finley gimmick was to have some trained dogs on the ground crew. In the fifth inning, they would run out onto the field with a base in their mouth and the crew would change the bases. "I have a line drive hit to me and I scooped it up and I guess the ground crew thought it was the last out and sent the dog on the field. I scooped the ball up and threw it to Dick McAuliffe at shortstop. The dog just shot out there and the ball went through his legs at the same time the dog went through there." The runner advanced a base, and the scorer couldn't charge the dog with the error so it was assigned to Demeter. He is gracious about it today: "I know in my own mind there were probably some balls on which I should have been given an error but they didn't." He had completed a total of 449 error-free chances. His string of error-free games by an outfielder stood as the major league outfielder record until the Giants' Darren Lewis broke it in 1993.

Always a team player, Demeter said he didn't pay attention to his batting average, preferring to emphasize his RBI totals. "That's the important one as far as I'm concerned. Ask anyone. Runs win ball games." He did most of his damage in 1962 while playing third base, stepping in when third baseman Andy Carey refused to play for the Phillies. He played 105 games at third, 63 in the outfield, and even one game at first base. His manager, Gene Mauch, went out of his way to praise Demeter's work ethic, saying "... he grinds it out every day, with the best disposition in the world. And now he's established himself in three positions—a greater value to himself and any team."

He traveled to Japan with Bobby Richardson in February of 1963 to spread the gospel, which he called one of the great spiritual experiences of his life. Demeter went on to have another solid season for the fourth-place Phillies in 1963, with a career high of 154 games. Once again, he played the outfield and both corner infield positions. His batting average was just .258, but he cracked 22 home runs and drove in 83 runs.

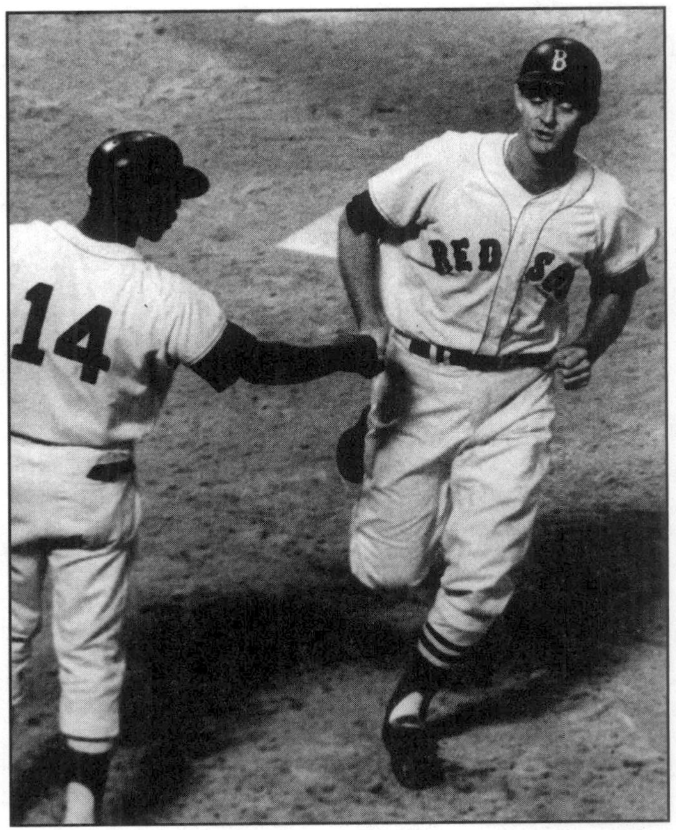

June 20, 1966. Don Demeter touches home plate after hitting a home run in his first game with the Red Sox.

After being prominently mentioned in trade talks with teams like the Chicago White Sox, on December 5, 1963, the Phillies traded him to Detroit along with Jack Hamilton (who later earned the undying enmity of all Red Sox fans when he beaned Tony Conigliaro during the 1967 season) for pitcher Jim Bunning and journeyman catcher Gus Triandos. Chuck Dressen, the Tigers manager, was pleased to get the more "consistent" Demeter to replace Rocky Colavito, who had been traded to Kansas City the previous month. "Don is a better all-around player than Colavito. He is a better runner and a better fielder."

Dressen went on with more praise for Demeter. "We simply had to get a top-flight outfielder. Actually, there were only two outfielders we considered. The other was Felipe Alou. I consider him [Demeter] one of the best outfielders in the game today." Bunning went on to win 74 games for the Phillies in the next four years, as well as pitching a perfect game (caught by Triandos).

Demeter had a tough time his first year in Detroit, as his playing time was sporadic. Shirley Povich of the *Washington Post* chided the Tigers on the trade after Bunning pitched his masterpiece, saying Demeter "has been a bench-warmer much of the season." Sid Ziff of the *Los Angeles Times* called Demeter a "washout and spends much of his time on the Detroit bench." His manager continued to support him, though, saying in July after a big series against the Angels "...I'll be surprised if he doesn't have a big year now." You could even buy a Don Demeter Rawlings baseball glove, on sale for $18.60. He ended up with very similar numbers to his 1963 campaign—.256 average, 22 home runs, and 80 RBIs, although his at-bats fell from 515 to 441 due to a series of nagging injuries.

Demeter continued to wear his faith proudly as a member of the "Fellowship of Christian Athletes." No less a luminary than Jim Murray of the *Los Angeles Times* wrote an article on Don's calm attitude and religious convictions. Fans would send him Bibles, which he would autograph with a proverb.

Going into the 1965 season, the Tigers showed renewed confidence in their centerfielder. "Demeter's hitting looked better than it did in the box score," said interim manager Bob Swift, serving due to Charlie Dressen's heart attack, "because he drove in the tying or go-ahead run in 28 games. He'll be getting a second-year look at American League pitching... and we still like the Demeter-for-Bunning trade." Dressen, the recovering manager, said, "What we need is to get good performances ... out of Don Demeter, who was hurt a lot."

He started the campaign strong, hitting .300 after the first couple of weeks. A highlight of the season came on August 12, when he drove in seven runs on a single, triple and grand slam in an 11-1 thrashing of the Kansas City Athletics. He finished the year hitting .278, but once again declined in at-bats, with only 389, home runs (16) and RBIs (58), splitting time between the outfield (82 games, at all three positions mostly in center and right field) and first base (34 games), as the Tigers finished fourth, 13 games behind the league leading Minnesota Twins.

Demeter began the 1966 season as a fourth outfielder and utilityman, as the Tigers had a logjam in the outfield, with Willie Horton, Mickey Stanley, and Al Kaline envisioned as the starting trio, and Norm Cash holding down first base. He played sporadically, appearing in only 32 games, batting a mere .212 for the Tigers, before being traded to the Red Sox on June 14. He accompanied minor league reliever Julio Navarro to Boston, as the Tigers got pitcher Earl Wilson and minor leaguer Joe Christopher. Haywood Sullivan was glad to get the versatile Demeter, "Although we regret giving up Earl Wilson, we think we have obtained a great outfielder in Demeter who has always hit well at Fenway Park." Manager Billy Herman echoed Sullivan's praise when he said, "This gives us a solid outfield. In Demeter, we have a right-handed hitter who can hit the wall in our ballpark."

However, once again, the trade would prove to be a lopsided one, as Wilson went on to star for the Tigers. One scribe went so far as to describe the trade as "the best deal Detroit has made since it got rid of the Edsel." Wilson even hit a grand slam against his former teammates on August 13, 1966, leading the Tigers to 13-1 victory. The trade was linked with Billy Herman's eventual firing as the Red Sox manager late in the season, as Wilson went on to go 18-11 (13-6 as a Tigers hurler) for the season while Demeter played only part time.

Demeter played mostly center field for the Red Sox in 1966, hitting .292 with 9 home runs in 73 games for them. His final statistics for the year were down once again, with only 14 home runs, 41 RBIs, and a .268 batting average. The Red Sox staggered to a ninth-place finish, a half-game ahead of the Yankees, but a whopping 26 games behind the eventual World Champion Baltimore Orioles. He ended the season by undergoing tests for a back ailment, which had contributed to his limited playing time.

Demeter was expected to compete with rookie Reggie Smith (called "the best looking rookie to come since Mickey Mantle") and José Tartabull for playing time in center field in the spring of 1967. He played all

three outfield positions, as well as one game at third for the team before being traded on June 4 with Tony Horton to Cleveland for pitcher Gary Bell, who went on to be an important hurler for the pennant winning Red Sox. His most memorable hit for the Impossible Dream team came on May 14 as his was the 28th extra base hit on the day, breaking a 62-year-old AL record for most extra base hits, combined, while the Red Sox swept the Tigers in a doubleheader, 8-5 and 13-9. He was hitting .279 for the Red Sox at the time of the trade, with only one home run and four RBIs.

"I enjoyed playing in Boston. Mr. Yawkey had the club at the time. He was very much a players' owner. Those were enjoyable times for us." Naturally, looking back, there is some disappointment that he wasn't there for the pennant run—but he believes there would probably not have been a pennant run if he'd stayed. "I tell Gary Bell this a lot when I see him at golf tournaments. Had they not traded me and got Gary, I don't think they would have won. Gary won 12 games for them. That's exactly the truth. He helped them far more than I would have." Don adds, "He always shows me his World Series ring and tells me it's mine."

For Cleveland, Demeter continued to play all three outfield positions, as well as one game at third base. But he hit only .207 for the Tribe, with five home runs and 12 RBIs. Two of the homers came in the same game, in a 5-3 loss to the New York Yankees. It would prove to be his final season in the majors, as nagging injuries and a suspect heart led to his retirement the next spring. In his last start, on August 27, he had two hits, including a single in his final at-bat. His last plate appearance in the major leagues came the next day, when he was hit by a pitch as a pinch hitter. He was sold to Detroit on August 31 but the sale was later canceled when a physical uncovered a heart problem, called "a disturbance of the athlete's coronary artery circulation," causing him to sit out the rest of the season. It was really an irregular heartbeat, and after he had returned home, Demeter received a better diagnosis. "It turned out it was just a dietary thing. I just needed to learn to eat right. I've had no problems since then. When I went to Cleveland, though, I knew I was just about finished although I was only 31 years of age. I couldn't get to balls that I used to get to. And I don't think I had the desire. Our kids were just about the age where you had to take them out of school and put them in another school, and I wanted stability for them at home. I had thought that if I could play five years in the major leagues, that would be wonderful, and it turned out that I played twice that much."

When he returned home and received the reassuring diagnosis, Detroit indicated they wanted to "buy me back", as Don puts it, but he decided it was time to call it a career.

After his baseball career ended, Don went on to become an insurance agent, as well as founding a swimming pool installation company which his son Russ now runs. He appeared in old-timers games for the Dodgers, while continuing to be very involved with his church, where he became pastor. He was named the president of the minor league Oklahoma City 89ers baseball team in November 1973, though that didn't work out too well; the owner really knew little about running a baseball team. Demeter had an unsuccessful run for the state legislature as a Republican candidate in 1976. In 1999, he was inducted into the Brooklyn Dodgers Hall of Fame.

His youngest son, Todd, was a highly sought-after high school first baseman, and was drafted by the New York Yankees in the second round. He set a bonus record, signing for $208,000 in 1979, as he threatened to go to college. That record stood until 1988. Unfortunately, Todd was stuck in the minors, and never appeared in the major leagues. He went to work in his father's pool installation business until Hodgkin's Disease tragically struck him down in 1996. The Demeters' daughter Jill has four children, two girls and two boys. The boys are currently playing high school baseball and Don deems them very good athletes.

Don still does some swimming pool sales for his son, but primarily devotes his life to the church. He pastors a small Southern Baptist church in Oklahoma City, the Grace Community Baptist Church, which he helped form a few years ago. Former Yankees pitcher Tom Sturdivant is a member of the church community, and a number of the boys he played high school ball with come to the church as well.

Today, many major league ballplayers hold chapel on Sunday morning. This is a change, Don notes: "When I was playing, there wasn't really much of that. There was a handful of guys—Bobby Richardson and myself, Dave Wickersham, Dalton Jones, Al Worthington, Albie Pearson—but it wasn't organized like it is now." Don has spoken at chapel in Kansas City and in Arlington, Texas. He enjoys keeping in touch.

Joe Foy

by Ray Birch

	G	AB	R	H	2B	3B	HR	RBI	BB	SO	BA	OBP	SLG	SB	CS	GDP	HBP
1967 RED SOX	130	446	70	112	22	4	16	49	46	87	.251	.325	.426	8	6	14	3

Joe Foy came to the Red Sox organization with an abundance of promise. He showed flashes of brilliance in the minors and during the 1967 pennant-winning season, but Foy's weaknesses, both on and off the field, kept him from being the player he was capable of becoming. Foy was eventually able to overcome some of his personal problems, but tragically died of a heart attack at age 46. Despite his failings, Foy remains a name that will be always be associated in a special way with the miracle 1967 Boston Red Sox, the team that revitalized baseball in Boston.

Joseph Anthony Foy was born on February 21, 1943 in New York City. Ironically, for a future Red Sox player, his home was only seven blocks from Yankee Stadium, although he professed to be a Dodgers fan in his youth.[1] Foy honed his baseball skills by playing stickball in his neighborhood, and from his earliest days in Little League, sandlot, and at Evander Childs High School in The Bronx, Foy, nicknamed Joey, showed versatility, playing first base, shortstop, and catching; eventually, though, Foy was moved to third base.

Upon graduating from high school in 1960, Foy was not selected by any major league team despite attending tryout camps held by St. Louis, Pittsburgh, and Philadelphia. He was selected to play in the Hearst Journal-American All-Star baseball tournament in New York in 1961. In a 1966 article in the *New York Times*, Foy remarked that "one scout told me to go to school; another said wait till next year; the others said nothing." The primary weakness noted by scouts was that he was too "roly-poly" at 5'9" and 200 pounds. This foreshadowed the weight problem that plagued him throughout his major league career.[2]

Eventually, Foy was signed by the Minnesota Twins, for "a very small bonus" in 1962, after a successful season with an amateur team in The Bronx, the New York Billikens. He was first assigned to Erie of the New York-Penn League. After an early attempt to convert him to catcher—he felt he "was a retriever, not a receiver"—he was moved to first base. After he hit .285 in 113 games in 1962, the Boston Red Sox selected him for $8,000 in the minor league draft on November 26. Foy went to spring training with Reading of the Eastern League, again as a catcher, but at the start of the season was a first baseman with Wellsville in the New York-Penn League. After a month of hitting .350, he spent the bulk of the season at Winston-Salem of the Carolina League, playing mostly shortstop, and hit .259. Following the 1963 season, Foy played in the Florida Instructional League on a combined team of the Boston Red Sox and the then Houston Colt .45s.

Foy began the 1964 season with the Seattle Rainiers of the Pacific Coast League, but on May 30 was sent to Reading of the Eastern League, after hitting only .225 in 14 games. At Reading, he firmly established himself as a third baseman. Foy was selected for the Eastern League All-Star team, along with future Red Sox teammate Mike Andrews, in part because of the .292 batting average Foy posted. Following the 1964 season, Foy again played for the Red Sox team in the Florida

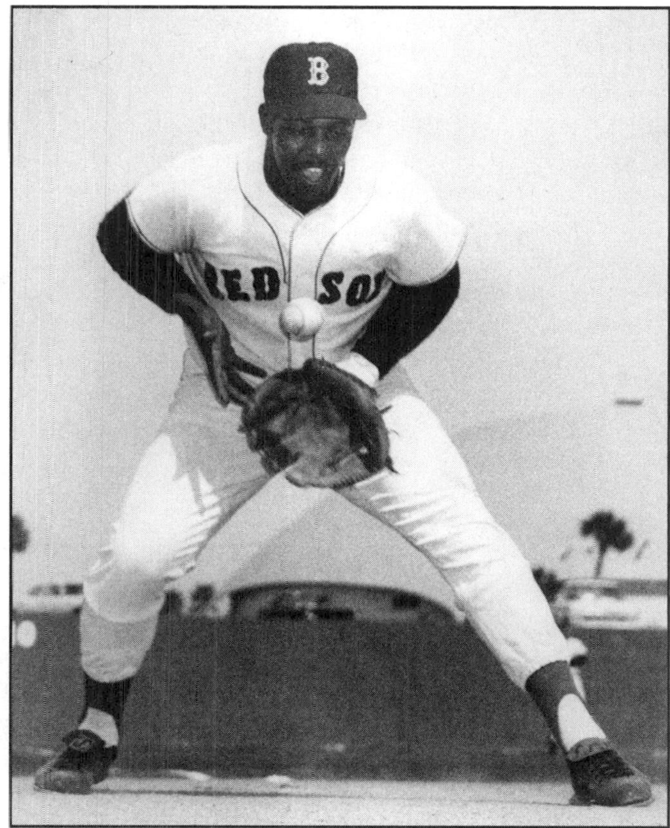

Ready for a hop. *On July 15, Foy was 3-for-4 at the plate with a triple, and started a first-inning 5-4-3 triple play on Paul Blair's liner to third.*

Instructional League, again primarily at shortstop.

His play earned him a spot on the Red Sox triple-A team, the Toronto Maple Leafs, to begin the 1965 season. After a slow start, Foy's batting average had improved by June to near .300. He was hitting for power and showing improvement in the field, and also displayed a knack for stealing bases. A hot streak of 23 hits in 43 at-bats helped to earn him a spot on the International League All-Star team. This improvement was noticed by Toronto manager Dick Williams and, more importantly, Red Sox skipper Billy Herman, who noted that both Foy and Toronto shortstop Mike Andrews were strong candidates to be infielders in Boston for the 1966 season.

At season's end, Foy was named the Minor League Player of the Year by *The Sporting News*, won the International League batting title, was chosen to the International League All-Star team as a third baseman, and was named the league's rookie of the year and Most Valuable Player. His main problem area, however, was in his fielding, where he made 26 errors, the most for third basemen in the league, mainly as a result of poor throws.[3]

On November 6, the Red Sox acquired Foy from Toronto; in the words of Manager Billy Herman, "he's our man at third." The prevailing feeling was that, as long as Foy did not try to pull everything as a hitter, given the short left-field fence at Fenway Park, he would become a good major league hitter.

Mike Andrews remembered Foy with fondness, from way back. "I remember Joe was a catcher then. We were together all the way up to 1965 in Toronto, the Red Sox Triple A team, when Joe won MVP of the league and was so great." He was, Andrews said, "the first black person I was ever close to, and soon he was my best friend. Joe Foy was more than baseball... He was so very special... you won't find anybody who doesn't feel strongly about Joe Foy the person." Andrews recognized the additional hurdles Foy had to overcome: "He had to rise above the racial problems, he and Reggie Smith and George Scott, when we were in the low minors. Those guys went through hell in spring training. You just can't overestimate what those guys went through. We'd be in a little town in Florida, and when we'd be done for the day, we'd have to drive to the other side of town and leave them off at one of those houses sitting on blocks." If an issue arose in the clubhouse, Foy could frequently help, Andrews offered: "If ever there were a black-white problem that needed to be solved, Joe was the bridge."[4]

In spring training 1966, Foy was installed as the

Foy receives The Sporting News 1965 Minor League Player of the Year trophy from Don Gillis of WHDH-TV.

regular third baseman, with Dalton Jones, who had been given a chance to audition for the job in 1965, as the backup. The long-time third baseman of the Red Sox, Frank Malzone, had been released following the 1965 season, so the job was Foy's to lose. To keep Foy focused during the preseason, coaches such as Eddie Popowski pointed out that Foy's many minor league awards were in the past, and fellow minor leaguer George Scott, the MVP of the Eastern League at third base in 1965, was in hot pursuit of his job, should Foy slump. Eventually, Scott was switched to first base, while fellow-rookie Foy batted .262 with 15 home runs and 63 RBIs in 554 at-bats, while playing mostly at third base with a few games at shortstop. His fielding average, though, was unimpressive at .953 with 21 errors at third base in 139 games. Foy had a great second half in 1966. He hit .213 with four home runs in the first half, then .306 with 11 homers in the second half, while the team played well. He hit second in the order most of the year.

The 1967 Red Sox, led by new manager Dick Williams, saw Foy as the number two hitter in their lineup. Foy's style of hitting was to hit line drives, with the occasional home run swing; he also was good at hitting behind the runner and did not strike out too often. Once the season began, though, Foy got off to his usual slow start, resulting in his occasional benching in favor of Jones and, later, the June 2 acquisition of Jerry Adair. Williams, as was his style, frequently brought up the issue of Foy's weight and also questioned his hustle on the field. Williams felt that Foy's fielding would improve if he lost some weight.

One highlight of the 1967 season was his fine fielding

play which helped preserve pitcher Billy Rohr's no-hit bid in the third game of the season. Joe also hit a two-run homer in the eighth to give Rohr a little breathing room in the 3-0 game. On June 9, despite going 3-for-9 with a home run in the June 8 doubleheader against the White Sox, Joe was benched again. Foy came back quickly, though. Called off the bench to pinch-hit for Jim Lonborg, he hit a fifth-inning homer and added another one later in the game to spark an 8-7 Red Sox win over Washington. There was speculation that manager Dick Williams was benching Foy from time to time as a tool to motivate the young infielder. Williams was also not shy about mentioning Foy's continuing weight problems as a reason for his disappointing performance.

On June 18, prior to a series in The Bronx against the Yankees, Foy spent the night with his parents, and arrived just as a fire broke out in their home. Fortunately, due to Foy's efforts, his parents and the rest of his family were able to get out safely, but Foy lost many mementos and keepsakes that he had earned over the years. On June 20, in the opener of the Yankee series, Foy hit a grand slam, helping the Red Sox to win 7-1. Later in the game, Foy was brushed back, upsetting his teammates on the Boston bench. The next night, after a Tony Conigliaro home run in the first inning, Foy was brushed back in the fourth inning by Yankee pitcher Thad Tillotson. Tillotson's very next pitch hit Joe in the helmet. When the Yankees came to bat in the bottom half of the inning, pitcher Lonborg hit Tillotson, who promptly began yelling at Lonborg. This prompted Foy to scream, "If you want to fight, why not fight me? I'm the guy you hit to start all this trouble." This ignited a major brawl between the two teams. A sidebar to the brawl was that the Sox' Rico Petrocelli and the Yankees' Joe Pepitone—who had grown up together in Brooklyn—were involved in the fight. Petrocelli raised Tillotson over his head, slamming him to the ground. Pepitone later left the game with an injury suffered in the brawl.

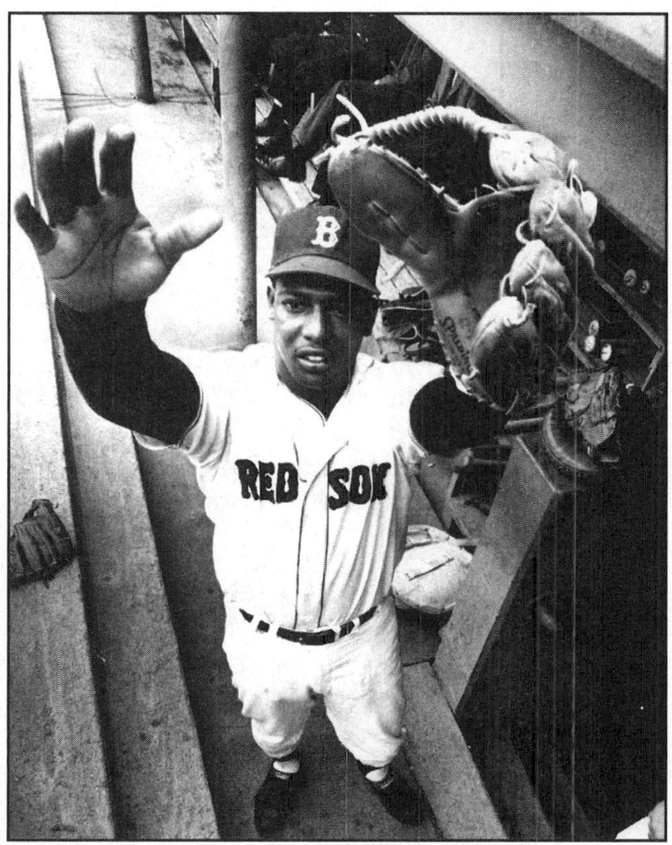

Reaching for the top. *Joe Foy on August 13, with the Sox just 2 ½ games out of first.*

In a game against the Baltimore Orioles on July 15, Foy started a triple play. He showed exceptionally solid play both on offense and defense for an extended seven-week stretch. Foy's easy-going nature around his teammates also helped in the clubhouse.

One of the players closest to Joe was Carl Yastrzemski. Yastrzemski told the *Boston Globe's* Michael Madden, "Joe would be so positive. Mr. Yawkey was the most positive guy who ever lived, but if it was possible, Joe was even more positive. I remember the last six weeks of '67, when we were getting down to the nitty-gritty, and maybe there had been a tough loss or something had happened. Mr. Yawkey would come down and Joe would be so up."[5] After the season, Yaz invited Joe out to his family's home in Bridgehampton, Long Island for several days.

In time, his bat cooled and he was platooned with Adair and Jones for the remainder of the season. In the World Series, Foy started three games and pinch hit in three other games, sitting out Game Two. He ended the Series with a .133 batting average with only a single and a double for his 15 at-bats. At season's end, manager Williams stated that the benchings during the season were because of Foy's poor fielding, but that Foy would be the starting third baseman for the forthcoming 1968 season and that he would have to prove that the job was not his in spring training.

Despite reporting to spring training in much better shape than the year before, the 1968 season was a disappointment for Foy, though, both on and off the field. His poor .225 batting average and 30 errors at third base, the most in the league, was further complicated by an off-field incident with pitcher Juan Pizarro involving drunk driving. According to

The Associated Press, Foy was the driver, Pizarro the passenger, in a car that collided with a taxicab. Boston police charged them both with being drunk. They were both fined $500 for curfew violations and suspended for a doubleheader without pay. This was apparently the last straw for the Red Sox who made Joe available for the expansion draft, which followed the season. Foy was picked high in the draft, selected by the Kansas City Royals as the fourth pick overall. Joe did not leave town quietly, however; he called Williams "a two-faced sneak" who enjoyed hurting people under the guise of making them better ball players.

In a new city for the 1969 season, Foy improved his game, hitting .262 with 11 home runs and, despite his weight issues, stealing 37 bases, while making only 12 errors at third base. The New York Mets needed a third baseman and offered the Royals both Amos Otis and Bob Johnson in a deal consummated on December 3, 1969. This trade has generally been viewed as one of the worst in Mets history, since Foy hit and fielded poorly during the 1970 season, while Otis became a star with the Royals, playing in the 1980 World Series and in three All-Star games. After the 1970 season, Foy was sold to the Mets' Tidewater Triple A team and then was selected, for $25,000, by the Washington Senators from the Mets in the Rule 5 major league draft on November 30, 1970. After only 41 games with the Senators, managed by Ted Williams, Foy was released by the Senators on July 16, 1971. Thus ended his professional baseball career.

Both during and after his pro baseball career, Foy struggled through a number of personal crises involving drugs and alcoholism. While with the Senators, Foy, when questioned about his marijuana use, was quoted as saying, "How many young people in New York do you know who haven't smoked grass?" Fortunately, he proved able to conquer those demons and counseled troubled youths, as well as pursuing a degree at Lehman College in the Bronx.[6] After a heart attack, Joe Foy died on October 12, 1989 at his home in The Bronx.

Looking back at Joe Foy's career, both a word and a phrase come quickly to mind. The word is "enigma," while the phrase is "what might have been." Foy was an enigma because, by all accounts, he was a good clubhouse presence and well-liked by his teammates. However, his conditioning throughout his career was poor, and incidents such as the 1968 drunk driving one made one question his dedication to the game. What "might have been" is even more interesting since he arrived in the major leagues in 1966 as a bonafide prospect, garnering multiple awards in the minors. His ability to get to balls in the infield, along with his good baserunning, complemented his more than adequate bat. But his relationship with Dick Williams soured somewhere between Toronto and Boston, and one is left to wonder if whether under a different manager, Foy's talents would have been better realized at the major league level. Foy's choice of friends outside the baseball arena may have also taken a toll on his personal life. Despite a disappointing major league career, though, Joe Foy will always hold a special place in the minds and hearts of Red Sox Nation for his accomplishments during the 1967 season.

Notes:

1. MacCarl, Neil, "Foy Cancels Early Flubs—Leafs Find He's Flash at Third" *The Sporting News*, May 29, 1965.
2. Millegan, Lloyd, "Stickballer Ready for Bigger Game" *New York Times*, February 26, 1966.
3. MacCarl, Neil, "Strong Man Foy: Durable Maple Leaf Mauler" *The Sporting News*, December 4, 1965.
4. Madden, Michael, "Fond Farewell to Foy," *Boston Globe*, October 13, 1989.
5. *Ibidem.*
6. Boswell, Thomas, "Opening Day: A Fading Memory" *Washington Post*, April 4, 1979.

Russ Gibson

by Tom Harkins

	G	AB	R	H	2B	3B	HR	RBI	BB	SO	BA	OBP	SLG	SB	CS	GDP	HBP
1967 RED SOX	49	138	8	28	7	0	1	15	12	31	.203	.263	.275	0	0	7	0

For baseball fans in New England, the 1967 season is known as the "Impossible Dream," and for Russ Gibson it was doubly a dream fulfilled. After toiling in the minors for ten years, 1967 was the year he achieved his dream of playing for the Boston Red Sox, his hometown team. Baseball writers of the time would refer to Gibson's long minor league career so often that one would think "10-year minor leaguer" or "28-year-old rookie" were part of his name.

Born May 6, 1939 in nearby Fall River, Massachusetts, Russ grew up a Red Sox fan (he was briefly a Boston Braves fan, but they left for Milwaukee when Russ was 13 years old). His family was of working class English-Irish stock. His father was a factory foreman for a jewelry manufacturer and his mother was a factory worker for an office supply company. Russ was the middle child of three brothers. Brother Jim was four years older and went on to a long career with IBM. His brother Paul, four years younger, attended MIT and is now a professor at nearby University of Massachusetts at Dartmouth.

At Fall River's Durfee High School, Russ was a three sport all-star, as quarterback and co-captain of the football team, a starting guard for three years in basketball (winning the New England Championship as a junior), and, of course, he was all-everything in baseball.

He was offered a baseball scholarship to Rollins College in Florida, and football scholarships to Boston University, Boston College, and Holy Cross as a punter, but soon after graduating from high school in June of 1957, the 18-year-old chose baseball as the most likely way to a professional career. The football offers were aided by his three sport Durfee coach, Luke Urban, who after an all-American career at Boston College played briefly in the NFL as well as catching for the Boston Braves in the late 1920s.

It was while in high school that Russ had his first experience with professional sports. In his freshman year Russ entered a polio fundraiser sponsored by the Boston Celtics where for a quarter one could take 25 foul shots. Russ made 23 of 25 and won the first prize, a road trip with the Celtics. He thoroughly enjoyed his trip to Madison Square Garden sitting on the bench with Bill Sharman and Bob Cousy.

Gibson's talents were brought to the attention of the Red Sox by Jumping Joe Dugan, a local "bird dog" of considerable baseball fame, a 14-year major league veteran. Dugan told farm director Neil Mahoney about Gibson's potential, and Mahoney eventually signed Gibson to a contract.

The Red Sox were not the only team interested in Gibson. The New York Giants checked Russ out when he visited the Polo Grounds as a Hearst All-Star. The annual tournament for high school seniors was run by Giants legend Carl Hubbell, and used by the Giants as a tryout camp. While Russ was in New York, his father summoned his son home because the Red Sox were preparing to make an offer. Due to the restrictive signing bonus rules of the times, Boston was not going to sign him to a bonus. That would require them to keep him on the roster and leave him sitting on the bench far too much. The Red Sox chose instead to sweeten the signing by offering to buy his parents a new car—a particularly tempting offer because the Gibson family car had died on the way to the contract discussions. To avoid invoking the bonus rule, the Red Sox instructed Russ's father to pick out a car and let the team know how much it would cost; soon his father received a check for the full amount drawn on the Yawkey Construction Company.

Immediately after signing, the 18-year-old prepared for his first minor league assignment. Before he left, his father arranged for Russ to talk with another Fall River local, Joe Andrews, who had made it as high as Triple A. Andrews was candid in telling Gibson what to expect and what was expected of him.

Right from the start, Gibson learned that both politics and business play a major part in baseball. In his first assignment, for Corning, New York, in the New York-Penn League, he appeared in only two games (he went 4-for-9) before he was summoned from his rooming house and told he was being shipped to Lafayette, Indiana, of the Midwest League. The move to Lafayette allowed him to play more or less regularly and in 41 games he batted a solid .312. His timely hitting produced 26 RBIs with 43 hits. Both the NYP League and Midwest Leagues were Class D, and Gibson's change could be considered a promotion.

The next season, 1958, found Gibson again in the Midwest League, this time for Waterloo, Iowa. He was the everyday catcher (102 games), but he suffered a sophomore slump as his average fell to .254. Two successful seasons in the Midwest League earned him promotion to the Class-B Carolina League, where he would spend the next three seasons. The first two were spent at Raleigh, where he played in over 80 games each year and hit .268 and .299. While at Raleigh he had the opportunity to catch the premier professional offerings of future Red Sox Hall of Famer Dick Radatz. Fresh off the campus of Michigan State, Radatz had a blazing, moving fastball that was nearly unhittable. In his first appearance, he was mowing them down but eventually a couple of batters caught up to him and singled. Gibson thought it was time to give the hitters another look so he signaled for Radatz's curve. After being shaken off a couple of times, Russ went to the mound to personally ask for the curve. Radatz replied that he didn't have a curve, so they stayed with the heater.[1] This "strategy" proved effective as the "Monster" went on to become baseball's best reliever for a few years in the early 1960s. Although Gibson and Radatz never played together in the majors, they remained friends until Dick's death.

After hitting .299 in 1960 and playing well in spring training 1961, Gibson felt he had earned and deserved a promotion, at least to Triple A, but it was not to be. In April he was sent back to the Carolina League, assigned to the new Red Sox affiliate at Winston-Salem. Once again, politics came into play as the front office was "loading" the new franchise to boost attendance in its inaugural season. Gibson's disappointment turned to discouragement and he has admitted that he didn't put forth a strong enough effort when he reported to Winston-Salem. Well into the season, he was just going through the motions and was batting well below .200. It took a visit from Red Sox roving trouble shooter Charlie Wagner to show Gibson that he was only hurting himself. Broadway Charlie encouraged Russ to buck up, and he did.

Playing hard every day, by season's end he had raised his average to a respectable .275, hitting 11 homers and driving in 71 runs in 110 games. This turnaround, coupled with an attitude adjustment, brought about a promotion for 1962, although only to York, Pennsylvania, of the Class-A Eastern League. Although it was not a Triple-A club, Gibson felt that this league was of a very high caliber. He had a good year even though his average dipped to .260. He showed some power with 37 extra-base hits, including a career high 24 doubles.

Russ Gibson helped the Red Sox hold first place with an RBI single and a sacrifice fly driving in two runs in Boston's 4-2 defeat of Detroit, September 20, 1967.

In 1963, after six years in professional baseball, Gibson finally was promoted to Triple A, and he remained at that level for the next four seasons. His first two Triple-A seasons he played for the Seattle Rainiers of the Pacific Coast League. He appeared in just 80 games in 1963, and his average slipped below .250 for the first time (.244). Although he didn't have a great year on the field, off the field he felt he had a very good year. In May he met a pretty young California native who was working as a secretary for the Boeing Corporation and by the next New Year's Eve she had become Virgie Ann Gibson. Married life obviously agreed with Russ, because the next season saw him raise his average to .276, achieving career highs in game played (130), hits (129), and home runs (17).

Gibson's manager at Seattle in 1963 was another Red Sox legend, Mel Parnell, whom he liked a great deal but felt was too nice a guy to be a manager. In 1965, the Red Sox moved their Triple-A affiliation to Toronto, and hired Dick Williams as the manager. Williams was anything but "too nice." Gibson suffered through some

injuries his first year under Williams, and he struggled, hitting only .215. However, he rebounded in 1966 to hit a healthy .292 and make a significant contribution to Toronto's championship season. The latter season, he served as a player/coach and teamed with future fellow Red Sox rookies Mike Andrews and Reggie Smith, and 1967 teammate Jerry Stephenson.

At the end of Toronto's season, Williams asked Gibson to join him for winter ball in Puerto Rico. Russ had played twice in Puerto Rico and enjoyed it; the money was good, too. As it turned out, though, Williams was unable to join him in Puerto Rico because immediately after the Red Sox season ended, the Boston front office tapped him to be the new manager of the Boston team. Even though his former manager was now the big league boss, that hardly guaranteed Gibson a slot for 1967. With Dick Williams one had to work hard to earn a place on the roster.

Still sharp from winter ball, Russ had a fine spring training in Winter Haven. Competing with the two catchers who had shared backstop duties for the '66 Red Sox, Mike Ryan and Bob Tillman, Gibson proved himself worthy of a major league roster spot. He easily outhit Ryan (.261 to .185) and, although Tillman hit an uncharacteristic .344, Gibson's hits were more timely, producing 12 RBIs to Tillman's four. In his last spring appearance, Gibson's three-run homer won the game for the Red Sox, assuring the team a winning Grapefruit League record, a distinction Boston had not achieved in several seasons.

As Russ headed for Boston, his dream had finally come true. After 10 long years in the minors, the Fall

Perseverance was the key to success for Massachusetts native Russ Gibson, who toiled for 10 ½ years in the minor leagues.

River kid was now playing for the Boston Red Sox. As the Red Sox bussed their way to New York for a three-game series, Russ quipped that after riding buses for ten years in the minors, he was now in the majors and still riding a bus. His major league debut will always be remembered because it was also the debut of another rookie, lefty Billy Rohr, who came within one strike of pitching a no-hitter in his first major league game. Suffice it to say that Russ called a great game and handled both his own nervousness and that of his fellow rookie like a seasoned veteran. He was the first to reach Rohr when he was hit by a batted ball and helped persuade Williams to leave the pitcher in.

At the plate Gibson went 2-for-4. He was put out his first two times up against Whitey Ford, before singling off Ford in the sixth and Thad Tillotson in the eighth. He still marvels that the catch Yastrzemski made in the ninth inning to briefly keep Rohr's no-hitter alive is the best catch he ever saw (a sentiment shared by others who saw it). He also asserts to this day that, with Rohr needing just one strike to close the game, the umpire blew the call on a 2-2 pitch to Elston Howard: "It was right down the middle." However, visiting rookies don't get the benefit versus a hometown veteran, so Howard lived to single off Rohr's curve.

For the rest of April, Gibson served as the regular catcher, significantly contributing to the team's 8-6 record, batting .300 with eight RBIs. But with Dick Williams, it was what have you done for me lately, and after a mini-slump (eight hitless at-bats over three games), Gibson was replaced by Bob Tillman. Gibson then developed a hand infection; unable to play, he was optioned to Pittsfield, Massachusetts of the Eastern League on May 10, when the roster had to be reduced to the 25-man limit. The move to Pittsfield was temporary and he played only once to make it official. Returning to Boston, he again shared time with Ryan and Tillman.

One of Gibson's favorite memories of 1967 involved "Russ Gibson Day" on July 30, organized by a number of his Fall River fans and friends. When it was first announced, Russ took some kidding from the veterans; Yaz said he had played for seven years and had won a batting title and had never had a "day" while here was Gibson, a rookie barely hitting .200 and he was getting one. In the days before the scheduled event Gibson had found himself in manager Williams' often-filled doghouse and hadn't been playing. However the night before his "day," Williams approached Gibson and told him not to worry because he was going to start. Gibson shrugged and replied that if anyone should be worried if he didn't start on Sunday it should be Williams himself. Russ didn't disappoint the 45 buses and more than 200 private cars that brought his fans to Fenway. He went 2-for-4 with two doubles, but the Sox lost to the Twins, 7-5.

Soon after the "day," another roster move took Russ back to Pittsfield. During this sojourn he played in 18 games and achieved what he hadn't in his first major league game: catching a no-hitter. The hurler for Pittsfield was Bob Guindon, who had been all-everything as a high school first baseman at Boston English and had signed with the Red Sox for a substantial bonus. An off-season accident to his hand had limited his hitting so he was in Pittsfield attempting to make a comeback as a pitcher. By coincidence, the Gibsons were renting the Guindons' Needham home during the 1967 season.

Gibson was back on the Red Sox roster with the September call-ups. By this time, veteran Elston Howard had been acquired from the Yankees and Bob Tillman had been sold to New York. For most of the September pennant race, Gibson played sparingly, with Howard and Ryan doing most of the catching. In the crucial final weekend series versus the Minnesota Twins, however, Dick Williams looked to the catcher who had helped him win it all the year before in Toronto. Gibson started both games, though he was pinch hit for early in each contest. The Red Sox won each game, and took the pennant on the final day. In his rookie season, Gibson hit .203 in 49 games.

It appeared that Russ might not be eligible for the World Series, because he had not been on the roster just before the September 1 deadline, but the Cardinals allowed the Sox to add him to replace the Army-bound Bill Landis. Against St. Louis, Gibson started Game One and was involved in two crucial plays, both of which he claims involved blown calls by umpires. The first call went his way. In the fifth inning, he took a Yaz throw and tagged out Julian Javier trying to score from second on a single. Russ claims, and Danny Gostigan photos published in the *Globe* the next day bear him out, that although he tagged Javier with his glove he had the ball in his other hand. The other missed call was much more important to the game's outcome. In the seventh inning, Lou Brock attempted a steal of second. Gibson made a perfect throw to Rico Petrocelli, beating Brock to the bag—but the umpire ruled the legendary base stealer safe. Brock eventually scored on Roger Maris's grounder. It turned out to be the margin of victory in the 2-1 game. For the rest of the Series, Williams went with the post-season experienced Howard. Gibson's only other Series appearance was in Game Seven as a late-inning defensive replacement.

Although 1967 will always be remembered as the

high point of his Red Sox career, Gibson played two more years with his hometown team. In 1968, he and Howard shared the catching duties. Mike Ryan had been dealt to the Phillies in the off-season. Neither catcher excelled at the plate in this "year of the pitcher." Howard in his last year batted .241 with five home runs and 18 RBIs, while Gibson raised his average to .225 with three home runs and 20 RBIs.

In 1969, Gibson had his best year statistically. He lifted his batting average to .251, with three homers and 27 RBIs. Appearing in only 85 games, he was backed up behind the plate by rookie Gerry Moses (.304 in 53 games) and Tom Satriano, acquired in midseason.

Even though Gibson was coming off his best year in the majors and had a good spring in 1970, the Eddie Kasko-led Sox chose to go with Moses and Satriano. Gibson credits GM Dick O'Connell with finding him a good place to go: O'Connell called San Francisco Giants owner Horace Stoneham and secured a place for Gibson.

How do we know which came first? Could it be that the manager reduced his playing time because he was hitting .232 or .193? Also Dick Dietz, the Giants regular catcher hit .300 and drove in 107 runs in 1970. He saw limited duty in San Francisco, backing up Dick Dietz. In his three years with the Giants his average dipped with his playing time. In 1970 he appeared in 25 games, hitting .232 in 69 at-bats; in 1971 in 25 games with only 57 at-bats he hit .193 and didn't appear in the Giants playoff loss; and in 1972 he spent most of the year in Triple-A Phoenix, hitting just .167 in five games and only 12 at-bats for the big club. Although he didn't play much, Gibson enjoyed being on the Giants with the likes of Willie Mays, Willie McCovey, and Bobby Bonds and catching future Hall of Famers Juan Marichal and Gaylord Perry. Although offered a contract and invited to spring training by the Giants in 1973, Russ decided to officially retire.

Gibson had played in the major leagues long enough to qualify for a pension. Wisely, he had also prepared himself for life after baseball. Through connections made in San Francisco, he landed a good position with Bank of America on the West Coast which he held for almost 10 years before he returned to the Fall River area. For the next 20 years, Gibson worked for the Massachusetts State Lottery covering the Fall River/New Bedford area.

While working for the Lottery, he was able to return to baseball activity part time. For two years he was head coach of a local junior college nine, Bristol Community College. He also spent some time as a local area scout for the Chicago White Sox, thanks to one of his former Red Sox teammates. Soon after Ken Harrelson was named White Sox general manager, he called Russ to offer him a job in the organization. Not willing to give up his steady Lottery position, he agreed only to accept a part-time scouting job. This was another good decision, as Harrelson's tenure as White Sox GM was brief. Since his scouting days, Gibson's baseball activities included his regular participation in Red Sox fantasy camps organized by his old friend Dick Radatz. Age and health concerns have recently limited his activity to an occasional Jimmy Fund golf tournament.

On the home front, Russ and Virgie Ann Gibson had a most successful marriage for 27 years until her death in 1990. Together they raised two boys, Gregg and Chris, both of whom still live in the area, allowing Russ to enjoy them and his three grandchildren on a regular basis. Gregg attended Worcester Polytechnic Institute, where he joined Air Force ROTC. After flying for the Air Force, he spent some time with United Airlines and is now a corporate pilot. Chris is located even closer, serving as a police officer in the neighboring town of Somerset.

As he approaches his 50th high school reunion and the 40th anniversary of that "Impossible Dream" season, Russ Gibson is able to look back at his life and say he has no regrets.

Notes:

1. Crehan, *Red Sox Heroes of Yesteryear*

Ken "The Hawk" Harrelson

by Alex Edelman

	G	AB	R	H	2B	3B	HR	RBI	BB	SO	BA	OBP	SLG	SB	CS	GDP	HBP
1967 RED SOX	23	80	9	16	4	1	3	14	5	12	.200	.247	.387	1	1	2	0

Kenneth Smith Harrelson was born on September 4, 1941, in Woodruff, South Carolina. In the sixth grade, he moved to Savannah, Georgia, where he and his older sister would grow up. Harrelson was the youngest child of a single mother, Jessie, who was his biggest supporter, closest confidante, and best friend. Jessie worked hard to support her son, and she held a difficult and poor-paying job as a secretary in order to provide for him. Fortunately, Ken had proved at a very young age that he was an extraordinary athlete, and when it came time for him to go to high school, the schools came to him, recruiting the athletic youngster by offering jobs, money, and financial support as incentives. Harrelson chose Benedictine Military School, because it was his mother's first choice. And despite Harrelson's strong aversion to the school's strict military code, he flourished as an athlete and obtained solid jobs through generous alumni. By the time he was 17, Kenneth had matured into a street-smart young man and become the family's primary breadwinner.[1] While he was still in high school, Harrelson met his first wife, Betty Ann Pacifi, whom he would marry that year. Harrelson was an excellent baseball player who hit three home runs in the first Little League game ever played in Savannah, but was by nature a competitor who also played football, basketball, and golf. Ironically, he regarded baseball as his worst sport.

Despite being an excellent baseball player and a Basketball Schoolboy All-American, Harrelson was fondest of football and he accepted a scholarship to play at the University of Georgia. His mother, making no more than $65.00 a week, asked him to reconsider, feeling that baseball would pay better, so her doting son decided instead to play baseball professionally. The two teams offering serious money were the Kansas City Athletics and the Los Angeles Dodgers. Los Angeles promised a larger bonus, but Harrelson signed with the A's because intrepid Kansas City scout Clyde Kluttz was able to convince him that he would reach the majors faster there.[2]

Ken Harrelson and Hawk Harrelson are two very different sides of Kenneth Smith Harrelson, and, in a 2004 article for *The State*, the newspaper in Columbia, South Carolina, Patrick Obely pinpointed the exact moment that the two sides met. It was a Gulf Coast Instructional League game in Florida in 1959, and one of Harrelson's teammates, Dick Howser, had come up with a new name for him. Harrelson's nose, which had been broken several times and had started to take on a distinctly beak-like aspect, was a point of great amusement for Harrelson's teammates and childhood friends. Howser, who thought that Harrelson looked like a character in a popular comic strip, took to calling him "Henrietta Hawk" in a mocking manner.

Aggravating the matter was the fact that Harrelson, one of Kansas City's most touted prospects, "wasn't doing squat as far as hitting goes,"[3] and the usually thick-skinned teenager from Savannah began to take offense to Howser's name calling, dubbing him "Slick" in retaliation. One day, after another especially disappointing effort at the plate for Harrelson, Howser again poked fun at the frustrated rookie, causing the latter to lose his cool. "Hey Slick, why don't you lay off?"

"I'll lay off," Howser retorted, "when you get a hit."

Disgruntled but inspired, Harrelson took the field the next day and hit two homers.

"Okay," said Howser, "I'll drop the Henrietta."[4] The name "Hawk" stuck.

After two more or less average years in the minor leagues in 1959 and 1960, Harrelson started to show promise in 1961, where he hit 25 home runs, with 114 RBIs, and had a .301 average in 135 games. The next year, Harrelson exploded; in a magnificent season with Binghamton, he set Eastern League records with 38 homers and 138 RBIs. In 1963, Harrelson continued to improve, and his solid play with Portland of the Pacific Coast League did not go unnoticed, as the Athletics promoted Harrelson to the majors, where he began to discover his more colorful side. In '64, Harrelson played only 49 games with the Athletics, who finished in tenth place. In 1965, the Hawk would play 150 games and slug 23 homers—though the Athletics would finish tenth again anyway.

Harrelson was a shrewd businessman and colorful hustler who always understood the value of a dollar, and before long he began to realize that the "Hawk" character was a persona that could make him lots of money. Harrelson was right, and as the outfielder began to hit home runs and grow more popular, "The Hawk" began to surface more often. Almost overnight, his flashy

alter-ego made Harrelson a fan favorite throughout the American League. After the 1964 season, Harrelson decided to play winter baseball in Venezuela, and it was there that he really discovered "The Hawk" personality.[5] "The Hawk was a character," says Harrelson's former Venezuelan winter ball teammate Billy Bryan. "He was a hell of a pool shooter and arm-wrestler, and a fun roommate besides."[6]

Harrelson also learned some lessons about relating to fans during his early years in Kansas City. One day, after a tough day at the plate, Harrelson, who was in a hurry to get to a party, rebuffed a bunch of kids requesting his autograph. While he was shoving his way through the overeager youngsters, he felt a firm hand on the back of his neck, pulling him back towards the clubhouse. Harrelson, by now incensed and ready to fight, turned towards the person who the hand belonged to, but felt his anger melt away when he found himself face to face with his mother's favorite player and his own childhood hero, baseball legend Rocky Colavito. Colavito pulled Harrelson aside, and let him have it, telling the rookie on no uncertain turns that he should always take the time to sign autographs for the people who paid his salary. Harrelson never forgot the lesson, and from that point on would treat the fans with respect and courtesy.[7]

Though "The Hawk" would soon make a name for himself on the baseball field, what really would put him on the radar in professional baseball was his prowess on the golf course. In 1964, just a year after his major league debut, Harrelson played in his first golf tournament for major leaguers. After he earned second place behind Albie Pearson, one of baseball's best golfers, many players, managers, and owners began to take notice of the sweet-swinging outfielder.[8] Golfing, besides being The Hawk's passion, would become part of his legacy—the popularization of the batting glove. One day in 1963 after two long rounds of golfing with Athletics teammates Ted Bowsfield, Sammy Esposito and Gino Cimoli,[9] Harrelson developed painful blisters on his hands. Arriving at the ballpark for that night's game, he found it would be easier to grip a bat if he wore the gloves he had used earlier that day to golf. When The Hawk stepped to the plate in the first inning against the New York Yankees, his teammates scoffed, but after Harrelson had a great night at the plate, both the Athletics and the Yankees showed up at the ballpark the next day wearing golf gloves. And thus, the batting glove was born.[10]

Growing up with little money, Harrelson could always sense when there was something to be earned. Raised in a rough-and-tumble area of Savannah, Harrelson chose his battles carefully and cautiously measured his actions. Despite his portrayal as an impulsive individual, the skinny baseball player learned how to maneuver his way out of unavoidable tight spots, using perceptive street smarts, the power of persuasion, and his extensive network of contacts and friends. Harrelson's autobiographical tome, *Hawk*, written with Al Hirshberg in 1969, detail pool hustling, golfing for money, and other episodes in the emergence of the outspoken Hawk persona from small-town Ken Harrelson, who took care of his mama and spoke with a Southern accent.

Not everyone was a fan of the flashy façade, and The Hawk ruffled a few people's feathers. Unfortunately, one such person bothered by the outfielder's flamboyance was Charles O. Finley, who owned the A's. Finley tried over and over to irk The Hawk, and refused him a raise; Harrelson had to call his mother for financial support.[11] In 1966, after 63 games, a series of heated public arguments and angry private exchanges, Harrelson was traded to the Washington Senators. He played there for the remainder of the season and some of the next before he was reluctantly reunited with Finley, who bought him back in the early months of 1967. Harrelson

Ken Harrelson, fashionista, with a couple of admirers.

never saw eye to eye with the eccentric owner, but he liked Kansas City, and thus patiently put up with Finley's shenanigans. Harrelson always cooperated with Finley, even when he was asked to take part in one of the baseball mogul's more infamous pranks—a donkey named Charlie O. that Finley repeatedly forced Harrelson to ride.[12] Finley's antics were usually rash and impulsive, often causing more harm than good, and Harrelson bore them with tolerance. "Charlie had some good ideas and some bad ideas," Harrelson says today, "but overall he was not a nice man."

After Finley suspended pitcher Lew Krausse on August 18, 1967, for what many viewed as a trumped-up offense, Krausse's teammates, led by Jack Aker, Harrelson and a half dozen other players, read a statement criticizing Finley. Manager Alvin Dark revolted, refusing to bench Krausse, instead choosing to voice his support for the pitcher.[13] Finley, not known for level-headed decisions, fired Dark, prompting Harrelson to publicly denounce the owner. On the morning of August 24, the Kansas City papers wrote that Harrelson had called Finley a "menace to baseball." Finley seethed, and all the extra effort The Hawk had employed to try to appease his boss was wasted when he was put on irrevocable waivers on August 25—because of his refusal to attend a press conference to apologize for a statement he says he never made.

Because Harrelson was having an excellent year (he had been hitting .273 at the time of his release), he found himself the subject of one of the first free agent bidding wars in modern baseball history. Among the bidders in the battle for Harrelson were the Boston Red Sox. The Red Sox were in the middle of a pennant race and had started the season with Tony Conigliaro as their right fielder. When Conigliaro, a popular and talented local sports hero, was tragically felled by a fastball on August 18, ending his season and curtailing a very promising career, the Sox began searching for a replacement. General Manager Dick O'Connell saw the release of Harrelson as an opportunity to fill the gap left by Conigliaro. After an intense struggle with several major league teams (and even the Tokyo Giants), O'Connell and the Red Sox finally signed "The Hawk" for $150,000 on August 28—approximately a $138,000 increase in salary.

In many ways, the signing of Hawk Harrelson marked the end of the age where the owner was boss, and the beginning of the era in which players controlled their own destinies. Harrelson was someone the Red Sox desperately needed, and while O'Connell knew it, so did The Hawk. The end result, an incredibly lucrative contract by the standards of the time period, was what Bill Reynolds called "a sneak preview of free agency" in his book *Lost Summer*.

The Red Sox and Hawk Harrelson were a perfect fit, and it was really in Boston that The Hawk took wing: the Red Sox needed a power-hitting right fielder, and Harrelson, who was having a great season, filled the bill perfectly. And not only did Boston love The Hawk, but The Hawk reciprocated that love.

"The Hawk was really a product of the fans of Boston," Harrelson says today, "The Red Sox were a great team, but they didn't have any real personalities up there... after some success, The Hawk evolved, and that is really how it happened. For many reasons, one of them being that, Boston will always have a special place in my heart." To Harrelson, The Hawk wasn't just some false persona to utilize for monetary purposes—though that was a very nice side effect—The Hawk was something that gave Harrelson, someone who always thought of himself as an overachiever, support when he was behind or slumping. He credits the fans with "bringing The Hawk to the forefront," and maintains that he never could have been successful in baseball without The Hawk backing him up.

In 1967, the fans were behind Ken Harrelson—and The Hawk—all the way, and the now-happy outfielder helped the Red Sox take the pennant. Besides being a solid outfielder, he was also a great clubhouse influence who could take the strain of a pennant race off other players, players like Carl Yastrzemski. Especially Carl Yastrzemski. In 1967, Yaz was, as Harrelson wrote in his book, "the greatest ballplayer who ever lived, in fact or fiction. Compared to him [fictional sports hero] Frank Merriwell was a piker." Harrelson provided great help in taking the press load off the media-conscious Yaz. Like every other member of the 1967 team, Harrelson recalls the Red Sox as having a great year, a magical, unbelievable, impossible year. Everyone did their part, even self-proclaimed Johnny-come-latelies like The Hawk. Harrelson did not have a good World Series, and the Red Sox lost in seven games. In the clubhouse immediately after the final game, Harrelson would finally lose his composure, sobbing uncontrollably as the victorious St. Louis Cardinals celebrated just down the hall. Harrelson had not played his best with the Red Sox, hitting just .200 with only 14 RBIs, and though Hawk had knocked out some clutch hits, including a key RBI in their October 1 pennant-clinching game, it was a definite possibility that his poor play would result in a trade.

Despite the rumored trade offers, by the spring of 1968, The Hawk was flying high. Harrelson had

Lonborg and The Hawk relaxing after the fifth game of the World Series. Harrelson drove in the first run in the Sox 3-1 win.

established himself as one of the baseball's best golfers, winning a number of golf tournaments in the off-season.[14] But soon as Spring Training started, The Hawk totally dedicated himself to getting ready for a good year, and even gave away his clubs so he could focus on baseball.[15] Red Sox fans, many of whom were initially upset at the thought of Harrelson replacing their beloved Conigliaro, had begun to open their arms to their flamboyant right fielder. Nonetheless, rookie Joe Lahoud was showing some promise in right, and with George Scott already at first base (Harrelson's second position), trade rumors regarding The Hawk abounded. Fortunately for Harrelson—and, as it would turn out, the Red Sox—Conigliaro's injury prevented him from returning and Lahoud proved to be too young. Shortly after Opening Day, it became clear that the Hawk would roost in right field at Fenway for at least one more season.

The 1968 season would become known as "The Year of the Pitcher," and in the American League, Detroit Tigers right-hander Denny McLain won 31 games and the MVP award. But despite the mastery of pitching that year, the Hawk excelled.[16] The Red Sox won no pennant in 1968, but Harrelson helped keep them competitive. He valued runs batted in above all other measures of individual success, and leading the league in RBIs in 1968 with 109 is something he remains proud of nearly 40 years later.

Again and again, The Hawk picked up the Sox, seemingly always getting a big hit when one was most needed. He hit 35 home runs during the season, 13 of them game-winners. Harrelson was enjoying Boston immensely and playing better than he ever had before, and his effusive, explosive alter-ego, The Hawk, was having the time of his life, earning more money then he ever had before—and spending that money just as quickly, which only helped build the "Hawk" persona.

The Hawk had become more than just a nickname, it was now a commodity, and lavish possessions

proliferated. A lavender dune-buggy. A sandwich shop, an insurance company, and travel agency. A song by a popular Boston band entitled "Don't Walk The Hawk." The emblem "Hawk" embroidered on every piece of clothing, including his trademark Nehru jackets. He attended an Academy of Professional Sports Show that was televised from Hollywood—and, reportedly, his attire made the movie stars "look like rag pickers."[17] The Hawk loved the attention, but Harrelson was overwhelmed by it. Carl Yastrzemski, who was no stranger to endorsements himself, offered some helpful financial advice: Hire Bob Woolf.[18] Woolf, a Boston lawyer who had become one of the world's best-known sports agents when he negotiated Larry Bird's contract with the Celtics in 1979, would manage The Hawk's finances for the rest of his career and serve as a voice of reason in times of trouble.

In the early stages of the 1969 season, in a shocking transaction, the Red Sox dealt Harrelson to the Cleveland Indians along with Juan Pizarro and Dick Ellsworth in exchange for Sonny Siebert, Joe Azcue, and Vicente Romo. George Scott and Dalton Jones would split time at first base, and Tony Conigliaro would try to making a comeback in right field. The move came as a paralyzing blow to Harrelson, who loved Boston and could not imagine leaving it. The previous season, Red Sox owner Tom Yawkey had announced in a newspaper article that he was thankful that the Red Sox had not traded Harrelson prior to spring training in 1968: "Often," Yawkey said, "the best deals are the ones you don't make." Harrelson's Red Sox teammates were distraught, and The Hawk himself was inconsolable. Angry fans picketed the front office protesting the trade. Despite Harrelson's public displays of disappointment, when Harrelson announced that he would retire rather than play for another team, jaws dropped across the country, and chaos reigned.

How could The Hawk nest anywhere else but Boston? He was loved by the fans, loved by his teammates, loved by sponsors, endorsers, businessmen, and consumers. Harrelson simply could not leave Boston—he would rather not play. On the other hand, baseball meant too much to The Hawk to simply leave it behind. For Red Sox General Manager Dick O'Connell, Cleveland Indians president Gabe Paul, and Baseball Commissioner Bowie Kuhn, the situation was a nightmare. Azcue and Siebert had already said they would not go back to Cleveland, and the other three players involved in the transaction were caught in limbo—freshly dressed in their new uniforms but not eligible to play. Meanwhile, Harrelson waited, in the middle of the frenzy, exhausted from lack of sleep and emotionally in shambles, The Hawk lay mostly dormant throughout the entire solemn ordeal, but shone through briefly when Harrelson met Kuhn for the first time. Though the distressed Harrelson had a serious matter on his mind, his flashy alter-ego was distracted by the finely-dressed commissioner's attire, and, unable to help himself, The Hawk commented extensively on the sartorial elegance of Kuhn's suit.[19] On April 21, Harrelson and his agent, Wolff, met with the commissioner, AL President Joe Cronin, Paul, and O'Connell at the MLB offices in New York, and resolved the situation. Harrelson loved baseball "too much to hurt it,"[20] and he reported to Cleveland the next day, reunited with friend and former manager Alvin Dark.

Despite Harrelson's reluctance to leave Boston, he was pleasantly surprised to be welcomed with open arms in Cleveland, and business deals abounded. He again endorsed products, and while in Cleveland his autobiography (written with Al Hirshberg) was published. The Hawk was huge again. But the style didn't lack substance, as Harrelson hit 30 homers and drove in 92 runs, en route to another great year.

In 1970, tragedy struck in the form of a debilitating injury. Playing in a spring training game on March 19 against his former team, the Oakland Athletics, Hawk slid into second base and immediately felt a shooting pain in his leg. It was broken. Harrelson was laid up for a long time, and while he was injured, rookie Chris Chambliss took his place. After the 1971 season, having played only 69 games since his injury, The Hawk felt an emotion that was entirely new to him. "I just lost my desire to play baseball," Harrelson says today. "I was still a competitor, The Hawk was still there, but I didn't want to play baseball anymore." Harrelson sadly announced that he would quit the game he had loved for so long to pursue a professional golfing career. That pursuit ended badly, and Harrelson turned back to baseball once more in 1975, coming back to Boston—this time as an announcer. Many Boston fans have fond memories of Harrelson's work behind the microphone.

In 1981, Harrelson was hired as play-by-play announcer for the Chicago White Sox, where he served until 1986, when he moved from the broadcast booth to the front office, serving as the White Sox executive vice president of baseball operations for a year. In 1987, Harrelson returned to the broadcast booth for good, taking a position doing play-by-play for the New York Yankees. He returned to the White Sox in 1991, and works there today in the same capacity. His Southern twang and enthusiastic catchphrases (like his distinctive

home run call "You can put it on the board... *yes!*") have made him a fan favorite—and also have led to some fans calling for his dismissal, claiming that his accent is unintelligible and his baseball phrases hackneyed.

Deep down, the competitive nature of The Hawk is still there and whether he is defending Lew Krausse or Jerry Reinsdorf, he never shies away from an issue. Today, The Hawk's opponent isn't an owner named Charlie Finley, but a journalist named Jay Mariotti. Mariotti, who constantly attacks Reinsdorf, has been affectionately nicknamed "Hiney Bird" by The Hawk. Harrelson explains: "The Hiney Bird is a creature that flies in perfectly concentric circles over and over again until it flies up its own ass and disappears forever."

Today, Harrelson resides in Chicago, with his wife, Aris, is the proud parent of two children, Casey and Krista, and a grandfather of one, Nicolas, with another grandchild on the way. Casey is a professional golfer trying to make the PGA tour, and his father is quick to point out that at 28, Casey is much better then his dad was at the same age. The Hawk usually lies dormant, and the Southern charm of Kenneth Smith Harrelson is usually what millions of White Sox fans hear every night when they tune in to the White Sox games on WGN-TV. But it still comes out occasionally, and though it's Harrelson's 54th year in baseball, he claims that he loves the game "more than ever."

Hawk Harrelson summarizes how he says he viewed the game: "Our two rules were play your ass off, and have fun. ... Sure, you wanted money... but that was third or fourth down the line."

Notes:

1. Interview with Ken Harrelson by Alex Edelman, May 4, 2006.
2. Reynolds, Bill, *Lost Summer: The 1967 Red Sox and the Impossible Dream.*
3. Ken Harrelson interview,
4. Reynolds, *op. cit.*
5. Or "El Hawko," as Caracas fans referred to him. There are many stories about Harrelson's adventures in South America. For instance, once, when Harrelson was tossed from a game in Venezuela, he charged out of the dugout to argue with the umpire, who immediately struck him in the jaw. Harrelson fought back, punching the umpire repeatedly. A newspaper article commenting on the event, written by George Minot Jr. of the *Washington Post* (June 10, 1966) remarked that Harrelson's jaw must have been a "prominent target."
6. Interview with Billy Bryan by Alex Edelman, May 23, 2006.
7. Ken Harrelson interview.
8. Harrelson, Ken, and Hirshberg, Al, *Hawk*. NY: Viking Press, 1969.
9. Harrelson interview.
10. Harrelson interview.
11. Harrelson and Hirshberg, *Hawk, op. cit.*
12. *Ibid.* Harrelson says he was paid $25
13. In *Hawk*, Harrelson claimed that Krausse got a "bum rap," and wasn't even slightly disorderly.
14. Harrelson and Hirshberg, Al, *Hawk, op. cit.*
15. "Harrelson: The Hawk Flies High With Boston" *Los Angeles Times*, May 30, 1968.
16. Harrelson won AL Player of the Year and came in third in the MVP race behind McLain and Bill Freehan of Detroit, garnering .37 shares of the vote. He also made his only All-Star appearance in a game that seemed typical of the year—a 1-0 pitchers' duel in favor of the National League.
17. Addie, Bob. "The Lavender Hawk" *Washington Post*, February 27, 1969.
18. Harrelson and Hirshberg, *Hawk, op. cit.*
19. Vecsey, George. "Williams Joins Lombardi's Fan Club" *New York Times*, April 27, 1969.
20. Harrelson and Hirshberg, *Hawk, op. cit.*

Tony Horton

by Mark Kanter and Mark Armour

	G	AB	R	H	2B	3B	HR	RBI	BB	SO	BA	OBP	SLG	SB	CS	GDP	HBP
1967 RED SOX	21	39	2	12	3	0	0	9	0	5	.308	.300	.385	0	0	2	0

The story of Tony Horton, the young and talented slugger for the Red Sox and Indians, is ultimately a tragic one from a baseball perspective. Just entering his prime seasons at the age of 25, he was forced to leave the game because of an emotional disorder and he never returned. Piecing together his story is not easy, because the person who knows the story best—Tony Horton—is keeping it to himself.

Anthony Darrin (Tony) Horton was born in Santa Monica, California, on December 6, 1944, almost three years to the day after the Japanese attacked Pearl Harbor. He got his athletic prowess from his father, Troy Horton, who played both football and basketball at UCLA.

Horton later said he did not play baseball at all until he was 10 or 11 years old. His friends were playing, so he decided to try to catch up. His father did not play, but read books on hitting and fielding and taught his son. Horton became a basketball and baseball star at University High School in Los Angeles and was byall accounts one of the best athletes ever to come out of the city; on the hardwood he averaged 27.3 points per game and was named Los Angeles City Player of the Year in 1962. (Other notables who won this prestigious award included future NBA players Joe Caldwell, Willie Naulls, and Gail Goodrich, as well as Earl Battey, a future All-Star catcher for the Minnesota Twins.) In baseball, Tony was a shortstop, starred in American Legion ball, and played for the championship Culver City team in the 1961 Connie Mack World Series.

The story of his signing with the Red Sox was told around Fenway Park for years. Scout Joe Stephenson strongly recommended him, despite the fact that the 17-year-old Horton had broken his leg his senior year in baseball and played only a few Connie Mack games that summer. Horton was ready to attend the University of Southern California in the fall on a basketball scholarship, so the Red Sox needed to decide before classes started in late September. He and his parents were flown to Fenway Park for a tryout in front of Red Sox farm director Neil Mahoney and assistants Ed Kenney and Milt Bolling.

Tony Conigliaro—a local 17-year-old slugger whom the Red Sox also wanted to sign—was there as well, and the two Tonys pitched to each other. As Kenney told *The Sporting News* two years later, Horton hit Conigliaro's first pitch into the center field seats, perhaps 430 feet away. The second pitch was driven to right field over the two bullpens. "To the day of my death, I'll never forget it," said Kenney. Kenney looked at the others, said "that's enough for me," and walked into the clubhouse.

The deal they struck was for a reported $138,000—a combination of bonus money and enough to cover four years of tuition. "The Red Sox offer was just too much money to turn down," Tony's father explained. "Tony feels a little bad because he had his heart set on going to school and playing there."

Horton enrolled at USC anyway, and began taking one semester of classes every off-season. By 1969, he was just two semesters shy of his degree in business administration.

Horton taking b.p.

Horton attended his first spring training with the Red Sox in Scottsdale, Arizona in 1963. There he worked with former Red Sox star Ted Williams, but played only sparingly that spring before being farmed out. After a 1963 season in which he hit .283 with 76 runs, 19 doubles, four triples, 21 home runs, and 88 runs batted in for Waterloo of the Midwest League, he was welcomed back "with opened arms" to spring training by the Red Sox the following year. Horton's 88 RBIs for Waterloo tied him for the league lead with Tommie Reynolds, a future major leaguer with the A's, Mets, Angels, and Brewers.

Entering the 1964 season, the Red Sox were excited about their two young teenage sluggers—Horton and Conigliaro. Both were right-handed hitting outfielders with just one year of minor league ball behind them, but both were considered candidates to make the club out of the spring. A rule of the time dictated that only one "first-year" player could be optioned out without being subject to a draft, so it was almost guaranteed that one of the Tonys would make the club.

The two players were not just rivals; they became instant friends, roommates in the spring, and constant companions away from the park. Conigliaro, in his 1970 autobiography, tells of many nights with Horton chasing women (with quite a bit of success, apparently). In a preseason game on March 28, 1964, both Horton and Conigliaro hit home runs to lead the Red Sox to a 12-10 victory over the Los Angeles Angels. Conigliaro and Horton were presented with trophies as co-rookies of the spring by the Charros Club of Scottsdale. In the end, Conigliaro's edge was that he was considered the better outfielder, an area where the Red Sox needed the most help. Horton was playing first base more and more, and would ultimately be shifted there, as the eventual successor to Dick Stuart. He was optioned to Reading of the Eastern League at the end of the spring camp.

Horton hit well for Reading, and by June he was named to the 1964 Eastern League All-Star team. For the season, he rang up a batting average of .297, with 60 runs, 29 doubles, five triples, seven home runs, and 62 runs batted in. In mid-summer, both Conigliaro and Lee Thomas suffered injuries, and Horton was summoned to "the show" in late July to shore up Boston's outfield. The comparisons with Conigliaro, who had started his career impressively, continued. "Horton is a different type hitter than Conigliaro," manager Johnny Pesky allowed. "Conigliaro pulls nearly everything he hits. Horton will hit the ball to all fields. He has good power to all fields, and goes with the pitch more than Conigliaro does." Horton was the prototypical slugger: 6' 3", and 210 pounds of muscle.

Horton's major league debut came at Dodger Stadium on July 31, starting in left field against his hometown Los Angeles Angels. Facing Aubrey Gatewood, he grounded out his first time up, but singled in the fourth inning and scored his first major league run moments later on Eddie Bressoud's double. Every run counted; the final was Boston 4, Los Angeles 3.

Horton was the Red Sox starting left fielder for most of the month of August. At Comiskey Park on August 8, Horton hit his first major league homer, off Fred Talbot of the Chicago White Sox. The Red Sox lost the game, 9-2. In 126 at-bats, this would be the only homer Horton hit that year. He hit safely in nine of his first 10 games, hitting .395 over that stretch, and was hitting over .280 as late as August 28, but slumped to .222 by the end of the season. He was unsteady in left field, a position he had not played in Reading, but he had gotten his feet wet in major league ball, and the future looked bright.

On November 29, 1964, the Red Sox traded first baseman Dick Stuart to the Phillies, opening up the first base job for Horton if he could claim it. But new manager Billy Herman chose to give the job to veteran Lee Thomas, and Horton began the season with Toronto in the Triple-A International League.

Horton was hitting .301 for Toronto in early June 1965 when Red Sox left fielder Gary Geiger broke his hand. The Red Sox recalled Horton to play first base temporarily, moving Thomas back to left field. Horton stuck with the team the rest of the season, eventually playing first base against left-handers, and hit a very solid .294 with seven homers in some 60 games. There was one stretch in which he truly made a difference. On August 31, his 10th inning homer beat the Senators. On September 8, he homered again in the 10th, beating the Indians. And on September 14, in another game against Cleveland, he tied the game in the bottom of the ninth, setting the stage for a walkoff 13th-inning homer by Carl Yastrzemski.

In December 1965, the Red Sox dealt Thomas to the Braves, and Herman announced that Horton would be his first baseman. Ironically, he ultimately fell victim to the Red Sox successful youth movement. After starting the first four games of the 1966 season, and playing in two others, he was sent back to Toronto after hitting a disappointing .136 (just three singles in 22 at-bats). The reason for the quickly terminated trial was the brilliant hitting and fielding of rookie George Scott, who won the job and ended up making the All-Star team. After being sent down to Toronto, Horton played

133 games and hit .297—with power, as evidenced by his 26 home runs.

Although Horton was still just 22 entering the 1967 season, he was now playing behind another young player fresh off an All-Star appearance. Nonetheless, new manager Dick Williams, who had managed Horton in Toronto for much of the past two seasons, was high on Horton and kept him on the club to open the 1967 season. In fact, many observers of the team felt Horton might force Scott to switch positions. After two months, Tony was mainly pinch-hitting, but hitting .308.

With the pennant race up for grabs, Williams implored GM Dick O'Connell to secure another starting pitcher. On June 4, the Red Sox traded Horton and Don Demeter to Cleveland for Gary Bell. Bell pitched well for Boston, winning 12 games and losing eight with an ERA of 3.16. The Red Sox would go on to win the pennant by one game over the Twins and Tigers and three over the White Sox.

Meanwhile, Horton was given the starting first

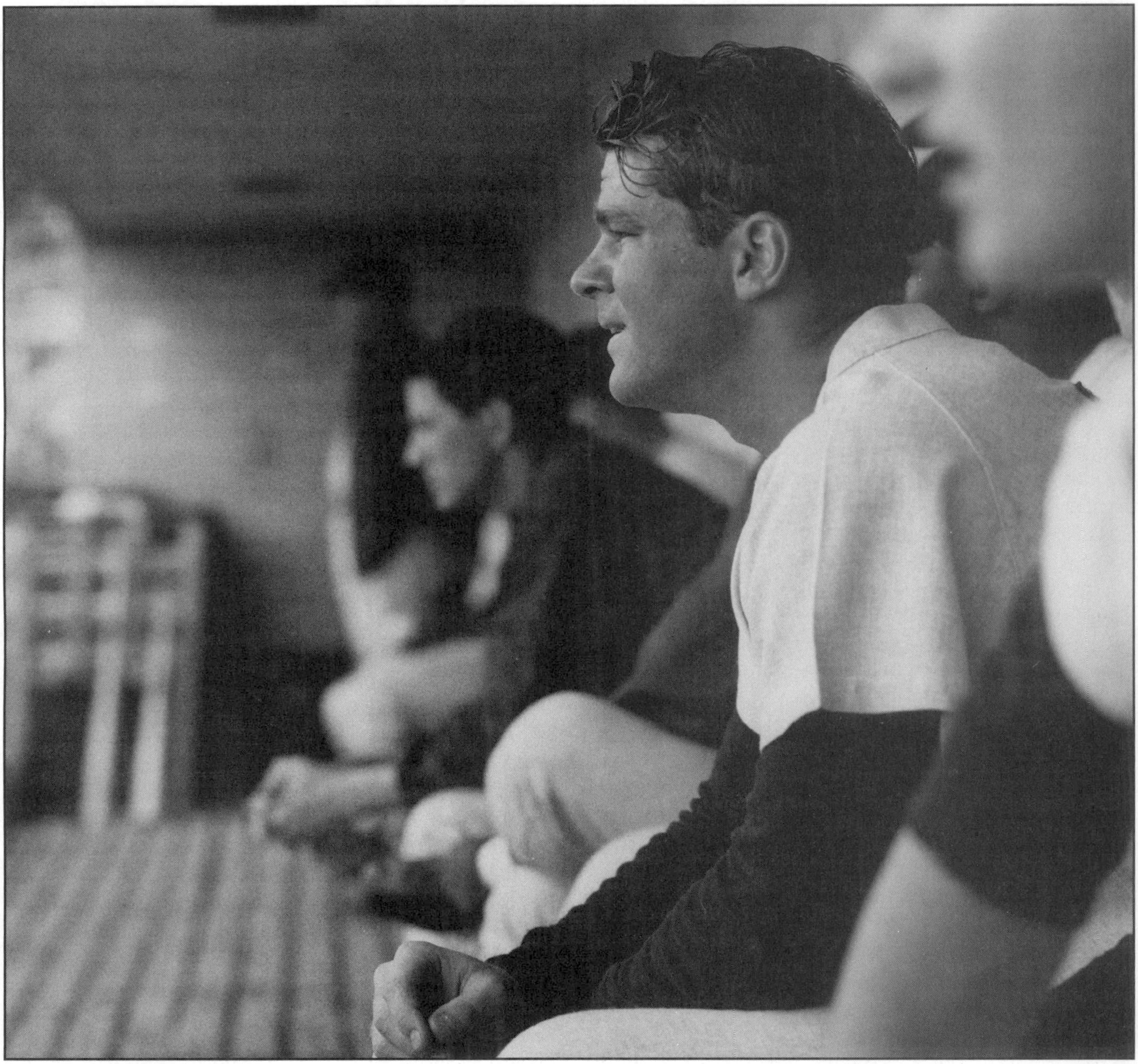

An intense Tony Horton watches from the dugout bench.

base job in Cleveland, and he kept it. In 363 at-bats, he tallied 35 runs, 10 home runs, and 44 RBIs while batting .281, with an on-base percentage of .321 and a slugging average of .421. For the first time, Horton no longer had to spend the off-season worried about his position on his team, and the 23-year-old slugger could look forward to many years of success.

In 1968, an extremely difficult year for hitters, Tony led the Indians with 14 home runs and 59 RBIs, while hitting .249 in 133 games. He missed three weeks in mid-summer when he injured his knee, but otherwise he was out there almost every day. The following season, 1969, the 24-year-old slugger had his best season, belting 27 home runs and driving in 93 while hitting .278—all team-leading figures—in 159 games.

Even then, Tony was described as extremely intense, a perfectionist who was never happy with his performance. In a June 29, 1968 story in *The Sporting News*, Tony admitted he was driven to succeed in anything he did, and he realized it was a problem. Recalling his years in Boston, Tony said, "If you're afraid—actually afraid—of missing a ball or having a bad night, you're going to worry and press, and all you can do is get worse."

In 1970, the stress of the game grew more difficult for Horton. After a three-homer game against the Yankees on May 24, a game the Indians lost, Horton was visibly down on himself for his failure to deliver in his last time up, angrily calling himself a "blockhead." He did not homer again for three-and-a-half weeks. He did go 4-for-5 with a grand slam on June 21, and hit for the cycle against the Orioles on July 2.

On June 24 against the Yankees' Steve Hamilton, Horton swung and missed on one of Hamilton's famed eephus pitches, so-called "folly floaters," then fouled the second one to the catcher. Returning to the dugout, Horton threw his cap and bat into the air, and crawled the last few steps to the dugout. The crowd roared, and everyone assumed it was a joke. Later, people wondered if it was.

At a game early August, the home fans booed the slumping Horton, but he turned the crowd around with a home run. Afterward, Tony admitted the boos bothered him. He worked himself tirelessly to overcome his hitting drought, and reportedly stopped eating and drinking, before finally suffering what was later thought to be a nervous breakdown sometime after his last game, which was on August 28. The *Los Angeles Times* on September 9 reported that Horton was sent home to Santa Monica due to "physical exhaustion." The slump was just a slump, though. By season's end, Tony had hit .269 with 17 home runs in 115 games, numbers very much in line with his fine statistics in 1968 and 1969.

Horton seeks some advice in the trainer's room.

Throughout the off-season, the Indians, and everyone else, believed that Horton was going to a big part of the team again in 1971. It was therefore a surprise when the team announced on January 21, 1971, that Horton would miss spring training and likely the entire season with an emotional disorder. He had been hospitalized since September. His father Troy insisted that he was doing well, and denied any speculation that his career was over. He reported that the doctors thought he needed some time off, but that he would be ready to play again in 1972.

Before the 1972 season, Indians general manager Gabe Paul visited Horton in Santa Monica, and reported that Tony was doing fine, though not yet ready to make a comeback. In July, Horton told *The Sporting News*

that he was 100% recovered, but not really thinking about baseball. He had a job with the stock exchange, played some golf, and read a lot.

For all practical purposes, that would seem to be the last anyone heard from Horton. There have been many theories as to what happened to him, but he has not talked about his career and his ending in the ensuing 35 years.

Author Bill Madden attempted to interview Horton about his breakdown and retirement from baseball in 1997. In an article in *Baseball Digest*, Madden wrote that Horton was working in telecommunications and living in Pacific Palisades, California, but would not talk about his baseball career. Madden wrote that Horton had tried to commit suicide while with the Indians, as reported by a Cleveland hotel owner where the attempt allegedly took place

Contacted in February 2006, to ask whether Horton could be interviewed for this book on the 1967 Red Sox, Madden replied:

"Tony Horton is a tragic story. If you read the piece I did on him, you'll understand that his breakdown was due to the pressure of never living up to his father's expectations. After the suicide attempt, I'm told doctors and psychiatric people told him he had to sever all ties to baseball and that part of his life. That's why his old teammates and managers never heard from him again and why he has become a bit of a recluse. ... I thought it was rather strange that Tony was still living with his father at the time of my article."

In July 2006, Mark Kanter presented his research on Tony Horton at SABR's annual convention in Seattle. A friend of Tony's was among those in attendance, and after the talk reported that Tony was in fact doing very well in business—but that the two had never discussed baseball. A couple of weeks after the convention, he asked Tony if he would be willing to talk about his time in baseball, but Tony was very clear that baseball is in his past, and he has no interest in revisiting that part of his life. We are happy to respect his wishes in this regard.

With three productive seasons behind him, Horton's baseball career ended at the tender age of 25. His early career performance suggests that he might have been a fine player for many years. We will never know.

Elston Howard

by Cecilia Tan

	G	AB	R	H	2B	3B	HR	RBI	BB	SO	BA	OBP	SLG	SB	CS	GDP	HBP
1967 RED SOX	42	116	9	17	3	0	1	11	9	24	.147	.211	.198	0	0	4	1

Elston Howard was born February 23, 1929, in St. Louis, Missouri, the son of Emmaline Webb and Travis Howard. A schoolteacher in Sikeston, Missouri, Emmaline fled to St. Louis when Howard, her principal, refused to marry her. She worked to become a dietician, and when Elston was five years old, she married Wayman "Big Poppy" Hill. Elston attended the Toussaint L'Ouverture school as well as the Mt. Zion Baptist Church. The church's pastor, the Reverend Jeremiah M. Baker, became Elston's godfather, and the boy was raised to work hard and eat right (thanks to his mother's dietician's know-how).

In the summer of 1945, Howard, then 16, was playing baseball in a sandlot when Frank Tetnus "Teannie" Edwards approached him. "The biggest kid on the field was hitting the ball so hard and far that it made [Teannie] mad," wrote Arlene Howard in her book *Elston and Me*. "When he got to the field he found out that the big kid was, in fact, one of the youngest on the lot." Edwards, a former Negro Leagues player himself, helped run the St. Louis Braves and he wanted Elston. Convincing Emmaline was the hardest part. Edwards had to promise that young Elston would eat properly. On Easter Sunday 1946 (April 21), Howard debuted in the Tandy League[1], catching in a game against Kinloch. He had two hits and threw out two runners trying to steal second in a 5-4 loss.

The following year, Jackie Robinson broke the color barrier in the Major Leagues. Now 18, Howard was working at Bauer's grocery store and finishing at all-black Vashon High School. After Robinson's debut, Vashon hastily formed a baseball team. Elston was already a star athlete at Vashon, playing football, running track, and making all-state in basketball. He was easily the best player in baseball, as well, and after graduating from Vashon, he played another summer with the Braves.

He was urged by Teannie Edwards to attend an open tryout for the St. Louis Cardinals at Sportsman's Park, but the Cardinals turned a blind eye. (Alas, the Cardinals would not field a black player until 1954—Tom Alston.) Meanwhile, college beckoned, with three Big Ten schools (Illinois, Michigan and Michigan State) asking for his services in football and several others interested in him for track, basketball, and baseball. Emmaline was hoping her son might grow up to be a doctor. But Edwards called in scouts from the Kansas City Monarchs, the elite Negro Leagues team Jackie Robinson had played for. The Monarchs were so impressed that they went to his mother to negotiate a professional contract. Elston would get $500 a month, mailed directly to her.

In Kansas City, Howard, like the rest of the Monarchs, was treated like a king. Player-manager Buck O'Neil and Earl "Mickey" Taborn, the Monarchs catcher and Ellie's roommate, showed him the ropes. They enjoyed tailored clothes, terrific food, and the best jazz music in the nation in Kansas City. Because Taborn was the regular catcher, Howard played left field, filling in at first base when O'Neil was out of the lineup. Then in 1949, Taborn left to play for the Triple-A Newark Bears. By the time he returned in 1950, Howard's new roommate was a young fellow named Ernie Banks.

The players could see what was coming. Monarchs owner Tom Baird had found that there was money to be made selling players to the majors. Ernie and Ellie made a bet: Whoever got to the majors first would call the other and tell him what it was like. Tom Greenwade, the legendary Yankees scout, soon came calling to look at a different player, but Buck O'Neil steered him to Howard. Within days, Elston Howard and Frank Barnes had been sold for $25,000 to the New York Yankees.

Now 21, Howard debuted on July 26, 1950, in left field for the Class A Muskegon, Michigan, Clippers. He would earn $400 a month. The Clippers had a 39-46 record when he arrived, and went 36-18 in the 54 games he played, making the playoffs. Howard batted cleanup and hit well, but the Clippers fell short of the league championship.

Returning to St. Louis for the off-season, Elston announced his decision to marry his high school sweetheart, Delores Williams. Just before the wedding, he was drafted into the Army, at the height of the Korean War. While he was in basic training, the marriage with Delores was dissolved—there are conflicting stories as to why. Howard was sent overseas, but he never fought in Korea. Once the Army realized it had a great baseball player on its hands, he was assigned to Special Services and sent to Japan. That was all Howard ever did in the army: play baseball.

By 1953 Howard was playing for the Yankees' top farm team, the Kansas City Blues. Another black player, Vic Power from Puerto Rico, was a teammate. Power batted .349 but because of the amount of trouble he stirred up was considered too much of a loose cannon to ever make it in pinstripes. Power was eventually traded to the Philadelphia A's. In August, *Jet* magazine featured an article with the headline "Howard May be First Negro With Yankees."

Shortly before Christmas, Elston proposed to Arlene Henley, whose sister he had gone to high school with. He spent February 1954 at "Yankee Prospects School" with 28 other ballplayers in Lake Wales, Florida, and March at spring training with the big club, sharing a locker room with Yogi Berra, Phil Rizzuto, Mickey Mantle, and Billy Martin. Bill Dickey, former Yankee great, worked with him to make him a major league catcher. Some newspapers, like the Baltimore *Afro-American*, criticized the Yankees, claiming the move to catcher was a manufactured setback to keep Howard in the minors. When the Yankees broke camp, they took three catchers north with them: Yogi Berra, Charlie Silvera, and Ralph Houk. They didn't want to send Howard back to the Blues, so they arranged for him to play with the Toronto Maple Leafs in the International League. Canada was a bit more welcoming to black players. Howard won the league MVP Award, hit .330, with 22 homers and 109 RBIs. At the end of the season, he gave Arlene an engagement ring, and they planned to marry in the spring of 1955.

Media reports that Howard would be a Yankee by spring increased, as did protests pressuring the Yankees to integrate. The Yankees won 103 games in 1954, but not the league pennant. Cleveland, featuring black outfielder Larry Doby, won the flag with 111 wins, a sign that the Yankees might need to integrate themselves. The Yankees decided to send Howard to winter ball in Puerto Rico.

The wedding to Arlene was rushed to December 4, 1954. Howard's godfather, Reverend Baker, married them in Arlene's mother's living room. They honeymooned in San Juan, where they lived in the same building as Willie Mays and Sam Jones. Then Howard was off to St. Petersburg for Yankee camp, Arlene back to St. Louis, pregnant with the couple's first child.

Casey Stengel batted Howard in the cleanup spot much of the spring, prompting Arthur Daley to write in the *New York Times*, "He seems certain to be the first Negro to make the Yankees. ... They've waited for one to come along who [is] 'the Yankee type.' Elston is a nice, quiet lad whose reserved, gentlemanly demeanor has won him complete acceptance from every Yankee." Daley was right. Ralph Houk went to the minors, Howard was given his uniform number (32), and on March 21 general manager George Weiss announced that Elston Howard would be coming to New York.

His New York City debut came the Sunday night before the season, when he appeared with Stengel and two other rookies on the Ed Sullivan Show. His on-field debut followed on April 14 at Fenway Park, subbing for Irv Noren, who had been ejected for arguing with an umpire. He got a base hit and knocked in a run. Perhaps the most memorable effect of Howard's presence on the Yankees that year, though, was that the team changed its hotel policy, staying only in hotels that would accept Howard as a guest. Yogi Berra, Phil Rizzuto, and Hank Bauer were Howard's best friends on the team. He hit .290 in 97 games his rookie season, with another five hits in the World Series, including a home run in his first World Series at-bat. That performance was offset by eight strikeouts, and the Dodgers won their first World Series. Howard made the final out of the Series,

Elston Howard dons catching gear before a Boston ballgame.

then traveled to Japan with the Yankees for a good will tour.

On the 25-game tour of the Pacific, Howard hit .468 to lead the team. Meanwhile, Elston Jr. was born. Howard's pay jumped in 1956 from $6,000 to $10,000, he bought a house in St. Louis, and then heard from Stengel that he would be doing more catching. Howard drove the family to Florida, planning to stay overnight with a friend of his godfather's, a preacher named Martin Luther King. But that night the King house was firebombed and they could not stay there. Almost as disastrous, Howard broke a finger in spring training. Then Norm Siebern went down, and Howard had to fill the gap in the outfield. So much for spending significant time behind the plate. He appeared in only 98 games, 26 at catcher, and finished the year with a so-so .262 batting average, 5 homers, and 34 RBIs. While he had started all seven World Series games in 1955, the team's acquisition of Enos Slaughter kept Howard on the bench for the first six Series games in 1956. Nonetheless, Stengel started him in Game Seven, and Howard homered and doubled in the 9-0 Yankee win.

The era of change continued to sweep New York. Jackie Robinson retired, and within a year the Giants and Dodgers went west, leaving New York to the Yankees and Elston Howard the only black major leaguer in town. In 1957, he returned to the Yankees once again hoping for more playing time. After Moose Skowron got hurt, Howard played more, and in midseason Stengel named him to the American League All-Star team. He ended the season hitting .253, with 8 home runs and 44 RBIs, still pining for more playing time.

As the 1958 season opened, hope for regular catching duties again flared. Stengel again hinted that Berra could not catch so much. The Howards bought a house in Teaneck, New Jersey. Howard was in left field again on Opening Day in Boston. Daughter Cheryl was bon on May 9, and Howard spent his first game behind the plate that season shortly after that, in the first game of a doubleheader on May 11. At one point Howard's batting average reached .350, but he would not have enough plate appearances to qualify for the title should his average hold up. Stengel was adamant about platooning his players; Howard ended the year hitting .314, with 11 homers, and 66 RBIs in 103 games, 67 behind the plate.

Elston's heroism as a Yankee was cemented in the 1958 World Series. Down three games to one in Game Five, Howard got the start in left, despite having dental work that morning. In the sixth, he made a game-saving dive in the outfield, then doubled off the runner, in a play that turned the Series around. "I knew I had to get the ball," Howard told reporters after the game. "I skinned my knee and my stomach doing it. I'm no outfielder. I'm a catcher, but the manager put me out there and I had to do the best I could." The next game the Yankees won again, 4-3, in 10 innings in which Howard had two hits and scored a run, and in Game Seven, with the score tied 2-2 in the eighth, Howard drove in the go-ahead run. The New York Baseball Writers chapter gave him the Babe Ruth Award as the outstanding player in the World Series.

In 1959, Casey's annual prediction that Berra would catch less was again wrong. In fact, Yogi caught 116 games, more than the previous year. Though Elston reached his career high in games played, the platoon system made him feel like a part-time player. One thing that did change was that the Yankees picked up another black player, Panamanian Hector Lopez, who came from Kansas City in a trade. But Mickey Mantle was hurt, Whitey Ford's elbow was balky, and it was all downhill that summer. The Yankees suffered bad losing streaks, including losing five straight at Fenway Park, and finished third in the standings.

Because the club had done poorly, general manager George Weiss tried to cut salaries in 1960. Howard's offer was $5,000 less than his previous year's wages, and he held out, missing the reporting date for spring training. Weiss relented, giving him $25,500, a $3,000 raise. Elston, like the rest of the team, had ups and downs that season, but eventually came out on top. Shelved by a few injuries, he nonetheless did get in 107 games, 91 catching, and made the All-Star team. He sprained a finger on the season's last day. Doctors said he wouldn't play until Game Three of the World Series, but Casey had him pinch hit in Game One. He hit a two-run home run in the 6-4 loss to Pittsburgh. He had a very good Series until he broke a finger batting against Bob Friend. He batted .462 in the Series, but the Yankees lost, on the famous Bill Mazeroski home run. The loss precipitated the ouster of both manager Casey Stengel and general manager George Weiss.

Ralph Houk, the former second-string catcher pushed back to the minors by Elston's emergence, became the manager in 1961. Preferring a more stable lineup than Stengel had, Houk plugged Howard in as his catcher 111 times, playing Berra more in left field. New hitting coach Wally Moses encouraged Howard to bat with his feet closer together, allowing him to spray the ball to all fields. Howard responded with a career year, hitting .348 with 21 home runs in 129 games. He again made the All-Star team and would have battled Norm

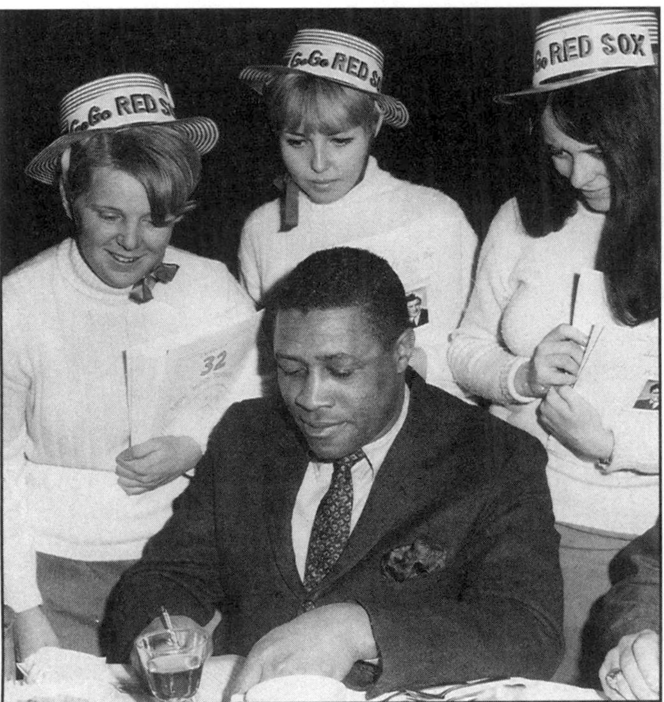

Arriving mid-season from the Yankees, the veteran Elston Howard was made most welcome.

Cash of Detroit for the batting title if he'd had the plate appearances (Cash won it, hitting .361). Between the revitalized Howard, an historic home run race between Roger Maris and Mickey Mantle, and terrific pitching (Ford won 25 games), the Yankees won 109 and took only five games to beat Cincinnati in the World Series. Howard caught all five games and was honored in the off-season as St. Louis' Man of the Year by the city.

1962 brought another improvement. Pressured to stop segregating their black players in spring training housing, the Yankees moved their camp to Fort Lauderdale. Howard's pay raise was significant, to $42,500, and he earned it. He hit another 21 home runs with 138 hits and a .279 average in a career-high 136 games. The three catchers, Howard, Berra, and Johnny Blanchard, combined for 44 homers that season. But Howard's batting average suffered a bit, down to .268 on June 30, though he made the All-Star team again. Most of the homers came in the late-season pennant race with Minnesota, and his and Mantle's surges insured that the Yankees captured the flag. They faced the San Francisco Giants in a pitching-dominated World Series that was drawn out by rain on both coasts. Elston was behind the plate when Ralph Terry secured the final 1-0 win in Game Seven.

The Howards bought a vacant lot in Teaneck on which to build a larger house. Mayor Matty Feldman begged them not to build in a white neighborhood. The Howards ignored him, and although they suffered graffiti and sabotage during building, they moved in toward the end of the 1963 season. Elston switched to a heavier bat, 38 ounces, that he said helped his power to right field. He hit a career high 28 home runs in 1963, many into the short porch in Yankee Stadium's right field, and with Mantle and Maris both hobbled by injuries, Howard batted cleanup often that year. He ended the season with a .287 average, and became the first African-American to win the American League MVP Award. He also took home the Gold Glove with his .994 fielding percentage. Howard appeared in his eighth World Series, and he hit .333, but Dodgers' pitchers Sandy Koufax and Don Drysdale kept the Yankees in check. The Dodgers swept in four.

The MVP Award meant off-season banquets and Howard gained 10 pounds speaking on the dinner circuit. The award also brought commercial endorsements, and Elston, his wife, and family were featured in ads for oatmeal, mustard, and beer. Howard also became the first black man to ever model clothes for *GQ* magazine. His salary for 1964 jumped to $60,000, making him one of the best paid players in baseball. (Mantle earned $107,000.) After the season, Ralph Houk moved upstairs to become GM; Yogi Berra became the field manager. Howard told reporters that he had set his sights on the batting title. "It takes planning," he told them. "That year I hit .348 ... I was a base-hit swinger, not a home-run swinger." He vowed to go with the pitch more and not be too pull-conscious. His efforts were successful. In a career-high 150 games, he tallied a career-high 172 hits for a .313 average, as his homer total dropped to 15. He also walked a career-high 48 times. He did not win the batting title, but did catch all nine innings of the All-Star Game. The Yankees went to the World Series once again, but Bob Gibson's Cardinals came out on top in seven games.

The loss precipitated major changes. Yogi Berra was fired as manager, replaced by Johnny Keane, and CBS bought the team and did nothing to improve the aging roster. Howard injured his elbow during spring training and it worsened over the next few weeks. By April 13 it was so swollen that he couldn't bend his arm enough to eat breakfast. Bone chips were surgically removed from his elbow and the Yankees slipped in the standings. Howard didn't catch again until June 13, and persisted catching 95 games after his return despite the sore arm. He ended with the lowest average of his career, .233, while the Yankees went nowhere. 1966 was not much

better. The arm still hurt, the now 37-year-old Howard hit .256, and the Yankees were stuck in the cellar.

Then came 1967. The Yankees offered a $10,000 pay cut. After a four-day holdout, Howard accepted only a $6,000 cut and a clause that if he performed well, he could earn the money back. But on June 26, Rick Monday fouled a ball off Elston's finger and his hitting suffered. On August 3, Houk telephoned to tell him he had been traded to the Red Sox. Boston was in second place at the time and, unlike the Yankees, had a chance to reach the top. Tom Yawkey called Howard to assure him how much they wanted him. Howard briefly considered retiring, but the chance to play in his 10th World Series was enticing. "If I can help the Red Sox win the pennant this year it would be the greatest thrill of my career," he told writer Jim Ogle.

He joined the Sox on the road in Minnesota and was greeted by manager Dick Williams, two years his junior. Elston played the next day in a nationally televised contest against the Twins. Not an auspicious beginning: He struck out with the bases loaded in the 2-1 loss. Boston mustered only three hits against Dave Boswell. Elston caught the next day, too, when Boston's best pitcher, Jim Lonborg, took the hill. But rain cut the game short, and Minnesota won it 2-0 in five innings, as Dean Chance did not allow a base runner and struck out four. They lost again after an off day, at Kansas City, the first time they had lost four games in a row since July 9.

The team sputtered along until August 18, when they beat the Angels 3-2 at Fenway, a game in which Howard caught Gary Bell's complete game four-hitter. The game would be most remembered, though, for the tragic incident that shattered Tony Conigliaro's eye socket. Perhaps inspired to win for Tony and helped by Howard's presence, the Sox reeled off a seven-game win streak, going 14-5 the rest of the month. Eleven of the games were decided by one run. In that span they played five doubleheaders and took three of four in New York. When Howard came to bat against his former team, the Yankee Stadium crowd gave him a standing ovation, one he later called "the best ovation I ever got in my life."

One of the memorable moments from the stretch run came when the Sox led Minnesota by half a game on August 27. That day the Red Sox faced Chicago, clinging to a 4-3 lead in the ninth. Ken Berry, the tying run at third, attempted to score on a shallow fly caught by right fielder José Tartabull. Tartabull's throw was high, but Elston leaped to snare the ball, then swept the tag down in the same motion—Berry was out and the game was over.

Howard's greatest contribution to The Impossible Dream, though, may be one that can't be measured, in his influence on the pitchers and in the clubhouse. His knowledge of the hitters in the league, his game-calling ability, and his calming presence helped the entire pitching staff. "He was like a pitching coach to Lonborg, Gary Bell, Gary Waslewski, Lee Stange, guys like that," Reggie Smith said. "No doubt Elston helped us win it. We were a young team. Our average age was 26. We needed someone like Ellie to show the way. He brought the Yankee aura of winning to the Red Sox." The Red Sox, of course, did pull off two amazing wins over Minnesota, while Detroit lost on the final day of the season, giving Boston the pennant.

How fitting that Elston Howard's tenth and final World Series would be against his old hometown, St. Louis. Unfortunately, the Cardinals beat the Sox; Elston mustered only two hits in the Series. That off-season he pondered retirement, and numerous possibilities. The Red Sox asked him to play and later coach. The Yankees suggested a minor league coaching job or scouting position. Bill Veeck said he wanted to make Howard the game's first black manager, if he could buy the Washington Senators. In the end, Veeck's bid to buy the Senators was rebuffed. Howard helped a New Jersey entrepreneur, Frank Hamilton, to market the doughnut—not the edible kind, but the weighted metal ring that batters today use in the on-deck circle. But when spring came, the Red Sox offered a $1,000 raise, and Howard decided to play one more year.

The Red Sox and Elston were banged up. Lonborg broke his leg skiing. Tony Conigliaro did not regain his full eyesight and sat out the season, his career apparently over. George Scott's average dropped to .171 as his weight rose. Meanwhile, Howard's elbow acted up again. At midseason, he couldn't straighten it and he did not want surgery. His playing time limited because of the chronic injury, Howard played in only 71 games. In his final game at Fenway, he received a standing ovation. He had hit .241, with five homers and 18 RBIs. He held a press conference on October 21 to announce his retirement from playing. Then on October 22, he was at another press conference, this one in New York to announce he was taking the first base coaching job with the New York Yankees.

Elston became the first black coach for an American League team, but never reached his goal of becoming the first black manager. (Frank Robinson would, in 1975 with the Indians.) While coaching, he took part in various side businesses, including

the ongoing involvement with batting doughnuts; a printing company; opening an art gallery with Arlene in Englewood, New Jersey, to sell Haitian and modern art; heading a division of Group Travel, for whom he was the star attraction on corporate tours and cruises; the Elston Howard Sausage Company concession stand at Yankee Stadium; and serving as vice chairman of the board of Home State Bank, an interracially owned bank that catered to the black community. George Steinbrenner, who bought the Yankees in 1973, would not make Howard a manager, but he did make occasional noises about wanting to move Elston from coaching to the front office. Meanwhile, at Yankee Stadium, he became the important counterbalance to the fiery Billy Martin in "The Bronx Zoo." He coached through the 1978 season.

In mid-February 1979, after nearly collapsing at La Guardia airport, Elston was diagnosed with myocarditis. The muscles of his heart were being attacked by the coxsackie virus and the doctors prescribed total rest. Elston could not participate in spring training. George Steinbrenner told him not to worry. Whenever he recovered, his coaching job would be waiting, and he stayed on the payroll. By August, Howard was still too weak to attend Thurman Munson's funeral. In February 1980, a year after his attack at the airport, Elston was appointed by Steinbrenner to join the front office staff. He would be an assistant to Steinbrenner, and his duties ranged from appearing at banquets to scouting talent in the Yankees minor league system. His health never recovered, though, and he was often too weak to travel. His heart was giving out, and on December 4, 1980, he was admitted to Columbia Presbyterian Hospital. Two weeks later, he died at age 51. In 1984, the Yankees retired his number 32.

Notes:

1. The "Tandy League" was founded in 1922 at Tandy Park in St. Louis and featured teams from local businesses including Union Electric, Scullen Steel, Missouri Pressed Brick, and Mississippi Tanning Company. According to Tweed Webb, it was the oldest "colored men's league" in St. Louis. [Oral history compiled by Bill Morrison, May 4, 1971, Western Historical Manuscript Collection, University of Missouri-St, Louis]

Dalton Jones

by Maurice Bouchard

	G	AB	R	H	2B	3B	HR	RBI	BB	SO	BA	OBP	SLG	SB	CS	GDP	HBP
1967 RED SOX	89	159	18	46	6	2	3	25	11	23	.289	.333	.409	0	1	2	0

In groups of twos and threes at first, and then in larger groups, the fans rose and cheered for their hometown team. It spread throughout Fenway Park until virtually every one of the 35,000 fans had joined in the spontaneous standing ovation. The top of the ninth inning on October 12, 1967, was about to start. The score was 7-2; the St. Louis Cardinals were leading the Boston Red Sox in the seventh game of the World Series. The way Bob Gibson was pitching, there was little doubt about the final outcome, but the fans wanted to say "Thank You" to their Red Sox, who had brought so much joy and excitement in the wild ride that was the summer of 1967. Dalton Jones, who was getting ready to play third base, remembered it well nearly 40 years later. "Talk about bringing a tear to your eye," Jones reminisced.[1] One could still hear the emotion in his voice four decades removed. Mississippi native Dalton Jones, still two months shy of his 24th birthday, had played on baseball's biggest stage—played and thrived.

Twenty-four summers before, Mrs. Louise Jones was concerned. Although they were living in Baton Rouge and had access to good medical care, Clinton and Louise Jones did not trust big city doctors.[2] The former Louise Purl had, in fact, lost a baby during her first pregnancy while in the care of Baton Rouge doctors. Not about to let that happen again, the Joneses moved back to their hometown in southern Mississippi to be in the care of a familiar, trusted doctor. James Dalton Jones was born on December 10, 1943, in McComb, Mississippi. Dalton, as he was to be known, was named for his father's brother, James Dalton, an Army Air Corps flier who had been killed in action in North Africa a year earlier.[3]

Dalton was the first child in the Jones family. A brother, Melvin, arrived three years later. While growing up in Baton Rouge, baseball was an integral part of young Dalton's life. Dalton's father loved baseball. Clinton H. Jones was then an assistant chemist for the Esso (now Exxon) Oil Company.[4] In addition to his official duties at work, he resurrected the company baseball team and help lead the team to a semipro championship. Previously, Clinton had been a star in the Class D Evangeline League. Clint, as he was known, played first base and was the batting champion in 1934 for the Opelousas (Louisiana) Indians.[5] Clint Jones led that league in runs scored and hits in 1934 as well. He moved up to the Class A Des Moines Demons in 1935 and would likely have gone on to higher-level minor league teams, perhaps beyond, had an arm injury not ended his baseball career.[6] In addition to Clinton's experience in the minors, Dalton's great-uncle Leroy "Cowboy" Jones played in the Texas League. Family vacations often centered on baseball. The Jones family would travel to St. Louis to see the Cardinals play; they traveled to Kansas City and even to Cleveland to see the Red Sox play on the road. Consequently, as a youngster, Dalton became a Stan Musial fan and a Ted Williams fan. The Jones family was present in Cleveland when Ted Williams tied and then passed Mel Ott for third place on the major league career home run list.

In addition, Clinton Jones coached Dalton from Little League up through American Legion ball. Dalton also benefited from countless one-on-one sessions with his father, who always had time to hit fungoes or throw batting practice. When scouts started flocking around the 14-year-old Jones, it was his father who kept everything in the "right perspective".[7] From an early age, Dalton wanted only to be a major league baseball player.

Dalton was a star shortstop for his high school team in Baton Rouge, the Istrouma Indians. In 1961, Jones led Istrouma to the Louisiana state championship game. (Future major league star Rusty Staub led the opposing team, Jesuit High School of New Orleans.) After graduation, Red Sox scout George Digby signed the 6'1", 180-pound, left-hand hitting shortstop for a $60,000 bonus, a considerable amount in 1961 but about half what some top prospects received. Still, Jones felt a responsibility to perform up to the high expectations of the Red Sox.

Jones immediately reported to the Alpine (Texas) Cowboys of the Class D Sophomore League, managed by former Red Sox pitching great Mel Parnell. In his first professional game, Jones hit two triples off the 425-foot fence at Tingley Field in Albuquerque. The second triple came with two out in the ninth inning. The hit started a three-run rally as the Cowboys beat the Dukes, 4-3.[8] After this promising debut, Jones went into a prolonged slump, the first time he had experienced mediocrity (or worse) in baseball. He

Dalton Jones brought a big bat to Boston.

was feeling the pressure, most of it self-inflicted. He seriously considered quitting baseball, thinking he could not make it at the professional level. However, after some soul searching, prayer, and calls home, Jones decided to persevere. He went on to hit .322 in 77 games, including 18 doubles, 8 triples, 6 home runs, 48 RBIs and 58 runs scored.

The next year, 1962, Jones was promoted to York (Pennsylvania) of the Double-A Eastern League. The teenager had a good year for the White Roses, hitting .309 in 127 games. The young shortstop led the league in triples with 13. He scored 77 runs and knocked in 52.

In 1963, after a very good spring training in which he nearly made the Red Sox opening day roster, Jones was promoted to the Seattle Rainiers of the Triple-A Pacific Coast League. Jones, switched to second base with the emergence of Rico Petrocelli (who would be Jones' roommate in the major leagues), had a decent year. His average dropped to .255 but he scored 78 runs while clubbing 7 home runs and 11 triples.

Spring training in 1964 was a very good one for the 20-year-old Jones, but he expected to be in the minors that year. As spring training marched on, however, Jones was still with the big club. One day late in the spring season, pitching coach Bob Turley found Jones working out in center field. As he walked by, the former Yankee pitching star joked to Jones, "I heard you're going to be rooming with me this season."[9] That was how Dalton Jones learned he was heading north with the Boston Red Sox.

Dalton with Rico Petrocelli.

Jones made his major league debut on April 17, 1964, the home opener at Fenway Park. He contributed his first major league hit, an RBI triple. It came in the third inning off White Sox hurler Joel Horlen. The Red Sox went on to beat the White Sox, 4-1, in a game that also featured another Red Sox rookie, Massachusetts native Tony Conigliaro, who hit the first pitch he saw at Fenway Park for a home run.[10] The next day, also at Fenway, Jones hit his first major league home run, a solo shot in the ninth inning off White Sox lefthander Don Mossi. After the game, Boston manager Johnny Pesky called Clinton Jones to celebrate Dalton's home run. Red Sox announcer Curt Gowdy gave Jones and Tony Conigliaro videotapes of the games in which each hit his first home run. In those days before VCRs and before universal TV coverage, that was a rare gift.

1964 proved to be an acceptable debut year for Dalton Jones. He was hitting over .300 late in May but then saw his average drop to as low as .218 in early August before settling at .230 for the year. Jones scored 37 runs and batted in 39 in 118 games for the eighth-place Red Sox. The highlight of his season came on May 19 at Fenway Park against the Los Angeles Angels. The Sox were losing 3-0 in the bottom of the ninth. Jones, who had not played in the game to this point, kept walking in front of manager Johnny Pesky to get noticed. Pesky relented and told Jones he would bat for (Red Sox pitcher Bob) Heffner.[11]

Heffner was due up seventh in the inning. After two quick outs, it looked as though Jones would not hit. Dick Stuart walked, however, and then went to third on Tony Conigliaro's double. A hit batsman and another walk produced a run and left the bases loaded for pinch-hitter Dalton Jones. As Jones would tell the *Boston Globe*'s Ray Fitzgerald three years later, "Pesky sends me up to pinch hit and I'm scared out of my mind."[12] Jones whistled a double past Angels pitcher Don Lee on a 3-2 count. The hit cleared the bases giving the Red Sox the walk-off victory, 4-3. It was Jones' most meaningful hit yet as a Red Sox pinch-hitter and it helped propel him into a role for which he would achieve some fame, at least among Red Sox fans.

While Jones had some success at the plate, he had some trouble in the field. Committing an error in each of his first three games, he was labeled, perhaps unfairly, as a defensive liability—a label that was to stick with him throughout his career. He played 85 games at second in 1964, sharing time with Chuck Schilling and Felix Mantilla. Second base was still a new position for Jones, and in 1964 he committed 16 errors for a .959 fielding percentage.

The next two years, 1965 and 1966, were lackluster seasons for the Red Sox. Tom Yawkey's so called "country club" may have been pleasant for the players, but it didn't do much for the winning percentage or the gate receipts. The Red Sox finished ninth in a 10-team league both years. Jones had a slightly better year in 1965 than in 1964. In '65, Jones was still batting over .300 in late August before finishing at .270. He also reached career highs in hits (99) and total bases (137).

Highlights for the season include a five-hit day against the Senators in Washington on July 9 and an RBI triple off Luis Tiant, providing the only run Dave Morehead would need when he pitched his no-hitter against the Cleveland Indians on September 16 at nearly empty Fenway Park. Nine days later, in another historic moment, Jones batted (and reached on an error) against the 59-year-old Satchel Paige in Kansas City.

Jones improved offensively despite tearing a hamstring muscle and moving to his third infield position in four years. He suffered the injury rounding first at Fenway while legging out a double against Luis Tiant in early May. Jones would play with his leg wrapped the rest of his career.[13] When Frank Malzone hurt his foot early in the season, manager Billy Herman put Jones at third base. Jones played so well at the position that he earned the starting spot against right-handed pitching after Malzone returned.[14] Jones played 81 games at third base and made 17 errors in 243 chances.

In 1966, Jones lost his starting job to rookie Joe Foy, and his offensive production dropped off. He batted only .234 in 252 at-bats, more than 100 fewer than in either of his previous two major league seasons. It was a struggle all year. Jones' average never reached .240; he was batting .200 on the Fourth of July. Jones played in 70 games at second base and just three at third base. He committed 10 errors in 260 chances, improving his second base fielding percentage from two seasons previous. Jones' batting highlight for the year came on July 6 in the first game of a doubleheader at Yankee Stadium. With the score tied, 3-3, Jones batted for the pitcher in the ninth inning and hit a one-out, two-run home run to make the score 5-3, which held up when the Yankees were retired in the bottom of the frame.

The Red Sox in the spring, summer, and fall of 1967 have been much chronicled. While most of the accolades deservedly go to Yaz, Jim Lonborg, Tony C, Boomer, Rico, and a few others, fans remember Dalton Jones' clutch hitting, especially pinch-hitting late in the 1967 campaign. In terms of raw offensive output, it was his least productive major league season so far. He played in only 89 games and had 159 at-bats. While he hit .289, he had only 65 total bases. Jones was a man without a position in 1967 and was relegated almost entirely to pinch-hitting. Rookie Mike Andrews was the starter at second, while Foy held down the hot corner. Freshman manager Dick Williams gave Jones a start when he could. For example, when Foy was in Williams' doghouse for being overweight late in April, Jones had five consecutive starts (April 21-25). Jones responded. He hit .368 during that stretch, scoring at least one run in each game as the Sox won four of the five games.

On May 24, in a rare start, Jones hit a solo home run off Denny McLain at Tiger Stadium. It was enough for Jim Lonborg, who blanked the Tigers, 1-0. Between June 8 and September 4, however, Jones started only one game. In addition to being forced out of the starting lineup for baseball reasons, there was also Uncle Sam to contend with. In 1967, the war in Vietnam was raging. The Red Sox and other teams were keen to keep their players out of the military draft. They made sure all of their eligible players were assigned to Reserve units. Lonborg, Jones, and other players did two-week stints during the season. Even though his playing time was limited, Jones made the most of his spot starts and pinch-hitting opportunities. He was especially productive late in the season as one of the closest pennant races in American League history unfolded.

Jones' average had dipped to .220 by August 17. Starting with a pinch hit on August 19, Jones went 24 for 59 (a .407 clip) the rest of the season, with one home run, 14 RBIs and six runs scored. On August 20, he came off the bench and had two key hits to help the Sox erase an 8-0 deficit against California as the Sox went on to win 9-8. On August 22, he broke a scoreless tie with a pinch-hit, two-run triple in the seventh inning off Phil Ortega of the Washington Senators. The Sox won, 2-1, which put them in second place, just a percentage point behind the White Sox. On September 18, the Red Sox played the Tigers in Detroit. Going into the game, the Sox were trailing the first-place Tigers by one game. Jones got the start at third because he hit well in Tiger Stadium and had hit a home run off

Always a fan favorite, Jones contributed substantially in the last two weeks of the '67 season.

McLain, the Tiger starter, earlier in the year. The move to start Jones paid off. He had four hits in five at-bats with two RBIs, including a 10th-inning home run off Mike Marshall. Jones speared Bill Freehan's line drive for the final out in the bottom of the 10th, giving the Red Sox a 6-5 victory and a share of first place. "This had to be the best game of baseball I've ever played in the big leagues," Jones told the *Boston Globe*'s Clif Keane.[15] On September 24, Jones got the start at third again. This time he went 4-for-6 with a double and triple and five RBIs as the Sox beat the Baltimore Orioles, 11-7.

When the Red Sox had to beat the Twins on the final two days of the 1967 season to ensure at least a playoff game for the American League pennant, Jones had a key role to play. In the penultimate game, with the Twins leading 1-0, Jones had a pinch-hit single in the bottom of the fifth inning, moving Reggie Smith to third. Jerry Adair knocked in Smith; Carl Yastrzemski drove in Jones for the go-ahead run. The Sox never trailed after that and won, 6-4, giving them a share of first place with the Twins. On October 1, the last game of the regular season, Jones got the start at third and batted in the second spot in the order. He had two hits in four at-bats, including a single to keep the rally going in the five-run sixth inning. Jones scored one of the five Red Sox runs as they beat the Twins, 5-3. The win and the Tigers' loss later that afternoon gave the Red Sox their first pennant in 21 years.

Given that Jones had so few starts in the regular season, it seems somewhat surprising he started four of the seven World Series games. Dick Williams wanted the left-handed hitting Jones in the lineup against St. Louis right-handers Bob Gibson, Dick Hughes, and Nelson Briles. With that vote of confidence, Jones responded. He hit .389 for the Series, second only to Yastrzemski among Red Sox hitters. Jones had a key pinch hit in Game Six, with the Red Sox facing elimination, down three games to two. Jones did not start even though the

right-handed Hughes was the starting pitcher for the Red Birds. (Jones unsuccessfully lobbied Dick Williams for the chance to start. At the time, he was the leading Red Sox hitter at .353. "I told him that I thought I deserved to play, I thought I had done the job.")[16] With one out in the bottom of the seventh inning, with the score tied 4-4, Jones was sent up to hit for John Wyatt. Facing former teammate Jack Lamabe, he singled to right field. The next batter, Joe Foy, plated Jones with a double to left for the go-ahead run. The Red Sox went on to score four in the inning, won the game, and forced a Game Seven the next day. Jones pinch hit in the eighth inning of the deciding game, with the Red Sox down, 7-1, and drew a walk. He stayed in the game to play third in the top of the ninth. It was the last time Jones would appear in a postseason game.

Dalton Jones thought, after the way he played third base in the World Series, he would compete with Joe Foy for the starting job in 1968.[17] Jones did start the first six games of the season at third base. He was batting only .071, however, when Joe Foy got the starting nod against White Sox lefty Gary Peters on April 18. Foy played well and became the regular third baseman the rest of the season. Williams gave Jones a chance to be an everyday player, but it meant learning a new infield position. By mid-season, first baseman George Scott was struggling at the plate (as were many players in the "Year of the Pitcher"). Jones started at first against Oakland on July 1 and played first base in 55 of the final 88 Red Sox games in 1968. He acquitted himself very well, handling 478 chances with only two errors.

While his fielding was improving, Jones' batting average was going in the other direction. He had decided he was going to hit more home runs and tried to pull everything.[18] Pitchers started pitching him outside. In the past, Jones would have taken the pitch the other way, to left field. Now he was hitting ground balls to second. Jones had 354 at-bats in 1968, nearly 200 more than in 1967, but his average plummeted to .234. One bright spot was his specialty, pinch-hitting; he had 11 pinch hits and a .407 average. Jones struck out 53 times, though, a career high.

As the offensive struggles continued, Jones put more and more pressure on himself.[19] The only person who could pull Jones out of his batting funk, Clinton Jones, was dying of leukemia 1,500 miles away. Clinton Jones would succumb to the disease the next year. Jones had more time at first in 1969, playing very well there, but his batting average dropped to .220. While he cut back on the strikeouts, he was not providing the offensive power major league teams expect from a corner infielder. The two-year experiment at first base was over and it was time for a change. On December 13, 1969, the Red Sox traded Jones to the Detroit Tigers for utility infielder Tom Matchick. Overall, Jones hit .243 with the Red Sox with 26 home runs and 186 RBIs. He hit well in pressure situations, compiling a .271 average as a pinch hitter. He remains the Red Sox all-time pinch hit leader with 55.

At first, Jones was happy about the trade.[20] He was ready for a change and he had always hit well in Tiger Stadium. When the 1970 season started, however, it was clear the Tigers' plans did not include Jones. The Tigers already had a left-handed pinch hitting specialist, Gates Brown. Jones was used sparingly as a utility infielder, appearing in only 62 games in the field, 89 overall. One "highlight" of the season came on July 9 against his former team. Jones came in as a pinch-hitter in the bottom of the seventh inning. With the score tied, 3-3, and the bases loaded, Jones hit what should have been the first grand slam home run of his career. Inexplicably, Don Wert decided to tag up at first and Jones passed him while rounding first. Jones was called out and given credit for a single. He did get three RBIs, however, and the Tigers went on to beat the Red Sox, 7-3. Jones hit .220 for the second straight year but he led all Tigers with 11 pinch hits and a .379 average as a pinch-hitter.

In 1971, Jones' playing time was reduced even further. He played only 32 games in the field, including, for the first time, the outfield. Jones was batting .375 when Al Kaline was slowed by a pulled hamstring. Jones hit .500 with a home run in three starts in right field. After maintaining a .300 average into mid-June, Jones finished the year at .254. Due to limited playing time however, he had career lows in most offensive categories, including runs, hits, RBIs, doubles and total bases. He was the team pinch hit leader again, though, with 13 pinch hits and a .289 average.

After going hitless in his first seven games of 1972 (seven at-bats), Jones was traded by the Tigers to the Texas Rangers for pitcher Norm McRae. It was a reunion of sorts for Jones, getting to play for manager Ted Williams. It was a difficult year for Jones. He was used sparingly again, getting only 151 at-bats for the last-place Rangers. He hit a career low .159 for "one of the worst teams in baseball history."[21] Although only 28 years old, Jones was running out of chances. In fact, his last chance had come and gone. On January 25, 1973, Dalton Jones was released by the Rangers.

Jones—who had married a Cambridge, Massachusetts, native and former Miss John Hancock,

Joanne Korezniowski[22]—moved his wife and two boys, Brian and Darrin, back to Baton Rouge. Jones could not find a job outside baseball. He contacted Mel Didier, director of scouting and player development for the Montreal Expos, and begged his way back into baseball.[23] Jones was given a minor league contract for the 1973 season. He reported to the Expos' Triple-A affiliate in Hampton, Virginia, the Peninsula Whips. Jones, by his own admission, was not very good. He appeared in 59 games and batted just .208 with seven doubles and two home runs. His stint in the Expos organization was over. Jones finished his nine-year, major league career with a .235 batting average, 41 home runs and 237 RBIs. He batted .262 in his career as a pinch hitter. When he retired, his 81 pinch hits placed him second all-time among American League pinch hitters.

After baseball, Dalton Jones has had several careers, including banking, mutual fund and investment sales, and finish carpentry. He worked for several years for his father's former employer, Exxon, as an electronic instrument technician. In the late 1980s, Jones and his new wife, Barbara, moved to Plymouth, Massachusetts, where Jones started a financial services company.

In 1989, he was an infielder and coach for the Winter Haven team in the Senior League, managed by former Red Sox pitcher Bill Lee. His teammates included Ferguson Jenkins, Gary Allenson, and Bernie Carbo. Jones also played in several softball games organized by the enterprising Bill Lee.

Barbara Jones, who has a Ph.D. in education, took a job in the Charlotte, North Carolina school system. After living in Charlotte for a few years, Dalton and Barbara moved to Liberty, Mississippi, where they live today, not far from McComb, where Dalton was born.

Notes:

1. Interview with Dalton Jones, February 28, 2006.
2. *Ibidem.*
3. Interview with Dalton Jones, March 29, 2006.
4. Fitzgerald, Ray. "Pressure Pinches Year-Round" *Boston Globe*, August 21, 1967:23.
5. www.nicholls.edu/baseball
6. Taylor, Sec."Demons Need Infield Material" *The Sporting News*, February 28, 1935:8.
7. Fitzgerald, Ray, *Boston Globe*, August 21, 1967:23.
8. Salazar. "Red Sox Scout Signs Prize, Then Manages Kid in Debut" *The Sporting News*, June 21, 1961:30.
9. Interview, February 28, 2006.
10. *Ibidem.*
11. *Ibidem.*
12. Fitzgerald, Ray. "Pressure Pinches Year-Round" *Boston Globe*, August 21, 1967:23.
13. Interview, March 29, 2006. The hamstring tear likely occurred May 7, 1965.
14. Keane, Clif. "Jones Hitting Wins Third Base Position" *Boston Globe*, May 23, 1965.
15. Keane, Clif. "'Best Game I Ever Played,' Proclaims Happy Jones" *Boston Globe*, September 19, 1967:27.
16. Anderson, Dave. "Second Guessers Are Left Up Tree", *New York Times*, October 12, 1967:60.
17. "Jones Feels Sure He Can Oust Foy", *Washington Post*, March 6, 1968: E2.
18. Interview, February 28, 2006
19. *Ibidem.*
20. *Ibidem.*
21. *Ibidem.*
22. White, Diane, "No more miniskirts for her", *Boston Globe*, August 21, 1967:27.
23. Interview, February 28, 2006.

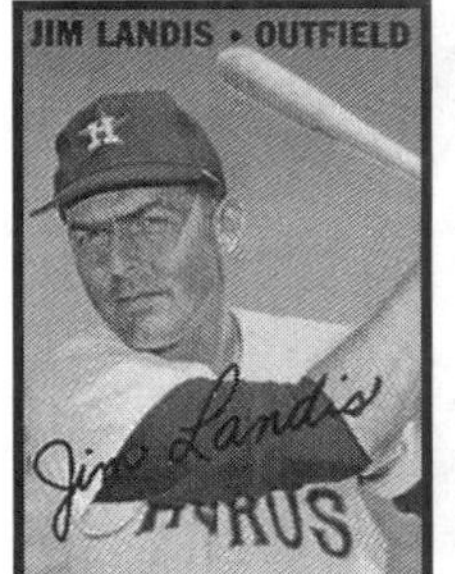

Jim Landis

by Mike Richard

	G	AB	R	H	2B	3B	HR	RBI	BB	SO	BA	OBP	SLG	SB	CS	GDP	HBP
1967 RED SOX	5	7	1	1	0	0	1	1	1	3	.143	.250	.571	0	0	0	0

Pop icon Andy Warhol once stated, "In the future everyone will be famous for 15 minutes."

In baseball terms, Jim Landis' Warhol moment actually lasted less than one week with the Impossible Dream Red Sox. He hit a home run in his second game with Boston, but soon faded into the gloaming faster than one of George Scott's long "taters."

The journeyman outfielder had a memorable stint with the Go-Go White Sox of the late 1950s, and is considered to be one of the best defensive center fielders in big league history. His .989 career fielding average placed him second only to Jimmy Piersall at the time of his retirement among major league outfielders.

James Henry Landis was born on March 9, 1934, in Fresno, California. He was signed by the Chicago White Sox as an amateur free agent in 1952, out of Contra Costa Junior College in San Pablo. Before that, he had a stellar career as a third baseman at Richmond (California) High School.

He was signed "after playing about four games at the junior college," he recalled. "I was approached by a White Sox scout named Bob Mattick who asked me about signing a big league contract and I said, 'Let's do it.'"

Landis began as a third baseman and outfielder with Wisconsin Rapids of the Class D Wisconsin State League in 1952, where he batted .274 in 92 games.

The following season he moved to Colorado Springs of the Class A Western League, where he posted a career-best .313 before spending two years with the Army.

"I was a lucky guy, I got stationed up in Alaska," he said with a chuckle. "I did get to play some baseball up there, but it wasn't a long season."

He returned to Colorado Springs in 1956, and in the same season was promoted to the Memphis Chicks of the Double-A Southern Association. In 1957, on April 16, he made his debut with the Chicago White Sox, for whom he played in 96 games that season. Chicago had Larry Doby in center and Minnie Minoso in left, and the speedy, sure-handed Landis nicely complemented the veteran outfield.

Chicago was just two years away from the memorable 1959 season. That year, the "Go-Go" White Sox became the first American League team since the Cleveland Indians (1948 and 1954) to wrestle the pennant away from the New York Yankees.

"It was a great year. We had a good ball club, we had four Hall of Famers on one team," he said, rattling off the names of Early Wynn, Luis Aparicio, Nellie Fox, and Larry Doby.

The White Sox also featured Earl Torgeson at first base, Bubba Phillips at third and catcher Sherm Lollar. Landis, Al Smith, and a platoon of Jim McAnany and Jim Rivera were in the outfield, while the pitching staff included Wynn, Bob Shaw, and Billy Pierce, with Gerry Staley and Turk Lown keys to the bullpen.

"One of the best things about the White Sox was the terrific group of guys I played with," he said. "Guys like Nellie Fox, Billy Pierce, Bob Shaw, Minnie Minoso, Jim Rivera. All these guys were true vets and I was the new kid. They were all like fathers to me."

Landis batted .272 for the pennant winners and received 66 points in balloting for American League Most Valuable Player, which was won by teammate Fox.

The White Sox were beaten in six games in the World Series by Los Angeles, which was led by the starting pitching of Johnny Podres and the bullpen work of Series MVP Larry Sherry, who won two games in relief and had two saves. In the Series, Landis batted .292 with seven hits for Chicago.

In 1960, Landis won the first of five straight Gold Gloves. A fan favorite in the Windy City, he was known for his many over-the-fence catches, stealing homers from Comiskey Park's center field bullpen.

"I knew how to play the game and I'm proud of my Gold Gloves," he said. "I think fielding was my forte, and I felt I knew the game well."

Landis' best year with the bat was 1961 when he had career highs of 22 home runs, 85 RBIs, and a .283 average.

"It was one of my best years. Everything kind of fell together for me," he said. "For a while I think I was hitting just around .300. I had a shot [at .300], but I blew it with a slump in May."

Landis was selected to his lone All-Star Game appearance in 1962.

In 1964, the White Sox had a chance to once again capture the pennant from the Yankees, falling one game shy.

After the season, Landis was involved in a three-

team deal between the White Sox, Kansas City, and Cleveland. He was traded with Mike Hershberger and Fred Talbot to Kansas City; Rocky Colavito went from Kansas City to Cleveland.

After one season playing 118 games for the last place A's, he was traded with Jim Rittwage to Cleveland for Phil Roof and Joe Rudi. His games dwindled to 63 outfield appearances with the Indians in 1966 and he was once again moved. In early January, Cleveland traded him, Doc Edwards, and Jim Weaver to Houston for Lee Maye and Ken Retzer. He began the 1967 season in Houston, but in late June, the Astros sent him to Detroit for Larry Sherry. There he played 25 games with the Tigers filling in for Al Kaline, who had broken his finger jamming his bat into the bat rack.

After Tony Conigliaro was lost to the Red Sox following his tragic beaning on August 18, the Red Sox needed some outfield help to go along with José Tartabull and George Thomas platooning in right field. On August 22, the Red Sox signed Landis after his release from Detroit, making Boston his fourth team that year.

His debut with the Red Sox was as a pinch runner for Norm Siebern on August 23. He took Tartabull's place in right field and struck out in the bottom of the ninth to end the game at Fenway.

The next day, Landis came on defensively late in the game against Washington; it was the day Conigliaro was released from Sancta Maria Hospital. With the Red Sox leading, 6-2, in the eighth inning, Landis homered off Darold Knowles providing a 7-2 cushion, but he made an even bigger contribution in the top of the ninth.

The Senators scored three runs and had the bases loaded with two outs in the ninth, when Ken McMullen hit a fastball from John Wyatt to deep right. A gust of wind caught the ball and, as Ken Coleman noted in his book *The Impossible Dream Remembered*, "Landis did a Tango under it: 'I nearly lost it in the sun,' Landis said. 'The wind slowed down and started to pull the ball away from me.'"

At the last second, Landis, running all the way, made a one-handed grab to end the game, lunging for the ball as the runners circled the bases. The victory put the Red Sox into virtually a first-place tie with Chicago, just a percentage point behind. It was one of the very few times since the 1940s that the Sox had been atop the standings this late in the season.

The heroics earned Landis a start the following night in right field against the White Sox in the first game of a doubleheader. He batted leadoff and went hitless in a 7-1 Red Sox victory. In the nightcap, Landis

Jim Landis' eighth-inning homer provided an insurance run in the August 24 win over the Washington Senators, bringing the Red Sox into a virtual tie for first.

was a late-inning replacement in right field as Chicago scored a run in the last of the ninth to win, 2-1.

His final appearance came on August 27, another late-game appearance replacing Thomas in right field in the second game of a doubleheader. Gary Peters out-dueled José Santiago, 1-0, as the White Sox scored a run in the last of the 11th inning.

The next day, Landis was released when the Red Sox signed Ken Harrelson, who had been released by the Kansas City A's after a well-publicized feud with owner Charlie Finley.

Landis' five-game totals read seven at-bats, with one hit—the solo home run—for a .143 batting average. He was reconciled to retirement and knew that the 1967 season would likely be his last in the majors, and relished his brief moment with the Red Sox.

"For me, knowing that I was going home the next year, it was nice to get to know some of those players," he said. "Being around Yastrzemski that year, even for a short time, was a nice ending to my career. I knew I'd be going out at the end of the year, so it was nice to be in the middle of a pennant race."

Ironically, the frantic 1967 American League pennant race featured three teams that Landis had played with in his career: Chicago, Detroit, and Boston.

"To be honest with you, I was pulling for Boston to win it down the stretch," Landis said. "It was the last team I was with. And to be honest, I didn't leave happily from the White Sox."

After he retired from baseball, Landis went into a safety sign business for about 15 years, catching on shortly after the creation of OSHA, the federal Occupational Safety and Health Administration. After he retired, he continued to stay active in baseball as a Babe Ruth League baseball coach in the Napa, California area for several seasons.

He and his wife, Sandra, live in Napa and are the parents of daughters Vicky and Michelle and sons Craig and Mike.

Craig, a shortstop, was the number one draft pick of the San Francisco Giants in 1977 and remained in the system through Triple-A. He was a standout baseball player and football defensive back at Stanford University. Today, Craig works as a sports agent, representing Paul Konerko, Randy Winn, and Aaron Rowand.

"Even though I only spent a week in Boston, it was a great place to be," Landis said. "Boston fans are great, and it was a good ending to my career. I had no complaints."

Rico Petrocelli

by R.R. Marshall

	G	AB	R	H	2B	3B	HR	RBI	BB	SO	BA	OBP	SLG	SB	CS	GDP	HBP
1967 RED SOX	142	491	53	127	24	2	17	66	49	93	.259	.330	.420	2	4	4	5

One of the most popular players to ever play for the Boston Red Sox, Rico Petrocelli will always be remembered for his familiar "Fenway Stroke" that sent many an opposing hurler's offerings into the net atop the Green Monster in left field. Although he was not physically imposing at 6' 0", 175 lbs., he hit 210 lifetime home runs (including a then-league-record for shortstops—40 in 1969) and his career total of 773 RBIs place him comfortably in the Red Sox top 10 in both categories. A two-time All-Star shortstop and veteran of two World Series with the Red Sox, Rico agreed to move to third base in 1971 to help fill a void in the Boston infield and enable the Red Sox to acquire shortstop Luis Aparicio. His 1976 season was his final one; Rico played in 1,553 regular-season and 17 postseason games in his 12-year career. Until 2006, he held the club fielding record for a season at two different positions in the infield, holding the third-base record and effectively tied for the shortstop mark with Vern Stephens (1950) and Rick Burleson (1980).

Americo Peter (Rico) Petrocelli was born June 27, 1943 in Brooklyn, New York, the youngest of the seven children born to Attilio and Louise. His father and cousins ran a shop specializing in sharpening tools used in the garment district. Rico developed his love for the game at an early age. At a time when there were three major league teams in New York, he was inspired by all of the great teams and players. As a youngster he was an avid Yankees fan, with his father taking him to both Yankee Stadium to see Mickey Mantle and the Bronx Bombers and to Ebbets Field to see the Brooklyn Dodgers.

Petrocelli started playing basketball at the age of six, but didn't play organized baseball until he was 12. By the time he started high school he was proficient at both sports, and would become an all-scholastic in both basketball and baseball at Sheepshead Bay High. When his family realized that he might have a chance at a professional career, he was allowed to concentrate on his athletic career full-time instead of getting a job to help support the family. His four older brothers all worked to bring in extra money, allowing him to pursue his dreams of becoming a pro baseball player. It was a sacrifice he has never forgotten.

A pitcher and a power-hitting outfielder in high school, he was considered a top prospect and a dozen scouts followed his progress his senior year. But while pitching in the city championship on an extremely cold day in 1961 he felt something snap in his right elbow. The scouts quickly disappeared until only four (Cincinnati, Philadelphia, Baltimore, and Boston) remained. The Red Sox were the first team to invite him to a workout after the injury, a gesture which made a favorable impression. He and his family made the trip to Boston and after a successful workout, stellar Red Sox scout Bots Nekola (the same scout who signed Carl Yastrzemski three years earlier) signed him.

Rico started his professional career in 1962 with Winston-Salem, North Carolina in the Carolina League—batting .277 with 17 home runs and 80 RBIs, but struggled in the field at his new position (shortstop), committing a league-high 48 errors. He was promoted to Reading in the Eastern League in 1963 and batted only .239, but he hit 19 homers and drove in 78 runs. The Red Sox brought him to Boston at the close of 1963, and the 20-year-old made his major league debut September 21 in the first game of a doubleheader against the Minnesota Twins at Fenway Park. In a portent of things to come in the future, Rico drove a Lee Stange offering off the fabled Green Monster for a double in his very first at-bat. The hit earned a standing ovation from the sparse crowd (only 6,469 in attendance) and would become one of his favorite memories.

By 1964, Petrocelli had been designated as one of the club's top prospects and was sent to the Red Sox Class AAA affiliate in Seattle. He managed to hit only .231 and, homesick and depressed over his poor play, began to doubt his ability. At the suggestion of his teammate Billy Gardner, he tried switch hitting, and when the Red Sox named him their starting shortstop at the start of the 1965 season he was encouraged to continue the experiment by then Red Sox manager Billy Herman with disastrous results—he hit only .174 through the first 20 games and the switch-hitting experiment was then scrapped. Red Sox coach Pete Runnels suggested he use his natural ability to try to pull the ball more and take advantage of Fenway's inviting left-field wall. Rico would spend the rest of the season refining his "new" swing, steadily producing results. He hit his first major

Rico Petrocelli in the clubhouse, Opening Day 1967

league home run June 20 against lefthander Gary Peters of the White Sox, and ended with 13 for the season.

His balky right elbow hampered his throwing for most of his rookie year and the problem persisted into the 1966 season, eventually landing him on the disabled list for the first time in his career. To add insult to injury, Petrocelli was not a favorite of Herman. The "old-school' manager had little patience for his brooding and insecurities and made life miserable for the young Sox shortstop. The situation came to a head when Petrocelli left the team in the middle of a game to tend to a family emergency. Herman demanded he be immediately suspended, but cooler heads in the Red Sox front office prevailed. Instead, he was fined the then-hefty amount of $1,000, but it did little to calm the conflict between manager and player. Things were finally resolved when Herman was fired in September, but even with his tormentor gone, Rico felt sure he would either be traded or sent back to the minors.

In 1967, new Red Sox manager Dick Williams took a different tack with Petrocelli. He brought longtime Red Sox minor league coach Eddie Popowski to Boston as the new third-base coach and gave him the locker next to Petrocelli. The good-natured Popowski had managed Rico at both Winston Salem in 1962 and at Reading in 1963, and helped to build the young shortstop's self-esteem with daily pep talks. Williams also helped Petrocelli to mature as a player by giving him the responsibility of being the leader of the club's young infield. Both moves resulted in giving him new-found confidence, and he blossomed as a player. He drove in the first run of the season with a single in the Red Sox 5-4 win over Chicago on Opening Day and later added a three-run homer for good measure. He earned the starting nod at shortstop for the American League in the All-Star Game, and finished with a solid all-around season batting .259 with 17 homers and 66 RBIs.

Petrocelli was a central figure in the famous Red Sox-Yankees brawl at Yankee Stadium on the evening of June 21. Both benches cleared after the two longtime

Rico works under mentor Frank Malzone.

rivals exchanged beanballs. Then Petrocelli and Yankee first baseman Joe Pepitone got involved in some friendly verbal jousting. The two were friends who had grown up in Brooklyn together, but somehow things escalated quickly into a full-scale battle. It took a dozen Yankee Stadium security guards, including Petrocelli's brother David (who pulled Rico out from under a pile of Yankee players), to help restore order. The fight was recognized as a defining moment that helped to bring the '67 Red Sox together as a team. Boston fashioned a league-best 60-39 record from that point on, winning the pennant on the final day of the season after a 5-3 win over the Minnesota Twins. It was Rico's catch of Rich Rollins' pop up that was the final out in Boston's "Impossible Dream" pennant race, a catch that would become one of the signature moments in the long history of the franchise.

Petrocelli had little success at the plate against the National League champion St. Louis Cardinals through the first five games of the 1967 World Series. Extremely run down by the long season, Petrocelli had a Vitamin B-12 shot prior to Game Six and proceeded to hit two home runs—a feat accomplished by only two other shortstops (Arky Vaughan and Alan Trammell) in a World Series game. His second homer was one of three home runs hit by the Red Sox in the fourth inning, a World Series record that still stands. Although the Red Sox lost Game Seven to the Cardinals, the future seemed bright for both the Red Sox and Petrocelli.

The success of 1967 soon dissipated as a series of injuries doomed the defending American League champions to a fourth-place finish in 1968. Petrocelli's batting average plummeted some 25 points as the chronic problem with his right elbow flared, causing him to miss 39 games. Rather than continuing to brood over his misfortune he took on a new positive attitude that winter. He changed his diet and gave up ice cream to help prevent the calcium deposits in his elbow from reforming. He also exercised his arms and wrists in the offseason. By the start of 1969 he felt stronger than at any time in his career, and the results were very evident. He began hitting home runs in bunches while hitting well over .300 for most of the first half of the season. He excelled in the field as well, threatening the record for consecutive games without an error by a shortstop by going 44 straight without a miscue. He would finish the season with a .981 fielding percentage, until 2006 the record for a Red Sox shortstop.

In July he was the overwhelming choice as the starting shortstop for the American League in the All-Star Game—his second such selection in three years. At the time he was hitting .309 with a remarkable 25 home runs. In the last year prior to the All-Star vote being returned to the fans, he earned more votes from his fellow players, managers, and coaches than any other player in the league. With the Red Sox out of contention since midsummer, his quest to break the American League record for home runs by a shortstop (39, by the Red Sox own Vern Stephens in 1949) became the big story in September. The record-breaker came on the evening of September 29 against the Washington Senators' Jim Shellenback at RFK Stadium. He finished the season with 40 homers and 97 RBIs while hitting .297. His .589 slugging percentage was second only to Oakland's Reggie Jackson in the American League.

Rico showed that 1969 was no fluke when he came through with another solid season in 1970. He hit 29 homers and knocked in 103 runs, becoming the first Red Sox shortstop to crack the 100-RBI barrier since Stephens in 1950. He also played in a career-high 157 games, showing his injury problems were a thing of the past. Over the winter, Red Sox general manager Dick O'Connell told him the Red Sox had a deal on the table for future Hall of Fame shortstop Luis Aparicio, but in an ultimate show of respect O'Connell told him he wouldn't make the deal unless Petrocelli would be comfortable moving to third base.

Rico readily endorsed the deal as being beneficial

Rico turns the double play, as Mike Andrews watches it unfold.

A number of Boston ballplayers had a passion for music—Rico played drums (and appeared on half the tracks of an album by organist John Kiley), while Tony Conigliaro, Sparky Lyle, José Santiago, and Reggie Smith were among the other singers and musicians on the team.

to the team and agreed to make the change. He reported early to spring training and worked for hours with former Red Sox All-Star third baseman Frank Malzone—the results were nothing short of amazing. Petrocelli set a major league record for third basemen with 77 straight games without an error. He also led the league in fielding percentage with a scintillating .976 mark (still the team record). He continued to produce on offense at a healthy clip, hitting 28 home runs and knocking in 89 runs while leading the team with what the Red Sox calculated as 12 game-winning hits. Between 1969-1971, his 97 home runs and 289 RBIs were the most by any Red Sox player.

Although his power output dropped significantly in 1972 (only 15 home runs) he continued to drive in runs at a consistent pace, leading the Red Sox with 75 RBIs despite hitting only .240. He was especially hot in August, hitting .344 with 23 RBIs to help the Red Sox surge into contention for the division title—they would finish a scant one-half game behind Detroit. He also led the majors in grand slams with three. He would finish his career with a total of nine grand slams, good for second on the Red Sox all-time leader list behind only the great Ted Williams.

The injury problems that had plagued him early in his career returned with a vengeance in 1973. He missed the last 47 games of the season with chronic elbow problems, and his loss was keenly felt. Boston was only 2½ games behind division-leading Baltimore when he left the starting lineup on August 12, but finished eight games off the pace. Off-season elbow surgery had him back and fit to start the 1974 season, but a series of new injuries set him back yet again. A nagging hamstring injury plagued him for most of the early part of the

season, and then disaster struck September 15 when he was hit in the head by a pitch thrown by Milwaukee's Jim Slaton. The beaning shelved him for the rest of the season, and the Red Sox ended up squandering a 7½ game lead near the end of August—staggering home in third place. Despite his time on the disabled list he still tied for the team lead in home runs with 15 and finished second with 76 RBIs.

Although Petrocelli was in the Opening Day lineup for the Red Sox at the start of the 1975 season, it was readily apparent that he was still suffering from the after-effects of the beaning. Although it was not public knowledge, he suffered from a severe inner ear imbalance that caused him a great deal of trouble with his sense of balance. While he continued to perform at his usual high level in the field, he had difficulty gauging the ball as it left the pitcher's hand and his batting average dropped significantly. Despite his shortcomings at the plate, his leadership ability came to the forefront with a new group of young players that drove the Red Sox to their first pennant since 1967. With the red-hot Baltimore Orioles coming on strong in the season's final month, Rico again demonstrated his ability to come through in the clutch. His solo homer off Baltimore ace Jim Palmer on the evening of September 16 accounted for the winning run in Boston's 2-0 shutout of the Orioles—a key victory that effectively put the Red Sox in firm control of the pennant race.

Thanks to medication that treated his inner ear imbalance, Petrocelli returned to his old form in time for the postseason. His seventh-inning homer off Oakland's relief ace Rollie Fingers in Game Two of the 1975 ALCS widened the lead in a one-run game and helped to propel the Red Sox to a three-game sweep of the defending champion A's. His stellar play continued in the World Series against Cincinnati, as he hit .308 and contributed some fine fielding plays at third base as Boston came within a run of winning their first World Series since 1918.

While Rico's play in the field continued to be above reproach, his lack of productivity at the plate became an issue in 1976. He began suffering reactions to the medication he was taking to correct his inner ear problems and he was forced to discontinue its use. The problems with his balance returned and severely hampered his ability at the plate. He hit a career-low .213 in 1976, and when Don Zimmer took over as manager shortly after the All-Star break he gave rookie Butch Hobson significant playing time at third. Rico was tried briefly at second base, but with little success. In a move that shocked New England, Petrocelli was cut at the end of spring training in 1977, ending his 12-year playing career in Boston.

Out of baseball for the first time in his life, he decided to remain close to the sports scene in Boston by writing a regular column in the *Boston Herald* that followed the progress of the Red Sox. He was also one of the early pioneers of the sports talk radio scene in Boston, co-hosting a show with Glenn Ordway. In 1979 he joined longtime Red Sox broadcaster Ken Coleman in the radio booth as the color commentator. On July 24 he had the privilege of calling former Red Sox teammate Carl Yastrzemski's 400th home run in a game against the Oakland A's at Fenway Park.

Petrocelli stayed only one year in the radio booth and after several years in the business world returned to uniform in 1986 as a manager for the Chicago White Sox Class A affiliate in Appleton, Wisconsin. He stayed in the White Sox organization a total of three years, eventually being promoted to manager of their AA club in Birmingham, Alabama in the Southern League, but left to return home as the new Director of Sports Programs for the Jimmy Fund between 1989-1991.

His love for the game moved him to accept the position as manager of the Red Sox AAA affiliate in Pawtucket in 1992. That began a six-year stay for him in the Boston organization as a roving instructor. On September 7, 1997, Petrocelli was rewarded for his outstanding Red Sox career when he and four other former players were inducted into the Red Sox Hall of Fame.

Since leaving baseball he runs his own private company, Petrocelli Marketing Group, based in Nashua, New Hampshire. He resides there with his wife of 40 years Elsie. They have four grown sons; Michael (39), twins James and Bill (38), and Danny (36). Rico remains active in the Boston sports scene as a frequent guest on Boston TV and radio sports programs.

Kicking off the 1967 season, Rico had a terrific Opening Day, going 3-for-3 with a home run and four RBIs. An airplane towing a banner reading "Go Rico" greeted him his first at-bat. Gibbs Oil of Saugus, the company he had worked for in the offseason, had hired the plane.

Ken Poulsen

by Charlie Bevis

	G	AB	R	H	2B	3B	HR	RBI	BB	SO	BA	OBP	SLG	SB	CS	GDP	HBP
1967 RED SOX	5	5	0	1	1	0	0	0	0	2	.200	.200	.400	0	0	0	0

After postponing his wedding when he was unexpectedly called up to the Boston Red Sox in June of 1967, Ken Poulsen collected one base hit in five at-bats during his brief two-week major league career. That lone base hit by Poulsen was witnessed by a SABR member, then 13 years old, who was at Fenway Park that evening and recorded the hit on a scorecard that he still has more than 35 years later.

The hit was Poulsen's one and only major-league moment. The ballplayer, after his cup-of-coffee American League experience in 1967, disappeared from public view. Little is known of his private life, either before or after his brief rise to the big leagues. Over the years, Red Sox officials, former teammates, and baseball historians have unsuccessfully attempted to track him down, to no avail. But for many Red Sox fans, his moment of glory in 1967 was reason enough to remember him fondly as a contributor to a dream season.

Kenneth Sterling Poulsen was born on August 4, 1947, in Van Nuys, California, a section of northern Los Angeles in the San Fernando Valley. His father, Ralph Poulsen, was a commercial airline pilot. Poulsen played three years of varsity baseball at Birmingham High School in Van Nuys, where his team won the championship of the West Valley League each of those three years.

In 1963, as a 15-year-old sophomore at Birmingham High, Poulsen started at shortstop on Coach Bob Zuber's championship squad. After Birmingham lost in the semifinals of the Los Angeles city high school baseball tournament, the *Los Angeles Times* ran a story on Birmingham's prospects in 1964, since seven starters would be returning to the team the following season. "Also in the infield will be shortstop Ken Poulsen, another sophomore, who only hit .167 in league play, but who smashed three for eight in the tournament," the *Times* noted.

At the beginning of his junior year in the spring of 1964, Poulsen had his picture appear in the *Los Angeles Times* as part of a preview story on the Birmingham High team. The caption read: "Holding handfuls of bats while waiting their turn in the batting cage are two Birmingham High veterans, Ken Poulsen, left, and third baseman Dave Drysdale, both juniors." Poulsen moved to the outfield that year, as his Birmingham High team not only won the West Valley League title but also the Los Angeles city championship. In the title game on June 2 at Bovard Field, Birmingham defeated Grant High, 2-0, as right fielder Poulsen went 0-for-3 while batting fifth in Coach Zuber's lineup.

Birmingham High went undefeated in the regular season during Poulsen's senior year in 1965. Under new baseball coach Hy Cohen, Birmingham High had a 26-game winning streak snapped in the quarterfinals of the city tournament when the team was upset by Polytechnic High. Poulsen was named a first-team all-star in the West Valley League and third-team all-star on the All-City team.

Although Poulsen wasn't the best player on his high school team, he was the highest draft choice in baseball's amateur draft in June of 1965 among high school baseball players from the city of Los Angeles. His play on American Legion teams during the summer may have helped his draft stock.

Because 1965 was the first year of baseball's amateur draft, Poulsen was unable to negotiate with major league teams or cop a big signing bonus like the $250,000 deal handed to Rich Reichardt in 1964. The Boston Red Sox saw major league potential in Poulsen, and selected him in the third round (45th overall).

Reflecting the vagaries of talent evaluation in 1965, Poulsen was selected ahead of many future major league stars in that year's amateur draft, including Andy Messersmith (53rd), Ken Holtzman (61st), Stan Bahnsen (68th), and Graig Nettles (74th). The fifth round choice of the Red Sox in 1965 was Amos Otis (95th), who went on to a 17-year major-league career, mostly with the Kansas City Royals. Poulsen was selected not long after future Hall of Fame catcher Johnny Bench, who was taken in the second round (36th overall).

Poulsen didn't immediately sign with the Red Sox, however, as he used the only leverage he had at the time—the threat to play college baseball. Poulsen played local ball that summer and then entered Pierce Junior College in Woodland Hills, California, where the baseball coach was Bob Zuber, his former coach at Birmingham High. Red Sox scout Joe Stephenson finally got Poulsen's signature on a contract in December 1965, just before the expiration of the six-month period that the Red Sox had to sign Poulsen.

The Sox assigned Poulsen to their farm team in Winston-Salem, North Carolina, in the Class A Carolina League for the 1966 season. Winston-Salem went on to have the best record in the Carolina League at 82-58, although the team lost in the playoff finals to Rocky Mount, North Carolina.

In 1967, Poulsen went to spring training with the Red Sox in Winter Haven, Florida. After going 0-for-3 in a March 13 exhibition game against the New York Mets, Poulsen was cut by Red Sox manager Dick Williams and sent to the minor league training camp for reassignment. Poulsen returned to Winston-Salem for the 1967 season.

On June 28, 1967, Poulsen was called up to the Red Sox to temporarily replace Dalton Jones, who had to report for two weeks of Army Reserve duty at Camp Drum in New York. The departure of Jones was a common occurrence during the Vietnam War era. Poulsen was unexpectedly promoted—the Sox reached down three levels into their minor league system for a left-handed hitter, bypassing righty-hitting infielders at both the Triple-A and Double-A levels— and caused turmoil in Poulsen's life. That weekend he had planned to marry his high school sweetheart, Vicki Swaton, whom he had met three years earlier at a high school track meet.

"Ken Poulsen, newly acquired infielder, yesterday called off his wedding to play for the Boston Red Sox," the *Boston Globe* wrote in a page one story about the cancellation of the nuptials. "His wedding was to have taken place in Winston-Salem, N.C., tomorrow morning. The bride was there, the guests invited, the parson engaged." Poulsen and Swaton had timed the wedding to coincide with the completion of her freshman year at Pierce Junior College.

"We can always get married...but how often does a guy get sent up to the big leagues," bride-to-be Swaton philosophically asked the *Globe*. "At first I was disappointed, but I've been so busy since we heard the news, that I've gotten over it. In fact, my mother took it worse than I did. She's been packed for a week at our home in California [getting ready to fly to Winston-Salem]."

"She was stunned, but she was happy too I got the chance to be with the Red Sox," Poulsen said at the time. "Vicki got to work on her phone and started calling off the wedding, canceling arrangements, and notifying guests." That evening, Swaton kissed her fiancé at the airport as he caught a plane to join the Red Sox. It is not certain whether Poulsen later married Swaton, and a check of marriage records at the Winston-Salem church where the wedding was expected to take place did not reveal any clues.

Poulsen's stint with the Red Sox occurred at a turning point for the team, which would eventually burgeon into the "Impossible Dream" season. He met the Red Sox team on its western road trip as the Bosox began their series with the Kansas City Athletics. After sitting on the bench for all the games in Kansas City, Poulsen saw his first on-field action in the next series, against the California Angels.

On July 3, Poulsen substituted for Jerry Adair at shortstop late in the team's 9-3 victory. The next day, in an evening game on the Fourth of July, Poulsen pinch hit for fellow rookie Sparky Lyle in the ninth inning in the midst of a Red Sox rally. With runners on second and third, Angels pitcher Minnie Rojas retired Poulsen for the second out on his way to saving California's 4-3 victory.

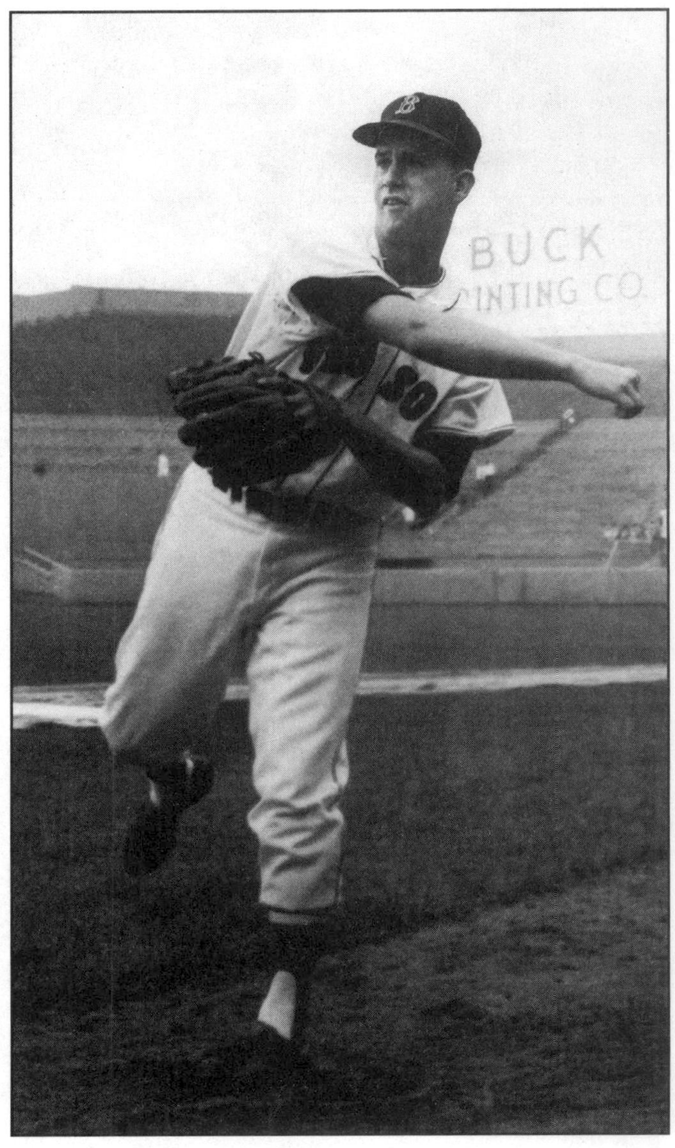

Poulsen keeps loose on the field at Fenway.

Since the Angels played in Anaheim, just 30 miles south of his hometown of Van Nuys, Poulsen's parents and friends may have witnessed his first major league game.

Poulsen got into two more games, at Tiger Stadium in Detroit, before the team headed back to Boston for a homestand following the All-Star Game. On July 8, Poulsen pinch hit again for Lyle and was retired by Tiger pitcher Denny McLain. On July 9, Poulsen substituted at third base for Joe Foy in the first game of a Sunday doubleheader and was unsuccessful in two at-bats against Tigers pitchers Earl Wilson and Mike Marshall.

Poulsen's last major league appearance came Friday night, July 14, at Fenway Park against the Baltimore Orioles. Jim Lonborg won his 12th game of the season in an 11-5 Boston victory, as Tony Conigliaro hit a two-run homer in the first inning and Carl Yastrzemski collected three hits. Poulsen played three innings in the field, entering the game in the top of the seventh inning to take the place of Foy at third base.

In the bottom of the seventh inning, Poulsen went to bat against Orioles pitcher Jim Hardin with two outs and no runners on base. Poulsen poked a hit over third base into the left-field corner in front of the Green Monster and stood proudly on second base with his first—and only—major league hit, a double. He was left stranded on second base, however, when George Thomas made the third out of the inning. The box score in the next day's newspapers showed two-base hits by Boston players Yastrzemski, Petrocelli, and Poulsen. In the Sunday newspapers, the Red Sox batting average table showed Poulsen with a .200 league batting average, sandwiched between Mike Ryan at .211 and Bob Tillman at .197.

Only briefly appearing in a Red Sox uniform, Ken Poulsen doubled in his final major league at-bat.

The July 14 victory started a 10-game winning streak that catapulted the Red Sox from fifth place in the standings (42-40 record before the game) to second place on July 23, just one-half game out of first place with a 52-40 record.

"It was the longest local winning streak in 10 years, and when the conquerors returned from Cleveland the night of July 23, there were 15,000 fanatics at Logan Airport," Dan Shaughnessy of the *Boston Globe* recounted in a 25th anniversary retrospective on the team. "This was the first gathering of what today is known as Red Sox Nation. Airport officials said the crowd was bigger than the one that greeted the Beatles. There would be no more crowds of 461 fans (September 1965). There would be no more battles for the basement with the likes of the Washington Senators. From this point forward, the Red Sox would be annual contenders, wildly popular at the gate and on the airwaves."

Poulsen didn't get a chance to bask in the fan adulation after the 10-game win streak. Dalton Jones returned from military duty and was in the Red Sox lineup July 16, as the Sox shipped Poulsen back to Winston-Salem. As the Red Sox magically wound their way to the AL pennant—with Yaz winning the MVP Award and Lonborg the Cy Young trophy—and then lost the World Series to the St. Louis Cardinals in seven games, Poulsen languished in baseball obscurity in the Carolina League.

By October, his Red Sox teammates had already forgotten about Poulsen when time came to vote on World Series shares. The players decided not to allocate Poulsen any part of the player proceeds, not even a small token gesture to serve as a wedding present. The *Boston Globe* on October 31 reported that the Red Sox players had voted a one-third share to George Smith, who was injured in spring training and never played an inning during the season, and a flat $1,000 to Ken Brett, a late-season addition from the minor leagues. Jim Landis and Gerry Moses, who both had short stints

with the team, received $250 apiece. But nothing was parceled for Poulsen. "Other recipients of Red Sox generosity were two bat boys, a clubhouse boy, two groundskeepers, and a parking lot attendant," the *Globe* story noted. "All received $750 each." There is no record to indicate why Poulsen was left out of the shares.

Four weeks after the players left him out of the World Series bonus pool, Poulsen was abandoned by Red Sox management when he was left unprotected in the minor league draft. The New York Yankees drafted Poulsen after taking Minnesota outfielder Andy Kosko. "The New York Yankees, who once dominated the game so thoroughly that they rarely drafted anybody, chose three players and got the pick of the litter," the *New York Times* reported on November 29. Besides Kosko and Dale Spier from the San Francisco farm system, "the Bombers also claimed Ken Poulsen, a 20-year-old third baseman, from Boston's farm system."

Boston hardly thought Poulsen was a "pick of the litter" player, according to the team's minor league director, Neil Mahoney. "I will not be surprised, though, if the Yankees return Ken Poulsen," Mahoney said after the draft, alluding to the fact that the Yankees could get half their money back by returning Poulsen. As the *Globe* reported, "According to Mahoney, Poulsen—who appeared in five games for the short-handed Sox in July—'retrogressed.' The Yankees seemed stunned by reports they heard after having paid $25,000 for Poulsen." Mahoney told the *Globe* that he had expected Poulsen to be demoted within the Sox farm system in 1968.

Early in 1968 spring training, the Yankees sent Poulsen to their minor league camp and eventually assigned him to their Binghamton, New York, team in the Double-A Eastern League. At Binghamton, Poulsen played against many of his former Winston-Salem teammates who were now with Pittsfield, the Red Sox Massachusetts-based farm team at the Double-A level. The next year, 1969, the Yankees sent Poulsen to Kinston of the Carolina League, where he tried to convert into a pitcher. He continued playing until 1973, briefly making it to Triple A as a pitcher with a decent ERA, but then called it a career.

The miracle Red Sox team of 1967 became part of New England sports lore. Since the Red Sox had lost contact with Poulsen shortly after the 1967 season, no one could locate Poulsen when anniversaries of the 1967 season and team reunions were celebrated.

When the 15th anniversary rolled around in 1982, "only two members of the team couldn't be tracked down," the *Boston Globe* reported. "One, curiously, is reliever Dan Osinski. The other, not so curiously, is Ken Poulsen, the then 19-year-old third baseman who had five at-bats in the week he came up from Winston-Salem when Dalton Jones had to go to National Guard [actually Reserve] summer camp. A couple of members of the team didn't even remember Poulsen, although his minor league teammates recall him mainly as Sally Field's high school boyfriend in Van Nuys, Calif." (Although the future "Flying Nun" attended the same high school as Poulsen, she graduated a year earlier. There is no confirmation that they had ever dated.)

Ken Coleman in his 1987 book, *The Impossible Dream Remembered: The 1967 Red Sox*, reported that Poulsen was working in residential construction in Simi Valley, California. At the team's 25th anniversary in 1992, the *Globe* again tried to track Poulsen down and at that time reported that he operated a cattle ranch in Oakhurst, California.

Poulsen became a nostalgic footnote to the Impossible Dream saga. In an August 4, 1985, column in the *Boston Globe*, Peter Gammons wrote: "Happy 38th birthday, Ken Poulsen, such a vital part of The Impossible Dream." In a May 20, 1990, story about an old-timers game at Fenway Park, Bob Ryan of the *Globe* wrote about the fielding prowess of first baseman George "Boomer" Scott: "When Frank Malzone's throw came up a foot and a half short, Boomer flicked his famed Black Beauty and the ball disappeared into the leather. At that moment, it was 1967 all over again and you can bet your autographed picture of Ken Poulsen that somewhere in the stands, a father poked a son or daughter in the ribs and said, 'Didn't I tell you? Nobody ever dug 'em out like the Boomer.'" In 1992, Gammons exhorted, "It might not be a bad idea for some current players to thank Lonborg for drilling Tillotson, ...remind Rico Petocelli how great he was, or remember Ken Poulsen."

The 1967 Impossible Dream team has attained mythical status in New England sports history. "If you were a contributor to the 1967 Red Sox, you will go to your grave knowing you were part of something special," Bob Ryan wrote in the *Boston Globe* in 2002. "Very few people in sport can say they helped change the course of a franchise's history, but that is precisely what the 1967 Red Sox did. We can speculate about a lot of things forever. But we *know* when modern Red Sox history began, and the year is 1967."

His lone major league base hit, on July 14, 1967, may have been a personal dream for Poulsen. Perhaps more importantly, though, Poulsen played a small role in the success of what became the "Impossible Dream" season for the 1967 Red Sox and as a historic footnote to a year that changed Red Sox history.

Finding Ken Poulsen

On the numerous anniversaries of the 1967 Impossible Dream season, there is one ballplayer who neither the team nor reporters ever seemed to be able to locate. He is Ken Poulsen, who filled in for Dalton Jones while Jones was on a two-week Army Reserve stint. Poulsen had five at-bats during his short stay with the Sox, played six more years in the minors but then seemingly disappeared. As early as the 15th reunion in 1982, the *Boston Globe* reported that Poulsen "couldn't be tracked down." Later researchers routinely struck out.

SABR members believe it is important to gather, document, and share information on all major league players, whether a Yastrzemski or a "cup of coffee" player who only had a handful of games in the big leagues, and it just seemed like Poulsen represented a loose end and a challenge to try and locate this former Red Sox player who had dropped off the map.

Charlie Bevis wrote an excellent biography based on available material. It nagged, though, the way Charlie was forced to conclude his piece. Ken Poulsen was out there somewhere. Was he reluctant to talk? Wanting to put baseball behind him like Tony Horton does? We learned through a mutual friend—a SABR member and former major leaguer—that Tony preferred not to open those pages in his life, which we respected. With Poulsen, no one seemed to know.

Web searches had turned up nothing. A private search firm turned up nothing. Finally, while the book on the 1967 team was literally being laid out by the designer, I decided to give it one last push and to try to take advantage of SABR's network of researchers. SABR's online membership directory found three members living in Van Nuys, California, where Poulsen attended Birmingham High School. I contacted them by e-mail and asked for help in perhaps locating a copy of his graduating class's yearbook, which would list the names of classmates. He was at one time engaged to be married to a Vicky Swaton; perhaps some Swatons could be found who could shed light on the "missing" Poulsen. There were 1,593 Poulsens with listed telephone numbers in the United States, but "only" 257 in California.

SABR member Barry Rubinowitz of Van Nuys came up with phone numbers for Poulsen's two high school baseball coaches, but neither had heard of him since the mid-1960s. This wasn't going anywhere, and I hit the point where there were maybe just 48 hours remaining before it would truly be too late to add anything to Charlie Bevis's bio. Then an idea popped off the typeset page of Charlie's work: Poulsen had had a father named Ralph. If living, he'd likely be in his 80's, but maybe there was a Ralph Poulsen listed. Yes, indeed there was. In Oakhurst, California.

Without wasting time, I called. Ken answered.

His father, a former pilot for Western Airlines, still lived on a 60-acre ranch but was progressively losing his sight. Ken's mother Betty had suffered a stroke in 1988 and a couple of years later Ken left his construction work in southern California to live on the ranch near Yosemite and take care of his parents. He was divorced (he did marry Vicky Swaton) and his daughter Kendra and son Brett were on their own, an investment banker and a design and aeronautical engineer, respectively, today.

Ken had been successful enough he could retire very early; expenses were low on the ranch. Betty Poulsen passed away in 2004. Ken is still looking after his father in early 2007. He remembers his baseball days with clarity, but modestly says, "Hell, I wasn't anything to begin with." He enjoys living where he does. They have about a dozen head of cattle and 40-50 fruit trees where they grow pears, plums, and apricots. "This is just about like paradise," he says.

–Bill Nowlin

Mike Ryan

by Dave Williams

	G	AB	R	H	2B	3B	HR	RBI	BB	SO	BA	OBP	SLG	SB	CS	GDP	HBP
1967 RED SOX	79	226	21	45	4	2	2	27	26	42	.199	.282	.261	2	0	8	1

Michael James Ryan was born on November 25, 1941 in Haverhill, Massachusetts, to parents John and Lorraine Ryan. He was born into athletic stock, his father John a tackle who nearly made the Boston Yanks of the National Football League. His grandfather's cousin Jack Ryan had been a major league ballplayer, breaking in with Louisville of the old American Association in 1889. Jack Ryan later caught for the National League Boston Beaneaters from 1894 through 1896, and finished his playing career with the Washington Senators, appearing in one game in each of the 1912 and 1913 seasons. Jack Ryan also served as a coach for the Red Sox for five years, 1923-27, working under both Frank Chance and Lee Fohl. Though Jack Ryan died in Boston in 1952, Mike does not believe he knew him.

Mike's father John was one of seven brothers to attend St. James High School in Haverhill, many of them active in school sports. Mike's uncle Paul Ryan pitched minor league ball but didn't advance past A-ball, and soon returned home to coach football at Haverhill High School. Mike's father played baseball in high school and in some semipro ball around town, but Mike himself never played baseball, or any other sport, at St. James because the school had dropped interscholastic sports in 1948. John Ryan insisted his son attend St. James anyway because he felt that getting "... a parochial education was more important than baseball."

John Ryan worked as a foreman at a shoe factory in Haverhill owned by his brother Dan. Lorraine Ryan was a homemaker. Mike was the oldest boy in a family of five boys and one girl. As it happens, none of the others showed much interest in playing baseball.

Mike did, though, and from an early age wanted nothing more than to play for the Boston Red Sox. He took in a couple of games at Braves Field as a kid, but the Braves moved to Milwaukee when he was 11 and it was the Red Sox that he always followed. Mike played town baseball in the Northeast League, an amateur league that consisted of teams located in Seabrook, New Hampshire and the Massachusetts communities of Newburyport, Amesbury, Salisbury, and Haverhill. He was a top player, and was one of the three New England players named to the Hearst sandlot team which played its 15th annual game at Yankee Stadium on August 18, 1960. Bob Guindon and Bill Harvey were the other two New Englanders on the club, which was pitted against a team of New York all-stars. Mike began to attract the attention of big league scouts. George Owen, on behalf of the Philadelphia Phillies, had his eye on Ryan and took him to a tryout camp in Milford, Connecticut. Mike had an off day and didn't perform well; Owen still had faith in him—"He was at my house at least once a week for a long time; he really wanted to sign me," Ryan says—but the Phillies passed.

Boston Red Sox scouts Larry Woodall and Fred Maguire had also noticed Ryan. They gave the 18-year-old the opportunity to fulfill his "lifetime dream"—to sign with the Red Sox. "They got hot on me and I went into Fenway for a workout. Tony was hitting them up in the screen like it was nothing, and they just took him upstairs and signed him right away." They told Mike they were interested in him, too, and asked him, "What's it going to take?" Mike remembers, "Money wasn't all that big a deal, even though it seemed like a ton of money to me. I said, "I'd like to meet Williams."" That wasn't too hard to arrange; they took him into the clubhouse where Ted was getting a rubdown from trainer Jack Fadden. "They introduced me to him, and we shook hands and he looked up and asked, 'Can you hit?' I kind of stammered; I didn't know what to say. He goes, 'F---ing right you can hit! Don't forget it!'"

Mike was given $5,000 to sign and the following spring, 1961, he began his professional career with Olean of the New York-Penn League where he struggled offensively, a pattern that would continue throughout his career, batting just .185 in 119 at-bats. He did prove to be a stand-out defensively, and caught Bobby Doerr's eye. Doerr was there at the right time. "It was the last series of the year as I recall, and I happened to hit a couple of home runs and throw out a couple of guys, and Bobby Doerr was in town. Bingo. Things started. When somebody like that says, 'Keep your eye on him,' it helps."

In 1962, while playing for Waterloo under manager Matt Sczesny, Ryan led Midwest League catchers in putouts, assists, and double plays. Playing under Eddie Popowski in Reading the next two years, and in 1964 led Eastern League catchers in fielding average and

double plays while being named to the All-Star team. That year he had the highest batting average of his professional career (.248). At the minor league season's end, he went home and spent several weeks hanging around with friends.

On Friday, October 2, Mike had come back home around midnight after spending a full day at New Hampshire's Hampton Beach. "I was down the beach having a good time. We were there every day for a month. My father was sitting there at the table and he said, 'The Red Sox called. They want you in the morning.' I'm standing there in the door and I'm looking at him. 'What?' He repeated it, and I kind of shook my head. 'Are you kidding?' He says, 'They want you there tomorrow.' I didn't go to sleep, really. I was at the ballpark at 8 o'clock in the morning, for a 1:30 game. They didn't know I was coming in; they wouldn't let me in!" The guard had to go in and ask around before they'd let him into the ballpark.

It had certainly been a call out of the blue. X-rays on Thursday had revealed that Bob Tillman fractured his thumb on a foul tip in Wednesday night's game, and the Sox wanted another catcher to back up Russ Nixon.

New manager Billy Herman (Johnny Pesky had been fired on Friday) asked Ryan if he was in shape. What was he going to say? "Sure." Of course he was, despite not having played for several weeks. Ryan made his major league debut on Saturday, October 3, 1964 on the next to last day of the season.

Bill Monbouquette was the pitcher, and Ryan was the starting catcher. After grounding out to third base to lead off the second inning, Mike singled in the third, driving in both Frank Malzone and Al Smith. Mike reached on an error in the fifth, and he was walked intentionally in the sixth. As Steve Ridzik threw a wild pitch, and Ken Retzer threw the ball wildly into center field, Ryan motored all the way around from first to home, but was tagged out at the plate trying to score. Unfortunately, he tore a ligament in his knee in the collision at the plate.

He had gone 1-for-3 with a walk and two runs batted in. He had been scheduled to catch in the Florida Instructional League later that fall, but due to the injury he could not crouch behind the plate. He did manage to go 6-for-8 as a pinch hitter in Florida, however.

1965 was split between Boston and Toronto of the International League. Ryan began the season with Boston, but his first appearance in a game didn't come until May 2. He made the most of it, though—his second major league ballgame—hitting a third-inning homer off Detroit's Julio Navarro and a fifth-inning homer off Johnnie Seale. He drove in three runs; this proved to be the only multi-homer game of his big league career. That was also one of the few bright spots at the plate in a season where he managed only a .159 batting average. In early July, he was sent to Toronto, where he played under Dick Williams, batting .236 in 161 at-bats. In mid-September, after the International League season was over, Mike was brought back up and got in another 12 games with the Red Sox.

Despite his lack of success as a hitter, he earned praise from Boston manager Billy Herman for his work behind the plate. Herman said of Ryan that he was "almost as good as Elston Howard. In fact, there is only a hairline difference between Ryan and Howard in defensive ability. Ryan has a great arm." Herman could not have known that Howard and Ryan would be teammates in 1967.

1965 was the last time Ryan saw the minor leagues as a player (though as a minor league manager in 1975, he inserted himself in a handful of games). In 1966, he won the starting catcher's job and appeared in 116 games for the Red Sox batting .214. He managed two three-hit games that year, but just two home runs and 32 RBIs. Bob Tillman served as the backup backstop.

Dick Williams took over the ninth-place Red Sox for the 1967 campaign. Williams was determined to run things his way and instill discipline into a ball club that historically had been known for its "country club" ways. At the start of the season, Ryan shared catching duties with Tillman and Russ Gibson. None of the three were known for their offensive contributions and Williams was hopeful that a trade could be made for a veteran catcher with some pop in his bat and experience in handling a pitching staff during a pennant race.

Ryan did the majority of the catching through July. However, there was some tension between Williams and Ryan because the two did not see eye to eye over pitch selection. On August 3, just two days after Ryan had connected for a three-run homer in a game against Kansas City, Williams got his wish and the Sox acquired a veteran backstop. The man they got was Elston Howard, with whom Ryan had been compared defensively, in a deal for Ron Klimkowski and Pete Magrini with the New York Yankees. Howard was 38 and had been a mainstay on several New York pennant winners. Williams was elated, commenting that Howard "is the best catcher I have ever seen for calling a ball game."

On August 17, Ryan was quoted in the *Boston Globe*, "We were in second place when he (Williams) took me out. Then we went all the way to fifth. He can yank me,

that's his privilege. But there's nothing that says I have to like it."

Ryan also let his opinion be known on September 1 in *The Christian Science Monitor*: "I know everybody thinks the Red Sox made a great move when they picked up Howard. I'd like to have his reputation and I wish him well. I hope he helps us win the pennant, because it's obvious he's going to play no matter what happens." Mike did have one more bright moment in the Sox chase for the pennant. In a September 10 game versus New York, he hit a bases-clearing triple in a 9-1 Boston victory, but Ryan watched most of the action the rest of the way from the bench. He did have two at-bats in the World Series, going hitless.

A short time after the World Series he married Suzanne Graham of Newburyport, Massachusetts. She was an athletic girl with long reddish hair and an attractive freckled face. She enjoyed scuba diving, skiing, roller skating, as well as collecting antiques. They were introduced by a mutual friend while Suzanne was working as a secretary with Western Electric in 1964. After their honeymoon in Antigua, Jamaica, and the British West Indies, they moved into an old colonial home in Kingston, New Hampshire. In a very short period of time, Mike had been to his first World Series, welcomed his brother Steven back from Vietnam, and gotten married to the woman who remains his wife nearly 40 years later.

That winter Mike was selling cars for Ryan Motor Sales in Haverhill, owned by his uncle Mike. Actually, he admits, he never sold a single car, but it gave him some work in the offseason—which soon took another turn. On December 15, he received news that he had been traded to the Philadelphia Phillies for Dick Ellsworth and Gene Oliver.

He shared catching duties in 1968 with Clay Dalrymple, appearing in 96 games and hitting .179 with 15 RBIs. Ryan did show a knack for hitting in the clutch--during a six-game period early in the season he knocked in the winning run in three of the four games the Phils won, with two of those hits coming in the ninth inning. After the season Dalrymple was traded to Baltimore, giving Ryan the number one catching slot.

He worked hard in the Florida Instructional League to improve his offensive production. He opened up his batting stance and choked up on the bat. According to Ryan, "I was always committing myself before, my first move with my hands was forward and when the pitchers changed up or took a little off I was too far out in front with my swing. Then, all I had left was my arms. Now my first move with my hands is back and that allows me to get a good look at the pitch before committing myself."

The results were mixed. He hit for more power in 1969, 12 homers and 44 RBIs, but his average was still just .204 in 133 games. He continued to receive recognition for his defensive prowess. Manager Bob Skinner's praise for his game calling struck a chord with Ryan as this was one of the raps against him leveled by Dick Williams.

"That was just Williams' excuse to get rid of me. I don't think I call a game any differently now than I ever did," Ryan remarked at the time. Veteran pitcher and teammate Dick Farrell said, "He's a great catcher. I pitched to [John] Roseboro and I think Ryan moves around back of the plate better than he did. I always thought Roseboro was the best. And Ryan's a great thrower, the best I've ever seen, not so much for strength, but getting rid of the ball and for accuracy."

Ryan's defensive ability not withstanding, Philadelphia acquired Tim McCarver from St. Louis after the 1969 season in the infamous Curt Flood deal. McCarver was an All-Star and World Series hero with the Cardinals and it was obvious that he would receive the bulk of the playing time. Ryan began the 1970 season on the disabled list and returned on April 19. On May 2, a Willie Mays foul ball broke McCarver's hand in the sixth inning of a game against the Giants at Candlestick Park. Ryan took McCarver's place. Mays singled, Willie McCovey doubled, and tried to score on Ken Henderson's single. Mike Ryan blocked the plate, but broke his finger tagging out McCovey at the plate. With two catchers lost in one inning, Jim Hutto took over. Ryan was activated on July 6 but was back on the disabled list for a third time on August 15. For the year he appeared in only 46 games, batting .179.

Ryan spent the next three seasons with the Phils seeing limited action as a backup. He batted .164 in 43 games in 1971, .179 in 46 games in 1972, and .232 in 28 games in 1973. He was traded to Pittsburgh for Jackie Hernandez at the end of January 1974 and saw limited action again appearing in just 15 games and getting three hits in 30 at-bats. He did not see any action for the Pirates in their NLCS loss to the Los Angeles Dodgers and he retired after the season.

Mike Ryan finished his career with a lifetime major league batting average of .193, but teams always saw value in his defense. In just over 5,000 innings of work, given a total of 3,832 chances, he made just 34 errors—a career percentage of .991.

The Pirates wanted him to stay with the organization and appointed him manager of their Class

Ryan's bases-clearing triple against the Yankees on September 10 took all the fight out of New York. The Sox held at a half a game behind the Twins in the standings.

A affiliate Charleston for the 1975 season. Charleston finished third in the first half season and fourth in the second. Ryan even filled in twice and pitched five innings, allowing three earned runs. The next season saw similar results for the Charleston ballclub, finishing fourth and third. He was let go following the 1976 season. The Phillies hired Mike as their minor league catching instructor for 1977, and midway through the summer, he was asked to manage their Triple A club in the American Association at Oklahoma City, beginning in July. Oklahoma City finished third that season with a 70-66 record.

Ryan finished his career in professional baseball as a bullpen coach with the Philadelphia Phillies from 1980 through 1995. His very first year, the Phillies won the NL pennant and, after a 97-year wait, their first World Series.

Montreal eliminated the Phils the following year in the Division playoff but in 1983, Philadelphia was back in another World Series. This time the Orioles beat them in five games. Ten years later, in 1993, the Phillies won the pennant again, but the Toronto Blue Jays beat them in six. Mike Ryan can look back on one Series as a player, and three as a coach. After the 1995 season, he elected to retire.

Mike and Suzanne Ryan have no children, and are currently fully enjoying Mike's retirement in Wolfeboro, New Hampshire. With 35 years in baseball, 27 in the majors, he has earned it.

George Scott

by Ron Anderson

	G	AB	R	H	2B	3B	HR	RBI	BB	SO	BA	OBP	SLG	SB	CS	GDP	HBP
1967 RED SOX	159	565	74	171	21	7	19	82	63	119	.303	.373	.465	10	8	13	4

George Scott's professional baseball career spanned 41 years beginning in Class D ball at Olean of the New York-Penn League in 1962. His travels were highlighted by his 14 seasons in the majors, starting with the Boston Red Sox in 1966. Scott also played for Milwaukee 1972-1976, Boston 1977-1978, and split his final year between Boston, Kansas City, and the New York Yankees. He served in various professional baseball capacities after his major league career, notably in the Mexican and Independent Leagues, finishing as manager of the Berkshire Black Bears (Northern League) in 2002.

George Charles Scott Jr., was born March 23, 1944 in Greenville, Mississippi, the youngest of three children. A brother, Otis, is now deceased. His sister, Beatrice, resides in Greenville. Interviewed at his Greenville home, George states that his first love was basketball, followed by football, and then baseball. His father worked as a laborer on a cotton farm and died when George was two. His mother, Magnolia, was forced to work three jobs to keep the family together. Because of work commitments, she never saw her son play baseball until he reached the major leagues.

When George was a young boy, he worked in the fields picking cotton. "That's all we knew," he relates. "The reason you did that, all of that money was turned over to your parents to make ends meet. Nothing can be worse than getting up at four in the morning waiting for a truck to pick you up to go pick and chop cotton from six or seven in the morning until five or six in the afternoon."[1]

Scott played Little League baseball, but was actually thrown off the team temporarily because he was "too good." He was so large and so much better than the others that local authorities investigated his background to determine if he was older than 12. In one stretch of six games, he hit either two or three home runs in each game. As a major leaguer, he was listed at 6'1 1/2" and 205 pounds, though he often had trouble staying at that weight.

George attended Coleman High School in Greenville, Mississippi where he was a three-sport high school star, lettering in baseball, basketball, and football. He quarterbacked the football team, and led both his football and basketball teams to state championships, but chose baseball "to make my living. I got tired of watching my mom struggle. I didn't have the mind that I could go to college and see my mother struggle for another four or five years."

Scott was discovered by major league scout Ed Scott (no relation) of Mobile, Alabama. Ed Scott, along with Red Sox scout Milt Bolling, signed George as an amateur free agent for $8,000 bonus money right out of high school on May 28, 1962. Ed, who had signed Hank Aaron to his first major league contract, described George as a better hitter when he graduated from high school than Aaron at the same age and stage of development.

George was assigned to Class D Olean of the New York-Penn League for 1962. In 63 games, he batted .238 with five home runs and 28 RBIs. Olean swept second-place Erie in two games in the 1962 NYP League Governors' Cup playoffs, but lost to Auburn in two straight in the finals.

In 1963, Olean's franchise and its players moved to Wellsville (Class A) which re-entered the NYP League. Scott stayed with the club, and batted a solid .293 that year with 15 home runs, 74 RBIs, and 200 total bases to his credit. Wellsville finished second to the Auburn Mets, establishing a new league home run mark of 153 round-trippers as a team.

Scott mostly played shortstop, but in 1964 moved to third base at Winston-Salem (Single A Carolina League). George did not start the season there, however, due to a knee injury and surgery in the off-season. Scott batted .288 while playing in only 55 games. He hit 10 home runs and drove in 30 runs.

Despite the shortened season, in 1965 George Scott was promoted by the Red Sox to the newly-established Pittsfield Red Sox of the Double A Eastern League. 1965 was a banner year for both George and Pittsfield. Scott iced a 3-1 Pittsfield victory over Springfield on the season's final day with an eighth-inning homer that gave Pittsfield the championship. That homer also won him the home run title, and the Triple Crown. Pittsfield finished 85-55, one game ahead of second-place Elmira. Scott finished with a .319 average, 25 homers, and 94 RBIs. He also led the league in total bases (290), hits (167), doubles (30), at-bats (523), and

With the power of his bat, George Scott soon attracted the nickname "Boomer."

games played (140). He was named the Most Valuable Player and received a unanimous vote from the National Association of Baseball Writers that named him to the Double A All-East All-Star team.

The Red Sox picked up Scott's contract from Pittsfield at the end of the 1965 season. Would Scott win a roster spot with the '66 Red Sox? "Only a sensational spring training could land Scott a job with the big club sooner than '67," wrote scribe Larry Claflin of the *Boston Herald Traveler*.[2] Scott was a third baseman, and the club had another third base prospect who was one level ahead.

Reporting on Boston's other rookie third-sacker prospect, Joe Foy, as Red Sox spring training opened in Winter Haven in February, 1966, Claflin wrote, "Third base is his if he can hold it."[3] The Red Sox brass, including Manager Billy Herman, all believed that Foy would replace departed veteran Frank Malzone. But Scott was determined to win a place on the team.

"They gave him [Joe Foy] the job, and right[fully] they should. Joe Foy was the MVP in Triple A in 1965, and I was the MVP in Double A in 1965. Joe Foy was ahead of me, and they really should have given him the job. I had no quarrel with that. But I wasn't going to settle for that. I was going to try to be on that roster come opening day. You know, it wasn't actually that I was trying to take Joe Foy's job. I was trying to win a roster spot for opening day," Scott said.

George not only made the roster but opened the season at third base. Full of confidence coming off a tremendous spring season, he played well in his first two games in Boston (including a pinch-hit single off Jim Palmer in the second contest), although the Red Sox lost both to Baltimore. But his first game in Cleveland turned into a rookie's nightmare. Scott encountered ace hurler Sam McDowell and went 0-for-5 with a walk, whiffing every at-bat (including three times against McDowell). He also made an error in the game. He struck out in his first at-bat the next day against Gary Bell, but settled down with three hits in his next four plate appearances.

"From that day on, Cleveland became one of my better clubs to hit against. I remember Leon Wagner making fun of me. Leon Wagner was in the outfield. Every time I would strike out, he would hold a finger up, and he told me he was glad I made contact because he was beginning to run out of fingers," Scott lamented.

On April 19, 1966—Patriots' Day in Boston—Scott hit his first major league home run, off Joe Sparma of the Detroit Tigers.

A week into the season, Scott was switched to first base, replacing Tony Horton. Scottie would make his mark as one of the finest first baseman to play the game, winning eight Gold Gloves. Herman used newly-acquired Eddie Kasko at third for a short while, but then replaced him with Foy who played across the diamond from Scott for the balance of the year.

On April 26 in New York, Scott hit a shot against the venerable Whitey Ford that may be remembered as one of the longest home runs in the history of the Stadium. Whitey later recalled that it was the longest home run he ever surrendered, and only Frank Howard and Walt Dropo had hit ones that traveled as far. When Ford asked Mickey Mantle what he thought the distance would have been if it hadn't first hit the seats, Mantle replied with a laugh, "Well, to pick a round number you could say 550 feet and not be exaggerating."[4]

By mid-May 1966, George Scott was among the batting leaders, hitting .330, behind Tony Oliva and Baltimore's Robinson boys, Frank and Brooks. He was leading in home runs with 11, and was the talk around the league, many projecting him for Rookie of the Year. Future Hall of Famer Rick Ferrell, who watched Scott during the spring and first part of the regular season, expounded on his talents: "In all my years in baseball, I have never seen a player have a debut like Scott. He's amazing."[5]

Scott was the majority choice of his peers to start at first base in the 37th All-Star game on July 12th at Busch Memorial Stadium. He beat out Norm Cash of the Tigers, 141 to 62. He proved a non-factor. He batted twice against future Hall of Famers Sandy Koufax and Jim Bunning, but popped out both times. The National League won the game by a 2-1 score in 10 innings.

Pitchers were beginning to catch up with George and his strikeout count began to mount. "What happened is the pitchers and teams adjusted on me, and I didn't adjust to them quick enough. After the [1966] All-Star break they started throwing me a lot of change-ups and curve balls, and I didn't make the adjustment. I don't even know whether I was capable of making the adjustment at that time. All the leagues I had come up through, they threw me a lot of fastballs and I could hit that fastball," Scott explains.

Herman was irked over his team's failure to perform well on a western road trip. With Scott swinging at bad balls and without a home run for a month, Herman announced on July 19 that he would bench Scott. George's batting average had dropped to .263, and he had fallen off the leaderboards. The day's game against California was rained out, though, and rescheduled as part of a twi-night double-header the next day. Scott

appeared in both games, and every game thereafter.

The benching incident turned out to be just a threat by Herman, but what followed seemed to stir the Hub city. A July 25 *Boston Globe* feature article called it "the George Scott case."[6] Scott was devastated, fans were confused, and Herman's back was to the wall to justify benching his rookie sensation. It made the local sports headlines for days. Speculation was rampant whether George was being treated fairly. Scott claimed he wasn't getting help from his manager or coaches, nor were his teammates showing much concern for him.

Scott was not about to languish in misery; he took action, watched film, made adjustments to his stance, and often talked to teammate Lenny Green who helped him the most. He began to emerge from his slump. On July 29, he hit his 19th homer, and the following day his 20th. Although he would continue to hit for power—an attribute much favored by the Red Sox—he did not hit for the high average that had accompanied his slugging during the first half. He finished the year with 27 home runs and 90 RBIs, but batted a mere .245. He also led the league in strikeouts with 152, setting a rookie record in the process.

On September 9, 1966, Billy Herman was fired by the Red Sox. They wasted little time in replacing him with Dick Williams, manager of the club's Triple A Toronto affiliate, hiring Williams on September 28.

During the off-season, the major league players, coaches, and managers honored George Scott with the most votes (532) in their selections for the eighth annual Topps All-Star rookie team, ranked the best of both leagues. Tommy Agee—who would later cop the AL Rookie of the Year Award—placed second with 517 votes. The Boston baseball writers elected George Scott and Joe Foy co-winners of the Harry Agganis Memorial Award as Red Sox rookies of the year.

Dick Williams, the sharp-tongued new Red Sox skipper, began posturing and making noises around Beantown right from the start. He announced he was stripping Yastrzemski of his position of team captain. There would only be one "'chief'" and that would be Dick Williams. He suggested Scott did not have a foothold on first base; it would be up for grabs between George and Tony Horton in Winter Haven. Williams was very high on Horton, whom he had managed in Toronto, and wanted to give him every chance he could to win the first-base job. He knew that Scott could play other positions. During the offseason, Scott declared publicly that he was no longer going to be a "dumb hitter." He was going to reduce his strikeouts and stop chasing bad pitches. Scott outplayed Tony Horton both at hitting and fielding—averaging .333 with four straight hits in the final exhibition game—and won the opening day start at first base.

The Red Sox were only six games into the 1967 season when Dick Williams took decisive action against three of his players, benching them for poor performance. He benched Scott first, on April 17, followed by Joe Foy and José Tartabull. Scott had struck out nine times in the first five games and was hitting only .182, once again chasing bad pitches. That angered the quick-tempered manager. He also accused Scott, Foy, and José Santiago of being overweight and ordered them to diet. Williams' concern for playing weight led to several more incidents between Williams and his players.

Tony Horton, who replaced Scott, failed to impress Williams, and Scott was reinstated nine days later. He began to hit again and raised his average to .271 by the end of May. Boston was in third place, four and one-half games out of first. In the third week of May, Scott put on a hitting display in a six-game span during a

Boomer had to work on his weight throughout the season, under Dick Williams' strict regime. He went 1-for-4 in this day's 3-2 win over the Angels.

homestand, rapping out eight base hits in 23 at-bats, including two triples, and one mammoth home run off Sonny Siebert of Cleveland. For that he won "Player of the Week" honors.

The annual All-Star Game was played on July 11 in Anaheim, California. Harmon Killebrew received the most votes from his peers for the first base slot. Scott failed to repeat, finishing fourth in the voting, and did not make the team.

Scott continued to play well following the All-Star break, both in the field and with the bat. By the first week in August, he was hitting .294 and was among the American League batting leaders. The Red Sox were in second place, two and a half games behind Chicago. But the Red Sox were about to start a worrisome western road swing.

Williams continued to keep pressure on his players, some say to a fault, by frequently changing lineups and, in particular, keeping close watch on his players' weight. Upon arrival in Anaheim, he again benched Scott for being overweight. Williams stood by his convictions keeping Scott out of the starting lineup for the entire Anaheim series. The Red Sox lost all three games, by scores of 1-0, 2-1, and 3-2. Williams retorted to the undercurrent that was building: "He is not going to play until he gets his weight down to 215 pounds. I have managed this way all season, and I am not going to change my methods now [just] because we are in a tight pennant race."[7]

Scott weighed in at 213 pounds before the Red Sox returned to Fenway. He was reinstated into the lineup. On his first appearance at the plate, a Fenway fan yelled, "C'mon Twiggy, hit one out of here." He did exactly that, sending a drive into the net off Joe Sparma.

The Red Sox went into the final days of the season neck and neck with Minnesota, Detroit, and Chicago. On September 28, Boston was tied for second with Detroit, trailing Minnesota by one game. Chicago trailed by one and one-half games. It came down to the final season-ending series against Minnesota, in Boston, on September 30 and October 1. The Red Sox beat the Twins in both games that were played in a well-fought and climactic "'showdown"' series. The Tigers double-header split on Sunday gave the Red Sox the pennant, their first since 1946. Scott was 2-for-8 in that series with a home run in the first game. He finished the regular season with a .303 average, 19 home runs and 82 RBIs.

The Red Sox went on to play in a memorable World Series against a strong St. Louis Cardinals ball club. Bob Gibson was the difference, winning three of the seven games. Gibson clinched the Series by making Scott his 10th strikeout victim of the game. Asked how he personally felt he had played in the Series, George answered, "I was probably a little off where I would have wanted to be. I felt that I swung the bat good against Bob Gibson." Scott managed four hits off Gibson, including a double and triple. He had six hits in the Series, batting .231.

In the days after the World Series, while speaking with reporters about the season past and ahead, Dick Williams said about George Scott, "I would have hated to put him on the scales during the World Series because I know his weight was way up again. But, George knows that when he lets his weight go up, he will pay for it."[8]

Scott was awarded his first Gold Glove, picked by better than a 2-to-1 margin over his nearest competitor. In this regard, Williams also gave him the ultimate compliment, describing Scott's fielding talents. "Until I saw George Scott, I thought Gil Hodges was the greatest defensive first baseman I ever saw. But Scott changed my mind."[9]

Scott played and hit very well in the spring of '68. But as bright as the spring was for George, the opening of the regular season could not have been more miserable. At the end of the first month of play, the team was in sixth place, five games out of first. Scott had only nine hits in his first 81 at-bats, hitting an anemic .111. He was in a woeful slump from which he never recovered. Several times he was benched and was a study in dejection. Williams replaced him with Ken Harrelson

Scott played for the Pittsfield Red Sox in 1965 and won the Eastern League Triple Crown, his eighth-inning homer in the final game winning the pennant for Pittsfield. Not surprisingly, he was named MVP.

at first, who proceeded to play well enough that year to make the All-Star team. Scott got closer to the end of the bench with each home run hit by Harrelson. Talk was brewing to trade Scott and keep Harrelson.

On September 8, while traveling in Anaheim, Dick Williams announced he would use Rico Petrocelli at first base that day, the eighth Red Sox first baseman of the season. Petrocelli was nursing an injury and had not played defensively in 18 days. Scott was humiliated and erupted in rage, ranting displeasure with his manager, claiming he would not play for him again, and asking for an audience with owner Tom Yawkey. The next night in Oakland, Scott, surprisingly, was back in the lineup.

There was much speculation that either Yawkey or GM Dick O'Connell had stepped in, and that Williams was losing his grip on the team. Dissension was evident and newsworthy, even though Ken Harrelson spoke out publicly to deny the accusation: "There is no dissension on this ball club that will hurt us on the field."[10] Word leaked out that other players were disgruntled with Williams, among them superstar Carl Yastrzemski and veteran Elston Howard.

Scott finished the 1968 year batting a woeful .171. He hit three home runs, none at Fenway Park. The Red Sox as a team finished the season in fourth place, with an 86-76 record, 17 games behind the Detroit Tigers. In spite of his poor year at the plate, Scott repeated with defensive honors, winning his second Gold Glove Award, despite playing just 112 games at first base.

Scott went to the Puerto Rican league over the winter, playing for Santurce under Baltimore's Frank Robinson. "I think what happened to me after the 1967 season, [and] 1968 when I was at my lowest point, I went to Puerto Rico and I met Frank Robinson. Frank Robinson was the manager in the winter-time down there. Having a chance to play for Santurce under Frank Robinson [was] the best thing that ever happened to my career. Because not only did Frank Robinson help me mentally, but he also helped me physically, and I became a better player." Scott had a strong season in winter ball under Robinson, batting .295. He led his league in home runs with 14, and RBIs with 45, well ahead of his competition.

In the wake of Joe Foy's departure to the Kansas City Royals in the expansion draft, Dick Williams announced that George Scott would be his third baseman in 1969, and Harrelson would move to first. Scott played the position with precision that spring and got his manager's attention. "I don't care how much he weighs, just look at him out there at third base and you can see what I mean about how he can field the position," Williams said with what seemed to be a change of heart over the matter of Scott's waistline.[11]

Scott had another excellent spring, batting well above .300, but once more flopped at the beginning of the regular season. He opened 1969 at third base, but at the end of May was hitting .193 with only four home runs. He was hot and cold throughout the year, finishing the season with a .253 batting average, 16 home runs, and 52 RBIs. He played 109 games at third base, but by the end of the season he was mainly back at first when Dalton Jones—who had been playing there—was not getting the job done. The Red Sox finished the year in third place with an 87-75 record, 22 games behind the Baltimore Orioles.

The platooning and constant juggling of lineups orchestrated by Williams, as well as discord that surfaced between him and his players led to his demise as Red Sox manager. On September 23, 1969 he was fired. On October 2, 1969 Eddie Kasko was named Red Sox manager.

Kasko was brought in to settle down the player ranks, vowing he had no plans to trade front-line players, and he would keep established players in their rightful positions. It was a message that worked for George Scott, who adjusted well to the new boss. Larry Claflin of the *Boston Herald-Traveler* summed it up best: "Suffice to say that George feels free of bondage now. It is up to him to prove his point that he was mismanaged by Williams. The only way he can do that is by hitting the baseball."[12]

The 1970 Red Sox were counting on rookie Luis Alvarado to handle third base and put Scott on first. Alvarado did not work out, so Scott was switched back to third, and Carl Yastrzemski was shifted to first. Both hit well, and Scott fell just short of hitting .300, at .296. It was a pleasant surprise for Kasko, thinking about 1971. Meanwhile the Red Sox finished third once more with an identical record to their previous year of 87-75.

The trade of Tony Conigliaro allowed Yastrzemski and Scott to return to their natural positions, but 1971 proved to be another year of dissension for the Red Sox. Players squabbled, Kasko became a target, and Boston scribes were speculating once again that a Sox skipper was in trouble. In the meantime, George was having a reasonably good year, finishing with a .263 average, 24 home runs, and 78 RBIs. The club finished third again with an 85-77 record. Scott won his third Gold Glove.

On October 10, 1971 the Red Sox pulled off a major trade, sending Scott, Jim Lonborg, Joe Lahoud, Billy Conigliaro, Ken Brett, and Don Pavletich to the Milwaukee Brewers for Tommy Harper, Marty Pattin,

Lew Krausse and a minor leaguer. This breathed new life into Scott, who was considered the "key," according to Brewers' GM Frank Lane. Scott batted .266 in 1972, with 20 homers. Milwaukee finished sixth with a 65-91 record. Scott won a fourth Gold Glove.

In 1973 and 1974, Scott had solid years batting .306 and .281, and hitting 24 and 17 home runs, respectively. He won two more Gold Glove Awards. He was becoming disenchanted with the Brewers, though, feeling they were not committed to winning. Milwaukee finished in fifth place both years.

1975 was a "career year," says George. He led the club in practically every key category, with 36 homers, 109 RBIs, 86 runs, nine game-winning hits, 318 total bases, and a .515 slugging percentage. He was the American League RBI and total bases leader, and he tied Reggie Jackson for the most home runs. He also won his seventh Gold Glove—fifth consecutively. He was named on the Associated Press' all-star team and selected Milwaukee's MVP. Once again, however, the Brewers were languishing in mediocrity, finishing fifth with a 68-94 record. On September 28, 1975 manager Del Crandall was fired, replaced by Alex Grammas.

George ascribed much of his success that year to Hank Aaron, who had come over to the Milwaukee club that season from Atlanta; "I attribute a lot of that to Henry Aaron. Hank was over there, and he talked to me a lot about sitting up, how to sit up straight on certain pitchers. He talked to me a lot. That was the only time I ever had anybody in my dugout to communicate with me like that at that level about hitting."

The 1976 season was not a happy one for George. The Brewers were once again mired at the bottom. General manager Jim Baumer pointed a finger at Scott as the reason, and Grammas temporarily dropped him to sixth in the order. This rankled Scott, and he asked to be traded. On December 6, 1976 he got his wish. Scott and Bernie Carbo were traded to the Boston Red Sox. According to Scott, he was returning to his "garden city."[13]

Scott walked off with his eighth Gold Glove—which

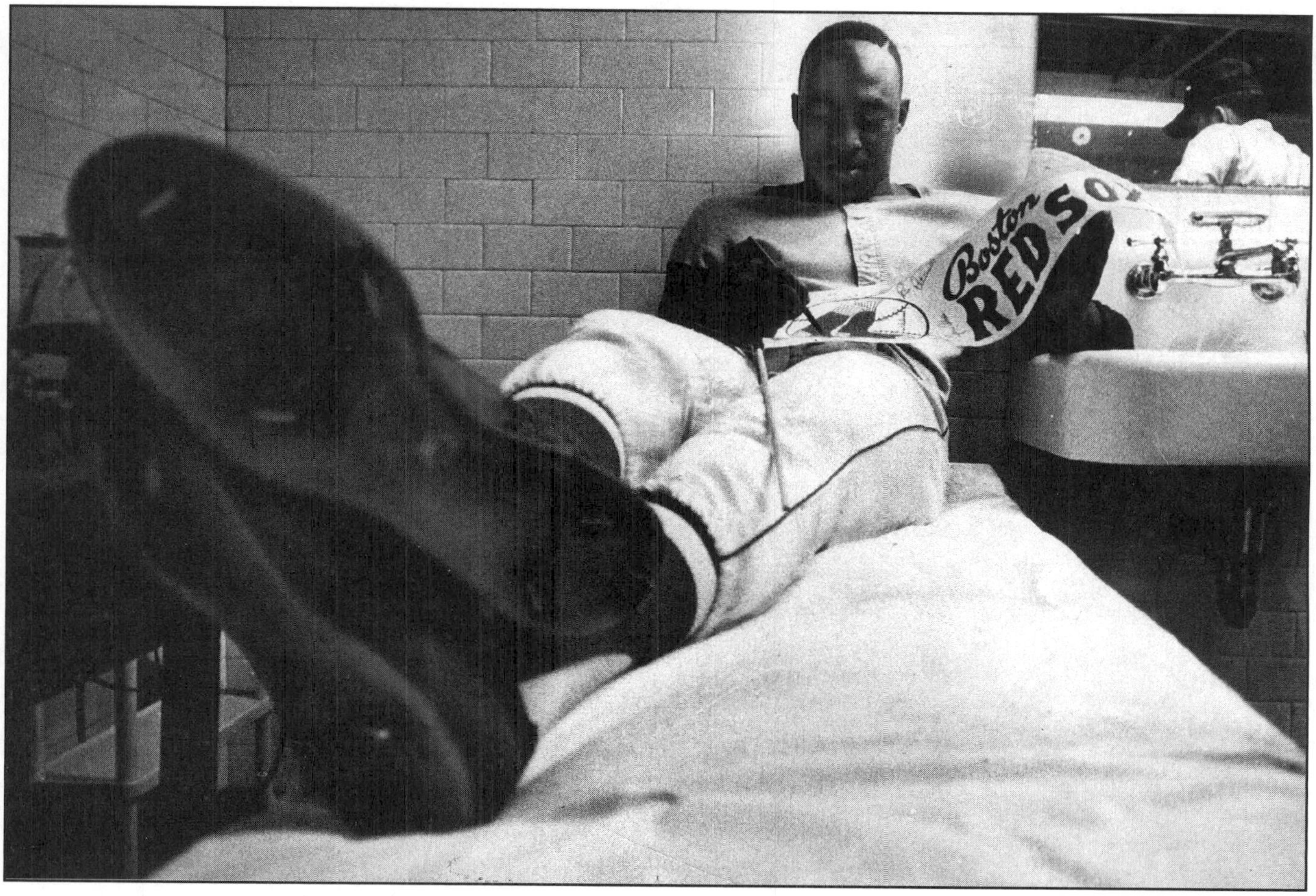

George Scott signs a pennant with the race neck-to-neck in late August.

would be his last—for his 1976 fielding performance. He batted .274 with 18 home runs. But he said that returning to Boston was a mistake. "I was very excited about going back. I don't think the Red Sox were that excited about having me back."

George had a good year at the plate for Boston in '77—batting .269 and clouting 33 home runs—but an uncharacteristic year in the field, making 24 errors. In spite of that he was barely edged out for a ninth Gold Glove by Jim Spencer of the White Sox. The Red Sox finished tied with Baltimore for second with a 97-64 record. Scott placed third behind Rod Carew in the All-Star voting, which was a fan selection that year. American League All-Star manager Billy Martin picked Scott as a sub and played him at first later in the game. Scott hit a two-run home run off Goose Gossage. He had 25 home runs at the All-Star break, and just eight thereafter.

In 1978, injuries slowed George down. He was on the DL early in the season, missing 17 games due to back trouble. On May 15, he was back in the lineup at first-base but promptly broke a middle finger on his throwing hand chasing a pop-fly. The finger healed slowly, and he never got a foothold on the '78 season, finishing with a .233 batting average and hitting only 12 homers. The Sox tied the Yanks for first place in their division, but lost the one-game playoff. Scott was 2-for-4 in the playoff game, with a double.

Scott started the 1979 season with the Red Sox but was traded to Kansas City on June 13. He played briefly, but was released on August 17. He was picked up by the New York Yankees as a free agent on August 26. George finished the year batting .254, but hit at a .318 pace while with the Yankees. New York released him on November 1, 1979.

On November 2, 1979 Scott was selected by the Texas Rangers—the only major league team to choose him—in the 14th round of the re-entry draft. Under the terms of the draft, players were free to negotiate with any club if they were selected by fewer than two teams. Texas announced their plans to use Scott as a "utility player"—if he was agreeable—to back up their established first baseman Pat Putnam. George balked at the idea and got an agent, whereupon he was offered a minor league job with Texas' Triple A Charleston club. He declined the offer, and left the major leagues.

Scott went to the Mexican League, playing there in the early 1980's and had some good years, especially in 1981 and 1982 when he finished high among the leaders, batting .355 and .333, respectively. He held various managerial positions starting with the Mexican League—where he was a player-manager—and went on to become full-time manager in Independent League baseball during the 1980s through 2002. Notable among these teams were the Saskatoon Riot in 1995, the Massachusetts Mad Dogs from 1996 to 1999, and the Rio Grande Valley White Wings of the Texas-Louisiana League in 2001. He also coached the Roxbury Community College baseball team from 1991 through 1995. He finished his baseball career managing the Berkshire Black Bears of the Northern League in 2002.

Scott is a recently-elected member of the Red Sox Hall of Fame and the Mississippi Sports Hall of Fame.

George Scott is now retired and lives in Greenville, Mississippi. He has three sons: Dion, a high school principal in Atlanta, middle son George III, in real estate in New Bedford, Massachusetts; and his youngest son, Brian, a sophomore attending Mississippi Delta Junior College. Brian plays on their baseball team and was batting over .400, said George, at the time of an early 2006 interview.

Notes:

1. Information source: George Scott / interviews: January 21 and 23, 2006, and March 3, 2006
2. Claflin, Larry; "Rookie Foy Winterbrook Choice To Nab Malzone's Post in Hub", *The Sporting News*, December 4, 1965, p. 30
3. Claflin, Larry; "Bosox Needlers Goading Flashy Joe Foy," *The Sporting News*, March 26, 1966, p. 5
4. McDonough, Will; "Scott's 420-Foot Homer Makes Ford's All-Time Hit Parade," *The Boston Globe*, p. 43
5. Claflin, Larry; "Big or Small, A.L. Parks Look Easy to Bosox Bombshell Scott," *The Sporting News*, May 21, 1966, p. 18
6. Unsigned Editorial; "Scott Changes Stance, Feels Slump Over," *The Boston Globe*, July 25, 1966, p. 17
7. Claflin, Larry; "Red Sox Boss Wins Weighty Argument With Slugger Scott." *The Sporting News*, September 2, 1967, p. 9
8. Claflin, Larry; "More Hurling Tops Bosox '68 Needs," *The Sporting News*, October 28, 1967, p. 16
9. Henkey, Ben; "Kaline A Gold Glover for Tenth Time," *The Sporting News*, November 11, 1967, p. 27
10. Horgan, Tim; "Hawk: Scott Wrong, Dick Right; Club Sore at Feud Talk," *The Herald Traveler*, September 19, 1968, p. 41
11. Claflin, Larry; "Tony C's First Homer Since '67: What a Tonic for the Red Sox!" *The Sporting News*, April 12, 1969, p. 9
12. Claflin, Larry; "Awake or Asleep, Scott Swinging Bat As Red Sox Terror," *The Sporting News*, April 11, 1970, p. 33
13. Whiteside, Larry; "Returning Scott Dubs Boston His 'Garden City'," *The Sporting News*, December 25, 1976, p. 47

Norm Siebern

by Doug Skipper

	G	AB	R	H	2B	3B	HR	RBI	BB	SO	BA	OBP	SLG	SB	CS	GDP	HBP
1967 RED SOX	33	44	2	9	0	2	0	7	6	8	.205	.300	.295	0	0	1	0

A former American League All-Star in the twilight of a productive career, Norm Siebern joined the 1967 Red Sox at midseason. He served as a pinch hitter and took an occasional turn in the field during Boston's pennant chase and in three World Series games. Siebern slugged 132 home runs during his 12 seasons in the major leagues, though none during two partial seasons in Boston. A strong, quiet and athletic 6' 2", 205-pounder who wore glasses, batted from the left side and threw right-handed, Siebern split time between first base and the outfield for six major league teams. Originally a Yankee, he played in two World Series for New York, and was part of the package the Bronx Bombers sent to Kansas City for Roger Maris. He was an All-Star first baseman for the Athletics and the Baltimore Orioles, and later played with California and San Francisco before he closed out his career in Boston in 1967 and 1968.

Norman Leroy Siebern was born on July 26, 1933, in Wellston, Missouri, in the St. Louis area. One of two sons of Milton, who later served as a scorekeeper for the Kansas City Athletics, and Iva Siebern, he was a baseball and basketball standout at Wellston High, and managing editor of the school newspaper. Lou Maguolo, Midwestern scout for the Yankees, spotted Siebern when the young slugger was 15, and signed him as soon as he graduated from high school in 1951. That summer, Siebern started his professional baseball career at the age of 17 at McAlester in the Class D Sooner State League. He appeared in 50 games, batted .331, and, though he homered just three times, he lashed 18 doubles, three triples, and drove in 31 runs.

He moved up to Joplin, Missouri, in the Class C Western Association in 1952, where he batted .324 and drilled 52 extra base hits, including 13 home runs, and drove in 95 runs in 137 games. He led the league with 33 doubles and 115 runs scored. That effort earned Siebern a promotion to Birmingham of the Double-A Southern Association in 1953, where he hit .281 with 21 homers and 97 runs batted in. But he wasn't busy just during the summer. Siebern and fellow Yankee farmhand Jerry Lumpe played basketball at Southwest Missouri State Teachers College (later Southwest Missouri State University and now Missouri State University) and helped the Bears win the 1952 and 1953 NAIA National Championship Tournaments. Southwest Missouri State posted a 10-0 record in the national tourney over the two seasons, including wins over Indiana State, Murray State, and Gonzaga, though both Siebern and Lumpe headed to spring training prior to the title games. The NAIA rule allowing athletes to play minor league baseball and college basketball was rescinded after the 1953 season, and Siebern set aside his pursuit of a degree in journalism.

Like many players of the era, Siebern entered the Army and missed out on the entire 1954 and 1955 seasons. He returned to baseball and was voted the first James P. Dawson Memorial Award by the New York writers as the outstanding Yankees rookie during spring training. Still just 22 years old, he joined the Denver Bears of the Triple-A American Association, the Yankees' top farm team, to start the 1956 season. In 36 games with the Mile High City squad, Siebern collected 30 hits in 100 at-bats, slammed eight homers and drove in 19 runs. The Yankees took notice and in mid-June, Siebern was called up to New York.

The youngster joined Yogi Berra, Billy Martin, Phil Rizzuto, Whitey Ford, and 24-year old Mickey Mantle, who was on his way to a 52-home run, 130-RBI MVP season. Mantle was entrenched in center field, Hank Bauer held down right field, and manager Casey Stengel was searching for a third outfielder to spell the injured 40-year old Enos Slaughter, using backup catcher Elston Howard in left field most often. Siebern wasn't quite ready. He made his debut on June 15 and in 51 games batted just .204 with four triples, four homers, and 21 runs batted in, while he quietly suffered in silence from knee and shoulder injuries incurred when he chased a fly ball into a concrete wall. Meanwhile, the Yankees cruised to their seventh AL pennant in eight years, and avenged their 1955 World Series loss to the Brooklyn Dodgers, four games to three. Siebern, now 23, was retired in his only appearance, a pinch-hit opportunity in Game Two, won 13-8 by Brooklyn. Siebern watched the remainder of the Series from the bench.

The following spring, the young thumper was farmed back to Denver, where he put together a spectacular season for manager Ralph Houk. Siebern batted .349 in 144 games, slugged 45 doubles and 15 triples, smashed

24 home runs, drove in 118 runs, and teamed with Marv Throneberry to lead the Bears to the American Association championship and a win over the International League champion Buffalo Bisons in the 1957 Little World Series. After the season, he was named the *Sporting News* Minor League Player of the Year. Despite leading the league in batting average, runs, hits, doubles, triples, and total bases, Siebern sat at home as the Milwaukee Braves bounced the Yankees in the World Series.

Siebern was back in New York's plans for 1958. The 24-year-old took over as the Yankees' regular left fielder. He played in 134 games and batted .300 with 19 doubles, five triples, and 14 home runs. He walked 66 times and stole a career-high five bases, but was cut down eight times. He also won a Gold Glove for his fielding, and solidified left field, a Yankee sore spot. He did everything the Yankees asked, although more quietly than they preferred. "I wish he would show a little more aggressiveness," Stengel said of his quiet young slugger. "He doesn't even show as much life as he did here last year. Maybe that's just as well. If he started hollering now he might forget some of the other things he does so much better."

For the fourth straight year and the ninth time in 10 seasons, the Bronx Bombers won the AL pennant, and for the second time, Siebern was World Series-bound, this time against the Milwaukee Braves. Stengel was faced with a dilemma. If Berra caught, then either Howard or Siebern sat. "Now what would you do?" Stengel said prior to the 1958 World Series. "For the first time in years I got a fellow who can play left field regular, and now you want me to start platooning?" But that's just what he did. Siebern sat the bench for Game One and the start of Game Two, while Berra caught and Howard played left field. But after the Braves tallied seven runs in the first inning of Game Two, Siebern replaced Howard and banged out a hit in three trips to the plate against Lew Burdette.

With the Braves leading two games to none, the Series moved to New York and Siebern started Game Three and walked twice in four plate appearances. The following day, Stengel slotted Siebern in the leadoff spot for Game Four. The youngster walked once in four trips to the plate, but struggled in the field. In the sixth inning of a scoreless pitching duel between Whitey Ford and Warren Spahn, Braves second baseman Red Schoendienst lifted a fly ball to left center field between Siebern and Mantle. Siebern, facing into the afternoon sun and lights turned on for the benefit of the color television broadcast from Yankee Stadium, lost the fly ball, and it fell for a leadoff triple. Moments later, Tony Kubek booted Johnny Logan's grounder, and the Braves scored the first run of the day. In the seventh, right after Stengel motioned the outfield in, Spahn's blooper dropped in front of Siebern to allow Del Crandall to score. And in the eighth, the Braves scored for a third time after Logan's fly fell to Siebern's right and bounced into the stands for a ground rule double. The Braves won 3-0 and led the Series three games to one.

Newspapers roasted Siebern. One headline stated, "Siebern Sunburn Singes Yanks," but the stoic youngster was toasted for his courage and honesty after he stood up to face the reporters and said, "I lost at least four balls out there, in the sun and against the lights." Stengel came to the defense of his left fielder. "I'll tell you one thing, I'm not asking waivers on him, and you can print that!" the "Old Perfesser" said. "He's a nice kid and I know he'll worry over this. He's playing the toughest left field in baseball, don't forget. He hit .300 for me. He's good at getting walks and he's good at going from first to third. I think he did real good in his first full year in the majors. He's not an easy man to get out."

But Stengel did not use Siebern again in the World Series, as the Yankees became just the second team to rally from a 3-1 deficit to win the Fall Classic. And he seemed to lose confidence in the youngster in 1959. Siebern played just 93 games in the outfield (and two at first base) as Stengel employed 13 outfielders during the season. He tried eyeglasses to help in the outfield, but batted .271, with just 11 home runs. The Yankees won 13 fewer games and slid to third place in 1959. The team wasn't close, and Siebern, Bobby Richardson, and Kubek, along with veteran Bobby Shantz, were referred to by Yankee insiders as the "Ice Cream and Popcorn Set" because they didn't drink, smoke, or swear. Stengel questioned his silent young slugger's effort, and whether the glasses would help him catch fly balls, recalling the youngster's World Series travails.

Several years later, Siebern was generous about Stengel's criticism in an interview with Leslie Lieber of the *Los Angeles Times*. "No, I don't remember Stengel making me feel bad," Siebern said. "What I do remember is the way he stuck by me when I needed him in the World Series. I had had a bad day, losing a couple of easy fly balls in the sun. Milwaukee beat us and we were down in the World Series three to one. I felt as low as anyone could. Stengel had every right to jump me, but he didn't. Instead he kidded me and cheered me up. I found out that day who my friends were. Anybody who says Stengel broke my heart is inventing fairy tales. What he did was give me heart. I'm happy I had the chance to play for him."

Siebern's bases-loaded triple in the August 19 game helped Boston to a 12-11 win over the Angels.

Nevertheless, on December 11, 1959, the Yankees traded Siebern, Don Larsen, Marv Throneberry, and Hank Bauer to the Kansas City Athletics for Roger Maris, Joe DeMaestri, and Kent Hadley. It was one of a series of trades that the two teams made during the late 1950s and early '60s, which went in New York's favor so much that Kansas City was referred to as a "Yankee farm team." New York clearly got the best of the trade as Maris won Most Valuable Player awards in 1960 and 1961, and eclipsed Babe Ruth's major league single-season home run record with 61. But the trade also worked out well for Siebern, who blossomed in Kansas City. Reunited with his old Yankee and Southwest Missouri State teammate Jerry Lumpe for the 1960 season, Siebern slugged 31 doubles, six triples, and 19 home runs—seven more than anyone else on the Athletics—for manager Bob Elliott. He split time almost evenly between the outfield and infield.

The A's started the 1961 season under manager Joe Gordon, but Bauer, a former Marine, took over at midseason. Siebern played 109 games at first base and 47 in the outfield, and enjoyed another fine season at the plate. He improved his batting average to .296, smacked a career high 36 doubles, and hit 18 home runs. The A's finished tied for ninth with the Washington Senators, 471/2 games behind the Maris- and Mantle-led Yankees. Mantle finished second to Maris in the MVP balloting. Siebern tied for 14th, with seven 10th place votes.

Under Bauer for a full season in 1962, the Athletics improved by 11 games, and Siebern flourished. He played all 162 games at first base, led the AL in putouts with 1,405, and steadied an infield that included Lumpe, shortstop Dick Howser, and third baseman Ed Charles. He batted .308 with 25 doubles, six triples, 25 home runs, and 117 runs batted in. He walked 110 times and led the league with 296 times on base, and with a .412 on-base percentage. In July, Siebern was the lone Kansas City player selected for major league baseball's two All-Star Games. On July 10 at District of Columbia Stadium in Washington, DC, he grounded out as a pinch hitter in the eighth inning, but he did not see action in the July 30 rematch at Wrigley Field in Chicago. At the end of the season, the bespectacled slugger placed seventh in the MVP race with 53 points.

Former Yankees pitcher Ed Lopat replaced Bauer in 1963 as Kansas City's field manager, the Athletics improved by one game, and Siebern, playing 131 games at first base and 16 in the outfield, slipped to a .272 average, but still hit 25 doubles and 16 home runs, and drove in 83 runs. Once again he was Kansas City's lone All-Star, and once again he played the role of spectator, this time at Cleveland's Municipal Stadium. At the end of the year, Siebern received one 10th place vote for MVP, the last he would collect. Despite his success, on November 27, 1963, the Athletics traded Siebern to the Baltimore Orioles for first baseman Jim Gentile and $25,000 cash.

Bauer had recently been named Baltimore manager, and Siebern's old teammate again played him exclusively at first base, for 149 games. Siebern joined an infield that included second baseman Jerry Adair, shortstop Luis Aparicio, and third baseman Brooks Robinson. Now 30 years old, Siebern slumped to .245. Though he did hit 24 doubles, he managed just 12 homers and 56 runs batted in. The Orioles contended for the American League title, winning 97 times to finish third, just a game behind second-place Chicago and two behind the pennant-winning Yankees. Despite his struggles at the plate, Siebern joined Robinson (the league's MVP) and Aparicio (who missed the game due to injuries), and his friend Lumpe, who was then with Detroit, at the 1964 All-Star Game at Shea Stadium in New York. Pinch hitting for Kansas City pitcher John Wyatt, his future 1967 Boston teammate, Siebern drove

a ball that National League center fielder Willie Mays tracked down.

The 31-year old Siebern saw his playing time decrease in 1965 when 23-year-old Boog Powell moved from the outfield to first base to make room for a pair of 21-year-olds in the outfield, Paul Blair and Curt Blefary. Siebern played first base in 76 games and pinch hit in 30 additional games, batting .256 with eight homers and 32 RBIs as the Orioles finished third again. On December 2, he was traded to the California Angels for Dick Simpson. The Orioles parlayed Simpson, along with pitchers Milt Pappas and Jack Baldschun, in a trade with Cincinnati for outfielder Frank Robinson. Robinson earned MVP honors in 1966, finishing ahead of teammates Brooks Robinson and Powell, and Bauer's Baltimore squad cruised to the AL pennant and a World Series sweep of the Los Angeles Dodgers.

Siebern, meanwhile, spent the 1966 season in California, and at 32 appeared in 125 games, 99 of them at first base. He batted .247 for Bill Rigney's squad, with five home runs and 41 RBIs, and was on the move again at the end of the season. This time, Siebern was swapped to San Francisco for Len Gabrielson in a December 14 trade. Starting the season as a backup to Willie McCovey, Siebern played 15 games at first base and returned to the outfield for the first time since 1963, handling three fly balls in two games. He also appeared in 29 additional games as a pinch hitter, but his brief National League tenure ended on July 16, when he was acquired by the Red Sox for the waiver price of $20,000. In order to claim Siebern on waivers, Boston also optioned injured outfielder George Smith to the Giants farm club at Phoenix.

Boston manager Dick Williams, a teammate of Siebern's at Kansas City in 1960, welcomed the well-traveled slugger. "I think Siebern can help us," Williams said. "I've played with him and I like his hustle and effort." But despite his hustle and effort, Siebern hit just .205 in 33 games for the '67 Sox. His only two extra-base hits were triples. He drew six walks and drove in seven runs. Siebern made one outfield appearance, recording an assist, and played 13 games at first base, where he handled 52 of 53 chances. But some of his appearances at first base were noteworthy. In Anaheim on August 11, Williams told first baseman George Scott, who had battled weight problems, that if he weighed more than 215 pounds, he would sit out the three-game series against California. Scott tipped the scales at 221, and Williams penciled Siebern into the lineup. Three weeks later, after Boston dropped the first game of a Labor Day doubleheader at Washington, Williams inserted Siebern into the lineup for the second game. Scott responded by throwing ice across the room and knocking down a row of bats, continuing a season-long feud with Williams.

Scott continued to boom out base hits through the season, while Siebern sat, making an occasional appearance as the Red Sox clinched the AL flag on the season's final day. For the third time, Siebern played in a World Series. He made three appearances, all as a pinch-hitter, and all against Bob Gibson. In Game One at Fenway Park, Siebern pinch hit for catcher Russ Gibson in the bottom of the seventh inning, but was left standing at the plate when Reggie Smith was caught stealing. He stayed in and played right field, then led off the eighth inning with a single, one of just six Sox hits. José Tartabull ran for Siebern, but was stranded in Gibson's 2-1 complete game win. Siebern pinch hit again in the eighth inning of Game Four, but was retired on a fly ball to centerfield. In Game Seven, he faced the Cardinal ace in the bottom of the eighth inning with a runner on third, and grounded out, plating the final Red Sox run of the Series in a 7-2 loss.

Siebern appeared in just 27 games—only four in the field—in 1968. He played a pair of games in the outfield and a pair at first base, and collected two hits in 30 trips to the plate. He played in his last major league game on July 30, and was released by the Red Sox on August 1, a week past his 35th birthday, and a week before Roger Maris announced his own retirement.

His playing days over, Siebern returned to Independence, Missouri, in the Kansas City area, where he and his wife, Elizabeth (Liz), had lived since he had been a member of the Athletics. The couple, who married in 1958, raised three daughters, Lisa, Jenny and Saundra (nicknamed Sondy), and made their home in a neighborhood that included several former Athletics, including Maris and Norm's old teammate, Whitey Herzog, who lived across the street. After his playing days were over, Siebern served as a scout for the Atlanta Braves and then the expansion Kansas City Royals, played in several Yankees Old Timers games, and joined his ex-Yankee teammates at several Roger Maris Memorial Charity Golf Tournaments in Fargo, North Dakota. He later moved to Naples, Florida, where he owned an insurance agency for several years. He sold the agency in 2000 and retired to Lady Lake, Florida. In 2002, he was honored by Missouri State University, where he is a member of the school's Athletic Hall of Fame, when the 1952 and 1953 NAIA championship teams held a 50-year reunion.

Reggie Smith

by Jeff Angus

	G	AB	R	H	2B	3B	HR	RBI	BB	SO	BA	OBP	SLG	SB	CS	GDP	HBP
1967 RED SOX	158	565	78	139	24	6	15	61	57	95	.246	.315	.389	16	6	7	1

Reggie Smith was a rookie in 1967 when the Boston Red Sox came back from a ninth-place finish to craft an extraordinary pennant-winning season. His All-Star caliber major league career was a great success that has been muddied by other people's expectations (too high) and Smith's media profile (too low).

Smith batted with power and average from both sides of the plate, was a fine center fielder, had superior base-running speed, and had a legendary throwing arm that may have been the best of his era. In the argot of the game, he was a "five-tool player." He took a scientific, analytical approach to the game. His teammates describe him as a man who relentlessly learned to do new things and who strived to be great at everything he did. And the discerning Dick Williams, who managed him in Boston, places Smith on his All-Dick Williams team, a team that includes players from 22 years of helmsmanship and five first-place teams, two of which won World Series.

According to pitcher John Curtis, a teammate of Smith's on both the Red Sox and St. Louis Cardinals, "I will always remember Reg as one of the most complete players I ever saw. ...I know he labored under the weight of everyone's expectations. In Boston, the sportswriters would wonder aloud why Reg wasn't playing up to his demonstrated abilities. ... He once told me that the worst word in the English language was 'potential.'"[1] At the same time, Smith was little-known because another outfielder named Reggie with a Hall of Fame career and a gregarious, exhibitionist personality overshadowed the more businesslike Smith in the eyes of national media. Curtis pitched against both and said, "On the basis of talent, I'd take Smith over Jackson any day. I played with both of them, and I wouldn't hesitate to take Smith's overall game over Jackson's showmanship."

In his 8,050 career plate appearances, Smith produced an OPS+ of 137, batting 37% better than his league's averages, with a batting average of .287, an on-base-percentage of .366, and a slugging percentage of .489. That OPS+ figure is tied for 91st all-time and through the 2005 season, only one previous switch hitter, Mickey Mantle, ranks higher.[2] He finished his career with 314 homers. He played in four World Series, and in 81 plate appearances in the Fall Classic, pounded the ball for a .521 slugging percentage with six home runs; his three homers in the 1977 Series were overshadowed by Reggie Jackson's five-homer performance.

Carl Reginald Smith was born on April 2, 1945, in Shreveport, Louisiana. His father, Lonnie, had been a catcher for a single season for the Jacksonville Red Caps, a Negro American League team that went under at the end of that season.[3] Both his father and his mother, Nellie, were capable musicians.[4] The family moved to Los Angeles when he was a child.

Their new neighborhood, then known by its residents as "Zone 61" but now as South Central, had many intensely competitive baseball teams, none more so than the eponymously-christened Chet Brewer Pirates. The Pirates were the mission of a man who had been one of the Negro Leagues' greatest pitchers. Brewer dedicated his post-playing career to working with children, using the game as a social magnet to involve them in the community (while kicking some serious axe on the field). Brewer recruited Smith when Reggie was only 15. The youngster played only Sundays for the Pirates—he worked the rest of the week assisting his father in the family's egg-delivery business. But his time with the team provided him some useful training for the life of a professional baseball player. Brewer's old pro teammates would drop by to work with the youngsters and chat with each other about the game and their experiences on and off the field.[5] Smith's post-playing career would parallel that of his early mentors.

Reggie went on to play sports at Centennial High School. There, he was an All-California baseball pick at shortstop and won the same honors in football.[6] After high school, he was signed as a free agent by the Minnesota Twins in June 1963. His father was very sick, and while his father wanted Smith to pursue his dream and go to college, Reggie himself wanted to help out the family immediately by earning the money he could make in baseball.[7] Smith started with Wyetheville in the Appalachian League. He was unprotected in the draft, and in December of that year was snared by the Boston Red Sox. He ascended the ladder of the Beantowners' farm clubs, playing for Waterloo (Midwest) and Reading (Eastern) in 1964, and Pittsfield (Eastern) in 1965. The following year he arrived in Toronto, the team's

top farm club, where he played for Dick Williams on a championship team. Smith led the league in batting average that year with a .320 mark.

"Smith had one hell of an arm, even for a shortstop," Williams said, "he could throw like the devil. He had such a strong arm, [then-Red Sox manager] Billy Herman wanted to make him a pitcher. He was my center fielder and he could really play. At that time he was just learning how to switch hit. He was a hell of player. He was moody then, but I had a good time with Reggie."[8]

Smith was a late season call-up to the big club in '66. In six games he showed little but had a chance to taste the major league experience. He played his first game on September 18, finishing 0-for-5 against the California Angels. Six days later, in Yankee Stadium, he got the first three hits of his career against Fritz Peterson. The Red Sox finished ninth, but Smith had secured a place in the team's youth movement.

Williams inherited the sorry franchise's manager position and planned to install Smith in center field, but Smith's rookie campaign was not to start that way. Williams had also brought in Toronto's Mike Andrews to play second base. Andrews, however, injured his back and Smith started the season by returning to his infield roots and playing second base for the team's first six games.

The rookie made important contributions at the plate during the 1967 tussle for the flag though he was only a league-average batter that season (.246/.315/.389 marks for batting average, on-base percentage and slugging average in 628 plate appearances). Through

Yaz, Reggie, and Tony—one of the most popular of all Red Sox outfields.

May 16, Smith managed only a .180 average and two homers in 89 at-bats and the team struggled, too, with a 13-15 mark that buried them in fifth place. Smith came on for the rest of the season, batting .258 with 13 homers while the team was playing 79-55 baseball.

On August 20, the switch-hitter crushed a homer from each side of the plate to lead his team to a 12-2 pummeling of the California Angels. In the bottom of a scoreless first inning, he came up with two outs and Carl Yastrzemski and George Scott on base. Facing starter George "Lefty" Brunet, Smith smoked a three-run homer as a right handed hitter, plating the runs that would stand up as the winners. In the sixth inning, with pinch runner José Tartabull on first base and the right-handed "Philly Pete" Cimino on the mound, Smith stepped to the plate left-handed and knocked one out, the first of six times in his career[9] he achieved the feat of hitting a home run from each side of the plate in a single game. Smith hit for power in the 1967 World Series, slugging .542 with a pair of homers in his 26 plate appearances (including two walks) while hitting for a .250 average.

In 1968, he led the league in doubles with 37, earned a Gold Glove for his work in the outfield, and clearly bettered the league average offense with a .265/.342/.430 line compared with the league's .245/.316/.343 level. And he made a game-altering catch Dick Williams calls one of the most impressive he's ever seen. On May 8, at D.C. Stadium in a scoreless second inning with the Senators' Ron Hansen on second, Smith ran down a Paul Casanova shot that was headed over the center-field fence, leaped to the top of the wall, speared the ball and teeter-tottered on his belt at the top of the fence without tumbling out of the field.

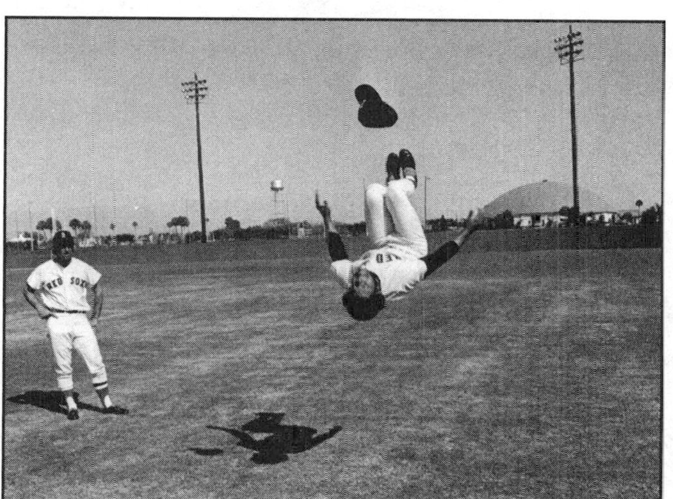

Reggie Smith is head over heels in early spring training.

In 1969, he had his breakout year. At the age of 24, Smith hit .309/.368/.527 for an OPS+ of 143, the American League's eighth best. He also had one of the best defensive seasons of his career.

His next four years in Boston progressed along a career path most players would envy, garnering ascending OPS+ marks of 128, 130, 143, and 150. In 1970, he tallied his career-high 109 runs, and gunned out runners rapid-fire, notching his rifle with 15 assists. In 1971, he launched 30 home runs, his best season total to date. In 1972, at the age of 27, he hit a new plateau for mastering the strike zone, garnering a new seasonal high for walks while trimming his strikeouts by 23 percent. The following year further trimmed his whiffs by an additional 22 percent.

But while Smith was maturing as a player, there were social challenges the home town threw at African-Americans, and in the big arena of Boston sports, the pressure was amplified. Boston had been the last major league team to integrate, and when Reggie Smith was a rookie in 1967, he was one of the very first African-American players the team had brought up with star potential. Black athletes were sandwiched from above and below by chronic racism and bigotry.

Above Dick Williams and the team's GM Dick O'Connell, the front office and ownership of the organization were notoriously prejudiced. Jackie Robinson, who had played alongside and mentored Dick Williams—even knowing Williams was not a bigot—publicly stated that he had to root against the Sox because owner Tom Yawkey was "one of the most bigoted guys in baseball."[10] *Boston Globe* op-ed page editor Marty Nolan referred to the Red Sox as "The Klavern."

The team itself was cliquish, but not cliquish by perceived ethnicity. Smith's closest friend and fishing buddy[11] was Yastrzemski, and Curtis suggested, "Race relations in the clubhouse actually weren't that bad. It was the front office where all the bigotry was festering. I don't recall any of my teammates making a racist remark about Reggie while I was in Boston."

Many of the fans in Boston shared Yawkey's racial views, but practiced a different, less refined way of expressing it. According to pitcher Bill "Spaceman" Lee, Smith used to receive hate mail that started with a racist epithet and then got worse. Playing in the outfield, he had to wear a batting helmet to protect himself from hard objects being thrown by his own team's fans.

Curtis elaborated. "He said some people in the bleachers would throw batteries, heated coins, and other

"Sign it where?" *Reggie Smith juggles items from fans at Fenway.*

projectiles at him. He also told me about a night when some hooligans drove up to his house and emptied the garbage cans he'd placed by the driveway all over his front lawn. That's when I began to understand that Boston was a different town for him than it was for me."

Smith hadn't been prepared for the intensity or texture of many Bostonians' primitive hate for people based on race. He'd grown up in Los Angeles when neighborhoods there were more integrated and social mores more relaxed. Like an anthropologist, he had the outsider's perspective on the behavior of this cultural island. Unlike other players, he didn't choose to suck it up and gut it out.

As Howard Bryant explained the situation in his 2002 book *Shut Out*, "There was no way, Smith thought, that he could not enter the fray... He was expected to produce winning baseball for the home fans, although some were the very people who sought to deny him rights as a person. He did not handle this conflict well, and he waged what was at times was a constant war with the home fans at Fenway."[12]

In late October 1973, the Bosox traded Smith to the Cardinals as part of a multi-player deal. There are always personal challenges in changing teams—new social structures, new processes, new rules and mores. In addition, by changing leagues, Reggie would meet baseball challenges in the form of a different strike zone, new pitchers to learn, and new parks to become familiar with. But neither the social nor the baseball challenges slowed down his career.

"St. Louis was a much friendlier environment for him," John Curtis opined, "because he had two talented and very proud individuals to look up to there—Bob Gibson and Lou Brock." Smith said he had always felt he was a National League player trapped in the American League.[13] And as perhaps the single most ferociously competitive African-American athlete in baseball, Bob Gibson was able to provide cover for Smith's intensity, even while reveling in it; according to Curtis, who later joined Smith in moving to the Cardinals. "Gibby used

to call him 'Spike,'" after the unyielding guard dog in the Bugs Bunny cartoon.

In his first season with the Cardinals, 1974, he totaled his best offensive year yet, an OPS+ of 157 over 598 plate appearances. Traditionalists could appreciate his .309 batting average and an even 100 RBIs. It was a very balanced team, too, with professionals like Gibson and Brock and Joe Torre, effective team-oriented role players like Ted Sizemore, Tim McCarver, and Orlando Peña, and a host of young talent that included José Cruz, rookie of the year Bake McBride, Ted Simmons, Bob Forsch, and Al Hrabosky. McBride's presence in center and Smith's superior throwing arm moved Reggie to right field, where he played most of the rest of his career. The Cards finished second to Pittsburgh by 1½ games, but this premier campaign established Smith in the league. He earned a roster spot in the All-Star game, his third of seven.

The 1975 and '76 seasons were more frustrating. In '75 his OPS+ of 137, while very good, was off his '74 mark, and the team was tumbling into third place. Smith played about half his games at first base. In '76, the team sagged further, and through June 15, his OPS+ at 95 was below league average. The front office people feared they might not be able to sign him as a free agent at the end of the season,[14] so they traded him to his hometown team, the Los Angeles Dodgers, for utilityman Joe Ferguson and throw-ins.

Reggie taking some cuts in the cage.

Red Sox owner Tom Yawkey and Reggie Smith in the Fenway clubhouse after Game Six of the World Series.

The Dodgers would prove to be the team that most benefited from Smith's impact. Back in the outfield, he picked up his offense with an OPS+ of 133. In 1977, he was the team's offensive leader, leading the league in OPS+ with a career best 167, and acting as the hub of an offense with four batters who notched 30 or more homers. His line of .307/.427/.576 is a little less gaudy than it looks—it was a high-offense year—but he was still adding to his game, earning 104 walks, a career high. On a team that had excellence all over the field but which had a lack of fire as its limiting factor, Smith's quiet intensity, even turned down a notch in his more comfortable environment, was a blessing. As teammate Dusty Baker said, "Reggie's a foxhole dude. If it was war or a baseball game, there wouldn't be another person I want [more] next to me".[15]

Things were changed, easier. According to Curtis, most teammates called him "Carl," his real first name. And he was finally in a place and at an age where his off-the-field life could exist in a more natural way. His passion for taking on new skills (he plays seven musical instruments[16]) and achieving a high level with them was obvious to his teammates.

Davey Lopes, the team's second baseman, described Smith's pursuits:

"He was very intelligent and everything he did, he wanted to become good at doing. He worked hard in the off-season at something new every year.

"He became a pilot. One year it was an airplane pilot, and he got his license. One year it was photography. He's got every lens there is in the world and he's become a master of photography. Then it's cooking. Amazing.... Every Spring Training, we'd ask ourselves, 'What's coming next?'[17]

"Reggie didn't ever settle for doing things half-assed."

The Dodgers won the pennant but lost the World Series to the Yankees, as they would the next season. Reggie Smith's 1978 campaign was close to his previous one; the league's numbers were down, as were his, but his OPS+ of 161 was good enough for second in the NL. At the age of 33, he'd started losing some of his range in the outfield, though his arm was still noteworthy around the league, and he was as close to well-known to casual fans as he would ever be.

In mid-July of 1979, he was injured, an event that truncated his season. His 125 OPS+, while well above average, was disappointing compared with his recent accomplishments. The Dodgers finished 79-83, mediocre enough for third place. But the 1980 season saw an uptick in his offensive production. His .322/.392/.508 line created an OPS+ of 153, which would have been second in the league if he had made enough plate appearances. His season had ended as a useful player in July, getting no starts afterwards, and only one pinch-hitting and two pinch-running assignments. His career as a regular in the majors came to an end. In 1981, he got 44 plate appearances. At the end of that season, he became a free agent and signed with the San Francisco Giants, where Frank Robinson was manager. Coincidentally, Robinson was the only other player in the history of the game who had appeared in both All-Star games and World Series for both leagues.[18]

In 1983, Smith played in Japan for the Yomiuri Giants and in a dark literary twist of fate, ended his playing career back in a racially hostile environment.[19] In spite of injury, he produced at a .285/.409/.627 rate in part-time play, with that slugging percentage rivaling the qualified leader's mark. According to the team's owner, Matsutaro Shoriki, it was Smith's contributions that led to the team's pennant. But beanball incidents, an on-field brawl, disputes with umpires' protean strike zones for African-American players, and racial epithets from fans that escalated to a physical assault on Smith and his son all cast a shadow on the contributions he made. The 1984 season was his last, cursed with injuries to wrist, shoulder, and knee, though he still slugged over .500 in his 231 at-bats.

In 1993, Smith became field coordinator for the Dodgers' minor league operations department. The next year he became the major league team's batting coach, a post he held through 1999. He coached the 2000 U.S. Olympic baseball team that won the Gold Medal, and was the batting coach for the 2006 U.S. entry in the World Baseball Classic.

According to a *Boston Globe* article, "When Smith is not working, he is doing charity work all over the country. Smith visits hospitals, youth centers, cancer centers and helps fund raising through golf tournaments and different activities. 'The community is very important to me and it's a way for me to share the gift that was given to me by being able to play,' said Smith. 'If I can inspire someone or provide a moment of enjoyment or pleasure for someone where I am with them and talk to them that's the least I can do. I try to encourage people and send positive messages.'"[20]

Smith has turned down major league coaching positions to focus on educational work. He's run a youth baseball camp since 1995 and opened the Reggie Smith Baseball Center in Encino, California in 1998. The center is an instructional facility for players of all ages and levels, based on scientific approaches to playing the game. And following in the footsteps of one of his key mentors, Chet Brewer, Smith is volunteering[21] to help MLB's 2006 launch of the Urban Youth Baseball Academy, a facility it is funding to attract inner-city youth to the National Pastime.

Notes:

1. E-mail interview with John Curtis, 2003.
2. Baseball-Reference.Com.
3. Riley, James A., *The Biographical Encyclopedia of the Negro Baseball Leagues*.
4. JockBio.Com profile.
5. Davis, David. "Remembering Mr. Brewer" LA Weekly, June 1997.
6. Baseball Library.Com article by Ed Walton.
7. JockBio.Com profile
8. Interview with Dick Williams by Jeff Angus, 2005.
9. The Baseball Page.Com
10. Bryant, Howard. *Shut Out*. NY: Routledge, p. 88.
11. JockBio.Com profile
12. Bryant, *op. cit.*, p. 91.
13. JockBio.Com profile
14. JockBio.Com profile.
15. Bryant, *op. cit.*, p. 90.
16. Baseball-Reference Bullpen entry by Mischa Gilman
17. Interview with Dick Williams, June 2005.
18. Ed Walton, Baseball Library.Com
19. Baseball-Reference Bullpen entry by Mischa Gelman.
20. Goode, Jon. "A Switch-Hitting Star: Catching up with Reggie Smith," *Boston Globe*, November 5, 2004.
21. Patton, Gregg. (Riverside) *Press-Enterprise* story, March 1, 2006.

José Tartabull

by Joanne Hulbert

	G	AB	R	H	2B	3B	HR	RBI	BB	SO	BA	OBP	SLG	SB	CS	GDP	HBP
1967 RED SOX	115	247	36	55	1	2	0	10	23	26	.223	.287	.243	6	6	4	0

It was Boston's eighth trade since the end of the 1965 season. In 1964, manager Billy Herman had vowed, "If I am ever made manager of this team and we have a losing club, I promise you one thing: We'll lose with new faces."

Herman lived up to his promise as the Red Sox occupied last place in the American League on June 15, 1966, despite earlier trades that had juggled the roster, shipped out players—Dick Radatz to Cleveland, Bill Monbouquette to Detroit, and Lee Thomas to Atlanta—and brought in Lee Stange, George Smith, and Eddie Kasko along with seven others in an attempt to improve pitching, increase hitting, and add speed. So radically had the Red Sox changed their roster that when owner Tom Yawkey attended his first game of the season, on June 15, there were 16 players he had never seen before. That eighth trade sent pitchers Ken Sanders and Guido Grilli and outfielder Jim Gosger to the Kansas City Athletics for pitchers Rollie Sheldon and John Wyatt. Then outfielder José Tartabull was added to make it a six-man swap, sweetening the deal and bringing to Boston a player known for speed, pinch hitting, and stealing bases, deficiencies suffered by Boston.

Tartabull was one of the fastest baserunners in the league, but during the three seasons he spent in Boston, he played in the shadows of Carl Yastrzemski, Tony Conigliaro, and Reggie Smith. He would be best remembered in New England for a throw to home plate in a crucial game during the late-season pennant race of 1967.

José Milages Tartabull Guzman was born November 27, 1938, at Cienfuegos, Las Villas, Cuba. He excelled at track and baseball during his school years, and attended La Universidad de San Lorenzo. "I tried all the other games," he said in a *Boston Globe* interview in 1967, "soccer, basketball, track. Don't really care too much for them. The kids in Cienfuegos used to make their own gloves from two pieces of leather, some thread and some rope, and bind up beaten-up old baseballs with tape. They'd nail together broken bats to keep them in service."

Tartabull also recalled how he and his friends used to wait outside the ballpark during winter league games looking for foul balls that were hit out of the park when many of the major league teams came to Cuba for exhibition games. "You bring the ball back," he said, "and they let you come in for nothing."

Watching the major league teams inspired him. Willie Mays was his favorite player, and the Yankees were the team he followed, but he also admired the Chicago White Sox because Minnie Minoso, a popular player among Cuban baseball fans, played for them at the time.

Tartabull first appeared with the Regina, Saskatchewan club, a semipro team in Western Canada, in 1957 after American scouts traveled throughout Cuba and offered outstanding players the opportunity to play outside Cuba. In 1958, having been signed to a pro contract by Giants' scout Alex Pompez, he was with the Hastings Club of the Nebraska State League and with Michigan City in the Midwest League, where he continued to improve. He returned to Michigan City in 1959, where he played in the outfield and led the league in fielding, putouts, assists, and double plays. He continued his minor league accomplishments in 1960 with the Giants' Eugene, Oregon, club of the Class B Northwest League, where he batted .344. In 1961, while with the Victoria club of the Single-A Texas League, he led the league in runs scored, triples, and stolen bases and was named to the league's All-Star team.

Also during that time, Tartabull had to make a life-changing choice—play ball in the United States or return to Cuba—a decision many Cuban players had to face when Fidel Castro cancelled the Cuban Winter League season in 1961. José's hometown, Cienfuegos, was a rural, sugar-factory town. His father worked for the government and was on the wrong side of the revolution when Castro took power. His family and that of his wife Maria—her father owned a sugar factory—were both affected by the regime change. Their families were well-to-do—José's father was a college professor, his grandfather a judge—and leaving Cuba and possibly never seeing them again was a heart-wrenching dilemma. "We talk to family as often as we can. We know what the situation is. We keep praying it will open up. But to keep talking by phone to parents and brothers and sisters that one hasn't seen for more than 30 years is heartbreaking," said Tartabull in an interview with Peter Gammons in 1992. "I was a ballplayer, that's what I had done all my life, so I really

had no choice. Of course, who would have ever thought in 1961 that I'd still never have been back or seen our families?"

With five years of semipro and minor league experience, Tartabull, described as an "obscure outfielder" and not expected to figure prominently in the Giants' plans for 1962, was dealt to Kansas City. At the Athletics' spring training in 1962, Tartabull, batting left and throwing left, demonstrated that he could do a good defensive job in the outfield, although he did not show much power. But he did have speed, he could go after the ball well enough, and his impressive year in the Texas League was proof enough of a promising future, thought Athletics manager Hank Bauer. Tartabull vied for an outfield position with Gino Cimoli, Bobby Del Greco, Manny Jimenez, and Bill Lajoie, and when Bauer completed the roster for the 1962 season, José Tartabull was in center field. He played his first game on April 10 as a defensive substitute in center field, got his first start the next day (going 0-4 against Minnesota ace Camilo Pasqual), and got his first hit on April 12, a single off the Twins' Joe Bonikowski. In the 1962 season, José started 67 games in center field, appeared in 107 games, with 310 at-bats and a batting average of .277.

In José's nine-year career he hit just two home runs, one off Barry Latman in Cleveland Stadium in 1963, and the other off the Senators' Phil Ortega in Kansas City's Municipal Stadium in 1965. "People wonder why I don't hit home runs, I tell them why," he explained in 1968 to Phil Elderkin, the sports writer for the *Christian Science Monitor*. He described how he swung the bat with a short stroke, while all the time he'd look for holes in the defense. "I slap at the ball. I either hit line drives between outfielders or I hit high hoppers." By the time the outfielders caught up with the ball, he said, he'd be crossing first base.

Bauer was optimistic that the Athletics would improve their performance over 1961 and felt they had a good chance to finish as high as sixth place. Kansas City ended up finishing ninth. Tartabull carved out a role as a reserve outfielder and pinch-runner for the Athletics, playing mainly left and center fields. In 1964, he appeared in 104 games but batted only 100 times. By the time he became part of Boston's eighth trade since the end of the 1965 season, Tartabull had established himself as a valuable major league player.

Meanwhile, the Red Sox were reeling from a 2-6 road trip in June 1966, a nightmare with no end in sight. The team returned to Boston, where it would showcase the newly acquired players in a game with Detroit and begin a 17-game homestand. They hoped to be an improved team from the one that left town on June 6. Manager Billy Herman commented, "When you're going as bad as we are, changes are necessary." Detroit hammered the Sox, 11-7, on June 15, and again the next day, 16-4. Tartabull's first action was in the latter game, when he pinch hit and grounded out against Denny McLain.

While the Red Sox languished near the bottom of the American League standings, the move from Kansas City to Boston was a boon for Tartabull's career. When he left the Athletics, his average stood at .236, but for the Red Sox he hit .277. He also led the club with 11 stolen bases, while the team as a whole had only 35. When he was not sharing the center field position with Don Demeter, he was pinch hitting, making some impressive hits at crucial moments, and assuring a place for himself at spring training the following year.

A firm believer in keeping his skills sharp with offseason work, he played for Caracas of the Venezuelan League during the winter of 1966-67, along with Bert Campaneris, Luis Tiant, Diego Segui, and Orlando Pena. "All this sitting around, though, it no good for ballplayer," Tartabull told Elderkin. He hated sitting around on the bench, as it made him rusty, and threw his timing off when he wasn't in the starting lineup every day. He played winter ball to keep his skills sharp, so that when spring training started, he was ready and ahead of everyone else.

With 1966 behind them—a year best forgotten—the Red Sox opened spring training in 1967 with a new manager, Dick Williams, and a distinctly different attitude. Strict curfews, wakeup calls, and rigorous workouts met the players as they reported in the last week of February. Manager Williams donned umpire's gear for the first intra-squad game at Winter Haven, Florida. Reggie Smith, George Thomas, and Tartabull hit home runs.

The team soon began a transformation. There was much work to do to change a few young stars and a bunch of players with a history as hapless losers into a team of disciplined players. Tartabull enjoyed a remarkable preseason, and was destined to continue his role backing up each outfield position. It was a young club, with many players under 25. Tartabull was one of the oldest at 28. Although working hard on his fielding and hitting, and still blessed with exceptional speed, Reggie Smith was set to take over the center field position, and there was no chance of deposing Tony Conigliaro or Carl Yastrzemski from their positions in right and left fields. Tartabull concentrated on providing solid pinch-hitting and outfield backup, situations where he would ultimately find himself in frequent demand. When Mike

Andrews developed a back problem in spring training, Williams decided to move Smith to second base temporarily, allowing Tartabull an opportunity to play center field at the end of spring training and for four of the first five games of the season. Tartabull grabbed the opportunity, running at top speed, and as Larry Claflin reported in *The Sporting News*, "getting on base so often and scoring so many runs that it seemed he was always sliding into home plate in a cloud of dust."

Tartabull was called the biggest surprise of all the players at spring training, and he may have been right about his time spent in winter ball. "I just didn't think he was as good a player that he has shown us," said Dick Williams. "José is a much better player now than he was two or three years ago. He had a fabulous spring. Every time he got in a ballgame he did something."

Opening Day at Fenway Park, April 11, 1967, was postponed by 40-degree temperatures and high winds. April 12 was only marginally better, but the game was played before just over 8,000 spectators. Fans were rewarded with a 5-4 win over the Chicago White Sox. Tartabull started in center field. As the leadoff batter, he had an infield single in the sixth, stole second, and then scored what proved to be the deciding run on a throwing error by Chicago shortstop Ron Hansen. "That's why I like to lead off for Red Sox," he told Phil Elderkin. "Nobody in front of me, I steal. I can't run whenever I want. Score has to be right and I have to get sign from bench. But all the time I study pitchers. Some pitchers they deliver slow to plate. I go when their throwing shoulder begin to fall. I also watch feet and hands. They tell me things. I play every day, I steal 25 base a year easy."

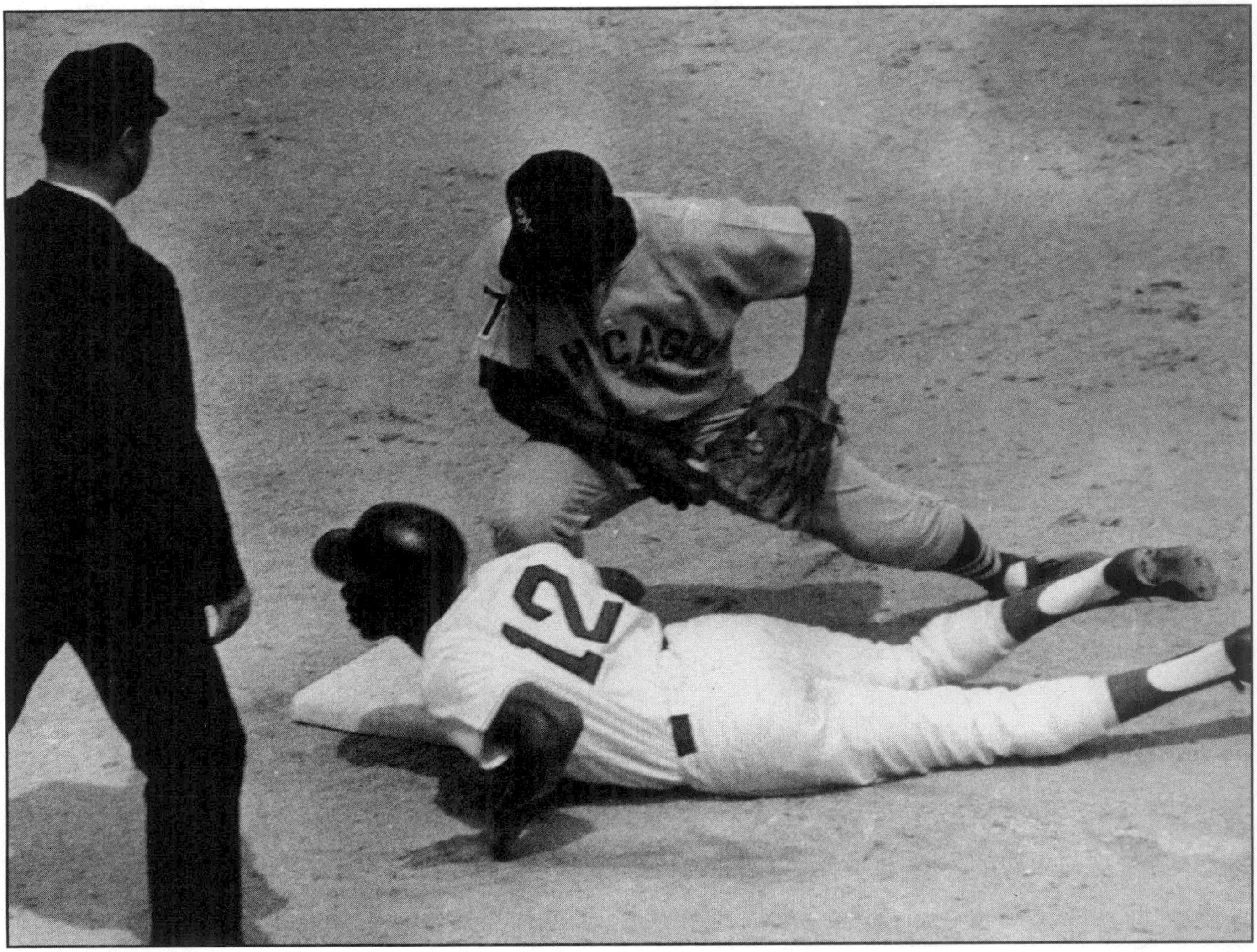

Tartabull stole second base on Opening Day, then did it again the following day. On August 27, his strike from right field reached Elston Howard at the plate and cut down White Sox rightfielder Ken Berry in a game-ending double play that secured a 4-3 win for the Red Sox.

Although he did not settle into a permanent place in the lineup, he filled in when Conigliaro suffered a hairline fracture of the shoulder when hit by a pitch from John Wyatt before a game against the Tigers during spring training, played center when Reggie Smith filled in at second as Mike Andrews battled muscle spasms, and he came off the bench to deliver a critical hit on April 29, in a game against Kansas City. The game was tied at 9-9 going into the 15th inning, but the Athletics took the lead with a run in the top of the inning. The Red Sox then loaded the bases, and Williams sent Tartabull to the plate to pinch hit for Mike Andrews. José singled to center, the ball shooting through the drawn-in infield as Conigliaro and Scott scored. The entire Red Sox dugout emptied out onto the field to congratulate him. Not only was it a dramatic end to a prolonged game, but the win also elevated the Red Sox to a first-place tie in the American League, an accomplishment not enjoyed by the team since 1963. Tartabull recalled he went up to the plate guessing what he might do. "Everyone in baseball knows I'm a high-ball hitter. [Pitcher] Jack Aker [knew it] too. When I was going up to the plate, I told myself that Aker would not pitch one high . . . so I started looking for a low ball to hit, and that's what I got."

On May 14, Boston occupied its more familiar place as part of a three-way tie for last place—six games out of first. Tartabull continued as a pinch-hitter and pinch-runner and provided relief in the outfield. An upbeat kind of guy, he showed no displeasure about his role as the consummate utility player. He was often heard singing in the clubhouse, accompanying himself on his set of bongo drums, a source of positive attitude, a sparkplug for the Impossible Dream Team.

Shuffling the roster frequently to keep the Red Sox in the running for the American League pennant, the Sox management continued to make trades throughout the summer, and on August 3, Tartabull was sent to the minor league team in Pittsfield. Two weeks later, he was back in the lineup when Bob Tillman was traded to the Yankees and Russ Gibson was sent down to Pittsfield.

"A spare outfielder—a man who can play center and right field in reserve and hit .275—is very much in demand," wrote Tom Monahan in the *Boston Herald-Traveler* on August 16. Just two days later, Tony Conigliaro was lost for the rest of the season after being struck in the face by a pitch from the California Angels' Jack Hamilton. Tartabull ran for Conigliaro after the beaning, and got most of the playing time in right field for the next 10 games.

On August 28, Ken Harrelson signed a free agent contract with the Red Sox following his release by the Athletics. Tartabull returned to his familiar role as the spare outfielder, but not before he provided a bit of memorable heroics for his team's fabled pennant drive. Home runs, double plays, and memorable drama were expected of players like Yastrzemski or Conigliaro, but the play many consider the signature moment of the season came from an unlikely source—José Tartabull.

Going into the games of Sunday August 27, the Red Sox were a half-game ahead of Minnesota and one over both Chicago and Detroit. In a double-header against the White Sox at Comiskey Park, Boston led the first game 4-3 in the bottom of the ninth inning. With one out, Chicago's Ken Berry was on third repreenting the tying run. Duane Josephson, batting for Hoyt Wilhelm, hit a soft line drive into right field off John Wyatt. José Tartabull, with a notoriously weak throwing arm, charged in, caught the liner, and fired home, on-line but high. Catcher Elston Howard leaped to reach the ball, kept his foot in front of home plate and tagged Berry out. Game over. Boston briefly took back first place in the pennant race, but dropped to second place after losing the second game of the doubleheader.

"If I make good throw and keep it low, I feel I throw him out," said Tartabull. "Then I see the throw go high and I say to myself, 'oh oh.' Then I watch him jump for the ball and when I see the umpire call him out, I say,

September 24, 1967. Returning to Boston from Baltimore where he'd gone 2-for-5 and scored two runs in an 11-7 win over the Orioles, Sox outfielder José hefts his son Danny while greeting his wife Marie. Thirty years later, in 1997, Danny wrapped up 15 seasons as a major leaguer.

'atta boy.' I caught the ball in the webbing of the glove and I have no chance to aim the throw."

Tartabull's Throw—one of only three assists he made that season—became part of Red Sox lore and was his primary contribution to the Impossible Dream. The Throw inspired the fans and galvanized the Red Sox. Williams figured it saved Tartabull's place on the team roster. In 2001, when Steve Buckley of the *Boston Herald* counted the 100 most significant moments in Red Sox history, Tartabull's Throw came in at number 59.

Four teams battled throughout September for the American League pennant. Sharing right field with Harrelson, who slumped after joining the club, Tartabull pinch-ran for Harrelson during the big sixth inning rally on the final day, and was on the field for the last three innings when the Red Sox clinched (at first) a tie for the pennant. When Rico Petrocelli caught Rich Rollins' pop fly to end the game, chaos broke out as the fans swarmed the field. "My glove slipped off and flew in the air," said Tartabull. "I reached up and grabbed it before anyone else could, and then I just hung on. It took fifteen minutes for me to get in."

There was chaos in the clubhouse as well. José administered champagne and beer showers to Jim Lonborg and Reggie Smith. He then took a handful of shaving cream and artfully painted the face of Carl Yastrzemski as Yaz posed solemnly, surrounded by frenzied teammates. These were the players who had been given a 100-to-1 shot at the pennant at the beginning of the season. A team described as a bunch of playboys, "Baby Bombers," rookies, "Cardiac Kids," misfits, and cast-offs, were in truth a team made up of players who had all at one time or another made a hit, a play, a save or a throw that had kept the team on its way to clinching a pennant.

The year 1967 was an extraordinary time for José Tartabull and his family, who spent the summer sharing a three-decker on Cypress Street in Brookline, Massachusetts, with José Santiago and his family. There was a park nearby where the elder Tartabull was often seen throwing underhand tosses to his son Danny, nearly 5 years old and destined to become a major league player. Although his counterpart in right field, Ken Harrelson, signed for a salary of $75,000, Tartabull was making $7,000. He was six years removed from his homeland and family, maintained a winter residence in Florida, and held precariously onto his job in Conigliaro's absence. He figured, "It's a good life."

Boston faced a tough World Series with St. Louis, and the oddsmakers offered little encouragement. In the first game, on October 4, Tartabull pinch-ran in the eighth and played an inning in right field. The next three games, he was the starting right fielder and leadoff batter. After two hitless games, he got two singles off Bob Gibson in Game Four, two of five hits the Red Sox achieved in the 5-0 loss. Harrelson was back in right field for the remainder of the Series, with Tartabull going in for defense in Games Five and Six, and striking out as a pinch-hitter against Gibson in Game Seven. José played in all seven games, hitting two singles in 13 at-bats.

José Tartabull remained with Boston for the 1968 season, appearing in 72 games. Despite his .281 batting average, he wasn't on the major league roster when the Red Sox started the 1969 season. "They had no reason for that," he said in an interview in September 1969. "I hit .281 the year before. I have no idea why they did that. I thought I was doing a great job."

On May 7, 1969, while playing for Louisville, he was purchased by the Oakland Athletics, returning to the club he had left three years earlier—albeit now in a different city. He was put to work as a pinch-hitter, and in left and center field. He appeared in 75 games with Oakland in 1969, and in just 24 games in 1970, and then went on to play two seasons with minor league teams. Thus concluded José's major league career.

Tartabull continued contributing to baseball as a minor league coach. He was the manager of the Houston Astros' Class A Sarasota farm team in the Florida State League. In 1984 he told Neil Singelais of the *Boston Globe*: "I'm everything here at Sarasota," he laughed, "I'm the manager, the coach and the hitting instructor. This is not the big leagues, you know."

He was also watching his son Danny, the kid who once used Fenway Park as a playground, on his way to making it in the big leagues. A right-handed hitter for Seattle, Kansas City, New York, and Chicago, as well as a brief stint with Philadelphia, Danny hit as many home runs in his debut year (two) as his father hit in his entire career. Danny's younger brother, José, Jr., was an outfielder in the Mariners minor league system from 1986-89.

José Tartabull secured his place in Red Sox history with his throw from right field on August 27, 1967. "If I meet someone from Boston today," he told Peter Gammons in 1992, "he usually says, 'I remember the throw.' It's nice, 25 years later, to be remembered in Boston. When someone recalls so fondly what I did in Boston, when I see what Danny has done for the Tartabull name, I realize that the decision I made in 1961 [to stay in the U.S. and play baseball] was the right one. But all I can pray is that all our families can soon be united and see what America has meant to the Tartabulls."

George Thomas

by Ray Birch

	G	AB	R	H	2B	3B	HR	RBI	BB	SO	BA	OBP	SLG	SB	CS	GDP	HBP
1967 RED SOX	65	89	10	19	2	0	1	6	3	23	.213	.255	.270	0	1	0	2

In the course of a major league baseball season, players assume certain important roles on their teams. Apart from whether they start or sit on the bench, a player's intangible qualities such as being a positive clubhouse presence can be essential to a team's success on the field. Throughout his major league career, and in particular during the 1967 season with the Boston Red Sox, George Thomas was invaluable to the teams he played for, not only for his versatility on the field but also for the quick wit and camaraderie that he brought to the dugout. This made him one of baseball's premier bench jockeys. His ability to play all non-pitching positions was complemented by his unique talent for being able to gauge the mood of the team and ease the tensions of the 162-game schedule.

George Edward Thomas Jr. was born on November 29, 1937, in Minneapolis, Minnesota. His father sold real estate and his mother was a homemaker who did occasional part-time secretarial work. The couple had three children; George was the middle child. His brother Jerry was two years older and was an all-American right-handed pitcher out of the University of Minnesota. Both Thomas boys came by their interest in baseball from their father, who had played semi-pro ball—a pitcher, too—but who had hurt himself while on a spring training tryout for the Minneapolis Millers, circa 1935. The boys had a sister as well, five years younger than George.

The elder George spent time with his sons, playing pepper with them and hitting ground balls to them. He coached the town team George Jr. played on in high school; George played midget ball, junior ball, and then American Legion ball.

Despite not being far apart in age, the two brothers never played even sandlot ball together, Jerry sticking with his older buddies and George with his own friends. George graduated from Bloomington High School where he played baseball, football, and basketball.

Like Jerry, George enrolled at the University of Minnesota, where he lettered as a sophomore shortstop for the Golden Gophers during the 1957 collegiate season. As he completed his sophomore year, Jerry prepared to graduate. Right after the College World Series, Detroit Tigers scout George Moriarty came to sign the older brother. "The next thing I know," George explained in a June 2006 interview, "he comes in from the car where they were talking, and asks me if I wanted to play!"

On August 5, George Thomas was signed by Moriarty as an amateur free agent, with the $25,000 he was given denoting him a "bonus baby." Under the bonus rule at the time, he had to stay with the Tigers, and so immediately joined the big league club, traveling with them the rest of the 1957 season. At the age of 19, he was the second-youngest position player in the American League that season behind Baltimore catcher Frank Zupo, although he appeared in just one game. The game was September 11 at Washington's Griffith Stadium, and Thomas struck out against Ted Abernathy as a pinch-hitter, then played two innings at third base. The Tigers saw Thomas as a shortstop or third baseman, although previously he had also pitched and played the outfield. The Tigers were impressed with his swing and with his "outstanding arm."[1]

That winter, the Tigers sent Thomas and other prospects to play Mexican League baseball, both for the Diablos Rojos in Mexico City and for the Puebla ballclub. The Tigers had a minor league manager and a pitching coach travel with them.

Thomas started spring training on the big league roster, but the bonus rule had been changed that winter, and as the season began, he was sent to the Tigers' Birmingham team in the Double-A Southern Association, where by year's end he hit .260 in 22 games as an outfielder. It was a year with a few changes of uniform. In May, he was assigned to Augusta, of the Single-A South Atlantic League. He played 71 games there, in two stretches, with a 24-game stint with Durham in between. While in Augusta, George and Jerry played for a while on the same team. Other than some overlap at the University of Minnesota, it would be the only time in their lives that they played together. George hit .294 for Augusta, seeing time at first base and the outfield. In September 1958, when the minor league season ended, he was called up to Detroit once more. Again, he appeared in just a single game, this time as a pinch-runner and then spending an inning in right field, not even getting an at-bat.

Jerry hurt his arm in A-ball. "I think he might have

gone to spring training with Birmingham," George recalls. " But he hurt his arm around 1959 or 1960, and that was about it."

The 1959 season found George back at Birmingham to start the season. On May 9, he was hit by a pitch at a game in Mobile and suffered a fractured jaw, sidelined until late June. Before the injury, he had been hitting .323. Thomas finished the season with a .274 batting average, and after the season he was once more added to the expanded Tigers roster, though he did not appear in a game.

After limited action during spring training in 1960, Thomas was sent to the Tigers' minor league complex. *The Sporting News*, in its April 13, 1960, edition, selected him as the "Likeliest to Improve" in the Tigers organization. Thomas played a full season in 1960 for Birmingham (.283 with 13 home runs in 124 games), also playing 14 games with Denver (American Association). That winter he served six months in the United States Army.

During the 1961 preseason, Thomas was paid a tremendous compliment when Triple-A Denver's manager, Charlie Metro, said that "Thomas can throw as good as Kaline," referring to the Tigers' All-Star outfielder.[2] Finally that season, Thomas stayed with the Tigers coming out of spring training, though he played just 17 games, 10 as a pinch-runner, and was hitless in six at-bats.

On June 26, 1961, he was sold by the Tigers to the expansion Los Angeles Angels. Chico Fernandez had been hurt, and the Tigers brought up Dick McAuliffe, putting Thomas on waivers. The Twins might have claimed the hometown player, but the last-place Angels had the first pick off waivers and grabbed him. With the Angels, Thomas played third base and the outfield, starting nearly every day, and hitting well. He got his first major league hit, a double off Chicago's Billy Pierce, on June 30. Two days later, he blasted his first home run off Warren Hacker. On September 9, Thomas hit his first grand slam off Frank Baumann, and finished with 13 homers and a .280 batting average in the 79 games he played for Los Angeles. His strong finish made him manager Bill Rigney's projected starter in center field for the 1962 season.

However, the Berlin Crisis was in full swing, and the United States Army had different plans for Thomas. In November 1961 he was recalled to serve a one-year hitch at Fort Lewis, Washington. Ultimately, because of Army policy regarding seasonal work and completion of service, Thomas and other major league players were discharged earlier than expected, and he rejoined the Angels on July 27, 1962. While playing all three outfield positions, he batted .238 over the final two months of the season. The nickname T-N-T was given to the combined talents of George Thomas and teammate Lee Thomas, as the Angels looked to their bats for needed power.[3] Combined, they hit 30 home runs, but 26 of those came from Lee (no relation) Thomas. "I never got myself going again," George admits. "And they traded me back to the Tigers." The trade came in mid-June the following year.

Going to spring training for the 1963 season, Thomas again was pegged for outfield duty. On May 1, he hit the second grand slam of his career against the Yankees' Ralph Terry (the first grand slam by the Angels at Chavez Ravine, their temporary home shared with the Dodgers). But at the trading deadline on June 15, Thomas, then hitting just .210, was shipped back to the Tigers, in exchange for pitcher Paul Foytack and infielder Frank Kostro. In Detroit, Thomas was mainly platooned with Bill Bruton in center field, playing against left-handed pitchers.

Before the 1964 season, Thomas was asked to come

Utilityman George Thomas spent a lot of '67 on the bench and quipped, "This is the best pennant race I have ever watched." The strong-armed Thomas proved to be a valuable addition due to his hustle, versatility and great attitude.

to spring training prepared to learn the catcher position in the event of injury to starter Bill Freehan and backup Mike Roarke. Still primarily an outfielder, Thomas did well as a pinch hitter (6-for-17 on the season), and platooned in left field. Eventually his steady play earned him additional playing time in center field, and he finished the season with a very strong .286 batting average.

During the offseason, Thomas married Dianne May, took courses at Wayne State University, and signed a new $15,000 contract with the Tigers. But after a dismal 1965 season, in which he batted only .213 in 79 games, the Tigers traded him with George Smith and a player to be named to the Red Sox in exchange for Bill Monbouquette. The Tigers had Willie Horton and Gates Brown coming up and saw more need in the area of pitching. Monbouquette was a Red Sox fan favorite for eight years, and many fans thought the Red Sox could have received more in return for him. But the team's management hoped that the trade for Thomas and Smith would improve the team's defense and make up for some of the wins that Monbouquette might have earned.[4] Thomas was surprised the Red Sox let Monbo go, but said, "I'd always played fairly well against the Red Sox, hitting-wise" and figured that's one of the reasons Boston made the trade.

In 1966, Thomas played in 69 games for the Red Sox and batted .237. But he had a sense of humor that was appreciated in the Red Sox clubhouse, and was a versatile, hustling player, a quality that earned him esteem in the eyes of manager Billy Herman. Many bench players complain about their lack of playing time, but Thomas accepted his role and came ready to play every day. He was comfortable in the role of utilityman. At one point a brief injury to another player gave him the chance to play four games in a row. When the hurt player was ready to come back, he jokingly demanded of his manager, "Dick, I can't play all these games. Bench me or trade me!"[5]

Before the 1967 season, New England fans were hopeful for a change in fortune for the Red Sox. In 1966, the Red Sox had finished with a dismal 72-90 record, but had played very well in the second half. A group of rookies from Toronto, the Red Sox Triple-A farm club, seemed poised to add more enthusiasm and life into the Sox lineup. Thomas made the 1967 club in his utility role, mainly backing up at the three outfield positions, and he added valuable experience in the dugout. However, on May 7, Thomas broke his finger attempting to catch a line drive and was sidelined for about four weeks. When he returned, Thomas resumed his utility role.

By this time, he'd played every position on the field except pitcher. He'd both pitched and played shortstop in high school ball. Did he ever talk to anybody about letting him throw an inning? "Not really. You didn't want to do that because you didn't want to make a farce out of the thing." He remembered, though, that while with Los Angeles, "Bill Rigney almost made me a pitcher after I had some trouble coming back after the service. He'd send me down to the bullpen to warm up and all that, but I never got in."

One of the ways that Thomas relaxed in the clubhouse was to be involved in a season-long bridge game with Carl Yastrzemski, Jim Lonborg, and other players. During the season, in the heat of the pennant race, Thomas quipped from the bench, "This is the best pennant race I have ever watched."

There was a role to be played even from the bench, though. Thomas always had a good rep as a clubhouse guy, helping keep others loose. He might have even helped a bit with Dick Williams. "Dick was a very strict guy, but he'd loosen up if you jabbed him a couple of times. That's kind of the thing. You sit on the bench, and you look at guys that are playing, and you try to be positive to them at all times. Some guys are tired, can't do any yelling and screaming out there, cheering along, so some of us did that."

George had been player rep for a year with Detroit. For the 1967 Red Sox, he roomed with Boston's player rep, Jim Lonborg. It helped that he could keep things light. Before the Series, at a team dinner, Thomas gave the following advice to Yastrzemski: "Don't get overconfident because right now we have the same average in the World Serie—.000." [6] Although the Red Sox lost the World Series to the Cardinals in seven games, Thomas, although hitless in two at-bats, had done his part.

After the 1967 season, during which Thomas became the father of a second daughter, he was left off the Red Sox' 40-man roster, and in April 1968 he was assigned to Louisville, the Red Sox Triple-A affiliate, where he played most of the season, appearing in only 12 games for the parent club in September. After the season, Thomas was not selected in the expansion draft by either of that year's two new teams, and it was a surprise to some that he made the Red Sox opening day roster for 1969.

As for himself, Thomas was just happy to have a chance to play in the major leagues. "And to be on a fairly competitive team, which the Red Sox became. You can be on a last-place team and get to play a lot, but

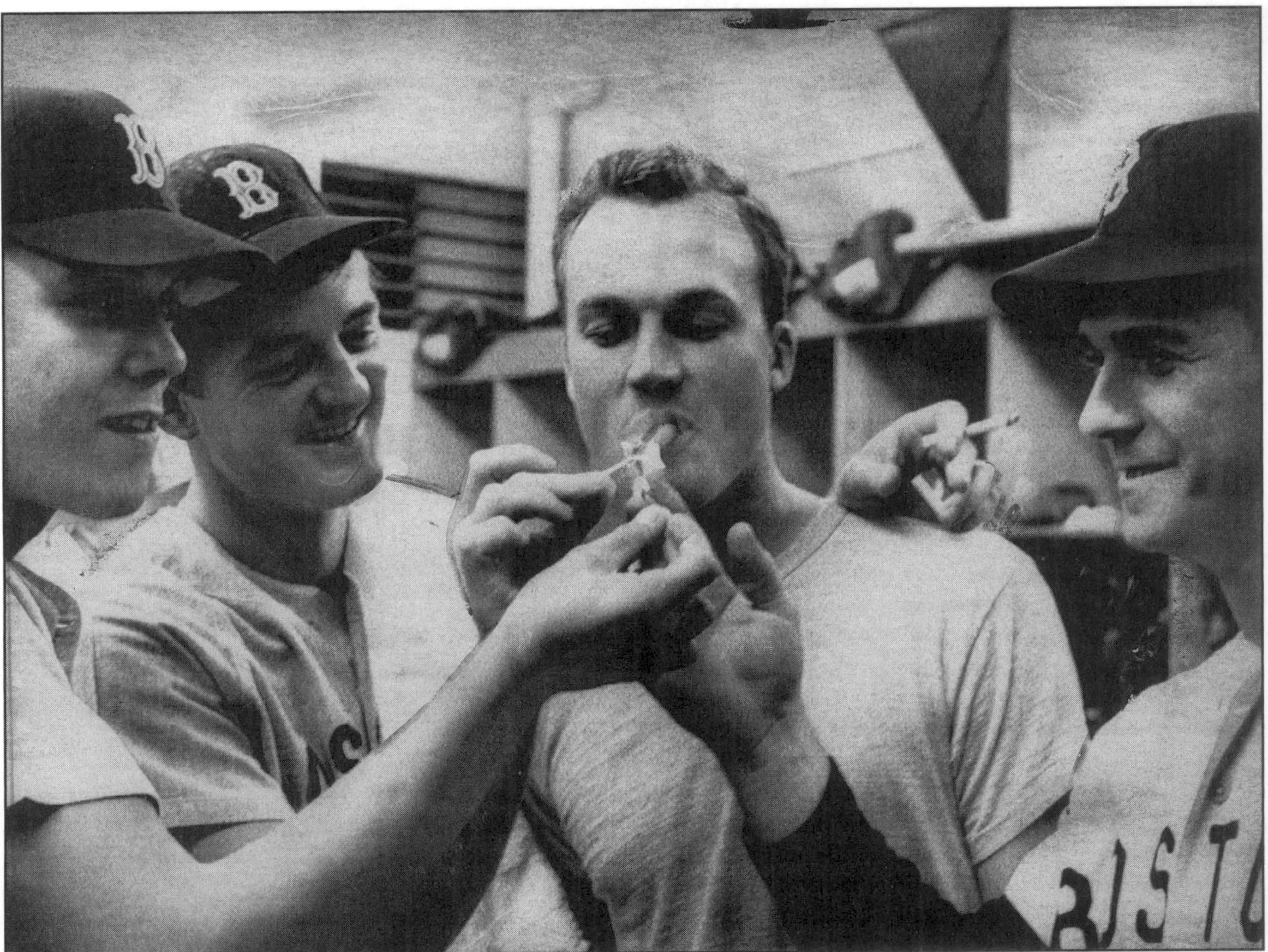

George Thomas lights up a cigar to celebrate the birth of a daughter.

you're not really going anywhere. I'd rather have been a part-time player on a winning team. You'd gear yourself up for being the fourth outfielder, fifth infielder, second third baseman, or whatever. Catcher. That was another thing that I really enjoyed doing."

George really appreciated Bill Rigney as manager, but gives Dick Williams the edge as the best he'd worked under. "He really got us into the World Series. He had some discipline... and he used a lot of people in the game. That was what made us a good team. He did keep you in the game. It gave some of the guys a rest, the guys who would be playing [nearly] full time."

In spring training of 1969, one of the other coaches had to return home because of illness. In June, Thomas was made a player-coach and remarked that "when I am out after the curfew, it is in my capacity as a coach, not a player."[7] In late June, Thomas tore ligaments in his knee and did not play again until the last game of the season. He had hit .353 in his 51 at-bats. He stuck with the team as a bullpen coach through the end of the season.

After the 1969 season, the Red Sox sent Thomas outright to Louisville. In spring training of 1970, he attempted to earn a spot on the roster, but broke his wrist. He was named a coach from March 30 to June 10 and was also available for active duty as a player in an emergency situation. When called upon to platoon at third base with Dick Schofield in June, Thomas, with mock disappointment, kidded that it was too bad he had to play because he had just been compiling a list of greatest games he had seen from the bench.[8] Thomas was also able to find humor in bleak situations. After an argument with umpires in Detroit, Thomas responded with crude language, which earned him a $200 fine and a five-day suspension. When the Red Sox won five out of the next six games, Thomas remarked, "It appears

Joe Cronin (then the American League president) has found the weakness in this club. Me!" He later added about his penalty, "Maybe I did the $200, but I don't think I did five days worth."[9] Thomas again played well in part-time work, hitting .343 in 99 at bats, with two home runs. Thomas's value was shown when he was honored as the team's unsung hero by the Boston baseball writers after the season. At the writers' dinner, he joked that his goal for the following season was to play in two games in a row for a change. [10]

Thomas played in only nine games for the Red Sox in 1971 (hitting 1 for 13) and was released on June 28. He signed with the Minnesota Twins two days later, but played in only 23 games and was released at the end of the season. Later, he became the assistant baseball coach at the University of Minnesota for ten years, resigning in 1981. He subsequently worked for an audiovisual company in the Minneapolis area until his retirement at the turn of the century. He now enjoys splitting his time between condos in Wisconsin and Florida, and getting in a fair amount of tee time.

Daughter Kristin is the one with the strongest interest in baseball, and she made national television during the 2004 World Series carrying a placard reading THE IMPOSSIBLE DREAM and GEORGE THOMAS FAN CLUB.

Clearly, George Thomas had a great effect on the teams he played for. Although his statistics did not compare with those of Yastrzemski or George Scott during the Impossible Dream season of 1967, his behind-the-scenes contributions helped to re-energize the New England region about Red Sox baseball. A quote from Thomas summarizes the feelings of almost every Red Sox fan about the 1967 season: "It's like having a child, or getting married. It's a part of your life. A golden moment that never can be duplicated. It just never will. People say they know how you feel. But they don't. They can't."[12] From those who lived through that magical ride to the World Series, through the Bill Rohr near no-hitter, the José Tartabull throw to nip Ken Berry at the plate, and the Rico Petrocelli catch of Rich Rollins' popup to clinch a tie for the pennant, George Thomas deserves thanks for letting Red Sox Nation be a part of the fun on that journey.

Notes:

1. Spoelstra, Watson. "Tigers Take Aim at First Top Four Finish Since '50" *The Sporting News*: September 18, 1957.
2. Falls, Joe. "Al Kaline Off to Flying Start on Comeback Trail" *The Sporting News*: March 1, 1961.
3. Dyer, Braven. "Thomas Boys Tie Package of T-N-T to Angels at Dish" *The Sporting News*: August 11, 1962.
4. Birtwell, Roger. "Smith, Thomas Fit Hub Plan for Speed" *The Sporting News*: October 23, 1965.
5. Fitzgerald, Ray. "What Baseball Badly Needs: Some First-Class Clowns" *The Sporting News*: March 21, 1981. Amplified in the June 2006 interview.
6. Coleman, Ken and Dan Valenti. *The Impossible Dream Revisited.* The Alpine Press, 1987.
7. Claflin, Larry. "Petrocelli's Hot Bat Wrote Year's No. 1 Story in Hub" *The Sporting News*: November 8, 1969.
8. Claflin, Larry. "Let George Do It...Red Sox Find That's Good Advice" *The Sporting News*: August 15, 1970.
9. Claflin, Larry. "Experiment Ends, Kasko Sends Rico Back to Shortstop" *The Sporting News*: June 27, 1970.
10. "Umpire Run-In Costs Thomas $200, Five Days" *Washington Post*: July 12, 1970.
11. Claflin, Larry. "Operation Big-Switch—Will It Boost The Red Sox?" *The Sporting News*: February 13, 1971.
12. Reynolds, Bill. Lost Summer—*The '67 Red Sox and the Impossible Dream.* NY: Warner Books, Inc., 1992.

Bob Tillman

by Barb Mantegani

	G	AB	R	H	2B	3B	HR	RBI	BB	SO	BA	OBP	SLG	SB	CS	GDP	HBP
1967 RED SOX	30	64	4	12	1	0	1	4	3	18	.188	.224	.250	0	0	2	0

A Tennessee native who played baseball and football on a football scholarship at Georgia Tech in 1957,[1] Bob Tillman caught the eye of Red Sox scout George Digby, who signed him out of Middle Tennessee State on January 18, 1958. Tillman, a 6'4" right-hander, earned a place in baseball history with his first official major league at-bat, which left the yard in a 6-5 Red Sox loss to the Los Angeles Angels on May 19, 1962.[2] Bob's career highlights also include being behind the plate for two no-hitters, Earl Wilson's in 1962 and Dave Morehead's in 1965. The latter no-no provided one of the few high spots in an otherwise dismal season (the Red Sox lost 100 games and finished ninth of 10 clubs) that also marked the last time Tillman appeared in more than 100 games in a season.

John Robert "Bob" Tillman was born in Nashville, Tennessee, on March 24, 1937, to Joseph Earl and Ruth Elizabeth Tillman, and graduated from Isaac Litton High School. After attending both Georgia Tech and Middle Tennessee State, he signed with the Red Sox in 1958. Tillman began his professional career with Raleigh in the Class B Carolina League, where he was named to the All-Star team as the starting catcher.[3] He progressed to Allentown in the Single-A Eastern League in 1959, where he was again named a starter for the All-Star team.[4]

In 1960, Tillman moved to the Triple-A American Association, where his Minneapolis Millers team included future major league teammates Carl Yastrzemski, Dick Radatz, and Earl Wilson.[5] Tillman's performance in Minneapolis included a two-home run, four-RBI game in July. The following year, with the arrival of the major league Twins in Minneapolis, the Red Sox franchise moved to Seattle in the Pacific Coast League. With the Seattle Rainiers, Bob played for manager Johnny Pesky, with whom he would be reunited in 1963 when Pesky took over as manager in Boston. Pesky, and the Red Sox, were impressed with his power numbers: in his four years of minor league ball, Tillman had slugged home run totals of 18, 25, 24, and 14.

In 1962, Tillman stuck with the big club out of spring training. With two other catchers, Russ Nixon and Jim Pagliaroni, on the roster, Tillman appeared in just over half of the games, including Wilson's no-hitter, one of two such games pitched by Boston hurlers that year.[6] His first action came on April 15, when he worked a pinch-hit walk off Steve Barber at Baltimore's Memorial Stadium. He then rode the bench until May 16, when he played a single defensive inning at Fenway Park against the Yankees. Three days later, Tillman got his first start when he was remarkably installed as the cleanup hitter against the Angels' Ted Bowsfield. After drawing a walk in the second inning, he hit a solo home run in the fourth—in his first official at-bat. This helped get him the bulk of the catchers' duties for the next six weeks.

Tillman ended the year with 14 home runs but batted only .229, and later admitted in a radio interview that as a rookie he "couldn't hit a curveball with an oar." As a result, Tillman was sent to the Florida Instructional League over the winter to overcome, in the words of general manager Mike Higgins, a tendency to "swing at many curveballs that are not in the strike zone."[7]

The 1963 season saw increased action for Tillman, whose new major league skipper, Johnny Pesky, was familiar with him and liked what he saw. When asked about Tillman's tribulations with the curveball, Pesky said many hitters had trouble with it, including him, and that Tillman would learn to hit it.[8] Not all observers were convinced, and longtime Boston sportswriter Larry Claflin observed, "The curveball is to Tillman what television is to movie theatres."[9] Nevertheless, over the winter it appeared that Tillman would be named the number one catcher in 1963; with Pesky showing loyalty to a player he once called "a right-handed Bill Dickey."[10] Tillman returned the favor by getting in early workouts with Bill Monbouquette at an indoor facility at Tufts University, before reporting to spring training in Scottsdale, Arizona.[11] While offseason conditioning is taken for granted now, in 1963 it was quite unusual and was considered an encouraging sign by Pesky. Unfortunately, despite the high hopes of the winter, 1963 was not a good year for Tillman at the plate, where he continued to struggle, hitting .225 with only eight home runs and 32 RBIs in 96 games.

Pesky did not lose faith in his catcher, however, installing him as the starter in 1964. Tillman responded with what would turn out to be his best year offensively. He hit .278 with 17 home runs and 61 RBIs in 131 games. His 17 home runs were a Red Sox record for a

catcher until Carlton Fisk hit 22 in 1972. To further put his performance in perspective, Tillman in 1964 was tied with Tim McCarver for fourth in the majors for catchers in runs created, behind future teammates Joe Torre and Elston Howard, and Bill Freehan. He ranked fifth in runs created/game, behind Howard, Freehan, and Torre. Pesky was fired before the end of the '64 season (another example of the classic Red Sox deck-chairs-on-the-Titanic managerial moves of the '50s and '60s). Billy Herman replaced Pesky for the rest of '64 and into '66, when Herman was in turn replaced by interim manager Pete Runnels for the final 16 games of the season.

With Pesky went much of Tillman's playing time, which dropped to 111 games in 1965, when he hit .215 with six home runs and 35 RBIs. For the third consecutive season he was the team's opening day starter, but his continued struggles with the bat caused Herman to give a great deal of playing time to Mike Ryan and Russ Nixon as well. Neither of them hit that well, either. Nevertheless, Tillman was behind the plate (and was 0-for-3 at bat) for Dave Morehead's no-hitter in September of 1965, witnessed by a reported crowd of 1,247 (perhaps not surprising for a team that lost 100 games). In 1966, Tillman played in 78 games as Ryan's backup, hitting .230 with three homers and 24 RBIs, while the Red Sox again finished deep in the AL standings, just a half-game ahead of the last-place Yankees in the 10-team league.

And then came 1967, which saw former teammate Dick Williams take the helm in the spring and lose faith in Tillman shortly thereafter. It was well known that Williams's doghouse was the size of a double-wide trailer, but Tillman's spot appeared to be set in stone on May 12, when, in an effort to cut down Al Kaline on a steal attempt, Tillman's throw to second was interrupted by relief pitcher John Wyatt's head, to the dismay of the 15,000 fans in attendance. After the ball struck Wyatt, it caromed to the on-deck circle, allowing Kaline to take third. Kaline then scored what proved to be the winning run on a sacrifice fly by Willie Horton. It was the first run allowed by Wyatt that year.[12] In a story reviewing the Red Sox's struggle to find a reliable signal caller, written after Carlton Fisk had finally been installed as the everyday catcher in 1972, Larry Claflin recalled Tillman's errant throw and noted that Tillman "became the prime tenant of Williams' doghouse" and was benched for 38 games thereafter.[13]

Tillman was one of manager Johnny Pesky's favorites, but didn't see much duty under Dick Williams. His June 25 homer off Tiant kicked off the scoring in an 8-3 Red Sox win.

After acquiring Howard, the Red Sox had four catchers. Someone had to go. In a move that would be nearly inconceivable today—there would be charges of trading with the enemy—Tillman was sold to the Yankees on August 8, 1967, after the Red Sox had traded Pete Magrini and a player to be named later (Ron Klimkowski) to the Yankees in return for Elston Howard five days earlier. Tillman, when he reported to the Yankees, said, "All I ask is a chance to play a little and prove myself. I've been to bat only 64 times all season and no one can prove anything in that time. I proved I could hit when I batted .278 in 1964 as the regular catcher in Boston."[14]

Backing up his words, Tillman started four games in his first week as a Yankee and had seven hits in 17 at-bats, driving in six runs in one game with a homer, a single, and a sacrifice fly. All told, Tillman appeared in 22 games as a Yankee, garnering almost as many at-bats in August and September as he had in the first 100 games of the season, and hitting almost 70 points higher (.254 to .188). Tillman's performance impressed manager Ralph Houk, who said in September that Tillman "fit right in" with his club, only to see Lee MacPhail send Tillman and Dale Roberts, a rookie pitcher, to Atlanta in December in exchange for future manager Bobby Cox.[15] In 1968, he again played a backup role, this time to another future skipper, Joe Torre. The change of league unfortunately did not improve Tillman's performance, as he hit only .220 with five home runs and 20 RBIs. He did achieve one career milestone, however, getting his first and only major league stolen base.

In the off-season, the Braves traded Torre to St. Louis for Orlando Cepeda, and Tillman got his fourth opening day assignment. Nevertheless, Tillman soon settled into a role as the backup to rookie Bob Didier,

playing 69 games. Despite the lack of playing time and a dismal batting average (.195), Tillman rediscovered his power, hitting 12 home runs in only 190 at-bats. Three of those dingers came on July 30 at Philadelphia's Connie Mack Stadium, in the same game in which Hank Aaron hit his 537th to move past Mickey Mantle into what was then third place on the all-time list.[16] All three of Tillman's home runs were hit off Grant Jackson. The Braves won the National League West that season, and Tillman saw his only post-season action, a single defensive inning in the final game of the Braves's three-game sweep at the hands of the Mets.

In 1970, Tillman's last year in professional ball, he shared the catching duties with Hal King and Bob Didier, appearing in 71 games and batting .238, with 11 homers and 30 RBIs. In December 1970, Tillman was traded to the Milwaukee Brewers in exchange for Hank Allen (brother of Dick and Ron Allen), Paul Click, and John Ryan, the latter two of whom never made it to the major leagues. After the trade Brewers manager Dave Bristol was quoted as saying that he expected Bob Tillman to play in 1971.[17] After a front-office shakeup, however, new general manager Frank Lane promptly placed Tillman on waivers and traded outfielder Carl Taylor, both of whom had just been acquired by his predecessor, Marvin Milkes.[18] No team selected him off waivers and so Bob Tillman's 775-game major league career was in the books.

He returned to his native Tennessee, where he lived with his wife, Dolores Cirillo (a Boston-area native he met in 1962 and married in 1963) and his two sons, Joel (born in 1967) and John (born in 1971). After a stint with a soft-sided luggage company, Bob worked for a food broker and food distributor until he retired on April 1, 1998. Sadly, his retirement was short-lived, as Bob Tillman passed away on June 21, 2000, of a heart attack at the age of 63.

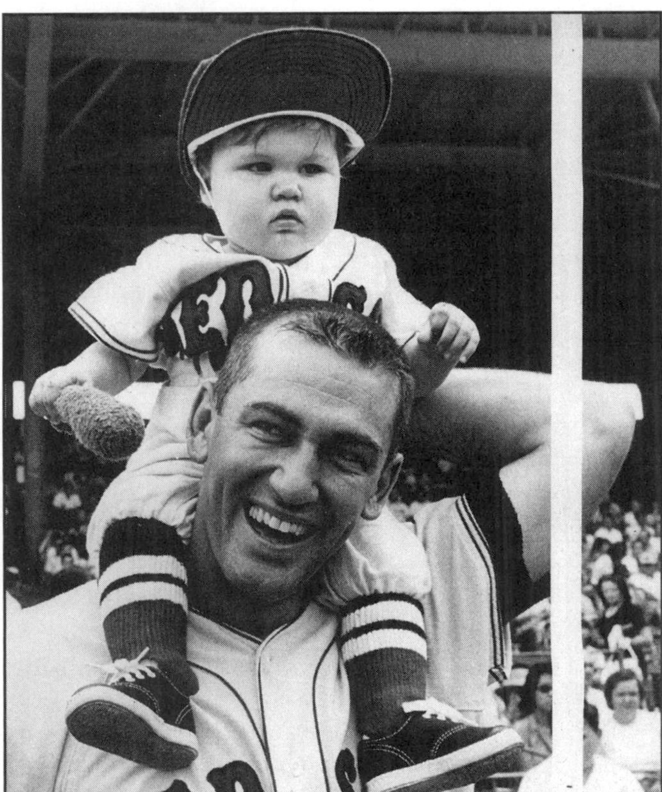

Bob Tillman with son Joel.

Notes:

1. Minshew, W. "Tillman Solves Tepee Quest for No. 2 Backstop," *The Sporting News* 12/30/67, p. 38.
2. All references to specific games are from www.retrosheet.org unless otherwise noted.
3. *The Sporting News* 7/16/58, p. 38.
4. *The Sporting News* 7/22/59, p. 39.
5. *The Sporting News* 4/27/60, p. 31.
6. Interestingly, Pagliaroni, who caught Bill Monbouquette's no-hitter in August 1962, also ended his career having caught two no-hitters, the latter being Catfish Hunter's perfect game against the Twins on May 8, 1968.
7. Holbrook, B. "Morehead and MacDonald Add Glitter to Hub Hose Hill Corps," *The Sporting News* 11/3/62, p. 17.
8. Holbrook, B. "Loafers, Playboys to Face Pesky Wrath," *The Sporting News* 11/24/62, p. 3.
9. Claflin, L. (in the Boston Record American) "Question-Mark Catchers Could Distress Pesky," *The Sporting News* 11/24/62, p. 4
10. Hurwitz, H., "Tillman Top Entry in Hub Mitt Tussle," *The Sporting News* 1/5/63, p. 15.
11. Hurwitz, H., "Early-Bird Tillman Tunes Muscles for Shot at Steady Job," *The Sporting News* 2/23/63, p. 34.
12. Claflin , L., "Throw to Second Base Konks Wyatt on Hill," *The Sporting News* 5/13/67, p. 19.
13. Claflin, L., "Bosox Catching Job-A Tale of Woe," *The Sporting News* 5/13/72, p. 19.
14. *The Sporting News*, 8/26/67, p. 18.
15. Ogle, J., "Power-Socker Cox Joins Yank Third-Base Tussle," *The Sporting News* 12/23/67, p. 36.
16. July 30, 1969, at home against the Philadelphia Phillies.
17. Whiteside, L., "Brewers Narrow Fan Gap During Winter Caravan," *The Sporting News*, 1/30/71, p. 34.
18. Whiteside, L., "Lane Obtains Kuenn Again—and Nobody Fires Rocks," *The Sporting News*, 2/20/71, p. 43.

Carl Yastrzemski

by Herb Crehan and Bill Nowlin

	G	AB	R	H	2B	3B	HR	RBI	BB	SO	BA	OBP	SLG	SB	CS	GDP	HBP
1967 RED SOX	161	579	112	189	31	4	44	121	91	69	.326	.418	.622	10	8	5	4

Before the 1975 playoffs began, Red Sox manager Darrell Johnson asked Carl Yastrzemski if he could still play left field. Yaz, who had played 140 games at first base that season, responded, "In my sleep." He played with both eyes wide open, and his outstanding fielding in left field was a key to the Red Sox sweep of the reigning World Champion Oakland A's.

Born August 22, 1939, in nearby Southampton, New York, Carl Michael Yastrzemski came of age in Bridgehampton, Long Island (population 3,000) where he often played alongside his father in local semi-pro games. Father Karol Yastrzemski (the name was Anglicized to Carl) and Yaz's uncle Tommy owned an inherited 70-acre potato farm, their work a "legacy from Poland, folks coming over here and doing what they knew from the old country."[1]

In his first of two autobiographies, Yaz wrote, "I'm told that when I was 18 months old my dad got me a tiny baseball bat, which I dragged around wherever I went, the way other babies drag blankets or favorite toys. I vaguely remember playing catch with him as a very small boy, but my first clear memory is hitting tennis balls in the backyard against his pitching after supper every night when I was about six. Later we played make-believe ball games between the Yankees and the Red Sox, my two favorite teams...."[2]

Yaz's dad loved baseball. He might have tried to make it in baseball himself, reportedly having offers from both the Dodgers and the Cardinals, but was "reluctant to leave the potato fields of Long Island to try baseball during the Depression."[3] Before Carl was born, Carl Yastrzemski Sr. actually formed a semipro baseball team, the Bridgehampton White Eagles; he played shortstop and managed the team. It was almost entirely a family team, with Carl Sr.'s four brothers on the team, as well as two brothers-in-law and three cousins. The team played on Sundays, and did so for years. By the time Carl himself was seven, he was the team's batboy, his first "job" in baseball. He first played for the team at age 14—young for a semipro player. Even at age 40, Carl's father was still "the guts of the ball club, a good shortstop and the best hitter of the team."[4] His father played with drive and determination, but channeled his ambitions to play professional baseball into his son Carl. Still playing (and out-hitting his son) at age 41, Carl's dad was doing it for his son. The younger Yaz wrote, "I could tell the only reason he played was on account of me, just as that had been the only reason he kept the White Eagles alive for so long."[5] From the very date Carl signed his first pro contract, the elder Yastrzemski never played again, but the memory lasted. "I loved his spirit and intensity when I played alongside him."[6]

Some of Carl's teammates with the Boston Red Sox saw the influence of Carl's father in his son's drive for success. Former Red Sox catcher Russ Gibson remembered one time early on: "Yaz and myself, and two other guys, shared an apartment in Raleigh [North Carolina] when his dad came for a visit. We were all just starting out, but Yaz was hitting about .390 at the time. We all went off to play golf while Yaz visited with his father. When we got back, all his things were gone. When I asked Yaz what had happened, he said, 'My dad thinks I'm distracted living with you guys. He's moved me into an apartment by myself.'"[7]

Carl's father was quite a man himself. In Yaz's words, though, "nothing ever topped the time he kicked the Yankees' scout out of our house while I shouted, 'Dad, what the heck are you doing?' But my father not only kicked him out but would never talk to him or the Yankees again."

While Yaz was still a senior in high school, the New York Yankees made a pitch. Though not allowed to sign Yastrzemski to an actual contract until after he graduated high school, Yankees scout Ray Garland was still welcomed into the household to talk hypothetically. He traded bonus numbers with Carl's father, writing $60,000 on a piece of paper at the dining room table. Carl's dad wrote out $100,000. Garland reacted dramatically, flipping his pencil in the air and hitting the ceiling as he exclaimed, "$100,000? Are you crazy? The Yankees will never pay that." The Yankees never got the opportunity, despite owner Dan Topping becoming involved. The elder Yaz told Garland, "Nobody throws a pencil in my house. Get the hell out and never come back." That was it for the New York Yankees.[8]

Yaz attracted a lot of attention playing ball on Long Island. His last couple of years in high school, he played semipro ball for Lake Ronkonkoma, a team based about 60 miles from home. His father played for this team, too,

Carl Sr. was a major influence on his son—and a fellow teammate—before the younger Yaz signed with the Red Sox. Father and son are shown here at 1961 spring training in Scottsdale, Arizona.

always after work on the farm was done. It was around this time that Carl's father began to boost him as a hitter more than as a pitcher—oddly enough, Carl learned this at a major league tryout camp for the Braves, where Carl faced nine batters and struck out all nine. The younger Yaz had the chance to sign on with a major league team before he even got out of high school, but Carl's dad had his eyes set on a sizable bonus and was prepared to turn down offers he saw as inadequate. Come his senior year, Carl's dad told his high school coach that Carl would not be playing football that year—there was too great a risk of injury, and that might hamper his development as a baseball player.

Red Sox scout Frank "Bots" Nekola had had his eye on Carl since he was a sophomore in high school. He never threw any pencils in the Yastrzemski household,

but he wasn't coming up with $100,000, either, and so Carl's father sent his son off to college. They'd fielded full scholarship offers from a number of colleges, but chose Notre Dame, playing on a scholarship that was half baseball and half basketball. Yaz completed his freshman year, without playing on the varsity team, but then the offers got more serious, even exceeding $100,000. The Red Sox didn't make the largest offer, but the admiration of the local parish priest for Tom Yawkey counted for a lot, and Yaz's father wanted him playing for an East Coast team, not too far from home. Yaz signed with the Red Sox in November 1958 for a $108,000 bonus, and their agreement to cover the rest of his college education. Sox GM Joe Cronin then met Yaz for the first time—and saw a 5'11", 160-pound kid. He couldn't help himself, blurting out, "We're paying this kind of money for *this* guy?"[9] Carl went back to finish up the fall semester at Notre Dame; his father increased his weekly allowance from $2 to $3 a week.

The first of many spring training camps came in 1959 and Carl was assigned to the Raleigh Caps in the Carolina League, a Class B team. The team switched him from shortstop to second base. He was struggling at the plate until manager Ken Deal got him in the box and told him to move up on the plate so he wasn't lunging at balls on the outer half of the strike zone. He says he batted close to .400 for the rest of the year. After Raleigh's season was over, he was invited to come to Fenway Park, not to play ball but to look in on the ball club. Ted Williams greeted him and told him, "Don't let them screw around with your swing. Ever."

Yaz then went on to Minneapolis to join the Millers as they entered the American Association playoffs. Wayne McElreavy notes that, oddly, Yaz was ineligible and there was a protest, but no forfeit was forced. The first time he faced Triple A pitching, and he went 7-for-18 in the six games it took to win the title. And then he traveled to Cuba to play the Havana Sugar Kings for the International League championship. Fidel Castro came to the ballpark, arriving by helicopter and landing near second base. The Sugar Kings won in the seventh game, but it was the last time (until the Baltimore Orioles played an exhibition game in 1999) that an American pro team played in Cuba.

In January 1960, Carl married Carol Casper. In February, they headed to Scottsdale so Carl could train with the big league ball club. Carl lockered right next to Ted Williams. But Ted rarely spoke to him. The main thing Carl learned from 41-year-old Teddy Ballgame was how hard he prepared himself to play. The Red Sox had Pete Runnels at second base (Runnels would win the batting title in 1960), so they sent Carl back to the minors for one more year, the purpose being to train Yaz to play left field and get ready to take over for Ted Williams after the 1960 season. Yastrzemski batted .339 for Minneapolis, just missing out on the title by three points, and began to show some skill in the outfield, recording 18 assists.

Ted Williams retired. Both the baton and the burden of replacing the great Williams was passed to Carl Michael Yastrzemski. Opening day 1961 was April 11 at Fenway Park, and Yastrzemski played left field and batted fifth. Replacing Ted Williams in left field and in the hearts of Boston Red Sox fans was a Herculean task for any player, let alone a 20-year-old with two years of professional baseball experience. Ted Williams was a larger-than-life figure on and off the field, and had played for the Red Sox since 1939. Yaz singled to left his first time up, but ended the day 1-for-5. His first and second homers came in back-to-back games on May 9 and 10, but all in all, he struggled at the plate. "I started off very slow. I actually think that was on account of Ted. I was trying to emulate him—be a home run hitter and not be myself: just an all-around player. I could never be a Ted Williams as far as hitting was concerned." When Yaz struggled, the Sox asked Ted to interrupt his fishing and come pay a visit. Williams complied, visited, and watched Yaz take extra batting practice. He told Yaz he had a great swing and to just go out and use it. "I think what dawned on me was that there can be a great swing that is not a home run swing at the same time."[10]

Yaz batted .266 in his rookie year, with 11 homers and 80 RBIs, a good first year once he'd gotten back on track. There was no sophomore slump: Yastrzemski boosted his totals to .296, with 19 homers (and 43 doubles) and 94 RBIs. His third year, he made the All-Star team for the first time, and improved dramatically again, to win the American League batting championship with a .321 mark. He led the league in base hits, doubles, and walks. All the while, Yastrzemski was improving in left field, honing the solid defensive play that he is remembered for today.

He continued to add to his totals, again making the All-Star team in 1965 and 1966. In 1965, he accomplished one of the rarest of hitting feats—Yaz hit for the cycle in the May 14 game, with an extra home run thrown in for good measure. Later that year, Yaz even faced Satchel Paige, who came back to pitch one last time at age 59. He threw three innings and gave up only one hit—to Carl Yastrzemski. Yaz's first six seasons in the major leagues had established him as one of the star players in the game. But his 1967 season would

Something we likely won't see again*—a Red Sox player feted by fans at Yankee Stadium. It was Carl Yastrzemski Night, hosted by friends from Yaz's home town on Long Island. The Red Sox won the August 28 game, 3-0.*

propel Carl Yastrzemski to a place among the elite players in the history of the game.

"One of the big differences in 1967," Yaz recalled, "is that I was able to work out the preceding winter. In earlier years, I was finishing up my college work. But I had completed my degree at Merrimack College so I had time to focus on my conditioning. I reported to spring training in great shape."[11]

By the time the 1967 All-Star Game rolled around, Yaz was among the top five in the American League in batting average, home runs, and runs batted in. The Red Sox were only six games out of first place at the All-Star break, and it was clear that the team had as good a shot at the American League pennant as anyone.

The 1967 Red Sox held New England fans spellbound all summer and into the fall, as they battled for first place in the most exciting pennant race in American League history. Their thrilling win over the Minnesota Twins on the last day of the season touched off one of the great celebrations in Boston history. While a different Red Sox hero seemed to emerge daily, the one constant was Yaz.

Former teammate George Scott remembers it this way, "Yaz hit 44 homers that year, and 43 of them meant something big for the team. It seemed like every time we needed a big play, the man stepped up and got it done." In the final 12 games of the season—crunch time—Carl Yastrzemski had 23 hits in 44 at-bats, driving in 16 runs and scoring 14. He hit 10 homers in his final 100 at-bats of 1967. He had 10 hits in his last 13 at-bats, and when it came to the last two games with the Twins—with the Sox needing to win both games to help avert a tie for the pennant—Yaz went 7-for-8 and drove in six runs.

Yaz was no slouch in the playoffs, either, batting an even .400 (10-for-25) with three home runs and five RBIs in the World Series against the St. Louis Cardinals. The storybook season came to an end when the St. Louis Cardinals won the World Series in Game Seven, but Carl Yastrzemski's place was indelibly etched in baseball folklore. Yaz came within one vote of a unanimous selection as the Most Valuable Player of the American League. He was selected by *Sports*

Yaz in the limelight after his heroics in the second game of the 1967 World Series.

Illustrated as the "1967 Sportsman of the Year" at year's end. And he achieved baseball's "Triple Crown," leading the American League in batting (.326), runs batted in (121), and home runs (44). In all the baseball seasons that have followed, no other player has been able to match his Triple Crown feat.

Yaz also led the league in hits (189), runs (112), total bases (360), and slugging percentage, not to mention on-base percentage. His On-Base plus Slugging (OPS) was 1.040. How did a Triple Crown winner who brought his team to the pennant miss the MVP by one vote? One voter cast his first-place ballot for Cesar Tovar of the Twins. Tovar batted .267, had six homers to Yaz's 44, and drove in 47 runs to Yaz's 121!

The next year, 1968, Yaz won his third batting title, with a .301 mark. This was, for sure, the Year of the Pitcher, and Yaz was the only batter in the league to crack .300, a full 10 points ahead of the second-best Danny Cater. Only four batters hit .285 or above.

Between 1965 and 1979, Yaz was named to 15 consecutive All-Star teams. The game he remembers best is the 1970 All-Star Game held in Riverfront Stadium in Cincinnati. Yaz had four hits, to go along with a run scored and a RBI, to earn him MVP honors that year. He and Ted Williams [1946] are the only two American Leaguers with four hits in an All-Star Game. Never one to focus on personal statistics, when asked about this record Yaz responded, "I never knew that before. To tell you the truth, I was so sick of losing to the National League that I didn't pay much attention to that stuff."

It is sometimes written that Yaz had a "career year" in 1967, but never again approached that standard. It should be noted that in 1970 he led the American League in runs scored, on-base percentage, total bases, slugging average, and—when rounded—he was .0004 out of the lead for the batting title. When coupled with his all-time high of 23 stolen bases, you have a year that would have been a career year for almost any other player.

Those 23 stolen bases made him only the second player in Red Sox history to steal more than 20 bases *and* hit more than 20 home runs in a single season. Former All-Star outfielder Jackie Jensen was the first Red Sox player to achieve this combination in 1954, and Jensen duplicated this feat during the 1959 season. Only three other Red Sox players have achieved this standard during the past 34 seasons.

In February 1971, Carl Yastrzemski signed a three-year contract that was reported to pay him $500,000 over the three seasons. At that time his contract was the largest in baseball history.

The year 1972 was a frustrating one. The season started late, due to struggles between players and owners. Teams agreed to simply play out the schedule without worrying whether one team played more games than another. As fate would have it, the Red Sox entered the final three games of the year playing the Tigers in Detroit. There was no chance of a playoff tie. The Tigers had a record of 84-69 going into the October 2 game, and the Red Sox were a marginally-better 84-68. Whichever team won two of the three games would win the pennant. The Tigers took a 1-0 lead in the first game, but Yaz doubled in the top of the third to tie it—and the Red Sox would have scored at least one more run (with Yaz safe at third with a triple) except that Luis Aparicio stumbled after rounding third and retreated

Always intense, Yaz grabs a quick bite under the stands.

to the bag where he met up with the oncoming Carl, who was called out. One never knows what might have been, but this was a pivotal play and the Red Sox lost the pennant by a half-game.

Yaz had a subpar year in 1975, batting just .269 with 14 homers and 60 RBIs, but his play throughout the postseason reminded fans that he had always been at his best in clutch situations throughout his career. His stellar play in the field and at bat carried over from the American League Championship Series against Oakland (he was 5-for-11, with a home run and two RBIs) to the World Series against the Cincinnati Reds. Although the Red Sox lost to the Reds in seven games in one of the greatest World Series ever played, Yaz had scored 11 runs, and batted .350 during the 10 postseason games. As in 1967, the Red Sox fell just short.

From 1976 to 1983, Carl Yastrzemski made the American League All-Star team six times. On July 14, 1977, he notched his 2,655th hit, moving past Ted Williams as the all-time Red Sox base hit leader. In 1979, he became the first American Leaguer to accumulate more than 400 homers (he reached the plateau on July 24) *and* over 3,000 lifetime hits (his September 12 single off New York's Jim Beattie was #3,000). Back on June 16, he'd banged out his 1,000th extra base hit.

On October 1, 1983, the next-to-the-last game of the season, 33,491 of the Fenway Faithful gathered to pay tribute to Carl Yastrzemski. The pre-game ceremony lasted for about an hour, and then came Yaz's turn to speak. After 23 years of never flinching in a pressure situation, Yaz broke down and cried when he stepped to the microphone.

Once he regained his composure, he asked for a moment of silence for his mother and for former Red Sox owner Tom Yawkey. After thanking his family and everyone connected with the Red Sox, he finished with the words, "New England, I love you."

Carl Yastrzemski had played in 3,308 major league ballgames—the record until Pete Rose topped it the next year—and played for 23 years for one team: the Boston Red Sox.

In January of 1989, in his first year of eligibility, Carl Yastrzemski was elected to Baseball's Hall of Fame. His vote total that year was among the highest recorded in the history of the Hall of Fame. On August 6, 1989, the Red Sox retired his uniform number and it still hangs today, #8, overlooking Fenway's outfield.

The baseball careers of Ted Williams and Carl Yastrzemski are inexorably linked. Their paths crossed directly for the last time when they were introduced before the 1999 All-Star Game at Fenway Park as two of the 100 greatest baseball players of the 20th century. The crowd reaction when Yaz was introduced shook the ballpark to its ancient foundations. The response of the crowd when Ted was driven in a golf cart from the far reaches of centerfield to a spot near the pitchers' mound nearly equaled the decibel count of the jet fly-by following the National Anthem. At the home opener in 2005, Carl Yastrzemski and Johnny Pesky joined to raise the 2004 World Championship banner that has flown over Fenway throughout the 2005 season.

Carl Michael Yastrzemski: the man we affectionately call Yaz.

Notes:

1. Yastrzemski and Eskenazi. *Yaz: Baseball, the Wall, and Me.* (1990), p. 7.
2. Yastrzemski with Hirshberg, *Yaz.* (1968), p. 37.
3. *Yaz* (1990), *op. cit.*, pp. 1, 8.
4. *Yaz* (1968), *op. cit.*, p. 46.
5. *Yaz* (1968), *op. cit.*, pp. 50, 51.
6. *Yaz* (1990), *op. cit.*, p. 11.
7. Personal interview with Herb Crehan, 1999.
8. *Yaz* (1990), *op. cit.*, pp. 19, 20.
9. *Yaz* (1990), *op. cit.*, p. 39.
10. Prime, Jim and Bill Nowlin, *Ted Williams: The Pursuit of Perfection.* Champaign, IL: Sports Publishing, p. 102.
11. Personal interview with Herb Crehan, 1999.

Yaz and the Triple Crown

by Bill Nowlin

In 1967, Yaz wasn't just the sparkplug for the Sox with his hitting and his fielding. He also posted stats that no one has matched for nearly 30 years, winning the last Triple Crown in major league baseball.

As the name implies, the Triple Crown is an indication of baseball royalty. Since 1903—the year many suggest was the first year of baseball's modern era—there have only been 10 batters to win the Triple Crown, accomplished by leading the league in batting average, home runs, and runs batted in.

Year	Batter	League	AVG	HR	RBI
1909	Ty Cobb	AL	.377	9	107
1922	Rogers Hornsby	NL	.401	42	152
1925	Rogers Hornsby	NL	.403	39	143
1933	Jimmie Foxx	AL	.356	48	163
1933	Chuck Klein	NL	.368	28	120
1934	Lou Gehrig	AL	.363	49	165
1937	Joe Medwick	NL	.374	31	154
1942	Ted Williams	AL	.356	36	137
1947	Ted Williams	AL	.343	32	114
1956	Mickey Mantle	AL	.353	52	130
1966	Frank Robinson	AL	.316	49	120
1967	Carl Yastrzemski	AL	.326	44	121

Clearly, the degree of competition matters. Cobb won the Triple Crown with just nine home runs, only Tris Speaker (7) and Red Murray (7) coming close. No one approached him in average or RBIs. Cobb not only won the Triple Crown in his league, but in all of baseball. Being the best in both leagues in all three categories is termed the Major League Triple Crown.

You'd figure that Hornsby's .401 was the best in the majors in 1922, but George Sisler hit .420 for St. Louis in the American League, and Ken Williams (also with St. Louis) led the AL in RBIs. Nonetheless, Hornsby led his own league by margins of 47 points in average, 20 runs in RBIs, and 16 homers—dramatically better than the second-place batter in each of the three areas.

Three years later, Hornsby won the Major League title outright.

1933 was quite a year—a Triple Crown winner in each league! Even more remarkably, both played for Philadelphia teams—Foxx for the Athletics and Klein for the Phillies. Foxx won the AL by 20 points in average, 14 homers, and 24 RBIs, but Klein was clearly better in batting average.

The very next year, there was another Major League Triple Crown winner—Lou Gehrig of the New York Yankees. Gehrig had healthy margins in HRs and RBIs, but he was just one percentage point above Paul Waner's .362 average. Nonetheless, Gehrig accomplished something Babe Ruth never did. Think of the many great hitters baseball has seen and realize that many never won the Triple Crown: Willie Mays, Babe Ruth, Stan Musial... The list is a long one, but those three names alone provide another indication of how rare a feat winning the Triple Crown truly is.

The last National Leaguer to win the Triple Crown was Joe Medwick in 1937. Medwick tied with Mel Ott in the home run race, but hit 10 points above Johnny Mize in average and drove in a full 41 more runs than the #2 man in the NL. Joe DiMaggio hit 46 homers and Hank Greenberg drove in 183 runs, but Medwick topped his own league in all three Triple Crown categories.

In 1942, Ted Williams saw his average plummet from 1941's .406, but he handily won the Major League Triple Crown, by 25 points in average, six homers, and 27 RBIs. Then after three years of military service, and a serious elbow injury that might well have cost the Red Sox the 1946 World Series, Williams won the Triple Crown again in 1947. In no category did he lead the majors, but against the competition in the American League, no one was better. He hit 15 points higher in average, hit three more home runs, and drove in 16 more runs than any other batter.

Williams and Hornsby are the only two players to ever win the Triple Crown twice—and Ted nearly won it a third time in 1949. Ted hit four more homers than teammate Vern Stephens, the #2 American Leaguer. He drove in the exact same number of runs as Stephens. But he lost the batting title to George Kell, even though both are shown with .343 averages. Kell's was .3429118 and Williams' was .3427561. That's a difference of .0001557, one ten-thousandth of a point. The slightest mistake in the calculations (a walk mistakenly listed as an at-bat) and the balance would have shifted in Ted's favor. And Ted walked 162 times in 1947; Kell walked 61 times. Ted reached base via hit or walk 356 times. Kell reached base 240 times. Ted's on-base percentage was .490 to Kell's .424.

Mickey Mantle took the Triple Crown in 1956, the last time any player has won the Major League title. He outhit Williams by eight points in average, but he hit 45

In this April 16, 1968 photo, Triple Crown winner Carl Yastrzemski receives his awards as MVP and 1967 AL batting champion, while Lonborg collects his Cy Young Award, Dick Williams gets a plaque as Manager of the Year, and George Scott gets a Golden Glove Award.

points more than Hank Aaron. His margin in homers was nine and in RBIs was 21.

Ten years later, Frank Robinson won handily against his AL peers, though Aaron drove in more runs in the NL and both Alou brothers hit for higher averages in the senior circuit.

Then came 1967, just a year later. Yaz had his sights set before the season began. Red Sox third base coach Eddie Popowski told Steve Cady of the *New York Times* in 1983, "He told me in spring training that year he thought he had a shot at it. He said, 'It's going to be great when every hit means something, when every putout means something.'" Yaz beat out Robinson for the AL batting total .326 to .311, and hit even more home runs than Hank Aaron (44 to 39), though he tied for the home run lead with Harmon Killebrew. Yaz's 121 RBIs topped Killebrew's 113, and was 10 above NL champion Orlando Cepeda. He didn't win the Major League Triple Crown, though, because the National League had some very hot hitters. Roberto Clemente hit .357, and there were four other National Leaguers who had higher averages than Yaz: Tony Gonzalez (.339), Matty Alou (.338), Curt Flood (.335), and Rusty Staub (.333). Against the competition that really counts, to get your team to the World Series, Carl led his league.

Yastrzemski also led the American League in runs scored, hits, total bases, runs produced, on-base percentage, slugging average, and a number of more sophisticated statistical categories. It was a very good year. Yaz also won batting titles in 1963 and 1968, but 1967 was the only year he led the league in either home runs or RBIs. It made a great deal of difference in the year of the Impossible Dream. Encompassing any number of stellar and timely defensive gems as well, 1967 will long be remembered as the Year of Yaz.

Can Stephen Jay Gould's theory explain why there has not been any batting Triple Crowns in Major League Baseball for the last 39 years?

by Andy Andres

The batting Triple Crown used to occur more often. There were nine Triple Crown winners in the 34 seasons preceding 1967, but there have been none in the 39 years since. One potential explanation for the lack of Triple Crowns since 1967 is suggested by Stephen Jay Gould's hypothesis explaining the disappearance of "the .400 hitter." Gould first published this idea as "Entropic Homogeneity Isn't Why No One Hits .400 Any More" in *Discover*, August, 1986; he later published it as a chapter in his book *Full House: The Spread Of Excellence From Plato To Darwin* (Harmony Books, 1996).

Gould begins by arguing an observable improvement in hitting, pitching, and fielding skills in major league baseball. Most people would agree that players are faster and stronger today than those of past decades, mainly due to better training methods, nutrition, lifestyles, and equipment. There has also been an expansion of the available talent pool. The American population has significantly increased and teams actively scout and sign more players internationally than ever before.

So, if there has been an improvement in baseball skills since the 1940s, what has caused the disappearance of the .400 hitter (and, by extension, the Triple Crown) since 1967? Even though the improvement of talent and skills may seem self-evident, perhaps there has been greater improvement in pitching and fielding skills than there has in hitting skills. Have league-wide batting averages actually declined since 1941, indicating better defense relative to offense? This question is testable, and Gould explains data that actually shows there has been no drop-off in league batting average since 1941. It has essentially hovered around .260. Note that this .260 value has not been precise; there have been fluctuations. In the pitcher's era of the 1960s, league batting averages were lower than .260, likely due to the height of the pitcher's mound and larger strike zone. Batting averages have been slightly higher since the mid 1990s, the start of the current power era. Overall, though, in the larger picture it is safe to conclude, as Gould does, that even with the different eras of baseball, batting averages have been fairly consistent.

Therefore, it is difficult to conclude that there has been a decline in batting average performance since 1941. In any event, the Triple Crown is a relative phenomenon. Should hitting skills decline (or increase) across the board, one hitter could still lead in all three diminished categories.

Gould then supposes that the decline in batting average peak (the .400 hitter, the outlier) is due to decreased variation in the population of hitters. In other words, as the skills of both hitters and pitchers improved, and as the pool of talented players to choose from increased, the variation in talent (the difference between the best to the worst batting averages) should decrease. Therefore, players in Major League Baseball in more recent period are arguably reaching the "wall" of human performance. Gould's analysis of the data supports this idea, as the standard deviation of league-wide batting averages has decreased steadily since the early 20th century.

Gould concludes that the .400 hitter has disappeared mainly due to decreased variability in the talent pool. Since his ideas have been published, other baseball analysts have considered Gould's work and have generally supported his conclusions. But Triple Crown Awards are of interest here. Can Gould's analysis and conclusions be applied to the disappearance of the Triple Crown since 1967?

First we should note the obvious: the .400 hitter is a "benchmark" offensive rate statistic that in recent times represents an extreme outlier among the pool of MLB talent. The Triple Crown indicates a best in league performance in three categories. These skills are different and a Triple Crown winner must own them all. Two of these categories measure intrinsic skills of the batter. Home runs are a measure of power skill, whereas batting average measures a skill dependent on strike zone judgment, pitch discernment, and hand-eye coordination. In addition, two categories of the Triple Crown statistics are dependent on external factors: playing time (to accumulate sufficient HRs and RBIs to lead all other batters), order position (RBIs), and team on-base ability (RBIs). Therefore a Triple Crown winner must be an extremely skilled batter with players who get on base in front of him in the batting order. A Triple Crown measures something

different than the .400 hitter.

Since the Triple Crown is a best-in-league performance in these three categories, its disappearance since in 1967 is either a statistical fluke or has been caused by something that has changed in baseball since the 1960s. If we accept Gould's hypothesis that a decrease in league-wide variation has led to a decrease in the probability of having an outlier, can we apply that to the disappearance of the Triple Crown since 1967? In other words, has the probability of leading a Triple Crown category in any given year decreased since the 1960s?

The overall hitting talent has probably increased since the 1960s; players are better trained and are selected from a growing pool of talented players. One might expect a decreased variation in hitting talent as major league hitters are reaching the posited "wall" of batting performance. Because of the combination of talent increase and variation decrease, it follows that the probability of leading the league in the Triple Crown categories decreases. A simple analogy might help: it is harder to stand out in a crowd when the crowd is bigger and more talented.

This increased "clustering" around the mean has been demonstrated to be the case in batting average. Dan Fox of *Baseball Prospectus* (danagonistes.blogspot.com/2004/08/where-have-400-hitters-gone.html) has shown that the percentage of players who have batting averages greater than 2.5 standard deviations from league average has decreased since the 1960s. From the 1900s to the 1950s, about 17% of players were at least 2.5 standard deviations above the average league batting average, in the 1990s, it was 9.7%.

Underlying skills are another factor. There are quite different batting skills required for the Triple Crown categories, namely power, batting "eye," strike zone judgment, pitch discernment, and hand-eye coordination. As player talent increases, it follows that variation in batting skills also decreases. Therefore, the chances are less that any one player could be the best in league in many different skills in one year (i.e., what would be required for a Triple Crown).

What about the pitching Triple Crown, defined as leading the league in earned run average (ERA), wins, and strikeouts? Looking at the same time frame as used at the start of this essay, there have been seven winners of the pitching Triple Crown since 1967 and seven winners in the 34 preceding years—something obviously different has happened with batters and pitchers since 1967. As with batters, training methods and the increasing pool of pitchers to choose from have most likely improved the skills and performance of pitchers. Has this improvement in pitching skills led to another decrease in variation, another clustering of performance? If so, the pitching Triple Crown does not reflect this "clustering" as it seems to in the case of the batting Triple Crown.

So what could explain the difference between the pitching and batting Triple Crown? The skills needed to lead the league in strikeouts include superior skills and playing time, something mostly under the control of the pitcher himself. The other measures of the pitching Triple Crown require less of personal pitching skills. ERA is certainly a reflection of skilled pitching, but is also dependant on fielding and park effects, especially home park effects. Wins as a measure of pitching performance are even less dependent on pitching skills—they are quite dependent on offensive run support. Since the winner of the pitching Triple Crown requires more of the players around him (offense and fielding helping ERA and wins) than the batting Triple Crown (players in scoring position while at bat helping RBI), it is might be that even though the pitching Triple Crown represents a great season, it may be easier to obtain than the many skills required for a batting Triple Crown.

So it seems as if there may be an explanation for the disappearance of the batting Triple Crown, and Stephen Jay Gould's baseball research may have provided some insight. Before the expansion of talent in baseball, before the decreased variation in skills and performance, it was easier to stand out in the crowd, easier to win the batting Triple Crown. It would take an exceptional year by a multi-skilled individual, placed in the right situation, to do it again.

White Sox manager Eddie Stanky snarled that Yaz "may be an All-Star, I suppose, but only from the neck down." Two days later, Yaz went 6-for-9 against Chicago in a doubleheader at Comiskey. As he rounded the bases after his home run in the second game, Captain Carl tipped his cap to the White Sox skipper.

Gary Bell

by Cecilia Tan

	G	ERA	W	L	SV	GS	GF	CG	SHO	IP	H	R	ER	BB	SO	HR	BFP
1967 RED SOX	29	3.16	12	8	3	24	3	8	0	165.1	143	70	58	47	115	16	683

Gary Bell was a wisecracking righthander who came up as a phenom in the Cleveland system, was traded to the Red Sox in early 1967, eventually winding down his major league career with stints as a Seattle Pilot and a Chicago White Sox.

His parents, Doris and Bill Bell, settled in San Antonio, Texas, in the 1930s. "My mom was the strength in our family. She was a hard-working gal from Kansas," says Bell. "My dad was a hell-raiser, liked to run around drinking and stuff, while she took charge and ran the house. He was always in the car business. During the Depression years when everyone was struggling and in World War II he sold cars and had a salvage yard. They would buy old cars and sell the parts, and then in World War II that was a good business since there were no new parts to be had."

The Bells raised twin boys, Billy and Bobby, plus Gary, who was seven years their junior, coming along on November 17, 1936. Although Gary was subject to the roughhousing ways of his elder siblings, they taught him to play baseball. There was no Little League in their area so "they worked with me until I got older," Bell says of his brothers' influence. "They showed me how to pitch, how to do everything."

Bell moved on to YMCA baseball, but Burbank High School in San Antonio did not have a baseball team. "I played football, basketball, and golf in high school. It's funny they had golf, but they didn't have baseball. I was shooting in the 70s when I was 14-15 years old," Bell explains. His best sport was basketball and he made all-conference basketball in junior college.

But a future in baseball beckoned when Bell was playing in American Legion ball. After beating out a base hit in one game, he took his lead off the bag. The first base umpire was a fellow named Ed Tech. "The umpire, he was a sort of bird dog scout. 'Boy,' he said, 'how'd you like to go up to University of Texas and play professional baseball?' Of course I said yes." Tech had thought to hook Bell up with Bibb Falk, the coach at UT who had been a major league player. In the end, though, Bell ended up spending one year at San Antonio Junior College before the major league scouts moved in.

In 1955, Bell landed with the Indians, despite the interest of several other teams. (This was in the days before the amateur draft.) "I know the Red Sox and Yankees were [among four or five teams interested]," he said. "If I'd been smart, and thought about the Yankees winning the World Series every year, I should have signed with them. But the scout that really scouted me the most was a Red Sox scout and he was the nicest one, and if I had any brains I would have gone with them, because they paid better than anybody else. But I signed with Cleveland, because all their big time pitchers were getting older—Feller, Lemon, Garcia, Early Wynn—so I figured that would be a good place to go, because by the time I was ready they would be on the way out That's pretty much how it worked out."

The Indians shipped him to Sherbrooke, Quebec, in the Class C Provincial League in 1955. "I did not do too well [0-4, with a 3.43 ERA]," Bell recalled. "I got banged around, and I was wild, nervous, scared, and young. I was only 18 years old. After a few weeks there, they sent me down to [Class D] Vidalia and I finished up pretty good." That winter he married Barbara Ann Jahn, his high school sweetheart. "We got married when I came home that winter, and she was with me my whole baseball career—then we went our separate ways. We got married too young and it's hard on baseball wives. They have to do all the packing and everything while you're doing your thing. School and all that stuff. It wasn't a good life for the wives."

In 1956 he was assigned to Reading, Pennsylvania, in the Eastern League, where he was teammates with Jim "Mudcat" Grant. Bell finished 13-8, 2.84, and led the league with 192 strikeouts, a league record that still stood as of 2006 and which has earned him induction into the Reading Sports Hall of Fame. He was on the way to repeating the strikeout feat in Double-A Mobile, Alabama, in 1957 when he was bumped up to San Diego in the Triple-A Pacific Coast League. The PCL was the big time as minor leagues went, though the San Diego Padres were far from the cream of the crop then.

"We probably sucked a little bit," Bell admits. "That was some league. San Diego, L.A., Hollywood, San Francisco, Sacramento, Portland, Seattle, and Vancouver. (The Padres finished 89-79, good for fourth in the eight-team league.) I got banged around pretty good [1-5, 4.95] the end of that year. [In Triple A,] the guys I was facing either had been to the major league

or were going there. They whacked me around pretty good." Nevertheless, in the spring of 1958, he found himself invited to spring training with the big club, and then opened the season with San Diego again. By the end of May he was 6-2 and leading the league with both a 1.21 ERA and 75 strikeouts in 60 innings and the two losses came courtesy of low run support, 1-0 and 2-0.

A *Los Angeles Times* story proclaimed "Padres' Bell No. 1 in PCL" on May 28. The next day, the Indians released the injured Mike Garcia and called Bell up to take his place.

Bell still remembers the phone call. "I was on a golf course in Seattle playing with our manager—George 'Catfish' Metkovich—and a couple other players. We had finished nine holes, and he got a phone call. He comes out and he says 'I have some bad news. You're going to the show.' It was bad news for him because he was losing one of his best pitchers. I went right to the Seattle airport and joined the team on the road in Kansas City."

That heady time as a rookie is still vivid to Bell. "The day I joined the team we were leaving after the game, flew from there to Boston, and then Baltimore, and back home. What a thrill. I was supposed to room with Herb Score in Boston, but he had a sore arm and stayed back in Cleveland so I had the room to myself at the old Kenmore Hotel right there on Commonwealth Avenue. Boston University owns it now. We could walk to the ballpark." Bell had his debut in relief on June 1 in Kansas City, in which he pitched three innings, struck out six, but gave up one run. Four days later he made his first start, in Boston, lasting only 5⅓ innings, giving up two home runs and leaving the game with the score tied 3-3. (Hoyt Wilhelm earned the loss after giving up two more runs in the eighth.) Bell did a bit better in his next start on June 10, and so did the Indians. Cleveland banged out 14 hits, including Minnie Minoso's eighth homer of the year, to sink Baltimore, 10-2. Bell worked six innings, allowing only three hits and two runs. He joined a rotation that included Ray Narleski, Mudcat Grant, and Cal McLish. Bob Lemon was on the downside of his career and with Garcia gone, Bell stepped in.

At that time he relied on his fastball and was considered a star phenom. He finished 12-10 his first season, good enough to place third in the 1958 Rookie of the Year voting, and the Indians finished fourth in the standings.

In 1959, the Indians had a better team and "that was the year we should have gone to the World Series," according to Bell. But the White Sox were better, and Cleveland slumped back into mediocrity after that

Right-hander Gary Bell delivered 12 wins to the 1967 Red Sox after coming from Cleveland for Demeter and Horton in early June.

season. Bell himself won 16 games, but with a 4.04 ERA. In 1960 Rocky Colavito was traded away, and the offense dwindled. During Bell's 10 seasons in Cleveland he pitched under at least nine different managers. "We weren't that good, you know, so somebody is going to get fired and it ain't the players," Bell says to explain the revolving door. "Great managers have great teams, you know. When great managers have lousy teams, they aren't considered great."

"We always had good pitching. Most of the years I was there we had real good pitching but not great defense and didn't score enough runs," Bell says. He himself was shifted in and out of relief and starting roles, and meanwhile the front office would spend little to shore up the team's weaknesses.

With no shot at the postseason, Bell's biggest thrills in Cleveland came in the regular season.

"There was one game where Rocky Colavito hit four home runs in a game and I was the winning pitcher," Bell remembers. It was June 10, 1959, the anniversary of his first win, again facing Baltimore in Memorial Stadium. This time Bell needed the run support as the

Dick Williams congratulates Bell after his Game Six save in the 1967 World Series, which evened the Series and set up a final Game Seven. Elston Howard is dugout bound, too.

Indians won it 11-8. "Another time I got four hits myself and that was kind of a fun thing to remember. You know we pitchers like to talk about our hitting. My best year I hit .240 and got like 70 plate appearances [Actually 75 at-bats -Ed.]—for a pitcher that's pretty good." His only career home run was hit on May 23, 1965 off Jim Lonborg.

But then came the fateful trade of June 1967, which sent Bell to Boston. "I was 1-5 before the trade and then I went 5-1 in the first few weeks after," he recalls. "I was not having a very good year in Cleveland and I wasn't too unhappy to be traded, but little did I know what was coming." He always felt he pitched well at Fenway, despite what other pitchers said. "Nobody really wanted to pitch there because the fence was so close, but it was just a beautiful old park."

Bell moved right into a brownstone in the Kenmore Square area and walked to the ballpark every day. "That was pretty exciting stuff. Every game was a drama, it seemed like, and new heroes all the time. Lonborg had a phenomenal year, Yaz too. Yawkey had traded his favorite boy for me, Tony Horton, but it turned out good." Bell ended up winning 12 games down the stretch. "We only won by half a game or what have you, so I guess those 12 wins helped a bit," he says.

After beating Minnesota on the final day of the season, the Red Sox went to the World Series against the St. Louis Cardinals. Bell was beaten 5-2 in Game Three, but nailed down the save in Game Six to ensure the Sox would live for one more day.

In 1968, Bell pitched well, with a 3.12 ERA, but the magic of the "Impossible Dream" had dissipated. "Lonborg had gotten hurt chasing Jill St. John down the slopes," Bell remembers. "That was a big part of it." Despite his good ERA and nine complete games, his record stood at 11-11. The next winter came the expansion draft, and the Seattle Pilots snatched up Bell, who had been left unprotected by Boston.

"I pitched Opening Day in Seattle, the first major league game in that city," Bell recalls proudly. "I pitched a shutout against the White Sox." But it was all downhill from there. "My ability to pitch was not that good anymore. I had lost something over the winter. I don't know where it went but it was gone. It was the beginning of the end for me." The Pilots traded him, he ended up finishing the year with the White Sox, and then thought about hanging up his spikes. "There weren't any injuries or anything, but as you get older you lose speed, and that's not good. A lot of other guys could depend on their other pitches. My curve was just average so when my fastball went, that was the end of me."

"But that winter I got a call from the fellow who owned the Hawaii Islanders. I wasn't going to play anymore, but they offered me a pretty nice deal. Didn't last the year there, though, but it was a nice experience. When your fastball disappears, so do you. Know what I mean?"

Life after baseball took Bell into two careers that seem apropos for a Bud-pounding ex-pitcher, the beer business and sporting goods. "I went to work for a Miller Beer distributor in Phoenix, for eight years or so, doing everything from driving trucks to delivery to heading a department, a little of everything. Never made any money, but it was good times." In 1978 he married a Phoenix native named Rhonda. Then a childhood friend who owned a sporting goods store contacted him about moving back to San Antonio. He went into sales there for about five years before Rhonda felt homesick, so Bell returned to the beer business in Arizona.

Four years later it was back to Texas and sporting goods, where an associate had a business in Fort Worth. "I wasn't there a year and the guy I went to work for died, that business went down the tubes, and I had to leave," Bell explained. "Then I was offered a job in San Antonio with the Double-A team here, owned by a friend of mine, Ethan Blackaby. I stayed with him a couple of years doing PR and that kind of stuff. But he ended up having to give up the club, so I went back to work for the original guy I was with in sporting goods again. Then HE ended up going out of business and I was starting to think it was me."

By then it was 1987 and Bell decided it was time to be his own boss. "I went out and borrowed $15,000 from the bank and started a sporting goods business of my own, calling on the same customers we used to. It's turned out good, I've been doing it for 19 years now. All I do is deal with coaches and schools and stuff like that."

Bell has five children, three from his first marriage, all daughters, Garriann, Cindy, and Lisa, and two children from his second marriage, daughter Casey and son Cody.

Dennis Bennett

by Mark Armour

	G	ERA	W	L	SV	GS	GF	CG	SHO	IP	H	R	ER	BB	SO	HR	BFP
1967 RED SOX	13	3.88	4	3	0	11	1	4	1	69.2	72	32	30	22	34	12	300

Dennis Bennett, a fun-loving character on baseball's stage for much of the 1960s, was blessed with a great left arm and a thirst for the good life. He also overcame several reckless brushes with danger, including a tragic accident, to forge a seven-year big league career, though he never reached the heights he likely could have.

Dennis John Bennett was born in Oakland, California, on October 5, 1939, to parents George and Ruth, of German-Dutch descent. There were ultimately five boys and a girl in the Bennett family. His family moved to Yreka, a heavily wooded town on the Northern California coast, when Dennis was 10 years old. His father liked to hunt and fish, and when a job with the phone company opened up nearer his beloved streams and forests, he took it. The elder Bennett started the boys' baseball program in Yreka, and Dennis soon became a star first baseman and hitter. He played Little League and Babe Ruth League baseball before entering high school.

At Yreka High School, he lettered in baseball, basketball, track, and football. His senior year, he won 15 of 16 decisions on the mound, and hit .458, playing first base when not pitching. He was, however, not fond of rules. "I can't remember a single season where I wasn't suspended for at least one game," he later recalled.

Dennis's off-the-field activities in his youth were atypical. Firefighting was a vital and lucrative occupation in his region, so he often skipped school to go off and join a fire crew (lying about his age). If that wasn't dangerous enough, he and some friends made extra money in the summers traveling around Northern California to various rodeos, riding saddleback and bareback bronco events. He later recalled, "I've been hit over the head with bottles and cut up some in fights at dances, but I still say I'm lucky. All those rodeos I rode in, I never got banged up."

Bennett did not throw particularly hard as a teenager, and few scouts showed any interest in watching the hurler. He garnered a partial scholarship to pitch for Mt. Shasta Junior College, pitching a single season for its baseball team. At that point, Bennett was offered a contract by Eddie Taylor, a scout for the Philadelphia Phillies. He was no bonus baby—he would get $500 if he stayed in the organization for 90 days, and $250 a month.

His professional career began in Johnson City, Tennessee, in the Appalachian League, where the tall left-hander finished 7-3 and led the league with three shutouts and a 1.52 ERA and struck out 92 in just 77 innings. The next year he finished 13-13 for Bakersfield in the California League, before spending the 1960 campaign with Asheville, North Carolina (South Atlantic League), where he finished 8-7.

He spent the start of 1961 in Chattanooga (4-2, 4.37), before tearing up his knee. Always a free spirit, the circumstances surrounding the injury typifies Bennett's personality. "There was a big hill in right field in Nashville. A bunch of us were standing around, and I challenged John Boozer to a somersault race downhill.

Dennis Bennett's three-run homer helped secure his 4-0 May Day shutout of the Angels.

It was for $10 and a steak dinner." He lost the bet and jammed the cartilage in his knee. An operation ended his season. He told his manager he got hurt jogging in the outfield.

The next spring Bennett was invited to major league camp, likely because the Phillies wanted to see how his knee was. Not only was his knee fine, but the rest had added several miles per hour to his fastball. He was sent to Triple-A Buffalo (International League), and started 3-1, 2.00 before his May recall to Philadelphia.

Bennett's first major league appearance took place at Chicago's Wrigley Field on May 12, 1962. The Phillies were leading 8-5 when he took the mound to start the bottom of the fourth inning. He walked his first batter, Lou Brock, before inducing a double play ground ball. After three scoreless innings, he could not escape the seventh, allowing three hits and a walk before being relieved.

After three mediocre starts, Bennett's first major league victory was a four-hit shutout that snapped the Los Angeles Dodgers' 13-game winning streak on June 2. He finished the season 9-9, leading the team with a 3.81 ERA and two shutouts. From August 12 to the end of the season, his ERA was 1.66, highlighted by three consecutive five-hit complete games. Bennett later recalled, "I figured I had a great career ahead of me. I knew I could throw. I wasn't a complete pitcher or the smartest guy out there, but at that time if you threw hard enough you learned as you went. I was real happy the way everything was going at that point."

The Phillies sent him to Arecibo, Puerto Rico, that winter to get ready for a big season. On January 7, 1963, returning to Arecibo from a team picnic, he was involved in a car accident that killed the driver. Bennett was thrown through the windshield, breaking his left ankle, pelvis, and left shoulder blade, and leaving severe lacerations all over his face. He had been sitting with his back against the door and leg up on the seat, talking to the people in the rear seat. According to Bennett, this was his fifth serious car accident, including the third time he had been thrown through the windshield. This was the first time he was seriously hurt.

The Phillies were most concerned with his ankle, but it was the shoulder injury that would linger, and cause problems throughout the remainder of his career. The doctor in Puerto Rico suggested he would never pitch again, and might not walk. After months in the hospital, he was working out by the end of May and, miraculously, joined the Phillies in late June. By July he was in the rotation, and he pitched very well the rest of the season, finishing the year 9-5, with a 2.64 ERA. For his efforts he won a local award as the most courageous athlete on the team. The shoulder seemed fine—then.

Bennett was cocky when assessing his chances for 1964: "There's no way I can't win 20. I always start good, but the past two years I haven't been out there early in the year." He elaborated in a July profile Stan Hochman wrote for *Sport*: "You can't go out there wondering whether you are going to win or lose. You can't look at the hitter and say, 'Geez, that's Henry Aaron ... or geez, that's Willie Mays.' Now, I don't care who's up there."

His manager, Gene Mauch, was also unconcerned: "He's got a big-league fastball and two breaking balls that are better than the average major-leaguer. And he believes in himself about 130 percent." Bennett later named Mauch as his favorite manager, a brilliant man whom people loved playing for.

Dennis was beginning to acquire a reputation as a free spirit who enjoyed the nightlife. He was single and spent his evenings doing what single men are wont to do. "You'll never catch me out the night before I pitch. But I figure a pitcher has two nights to fool around."

Bennett started strong in 1964, winning eight of his first 12 decisions through June. The personal highlight took place on June 12 in a game in which he was knocked out of the box by the Mets in the third. Later in the game, his brother Dave Bennett made his major league debut, pitching the ninth inning for the Phillies in what turned out to be an 11-3 loss. Dave was just 18 years old, a 6' 5" right-hander who possessed none of his older brother's swagger or brashness. Alas, this was to be Dave's only major league appearance.

In the second half of the 1964 season, Dennis's shoulder, and its still undiagnosed injury, started to bother him, and the pain never really went away again. He managed just a 1-7 record in July and August, ironically as his team started pulling away in the pennant race. On September 7, he beat the Dodgers 5-1, and followed with a 1-0 victory over Juan Marichal and the Giants. After he followed with a 1-0 victory over the Astros on the 15th, the Phillies had a six-game lead over the Cardinals with 17 games to go. He started three more times, losing two, and the Phillies lost a heartbreaking pennant race. By season's end, the pain in his shoulder was constant and tremendous. Bennett finished 12-14, with a 3.68 ERA.

The 1964 Phillies are one of the more famous teams in Philadelphia history, and Bennett's injury was likely the biggest element in their collapse. He was the club's Opening Day starter, and an ace hurler for the first half of the season before the sore shoulder set in. Bennett believes the team would have won the pennant "hands

Through early June 1967, Bennett was 4-1 (2.97 ERA) but he was in Dick Williams' doghouse and three weeks later he was traded to the Mets.

down" had his arm stayed healthy, and lists it among his biggest disappointments. He later recalled his shutout of the Giants in September as the best of his career, a game notable for his three strikeouts of Willie Mays. Mays hit just .111 (3-for-27) off Bennett in his career, and Willie McCovey was 0-8 with five strikeouts, while their teammate Jim Ray Hart, who Bennett recalled decades later as a nemesis, managed a more robust .533 with three home runs.

On November 29, 1964, the Phillies dealt Bennett to the Red Sox for slugger Dick Stuart. Bennett was angered by the deal because he felt the team had promised him he would be back with the club. More than that, he knew he was injured and felt the Phillies knew so. Bennett was speaking at a banquet in Boston that winter and surprised the assembled media and team personnel when he casually mentioned that his sore arm might not be ready for the opening of the season. In fact, it was "50-50." The Phillies offered to nullify the deal, but the Red Sox were happy to be rid of the enigmatic and controversial Stuart and didn't argue.

As a left-hander moving to Fenway Park, Bennett admits that the wall in left field "messed with my mind a little." Balancing that, he believed there were far fewer tough outs in an American League lineup compared with his National League opponents. Bennett pitched adequately for the 1965 Red Sox, starting 18 games and relieving 16 others, finishing 5-7 for a team that lost 100 games. He started the season on the disabled list, joining the club in early May. During his recuperation, he vowed to host a champagne party for the writers after his first victory, a promise he kept after topping the Athletics at Fenway Park on May 31. The thankful writers allowed that they would return the favor after his first shutout.

His reputation for zaniness grew. For one thing, he carried several guns with him on the road, and often on his person. He tells the story of shooting off several rounds with a gun one quiet spring just over the head of *Boston Globe* writer Will McDonough, who had written a story Bennett did not like. "Just trying to scare him," he recalls, allowing that McDonough gave him a wide berth thereafter. Then there was the time Bennett shot out the lights in his hotel room instead of getting up and flipping the switch.

After the 1965 season, Bennett finally underwent shoulder surgery, keeping him on the disabled list until mid-July. A doctor finally isolated the problem—calcium had built up in a crack in the shoulder blade caused by his 1963 accident. Bennett recalls that pitchers tended to throw through such problems back then, but the Red Sox supported his decision to have surgery. Upon his return, he was actually one of the more steady members of the rotation, finishing 3-3 with a 3.24 ERA in 13 starts for an improving club that played .500 ball in the second half.

The next spring, Bennett was involved in an incident in Florida that was part of a sad lineage of race relations with the Red Sox. He entered a club in Lakeland with pitchers Dave Morehead and Earl Wilson. While Bennett and Morehead were asked for their drink orders, the bartender turned to Wilson, an African-American, and said, "We ain't serving you. We don't serve niggers here." The players left, but word of the incident soon leaked out. The club did not strongly back Wilson, who was traded in June. He won 13 games in the latter half of the season for the Tigers, and 22 the next year.

Bennett later related to Peter Golenbock what these Red Sox teams were like: "You'd have four or five players and some girls, and you'd have a party. And it might go until six, seven in the morning, and maybe you had a day game that day. And the thing was, you'd get on the bus, and [manager] Billy Herman would be sitting in the front seat, and everybody would talk about the party the night before, and Billy would sit there hearing it all, but there wasn't too much he could do about it because some of your stars were the ones doing the talking, and he didn't have any control over the ballclub whatsoever."

The new manager for 1967, Dick Williams, was different. When Bennett and another pitcher showed up late one day in the spring, Williams publicly called them out and fined them. When Bennett blamed the hotel for failing to give him his wakeup call, Williams ridiculed the players, and Bennett never got out of the new skipper's doghouse.

Dennis continued to pitch well early in the 1967 season. He started the fourth game of the season, following Billy Rohr's one-hitter in Yankee Stadium with a five-hit, 1-0 loss to the same Yankees on April 15. On May 1, in Anaheim, he shut out the Angels with a six-hitter, and also hit a three-run home run off Angels' starter Jorge Rubio. After surrendering the round-tripper, Rubio hit Reggie Smith with a pitch, then was removed from the game. This was Rubio's 10th major league game, and his last. Bennett was doubly happy about the shutout, as the local writers had promised him a champagne party two years earlier. "I got to hand it to them, especially Larry Claflin and Clif Keane," Bennett recalls. "We had it upstairs at the Playboy Club in Boston."

When Bennett beat the Indians' Gary Bell on June

3, he brought his record to 4-1, with a 2.97 ERA. After a couple of rough starts, he fell to 4-3, and his relationship with Williams deteriorated further. On June 24, the Red Sox traded Bennett to the Mets for minor leaguer Al Yates, who would never pitch for the Red Sox. According to Bennett, Williams had not spoken to him for weeks prior to telling him he had been dealt. The pitcher expressed disappointment at the trade, telling the New York writers that he thought a good ballclub was coming together in Boston.

Bennett split two decisions with the Mets, also spending time with their Jacksonville affiliate in the International League. After two appearances for Jacksonville in April 1968, he was sold to the Chicago Cubs organization, which placed him with Tacoma in the Pacific Coast League. He was 9-8 in 19 starts out west, and at the end of July was sold to the California Angels. He finished the season, and his big league career, by dropping all five of his decisions for the Angels.

But he wasn't through pitching just yet. He spent the next five years in the Pacific Coast League, much of it far removed from the continental United States. He played for Hawaii in 1969 and 1970, tying for the league lead each year in victories (13 and 18) and making two All-Star teams. These Hawaii clubs were great teams, filled with ex-major leaguers. The 1970 team finished

Hope springs eternal. *Bennett, Jerry Stephenson, and Dave Morehead were all sidelined most of '66 with ailments, but all got off to good starts in spring training 1967.*

98-48, and was led by Bennett, Gary Bell, Juan Pizarro, and several other former big leaguers.

Bennett spent a year and a half with Salt Lake City before returning to Hawaii for parts of the 1972 and 1973 seasons. At the conclusion of the latter campaign, he finally walked away from the game.

Bennett married Terry, whom he had met in Boston, on January 3, 1970, and the two have raised nine children. Having settled in Klamath Falls, Oregon, Bennett operated a restaurant and bar for a few years, worked for several years in a mill, operated another bar, and finally opened a more elaborate club with banquet rooms in 1998.

In the 1990s, Bennett was the victim of identity theft—a man in Texas successfully passed himself off as the former major league pitcher, sticking the real Bennett with tens of thousands of dollars in bills, including $77,000 for open heart surgery. As he later told researcher Todd Newville, "It caused me a lot of misery for several years. It's all water under the bridge now, but for about five years, I couldn't even buy a pack of gum on credit. That's how bad that guy ruined it."

Klamath Falls is a small community when compared with the big metropolises in which he spent his pitching career. Bennett's businesses and big family have kept him at home most of the time, but he has attended many reunions and fantasy camps over the years. He kept many dear friends from his playing days, including Jim Lonborg, his roommate with the Red Sox, and Chris Short, his best friend on the Phillies, who died too young in 1991. He values all his old baseball memories, and loves getting together with his old teammates and opponents.

"Baseball was the best time of my life," Bennett later recalled. "I couldn't throw without pain for most of the time after the wreck. If I hadn't cracked my shoulder blade in the accident, I think I would have had one hell of a career." Asked many years later to recount the highlight of his big-league career, he said simply, "Just being there was the highlight. Playing against all those great players."

Darrell "Bucky" Brandon

by David Laurila

	G	ERA	W	L	SV	GS	GF	CG	SHO	IP	H	R	ER	BB	SO	HR	BFP
1967 RED SOX	39	4.17	5	11	3	19	11	2	0	157.2	147	86	73	59	96	21	683

Darrell Brandon grew up rooting for Joe DiMaggio and Mickey Mantle. On July 5, 1966, the right-hander earned his first big league win, striking out Mantle twice as the Red Sox defeated the New Yorkers, 7-1, in Yankee Stadium. Brandon went on to win 12 more games for Boston, including five for the 1967 pennant winners. Overall, he posted a record of 28-37 in a seven-year major league career that included stops in Seattle, Minnesota, and Philadelphia.

Born on July 8, 1940 in Nacogdoches, Texas, Brandon had what he called "a good childhood, always playing sports." He primarily followed the Yankees, who made regular appearances on *The Game of the Week*, and the Cardinals, whose games he heard via the strong signal of St. Louis radio station KMOX. Turn the dial ahead to 1967, and Brandon would be part of a New England Summer of Love that saw the airwaves filled with both the Beatles and the voices of Ned Martin and Ken Coleman on WHDH. It was a long and winding road that brought him from the Lone Star State's oldest city to his place in Red Sox history.

After graduating from Nacogdoches High School in 1958, Brandon signed with the Pirates and began an eight-year journey to the big leagues the following season. "I made it through perseverance and faith in myself," said Brandon. "Starting out as an outfielder, and getting released a few times, I almost should have given up."

Primarily a shortstop in high school, Brandon spent 1959, his first professional season, in the outfield. He appeared in only one game as a pitcher, allowing seven runs in five innings for Salem in the Appalachian League. He was subsequently released, but signed with the Cardinals the following year after attending a tryout camp in Tulsa. He played the entire 1960 season with Dothan in the Alabama-Florida League, again mostly as an outfielder. He got into five games as a pitcher, allowing eight earned runs in 10 innings. The next year, in spring training, he asked if he could pitch full time, but the Cardinals weren't interested. Instead, he found himself released for the second time in two years.

Out of organized baseball in 1961, Brandon pitched on a semi-pro team near his home in Texas and worked as a milkman to earn his living. "I actually did that in the offseason for three or four more years," explained Brandon. "In those days, I made more money driving a milk truck than I did as a minor leaguer."

But driving a milk truck wasn't Brandon's career goal, and a good showing at another tryout camp landed him a job in the farm system of the expansion Houston Colt 45s in 1962. It was there that he acquired the nickname that would stay with him throughout his baseball career.

"When I was in Class D ball," Brandon explained, "there was this little Indian kid from California on the team, and he had buck teeth. He had 'Bucky' carved into his glove, and I ended up buying it from him. A few years later, when I went to spring training with Houston, I had it with me. It was really beaten up, so the guys on the team gave me a hard time about it and started calling me 'Bucky.'"

Along with a new nickname, Bucky Brandon also went into the 1962 season with a new position. Finally given an opportunity to pitch full time, he posted a record of 9-5 in 17 games with Modesto in the California League, establishing himself as a legitimate prospect. He followed that by going 14-6 for Durham in the Carolina League in 1963, 15-7 for San Antonio in the Texas League in 1964, and 13-6 for Oklahoma City of the Pacific Coast League in 1965. When his Triple-A season in Oklahoma City came to an end, Brandon was told he would be getting called up to Houston for the final month of the season. However, "See You in September" by The Happenings wouldn't hit the Top 40 until the following year, and Brandon's big league debut would likewise have to wait.

"I was told to report to the Astrodome," Brandon explained, "which meant I was going home to play in the big leagues. But while I was loading my trailer, I got a call saying I had been traded to Boston for Jack Lamabe. That was disappointing, because I barely knew where Boston was at the time, and they didn't bring anyone up from the minor leagues that year."

The Red Sox were coming off a 100-loss season when Brandon reported to spring training in 1966. One of several new faces on the team—George Scott, Joe Foy, Reggie Smith, and Mike Andrews all saw their first big league action that year—he pitched well, earning himself a spot as a reliever. On April 19 at Fenway Park,

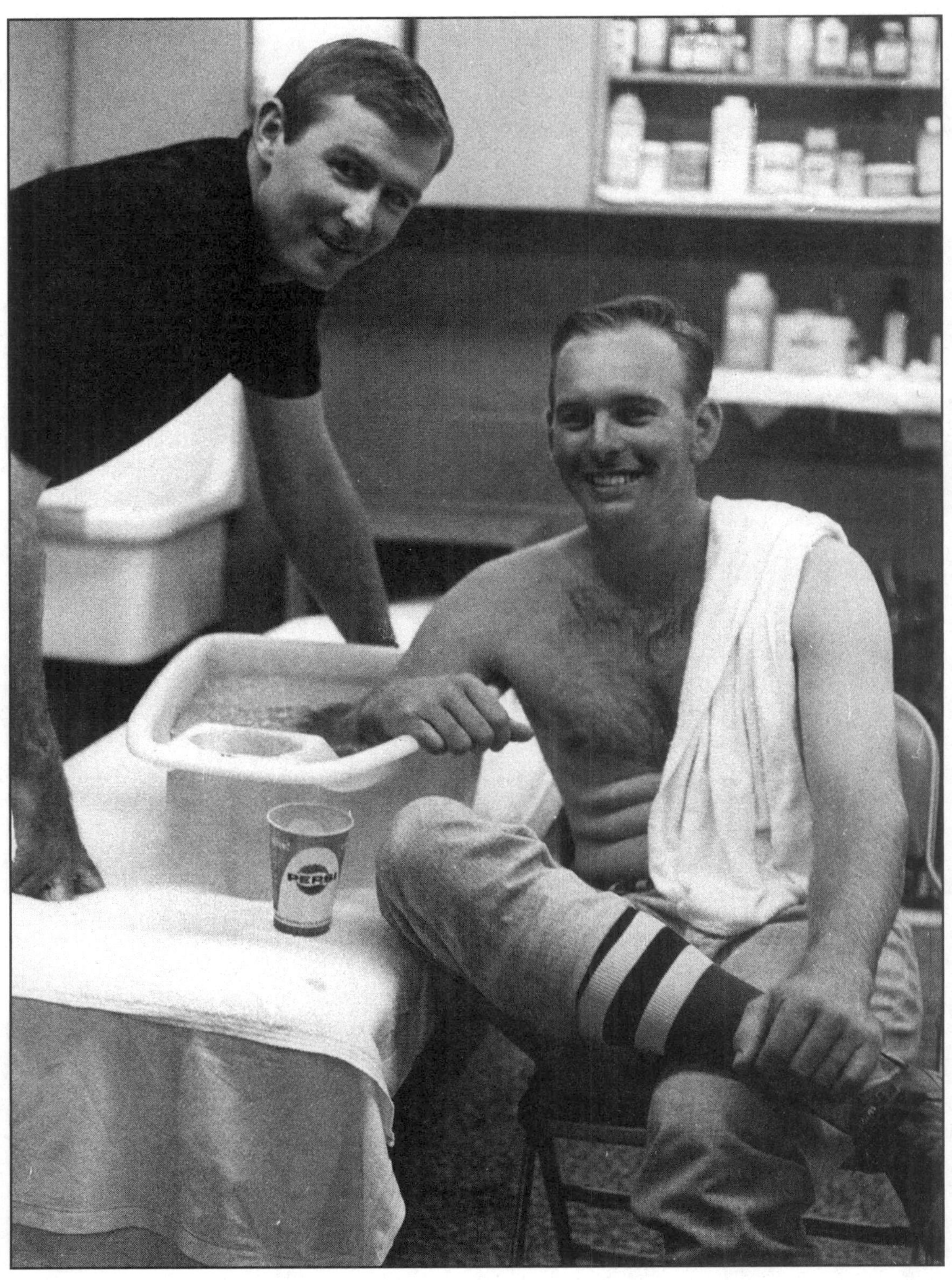

Brandon pitched 3⅓ innings of two-hit relief, saving the August 26 game for Jerry Stephenson and propelling Boston into first place.

wearing the number 27 on his Red Sox uniform, he made his major league debut against the Tigers.

"We were losing 6-0 when the phone rang in the bullpen," Brandon remembers, "and the first hitter I'd be facing was Bill Freehan. Dick Radatz was the bullpen spokesman, and he told me Freehan likes the ball out over the plate, so I should pitch him inside. That's what I did, and Freehan hit my first pitch off the wall in left. Afterwards, Radatz said, 'I meant high and inside, not inside at the belt.'"

Brandon proceeded to strike out the next batter, Denny McLain, recording the first out of a career that would see him pitch in 228 major league games, 43 as a starter and 185 in relief. The following month, in his 13th appearance of the season, Brandon again pitched in relief as Lamabe, now with Chicago, pitched a one-hitter at Fenway Park in an 11-0 White Sox win.

Moved to the rotation on July 1, Brandon pitched well, finishing the season with a record of 8-8, 3.31. After his inaugural win against the Yankees on July 5—a complete game in which he contributed to his own cause with two hits, including a triple—he threw another complete game on July 9, beating Gary Peters and the White Sox, 4-2.

He went on to earn wins in four of his last five starts on the season, one of them a 5-4 decision against Lamabe at Fenway Park. He threw two shutouts in September, one in his final appearance, and went into 1967 with high expectations. His ERA was the best on the team amongst pitchers with 100 innings pitched.

Going into the season, Brandon was considered to be one of the set members of the rotation, along with Jim Lonborg and José Santiago. While a solid contributor to the '67 pennant winners, Brandon was unable to replicate his promising rookie season, finishing a disappointing 5-11, 4.17. He began the year in the starting rotation, but was inconsistent and by early August pitched only in relief.

"I pitched well in spring training," Brandon remembers, "but then didn't have the year I hoped to. I made the mistake of getting cute rather than going after hitters like I did the year before. I was trying to pitch to weaknesses, and just wasn't making the pitches like I did in '66."

Brandon started the second game of the 1967 season, and got a no-decision as the Red Sox lost at home to Chicago. Ironically, the winning pitcher was again Lamabe. Brandon went on to lose his first four decisions, but pitched better than his record indicated as he allowed only nine earned runs in those outings. The toughest of the four defeats came on April 30, as he lost to Jim Nash and Kansas City 1-0 on a Danny Cater home run. His first win finally came on May 21 when he outpitched "Sudden Sam" McDowell as the Red Sox defeated Cleveland 6-2 at Fenway Park. That effort was followed, however, by a 10-0 shellacking in Baltimore that saw him give up two home runs to Frank Robinson.

"I remember thinking that I had good stuff that day," recalls Brandon, "but Frank hit it harder than I threw it. He was probably the toughest hitter I ever faced, and I think he hit six home runs against me in my career." [*Editor's note: Robinson had five home runs and was 10-for-23 off Brandon.*]

Brandon was still in the starting rotation when the Red Sox went on their longest winning streak of the season—10 games—establishing themselves as serious pennant contenders and eliciting more than a few exclamations of "Oh Mercy!" from Ned Martin in the broadcast booth. He won twice in that stretch, including a complete game 6-2 triumph over Luis Tiant and the Cleveland Indians on July 21 that moved the Red Sox into second place. It was to be Brandon's final big-league win as a starter. He started three more times in 1967, twice losing to the Twins and Jim Merritt, and spent the remainder of the season in the bullpen.

Two of Brandon's best relief outings came in August, a month that saw The Hub gripped by pennant fever and the Buckinghams reach the top ten with "Mercy, Mercy, Mercy." On the 16th, he relieved Lee Stange early in the game and pitched seven shutout innings to earn what would be his last win in a Red Sox uniform. On the 29th, he went five strong innings but gave up a run in the 20th inning to lose in Yankee Stadium, a game in which New York's starter was former Red Sox ace Bill Monbouquette.

The low point of Brandon's season came on September 24 in Baltimore, a game that saw Jim Lonborg win his 21st game and José Tartabull steal home. While throwing a pitch to the Orioles' Boog Powell in the ninth inning, Brandon suffered a shoulder injury that ended his season and forced him to miss the World Series. Despite being unable to pitch in the Fall Classic, Brandon did, however, make a contribution—albeit a unique one—to the team's effort against the Cardinals.

"A fan sent me a paper horseshoe in the mail," Brandon explained, "and I gave it to Lonnie (Jim Lonborg) before he threw the shutout in Game Two. It worked pretty well... until Game Seven, anyway."

The Supremes had a hit with "Reflections" as the Red Sox and Cardinals did battle in the fall of 1967,

and Brandon has mixed feelings when he looks back at his role in one of the most exciting seasons in team history.

"It really hurt not to pitch in the World Series," Brandon said. "And while it was the thrill of a lifetime to be part of the team that turned baseball around in New England, on a personal level it wasn't as satisfying. I always tell people that I helped contribute to an exciting season, because we'd have won going away had I pitched better."

When the 1968 season got underway, Brandon's arm was still less than 100 percent. Unable to earn a spot on the Red Sox pitching staff out of spring training, he ended up spending most of the year with Triple-A Louisville, going 13-11, 3.32 as a starter. Simon and Garfunkel topped the charts with "Mrs. Robinson" that summer, but they could just as easily have sung "Where have you gone Darrell Brandon?" as Brandon pitched in only eight games with the big league club, all in relief, going 0-0, 6.39 in $12\frac{2}{3}$ innings. His final game in a Red Sox uniform came on September 24 in Washington, as he pitched two innings in a 10-2 loss to the Senators.

After the season, Brandon was truly gone, taken by the Seattle Pilots in the 1968 expansion draft.

"Sal Maglie was the pitching coach there," Brandon explained, "and he recommended they draft me. He had been my pitching coach in '66 and '67, and liked me as a pitcher. A few other guys came over from here too, like Gary Bell, but going there wasn't good. I'd have liked to have stayed in Boston."

Brandon began the 1969 campaign in Triple-A Vancouver and won his first three games as a starter. He was called up to Seattle by the end of April, but appeared in only eight games out of the bullpen for the expansion Pilots, two of them against the Red Sox. On May 6, at Seattle's Sick's Stadium, Brandon gave up a home run to Syd O'Brien in the ninth inning of a 12-2 Boston win. On May 17, he pitched three scoreless innings in a game the Red Sox won 6-1 behind Mike Nagy. On July 8, Brandon's 29th birthday, the Pilots sold him to Minnesota. He pitched in only three games with the Twins, seeing most of his action in Triple-A Denver where he went 4-2, 3.17.

Released by the Twins at the end of spring training

The Brandon family gathers around the starter-turned-reliever as the Impossible Dream season unfolded.

in 1970, Brandon was signed by the White Sox and spent the entire season with their Triple-A team in Tucson. Again a starter, Brandon went 15-10 and led the Pacific Coast League in strikeouts.

"Looking back, it was hard going back and forth," Brandon said. "These days you're either a starter or a reliever. Back then you'd be a starter in the minors, and when you got called up they would stick you in the bullpen. That didn't make sense to me. I should have been a starter, because I was getting the job done when I was."

In January, Brandon was sold to Philadelphia where he spent the final three years of his major league career. Finally comfortable pitching out of the bullpen, he enjoyed two of his best seasons. In 1971 he appeared in 52 games for the Phillies, going 6-6, 3.90 with four saves. In 1972 he finished 7-7, 3.45 with two saves in 42 games. On a team that won only 59 times all season, Brandon's seven wins were second on the team to Steve Carlton's 27.

In 1973, Brandon returned to the City of Brotherly Love and went 2-4, 5.43 in 36 games. He also recorded two saves, which ironically came in relief of former Red Sox teammates Ken Brett and Jim Lonborg on consecutive days in July. In what was to be his last season in a big league uniform, Brandon also made eight appearances for Eugene in the Pacific Coast League. After spending 1974 with Toledo in the International League, and 1975 with Coahuila in the Mexican League, his pitching days were over.

After retiring, Brandon started a pitching school in Cherry Hill, New Jersey, where his second pupil was 16-year-old Orel Hershiser, who would go on to win 204 games in the big leagues. In 1976, Brandon moved to Hanover, Massachusetts, where he continued to teach young pitchers for over 20 years. Nearly four decades after being a part of the 1967 Impossible Dream Red Sox, Darrell "Bucky" Brandon now works in the insurance business.

Ken Brett

by Jonathan Arnold

	G	ERA	W	L	SV	GS	GF	CG	SHO	IP	H	R	ER	BB	SO	HR	BFP
1967 RED SOX	1	4.50	0	0	0	0	1	0	0	2	3	1	1	0	2	0	8

One longtime scout called Ken Brett "a combination of George Brett [his brother], Fred Lynn, and Roger Maris. He was the best prospect that I ever saw." Ken Brett's numbers never quite lived up to the reputation. "The worse curse in life," Brett would later offer, "is unlimited potential." Only 19 years old in 1967, he was the youngest pitcher to ever appear in a World Series. He then went on to hurl for a then-record 10 different teams, appear in (and win) one All-Star game, carry a no-hitter into the ninth inning twice, and set the record for most consecutive games with a home run by a pitcher at four.

Kenneth Alven Brett was born on September 18, 1948, in Brooklyn, New York. He was the second of Jack and Ethel Brett's four sons. All four brothers played professional baseball. Baby brother George is, of course, enshrined in the Hall of Fame. The eldest, John and third son Bobby, played in the minors until injuries derailed their careers.

John, Ken, and Bobby were all born while the Bretts lived in Brooklyn. George was born in West Virginia, and the family finally settled in El Segundo, California. Nestled by the Pacific Ocean, the Los Angeles airport, the 405 San Diego Freeway and oil refineries, this LA suburb was a bedroom community, and is now home to many aerospace companies. Jack was an accountant, eventually becoming a finance director for Datsun. He had a no-nonsense attitude as a father. Ken would later say, "Dad was stern and strict, a tough disciplinarian. He expected us to do well in school and he expected us to do our work around the house. He made me go to summer school once to improve what was a better-than-average grade to start with."

Even when Ken was a little boy, his father was impressed with his physique. "He looked like the statue of David when he was growing up." Jack once said. "When he was just a little boy, his stomach was so strong that you could see the plates, the muscles." His father recalled the 10-year-old Ken hitting two home runs over a 220-foot fence.

Kemer (pronounced "kemmer," a family nickname derived from his brother James' pronunciation of Kenneth) had a 33-3 record in high school, to go along with a .484 batting average. He played first and shortstop (despite being a lefty) in Little League, but later switched to the outfield when he wasn't pitching. He also played football and basketball in high school until he broke a leg in his junior year. He was the California Interscholastic Federation Player of the Year in 1966, drawing the attention of many baseball people. Casey Stengel, Yogi Berra, Carl Hubbell, and Bobby Doerr were among the parade of those who went to see him play. His dad dreamed of him replacing Mickey Mantle in the Yankees' centerfield, but Ken was selected by the Red Sox with the fourth pick of the 1966 June amateur draft.

The other organizations interested in Brett would have selected him as an outfielder, but the Red Sox, still mired in the second division, needed live arms. Jack Brett negotiated for his son, in those days before agents. He talked to the father of Steve Chilcott, who was the No. 1 pick that year, selected by the Mets, to get an idea of what Ken's signing bonus should be. It took Red Sox scout Joe Stephenson three visits to the Brett house to sign him; Ken had an out—he could go to college. But he really wanted to play and they agreed on a $100,000 bonus, plus money for college.

He struggled his first season with Oneonta in the New York-Penn League, going 1-4 with a 5.81 ERA with 62 innings pitched. He went on to play winter ball in the Florida Instructional League.

In 1967, Brett pitched for Winston-Salem of the Carolina League and Pittsfield of the Eastern League, putting up some strong numbers—189 innings pitched, a combined 14-11 record with 219 strikeouts and an ERA of 1.95—before being called up in late September by the Red Sox. Even though the left-handed fireballer had only recently turned 19, the big leaguers were already impressed with his fastball. Carl Yastrzemski told a reporter, "That's the new Sam McDowell. Russ Gibson says that kid throws harder than anyone he's ever caught." Elston Howard said, "This boy Brett is as fast as Bob Turley was in his prime. I also think that he's as fast as Koufax was."

The Red Sox were deep in what many consider the greatest pennant race of all time. On September 27, Brett made his major league debut, pitching two innings to finish up a game against the Cleveland Indians. He gave up one run on three hits, walking none

and striking out two in his only appearance during the regular season.

The Sox prevailed and faced the St. Louis Cardinals in a rematch of Boston's previous World Series appearance 21 years ago. Because he was a September call-up, Brett did not qualify for the postseason roster. But one bullpen lefty (Bill Landis) went into the service, while another (Sparky Lyle) developed late-season arm trouble. The Sox secured approval from both Commissioner William Eckert and the Cardinals to add Brett to the roster.

Brett pitched twice in the World Series. At age 19 years and one month, he was the youngest pitcher to ever appear in the Fall Classic. He pitched 1⅓ innings, with no runs, one strikeout and one walk. That short stint was enough for the opposing manager to praise the phenom. "Where has he been?" asked Cardinals skipper Red Schoendienst after his first appearance. "With the kind of stuff he showed us, you wonder why he isn't starting the Series. But don't let me give the Red Sox any ideas."

Brett was a teenager in the spotlight, dubbed "the next Lefty Grove," but this was the Vietnam era and not two weeks after the World Series, he started a six month tour of duty with the Army Reserve. "That was a humbling experience," he later recalled. "Those guys in the Army didn't care about the World Series. They wanted me in the kitchen with a shovel in my hand." In his hilarious biography, *The Wrong Stuff*, Bill Lee described Brett in the same unit as himself, Dalton Jones and Jim Lonborg. Lee was a clerk typist while the other three served as medics.

After his military tour, Brett returned too quickly and hurt his elbow, an injury that plagued him the rest of his career. He sought relief through a variety of methods, including drugs, acupuncture, chiropractic therapy and finally surgery in 1974. He threw 29 innings at triple-A Louisville in 1968, striking out 20 and finishing with a 3.10 ERA. Despite the injury, the Red Sox protected him for that winter's expansion draft, hoping he would fulfill his potential.

1969 saw Brett open the season with the Red Sox, but he was sent down to the triple-A Louisville Colonels after three rocky starts, and was not called back up until the rosters expanded in September. The International League adopted the DH rule that year, so he could not show his prowess with the bat. He fell a triple short of the cycle in a September 12 game against the Yankees, while garnering his first big league victory. His pitching at Triple A was solid, with a 7-5 record, 81 strikeouts, and a 3.28 ERA in 129 innings. His major league statistics were lackluster: a 2-3 record, with 23 strikeouts, 22 walks, and a 5.26 ERA in 39⅓ innings. He returned to the Florida Instructional League that winter to work on his curve and changeup to complement his fastball

Ken Brett came from a family that saw four brothers play professional baseball. Injuries in the minor leagues curtailed the careers of John and Bobby Brett; George Brett is in the Hall of Fame.

In 1970, Brett spent the entire year on the Red Sox major league roster, and he spent more time in the Reserve. He started 14 games and also worked out of the bullpen, pitching 139⅓ innings in 41 games, compiling an 8-9 record with two saves, 155 strikeouts, 79 walks, and a 4.07 ERA.

He again played winter ball, this time in Puerto Rico for the San Juan Senators, skippered by Roberto Clemente, and was named to the Puerto Rico All-Star team.

Brett's winter ball success failed to carry over into the 1971 season. He found himself in manager Eddie Kasko's doghouse, appeared in only 29 games, starting two, going 0-3 with one save and a 5.34 ERA. He devoted another two weeks to Army Reserve duty. The Red Sox finally gave up on him, trading him to the Brewers in October as part of a 10-player deal that saw 1967 Cy Young winner Jim Lonborg, first baseman

George Scott, Billy Conigliaro, Joe Lahoud, and Don Pavletich go to the Milwaukee Brewers for speedster Tommy Harper, two seasoned pitchers, Lew Krausse and Marty Pattin, and minor leaguer Pat Skrable.

Ken pitched one season for the Brewers, mostly as a starter, finishing with a 7-12 record, 133 IP, 74 strikeouts, 49 walks, and an ERA of 4.53. He spent three weeks on the disabled list with lower back pain in July and August.

On October 31, 1972, Brett was traded to the Philadelphia Phillies along with fellow hurlers Jim Lonborg, Ken Sanders, and Earl Stephenson for Don Money, John Vukovich, and Billy Champion. The last place Phillies were looking to rebuild their pitching staff. Brett and Lonborg joined Steve Carlton in the Phillies rotation. "We had to improve our pitching staff," General Manager Paul Owens said, as Carlton's 27 victories were nearly 50% of the total number of Phils wins.

Brett's 1973 season with the Phillies was one of his best in the major leagues. He started the year in the bullpen, but soon replaced Lonborg in the rotation. Brett ended up with a 13-9 record and a 3.44 ERA in 211⅔ innings pitched, striking out 111 while walking 74. He also set the major league record for a pitcher by hitting home runs in four consecutive games. He later said that it should have been five except for a blown call that turned a home run into a double. He missed a couple of weeks in July after hurting his shoulder in a collision with St. Louis catcher Tim McCarver while being used as a pinch runner, a move manager Ozark later said he was "kicking myself" over. Brett also led the league in fielding by handling 52 chances without an error. He gave up home run No. 700 to Hank Aaron on July 21, 1973 in an 8-4 Phillies victory over the Braves.

Despite his solid season, the Phillies traded Brett to the Pittsburgh Pirates on October 18, 1973, getting slick-fielding second baseman Dave Cash in return. Said Pirates manager Danny Murtaugh, "Brett is a good [arm] who can step right into our starting rotation." Phillies pitcher Steve Carlton, though, said about the trade, "When you talk about Brett, you're talking about a pitcher going on 25 years old with a questionable arm... If Kenny's arm never bothered him I wouldn't have liked the deal. A lot of times he went out there and his arm wasn't 100 percent. ... Kenny has a lot of courage. He'll battle you. But a chronic elbow can be a factor as a pitcher gets a little older."

The 1974 Pirates were picked by many preseason prognosticators to win the National League East, with newly-acquired pitchers Brett and Jerry Reuss filling out a solid pitching staff that also included Dock Ellis and Jim Rooker. Brett went on to have another excellent season, finishing 13-9 with 10 complete games and three shutouts while starting 27 games. He struck out 96, walked 52, and had an ERA of 3.30. He also contributed two home runs (in consecutive games) and led all major league pitchers with 15 RBIs and a .310 batting average. (He had only 87 at-bats, but had at least 60 at-bats more than the pitchers with higher averages.)

On May 27, Brett set down the first 24 San Diego Padres to face him until Fred Kendall, a former California high school football and baseball opponent, lined a solid single to open the ninth. He ended up winning, 6-0. "I was thinking about a no-hitter after the fifth inning," Brett said. "You sit on the bench and think about what it means. You realize what you've got to do to get it." After Kendall's single, Brett broke into a half-hearted smile and shrugged his shoulders. "I just told myself 'Forget it, that's all you can do.' That's a shining achievement. But I didn't get it, and I can't do anything about it now." In the second game of two that day, he drove in the tying runs with a two-run pinch-hit triple in the bottom of the seventh, in a game the Pirates went on to win 8-7.

Brett was named to the All-Star team that year. He pitched two innings in front of the Pittsburgh crowd, giving up no runs and earning the win. Said Brett about the All-Star game, "I started getting nervous at 6:35, that's two hours before they threw the first pitch. The ovation at my introduction gave me goosebumps. It was one of the biggest thrills of my life." Later in the season he blamed that appearance for his elbow woes. "I got out of my normal routine because of the All-Star Game. Then when I got into the game I was all tensed up. Consequently, I think I overthrew the ball." He missed more than a month of action, between August 6 and September 10, as the Pirates clawed their way back into pennant contention.

Brett didn't pitch all that well upon returning to the starting rotation, giving up 18 earned runs in 22 ⅔ innings. The Bucs made it to the postseason, losing to the Los Angeles Dodgers, 3-1, in the NLCS. Brett appeared in only one game, giving up 2 earned runs in 2⅓ innings in relief of Game 4 starter Jerry Reuss. He underwent surgery to remove chips and a bone spur from his left elbow during the following offseason.

Brett signed back on with the Pirates for the 1975 season. His elbow continued to be a problem, as he re-injured it during a spring training game and began

the season on the disabled list. He appeared in only 23 games, 16 of them starts, going 9-5 in 118 innings pitched, with 47 strikeouts and a 3.36 ERA, while the Pirates repeated as the NL East division champions. The Bucs once again lost in the opening round of the postseason, falling to the Reds in three straight games. Brett appeared in two games, both in relief, giving up no runs while striking out one during his 2⅓ innings pitched.

Brett was traded to the New York Yankees on December 11, 1975, along with fellow starting pitcher Dock Ellis and rookie second baseman Willie Randolph, for pitcher Doc Medich. He did finally face his younger brother George. In their first meeting, a spring training game, George took Kemer long and deep with a booming 425-foot home run. Ken began the season in the Yankees' bullpen but was traded to the White Sox on May 18 after just two appearances. Also going to the White Sox was Rich Coggins, in exchange for outfielder Carlos May. Brett immediately joined the starting rotation in Chicago.

All this moving around was getting to Brett. "I became a pitcher instead of a thrower. And I still got traded three times. I'm a little bitter about that," he said in an interview after the White Sox trade. When asked about becoming a full time hitter, he answered, "I think about it all the time. If something were to happen to my arm I wouldn't mind going to the minors for a year and trying to make it as a hitter. I'm single and have no ties, and I'd do it just for the fun of playing just to see if I could do it." The trade also upset brother George, who said before the Royals faced the Yankees in the 1976 playoffs, "I have a killer's instinct against that team. I want to beat them bad every time I play them, not only for the team but for my brother, too."

Brett's 1976 season for the White Sox was solid, if unspectacular. Appearing in 27 games (26 starts), he finished the season with a 10-12 record in 200⅔ innings, with a 3.32 ERA and 91 strikeouts. His year in Chicago also included 16 complete games (a career high), one shutout, and one save, as well as 12 at-bats, with only one hit, though. The 12 at-bats are the most by any American League pitcher in a single season since the DH began in 1973, even including interleague play.

The season highlight came on May 26, when he mowed down the first 24 Angels he faced and took a no-hitter two outs into the ninth inning before giving up a controversial single to Jerry Remy. Remy's half-swing, half-bunt bouncer to third was misplayed by charging third baseman Jorge Orta, who let the ball get by him. It was ruled a hit by the official scorer, bringing down Brett's ire, who later said, "I think the call on me was brutal, I think it stunk, but I understand the guy who made it is short, so maybe he couldn't see out of the press box. But what the hell, we won." It took 11 innings to win, 1-0, Brett pitching 10 innings and getting credit for the victory, after giving up one more hit in the tenth.

Brett began 1977 locked in a contract battle with the White Sox, and the player representative struggled on the mound. He did start the very first regular season game ever played in Toronto, although he lasted fewer than four innings in the frigid (32 degree) snowy weather at Exhibition Stadium as the White Sox lost to the fledgling Blue Jays, 9-5. His left elbow continued to bother him, and he was forced to leave his third start of the year with elbow problems. "It's an ache, and it's more than slight," he said after the game, but he missed only one start.

On June 15, the trading deadline, the still unsigned Brett, sporting a 5.01 ERA and a 6-4 record, was traded once again, this time to the California Angels, for three players, pitchers Don Kirkwood and John Verhoeven, and minor league utility infielder John Flannery, plus cash (rumored to be as much as $400,000). "I have mixed emotions," said Brett after the trade. "I'm sort of in complete turmoil. My entire family is in LA and I have a ton of friends there. I wouldn't have been unhappy to stay in Chicago but I don't think they were going to sign me. If they could afford to lose anyone it was me [since they were going to lose him to free agency in the winter –eds.]. I can understand why they did it and I'm surprised it didn't come sooner."

Brett took a regular turn in the rotation for the struggling Angels, finishing the season with a combined 34 starts, a career high. His record for the Angels was only 7-10, but included five complete games. His strikeouts were down again, totaling only 80 for the year, while his ERA was a respectable 4.53. He was in the top 10 in all the wrong lists for the year, though—sixth in hits allowed, fourth in earned runs, seventh in home runs against, and seventh in walks per nine innings.

The 1978 season opened with Brett in the starting rotation as part of an optimistic Angels team. His first start was a five-hit shutout against the Minnesota Twins, but as the fifth starter he didn't get a regular turn in the rotation. He continued to alternate between starting and relieving for the entire 1978 season, appearing in 31 games, 10 starts. In 100 innings, he struck out 43 while walking 42, finishing with an ERA of 4.95.

Brett's position as a team leader was emphasized when he spoke for the Angels at the funeral for

Brett, a 19-year old with only two innings of prior major league experience, became the youngest pitcher in a World Series game in Game Four of the 1967 fall classic. Afterwards, a thrilled Brett said, "I wasn't half as nervous as I was when I pitched against Cleveland. When I got the call that game, my foot started twitching."

teammate Lyman Bostock, the gregarious outfielder who was killed by a shotgun blast during the season. "There's only one consolation: we're all better persons for having had him touch our lives," he concluded, struggling for his composure. He later participated in Bostock charity baseball games.

During the winter of 1978, Brett took instruction in throwing the screwball from the great Warren Spahn. He began spring training in 1979 rumored to be either traded or released. His balky back, which limited his spring playing time, didn't help, and he was waived in April by the Angels, who ate Brett's guaranteed $165,000 contract. Later that month, he signed with the Minnesota Twins. He appeared in only nine games with the Twins, all in relief, throwing 12⅔ innings, while striking out only three and walking six, and was released on June 4.

Brett was back in the Los Angeles area when he signed on with the Dodgers on June 11, his ninth major league team. "I'm happy to be here and I'm going to go out and pitch as well as I can. This is not the end of the world for me," Brett said of his precarious roster spot as a middle reliever. He pitched out of the bullpen for the Dodgers, going 4-3 in 30 games with a 3.45 ERA, throwing in 47 innings with 13 strikeouts, 12 walks, and two saves.

Brett began 1980 spring training as part of the Dodgers bullpen plan, but he hurt his arm in his first spring outing and was released before pitching again. "I tried to throw too hard. My elbow locked so badly I couldn't move it," Brett said later. "I'm tired of all the traveling," he added. "I'm going home to California to rest. I'll have an operation on my arm and then go back to college to study business."

He was out of major league baseball for most of the summer, playing for the semi-pro Orange County A's, until he signed to play with brother George's Kansas City Royals on August 11. He began at Triple-A Omaha, but joined the Royals on August 29 and pitched in eight games. He didn't allow a run in 13⅓ innings pitched, striking out four, walking five, and saving one game.

The brothers Brett enjoyed their time together in Kansas City. George by now was a big star, as 1980 was his run at batting .400 (he ended up at .390), but Ken wasn't above needling his younger brother, saying, "If it hadn't been for the DH rule, I'd have been the first in the family to hit .400." George was particularly candid in discussing how much an influence his brother Ken had on his playing future, saying "I decided to make baseball my goal when we went to see Ken pitch in the '67 World Series between Boston and St. Louis. I was 14 and Ken 19. It was a real thrill. He could really bring it then. And he'd always come home with a new car, a new girl and a new roll of bills. I said to myself, 'That's for me.'"

Ken helped George with the media pressure during the youngest Brett's drive to .400, but he didn't want it overstated. "People think I'm here to have a mature influence on George," said Ken, unused to being a good influence. "George doesn't need me. He's been grown up for a long time. If anything, I just hope I'm not a hindrance to him."

The 1980 Royals went on to sweep the Yankees in the ALCS, 3-0, but lost to the Phillies in the World Series, 4-2. Ken was on the roster for both the Championship Series and the World Series, but didn't appear in a game during the postseason.

Ken Brett finished his major league career with the Royals in 1981, appearing in 22 games as a lefty specialist. He pitched 32⅓ innings, with a 4.18 ERA but an unimpressive 14-7 walks-to-strikeouts ratio. He won one game, lost one game and had two saves. He was waived by the Royals in November of 1981, ending his pitching career. He did try to hook back on with the Pirates the following spring, but was released on March 22.

Ken pursued varied career paths after baseball, including co-owning a minor league baseball team (Spokane Indians) and a minor league hockey team (Spokane Chiefs), serving as television color commentator for the Seattle Mariners and the California Angels, and appearing in various beer commercials. One commercial took advantage of his much-traveled career. In it, he stood at a bar, confused as to what city he was currently in, finally guessing "Utica." Brett later visited Utica and was given the keys to the city, where he remarked it was as close as he would ever get to Cooperstown. This appearance led to a year as the manager for the New York-Penn League Utica Blue Sox.

Ken Brett married Teresa Smogyi, who worked in movie productions, in 1985. He was also involved in restaurants with his brothers. He appeared in the 1994 movie The Scout as himself.

Ken Brett died on November 19, 2003 at the age of 55 of brain cancer, the same tragic disease that took his father's life.

Galen Cisco

by Les Masterson

	G	ERA	W	L	SV	GS	GF	CG	SHO	IP	H	R	ER	BB	SO	HR	BFP
1967 RED SOX	11	3.63	0	1	1	0	6	0	0	22.1	21	10	9	8	8	4	90

Though Galen Cisco pitched in nearly 200 games over his seven-year major league career, his athletic accomplishments were much more substantial than that, appearing in the Rose Bowl as a young man, and still helping major league pitchers four decades later.

Galen Bernard Cisco was born on March 7, 1936, to Beryl and Esther Cisco in St. Marys, Ohio, a small town near the Indiana border, halfway between Dayton and Fort Wayne. The Ciscos owned their own farm, and Galen and his three brothers and one sister spent hours working in the family business. "We kind of had a really great family life," Cisco recalled. "We were brought up on the farm. Everyone had their chore and we all did the things that we needed to do growing up on the farm."

When young Galen wasn't taking care of livestock, he squeezed in time playing sports, namely football and baseball. Cisco attended Memorial High School in St. Marys, where he played both sports for the Roughriders. His football coach was Jack Bickel, who had been a running back at Miami (Ohio) University for Woody Hayes. Cisco recalled that many of the plays in the Memorial playbook were the same ones Hayes later ran at Ohio State.

Like most young Buckeyes, Cisco dreamed of playing for Ohio State University. After graduating from high school in 1954, he enrolled at Ohio State with a major in education. Freshmen were not allowed to play on varsity teams in that era, so the pride of St. Marys spent a year practicing with the varsity. Once Cisco got the chance to play, he excelled in both sports. He sported a 12-2 collegiate pitching record and was named a third team All-American in 1956. But he gained greater acclaim in college, as a running back and linebacker.

In his senior year the Buckeyes went to the Rose Bowl on New Year's Day 1958. Before a big game, many athletes focus strictly on the showdown, but that wasn't true for young Galen Cisco. Preparing for the biggest (and final) gridiron game of his college career, he made a life-changing decision. Hayes told his players that anyone who was married could bring their wives free to Pasadena to attend the Rose Bowl game. Cisco was engaged to his longtime girlfriend, Martha. With this Rose Bowl-colored carrot dangling over their heads, Galen and Martha decided there was no reason to wait until after the football season to tie the knot.

"She married me and got a free trip to the Rose Bowl," recalled Cisco.

The 8-1 Buckeyes were a 21-point favorite over 7-3 Oregon in the Pasadena classic, Cisco recounted, but the Ohio State offense just couldn't get started that day. In fact, Oregon gained more yards and collected more first downs than the favorites. Ohio State still prevailed, 10-7, thanks to a 34-yard field goal by Don Sutherin in the fourth quarter.

While some players suffered under Hayes' rough nature, Cisco enjoyed playing for him. "He was a very, very fundamentally-minded coach. He didn't get too fancy. He didn't pass a lot. He seemed to think that if you take a few plays and play them better than anyone else, you're going to be successful," said Cisco. "He was a no-nonsense guy. He probably was one of the most prepared people I have ever been around."

Cisco's collegiate career was coming to an end in 1958, but he didn't need any help choosing which sport to pursue. He recalls that a few professional football teams called Hayes about the two-way star, but were told the running back/linebacker was interested in throwing baseballs—not throwing tackles. "The closer I got to the latter years in college, I thought baseball would have more longevity than football. I had an opportunity to sign, so I did," said Cisco.

Signed in 1958 by Red Sox scout Denny Galehouse, Cisco wasted no time hurling the horsehide in the minors. He pitched in 32 games for Raleigh of the Class-B Carolina League and Corning of the Class-D New York-Pennsylvania League that summer, with a composite record of 6-12.

Since he still was short two quarters of receiving his bachelor's degree, he spent the 1958-59 offseason back in Columbus to finish his schooling, and Hayes hired him as the backfield coach for the freshman football team. He stayed in that position for four off-seasons, coaching future NFL stars Paul Warfield and Matt Snell, among other players.

While teaching young running backs how to find holes each autumn, Cisco spent his springs and summers

becoming a more accomplished pitcher. Along with brief 1959 stops in Raleigh and Allentown (Eastern), he won 15 games with a Midwest League-leading 2.23 ERA for Waterloo. The next year he finished 3-7, but with a fine 2.93 ERA, for Minneapolis in the American Association in 1960, and joined the Seattle Rainiers of the Pacific Coast League in 1961.

Along with teammates Dick Radatz and Don Schwall, Cisco pitched for manager Johnny Pesky in Seattle. In his nine games with the Rainiers that year, Cisco finished 6-1, compiled a 1.54 ERA and completed five of his starts. Cisco was clearly ready for the call, and he quickly followed his teammate Schwall to Boston.

The Red Sox team Cisco joined had suffered through a decade of mediocrity, and in 1961 Ted Williams no longer patrolled left field for the Olde Towne Team. If fans hadn't attended games at the nearly 50-year-old park with the great Williams in the lineup, they surely stayed away from a team made up of unproven players like Carl Yastrzemski. "The product we put on the field was not that great," said Cisco. "It was a tough place to play. The writers there were tough."

Cisco's first game was a Fenway Park start on June 11, and he allowed five hits and five runs in just 2⅓ innings against the Twins. Six days later he won a start against the Senators, but by mid-July he was out of the rotation. Cisco struggled with the second-division team (2-4, 6.71), but Red Sox management was excited about the future of their rotation with Schwall, Tracy Stallard, Bill Monbouquette, and Cisco. His former manager, Pesky, predicted Cisco was "another Schwall," who had won the Rookie of the Year in 1961.

Schwall himself said that the Galen Cisco who pitched in Boston was not the same guy who was his teammate in the minors. "When he came up here, he got off to a bad start. Then he began to press. He wasn't pitching normally and as a result he didn't look like the pitcher he was when I was with him in Minneapolis and Seattle," Schwall told *The Sporting News* after the 1961 season.

But Cisco showed great improvement in spring training before the 1962 season. In 28 innings, he allowed only three earned runs for an 0.86 ERA, while scattering 23 hits. Shortly before Opening Day, Red Sox manager Pinky Higgins told the press, "Nobody can believe Cisco is the same guy who was with us for the last half of 1961."

Alas, his 1962 season with the Red Sox mirrored his struggles of the previous year. On July 27, Higgins even left Cisco on the mound to allow 16 hits and 13 runs against the Senators, finally taking him out of the game in the sixth inning. Two relief appearances later, the Red Sox placed Cisco on waivers, and he was claimed by the New York Mets.

The right-handed pitcher went from a mediocre team to one of the worst in the history of baseball. "We had guys who couldn't hit the ball and didn't catch it," Cisco recalled. Cisco now played for Casey Stengel, a learning experience for the young pitcher. After splitting two decisions in September 1962, Cisco was 7-15, 4.34, in 51 games in 1963.

While in New York, "Ohio State" (Stengel's name for Cisco) started and relieved. Despite the team's futility, he was able to discuss the art of pitching with teammates Roger Craig, Al Jackson, Don Rowe, Bob Miller, and Larry Bearnarth, all of whom later became pitching coaches in the major leagues. "I think everybody used to talk more [then] about the game than they did later. I'm talking about in the 1990s on. I think they talked about the game much more then," said Cisco.

While the team did not perform well, Cisco was likely the best pitcher on the 1964 Mets' staff. Pitching in the new Shea Stadium, the right-handed hurler finished with a 3.62 ERA, while going 6-19 for the still-hapless team. In that season, Cisco's pitching forced a future Hall of Famer to try a new pitch.

Cisco came in to the 14th inning of the second game of a doubleheader against the San Francisco and proceeded to shut down the Giants. His mound opponent late in the game was Gaylord Perry, who was struggling to stay in the major leagues, but who would ultimately win 314 games and a plaque in Cooperstown. Perry was called into the game in the 13th inning, and Perry later acknowledged throwing his first spitball in this game. Cisco and Perry traded scoreless innings until Jimmy Davenport tripled in the winning run for the Giants in the 23rd inning.

Undeterred, Cisco came back in his next start and four-hit the world champion Los Angeles Dodgers, 8-0, in front of 55,000 fans at Shea. Cisco's performances made an impression on his manager. During the 1964 season, Stengel acknowledged that the Mets had debated whether to even keep Cisco on its roster in the spring. "Then he got a little bit better and a little bit better and a little bit better. Now he's about as good as anyone we have," Stengel told *The Sporting News*.

Unfortunately, he followed this fine season by limping to a 4-8 record and a 4.49 ERA in 1965. After the season, Cisco was sent to the minors, finishing his four-year Mets career with an 18-43 record and 4.04 ERA.

After starting the 1966 season with the Mets Triple-A Jacksonville affiliate, in June he was sold back to the

A bit player on the team, Cisco was primarily used in mop-up work.

Red Sox, and he finished the season with their Toronto club. Dick Williams, manager of the Red Sox's Toronto Maple Leafs team in the International League, knew Cisco was only about 60 days of service time away from his pension, and wanted to help the soft-spoken Ohioan. For the season, Cisco finished 11-6 in 157 innings in his two International League stops.

Williams, who was named skipper of the 1967 Red Sox, told Cisco he would try to get him his pension. "He told me if he had a chance he would give me a look or maybe bring me up even for two years the last 30 days when teams could expand the club," Cisco recalled. If he'd been hurting the team, Williams would have sent him down, but Williams stuck to his word in 1967 and gave him a shot. Cisco started the year with the Red Sox as a reliever. Looking back 40 years later, Cisco said the team didn't seem special at the start.

"I think we thought we had a pretty good club. What it boiled down to was what kind of pitching staff you had," said Cisco. "I don't think anybody expected us to do anything like [the 1967 Red Sox eventually] did." Cisco was used mostly in mop-up work. He pitched in 11 games and threw 22⅓ innings for the Impossible Dream team. But shortly after the All-Star break, the Red Sox saw an opportunity to improve their bench and picked up Norm Siebern, and sent Cisco to the minors to free up the roster spot.

A number of players chafed under the pressure of playing for Dick Williams, but not Cisco. "I learned a lot of baseball as a player from Dick," he says. "He was a no-nonsense guy. You didn't have to wonder what he was thinking about." In this regard, Cisco added, Williams was much like Woody Hayes. "He was honest with me always. I got along with him just fine."

For the remainder of the 1967 season, Cisco pitched for Pittsfield (0.82 ERA in 11 innings) and Toronto (2.08 ERA in 65 innings). Cisco enjoyed a renaissance in 1968 for the Red Sox new International League affiliate in Lousiville. He led the league with a 2.21 ERA while winning 11 games for the Colonels, at one point throwing 22 consecutive scoreless innings.

After the season, Cisco was sold to the expansion Kansas City Royals, who would begin play the following spring. Unlike the Mets in 1962, though, the Royals were more mediocre than atrocious. "The Royals I think had a little bit better draft. The way the draft was set up I think the Royals had a little bit better advantage than the Mets," Cisco said, comparing the two expansion clubs.

Despite struggling with Omaha in the early season (5.00 ERA in 10 games), Kansas City recalled Cisco in June and the Buckeye finished the season in the Royals' bullpen. Cisco finished with a 3.63 ERA in what would be the last 22⅓ innings of his major league career. He was 33 years old.

The following year Omaha hired Cisco as a player-coach. The plan was to work as the pitching coach, but to take to the mound if there were injuries or the team was in dire need of an arm. He threw 76 innings and finished his final year as a player with a 2.49 ERA. Cisco also won his final six decisions, which was the longest streak in his pro career.

Just 35 years old, Cisco became the pitching coach for Bob Lemon in Kansas City in 1971. During his tenure with the Royals, he worked with such top-notch starters as Dennis Leonard, Steve Busby, and Paul Splittorff. All three credited Cisco for their successes. "I had been dropping too much on my slider and Galen got on me about throwing more over the top," Busby told *The Sporting News* in 1973, after the publication named him the American League Rookie Pitcher of the Year. "I guess I was doing the same thing with my fastball. I know I felt better and threw better when I went back to the old way." The following year he would win 20 games.

Mound ace Leonard told *The Sporting News* in 1976, "When I struggled last season, Galen worked with me. He told me I was dropping down too much and everything I was throwing was flattening out. He worked with me for hours and hours."

When Splittorff contemplated quitting in the minors, Cisco talked him out of it. "I told him 'you're left-handed and your time will come when you're going to get a shot at the big leagues. You have spent three full years playing this game and you should give it one or two more years before retiring,'" Splittorff won 166 games over 15 seasons in the majors.

Cisco was the pitching coach for the Royals' division championship teams in 1976-1978 before being let go when Whitey Herzog was fired after the 1979 season. The experienced pitching coach quickly found work as his old friend Dick Williams hired him to lead the pitchers in Montreal.

A few years later Cisco worked with Williams in San Diego. In 1987, the Toronto Blue Jays hired Cisco as their pitching coach, and within four years, his staff included Jimmy Key, Dave Stieb, Todd Stottlemyre, and David Wells. Wells, not known for his love of management, appreciated Cisco's assistance. "Galen Cisco helped me a lot. He would help me correct little things if he saw me doing something wrong, and we would talk pitching," Wells said in 1988.

Cisco led the Jays' pitchers during their world

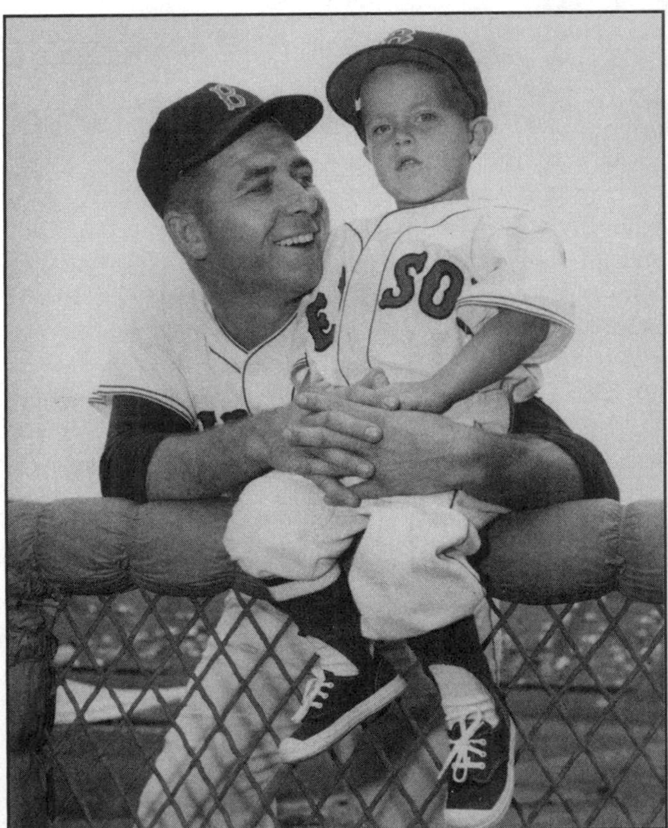

Cisco and kid.

championship years of 1992-1993, the first team to win back-to-back World Series in 15 years. In addition to Key, Stieb, Stottlemyre, and Wells, pitchers who threw for him during those two years included Jack Morris, David Cone, Dave Stewart, Tom Henke, Duane Ward, and Mike Timlin. "I have to give [Pat] Gillick a lot of credit, and the scouting department," Cisco says of the organization's two wins. "After the first [championship], most teams would have stayed pretty much pat, but they brought in two or three key players... Without those players, I wonder if we would have won it back to back."

Toronto did not re-sign Cisco after the 1995 season, but the year wasn't all bad for the Ohio State graduate. He was inducted into OSU's Varsity Hall of Fame.

Two years later, Cisco accepted his final major league job—pitching coach of the Philadelphia Phillies—under new manager Terry Francona, who would lead the Red Sox to its first World Series win in 86 years in 2004. The two friends still stay in contact via email, he said. After being let go by the Phillies, Cisco worked in the Blue Jays' minor league system before retiring after 45 years in pro baseball.

Looking back on his successful career as a pitching coach, Cisco says he doesn't have one favorite hurler. "I think that two starters had as good stuff as anybody: one was Dave Stieb and one was Steve Rogers." The smartest pitcher? Busby. "He studied [hitters'] weaknesses and was a student of pitching. If this guy stayed healthy, he would have been something," Cisco said of his former pupil, whose career was cut short by injuries.

Cisco points to Willie Blair as a pitcher of borderline talent stuck in Toronto's Triple-A farm club, who worked hard on his game with Cisco. Blair won 60 games in the major leagues, including 16 for Detroit in 1997. "I don't know if I had a lot to do with it or not, but he went on and had some pretty good years," said Cisco modestly.

In 2006 he was enjoying retirement in Celina, Ohio, only a few miles from his hometown of St. Marys. Though he doesn't live in town any longer, St. Marys still gives the Galen Cisco Award to the Little League MVP. The award has been given since 1965 and was won by Galen's nephew Ty in 1980. Though Galen is out of the game now, the Cisco baseball legacy continues. Cisco's grandson, Mike Cisco, was a pitcher at South Carolina in 2006, and Grandpa Cisco would travel to watch Mike pitch for the Gamecocks. Galen and Martha Cisco have been together 49 years and enjoy spending time with their two boys, Galen Jr. and Jeff (both of whom played minor league ball), and their families.

After two decades, and two championships as a coach, Cisco's memories of his own playing career have faded. Speaking of his time with the 1967 Red Sox, he says, "I wish I could remember more, but there's been a lot of water over the dam since then."

Hank Fischer

by Mike Richard

	G	ERA	W	L	SV	GS	GF	CG	SHO	IP	H	R	ER	BB	SO	HR	BFP
1967 RED SOX	9	2.36	1	2	1	2	2	1	0	26.2	24	15	7	8	18	3	114

When the Red Sox arrived at their spring training camp at Chain-O-Lakes Park in Winter Haven, Florida, in 1967, manager Dick Williams seemed to have a pretty good idea who would comprise his pitching staff. However, in its preseason outlook, *Sports Illustrated* was not impressed with the group, which the magazine mocked as a "prospect that won't cause too many hitters around the league to lose sleep." One of those hurlers was Hank Fischer.

Henry William Fischer was born in Yonkers, New York, on January 11, 1940, and from his early youth seemed destined for greatness—but it was in basketball, not baseball, that he first drew attention. He led the St. Paul's Midget League basketball team through three undefeated seasons and poured in a record 53 points during a playoff game. He earned the nickname "Bulldog" for his aggressive demeanor on the basketball court, and at Roosevelt High School, he led the city in scoring during his senior year in 1957.

That same year, playing baseball for coach Joe Seidell, Fischer led the team to the city crown, pitching three no-hitters en route to the title. He was the first recipient of the Louis J. Flowers Memorial Award, still given annually to Yonkers' outstanding high school athlete. In his late teens, he also pitched for an American Legion baseball team that advanced to the national finals in 1957. Fischer also pitched two years for the Connie Mack Eastern Championship team, which put together an unbeaten string of 35 games.

After graduation, Fischer enrolled at Seton Hall University, where the 6-foot 190-pound freshman led the frosh basketball team with an 18-point-per-game average. His college basketball coach, John "Honey" Russell, was also a scout for the Milwaukee Braves, and recommended that the club sign his hoop hotshot. Before the 1959 baseball season, Fischer signed with the Braves. That year, he pitched for two Braves farm teams, Eau Claire of the Class C Northern League and Cedar Rapids of the Class B Three-I League. In 1960, with Cedar Rapids, he led the Three-I League in strikeouts (217) and earned run average (2.01).

Fischer appeared to be on the fast track, moving up to Triple-A Louisville in 1961, where he had 163 strikeouts and pitched in the American Association All-Star Game. The following year, Fischer split his time between Louisville and the parent Milwaukee club, making his debut with Milwaukee on April 16, 1962, pitching a scoreless inning against Cincinnati in Crossley Field. Although Fischer was a starting pitcher in the minor leagues, he relieved in all 29 of his appearances for Milwaukee in 1962, and posted a record of 2-3, and a 5.30 ERA, in 37⅓ innings. The next season, six of his 31 games were starts, and he improved to 4-3 and 4.96 in 74⅓ innings.

The Braves of this era were attempting to transition from their great teams of the late 1950s—a pitching staff led by Warren Spahn, Lew Burdette and Bob Buhl—to a more youthful mid-1960s group. The Braves had thought of Fischer as a reliever until manager Bobby Bragan gave him a few starts in 1963. "I like starting much better," said Fischer. "You live differently when you start. You know what day you're going to pitch and you can gauge your pitching accordingly. You clutch up a little before you start and that gets you in the right frame of mind for competition. You can't do that in relief." After the 1963 season the club traded starters Bob Shaw and Bob Hendley to the Giants, opening a spot in the rotation for Fischer, who started 24 games that season.

Fischer began the 1964 season by winning his first two starts, despite serving up two home runs in ⅔ of an inning during his debut. Later, he pitched a two-hit, 1-0 masterpiece on May 3 against the Phillies, driving in the only run himself. Fischer went on to complete the best season of his career, finishing 11-10 with a 4.01 ERA. He had five shutouts among his 11 victories, finishing second in the league to Sandy Koufax, who threw seven. At the end of July he was 9-5, 2.90, before struggling the last two months. The low point was in early August when he was knocked out of the box in the first inning against the Reds on August 6, then came back the very next night to get knocked out in the first again, this time by the Dodgers. But this bad stretch did not ruin his breakout season.

"I've got confidence now," Fischer reported. "I go out there knowing that even when I get bombed, I'll be starting again in five days. Now I am a pitcher instead of a thrower. I've started to try to control the ball, rather than try to strike everyone out. Now I can throw the slider and curve and I can get them over the plate."

In 1965—the final year for the Braves in Milwaukee—

Fischer was in and out of the rotation all year, and recorded an 8-9 record and a 3.89 ERA. He moved with the team when it headed to Atlanta in 1966, where he was 2-3, 3.91 in the early going. On June 15 of that year, he was traded to Cincinnati for fellow right hander Joey Jay. He spent exactly two months with the Reds, appearing in 11 games with a 0-6 record before being traded to the Red Sox on August 15 for cash and two players to be named later.

He pitched well for the Red Sox at the end of the season, finishing 2-3, 2.90, including a complete game 4-1 victory over the Athletics on August 25 at Fenway Park. After his victory, Fischer allowed, "I think I have proved I can do something for this club."

In the spring of 1967, Fischer reported to the Red Sox and new manager Dick Williams ready to fight to make the roster. His strong 1966 finish likely gave him an edge, though his manager was in Toronto at the time. In his first Grapefruit League outing, on March 17 against the Reds, Fischer threw three perfect innings. Four days later, he came on in relief and gave up five runs on six hits over two innings in a 10-5 loss to Philadelphia.

Fischer continued to seesaw his way through the spring. He went six innings against Atlanta, allowing eight hits and four runs while striking out four in a 6-1 loss. Finally, on March 30, in his best outing of the exhibition season, he relieved Lee Stange, pitched four shutout innings, and almost assuredly won a spot on the roster. He allowed just one hit and one walk and struck out two as the Red Sox beat the Orioles, 1-0.

Fischer's ERA was just 2.36 but arm troubles limited his ability to contribute in 1967.

In the end, Fischer made the team but was considered the last man in the bullpen. A few highlights from his season do stand out. On April 13 Fischer relieved starter Darrell Brandon in the sixth and did not allow a runner past second in his first three innings. In the ninth, the Red Sox committed three errors (and a total of five for the game), allowing five unearned runs and handing Fischer the loss. Three days later Fischer pitched shutout ball in the 16th and 17th innings against the Yankees, allowing one hit and striking out two. The Yankees won the game in the bottom of the 18th when Joe Pepitone's two-out single ended the five-hour, five-minute marathon.

Fischer's best effort of the season was on April 25, a complete-game 9-3 victory over the Senators at D.C. Stadium, to even his record at 1-1. He threw a five-hitter, walked three and had five strikeouts, aided by home runs by Reggie Smith, Mike Andrews, and Tony Conigliaro. However, Fischer earned the wrath of manager Dick Williams for his failure to knock down Senator reliever Bob Humphreys, who had hit Rico Petrocelli with a pitch after Conigliaro's home run.

Fischer's only other start of the season was on May 2, when he pitched five innings, allowing all three California runs in a 3-2 loss. He made three more relief appearances before going on the disabled list with a sore pitching arm. On August 8 Fischer was reactivated from the disabled list, and he wound up pitching in both ends of a doubleheader split in Kansas City, pitching three scoreless innings.

Although Fischer had come off the disabled list, assistant general manager Haywood Sullivan said he was not throwing hard and was still having arm troubles. A week later, Fischer was sent to the team's Toronto farm club, where he finished the 1967 season. For the Red Sox, he finished 1-2 with a strong 2.36 ERA for the season, in a year when the outcome of every game was crucial to winning the pennant. At the end of the season the Red Sox released him, ending his career.

The following season he was on the Louisville roster, but in early May chose retirement rather than another trip to the disabled list. Over his major league career, Fischer pitched in 168 games with the Milwaukee Braves, Atlanta Braves, Cincinnati Reds, and Boston Red Sox. He had a total of 546 ⅔ innings pitched and a career strikeout total of 369.

Only 28 at the time of his forced retirement, Fischer and his family relocated to West Palm Beach, Florida, where he worked in the restaurant business. While his current whereabouts are unknown, he was last known to be living in Hiawassee, Georgia.

Bill Landis

by Bill Nowlin

	G	ERA	W	L	SV	GS	GF	CG	SHO	IP	H	R	ER	BB	SO	HR	BFP
1967 RED SOX	18	5.26	1	0	0	1	5	0	0	25.2	24	16	15	11	23	6	110

To many, there can be no greater honor than to serve one's country, but occasionally the call to duty comes at an inopportune time. Bill Landis expresses no regrets, but history should nonetheless note that he played the full 1967 season for the 1967 Boston Red Sox—perhaps the most beloved of all Red Sox teams—yet was called into the Army just days before the end of the regular season, departing the team when they had just four games to play.

Landis was a relief specialist who won just a single game in 1967—in a season where one win made all the difference. Yet he had to watch the World Series from Fort Polk, Louisiana—and then was only allowed to watch because the commanding officer of his unit was from Boston.

William Henry Landis was born October 8, 1942 in Hanford, a largely agricultural community of some 10,500 in California's Central Valley. One of the largest flour mills in the valley was located in Hanford, and fruit processing and shipping were major industries in Hanford as well. Bill's parents were Robert and Betty Landis, Robert handling employment matters for farms in the area for the California Agriculture Department while Betty collected taxes in the Kings County Treasurer's Office. Bill also had a brother, Rick, some six years younger.

Bill's first memory of baseball is of playing catch with his grandfather Fred Donahoo. "He was the one baseball fan in the family," Bill recalls. As a youngster, Bill played sandlot ball, first getting involved in organized baseball with Little League at the age of 11. He did pitch some as a youth, but mostly played first base. He batted left and threw left.

The first professional games he saw were in Visalia, about 20 miles east of Hanford, where the Visalia Oaks played in the California League. When the New York Giants relocated to San Francisco in 1958, Bill followed them quite often on radio. The first major league ballgame he ever saw, though, was in Philadelphia. He was a freshman in high school at the time, and had traveled to Pennsylvania for the 1957 Boy Scouts' National Jamboree in Valley Forge. He saw the Phillies host the Milwaukee Braves.

Bill played for Hanford High School, pitching some, but also playing first base and the outfield. "We had an exceptionally talented high school team," he explains. "We had two other pitchers that signed with significant bonuses off our team. Chuck Nieson with the Twins was up for a very short time. The other one was Randy Davis, who signed with the Phillies. Eventually, I think there were six guys off that team who signed. I signed out of college, Coalinga. I signed after my freshman year." Coalinga was a junior college located about 60 miles from Hanford; the school is now known as West Hills Community College.

California offered the chance to play more baseball than colder climes, and Hanford High played a 46-game schedule. Landis later told the *Boston Globe*'s Roger Birtwell, "My three years there, we won the Central Yosemite Valley Championship all three years." Bill's role at the time was exclusively as an outfielder. In college, he became a pitcher. "They didn't have any pitchers. The coach thought I could throw pretty hard. So he made me a pitcher." Landis later went back and got his degree, both at Coalinga and at College of the Sequoias in Visalia. While at Coalinga, Bill made California's All-America Junior College All-Star team as a pitcher on the first team—and as an outfielder on the second team.

The scout who signed Landis was former Red Sox player Al "Zeke" Zarilla, and he was able to offer a $35,000 bonus for signing with the Kansas City A's. Zarilla's interest wasn't surprising; *The Sporting News* reports that Landis had struck out 151 batters in just 80 innings with Coalinga. As it happened, Visalia was a Kansas City farm team so Bill was able to play ball close to home in the same city he'd first seen pro ball, appearing in 21 games pitching for the Visalia Athletics in 1961. "I think they wanted a local boy to play close to home, frankly for the tickets," he says.

After signing, he made the transition to pitching full time. His debut was far from promising. On June 14, he gave up eight runs on six hits, a hit batter, and two wild pitches. By season's end, the left-handed Landis had thrown six complete games and 121 total innings, but wound up with a disappointing 4-11 record and a 6.47 ERA. He walked 128 batters that season, but it was teammate José Santiago who led the league.

The A's brought him to their West Palm Beach big

In the right place at the right time, Bill's one decision in 1967 was a win, but he had to watch the World Series while serving in the Army.

league camp for spring training in 1962, then assigned him to Lewiston, Idaho, in the Class-B Northwest League where he improved his ERA to 5.76, with 152 strikeouts. He led the league in walks, though, with 151, and he lost his first eight decisions. His 4-15 record gave him the league lead in losses. The A's moved to Bradenton for spring training in 1963, and Landis performed well, earning a promotion to Binghamton in the Eastern League. He posted a 3.67 ERA with a 9-11 record, and struck out 147 while bringing his bases on balls down to 76, despite a heavy workload of 184 innings. At the very end of the year, Bill was called up to the majors and got his first taste of the Show. He'd been rated one of the Eastern League's most improved pitchers and had walked three or fewer batters per game in his last 17 games.

He worked out with the team for a week or so; the first trip he went on with the A's brought him to Boston. Landis got in just one game, a mid-game relief appearance for manager Eddie Lopat against Cleveland on September 28, 1963. Landis threw 12/3 innings, walking one but striking out three and yielding neither a hit nor a run. It would nonetheless be more than three years before he returned to the majors.

In 1964, the A's sent him to Dallas, which, despite its location, was part of the Pacific Coast League at the time. He is pretty frank about his miserable season: "I had a terrible year at Dallas. I had a tremendous control problem." The record shows a 4-17 mark, with a 5.71 ERA and more walks than strikeouts (108 to 101). He always relied on his fastball, but in 1964 he had a hard time locating it. The A's stuck with him, though, and in 1965, working for Birmingham in the Southern League, Bill bounced back with a 4.02 ERA and his first winning record in pro ball (8-5), with seven complete games.

In 1966, Landis, still in the Kansas City system, pitched for the Vancouver Mounties in the PCL, and posted a record of 11-10, with a 3.40 ERA. The Boston Red Sox must have seen something, because they claimed Bill Landis in the Rule 5 draft after the 1966 season and invited him to Winter Haven. Bill was playing winter ball for Licey in the Dominican Republic when he received a letter from Red Sox general manager Dick O'Connell informing him of the transaction. He'd been the fourth pick overall in the first round. Landis was soon traded from Licey to the Estrellas Orientales in Dominican League play. A few weeks later, he shut out Licey on two hits. Landis had pitched briefly for Haywood Sullivan at Vancouver, and Red Sox scout Glenn Wright highly recommended him.

It might have seemed like a step down; Boston had played even worse than the A's in 1966. But at least Landis had a better shot to play, since Rule V draftees must be kept on the major league roster for a year or returned to the club from which they were acquired. The Red Sox had tried to sign Landis when he was an amateur. Scout Charlie Wallgren had even given Landis his choice—he could sign either as a pitcher or as an outfielder. Despite the flexibility, not offered by any other scout, Landis signed with Kansas City because he felt that the organization offered him a better opportunity to advance, given its evident need for good pitchers.

Landis pitched well in spring training, and the Red Sox chose to keep him on the roster. Bill was with the team for the entire season, until military service called at the very end, appearing in 21 scattered games. His first appearance came at Yankee Stadium on April 16, a Sunday game that ran 18 innings and ended in a 7-6 Yankees win. Jim Lonborg had started for Boston, but was taken out for a pinch-hitter in the top of the sixth. Landis took over, and showed some control problems, walking the first two batters, then allowing Ruben Amaro to bunt safely to load the bases. He struck out pinch-hitter Bill Robinson, but when he walked Tom Tresh to force in a run, Dick Williams had seen enough and called on Don McMahon. "I thought Dick was a *very* good manager," he offers. "He was hard-nosed. My first game, I walked some guys and I don't think I pitched for three weeks after that. He didn't play favorites. He actually turned that organization into a winning organization—not by himself—I think that had a lot to do with Dick O'Connell, too, the general manager—but he certainly was the manager who came in and it's been a winning organization since he was there."

Hard-nosed wasn't the half of it. Williams, in his 1990 autobiography, pulled no punches. His take on the game: "Bill Landis was pitching for us like he had no brain—meaning he was walking people. I guess he'd forgotten that the first step to building a winning baseball team is taken when pitchers stop walking people. Just throw the fucking ball over the plate. How hard is that? After Landis had walked three batters, I strolled to the mound, carefully, because he had shit all over himself, and I didn't want to step in it. I told him that if he didn't straighten up, his next pitches would be from the back of my doghouse. No sooner did I return to the dugout than he walked another guy. Needless to say, I didn't pitch him for another 28 days."

Williams misremembered, in that Landis walked three batters total, not four. And it wasn't 28 days, but it was nearly three weeks before Landis got another chance. When he did, he acquitted himself well,

retiring the Twins in order in the eighth inning of the May 6 game.

Landis was used from time to time, save for a two-week stint with the Army Reserve in late June. He completed his season with a 1-0 record, the one win coming at Fenway Park on July 26 against the California Angels. Bill pitched the top of the seventh, taking over for Darrell Brandon and allowing just one hit and no runs. The Angels were leading, 4-1, but Boston scored six runs in the bottom of the seventh and took a lead that held up. Three Red Sox pitchers closed out the game, but Landis got the win. He says, "When you pitch relief, that's your job. You hope your team does something, or you stop the other team."

Used three times as a pinch-runner (twice for Dalton Jones), Landis' stats show that he scored one run in the major leagues. It came on July 5, 1967, when he ran for Jerry Adair in the top of the ninth in a game at Anaheim Stadium. Landis was on first, but was able to trot around the bases and score the tying run when George Thomas homered, giving the Red Sox a 3-2 lead in the game. He also pinch-ran once in 1969.

Landis enjoyed working with pitching coach Sal Maglie. "We got along great. He was a quiet guy. He'd help you when he could." Bill got his one and only start of the year on August 3; three times before, he'd been scheduled to start and three times the game had been rained out. He was bombed for three hits and three runs in just two innings. Fortunately, Dave Morehead came on, the Red Sox bats went to work, and Morehead won the game, 5-3.

From his next appearance, August 13, to the end of the year, Landis appeared in just seven games. He held the Yankees scoreless for 21/3 innings on August 29. He didn't pitch again until September 19, when Dick Williams welcomed Landis to the mound in relief of José Santiago. Williams reportedly asked his reliever, "Do you know what the oblong thing is there?" It was the bottom of the ninth in a 4-3 game, with two runners on base. Bill correctly identified the pitching rubber, took the ball, and struck out Detroit pinch hitter Eddie Mathews. Some writers, such as Bill Reynolds of the *Providence Journal-Bulletin*, put the strikeout of Mathews right up there with the Tartabull throw and the Elston Howard tag of Ken Berry. After the strikeout, Russ Gibson told Bill, "You just struck out 500 home runs. If you want to faint now, it's OK." (*The Sporting News*, April 6, 1969) Gary Bell came in to get the last out of the game.

Not once in those final six appearances, though, did he give up even one earned run, allowing just four scattered hits over 6⅔ innings of work. In a year when the Red Sox won the pennant by a single game, one might argue that Landis's efforts made a difference. Every player dreams of making the World Series. The Red Sox truly lived the Impossible Dream in 1967, and with his strong finish, Bill Landis surely would have been on the postseason roster.

But he wasn't. He didn't have a choice. He'd previously signed up for the Army Reserve and it was a six-year commitment involving two weeks of training each summer and a weekend once a month. There was also a six-month training requirement that needed to be filled, and when the Army had beckoned earlier in the season, Landis went to Massachusetts' Fort Devens and argued as a professional athlete for an extension. He was granted one, but the next date that came up saw him leave just before the season ended. He would miss out on the wild celebration on the field at Fenway and the World Series, too.

Landis was sent to Fort Polk, Louisiana, but

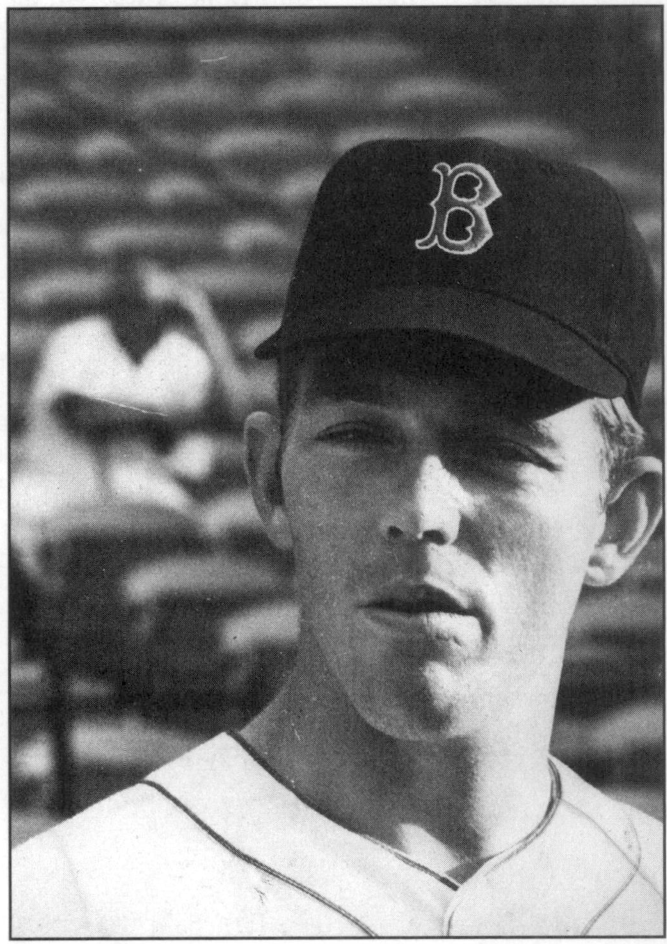

"The whole time I was in Boston, it was very enjoyable," Landis remembers. "There wasn't one thing I didn't like about it."

was lucky to at catch the games on television. "My commanding officer was from Boston and he let me watch all the games on television in the rec room," Bill explains. Maybe if he'd been on the team...? "You never know," he says philosophically.

Bill got out the day before spring training began in 1968, his service commitment fulfilled. In 1968, Landis more than doubled his workload from the year before, appearing in 38 games and throwing a full 60 innings in relief. His ERA was an excellent 3.15 and his record an even 3-3 with a strikeout-to-walk ratio of almost 2 to 1. The following winter, he played ball in San Juan, Puerto Rico, his second experience with winter ball.

In 1969, Bill won five and lost five. In fact, the first three wins the Red Sox had in 1969 were all Bill Landis wins—on April 8, 11, and 12. He gave up just one hit in 7⅔ innings over the three games. The Sox had lost the second game of the season, so Landis told Williams that his personal goal was 161 wins. In the end, he upped his innings to 82⅓ getting into 45 games. The walks went up and the strikeouts came down, and his ERA bumped up to 5.25. After '69, he pitched some winter ball with the San Juan Senators in Puerto Rico. The Red Sox asked him to pitch in Louisville in 1970, and he complied. He had been expecting a trade to the San Francisco Giants along with Russ Gibson, but as it turned out, Gibson was the only one who went, in April 1970. In 101 innings, Landis posted a 4.46 ERA in the International League, with a 5-9 record. In October, he was traded to the Cardinals for Billy McCool.

Landis spent spring training 1971 with St. Louis, but he had a sore arm that refused to get better. The Cardinals left him in Florida in hopes the arm would come around, then sent him to their Tulsa affiliate in the American Association to try to rehab it, but he got in just 10 innings as the arm never improved. He'd worked in Boston in the off-season in sales for the Arrow Shirt Company and was offered a full-time job with the company. Bill wrote St. Louis, told them that his arm was just not responding, and that he would not be going to spring training. That was it.

"The whole time I was in Boston, it was very enjoyable," he remembers. "There wasn't one thing I didn't like about it. I liked the organization. I liked Massachusetts. Well, there was one thing. I didn't like the snow."

Landis worked for Arrow Shirt for three years, then a year for Buxton Leather out of Springfield, Massachusetts. Then he moved back to California. On his return to the Golden State, Bill switched careers completely, to law enforcement. He worked a full 25 years for the Kings County Sheriff's Department, starting as a patrolman and working his way up to Assistant Sheriff when he retired. Now he has the opportunity to play golf almost every day.

Bill and his wife, Vicki, had met at Hanford High. They married in 1962 and had an infant daughter who passed away a few days after birth. Bill did eventually father two sons. Both played baseball and soccer, but neither pursued baseball actively. Brady Landis competed seriously in BMX bicycle racing, winning in the nationals in Texas. Bill's younger son, Justin, played professional golf for a while. Both ultimately pursued other careers. Justin's mother is Bill's second wife Mary Ann. She and Bill have been married 31 years; Mary Ann is the retired Jury Commissioner of Kings County, California.

Bill felt particularly close to a number of players on the 1967 Red Sox, including Mike Andrews, Jim Lonborg, Russ Gibson, and Sparky Lyle. There was one last question put to him in the interview for this book. We saw that Bill only became a full-time pitcher when he signed professionally. He must have been a pretty good hitter in high school and college to have attracted the attention he had. Yet he had 19 major league at-bats and but didn't get a hit in the major leagues. "I know!" he laughs. "When you focus on your pitching, you just don't get to practice as much, and consequently your timing's not as good as it was. It happens. I just call it 0-for-3. 0-for-three years!"

Jim Lonborg

by Saul Wisnia

	G	ERA	W	L	SV	GS	GF	CG	SHO	IP	H	R	ER	BB	SO	HR	BFP
1967 RED SOX	39	3.16	22	9	0	39	0	15	2	273.1	228	102	96	83	246	23	1130

He made his big-league debut on a day when the Reverend Martin Luther King Jr. addressed thousands of civil rights marchers on the Boston Common, and flourished as a pitcher during the Summer of Love. As he struggled with injuries, Americans grappled with the strain of assassinations, racial riots, and the escalating Vietnam War.

Jim Lonborg's all-too-brief tenure with the Red Sox coincided with some of the most turbulent years of the 20th century, and he was traded just as his full strength was returning and the war was winding down. But the soft-spoken, cerebral hurler will always be remembered—and revered—for what he accomplished during a two-week span in 1967 when New Englanders put other cares on hold and attached their Impossible Dreams to his powerful right arm.

The first Cy Young Award winner in team history was born on April 16, 1942 in Santa Maria, California and raised in nearby San Luis Obispo. The coastal community was home to the California State Polytechnical College, where Lonborg's father Reynold worked as a professor of agriculture.

A straight "A" student, Jim dreamed of being a surgeon rather than a World Series star. The Lonborgs were an athletic clan—Reynold was a top hurdler at Fresno State, where Jim's older brother Eric would later star in football and track—but the family's primary focus was on academic achievement and good citizenship. While Reynold was teaching or working the fields with his students, his wife Ada took care of Jim, Eric, and their little sister Celia; when Reynold returned home at night, Ada was often off to host a local TV talk show dedicated to current events.

Lonborg was 10 when the town built a Little League and softball field just a block from his house. His first team was the Kiwanis Red Sox, and he participated in the town's first-ever Little League game. "Those were the days when you'd come home from school, drop off your books, and just go out and play ball all day," he says. "After the Dodgers moved from Brooklyn to LA, I became a big fan of Don Newcombe and Sandy Koufax, and so I was a pitcher, too."

Too skinny for the gridiron, Lonborg focused on baseball and basketball at San Luis Obispo High. The right-hander didn't make the varsity pitching squad as a sophomore, but by his senior year was its ace. Coaches later remembered him as "the hardest-working kid on the field," but his talent had not yet taken full bloom.

"I was very good at times, but at other times just mediocre," he recalls. "We had a shortstop, Mel Queen, who was my best friend growing up. He was our star, and signed for something like an $80-90,000 bonus with the Reds out of high school. He married my sister and eventually became a pitcher in the big leagues."

Scouts were often in the stands at San Luis Obispo games to look at Queen, and made inquiries about Jim when he pitched well. "But they knew I was academically oriented, and I was going to be a pre-med student in college. From what I understood, they were afraid of signing me to a bonus and then having me quit after a couple years."

Young, strong, and signed

Good enough as a 6-foot-5 basketball center to be "quasi-recruited" by Stanford, Jim earned an academic scholarship from the school. He played on the freshmen hoops squad—NCAA rules then barred first-year collegians from varsity teams—but was stuck behind 6-foot-9 future All-American Tom Dose on the depth charts.

Then spring came around, and baseball tryouts. Jim made the freshman team and was on his way. He had a decent season, and, leaving basketball behind, graduated to the varsity pitching staff in '62. "I had a really good year, and by that summer, the Orioles were starting to take a real strong interest in me."

Baltimore was in the midst of building an American League powerhouse through its farm system, and funded summer-league teams where promising youngsters could perform under their watch while maintaining their amateur status. Lonborg was assigned to the Everett (Washington) Orioles of the Northeast League, where he suited up for five to six games a week and lived with a host family.

"That was my first summer living away from home, and it was a great experience," he remembers. "I was young and strong and had a rubber arm. In a playoff doubleheader against Bellingham I won the first game, told the manager I felt good, and wound up pitching the second one too—18 innings in one day."

After an MVP junior season at Stanford—where he was majoring in Biology—Jim was invited by the Orioles to join the highly competitive Basin League in the summer of 1963. Playing in rural South Dakota on a team with future big leaguers Jim Palmer and Merv Rettemund, Lonborg stood out. Baltimore scout Phil Galvin was overseeing his progress, but scouts from other major league clubs often made the trip to the woods as well.

"I was throwing an awful lot, two games a week plus between starts, and one day Red Sox scout Danny Doyle recommended to the manager that they rest me up a little more. We tried it out, and the next start I struck out something like 17 guys. Bobby Doerr was in the stands that night for Boston, and that's when the Red Sox started to make a strong move."

These were the days before the annual major league draft. Although he felt a strong allegiance to the Orioles, Lonborg wound up signing with the Red Sox for a bonus of $25,000 at summer's end, reportedly much higher than what the O's offered. "The Orioles couldn't believe it, but I guess the Sox had had a good year financially, and Mr. Yawkey told his scouts to go out and get some guys. It was a hard decision for me, but one that amounted to economics."

After two more quarters at Stanford (where he would later complete his degree in the off-season), Lonborg reported to Deland, Florida for spring training with the Triple A Seattle Rainiers. He split the year between Seattle and Single A Winston Salem, and was a combined 11-9. The next spring he was invited to Boston's big-league camp.

The "doctor" is in

The perennial second-division Sox were desperate for pitching help in 1965, and the 22-year-old was given a strong chance to make manager Billy Herman's club. Almost immediately, reporters began playing up his background. While in college Jim had developed a taste for symphony music, and this became a frequent reference point for sportswriters. "I remember at Stanford in a fine arts course, we were studying the Brandenburg Concertos," he told the *Boston Globe*. "There was a bunch of us, guys and coeds, listening to it at the Phi Delta Theta house. And this Bach thing really got to us. We started dancing to it, twisting."

The image seemed to capture the handsome young bachelor—a perfect meld of culture and cool. He was capable of taking the short stroll from Fenway Park to Symphony Hall one night, then hitting the rock-oriented nightclubs of Kenmore Square the next. He also had pitching sense and confidence well beyond his years, and in a surprising move to start the season, Herman named Lonborg as one of his four starters along with ace Bill Monbouquette, Earl Wilson, and Dave Morehead.

With a then-familiar Boston blend of strong hitting, thin pitching, and suspect defense, the Red Sox were a consensus pick to place ninth in the 10-team American League. After six straight losing campaigns, fans of the club were looking for reasons to hope. The lanky right-hander with the high leg-kick provided one immediately.

In his big-league debut at Baltimore on April 23, Jim let up just two hits over six innings, while notching four strikeouts. He did allow five walks and three runs while taking the loss against Hall of Famer Robin Roberts, but it was a strong first impression. Back in New England the big news was King's speech on Boston Common promoting racial harmony, but buried in the sports pages of the *Globe* was a prophetic opening line from Roger Birtwell's account of the Orioles' 4-2 victory: "The Red Sox Friday night lost a ball game, but found a pitcher."

More strong starts followed, including a pair against the defending AL champion Yankees for his first two major league victories. Jim today credits veterans like his locker-room neighbor Wilson for providing the pitching wisdom necessary to survive in the majors, and Herman for assuring him he had the stuff to do so. The manager was right; Lonborg possessed an explosive fastball, along with a strong breaking ball he could throw for strikes and which hitters often sent into the dirt. Unfortunately, a ground-ball pitcher and irregular defense didn't mix, and the end result was a 9-17 record and 4.47 ERA for the Sox, who met expectations with a ninth-place finish.

Asked if all the "Dr. Lonborg" and "Stanford slinger" stories that first year got to him, he laughs. "Sure, there was a lot of ribbing because of it, but you learn how to have very thick skin. And if you're healthy and pitching well, a lot of that stuff falls off. My parents instilled strong self-esteem in me. It would have taken a lot for me to break."

With the Red Sox coming together as a team in 1966, Jim's pitching record improved. Shortstop Rico Petrocelli and first baseman George Scott, young players with great gloves, were now gobbling up his grounders, and Lonborg was a solid 10-10 with a 3.86 ERA for the season. Hoping they had the makings of a big winner, Boston management sent him to work on his breaking ball in the Venezuelan winter league. After play there

The most important base hit in the history of the Red Sox? *Down 2-0 to Minnesota in a game Boston had to win or be eliminated, Lonborg led off the sixth inning with a bunt single and scored the first run of a five-run rally that won the October 1 pennant-clinching game.*

ended around Christmas, he went back to California and one of his off-season passions: skiing.

"The team didn't even know I skied then. It was just something I liked to do, and I figured that there couldn't be anything better for your leg and shoulder strength and your overall conditioning. I left Heavenly Valley [resort] on a Friday morning, and I was in spring training on Saturday in the best shape of my life."

Best in his business

Awaiting the Red Sox in Winter Haven was new manager Dick Williams, a stern disciplinarian who had managed many of the team's young players at Triple A Toronto. "Dick came in with very strong ideas about the way things should be done," says Lonborg. "He knew he had some great athletes, but a lot of them were doing their own thing. He really helped everybody congeal with his personality. If you made mistakes, he'd let you know about it. If you continued to make them, he *really* let you know about it."

Williams was out to alter the "country club" image of the team, and Jim welcomed the change. No pitcher looked better in camp, and Lonborg made headlines when he stated his goals were to win 20 games, make the All-Star team, and pitch in the World Series. While few imagined all three could happen *that year*, big things were expected of the man tabbed by Williams as the team's No. 1 starter.

And after frigid, windy weather forced a one-day postponement of the team's home opener, Lonborg got the season off to a good start. On Wednesday, April 12, he hurled six-plus strong innings in a 5-4 victory over the Chicago White Sox. Just 8,324 fans turned out at Fenway Park that bitterly cold day, but sparse home crowds in any weather would soon be a thing of the past.

With Jim compiling a 6-1 record during the first two months, the surprising Sox ended May in third place. Emerging as a certified power pitcher, he had a 13-strikeout, zero-walk shutout against the A's in one April game and 71 strikeouts overall in his first 70 innings. Forced several times to leave the team between starts for Army Reserve duty, he would fly in

on a private plane sent by Tom Yawkey in time to pitch another gem.

By early summer, the American League pennant race was shaping up to be a four- or even five-team affair, and just as Carl Yastrzemski guided the offense, Lonborg set the tone for the mound corps.

Jim's low-key, friendly demeanor in past seasons had earned him the nickname "Gentleman Jim," but with the help of Red Sox pitching coach Sal Maglie, he was asserting himself more on the mound by throwing high-and-tight fastballs to keep hitters on edge. His 19 hit batsmen would lead the AL in '67, but many were in "retaliation" for a plunked teammate. And even in these situations, he always seemed to keep his cool.

The evening of June 21 at Yankee Stadium provides an example. Sox third baseman Joe Foy had hit a grand slam the previous night, so New York starter Thad Tillotson beaned him on the helmet in the second inning. Lonborg responded by hitting Tillotson when he came up, and a five-minute, bench-clearing brawl ensued. Tillotson next sent Jim sprawling with a pitch in the fourth, leading to more heated words and shoving between the teams. But while the melee rattled Tillotson, who was gone by the fourth, Jim pitched a complete-game victory and allowed just one unearned run.

Named an AL All-Star, Lonborg was 11-3 and leading the AL in victories by early July. Just before the break, he pitched one of the forgotten gems of the season—a 3-0 win in which he lost 12 pounds over seven stellar innings on a hot, muggy day in Detroit. The win

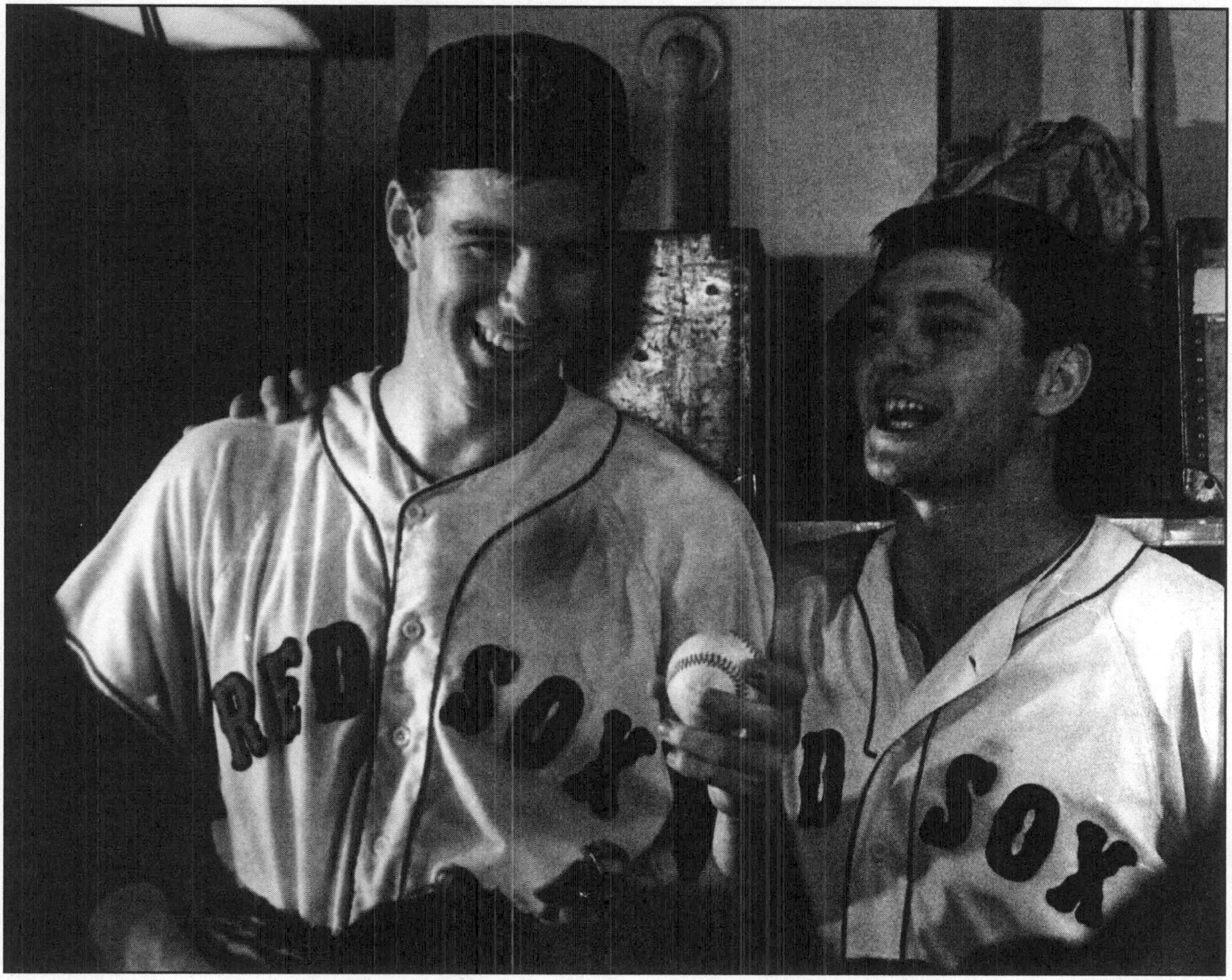

After Jim shut out St. Louis with a one-hitter in Game Two of the World Series, Yastrzemski said, "When I hit the first home run, I told Jim, "You have enough, big guy. Go get 'em!' And he sure did."

halted a stretch of five straight losses by the team and was quickly followed by a 10-game winning streak.

From late July on Boston would never be more than 3½ games out of first place, and usually much closer. Knowing his youthful team was still considered the underdog in a race against veteran clubs like the Twins and Tigers, Sox general manager Dick O'Connell made a key move on August 3 by acquiring Yankees catcher Elston Howard. A former MVP and a veteran of nine World Series, Howard had a huge influence on his new team—especially its ace pitcher. "Mike Ryan and Russ Gibson were great young catchers," Lonborg says, "but when Elston got there, he took a lot of pressure off of me in trying to figure out the best way to get hitters out."

When Lonborg earned his 20th win over Catfish Hunter and the A's on September 12, it put the Red Sox in a tie for first place. A usually weak hitter, Jim aided his own cause with an eighth-inning triple and moments later scored the winning run on a sacrifice fly. Two of his pre-season goals had now been accomplished. The biggest remained.

One for the money

Dick Williams had his pitching rotation set so Lonborg could start twice during the last week of the year, including (if necessary) in the season finale. When Jim was hit hard in a loss at Cleveland on Wednesday, September 27, the Sox fell a game behind first-place Minnesota. But fate and the schedule had the Twins at Fenway for the last two games of the season, and after a 6-4 win by the Sox on Saturday the teams were tied again at the top. Sunday's winner-take-all affair would feature a duel of aces: Dean Chance (20-13) against Lonborg (21-9), who was 0-3 that year and 0-6 lifetime against Minnesota. A few months earlier, Chance had beaten Lonnie with a no-hitter halted by rain after five innings.

Jim pitched better on the road throughout the 1967 season, but this wasn't the only reason he decided to stay in teammate Ken Harrelson's hotel room the night before the biggest ballgame of his life. "I was living at Charles River Park, a very active complex," Lonborg explains. "There was a lot of traffic going in and out, and I really needed a quiet place to get ready for the game. I stayed at the Sheraton right near the Hynes Auditorium, had a nice dinner and some wine, slept well, and woke up a lot more relaxed than I would have had I stayed at home."

Although he was later quoted as saying, "I just knew I was going to win," Lonborg gave himself added incentive before the contest by writing the figure "$10,000"—what he estimated to be each player's World Series share were the Sox to make it—into the palm of his glove. When uncharacteristic defensive miscues by Gold Glove teammates Yastrzemski and Scott led to two unearned runs and a 2-0 Twins lead entering the bottom of the sixth, Jim grew concerned. But then came what might have been the biggest of Boston's 1,394 regular-season hits, from the unlikeliest source in the lineup.

"For some reason I always hit Chance very well," says Lonborg. "He was having a great year, but I just seemed to pick up his ball well and had gotten a single my first time at-bat that day. Going up to the plate in the bottom of the sixth, I looked down to third base for a 'take' sign from coach Eddie Popowski, and he didn't give it. I had bunted a lot during the course of the year, and could run pretty well for a big guy. [Cesar] Tovar seemed back a little further at third base than normal, and I had an opportunity on the first pitch to lay one down. Tovar couldn't handle it, and that just started things off."

Given his blue warm-up jacket at first base, Lonborg quickly came around to score as the next three batters—Jerry Adair, Dalton Jones, and Yastrzemski—all followed with first-pitch singles. A few botched grounders and wild pitches later, and Boston had the crowd on its feet and a 5-2 lead going into the seventh.

Minnesota got one run back in the eighth, but lost a chance for more when Yaz deftly handled Bob Allison's liner to the left-field corner and threw him out at second base. It was still 5-3 with two outs and one on in the Twins ninth when pinch-hitter Rich Rollins hit the first pitch he saw from Lonnie high into the air behind shortstop. Rico Petrocelli grabbed it, and Red Sox broadcaster Ned Martin perfectly summed up what happened next when he told listeners, "And it's pandemonium on the field!"

As Jim leaped up and down, Andrews and Scott came over and lifted him onto their shoulders. Other players from the field and dugout quickly swarmed around them, as did many of the 35,770 fans on hand who for the first time in decades had a reason to jump the low walls separating them from their heroes. One photograph shows a beaming Lonborg literally riding above a sea of revelers, many of who are reaching out to touch him and "grab" a souvenir.

Then, as he recalls, "the crowd starting moving toward the right-field foul pole, and I was trying to get back to the dugout. A lot of articles of my clothing were starting to disappear; the moment of jubilation had passed, and now the moment of anxiety had started to set in." By the time he reached the dugout, Jim had

lost the buttons on his uniform jersey, the undershirt beneath it, a shoelace, and his cap.

Now assured of a tie for the AL pennant, the Sox claimed the flag outright a few hours later when second-place Detroit lost the second game of a doubleheader to California. Owner Tom Yawkey, in an unusual public display of emotion, gave his champagne-soaked ace a bear hug and broke down while telling Lonborg how terrific he had been. The numbers bear Yawkey out: Jim finished the regular season 22-9 and led the league in wins, strikeouts (246), and starts (39) while placing second in complete games (15) and innings (273.1).

As Bostonians partied hard into the night, high school senior Rosemary Feeney struggled to get some sleep. In town with her mother to visit Garland Junior College, she was staying across the street at the Hotel Somerset. Both establishments were around the corner from Fenway Park, but despite the noise Rosemary wound up going to school at Garland. Lonborg met the New Jersey native at a party in Boston three years later, and they married in November 1970. Six kids and several grandkids later, they are still going strong.

Mastery and misery

The thrilling finish left Jim unavailable to start Game One of the World Series against heavily favored St. Louis at Fenway three days later. After the Cardinals and their ace pitcher Bob Gibson had taken the opener, 2-1, Lonnie was near perfect in evening up the series.

Facing a lineup featuring Hall of Famers Lou Brock, Orlando Cepeda, and several other All-Stars, he set down the first 19 men in order before walking Curt Flood in the seventh. The Cards had no hits until Julian Javier's double with two outs in the eighth, and they did not get another as the Red Sox evened the Series with a 5-0 win. Yaz had two homers and four RBIs, but Jim's one-hitter was the big story. In from California, Lonborg's mom and dad watched proudly.

Boston's other starters could not maintain Jim's momentum, however, and St. Louis won the next two games (including a Gibson shutout) to put the Sox on the brink of elimination. Then, starting his third crucial contest in eight days, Lonborg in Game Five nearly matched his previous masterpiece. Pitching a three-hitter, he had a shutout until Roger Maris homered with two outs in the ninth inning of a 3-1 Sox victory at Busch Stadium. Through 18 innings, Lonnie had now allowed four hits and one walk, the greatest back-to-back pitching performances in World Series history.

Jim credits "great physical stuff and great emotional concentration in those two games" as the key, along with some advice he got from his boyhood idol, Sandy Koufax. "Sandy was one of the TV announcers for the Series, and we had a wonderful conversation about preparing for a game in the bullpen—visualizing which hitters were coming up to the plate and almost pitching a game in your mind before you've even walked out on the field. That was very, very helpful."

In athletics, however, optimism and talent can sometimes be trumped by physical exhaustion. This is what happened after the Sox won Game Six and Jim started the finale at Fenway on just two days rest against Gibson—who had enjoyed his normal three-day break after Game Four.

Lonborg remembers feeling strong and comfortable before the game, but Sox coach Bobby Doerr noticed early that his pitches lacked the "snap" of his previous three starts. Jim also wasn't locating the ball the way he wanted to, and in the third inning the Cards went up 2-0 on three hits and a wild pitch.

"I was hoping we could score some runs early, because I didn't know how long I could keep my energy level up," Lonborg says. "I was still throwing decent, but then in the third I gave up a [leadoff] triple to [.227 hitter] Dal Maxvill off the center-field wall. That's when I knew I was in trouble and that my stuff was starting to flatten out."

Gibson homered in the fifth, Julian Javier added a three-run blast an inning later, and it was 7-1 St. Louis when Jim struck out Curt Flood to end the sixth. Lonborg doesn't remember crying as he walked off the mound, but teammates and fans near the Sox dugout could see his tears. It was probably one of the few times a pitcher who had just allowed 10 hits and 7 runs received a standing ovation.

Headlines the next day revealed that Lonborg had asked Williams to keep him in the game just before Javier's homer (pitcher and manager had both expected a bunt), but there was surprisingly little second-guessing in the days and decades to come. After 297 innings and 24 wins, it was accepted that Lonnie had simply run out of miracles. Nine outs later, so had Boston.

Ski slopes and sunken hopes

What happened next is forever woven into Red Sox lore alongside Bill Buckner's muff and Bucky Dent and Aaron Boone's homers. After picking up the American League Cy Young Award in a near-unanimous decision, Lonborg signed a 1968 contract for $50,000 (a $30,000 raise), then went to Lake Tahoe, California for some Christmas-time skiing a week later.

He still defends the decision, to a point. "There was

nothing in my contract that said I couldn't ski, and I felt it was the main reason I had been so successful in '67—because I was in such great shape. But looking back on it, I didn't have enough experience to know when it was time to go inside and say you've had enough for the day."

On December 23, making perhaps one run too many, Jim wiped out while attempting a snowplow stop and severely tore ligaments in his left knee. Flown back to Boston with his knee in a cast, he was examined by Red Sox team physician Dr. Thomas Tierney. The doctor recommended surgery to patch the torn ligaments with sutures, but predicted Jim would be back for the start of the 1968 season. It would turn out to be wishful thinking.

Tierney and orthopedic surgeon Dr. John McGillicuddy performed the operation on December 27, and found the injury to be much worse than feared: two ligaments were damaged instead of one. While the surgery was deemed successful, Jim's pitching future was now more in doubt. He was in a waist-high cast for six weeks, then reported with the team to spring training and a rehab regimen of weightlifting each morning and 27 holes of golf each afternoon.

Lonborg met his goal of a May return, but at a heavy price. In compensating for his knee, he unknowingly altered his pitching motion slightly and placed added stress on his right shoulder. The resulting muscle and tendon damage would plague him the rest of his career.

"They were able to diagnose it as rotator cuff problems, which they really didn't know how to treat back then," he says. "I had tons of cortisone shots, and I tried to come back too soon without building up my arm strength properly. It was just a case of youthful energy, and wanting to get back on the field."

Jim Lonborg had a passion for skiing and cites how well it kept him in condition, until a 1967 post-season accident threatened to end his career.

The long goodbye

Lonborg made his 1968 debut with a short relief stint on May 28 at Oakland. After four such appearances, he drew his first starting assignment on June 16 in Cleveland. The results were encouraging—five innings, three hits, one run allowed—but he also walked four. His once-stellar control was off; even in throwing six one-hit innings against the Yankees in July for his first win since the World Series, he walked eight. By the start of August, he was just 1-3 with a 5.06 ERA.

There were some encouraging signs down the stretch, including a three-hit shutout of Cleveland in which he struck out nine and walked none. But Jim's final record of 6-10 and team-worst 4.29 ERA were seen as a major cause for Boston's fall to fourth place, 17 games behind pennant-winning Detroit. Lonborg hoped another winter of rest would help him turn things around.

For a while, this looked to be the case. Although he had to leave the 1969 season opener after 2⅔ innings due to shoulder pain, he returned to the rotation three weeks later and by early June was 6-0 with a 2.33 ERA. But he missed three more weeks after breaking his toe on June 21, and then encountered more shoulder woes when he came back. He lost his last eight decisions to finish 7-11, and the Sox wound up third.

The 1970 season was even more frustrating for Jim. He had three strong starts to begin the year, but then his shoulder landed him on the disabled list again. When it failed to come around, management put him on waivers and then sent him to Triple A Louisville on July 23. He made a few starts there, with middling

results, and in August was told to go home for the year. Pitching just nine times for the varsity overall, he was 4-1 with a 3.18 ERA.

"Most everybody was hopeful that I would be able to get back to my initial form," he says in retrospect. "I always felt very good around the clubhouse; my teammates were great, and the Red Sox were very patient with me. I did have flashes of the old stuff, but had not yet learned what it took for my body to heal properly."

When he was brought back up from Louisville midway through the '71 season, it appeared Lonborg had figured it out. He went 7-4 the last three months, including 3-1 (with three complete games) in September. His final record of 10-7 with 167⅔ innings and 100 strikeouts marked his highest totals since 1967, and he felt he was finally "getting a handle on getting healthy." He was also still just 29 years old.

The Red Sox, however, finished a distant third for the third straight year. Yawkey wanted changes, and on October 10 Boston engineered a 10-player deal with the Milwaukee Brewers in which George Scott, Billy Conigliaro, and Lonborg were among those sent packing for a quartet including pitcher Marty Pattin and speedy leadoff man Tommy Harper. Fans polled mostly felt it was a bad deal, in part because of Lonborg's promising comeback summer.

"We got the phone call and it was a shock," recalls Jim. "We loved it in Boston and wanted to stay, and I thought I was really coming around." He was, but it was not the Red Sox who would benefit.

Far from finished

Lonnie's last seven full years in the majors are usually an afterthought to armchair historians encapsulating his career, but those who simply say he "never came back" from his ski mishap are neither fair nor accurate. He never again won 20 games, but he was a successful and at times stellar pitcher.

His 1972 season with Milwaukee was a case in point. Pitching 223 innings, often still in pain, Lonborg had a 14-12 record on a last-place team. He had 11 complete games, a 2.83 ERA (the best of his career), and 143 strikeouts. Some of his top performances came against the Red Sox, including a 7-hitter on June 24 in which he registered 11 strikeouts—his most ever for a game not pitched in 1967.

Lonborg enjoyed his year in Wisconsin and was surprised when he was traded to the Philadelphia Phillies on October 31, 1972 as part of another massive deal. The Phils had the National League's worst record in '72, despite a 27-10 season from Cy Young awardee Steve Carlton. Future All-Stars like Mike Schmidt, Greg Luzinski, Bob Boone, and Larry Bowa were joining the lineup, however, so the promise of better days lay ahead.

Philadelphia wound up improving each of the next four years, and Lonborg played a key role. In 1974 he was 17-13 with a 3.21 ERA over a career-high 283 innings, and was third in the NL with 16 complete games as he and Carlton formed one of the league's best one-two duos. His hard sinking fastball gone, he became a crafty pitcher who worked the corners and developed a better slider and change-up.

More shoulder woes set Jim back a bit in 1975, but with an 18-10, 3.08 season in '76 he helped the Phils complete their four-year rise with an NL East championship—their first title of any kind since 1950. He had a sparkling 13-3 mark in home games at Veterans Stadium, and notched the East-clinching victory with a four-hitter at Montreal on Sept. 26.

Nine years after hurling the Red Sox to a title, Lonborg had come full circle. He later called it his best year as a "pitcher" rather than a "thrower," but it didn't top '67. "It was exciting, but it didn't have nearly the same aura about it. We knew we were going to win the division, and I just happened to be the guy on the mound that night. It wasn't a 'win or you're out' situation." Soon Philadelphia was out, however; the Phils were swept 3-0 in the NL Championship Series by Cincinnati, with Lonborg taking the 6-2 loss in Game Two.

The older he got, the harder it was for Jim to shake off his shoulder pain. But he knew when and how to rest now and could still win with consistency. Limited to 25 starts in 1977, he made the most of them with an 11-4 record that included a 10-2 mark in the season's second half.

One game from this stretch drive stands out. Facing the two-time defending world champion Cincinnati Reds at the Vet on Friday night, Sept. 2, Lonborg learned early in the contest that his wife had gone into labor with their fifth child. Given extra incentive to work quickly, he shut down Bench, Morgan, Rose, and the rest 3-0 and rushed to the hospital in time to see daughter Nora born.

Unfortunately, he didn't have time to ice down his arm properly after the contest. "I had to sleep at the hospital with my arm propped up in bed, and when I came out to the ballpark Saturday night I could hardly throw a baseball." In the NLCS a month later, he lost Game Two 7-1 as the Phillies fell in four to the Dodgers. There would be no return trip to the World Series for Jim Lonborg.

Final uniform change

The Phils won the East again in '78, but Jim slipped to an 8-10 mark with a career-worst 5.23 ERA and did not pitch in the postseason. He didn't expect to even make the team in 1979, but injuries to younger pitchers kept him on the roster for a few months. Appearing in just four games, he made his final major league appearance on June 10—a three-inning relief stint against Atlanta in which he allowed five hits and three runs.

When Lonborg was released six days later, the event registered just a single line in Boston newspapers. He might have helped another team down the stretch, but didn't pursue it. He wound up with a fine 157-137 lifetime record in the majors, along with a respectable 3.86 ERA over 425 games. Ironically, his post-Red Sox record (89-72) had been considerably stronger than his Boston slate of 68-65.

New England, however, had been where he made his mark—and his home. Even as a rookie, Jim had been looking to his life after baseball and the opportunity to fulfill his childhood ambition of a medical career. Now, at 37, he returned to Boston to act on those dreams. Taking the advice of his wife Rosie, who "always thought I looked great in uniform," Lonborg decided to trade his flannels for a white coat and become a dentist.

He put in a year at UMass/Boston boning up on chemistry and other related subjects, then spent three years at Tufts University Dental School, one of the nation's premier programs. Occasionally he turned heads when younger students recognized him or heard his name called in class.

Still immensely popular in his adopted state, Dr. James Lonborg, DMD, had no trouble finding veteran dentists willing to bring him on. He honed his skills with several, and by the mid-1980s had established his own thriving practice in Hanover, Massachusetts—a small, quiet community between Boston and Cape Cod. He's still working there today, and he and Rosie live "about 12 minutes away" in Scituate, in the same house they've had since 1975.

Philanthropy has always been important to the Lonborgs, and with old Red Sox teammate Mike Andrews serving as chairman of the Jimmy Fund at Boston's Dana-Farber Cancer Institute (DFCI), they have been longtime supporters of this charity. Jim has earned recognition as one of DFCI's leading celebrity fundraisers, and Rosie works part-time in the hospital's Jimmy Fund Clinic soothing the needs of pediatric cancer patients and their families.

Lonnie has also reestablished strong ties to the Red Sox, and was named to the team's Hall of Fame in 2002. He enjoyed watching from home with his family as the 2004 club made its run to the World Series title, and says seeing them beat the Yankees "was just the best thing in the world." It was not, however, a case of déjà vu. He knows no matter what happens, '67 will always be unique.

"People I meet at charity events still tell me they were there when we beat the Twins," he says. "It doesn't matter where I am, really. Rosie and I were out in Jackson Hole, Wyoming, this winter skiing, and a guy came up to me and said, 'I'm sorry to bother you, but I couldn't help notice the 'B' in your ring. That isn't a World Series ring, is it?'

"It turns out he was just the greatest Red Sox fan in the world. My friends from Arizona watched this young guy of about 38 talk to me about the old days, which he only knew about from stories, and they couldn't believe it.

"I had to explain to them afterwards that it was something like folklore."

In MLBPA's infancy, Lonborg was in there pitching

by Saul Wisnia

In addition to playing a key role in the rebirth of the Red Sox during the 1966 and '67 seasons, ace pitcher Jim Lonborg was also instrumental in helping all major leaguers make off-the-field gains as the team's official player representative.

It was the early days of the Major League Baseball Player's Association (MLBPA), and each of the 20 teams had a rep. Jim Bunning of the Phillies, a Hall of Fame hurler and future United States Senator, was then heading up the player's union, which appointed a labor attorney/economist named Marvin Miller as its executive director in '66.

"We would meet at a hotel in New York during the All-Star Game and World Series," Lonborg remembers. "The major topics were the language in contracts and the minimum player's salary–which was $6,000 when I started in '65. We wanted better benefits for the ballplayers; the healthcare was already pretty good. There was discussion about the dispersion of World Series and All-Star money, and how much was given to the players for their pension fund."

Lonborg recalls that the meetings grew longer and more frequent over the next few years. The MLBPA got the minimum player salary raised from $6,000 to $10,000 by 1968 (the first such raise in two decades), and sought to challenge the reserve clause, which for nearly a century had given team owners complete control over where and when players were traded, signed, or released, regardless of their seniority.

After veteran St. Louis Cardinals outfielder Curt Flood refused to accept a trade to Philadelphia in 1969, and then privately sued the MLB with the union's support, Miller fought the case all the way to the United States Supreme Court. Although Flood lost, the action paved the way for free agency to emerge in 1975. "Curt was a very strong individual, and we were lucky to have someone with his strong conviction to see that through," says Lonborg, who also developed a close friendship with Miller during this period.

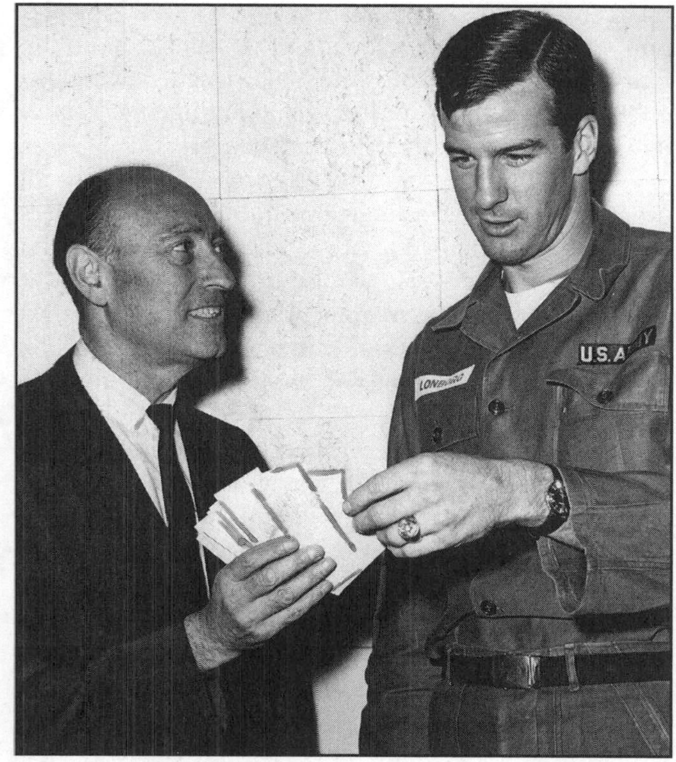

A number of Boston ballplayers did duty in the Reserves during the course of the 1967 season. Lonborg takes time out from his Army duties to purchase some tickets from Bill Koster, director of the Jimmy Fund, for the premiere of Walt Disney's The Happiest Millionaire.

Sparky Lyle

by Diane MacLennan

	G	ERA	W	L	SV	GS	GF	CG	SHO	IP	H	R	ER	BB	SO	HR	BFP
1967 RED SOX	27	2.28	1	2	5	0	11	0	0	43.1	33	13	11	14	42	3	173

"Why pitch nine innings when you can get just as famous pitching two?"—Sparky Lyle

He did just that. Albert Walter "Sparky" Lyle never started a game in his 16-year major league career, amassed 238 career saves, and was the first American League relief pitcher to win a Cy Young Award (1977).

"I wonder what Ben Shingledecker thinks of my winning the Cy Young," says Lyle. Born in DuBois, Pennsylvania on July 22, 1944, Lyle tried out for the hometown teener league team at the age of 13, and was told by Shingledecker, "You can't throw hard enough to be a pitcher." Crushed, Sparky played only pickup baseball around his neighborhood for the next few years.

In the small coal-mining town of Reynoldsville, 100 miles northeast of Pittsburgh, Albert "Sparky" Lyle was known as a Reynoldsville High School football and basketball star, named as an All-Conference end in football and recognized with an honorable mention on Pennsylvania's All-State basketball team. In the spring of his junior year in high school, he started pitching for the DuBois team of the Legion league because Reynoldsville did not have a Legion team.

While pitching for DuBois, it seemed he was always striking out 16 or 17 batters a game. This accomplishment made local headlines and in one game during that summer, he struck out 31 batters. He threw mostly fastballs and curve balls and ended up walking eight or nine men. It was a 17-inning game, yet Lyle only pitched 14 of those 17 innings; he handled first base duties for three innings in the middle of the game. That caught the attention of Baltimore Orioles' scout George "Stopper" Staller and earned him a contract.

"Stopper" Staller had just one year of major league experience under his belt, playing outfield for the Philadelphia Athletics during the wartime 1943 season. Twenty-one years later, he signed the man who became one of the most dominant left-handed relief pitchers in all of baseball to a Baltimore Orioles contract on June 17, 1964. Lyle did not receive any signing bonus and earned only $400 per month.

Lyle was assigned to Bluefield in the Appalachian League and threw 33 innings there in 1964 (3-2, 4.36 ERA) before he was moved to Appleton, Wisconsin, where he finished the season for Fox Cities, the championship team in the Midwest League. There he posted an excellent 2.31 ERA, with a 3-1 record in 35 more innings of work, with a strikeout to walk ratio of nearly 3 to 1.

On November 30, 1964 the Red Sox drafted Lyle from Baltimore, placing him on their major league roster, though by the start of the 1965 season, they had assigned him to the minors. He started his second year of pro ball at Winston-Salem, North Carolina at the Double-A level. It was his toughest year in baseball, pitching only in relief, and his control was ghastly—walking in runs and having difficulty getting anyone out. Working extremely hard on his control and getting 87 innings of work (5-5, 4.24 ERA), with 79 strikeouts, he earned a promotion to Boston's Eastern League farm club at Pittsfield.

After having a 5-5 season with Winston-Salem, Lyle was sent to Ocala, Florida for spring training where he met Ted Williams. After watching him pitch one afternoon, Williams asked Sparky what he thought was the best pitch in baseball. Sparky didn't have an answer; Williams told him it was the slider, because it was the only pitch he couldn't hit consistently even when he knew it was coming. He went on to explain to Sparky how the pitch broke and what the ball was supposed to do. The ball should come in at a right-handed batter and drop down. Williams, though, was not a pitcher and could not tell Lyle how to make the pitch happen, but his words gave Sparky the determination to figure it out for himself. Lyle often tells of how this meeting changed his life. He worked exhaustively on making the ball spin the right way and break. The spin wasn't as much of the challenge as the break was, but he perfected his slider, and it remained his signature pitch for most of his career.

His manager at Pittsfield in 1966 was Eddie Popowski, who saw Sparky strike out 72 men in 74 innings and record a 3.65 ERA (4-2).

Lyle began the 1967 season with Boston's Triple-A club in Toronto, but when the Red Sox sold Dennis Bennett to the New York Mets (receiving Al Yates along with cash), on June 24, 1967, they called up Lyle. Lyle's 1.71 ERA and Popowski's praise no doubt factored into

the promotion as well, since Eddie was now the Red Sox third base coach.

Breaking into the major leagues on July 4, 1967, in the seventh inning at Anaheim Stadium. Al "Sparky" Lyle made his debut just 18 days before his 23rd birthday, facing the California Angels. After Russ Gibson batted for Sox pitcher Darrell Brandon in the top of the seventh, Lyle came in to pitch in the bottom of the inning with the Red Sox down, 4-1. He gave up a base hit to Jimmy Hall, but then struck out Rick Reichardt, got Buck Rodgers on a ground out (catcher to first), and struck out Tom Satriano. In the eighth inning, he walked a batter and threw a wild pitch, but escaped other damage. Ken Poulsen batted for Lyle in the ninth, but the Red Sox lost the game, 4-3. In the two innings he pitched, Lyle gave up one hit, walked one, allowed no runs, and struck out three. From then until season's end, he pitched 43⅓ innings, gave up 33 hits and struck out 42, and had a 1-2 won-lost record. He did not appear in the World Series due to a sore arm.

In 1968, Lyle was 6-1 with 11 saves, settling into a role as the team's primary left-handed reliever. The following season, he pitched 102 ⅔ innings, chalked up 17 saves and had 93 strikeouts, along with his 8-3 record. This season made him one of the best relief pitchers in baseball. In the next two seasons he logged 36 more saves, leading the team in that category three straight seasons. His future looked bright.

Lyle became one of the game's dominant relievers of the 1970s, but most of his best seasons came with the team's hated rivals. In what many Red Sox fans consider the team's worst trade of the past 50 years, during spring training in 1972, Lyle was sent to the New York Yankees for first baseman Danny Cater and

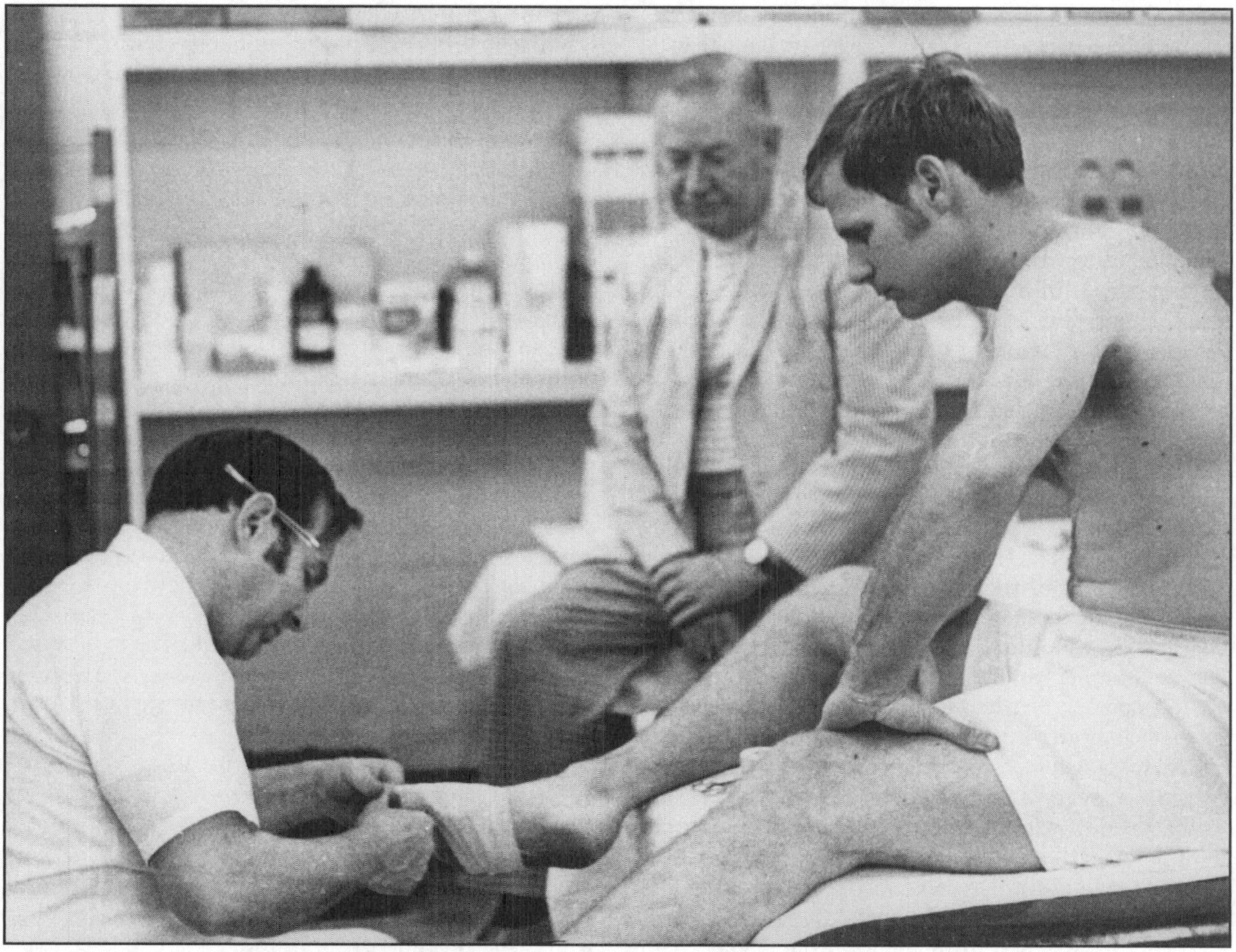

Red Sox trainer Buddy LeRoux works on Lyle's right foot.

a player to be named later (Mario Guerrero). Cater batted an abysmal .237 in his first year with the Red Sox, although he rebounded in 1973, hitting .313 in 63 games. Meanwhile, the Dominican shortstop Guerrero struggled with a .233 batting average in 1973.

By contrast, from 1972 through 1978, Lyle established himself as the Yankees' bullpen ace. He helped lead the Yankees to three straight pennants from 1976-1978 and World Series titles in 1977 and 1978. Saving 35 games in 1972, he set a major league record for left-handed relievers. (Just the next year, John Hiller of the Detroit Tigers surpassed Lyle's total, recording 38 saves.) In 1972, Lyle had become the first lefty to compile 100 saves in the American League, helping him earn the 1972 Fireman of the Year award from *The Sporting News*.

Leading the league again in 1976 with 23 saves, he broke future Hall of Fame pitcher Hoyt Wilhelm's American League record of 154 career saves, and proceeded to break Ron Perranoski's major league record for left handers of 179 career saves. By 1977, Lyle had collected 201 career saves and was fast closing in on Wilhelm's career record of 227. Lyle did briefly hold the record when he tied Wilhelm on May 26th at 227. That record was itself equaled by Rollie Fingers of the San Diego Padres a few days later on May 31. Lyle went to 228 on June 4; Fingers tied him June 7. Lyle then went up by two with saves on June 13 and again on June 16. Fingers tied him at 230 on June 25, but Fingers then went ahead for good June 1.

In 1973, he was named to his first of three American League All-Star teams. He pitched one full inning, giving up one hit and striking out one. He was again named to the AL All-Star teams in both 1976 and 1977;

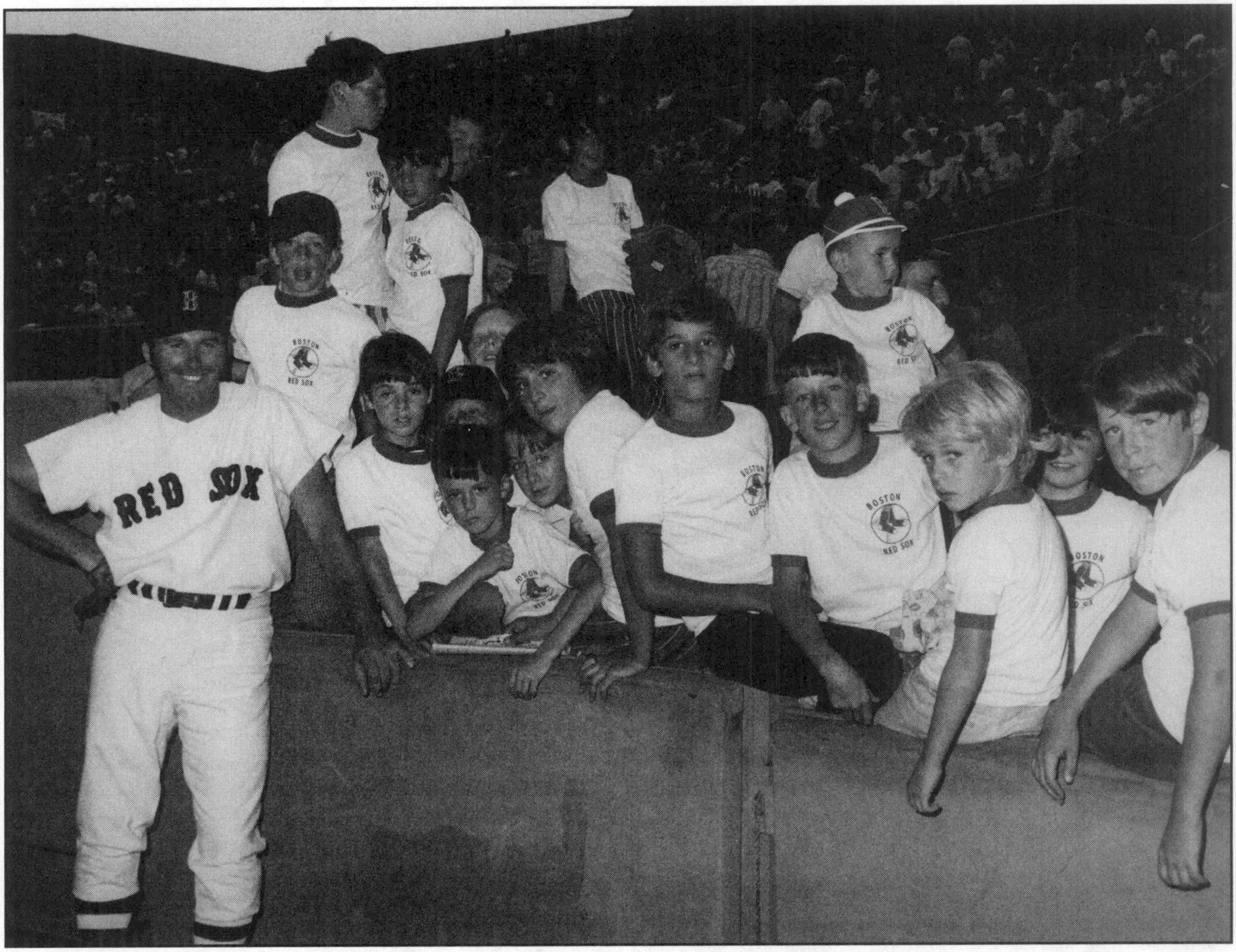

Sparky Lyle began his 16-year major league career with the '67 Sox and worked out of the bullpen with a 2.28 ERA.

he didn't appear in the 1976 game and pitched two innings in the 1977 game.

Sparky Lyle's contributions to the New York Yankees from 1972 through 1977 were so paramount to their success that the team played "Pomp and Circumstance" as theme music at Yankee Stadium each time he entered from the bullpen. Primarily using his superb slider, he also had a great fastball and a very impressive curve ball in his arsenal. His career year, 1977, produced a 13-5 record, a 2.17 ERA, 26 saves and the first American League Cy Young Award for a relief pitcher. Lyle worked 137 innings in 72 appearances.

After the season, Lyle and Yankees owner George Steinbrenner were unable to reach easy agreement on a new contract. The controversial Yankees owner was reluctant to give Sparky what he wanted, because Lyle would be 35 years old in the third year of a three-year deal. The Boss thought that was too old to be earning $100,000 to pitch. But one early morning in Tampa, the phone rang. Sparky had no idea who was on the other end when the voice asked, "What do you want?" Once Lyle finally figured out who was calling, he and Steinbrenner came to an agreement on roughly $425,000 for three years.

Then in late 1977, George Steinbrenner decided to take out his checkbook and sign Rich "Goose" Gossage and Rawly Eastwick, despite Lyle's established presence in the Yankees bullpen. While Lyle stewed all season, Gossage became the new Yankee closer, and on November 10, Lyle was part of a 10-player deal with the Texas Rangers.

Now in his mid-30s, Lyle was unable to attain the level of success of previous years. During his first year with the Rangers, 1979, he threw 95 innings, posting a 3.13 ERA, going 5-8. Texas finished five games out of first in the AL West. In 1980, Kansas City tore up the West, and Texas finished 20½ games out of first. Sparky had a 3-2 record in 80⅔ innings of relief, with a 4.69 ERA, the first time his ERA had exceeded 4.00.

In 1980, Rollie Fingers broke Lyle's AL record for career saves, and in 1991 Dave Righetti (who had come to the Yankees from Texas in that 10-player deal) passed him at the top of the list of career saves by a left-hander.

Late in the season, on September 13, he was once again involved in a trade for a player to be named later (Kevin Saucier), ending up with the Philadelphia Phillies. Lyle threw just 14 innings but with a good 1.93 ERA and helped the Phillies reach the postseason. Though the Phillies went on to win their first World Series title that year, Lyle was not eligible to pitch in the postseason. Sparky played out the full season with the Phillies in 1981, appearing in 48 games and throwing 75 innings. He posted a 9-6 record, with an ERA of 4.44.

His last year pitching in the major leagues was 1982. With Philadelphia, he was 3-3 in 36⅔ innings of work, and a disappointing ERA of 5.15. The Phillies felt he was finished, and sold his contract to the White Sox on August 21. Lyle closed out his career appearing in 10 more American League games, with an even 3.00 ERA (no decisions in 12 full innings of work). On September 27 he played his last major league game.

He was released on October 12, 1982, finishing his 16-year career with 238 saves, a 2.88 ERA, and a win/loss record of 99-76 in 899 games pitched—every one of them in relief.

After the Yankees had signed Gossage, Sparky's workload dropped, affording him the opportunity to take a closer look at what was happening around him. He proved to be a much more astute observer than anyone could have predicted. The 1978 season was a roller coaster of a season for the Yankees, with any number of dramatic dimensions, and proved one of their most sensational and controversial ever. Working with author Peter Golenbock, Lyle wrote a best-selling, highly acclaimed book cleverly titled *The Bronx Zoo*, published in 1979. In 1990, he wrote another humorous tale: *The Year I Owned the Yankees: A Baseball Fantasy*. This fictitious account of a year in which he ran the Yankees organization spoofs the first 15 years of the Steinbrenner era.

Some years after his unconditional release from the Chicago White Sox in 1982, Sparky Lyle once again found himself in an important role. He became the manager of an independent league baseball team in Bridgewater, New Jersey, the Somerset Patriots. It was a role he fell into pretty much by accident. One day he was looking to buy a new truck and his good friend, former major leaguer John Vukovich, took him to one of John's friends, Steven Kalafer, the owner of the Flemington Car and Truck Country Family of Automotive Dealerships. Lyle was looking for a good deal and Kalafer gave him one. In the six weeks it took for the new truck to arrive, Kalafer happened to buy a new baseball team in the Atlantic League of Professional Baseball and told Vukovich that he was looking for a Yankee to manage his new team. He wanted "somebody with a name," so Sparky Lyle's name came up. On the day Sparky and his wife went to pick up the new F-150, he not only got his new truck, but a job offer to manage the Somerset Patriots.

Lyle has been manager of the Somerset Patriots since the team started in 1998. He boasts a very impressive managerial record, leading his Patriots to three League Championship titles—a league record—

Celebrating the pennant are Sparky Lyle, Russ Gibson, and Dick Williams. The rookie Lyle was set as the sole left-hander in the Series from the Red Sox bullpen until Boston was given permission to add Ken Brett.

seven Half Championships, and six South Division Championships.

In 2003, Lyle led the Patriots to the team's second Atlantic League Championship. They started out the first half of the season at the bottom of the South Division standings. Under Lyle's leadership, the team made a remarkable comeback to win the Second Half Championship and move into the post-season. Shutting out the Camden Riversharks in back-to-back games, the Patriots then defeated the Nashua Pride for the Atlantic League championship. Lyle was named Manager of the Year, the second time that honor was bestowed on him. (The first time was in 1999.)

In 2005, Sparky Lyle earned his 500th win as the Somerset Patriots manager and to this day is the winningest manager in the league. In 2006 he signed a contract extension keeping him with the team through the 2007 season.

In the winter, Sparky spends his spare time listening to The Eagles while shooting pool, golfing, cooking, and just hanging around the house. He says, laughing: "I think I've actually been on one vacation in my whole life. I went to Sedona, Arizona, for ten days, and I was back in four. I couldn't take it anymore. I saw enough of them (freaking) red rocks!"

Don McMahon

by John Vorperian

	G	ERA	W	L	SV	GS	GF	CG	SHO	IP	H	R	ER	BB	SO	HR	BFP
1967 RED SOX	11	3.57	1	2	2	0	6	0	0	17.2	14	8	7	13	10	4	79

History has not been kind to Don McMahon. Now largely forgotten, McMahon had a very long, often excellent career, pitched in the postseason four times, helped win two World Championships, and was clearly one of baseball's best relief pitchers in a number of seasons.

Playing in the days before the closer became such a highly-prized position, Donald John McMahon worked for seven teams in 18 major league seasons. Upon his retirement at the age of 44, records show that only three pitchers (Hoyt Wilhelm, Lindy McDaniel, and Cy Young) had appeared in more games. The two-pitch (fastball and overhand curve) right-handed McMahon pitched in 874 games, racking up 1,310⅔ innings and 1,003 strikeouts. He notched 153 saves, posted a 90-68 won/loss record (.570), with a career 2.96 ERA.

Born on January 4, 1930, in Brooklyn, New York, McMahon grew up there as well. The youngster of Irish-American descent went to St. Jerome's elementary school and Brooklyn Prep. In 1948, he graduated from Erasmus Hall High School. McMahon played baseball for the local Flatbush Robins in 1949. He was signed by Boston Braves scout John "Honey" Russell before the 1959 season.

Although mainly a third baseman in high school, McMahon was converted by the Braves into a pitcher. In 1950 at Owensboro, Kentucky (Kitty League), the 20-year-old won 20 games, with 143 strikeouts and a 2.72 ERA. He led the league in all three categories. The next year, he was sent to Denver (Western League) but appeared in only four games—in relief—before entering the Army, where he served from May 22, 1951 to May 14, 1953. After completing his service time, McMahon remained in the Braves organization—though the club had relocated to Milwaukee just before the 1953 season.

McMahon was assigned to Evansville in the Three-I League and pitched 114 innings in 1953 for a 6-5 win-loss record with 91 strikeouts and a 4.50 ERA. In 1954, he was assigned to the Atlanta Crackers (Southern Association) where he improved his game and got his ERA down to 3.56.

On the personal front, 1955 was a big success: he married Dolores Darlene Sater on February 5. But it was a dismal baseball year. Now with Toledo (American Association), McMahon finished 2-13 with an ERA that ballooned to 5.01. He returned to Atlanta the following year. Incoming Braves pitching coach Charlie Root acknowledged the 2-13 record, but said, "I don't see how anybody ever hits him. He throws so hard that catchers have a hard time hanging onto his pitches."

McMahon always credited the Atlanta Crackers' field manager, former Brooklyn Dodger hurler Whitlow Wyatt, for moving him from the rotation to the bullpen in 1956. It was a switch which proved very successful. That year, McMahon posted a 4-2 mark in 36 innings, struck out 34, and recorded a low 2.00 ERA and earned a mid-season move to Wichita in the American Association. He took a while to adapt to the new league, but led off 1957 with a 2.92 ERA in his first 71 innings of relief and got himself a call-up to the big leagues in June. Clyde King also was credited with helping McMahon develop. By this time, McMahon was pitching exclusively in relief.

On June 30, 1957, McMahon made his major league debut against the Pittsburgh Pirates in a Sunday nightcap game before 36,283 in Milwaukee's County Stadium. Called upon in the top of the ninth to replace southpaw Taylor Phillips, he entered a game the Pirates were leading, 4-2. McMahon set down the three batters he faced. In the bottom of the ninth, the hometown Braves knotted the score on a Felix Mantilla home run with Joe Torre on board. In the Braves 10th, McMahon popped out to first in his first major league at-bat. Taken out in the 12th for a pinch hitter, McMahon ended his part of the game with four innings pitched, giving up just two hits and striking out seven. Milwaukee won the match in the 13th by a come-from-behind score of 6-5 when Eddie Mathews hit a two-run home run.

In his first eight appearances, he threw 14 scoreless innings. Milwaukee captured the 1957 National League pennant with a 95-59 record. McMahon ended a great first season with nine saves and a 1.54 ERA. He made three appearances in the 1957 Fall Classic against the Yankees, which the Braves won four games to three. McMahon threw five innings in relief without allowing a run. After the season, he played winter ball for San Juan in Puerto Rico. In December, though, he was traded to Estrellas Orientales in the Dominican League.

The "trade" was put in quotation marks because the idea was to place him with a team that didn't need as much relief help, so he wouldn't get overworked.

McMahon pitched very well to open the 1958 season and was named to the 1958 All-Star team. He won seven games and lost two, with an ERA of 3.68. It wasn't until June 6 that he gave up his first home run in major league ball, to Don Zimmer, after 47 appearances without one. McMahon reportedly became a baseball factoid sometime in 1958 at Milwaukee's County Stadium when he was the first pitcher driven from the bullpen to the mound; he arrived in a motor scooter with sidecar. McMahon saved the pennant clincher for Warren Spahn on September 21 and the Braves repeated as NL champs. McMahon again made three appearances in the World Series but this time Milwaukee fell in seven games to the Yankees.

In 1959, relief specialist McMahon led the National League in saves with 15 and had a very good year with a 2.57 ERA. He claimed to have counted 132 times he was up and throwing in the bullpen; accurate or not, he was used in 60 games. He helped keep the Braves in it, but the hitting wasn't quite sufficient and the Braves finished the year tied with the Dodgers. The Dodgers took the first two games of the best of three playoff.

He got a good pay raise but had a disappointing year in 1960, with a 5.94 ERA and a 3-6 mark. The Braves still contended, finishing second, seven games behind the Pirates. Bob Wolf wrote in *The Sporting News* that "the Braves' relief pitching was far short of championship caliber. The failure of Don McMahon to regain his form of the last three years was becoming more costly as the season wore on."

Bouncing back from his "season-long slump" (Wolf) in 1961, McMahon brought his ERA back under 3.00 and finished a decent season with a 6-4 mark and a 2.84 ERA. He'd started 1961 very well indeed, but tailed off significantly in August and September, and the team was not convinced that he'd entirely returned to form. They chose not to protect him in the expansion draft as the New York Mets and Houston Colt .45s both joined the league for 1962. Neither team picked him up, and Bob Wolf wrote in February that he "doesn't seem to have the old hop on his fastball, but he does have a good slider and a pretty fair curve."

On May 9, 1962, though, Houston was ready to make a move and though he'd not worked much and not pitched well, the 32-year-old right hander was purchased by the Colt .45s for a relatively modest $30,000. When the Braves came to Houston for the first time, he unleashed a barrage at his old manager

Lee Stange and Don McMahon may be wondering if the team can turn the season around. Both came from Cleveland in a June 1966 trade for Dick Radatz.

Birdie Tebbetts, bitter over the fact that he'd hardly been used by Milwaukee (three innings of work in the first month) and that Tebbetts had told him not to use his fastball except as a waste pitch. He blazed several fastballs past Braves batters and got credit for beating his old team on June 7. A *Sporting News* account in the June 23 issue makes it clear there was no love lost between Tebbetts and McMahon. Don later admitted he got a letter from his mother admonishing him. "She told me to quit saying things against Mr. Tebbetts," he reported. He'd also had a flare-up over salary with Braves GM John McHale, so a change of scenery was probably in order.

Looking back on the year, McMahon was able to tell reporter Clark Nealon that 1962 was "the most gratifying year I've had since I came up to the Braves in 1957, helped them win the pennant and pitched in the World Series." (*The Sporting News*, March 16, 1963) He'd found his fastball again, liked the hot weather, and felt Houston treated its players better (and had a better philosophy of sharing relief work). He appeared in 51 games for Houston and contributed a stellar 1.53 earned run average.

In 1963, McMahon put in a full year for Houston, but it wasn't nearly as strong as '62. His ERA ballooned

to 4.05. He did witness teammate Don Nottebart's no-hitter. It was the eighth no-hitter McMahon had seen. McMahon had been the one to recommend signing Nottebart to GM Paul Richards. Right at the end of the 1963 season, McMahon was bought by the Cleveland Indians, reuniting him with Birdie Tebbetts, now the Tribe's manager. It was Tebbetts who recommended getting McMahon, though it was a cheap enough acquisition at the $20,000 waiver price. The Indians weren't desperate for bullpen help, but Birdie spotted something in Hoot Evers' scouting report on McMahon and thought he saw a bargain.

McMahon lamented leaving Houston, saying that a bad shoulder had hampered him during a large part of the '63 season. After the winter off, he established himself as Cleveland's bullpen ace right out of the gate. Coming to a new league gave him a bit of an advantage at first. He still relied mainly on his fastball. "My control isn't so sharp that I can pitch to the inside corner on one guy and the outside on another. All I want to know is whether I should pitch him high or low." (Regis McAuley, *The Sporting News*, June 6, 1964) By mid-year, he had a 1.71 ERA. By year's end, he'd made 70 appearances in relief, breaking the previous club record of 63 appearances. He was 6-4 with 16 saves. In November, he was named Man of the Year for the Indians.

He was a holdout in the spring, and it took a while before Cleveland GM Gabe Paul and his pitcher came to terms—while seated at the February writers' dinner. He contributed a solid and respectable '65 season (3.28 ERA), though not nearly as spectacular as in 1964.

He wasn't being used quite as much in early 1966, throwing a little over 12 innings in 12 games through the end of May. His ERA was good, though, at 2.92.

In early June, the Indians traded McMahon and fellow pitcher Lee Stange to the Red Sox for Dick Radatz. In *Lost Summer: The '67 Red Sox and the Impossible Dream*, author Bill Reynolds described Radatz as the "...most dominant relief pitcher in the game, a large hulking man nicknamed 'the Monster'..." He'd really had a disappointing year in 1965, losing 11 games, and wasn't off to such a hot start in '66, losing his first two decisions. Dick Stuart called him "that former fastball pitcher" and unforgiving Fenway crowds weren't making his life easy. The Red Sox were on a bit of a swapping spree; the trade was the seventh the team had made since September '65, as Dick O'Connell moved to remake the team.

Despite The Monster's struggles, the trade was condemned by many in Boston. Stange was acquired for long relief and spot starts; McMahon was seen as the short relief specialist—though his first appearance was a four-inning stint against the Yankees on June 4, and he faced the minimum 12 batters in the seventh through the tenth innings in a game the Sox won on a three-run homer by Jim Gosger in the bottom of the 16th. He put out a fire the following night, also against the Yankees. On July 6, he earned wins in both halves of a doubleheader at Yankee Stadium and began to win hearts and minds in Boston. The last pitcher to win both ends of a doubleheader from the Bombers was Dave Davenport of the St. Louis Browns a half-century earlier, in 1916.

McMahon took over the fireman role leading the 1966 pen with nine saves and a 2.65 ERA. Stange won seven games, but lost nine. Radatz had had his day; he disappointed Cleveland with an 0-3 record and a far higher ERA than either Stange or McMahon. Stange won 15 games and Radatz not one. Radatz had another mediocre year in Cleveland and, in the end, Larry Claflin wrote that the Sox felt they "jobbed" the Indians and may have cost Birdie Tebbetts his job. But Boston still wound up just a half-game out of last place. The Boston baseball writers noted McMahon's contribution nonetheless and voted him the club's most valuable pitcher for 1966.

April 29, 1967. Don McMahon gave up a run to Kansas City in the top of the 15th, but José Tartabull's single drove in Conigliaro and Scott for a 5-4 Red Sox win. McMahon shows Tartabull some post-game appreciation.

At the start of 1967, Don, his wife Darlene, their six kids, and two dogs all drove across country from his home near Anaheim for Red Sox spring training. He and John Wyatt were seen as the core of the Boston bullpen. McMahon didn't pitch as well, though, running up a 3.57 ERA in April and May.

Exactly one year from the day he was acquired by the Red Sox, they sent him to Chicago. It was June 2, 1967, as Red Sox management sought to bolster their infield by trading for veteran utilityman Jerry Adair. McMahon was not getting a lot of work, having thrown just 17⅔ innings. The White Sox had lost their primary reliever, Dennis Higgins, who suffered a detached retina, and were anxious to make a trade, anxious enough to give up a player like Adair. O'Connell found it a very attractive deal, and he pounced on it, throwing in highly-touted minor league pitching prospect Bob Snow (who'd gone 20-2 for Winston-Salem the year before).

'67 Red Sox skipper Dick Williams told SABR interviewer Jeff Angus that it was "a trade that helped both clubs." He added, "McMahon was disgruntled to leave, but he was just bouncing the ball off the plate with us. When he went over to Chicago, [he] pitched very well for them ... [while] Adair played short for us for three weeks when Rico was hurt, and contributed...." The shift agreed with McMahon—he finished the year with a 1.67 ERA for the White Sox and a 5-0 record, making a key contribution to Chicago's pennant drive. Adair contributed in a number of ways, and a number of writers felt his acquisition one of the key moves the Sox made in 1967.

McMahon didn't last much more than a year in the Windy City. The White Sox really needed another starter, and in a straight-up swap on July 26, 1968, they sent McMahon to the Detroit Tigers for right-hander Dennis Ribant. Chicago was worried about Gary Peters' health and wanted a pitcher with starting capabilities. McMahon again posted a final 1.98 ERA (consistent throughout the year, he was 1.96 for Chicago and 2.02 for Detroit). He'd missed being in the 1967 World Series with the Red Sox, but he found himself with another pennant-winning team as Detroit won the pennant in 1968. McMahon collected his second World Championship ring, as the Tigers beat the St. Louis Cardinals in the Fall Classic, he himself appearing twice, though briefly and not effectively.

McMahon returned to the National League later the following year, joining his seventh major league team, when the San Francisco Giants purchased him from the Tigers on August 8. Playing with Cooperstown-bound Willie Mays, Juan Marichal, Willie McCovey, and Gaylord Perry must have agreed with him. He was 39 at the time of the transaction, and he still kept getting batters out. He posted a 3.04 ERA for the remainder of 1969 and a 2.96 ERA in 61 appearances in 1970. In 1971, he was still relying on his fastball but admitted he hadn't used his slider for a couple of years. He was getting his breaking ball over the plate better than ever, and so featured that more.

In 1972, when the Giants signed him, they did so in two capacities. He was to be a pitcher, of course, but he also served as pitching coach, taking over from Larry Jansen. He still got into 44 games, throwing 63 innings and tallying a 3.71 ERA.

Over 3½ seasons, McMahon posted an overall 25-15 won-loss record with 30 saves. After the 1972 season ended, the Giants released him as a player. He continued with his duties as pitching coach. When San Francisco's bullpen began to falter in mid-1973, McMahon was reactivated on June 25. He'd been throwing batting practice. all year, so was in excellent shape, and hopped into a game against Atlanta on July 2. The score was 6-5 Giants, there was a runner at first and no one out, with Hank Aaron due up. McMahon closed the game, setting down six straight batters. He notched a 4-0 won-loss mark with six saves, with an excellent 1.48 ERA. The following year, the same situation presented itself. He was the team's pitching coach, returned to the active roster on May 21, and the following day shut down the Braves in two full innings of work. He threw only 11⅔ innings, though, appearing in nine games with no decisions and a 3.09 ERA. Six weeks later, San Francisco called up Phoenix (Pacific Coast League) farmhand right-hander Ed Halicki and placed McMahon on waivers. Once he cleared waivers, McMahon returned as the pitching coach. His last appearance as a pitcher had been on June 29, 1974, in a home game against the Dodgers. He threw two innings in relief.

McMahon coached for San Francisco through 1975. In 1976-1977 he was a coach with the Minnesota Twins. For a couple of years, Don worked in sales for the Rawlings Sporting Goods Company and turned up at Anaheim Stadium to present Rick Miller with a Gold Glove.

He returned to the major league ranks in a reprise as pitching coach with the Giants for three more seasons, 1980-1982. Within a few weeks after he was released, he was hired by the Cleveland Indians in the same capacity from 1983-85. In November 1985, he was hired by the Los Angeles Dodgers "to position players

from the press box" as the team's Eye in the Sky. He even worked some in the offseason as a football scout for several years, helping out the Oakland Raiders even while still an active player. Al Davis and he had both gone to school at Erasmus High in Brooklyn.

On July 22, 1987, at Dodger Stadium, while pitching batting practice, the 57-year-old McMahon suffered a heart attack and died a few hours later in a local hospital. He had been working for Los Angeles as an instructional coach and scout and threw batting practice almost every Dodgers home game.

Hall of Fame outfielder Duke Snider said of Mac, "I played against him. He never gave in to a hitter. He was a great competitor." The *New York Times* ran a heartfelt appreciation of Don McMahon by Ira Berkow, headlined "He Died With Spikes On." The Dodgers wore an arm band reading "MAC" in his memory.

Survived by his wife and six children, Don McMahon was buried at Good Shepherd Cemetery, Huntington Beach, California with a baseball in his hand.

Dave Morehead

by Andrew Blume

	G	ERA	W	L	SV	GS	GF	CG	SHO	IP	H	R	ER	BB	SO	HR	BFP
1967 RED SOX	10	4.34	5	4	0	9	0	1	1	47.2	48	24	23	22	40	0	208

While Red Sox fans remember Dave Morehead mostly for the no-hitter he threw in 1965, Morehead played a role on the '67 dream team by contributing five wins in the August-September stretch drive. Although he had a career major league record of only 40-64 with a 4.15 ERA, he showed flashes of brilliance, particularly early in his career, but extended success was thwarted by arm trouble.

David Michael Morehead was born to Charles and Patricia Morehead on September 5, 1943 in San Diego, California. A self-described "gym rat," he always enjoyed sports as a youth and hung out at the local recreation center where he would play games and sports ranging from ping pong to pinochle. As a nine-year-old, he played in the first Little League program offered in the San Diego area. Morehead's two-year-younger brother played in Little League with him. Two former professional ballplayers, Lee Singleton and Jim Gleason, were instrumental in his early development in baseball. His parents actively supported and encouraged his sports development, attending all his games.

Morehead recalls both going to watch the Pacific Coast League San Diego Padres and listening to them on the radio, always rooting for his favorite Padre, Max West. Morehead graduated from Herbert Hoover High School in San Diego, the same school that produced Ted Williams and ex-major leaguer and premier talent scout Ray Boone. The Cincinnati Reds, Kansas City Athletics, and Los Angeles Angels were among the teams competing with the Red Sox to sign him to a professional contract. Right after his 1961 graduation, he signed as an amateur free agent with Boston.

It was Boone who signed Morehead, the first player the former infielder secured as a Red Sox scout. Boone would later sign, among others, Curt Schilling. Morehead earned a bonus of $85,000, based on his 16-0 senior season credentials, an average of 15 strikeouts a game, and all-league honors (he also made all-league in basketball).

"I saw the Red Sox weren't playing very well, and I saw it as an opportunity to advance fast," Morehead told Peter Golenbock, author of *Red Sox Nation*. Morehead considered attending USC but was encouraged to sign with the Red Sox by former Boston Brave Bob Elliott, who sang the praises of owner Tom Yawkey. Morehead recalls having first met Ted Williams as a high school senior when Williams looked him over for the Red Sox (Williams grew up three or four miles east of him in the University Heights section of San Diego.).

Morehead was originally slated to start out in Alpine, Texas, in the rookie league. First, though, he was summoned to Seattle to pitch in an exhibition game for the Red Sox against their Triple-A Seattle Rainiers club. Morehead was given five innings to show the Sox what he had, opposing fellow prospect Stew McDonald. Morehead impressed the parent club, tossing five shutout innings. Instead of Alpine, the Sox assigned him to Johnstown of the Single-A Eastern League where he went 4-8 with a 4.80 ERA.

In 1962, the 18-year-old was promoted to the Rainiers, managed by Johnny Pesky. Now at the doorstep of the major leagues, Morehead improved significantly on his first-year numbers, posting a 10-9 record, 3.72 ERA with 159 strikeouts. His fast track to the majors was completed the next season as both he and his manager, Pesky (succeeding Mike "Pinky" Higgins as Boston manager), were promoted to the big leagues.

Morehead was originally set for a return to Triple A in 1963 but was called up to Boston when Gene Conley and Ike Delock experienced arm troubles. The 6-foot, 185-pound, right-handed Morehead began his major league career in phenom style on April 13, 1963, at D.C. Stadium against the Washington Senators, shutting out the Senators, 3-0, striking out 10 (the first of 10 double-digit strikeout games in his career), and allowing only five hits. His shutout was the first by a Red Sox pitcher making his debut since Dave "Boo" Ferriss in 1945. Morehead pitched 6⅔ innings of one-run, four-hit ball in his next start, on April 20 against the Tigers, but recorded a no-decision in a 15-inning Red Sox victory. In his third start, on May 5 at Kansas City, Morehead allowed only four hits in 7⅔ innings in a 3-2 Red Sox win.

Continuing his early mastery of major league hitters, Morehead pitched a one-hitter against the Senators on May 12, 1963 at Fenway Park, raising his record to 3-0 in the 4-1 win and lowering his ERA to 1.11. Alas, this was the major leagues, and his ERA ballooned to 4.19 in the process of losing his next five starts.

On July 2, Morehead threw a complete-game two-

hitter against the Indians in Cleveland, a 6-1 Red Sox win in which he had a no-hitter that was broken up in the eighth inning by a grounder that bounced off something in the infield and went into right field. He followed this up with a three-hit 6-2 win over the White Sox on July 6 at home.

Morehead's final numbers in his rookie campaign were 10-13, 3.81, with 136 strikeouts, 99 walks, and only 137 hits allowed in 174⅔ innings. He threw six complete games and one shutout (his debut). It was an excellent start for a 19-year-old rookie on a poor team.

Morehead's numbers slipped in 1964. On a team that lost 90 games and had only one pitcher with a winning percentage over .500 (ace reliever Dick Radatz, who had a remarkable 16-9 season), Morehead was 8-15 with a 4.97 ERA. In 30 starts, he struck out 139, walked 112, and allowed 156 hits in 166⅔ innings. On June 12, he struck out a career-high 12 Orioles in a 7-3 Red Sox win.

The 1965 Red Sox were worse than the year before, posting a 62-100 record, the team's first 100-plus losing season since the 1932 team lost a franchise-record 111. Earl Wilson led the staff with 13 victories. Morehead and Bill Monbouquette each posted 10-18 records. In 192⅔ innings, Morehead struck out 163, a career high, and allowed only 157 hits, but walked 113 and posted a 4.06 ERA. He finished the season strong. On August 26, he threw a three-hit complete game win over the Senators, 4-2. Five days later, he gave up two hits in six innings in a 4-0 shutout of the Senators. On September 4, he threw a complete game, three-hit, 1-0 shutout at Yankee Stadium for his third straight win. On September 10, he was charged with the 8-5 loss to the Twins. Next came his gem.

On September 16, Morehead took to the Fenway Park mound against Luis Tiant and the Cleveland Indians before a paid crowd of 1,247 with another 1,123 present on passes, the smallest crowd of the year at Fenway. In the Indians' second, Rocky Colavito drew a

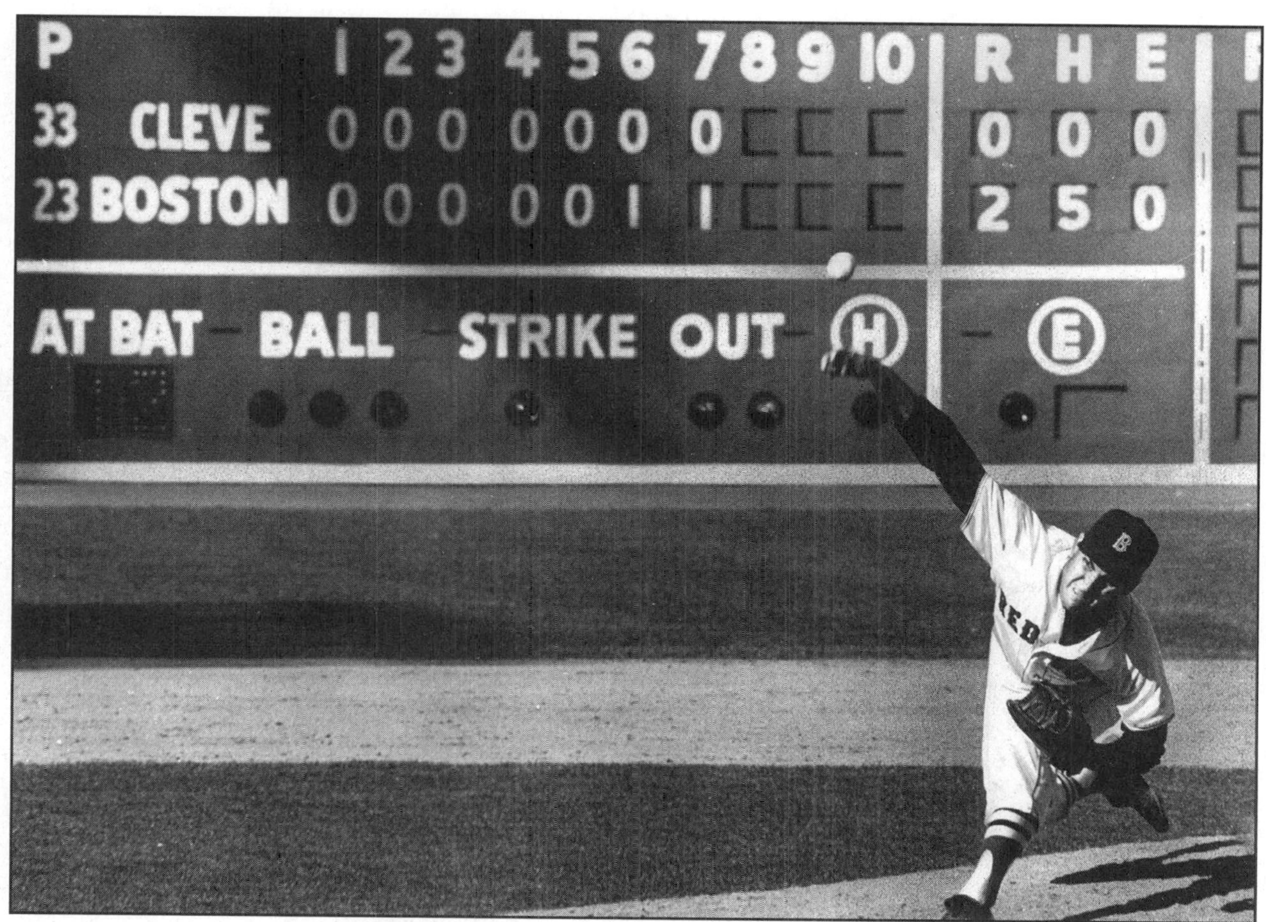

September 16, 1965. With two outs in the top of the eighth, Morehead fires a pitch to Bill Davis, pinch-hitting for Cleveland second baseman Pedro Gonzalez. Davis flied out to Jim Gosger in center field and Morehead's no-hitter remained intact.

leadoff walk on a 3-2 pitch. Colavito was the only batter to reach base for the Indians that day.

Meanwhile, Luis Tiant, Morehead's mound opponent, matched Morehead zero for zero until the sixth, retiring 17 batters in a row at one point. With two out in the sixth, Boston's Jim Gosger beat out his second hit of the day off Tiant and scored on a triple to the Boston bullpen in right-center by Dalton Jones. Lee Thomas added an insurance run in the seventh with his 20th homer of the year down the right field line.

With two outs in the top of the ninth, Vic Davalillo batted for shortstop Dick Howser. Morehead got two quick strikes on fastballs. After some angst—Indians manager Birdie Tebbetts was trying to disrupt his rhythm, Morehead told Golenbock—he threw a curve that Davalillo hit back to him. "I went to catch it, and I was going to run over to first the way Mel Parnell did in his no-hitter, either step on the bag myself or hand it to the first baseman so I wouldn't take the chance of throwing it away. In my haste, the ball hit the heel of my glove and I started to run without the ball. The ball lay on the mound. I went back to pick it up and threw it to first base real quick. The throw was low in the dirt, and Mad Dog Lee Thomas scooped it out. I had my no-no."

It was a brilliant effort—nine hitless innings with just a single walk and eight strikeouts. Ultimately, what made this event so remarkable is that no Red Sox pitcher would throw another no-hitter until Hideo Nomo in 2001. For the next 35 years, Dave Morehead's name was remembered around Fenway Park as the last Red Sox pitcher to have thrown a hitless gem.

Morehead's pitching feat was overshadowed by a post-game press conference announcing the firing of Red Sox general manager Mike "Pinky" Higgins. This would prove a key move as executive vice president Dick O'Connell, who had until then handled the business end for the Sox, took over the all-around operation of the team and proceeded to put together

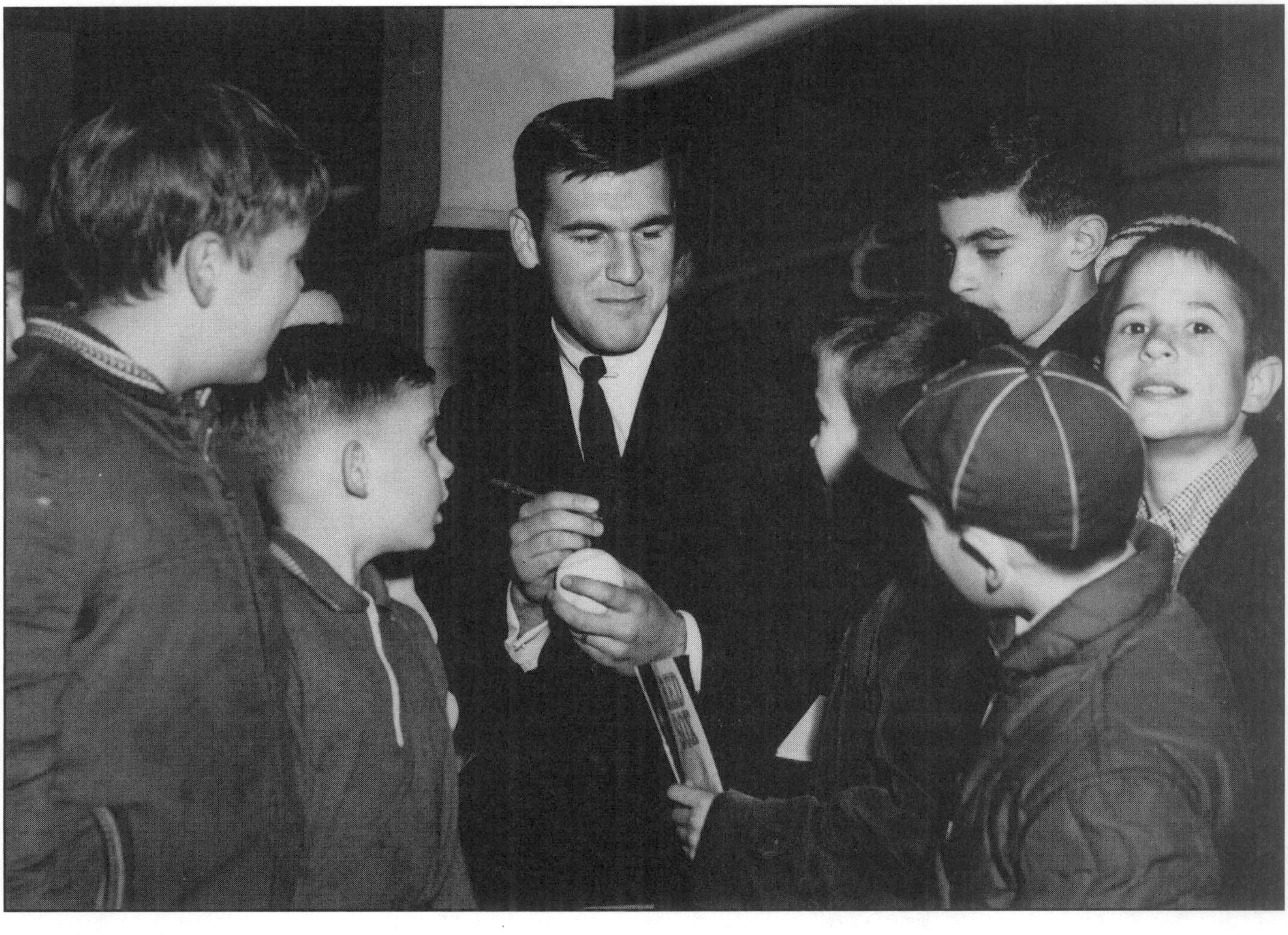

Dave Morehead surrounded by some young fans.

the '67 Impossible Dream team.

Morehead was immediately rewarded for his pitching gem with a $1,000 bonus by owner Tom Yawkey. But the optimism engendered by his late-season success in 1965 turned to disappointment in 1966. In his first start of the season, he lasted only three innings and gave up three home runs in an 8-1 loss to the Orioles on April 13.

On April 19, he pitched five innings at Fenway against the Tigers, his longest outing of the year and one that may have had an effect on the remainder of his career. It was cold and drizzly and the footing on the field was poor. Morehead was cruising along, striking out six Tigers with a 7-0 lead through four innings. In the fifth, he threw a pitch and his left foot gave out as he landed on the mound. He felt something pop in his arm. He completed the inning, but was unable to lift his arm to take off his jacket and start the sixth. He would not win another game in 1966 and would not make another appearance until May 30.

According to Morehead, his whole shoulder turned black and blue within five to six weeks after the injury. He was treated with cortisone shots, and was instructed by trainer Buddy LeRoux to hold a 2½ pound steel ball shoulder-high. He pitched only 28 innings through July 23, his last appearance of 1966. He completed the season 1-2 with a 5.46 ERA. Morehead, who threw a low 90s fastball, a quarter curve (similar to a slider) and an overhand curve (his out pitch), believes the April 1966 injury had an effect on the balance of his career. He altered his delivery to compensate for the pain.

Morehead began the 1967 season with Toronto of the International League, posting an 11-5 record with a 3.10 ERA with 109 strikeouts and 105 hits allowed in 122 innings, including five complete games. He was recalled by the Red Sox in late July. He started his first game on August 1 against the Athletics at Fenway Park. He allowed four runs in the third, giving a bases-loaded triple to Bert Campaneris, was taken out with nobody out, and was charged with the 4-3 loss. Two days later on August 3, he picked up the win in his only relief appearance of the 1967 season in a 5-3 victory over the A's. In five innings of scoreless relief of starter Bill Landis, he gave up only four hits.

Morehead continued what would be a seesaw season

Morehead's 1965 no-hitter happened on the same day the Sox finally kissed Pinky Higgins goodbye, enabling Dick O'Connell to become general manager.

for him on August 8 in Kansas City. In a 5-3 loss to the A's, he allowed five runs, four earned, with seven hits in 4.1 innings. But at home on August 15, he shut out the Tigers 4-0 for his first complete game since his no-hitter nearly two years earlier. Then on August 20, he lasted only 1⅔ innings against California, allowing six runs. The Angels increased their lead to 8-0 before the Red Sox made a memorable comeback and won, 9-8.

On August 24 at home, Morehead ran his record to 3-2 with 6⅓ innings of five-hit, two-run, seven-strikeout pitching in a 7-5 win over the Senators. On August 28 at Yankee Stadium, Morehead paired up with Sparky Lyle to shut out the Yankees, 3-0.

On September 4, Morehead lost to the Senators, 5-2, but on the 9th he again teamed up with Lyle to shut down the Yankees, 7-1, at Fenway. It was Morehead's fifth victory. His last regular season appearance of 1967 was on September 15 at home against the Orioles. He gave up three runs in a 6-2 loss to Baltimore. The last of his 10 appearances, the loss brought his regular season to a close with a record of 5-4 and a 4.34 ERA. In 47⅔ innings, he struck out 40 and walked 22, allowing 48 hits. Morehead no longer recalls why he was not used the final few weeks of the season other than remembering that the starters went on a good run and his services were not necessary down the stretch.

Morehead made two appearances in the 1967 World Series against the Cardinals. In Game Four in St. Louis, he pitched an impressive three innings of hitless relief in the 6-0 loss. In the seventh game 7-2 loss on October 12, Morehead took to the hill to start the ninth inning. He struck out Bob Gibson but walked the bases loaded before giving way to Dan Osinski and Ken Brett who retired the Cardinals without a run.

Morehead enjoyed the 1967 experience. He told Golenbock, "There was no pressure in '67. It was fun." Morehead reports that he still keeps in touch with fellow dream-teamers, including Darrell Brandon, Mike Andrews, Gary Bell, and Lee Stange. "You had the camaraderie and no bitching and moaning, 'cause you're pulling for one thing, to win, and that's what was really exciting. I tell you, it was fun to be wrapped up in a pennant race, probably the most exciting pennant race that has ever been." Morehead expressed respect for manager Dick Williams, having played alongside him in his early years and having commuted to the ball park with Williams and Lee Thomas. Despite Williams' "sarcastic" style of getting in a player's head, Morehead said he learned a lot from him and said you "always knew where you stood with Dick."

Morehead again began the season in Triple A in 1968, pitching for Louisville of the International League. In 18 games, he was 6-7 with a 3.18 ERA. He made the first of his 11 appearances for Boston in 1968 on July 27 in Washington. After two one-inning relief appearances, he made nine starts for the Red Sox, compiling a record of 1-4, with a 2.45 ERA. He threw three complete games. In 55 innings, he allowed 52 hits, walking 20 and striking out 28.

On October 15, 1968, Morehead was selected by the Kansas City Royals in the expansion draft. In 1969, he appeared in 21 games, making only two starts. In 33 innings, he compiled a 2-3 record with a 5.73 ERA. In 1970, Morehead appeared in 28 games for the Royals, starting 17 (including one complete game). He was 3-5 with a 3.62 ERA. On August 7, he made his last career start, pitching five innings and allowing one run on seven hits and earning his final career win in a 10-2 victory in Kansas City against the visiting Milwaukee Brewers. On September 29, he appeared in his final major league game, a 4:05 twelve-inning contest won by the Royals 14-13 over the Twins. Morehead allowed one run and three hits in 1⅓ innings. He was called out on strikes against Jim Perry in the third in his final career at-bat. In the third, Morehead faced his final batter, shortstop Leo Cardenas, getting him to ground to second, forcing out Cesar Tovar. Morehead was released by the Royals on March 30, 1971, bringing his baseball career to a conclusion. He briefly pondered his professional baseball options but ultimately decided to begin his post-baseball life; he'd been attending San Diego State in his offseasons.

Morehead enrolled at S.D.S.U. in 1961 and persevered to earn his B.A. in marketing in 1973. In 1972, he went into the retail business and worked for Gemco through his college management training program. In 1990, Morehead started a business in which he is still active: Pacific Crest Marketing. He is a manufacturer's representative engaged in the sale of primarily sporting goods to retail chains. He still enjoys professional baseball and follows the Red Sox from a distance. As a season-ticket holder for the local Angels, he attends approximately 15-18 games a year.

Morehead married the former Patricia Morse in 1963 and has resided in North Tustin, California, since 1975. His son Michael was born in June of the 1967 season and is an attorney in Northern California and a big Red Sox fan. His daughter Crista was born in September 1969 and is a director of marketing for Goldman Sachs investment firm in San Francisco. Morehead has two grandsons, Spencer and Rhys.

Dan Osinski

by Ron Anderson

	G	ERA	W	L	SV	GS	GF	CG	SHO	IP	H	R	ER	BB	SO	HR	BFP
1967 RED SOX	34	2.54	3	1	2	0	12	0	0	63.2	61	19	18	14	38	5	268

He was known among his colleagues and sports scribes as "The Silencer," a name—acquired from a Pacific Coast League sports writer in 1962 while playing for Portland—that followed him through his professional baseball career. Dan Osinski, who would later pitch for the Boston Red Sox, was an original "fireman," as the term was coined during the early 1960s when the relief specialist role was becoming fashionable in professional baseball. The timing couldn't have been better for Osinski, and may have extended his career.

Daniel Osinski was born on November 17, 1933, in Chicago. In his major league playing days, he was listed as 6 feet 1½ inches tall, and weighing 200 pounds. In his first two high school years, in Wauconda, Illinois, Osinski played basketball, baseball, and one year of football. His family moved to Barrington, Illinois, where he starred in the same three sports at Barrington High School in his junior and senior years. He threw two consecutive no-hitters in his senior year in 1951, and remembers that there were baseball scouts everywhere watching his games. Interviewed at his Sun City, Arizona, home, Osinski recalled his early days. "Baseball wasn't my main sport," he recalled. "When I was in high school it was basketball and football."[1]

A brief flirtation with the U.S. Naval Academy was scuttled when the media accused them of favoring athletes by clearing Osinski for admission though he failed his physical. Osinski wanted no part of the media or the controversy and chose instead to play pro baseball. "I went to St. Louis and worked out with the St Louis Browns, and the Cleveland Indians were [also] down there at the time. They ended up signing me when I was down there," he recalled in an interview.

Wally Laskowski, an Indians scout, signed Osinski to a major league contract in 1951. Osinski was 17 years old. He signed for $4,000, the most he could get and not be considered a "bonus baby" which would have required him to spend a year with the big league team.

In 1952 Cleveland assigned Dan to Fort Smith, Arkansas, of the Western Association (Class C). He recalls pitching to John Blanchard of the Yankees organization: "I can remember throwing him a fastball and he hit that thing up the light tower in right-center field. I never had a ball hit that hard off me ever."

Osinski had an 11-16 record with Fort Smith, with a 3.58 ERA. He struck out 155 batters, but led the league with 171 bases on balls. He gave up 188 hits in 221 innings.

In 1953 Osinski pitched for Sherbrooke, Quebec, of the Provincial League (Class C), an experience he described as being "a little wild." He racked up a good record of 18-7 with a 2.80 ERA, giving up only 149 hits over 196 innings pitched. He struck out 135 batters—a team record—but issued 138 walks.

Dan described with amusement a unique pitching experience at Sherbrooke. "I was out to Lake Magog, a little place I remember going swimming out there one time, and I never got sunburned so bad. And then I had to come back and pitch the next day. I had sunburn all over and I just covered myself up with this Noxzema, and I had a wool sweatshirt on, and I went out there. I was loose, don't get me wrong, I got very loose. I walked 17 batters and I still had a shutout going in the eighth inning. I won the ballgame 5-1."

From Sherbrooke, Osinski went to Keokuk, Iowa of the Class B Three-I League in 1954. "My roommate there was Roger Maris," said Osinski. "Roger and I were roommates at Keokuk, Reading, and Tulsa."

Osinski laments his season at Keokuk, where he won 13 games and lost 10. He made a great start the first half of the season, and was the starting pitcher in the All-Star game. But he became inexplicably tired, weak, and ineffective during and after the All-Star break. Though he pitched in his normal rotation, he struggled the balance of that year. He was later diagnosed with infectious mononucleosis, which plagued him for a long time.

For 1955, he and Maris were assigned to Tulsa of the Double-A Texas League. One day, a day before he was to start, Osinski was running a fever and not feeling well. As he warmed up for a relief stint, the team doctor paid him a visit. "Boy, he came out and got me. He wouldn't let me in there because I had too high a fever. That's when I really found out I had the mononucleosis. That's from the year before. I had it all that time, I couldn't shake it. I didn't find out about it until I was on the road trip. I wasn't sure what happened, you know, what it was. They sent me to Reading, Pennsylvania. I

got into the hotel and then I just passed out. The maid found me in my room."

Osinski spent the better part of two months in and out of a hospital recovering, and saw little action while in Reading. He was then sent to Spartanburg of the Tri-State League (Class B), where he made his first start for the Peaches on July 9, 1955, allowing only five hits and two earned runs. "My weight was down, too, at that time, probably, if I was 175 pounds I was heavy. I was getting over [the mono]. I was still kind of shaky with it."

From Spartanburg, Osinski was sent to Fayetteville of the Carolina League (Class B) in 1956. Still recovering from his illness, he pitched anyway. He posted a 10-11 won-loss record that year with a 3.75 ERA.

In 1957 Osinski was drafted into the Army and served for two years. (He failed his first physical because he still had mononucleosis, but passed a second physical.) He suffered doubts about continuing in baseball. "At that time I was just thinking about hanging it up. I just wasn't moving at all going from Double A to A, to B again, and then to B again which was not considered as strong a league as the Three-I League. You think, oh, you're done." Meanwhile, he wound up at Fort Campbell, Kentucky, where he received a "special assignment"—playing baseball—for the 187th Battle Group.

Osinski returned to baseball in 1959 as a free agent. "I never knew what my status was," he recalls. "Nobody knew that I was in the service. If you see all my records, they show 'out of baseball.' I didn't tell anybody. I just thought I was done anyhow, so when I got out I went to see somebody at the White Sox, and they ended up [asking me to] come to spring training. We went to spring training in the minor leagues at Hollywood, Florida, and I made the ball club for the Class C team there."

The White Sox sent Osinski to the Duluth-Superior club of the Northern League (Class C), where he made a conscious effort to craft himself into a relief specialist, as a strategy for reaching the big leagues. "When I got there I decided, well, the best way for me to do it is to become a relief pitcher, and forget about the starting."

Osinski made a league-leading 54 appearances, all in relief, at Duluth-Superior in 1959. He was among the leaders with a 2.41 ERA, an 8-9 won-loss record, and 129 strikeouts. "Duluth was just a stop to see if I could play again," he says.

From Duluth, in 1960 Osinski traveled to Charleston, South Carolina, in the South Atlantic League (Class A), where he played briefly, posting a 2.31 ERA. Before the season ended, he was sent to Lincoln, Nebraska, of the Three-I League, and posted a 9-2 won-loss record with an impressive 2.89 ERA. He pitched in 61 games between the two clubs, mostly in relief roles. In 1961 Osinski returned to Charleston and pitched a full season there. Once again he led his league for most appearances with 56 that year, with an 8-6 won-loss record and a solid 2.50 ERA. Osinski was taking on the "workhorse" label and being noticed by major league clubs.

The Kansas City Athletics acquired Osinski's contract from the White Sox and invited him to spring training for 1962. Osinski made a strong showing, and went north with the club. He made his major league debut on April 11, 1962 against the Minnesota Twins in a losing ball-game, 8-0. Dan had a somewhat inauspicious start pitching one inning, yielding three runs on three base-hits, including a two-run homer by Earl Battey. He pitched in four games, allowing nine runs on eight hits, eight walks, and four strikeouts in 4⅔ innings. On May 10, Osinski was shipped to the Athletics' Albuquerque, New Mexico affiliate in the Texas League, where he posted a 3.00 ERA with a 3-1 won-loss record.

The Athletics' manager, Hank Bauer, was engaged in a youth movement and gave up on many of his older players, Osinski among them. The organization rated him "promising" but wild. He was sold outright to the Portland, Oregon club of the Pacific Coast League (Triple A). Osinski was a workhorse from the outset. He arrived in Portland on May 29, pitched that night, and relieved twice the next day. Sports writers labeled him "rubber-arm" for his endurance. By June 17 he had made 16 relief appearances in 20 days, posting a 1.06 ERA in that stretch.

Osinski made the PCL All-Star team which played an exhibition game against the Los Angeles Angels in Portland on August 11, 1962. "I made the All-Star team. I wasn't there more than 22 days, or something like that, and made the All-Star team. Not very long. Les [Peden, All-Star manager] says come on out, get a little gift or something while you're there, get in uniform and just go out and get dressed, go back and just [make an appearance]. My brother came in town, we had a couple of beers, played golf that day and I went to the ballpark," Osinski recalls.

"I said, well, I'll sit out in the bullpen. [Tom] Lasorda's pitching and he's got the bases loaded, or something like that, and Les calls up the bullpen and he says, 'Dan, can you get somebody out?'" Osinski says with a chuckle. "And that was my big break, really. I said, 'Yes I'm loose. I had a couple of beers, is that all right?'

Osinski was a workhorse, relieving in 34 games and posting an earned run average of 2.54.

I went in there, I don't know who they [Los Angeles Angels batters] were, but I struck out the side and got out of the inning without giving up a run." He went on to pitch another inning against the Angels. "I think I just about struck out everybody I faced. That was the whole turning point [for me]," said Osinski, who won the game in relief.

Fred Haney, the Angels' general manager, attended that All-Star game and liked what he saw. Haney acquired Osinski's contract from Kansas City for $25,000 and a player to be named.

Osinski joined the Los Angeles team on July 24, 1962, making an immediate impact, and established himself as a reliable major league reliever. He was called upon one month later to pitch in a New York Yankees series and distinguished himself by appearing in all three games, shutting down the Yanks for five innings in the final game and winning it in the 13th. He had five wins and two losses through August, and appeared in 18 games over a five-week span. He finished the season appearing in 47 games with a 6-4 record and 3.97 ERA.

Osinski gives a lot of credit to Angels pitching coach Marv Grissom, who molded several Angels throwers into quality moundsmen. "Marv was the first real pitching coach I ever had in the big leagues. I really liked him because you got them out any way you could. If you had to knock someone down you knocked them down. They got me to be what they called the 'hatchet man.' If someone knocked one of our players down, I knocked two or three of theirs down. They played me in games sometimes just to do that. And that was from Marv. [It was the] same way he was. You'd be wild enough to be effective."

He pitched for the Angels in both 1963 and 1964, posting 8-8 and 3-3 records, with 3.28 and 3.48 ERAs, respectively. He recalls an injury in 1963—when he was hit by a line drive off the bat of J.C. Martin of the White Sox and broke a finger on his pitching hand—as being his downfall with the Angels. "That's [when I] ended up not being effective for the Angels, really."

The Angels traded Osinski to the Milwaukee Braves on November 29, 1964. One of Osinski's lasting—and not very fond—memories of his experience that 1965 season with the Braves was an event that could have jeopardized his baseball career. Describing manager Bobby Bragan's actions, he said: "He got me in a little trouble. How would I say it, he wanted to always prove a point [about] something. I remember [on] that day, Ken Silvestri was our bullpen coach. He was a catcher, [and] Bragan calls up [the bullpen]. We're playing the Giants, I believe it was, and Shaw was pitching for the Giants and throwing nothing but spitters. I remember [Bragan] calling the bullpen and asking if anybody down there threw a spitter, and I got elected."

Osinski says Bragan handed him the ball upon his arrival from the bullpen and ordered him to throw spitters. "'Dan, I want you to throw every pitch a spitter and make it obvious. So I said okay, and that's what I did. And I threw, I think it was, 81 straight spitters. I only got called on it, I think, twice and they said 'just wipe it off.'"

The following day Howard Cosell, who was covering the game for a TV network that day, asked Bragan before the game if Osinski would demonstrate the spitter. Osinski was reluctant, realizing the threat to him that that kind of exposure would bring, but Bragan prevailed and Osinski was featured on national television.

"From that day on I never got another strike [called that year] in the big leagues. If they didn't swing at the ball they were walked. I still ended up pitching in 61 ball games that year." There is clearly some hyperbole here, in that Osinski did not pitch more than two innings against the Giants that year; and, no one appears in 61 ballgames without a single strike being called by an umpire, but his point remains.

Remarkably, Osinski still posted a 2.82 ERA that year with Milwaukee. He and Billy O'Dell surpassed the club record of 60 pitching appearances. O'Dell pitched in 62 games and Osinski in 61.

On December 15, 1965 Osinski was traded to the Red Sox along with pitcher Bob Sadowski for Arnold Earley, Lee Thomas, and a player to be named (it turned out to be Jay Ritchie). The Red Sox intended for Osinski to be a short relief pitcher backing up their ace reliever, Dick Radatz. Manager Billy Herman was high on Osinski.

Sizing up the Red Sox's chances in spring training, future Hall of Famer Ted Williams made the comment that their strong suit in 1966 would be pitching. Analyzing the pitching corps, Williams spoke about the new kid, Dan Osinski: "I'd hate to hit against that guy. What a motion he's got. He's got to help this club."[2]

In 1966 the Red Sox finished ninth—next to last—in the American League, 26 games out of first place. Osinski appeared in 44 games with a 4-3 won-loss record and a 3.63 ERA. Since he had a one-year contract in '66, he had to once again earn a place on the roster in 1967, which he did.

1967 was a memorable year for the Red Sox and for Dan Osinski. That year he became a five-year man and qualified for a major league pension, played on a league

champion, and played in a World Series. An article in the *Boston Herald Traveler* described Osinski this way: "Osinski is not a sentimentalist. Rather, he's a pro's pro. Though he has only five years in the major leagues, he has the qualities—maturity, judgment and a dogged competitiveness—that often are never found in men with twice his longevity."[3]

The Red Sox won the pennant—their first since 1946—in the final season-ending series against Minnesota. They went on to play the St. Louis Cardinals in the World Series but lost in seven games. Osinski pitched in two games. In Game Three, Osinski came in to pitch in the eighth inning and gave up two hits and one run. In Game Seven, he relieved Dave Morehead, who had walked the bases full in the ninth inning. He pitched to one batter, Orlando Cepeda, who fouled out. He remembers the seventh game vividly. "Lonborg couldn't break a pane of glass in the bullpen when he was warming up," said Osinski, "We all knew that, and [Dick Williams] still started him. You know he could have pitched the bullpen an inning apiece, or something. It just gave Gibson too big a lead against us that we couldn't come back from."

Osinski finished the 1967 regular season with a 3-1 record and a 2.53 ERA. In spite of a pretty good year, the Red Sox released him on April 3, 1968. He said he never heard from management, but found out from a Boston sports writer. He was picked up as a free agent by the Chicago White Sox on April 29, and was sent to Hawaii of the Pacific Coast League.

Osinski once again became the workhorse, pitching often and winning games. In one stretch in May, he worked more than 25 innings of scoreless ball. By mid-July he had a 5-0 won-loss record and a 1.44 ERA, and was named to the first team PCL All-Star squad. For the season, he appeared in 51 games with an 8-2 won-loss record and a 2.39 ERA.

The White Sox invited Osinski to their 1969 spring camp. He didn't have a major league contract at the time, so he had to earn his way onto the roster. Osinski earned a roster spot with the White Sox and played the entire 1969 season with them, posting a 5-5 record with 51 appearances and a 3.54 ERA.

At the end of the '69 season, the White Sox assigned Osinski to their Tucson affiliate. He was then sold to the Houston Astros and invited to their spring camp as a nonroster player. He made the Astros club and pitched in three games, but was ineffective. He was optioned to Oklahoma City of the American Association (Triple A) on April 22, 1970, and made 45 appearances with a 6-8 record and 2.42 ERA.

Jim Lonborg and Dan Osinski compare notes in this spring training shot.

On November 30, 1970, the San Diego Padres made Osinski their first selection in the Triple A draft at the baseball winter meetings, and planned to assign him to their new Hawaii franchise. But he decided to end his baseball career and stick with his offseason job at a bank full time. "In the offseason I was usually selling tickets for the White Sox or working for the bank, and my boss at the bank [it was thought] had a heart attack," he says. "I was one of the few guys that knew all the accounts and was able to wine and dine its customers. If they needed money, I could go out and get the money for them, and I ended up staying at the bank."

Dan currently works in a sales capacity for a used car dealership in Sun City, Arizona, where he resides. He is married to wife Peggy, and has one son, age 43.

Notes:

1. Interviews with Dan Osinski, March 3 and 12, 2006
2. McDonough, Will; "Pitching to Be Sox Strong Point—Williams," *Boston Globe*, March 4, 1966, p. 22
3. Unsigned Editorial; "Danny O. Won't Forget This Year," *Boston Herald Traveler*, October 4, 1967, p. 51

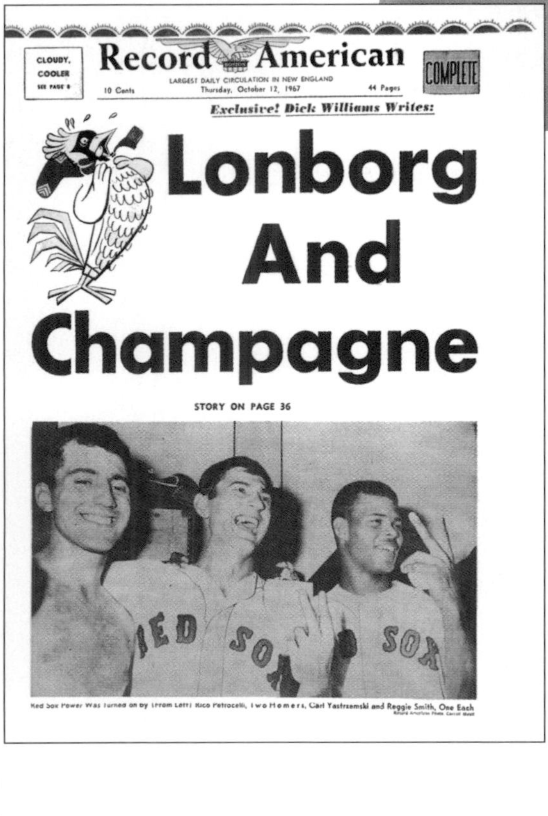

CLOUDY, COOLER
SEE PAGE 8

Record American

LARGEST DAILY CIRCULATION IN NEW ENGLAND
10 Cents Thursday, October 12, 1967 44 Pages

COMPLETE

Exclusive! Dick Williams Writes:

Lonborg And Champagne

STORY ON PAGE 36

Red Sox Power Was Turned on by (From Left) Rico Petrocelli, Two Homers, Carl Yastrzemski and Reggie Smith, One Each

Dick Williams – The tough Red Sox skipper played 13 seasons in the major leagues at every position but shortstop, catcher, and pitcher. In his rookie year as manager, he brought the Sox to the World Series in the first of 21 seasons as a major league manager. Williams would taste World Championship champagne in both 1972 and 1973 as manager of the Oakland Athletics.

Jim Lonborg had a Cy Young year in 1967, with a 22-9 record. In the World Series, he threw a one-hit shutout in Game Two (see the no hits on the Fenway scoreboard in the sixth) and a three-hit Game Five marred only by a Roger Maris solo home run in the ninth. Pitching Game Seven on short rest, he just ran out of steam.

CAN
16
WASH
N.Y.
BALT
K.C.
DET
MINN

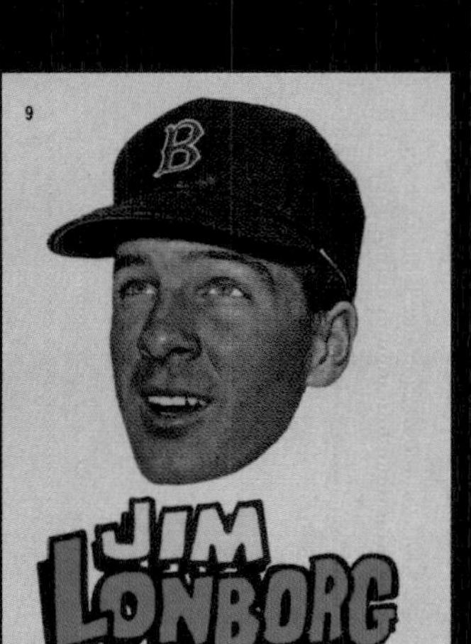

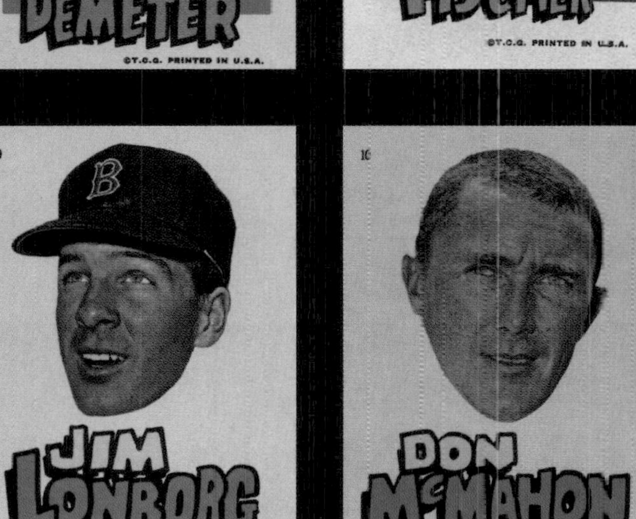
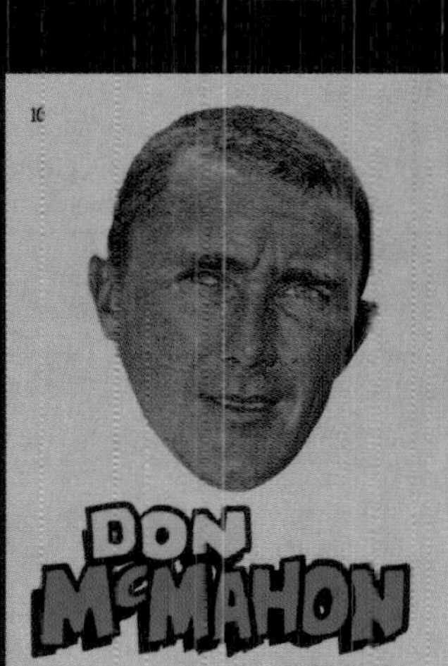
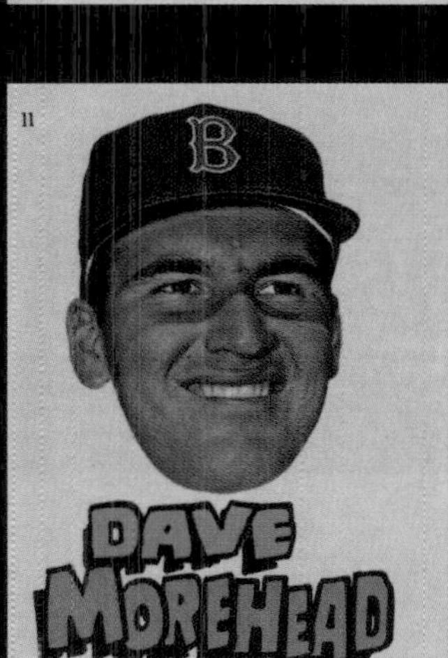

7
MIKE ANDREWS
©T.C.G. PRINTED IN U.S.A.
1
DENNIS BENNETT
©T.C.G. PRINTED IN U.S.A.
2
DARRELL BRANDON
©T.C.G. PRINTED IN U.S.A.
3
TONY CONIGLIARO
©T.C.G. PRINTED IN U.S.A.
4
DON DEMETER
©T.C.G. PRINTED IN U.S.A.
5
HANK FISCHER
©T.C.G. PRINTED IN U.S.A.
6
JOE FOY
©T.C.G. PRINTED IN U.S.A.
8
DALTON JONES
©T.C.G. PRINTED IN U.S.A.
9
JIM LONBORG
©T.C.G. PRINTED IN U.S.A.
10
DON McMAHON
©T.C.G. PRINTED IN U.S.A.
11
DAVE MOREHEAD
©T.C.G. PRINTED IN U.S.A.
13
RICO PETROCELLI
©T.C.G. PRINTED IN U.S.A.

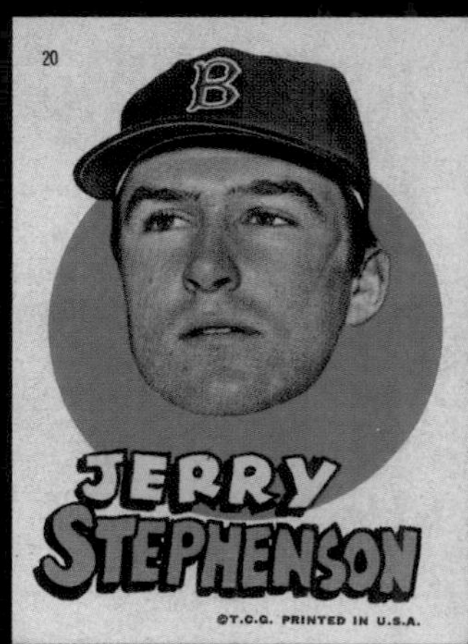

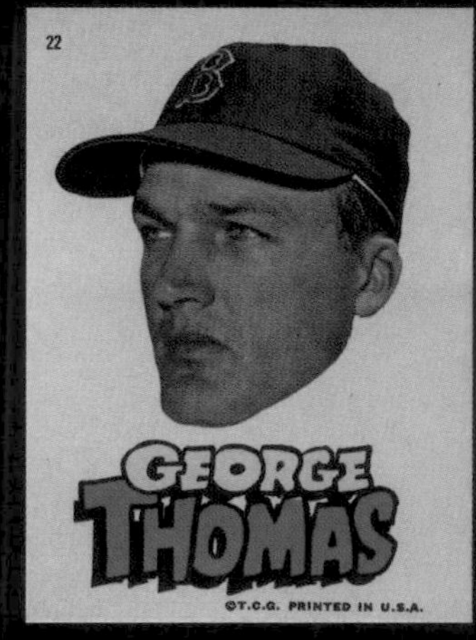

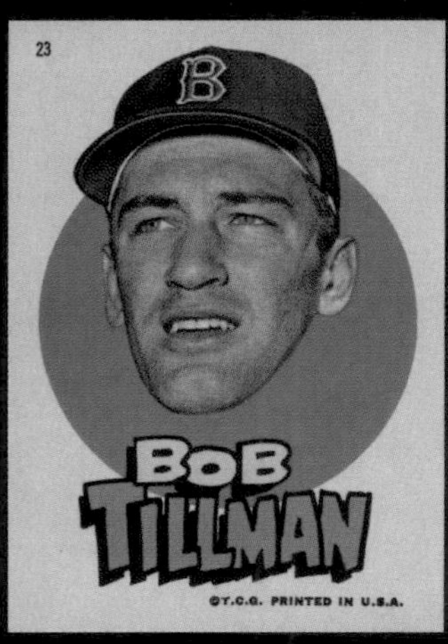

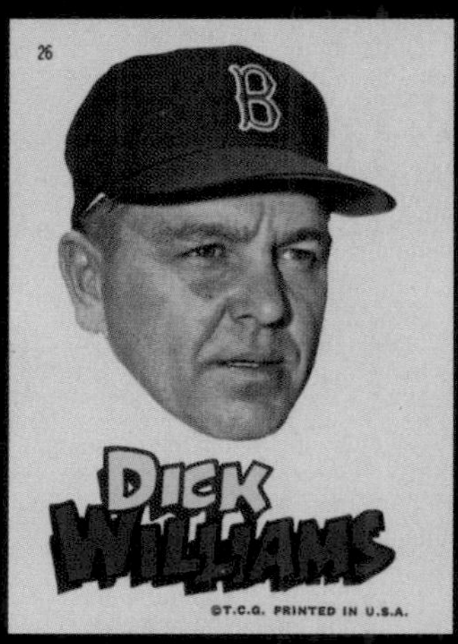

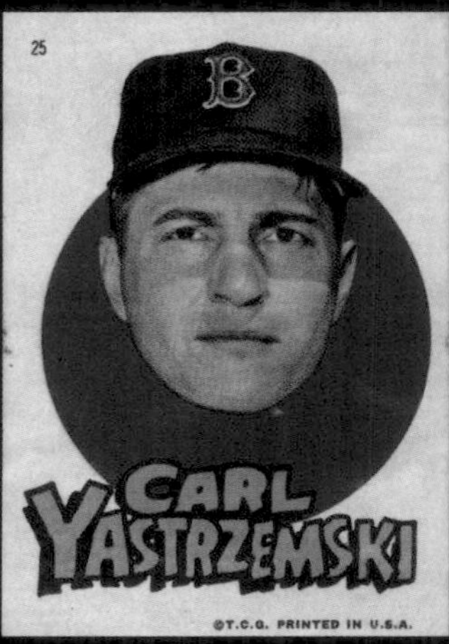

In 1967, Topps issued a series of "test stickers" which featured players on the Red Sox team and also included themes, such as "Happiness Is A Red Sox Win."

George Scott, "Boomer," played almost every game and batted .303 while driving in 82 runs under tough manager Dick Williams. Scott played nine of his 16 seasons with Boston.

Mike Andrews starts to uncoil his swing.

The Red Sox acquired nine-time World Series veteran Elston Howard for the pennant drive.

Ken Harrelson brought a colorful personality to Boston.

Jerry Adair turning the double play.

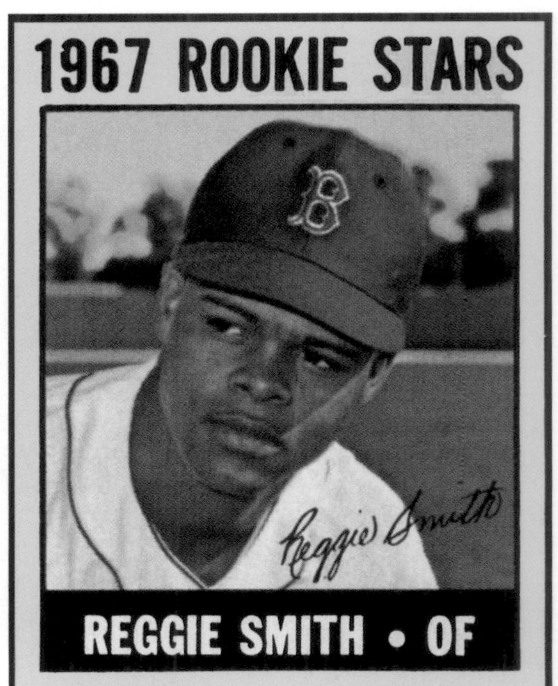

The Sox take the field, with Mike Andrews jogging out to his position at second while Gary Bell tugs his cap on his way to the mound.

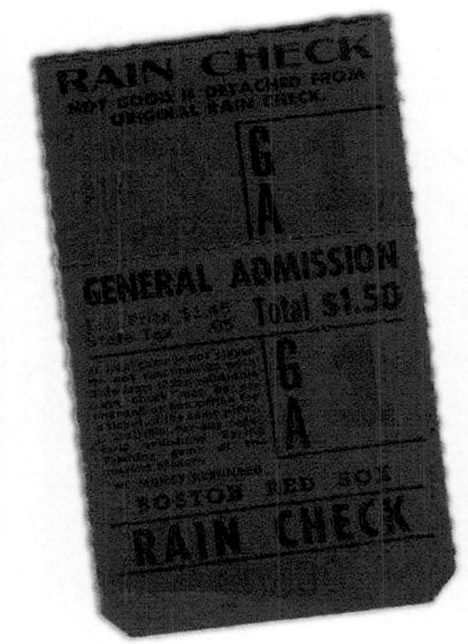

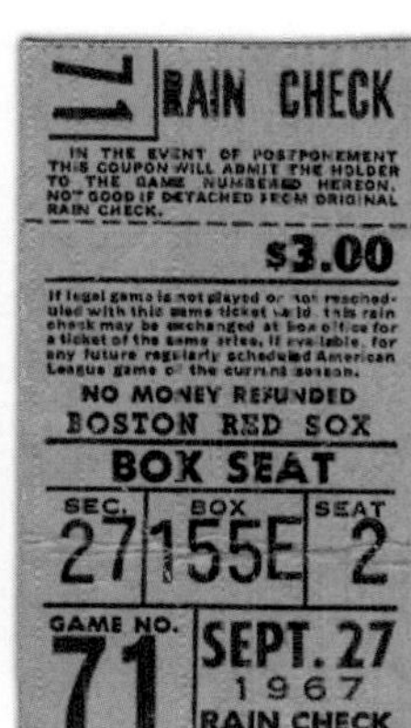

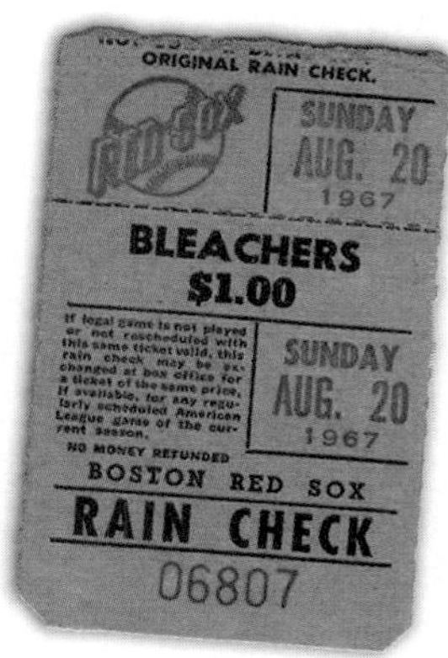

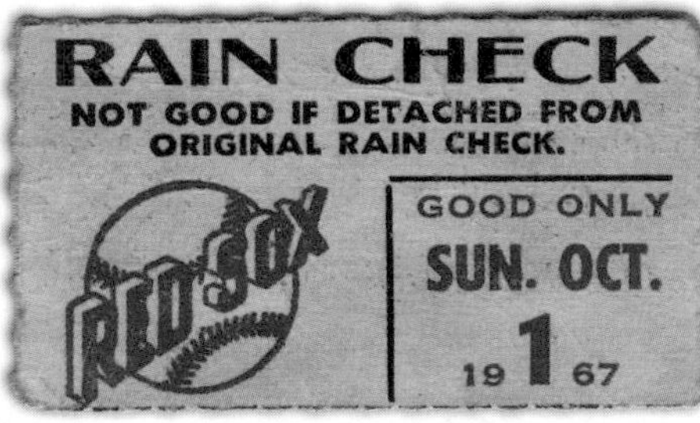

Red Sox fan Paul Shannon turned around and snapped this photograph of the scoreboard behind the bleachers just one minute before the end of the October 1 ballgame. At 4:36, Lonborg induced a popup, Rico caught the ball, the Red Sox secured at least a tie for first place, and pandemonium broke out on the field.

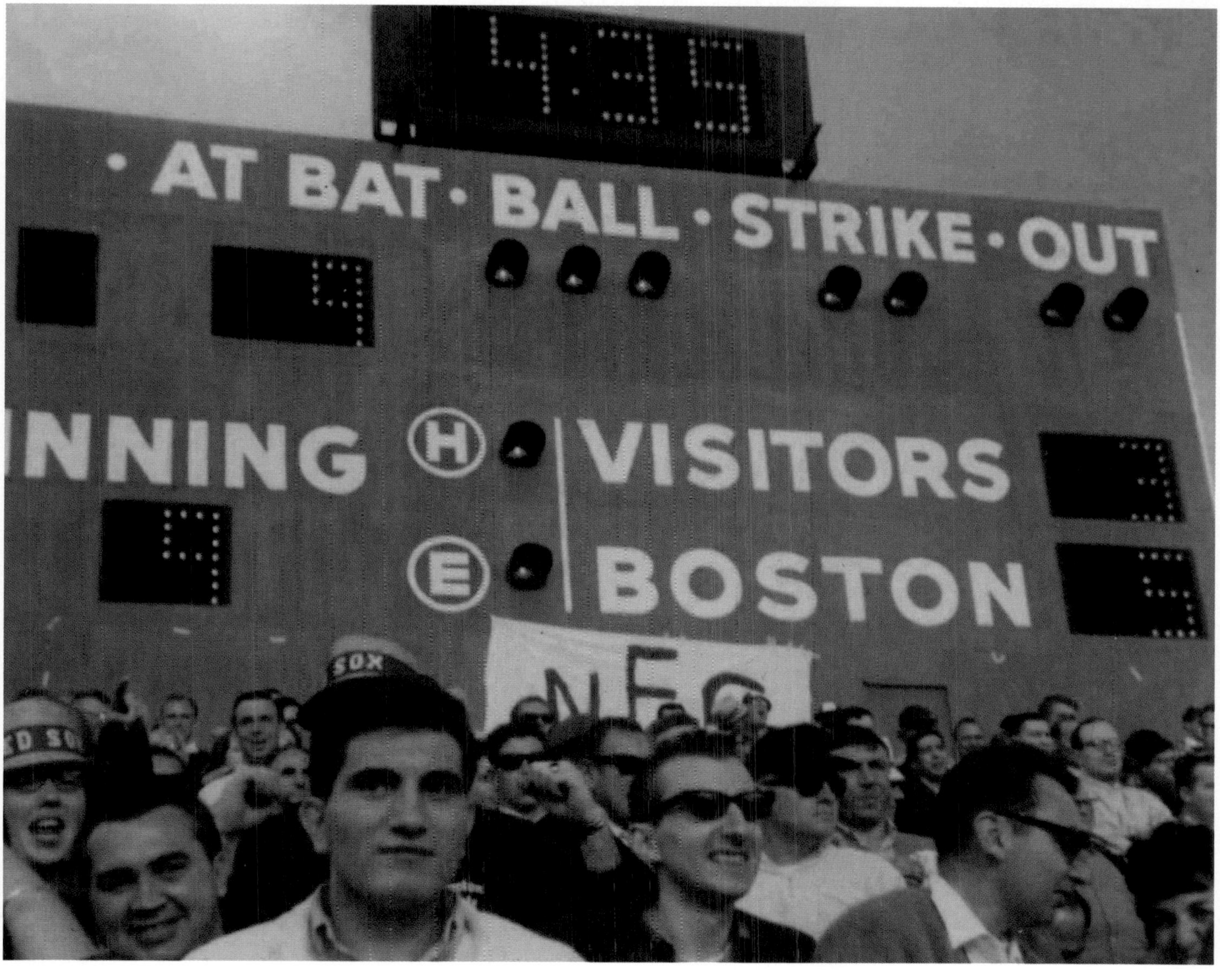

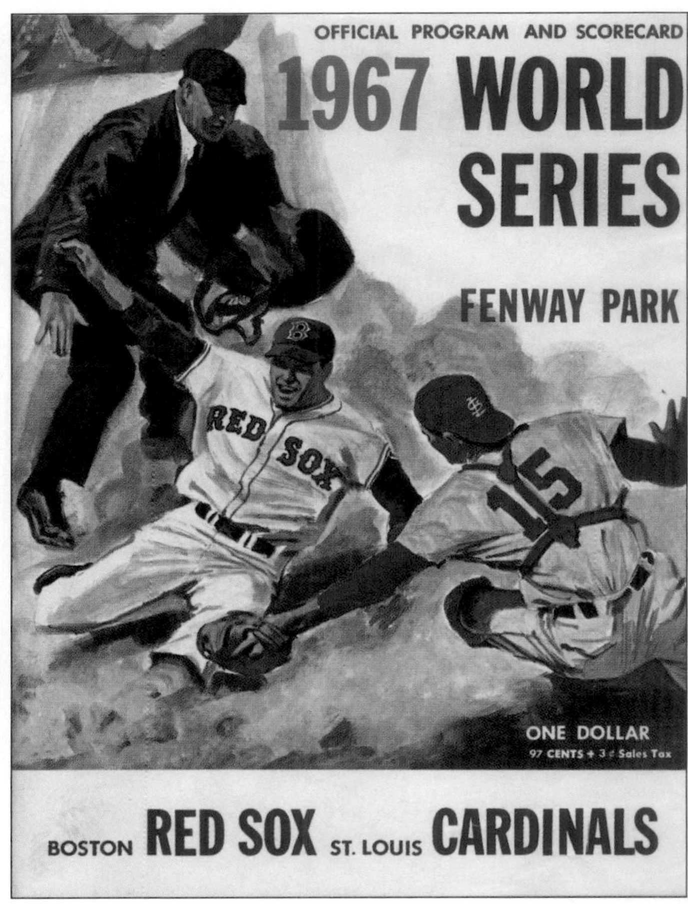

Record American

COMPLETE

LARGEST DAILY CIRCULATION IN NEW ENGLAND

Monday, October 2, 1967

44 Pages

10 Cents

SUNNY, WARM SEE PAGE 12

CHAMPS!

STORIES, PHOTOS ON BACK PAGE AND PAGES 2, 3, 4, 6, 8, 22, 23, 32, 33, 34, 35, 36, 38

Regular season and World Series programs, and the front page of the Boston Record-American the day after the Impossible Dream became a reality; the Cardiac Kids had won the pennant.

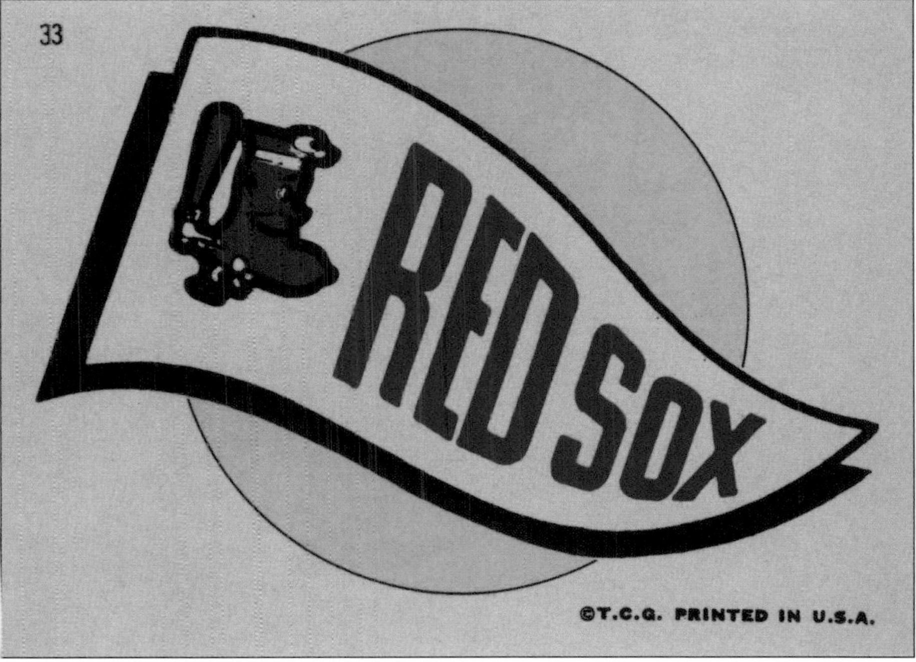

A selection of theme and sentiment graphics produced by Topps in its 1967 test sticker series.

BILL ROHR • P

Billy Rohr

by Alex Edelman

	G	ERA	W	L	SV	GS	GF	CG	SHO	IP	H	R	ER	BB	SO	HR	BFP
1967 RED SOX	10	5.10	2	3	0	8	0	2	1	42.1	43	27	24	22	16	4	195

William Joseph Rohr was born on July 1, 1945, in San Diego, California, right in the middle of the baseball season. Rohr began playing baseball when he was 8, and despite weighing only 145 pounds in high school, he finished his career at Bellflower High with a 26-3 record,[1] pitching four no-hitters for his varsity team. After graduating in 1963, Rohr was signed by Jerry Gardner of the Pittsburgh Pirates on June 15, 1963, paid $25,000, and sent to rookie ball in Kingsport, Tennessee of the Appalachian League.

The Pirates tried to keep Rohr away from other teams, hiding his obvious talent by placing him and some other promising prospects on the disabled list the entire 1963 season—leaving them inactive when they were perfectly healthy. The strategy failed miserably. Mace Brown, a Red Sox scout whom Rohr would later call "one of the nicest men I have ever met... as well as a great pitching coach," was alerted, and in November, Rohr was drafted by the Red Sox.

Starting out with Wellsville of the Class-A New York-Pennsylvania league in 1964, Rohr finished 10-9 and pitched eight complete games, demonstrating the endurance the world would glimpse briefly three years later. The next season he started out with Winston-Salem, and after dazzling Carolina League batters for two months (7-3, 2.93), he was promoted all the way to Triple-A Toronto, where he finished 6-10 but with a fine 2.73 ERA. Pitching for manager Dick Williams, Rohr remained at Toronto in 1966, logging a 14-10 record and tossing 10 complete games.

His accomplishments led to a spring training invitation from the parent Red Sox in March of '67, under the direction of Williams, recently promoted himself. With a great changeup added to his repertoire,[2] Rohr easily nailed down a berth on the major league team on April 6, pitching six innings in a 4-1 win against the Tigers in Winter Haven.[3] Heading into the season, Rohr was the team's third starter.

On the night of April 13, 1967, 21-year-old Billy Rohr tossed and turned in his bed in a New York hotel room, so nervous about his major league debut the next day against Yankee great Whitey Ford that, instead of sleeping, he spent time analyzing the Yankees lineup with Jim Lonborg.[4] Just as nervous as Rohr was rookie Russ Gibson, who had taken a decidedly different path to the majors. Gibson, a 28-year-old catcher who would also be making his major league debut the following day, had toiled away in the minors for 10 years and had been contemplating hanging up his spikes when the Red Sox called to invite him to spring training in 1967. Though they had taken disparate journeys to the majors, Rohr and Gibson's paths converged at a 60-foot 6-inch stretch of land on the infield at Yankee Stadium.

April 14 was Opening Day at Yankee Stadium. The monuments in left-center field stared across the diamond into the Yankees dugout, where Mickey Mantle, who would be honored in Monument Park himself two years later, sat on the bench, waiting for the game to start. Whitey Ford, one of the most fearsome pitchers in Yankee history, but nearing the end of his great career, was warming up in the bullpen. Rohr was set to make his first major league start that day, while Ford would be making his 432nd. But Mantle and Ford were aging, the Yankees weren't favorites to finish high in the American League that year, and those monuments in the outfield only seemed to mock the Bronx Bombers, as a small crowd of about 14,000 entered Yankee Stadium.

Rohr says he can only remember being extremely nervous, and announcer Ken Coleman told fans that the rookie pitcher looked a bit scared as he stepped to the mound, ready to begin the bottom of the first inning, working with a 1-0 lead that came from Reggie Smith's leadoff homer. Dennis Bennett, a Red Sox pitcher who, a day later, would lose the second game of the series, 1-0, to Mel Stottlemyre,[5] told Coleman, "If he gets by the first inning, he'll be okay. But he's a nervous wreck right now."[6]

However nervous Rohr may have been, the first inning was uneventful, and the lanky southpaw showed no sign of nervousness as he coolly retired Horace Clarke, Bill Robinson, and Tom Tresh. The second inning saw Rohr's first major league at-bat, a groundout. In the second and third innings, Rohr retired the Yankees in order again, and the crowd began to stir. In the fourth, Rohr walked two but stranded them on the bases, and the murmurs began to come from the stands. "I knew I was catching a no-hitter," Russ Gibson said, "and he knew he was throwing one."[7]

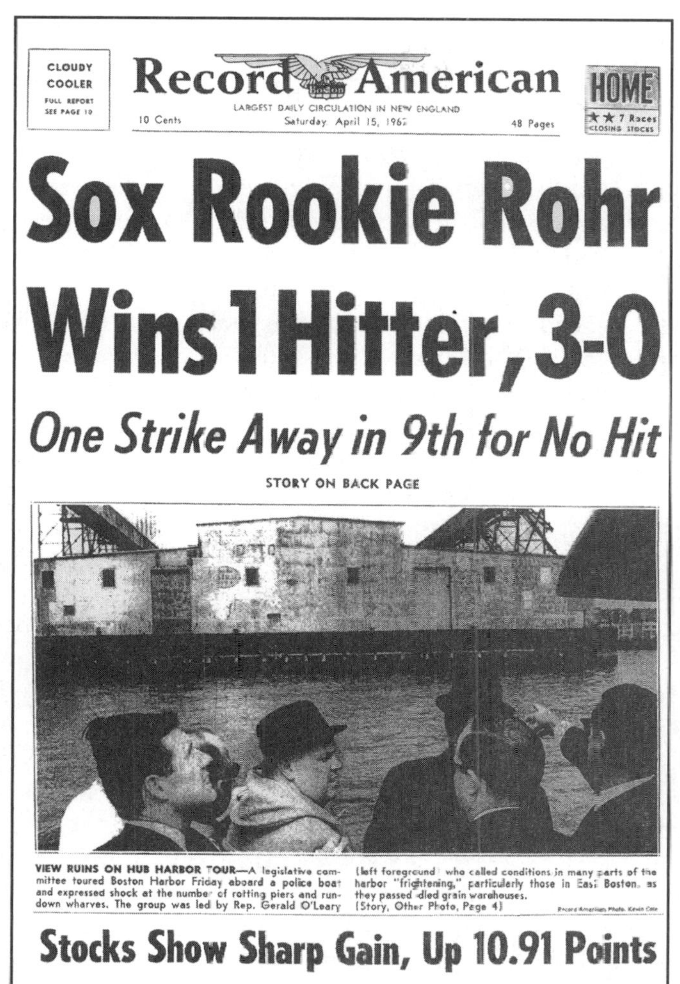

CLOUDY
COOLER
FULL REPORT
SEE PAGE 10

Record American

LARGEST DAILY CIRCULATION IN NEW ENGLAND

10 Cents Saturday April 15, 1967 48 Pages

HOME
★★ 7 Races
CLOSING STOCKS

Sox Rookie Rohr Wins 1 Hitter, 3-0

One Strike Away in 9th for No Hit

STORY ON BACK PAGE

VIEW RUINS ON HUB HARBOR TOUR—A legislative committee toured Boston Harbor Friday aboard a police boat and expressed shock at the number of rotting piers and rundown wharves. The group was led by Rep. Gerald O'Leary (left foreground) who called conditions in many parts of the harbor "frightening," particularly those in East Boston, as they passed idled grain warehouses. (Story, Other Photo, Page 4)

Record American Photo, Kevin Cole

Stocks Show Sharp Gain, Up 10.91 Points

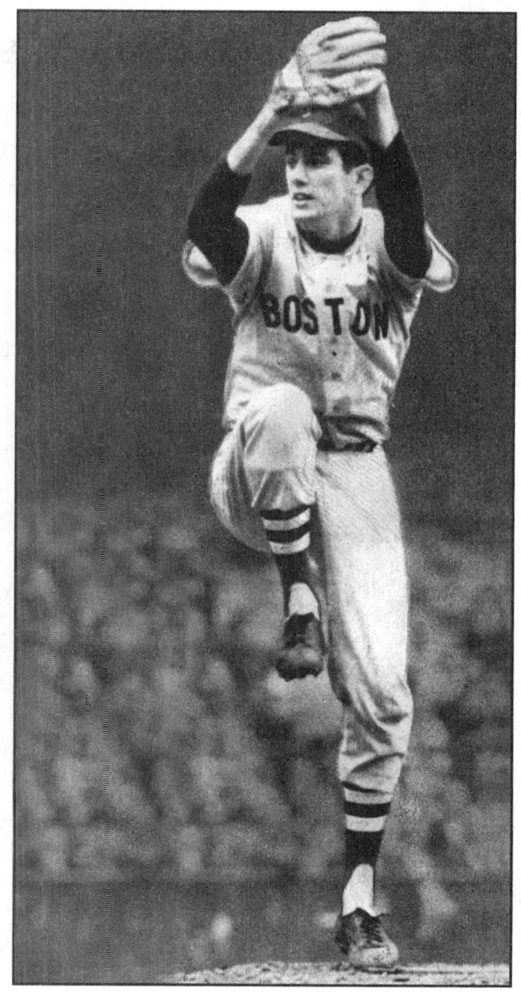

By the sixth inning, with everyone fully conscious of what Rohr was doing, Yankee right fielder Bill Robinson slashed a hard grounder up the middle, striking Rohr in the left shin, which he clutched in pain as the ball ricocheted directly to Joe Foy at third base. Foy threw to Scott at first in time for the out, and it was Rohr's first major league assist, but it left him walking gingerly for a good five minutes. Trainer Buddy LeRoux rushed out with manager Dick Williams, ready to pull the young pitcher from the game. Rohr told his manager that he felt all right, but Williams worried that Rohr would hurt his arm by favoring his leg. He told Gibson that if Rohr showed any signs of deviating from his usual pitching motion, to have the rookie yanked immediately. An inning later, Gibson informed Williams, "The kid has better stuff than he had before he got hurt."[8] Rohr limped for the rest of the game.

As Rohr got the last out in the sixth inning and headed to the bench, he found himself sitting in solitude. No one talked to him as he iced his leg by himself on the right-hand side of the dugout. It is baseball superstition: no player talks to teammate throwing a no-hitter—or mention it to anyone else, lest he jinx it. And so, in his first major league start, Billy Rohr sat, by himself, marooned in a sea of people, all alone to absorb what was taking place.

In the top of the eighth inning, third baseman Joe Foy's two-run homer gave Rohr a three-run lead, and, with tension mounting in the stands, he took the mound as the now-desperate Yankees struggled to find a way, any way, to get a hit. Yankees manager Ralph Houk sent up Mickey Mantle as a pinch-hitter to lead off the bottom of the eighth, hoping to crack Rohr's aura of calm assuredness. Mantle received a huge ovation from the Yankees fans—but paradoxically an even greater one after he flied to Tony Conigliaro in right.[9]

The next batter, Lou Clinton, gave the Sox a scare when he reached on a throwing error by Rohr and advanced to second on the walk that followed, but Bill Robinson grounded into a double play, and Rohr was only three outs from baseball history.

"We wouldn't bunt on him when the game got into late innings," Ralph Houk said later. "It was going to be a clean hit or nothing."[10] As Rohr got ready to face Tom Tresh to start off the ninth inning, a funny thing happened, something that, for some odd reason, seemed to stick in the heads of all those watching. He paused, looking around the infield. Ken Coleman thought that he was "establishing a magical bond with each of his teammates, a connection that, in some wordless way, help preserve the no-hitter."[11] Writer Ed Linn said that Rohr "turned slowly around as if he were checking his defense."[12] Sportswriter Bill Reynolds was listening on the radio, but even he remembers Rohr "looking around at his teammates."[13] Rohr laughs at the idea that he was checking his defense. What could he do? Reset them? The truth is, Rohr says, he was soaking in the moment. Turning back to the task at hand, Rohr ran the count to 3-2, and the play of the game took place. Tresh, looking for a pitch to hit, got a good one, and lined it to deep left field. Behind the plate, Russ Gibson cursed silently, thinking "Well, there goes the no-hitter."

Among all the people who saw the play, there remains a consensus that there is no way Carl Yastrzemski, who was playing shallow to prevent a Texas-league single, could ever have been expected to catch it. Ken Coleman provided the best description of the event in his diary.

> [Tresh's] drive to left over the head of Carl Yastrzemski left a rising trail of blue vapor... At the crack of the bat, Yaz broke back, being guided by some uncanny inner radar. Running as hard as a man fleeing an aroused nest of bees, Yaz dove in full stride and reached out with the glove hand in full extension, almost like Michelangelo's Adam stretching out for the hand of God. At the apex of his dive, Yaz speared the ball, and for one moment of time that would never register on any clock, stood frozen in the air as if he were Liberty keeping the burning flame aloft. [14]

In a record album released after the 1967 season entitled *The Impossible Dream*, Coleman's call of Yaz's catch is immortalized forever in black vinyl. "Fly ball, to deep left...Yastrzemski is going hard... way back... way back... and he dives and makes a tremendous catch! One of the greatest catches I've ever seen! ... Everybody in Yankee Stadium on their feet." All eloquent imagery aside, Yaz ran toward deep left, dove with his back to the plate, caught the ball with his glove extended, hit the grass with his left knee first, somersaulted once, came up with the ball in his bare hand held high, and fired the ball back to the infield. For Will McDonough of the *Boston Globe*, the catch was a moment that defined the entire rivalry between the Yankees and the Red Sox: "When I think of the Yankee-Red Sox rivalry, I don't think of Williams or DiMaggio. I think of the catch Yaz made in the Stadium to save the no-hitter for Billy Rohr."[15]

For a brief moment, the crowd of Yankee fans turned completely bipartisan, rooting for their own player to record an out, something that probably has not happened since and may never happen again with the enemy Red Sox in town. When Joe Pepitone flied out on the next pitch, the cheers reached a fever pitch for Rohr. A month before the Pirates drafted him, on May 11, 1963, Rohr had looked on as Sandy Koufax no-hit the Giants at Dodger Stadium. Now, four years later, he was one out away from joining Koufax.

As Elston Howard stepped to the plate, Dick Williams trotted out to the mound, as Rohr took a little breath and was reminded by his manager that Elston Howard loved to swing at the first pitch. As play resumed, Rohr heeded his manager's advice, and Howard swung at a bad pitch, low and away. After two more pitches, and the count at 1-2, Rohr split the plate with a fastball. Umpire Cal Drummond called it a ball, but to this day, Russ Gibson maintains that the pitch was most certainly a perfect strike. After another ball that ran the count full, Gibson called for Rohr to throw Howard a curveball, hoping that Howard, having seen only fastballs all day, would be looking for a heater. But with one swift, sad stroke, Howard looped a shot over second baseman Reggie Smith's head, where it softly landed in front of a disappointed-looking Tony Conigliaro. When Howard reached first base, he was surprised to hear boos and hoots. It was, he noted wryly, the first time he had ever been booed for a base hit in his home park. Howard was stranded when Charley Smith flied out on the first pitch he saw, ending the game.

Later on, Williams would agonize over his decision to go out to the mound. "I told him I've beaten myself over the head about that trip to the mound.... He had one shot at fame, and my meddling may have blown it for him."[16] Rohr's opinion was that while Williams had no business coming to the mound at that moment, the

hit was not his fault—the manager isn't the one who throws the pitch. Rohr was good humored about the moment, for it wasn't the first time glory had slipped from his grasp. In 1966, pitching for Toronto in the International League against the Yankees Toledo farm team, Rohr had a no-hitter going with two out in the ninth—but was unable to close out the game, giving up a hit to a Yankees prospect named Mike Ferraro.[17]

After the game, congratulations began to flood in. Jacqueline Kennedy, who was in attendance with her son John-John, came by the clubhouse to meet Rohr, who happily signed a ball for the former First Lady's son, to the child's great delight. It was a proud moment as well for Rohr, who had been deeply affected by the assasination of President Kennedy. "After I pitched the game," Rohr remarks, "I got to speak on the phone with Koufax and Drysdale. That was a huge thrill for me, because I had seen Koufax throw his own no-hitter and I was a Dodgers fan growing up. Andy Warhol once said that everyone has their 15 minutes of fame—that was my 15 minutes." Indeed it was.

On April 16, Rohr made a brief appearance on the Ed Sullivan show, appearing with Nancy Sinatra, Tony Bennett, and Count Basie. He also received a new contract from the Red Sox, upping him from $8,000 to $9,000 a year. The box score in the *Boston Globe* the next day was entitled "And The Crowd Rohr-ed." Boston Mayor John Collins sent a telegram: "You gave Boston an unforgettable day. Red Sox fans everywhere salute you on a fine pitching performance. May today's victory be the first of hundreds in your major league career."[18]

Unfortunately for Rohr, it was not. He followed with another solid win on April 21 in which he nearly pitched a shutout (only to have it broken up in the eighth, when his personal tormentor, Elston Howard, singled in the only Yankees run). In his next three starts, though, he was knocked around by opposing batters, giving up 12 runs and 15 hits in 7⅔ innings. After a relief appearance on May 16, he threw another excellent game on the 21st, allowing just one earned run in 7⅓ innings without earning a decision. Two ineffective starts later, he was sent to Triple-A Toronto and never started another ball game for the Red Sox. In September, back with Boston, Rohr pitched poorly in one game in relief, was demoted to Louisville after the year ended, and soon after the start of the 1968 season, was sold to the Cleveland Indians.

His tenure with the Indians was short, and after 17 games with them in 1968, finishing 1-0 but with a 6.87 ERA, Rohr was again sent to the minors, where he bounced from team to team in the Eastern, Southern, International, American Association and Pacific Coast Leagues before retiring in 1972.

Rohr's first two starts against the Yankees seemed to foreshadow a great career. That was not to be, but the promise of his performances helped ignite fan interest early in the young season.

Today, Rohr is a medical malpractice attorney in California, near his hometown and Western State University where he attended law school after his career ended. Every year on April 14, he gets a call from some reporters, and his name inevitably appears in a "This Day in Baseball History" article. Rohr is different from some ballplayers. Many athletes who have had near brushes with history are bitter about the fleeting touch of fame, hating the memory of the bad break that made them a footnote instead of one of the sporting world's greatest heroes. Not Rohr.

Today, Bill Rohr (yes, it is Bill now) revisits the memory with a quiet clarity that is pleasant to be exposed to. Nothing fazes him, not Mickey Mantle at the plate in the eighth inning, or an unhappy memory of a mediocre season with the Toledo Mud Hens. When he has a quiet moment at home on the evening of April 14, he does get a bit nostalgic, but it's on his own time, and the experience of that Opening Day is something that he remembers with pleasure, even 40 years later. People always tell him that they remember the game, and knew people who were there. This is a humorous

point for Rohr, who laughs that if all those people had indeed been there, there would have been "175,000 people in Yankee Stadium instead of just 14,000."

Rohr has been back to Fenway a few times since the end of his playing days. He remembers one time in particular. It was June 6, 1983, Tony Conigliaro Night at Fenway Park, a reunion for the 1967 team and a fundraiser to help defray the rising medical costs of their former right fielder, the man who had played behind Rohr on that Opening Day at Yankee Stadium.[19] Later that evening, Buddy LeRoux, the former trainer who had tended to Rohr on the mound in the sixth inning when he was hit by Robinson's grounder, stood up and announced that he and limited partner Rogers Badgett had taken over the Red Sox front office from principal owners Jean Yawkey and Haywood Sullivan, and that he was now in charge. Rohr and the other players gaped. A confrontation erupted inside the organization, one that would be resolved by a long, drawn-out legal battle.

Rohr's moment in the sun, though not unheard of in baseball, was considerably more significant than any other. Rohr's moment of masterful pitching in the national spotlight is viewed by many as a catalytic stimulant to the Red Sox season, which was initially projected as just another typical Red Sox season in the '60s—one that promised to deliver failure and frustration. Despite the fact that the Yankees were steadily declining, there was always something special about beating their East Coast rivals, and by winning in the Bronx, the Red Sox gained the self-confidence they lacked as the season got under way.

"Billy Rohr *was* 1967," Peter Gammons once wrote, "even if he only won two games and was out of town by June."[20] To casual baseball fans who witnessed the year of 1967, Billy Rohr truly was a one-hit wonder, but to more philosophical fans, Rohr's moment of magnificence symbolizes so much more than a moment in the sun, or a very near miss. To a Red Sox fan who suffered through years of near misses, Billy Rohr's one-hitter typified the experience of supporting the Red Sox: standing on the brink of perfection, but somehow falling just short.

Notes:

1. Reynolds, Bill, *Lost Summer: The 1967 Red Sox and the Impossible Dream*. Warner Books, 1992.
2. Rohr credits Mace Brown with this development as well. Interview with author, February 2006.
3. Coleman, Ken, *The Impossible Dream Remembered: The 1967 Red Sox*. Stephen Greene Press, 1985.
4. Who, Rohr notes, was probably up a little later then he liked. Interview with author, February 2006.
5. He would wind up losing 1-0 to Mel Stottlemyre in what many remember as an epic pitching duel.
6. Coleman, *op. cit.*
7. Interview with Russ Gibson, March 20, 2006.
8. Coleman, *op. cit.*
9. *Boston Globe*, Henry McKenna, 4/15/1967. "Rohr One-Hitter Tops Yanks, 3-0"
10. Mckenna, *op. cit.*
11. Coleman, *op. cit.*
12. Linn, Ed, *The Great Rivalry: The Yankees and the Red Sox 1901-1990*. Ticknor & Fields. 1991.
13. Reynolds, *op. cit.*
14. Coleman, *op. cit.*
15. Linn, *op. cit.*
16. Dick Williams, *No More Mr. Nice Guy: A Life of Hardball.* Harcourt, 1990.
17. "Narrow Miss Doesn't Disturb Red Sox Rookie." *Los Angeles Times*. April 15, 1967.
18. Coleman, *op. cit.*
19. In August, months after Rohr's one-hitter, Conigliaro was hit in the face by a fastball from California Angels pitcher Jack Hamilton, an incident that was the first of a string of many medical problems.
20. Gammons, Peter, "Musical Chairs on Yawkey Way," Glenn Stout and Richard A. Johnson, *Red Sox Century*. Boston, Houghton Mifflin, 2000, p. 424.

José Santiago

by Edwin Fernández and Bill Nowlin

	G	ERA	W	L	SV	GS	GF	CG	SHO	IP	H	R	ER	BB	SO	HR	BFP
1967 RED SOX	50	3.59	12	4	5	11	16	2	0	145.1	138	61	58	47	109	14	605

In José Santiago's first appearance on a major league mound, he entered a 6-6 tie game against the New York Yankees to pitch the eighth inning. It was September 9, 1963 and he got Elston Howard to ground out back to him on the mound, Joe Pepitone to line out, and Clete Boyer to strike out. When Kansas City scored in the bottom of the eighth, Santiago picked up the win. It was a nice way to start an eight-year career in major league ball, three years with the Athletics and five with the Red Sox.

José R. Santiago-Alfonso was born in Juana Diaz, Puerto Rico on August 15, 1940. Known as "*la ciudad de los poetas*" (the City of Poets), Juana Diaz is a community roughly ten miles northeast of Ponce in south-central Puerto Rico. The city is also known as "*la Ciudad del Jacaguas*" after the river of the same name which flows through its fields on the way to the sea. Juana Díaz produces sugar cane and beige marble, considered one of the finest marbles in the world.

His father Alejandro Santiago, ran a kind of general store that served workers on the sugar cane plantation. "He'd sell all kinds of products in it. He would sell the beans and the rice and everything you can think of," José recalls. Alejandro Santiago ran the store with his wife, Merida Alfonso. The two raised three children: Betty, José, and a younger boy, Alejandro Junior.

Juana Diaz was a good-sized community back then, around 30,000 to 40,000 people, and has grown to about 50,000 today. The Santiagos were well-off economically relative to others, but José still learned humility as a young boy. His first memories of baseball date back to being five or six years old. As he grew older, the kids in the Lomas neighborhood where he was born benefited from José's father's passion for baseball. Alejandro had played amateur baseball, a third baseman. "At the time, it was tough to play baseball," José remembers. "We didn't have any equipment. We had to get the sacks that they bring the wheat in, and wash it for about three or four days and then try to make a uniform out of that. My dad bought some bats and baseballs and some gloves for us, and that's how we started. We didn't even have a ballpark to play. We have to go either to another city to play or to go across the river and play... it was a cow field. Cut the grass and go ahead and then just play."

As a child, José was a very skinny boy. That caused some friends to called him "*Palillo*," the Spanish word for toothpick. He played his first game on the shores of the Jacaguas River near Lomas. "We played some other barrios, some other sectors of Juana Diaz." In high school, when classes were over on Fridays, the team would travel by bus and play in Ponce, Mayaguez, or elsewhere.

José wasn't always a pitcher, though. That came in college. Right through high school, Santiago primarily played center field. "I just had a great fastball, great arm, but I didn't know anything about pitching. I couldn't curve nothing." It was his father who saw him pitching one day, and said, "I think you've got a better chance to be a pitcher than an outfielder." In college he was able to benefit from some real coaching from Carlos Negron and Gonzalez Pato at the Pontificia Universidad Católica de Puerto Rico (Catholic University of Ponce). Another man he is quick to credit with help in pitching is Cefo Conde, who was a pitcher in the old Negro Leagues. Conde's nephew is Santos (Sandy) Alomar Sr.

José Santiago's final accomplishment as an amateur player was for a Class A team in a neighborhood called Romero. He threw a 16-inning game that he lost 3-2 against Santa Isabel. But the young *juanadino* was on his way.

José Santiago became a professional baseball player in 1957. It happened when finishing his freshman year at Catholic University. According to his sister Betty, one morning José was working with her in the family store, when he suddenly disappeared. At 3:00 pm, he returned from the town's ballpark, sweating and apprehensive, announcing there were three baseball scouts from the New York Giants organization asking to see his father because they want to sign him to play pro ball. His father said, "I am the one to sign you." An hour later, Alejandro Pompez came to the home to talk.

This was the same Alex Pompez named to the Hall of Fame in 2006. José was on shaky ground here with his father, because he knew that his father wanted him to finish university before thinking of playing professionally. One of José's friends, knowing there was a tryout being held, had convinced him to try out. "Hey, this is a good chance to show them what you can do. I'll

Record American *sportswriter Larry Claflin twists Jose Santiago's arm during San Juan's winter ball season, December 28, 1966.*

tell you what I'll do. I'll go to your place. I'll pack your bag, and then I'll meet you someplace else." José made up an excuse and left the store for the rendezvous. "My dad almost killed me when I came back! (laughs) I told him, 'Hey, they liked me. They want to sign me...'"

So began the saga of Santiago's signing. Both Pompez and Pancho Coimbre of the Pirates were interested, but Coimbre deferred to Pompez, just letting it be known that if things didn't work out, he'd be interested. Pompez offered $25,000 but José's dad wanted him to finish college first. That would mean waiting three years, not what the youngster wanted to hear. He pleaded with his father. Both scouts agreed on José's potential, Pompez saying, "He's got a lot of tools. He can play professional and I'm pretty sure he can get to the big leagues."

Alejandro asked Pompez, "Well, all right, do we get the money now or he's going to get the money later? What's the deal on that?"

"Oh no, as soon as he gets to spring training, we're going to send you the money." It was worked out and José signed. After that, he reports, "I went to spring training. I went through the whole spring training. Never got the money." His father called. They talked. The Giants said not to worry, and sent him to D-ball. He was slated to pitch the opening night game, but stood fast. "I told them, 'I'm not going to pitch until I get my money.' They said, 'You're going to get it. You're going to get it.' My dad called me up and said, 'I'm going to send you a ticket. You come home.' So I came home. They tried to get me back, and I said, 'No.' They lied to me." His father was a man of his word, and José and his father were united.

He had a written contract and could have consulted a lawyer, but his father didn't want to go that route, and José determinedly headed back to school. At that

point, Kansas City scout Félix Delgado saw José pitch a 12-strikeout game against a team from the University of Puerto Rico. Delgado called Sr. Santiago, and they talked, with José and his father explaining about the experience they'd had with the Giants. Delgado offered $15,000—but paid in advance.

Playing later for owner Charley Finley, and well aware of the reputation Finley had, José interjected a memory of the time he tried to help out some fellow players: "To me, he was outstanding. He treated me great." A humorous story followed. "The only thing bad that I did... at the time, Orlando Peña, Diego Segui, Monteagudo, Campaneris, and all those guys... they didn't know how to speak English at all. I made a big mistake. They talked to me about it. I went to the office to see Mr. Finley about it. First thing he said: 'Are you a baseball player or are you an agent?' I said, 'Wait a minute. I'm just trying to help these guys.' 'All right. What do you need?' 'They want a raise and...'"

Finley agreed on the spot and said, "All right, I'm going to give them a raise." He arranged for a new contract, and as they all got up to leave, but Finley said, "José. You stay here." "What is it, Mr. Finley?" "You know how much I like you and all that, but never... never do that again. Let their own people... they can take care of their own business, even in Spanish, but don't get involved with this, because this is not your job. You're here because you want to do a job. So you go out on the field and do the job. I'm glad you did this for those kids. I appreciate that, but this is a business. All right. You got what you wanted. Now get the hell out of here." José laughs, telling the story, adding, "He was tough, but he was a great guy. To me, he was great."

José started his pro career in 1959 with Olean in the New York-Penn League, with a 6-3 or 5-3 record (accounts differ) and a 3.24 (or 3.34) ERA in 62 innings. The same year, he moved on to Grand Island in the Nebraska State League, going 3-6, with a 3.91 ERA. He pitched for Albuquerque in 1960 and on June 13, José threw a 2-0 no-hitter against Hobbs. It was the first no-hitter in the 28 years of the Albuquerque franchise. Just a walk and two errors—all in the sixth inning—prevented the perfect game. With the bases loaded, José struck out the final batter. At the time, *The Sporting News* made it clear that José "Palillo" Santiago was no relation to the older Puerto Rican pitcher José "Pantalones" Santiago, pitcher for Cleveland and Kansas City 1954-56. With Albuquerque, the young "Palillo" had an excellent 15-6 record with a 3.30 ERA.

In 1961, he pitched for both Visalia and very briefly for Shreveport, leading the California League with 218 strikeouts but also leading in walks with 130. Back in Albuquerque in 1962, he won a league-leading 16 games against just nine losses. For most of 1963, he played for the Portland Beavers in the Pacific Coast League (12-15, 3.66 ERA), and near the end of the year got his first chance in big league baseball.

As noted at the start, José broke in for Kansas City with a perfect eighth inning in relief in the September 9, 1963 game at Municipal Stadium against the Yankees. He was pulled for a pinch-hitter in the bottom of the eighth but the Athletics pushed a run across and José got the win. He next appeared in a game just two days later, also against the Yankees, pitching the final two innings of a game he entered with the Yankees ahead 5-1. He let in three runs on three hits, one of them a two-run Pepitone homer. Santiago appeared in two more games in 1963: Boston's Dick Stuart hit a solo homer off him in a game Orlando Peña started (and lost), and he threw the final two innings of a game lost to the Indians, 7-0. All four appearances were in Kansas City. Santiago ended the year with a record of 1-0, but an ERA of 9.00 in seven innings. He'd yielded four home runs in those seven frames.

In 1964, José started the season with Dallas in the Pacific Coast League but only pitched two innings in one game. After a stretch on the disabled list for half of April and most of May, he returned to the Athletics in early June and appeared in 34 games throwing a total of 83⅔ innings, including eight starts. Kansas City finished in last place, with a record of 57-105, some 42 games out of first place. Santiago posted a 4.73 ERA, but an unfortunate 0-6 won-loss record. Five of the six losses came in games he'd started, the last one being a 3-2 loss to the White Sox on October 2.

In 1965, he started the season with the big league club, but only appeared in four games. The May 2 game against California was his last one of the year, and the last one for the Athletics. He spent most of the year with Vancouver in the Pacific Coast League, and got some innings in, 119 of them, with an excellent 2.19 ERA. The Red Sox took note and purchased him from Kansas City on October 15 for a reported $50,000 in cash. "I enjoyed my time with the A's," José told his friend, author Herb Crehan. "I got along well with Charlie Finley, and I met my wife Edna there. I also got to know Sully [Haywood Sullivan] very well."

After a full year with the Red Sox in 1966, he found himself looking up at Kansas City in the standings. The Red Sox finished in ninth place, a half-game ahead of the last-place Yankees, while KC was three games higher up in seventh place. But José got in a full 28

José's 12-4 season made a tremendous difference in 1967.

starts and, despite pitching for a ninth-place team, won 12 games with a 3.66 ERA. His record was 12-13, with seven complete games to his credit and 119 strikeouts. "We played very well in the second half of the season, but hardly anybody noticed," José recalled to Crehan. José was selected as Red Sox Pitcher of the Year. The Red Sox investment had already paid off nicely.

In 1967, Santiago's first three appearances came out of the bullpen, allowing just one earned run in four innings, winning one and losing one—both against the Yankees. He then made five starts in a row, again winning one and losing one. After the May 30 start (he was hit for four earned runs in three innings, though the Sox won the game in the end), it was back to the bullpen until August 19 when he started against California. His record was 6-4 at the time. He wasn't involved in the decision, but pitched again in relief the very next day and earned a win, throwing the final two innings in the game the Red Sox won 9-8, overcoming a 6-0 deficit.

For the rest of the regular season, he was used both as a starter and reliever and he won five more games while losing none. He threw a complete game win against the Orioles on September 22 and Dick Williams gave him the ball to start against the Twins on the next-to-last game of the year on September 30. A loss would take the Red Sox out of the race, but José won a hard-fought game, going seven innings while allowing just two runs, and leaving to a standing ovation from the Fenway faithful. The Red Sox won the game, and won the pennant the next day. As Herb Crehan once wrote in *Red Sox Magazine*, "Every Red Sox fan recalls the scene of Jim Lonborg being carried off the field... when his victory clinched at least a tie for the American League pennant. But it was Santiago's gutsy seven-inning stint on Saturday that set the stage for Lonborg's triumph."

Dick Williams named José Santiago his starting pitcher in the first game of the 1967 World Series. Santiago pitched a solid game, allowing the Cardinals just two runs in seven full innings. It was his misfortune to be paired against Bob Gibson, who allowed but one Red Sox run—a third-inning solo home run by José himself in his first World Series at-bat. His only other major league homer had come off Mickey Lolich in the second inning of the May 14 game against the Tigers, a 13-9 Red Sox win. Lifetime at the plate he was .173 with six doubles and seven RBIs. In World Series play, be batted .500.

He got another start, in Game Four, but this one was a disaster. Again facing Gibson, who shut out the Sox, José was bombed for four runs on six hits and never made it out of the first inning. José appeared one more time, throwing two innings of perfect relief in Game Seven. But Jim Lonborg had imploded, and the Red Sox were losing 7-1 by the time José had entered the game. The Red Sox lost Game Seven and lost the World Series. José's record shows 0-2, but Game One against Gibson was a strong effort. José finished the regular season with a 12-4 record and a 3.59 ERA. He forever holds the distinction of being the first Latin pitcher to start the opening game of a World Series. Santiago praised both his teammates and Dick Williams to Herb Crehan: "Williams kept us focused from start to finish. He deserves a lot of credit."

In 1968, Santiago appeared in just 18 games, every one as a starter. His record was 9-4 with a sterling 2.25 ERA. He was on a roll from the 1967 season, and won his first four decisions, a string of 12 straight wins without a defeat. In his first four games, he gave up a total of just 14 hits. The first game he lost was a hard-luck 1-0 defeat by Mel Stottlemyre and the Yankees on May 11. He lost another 1-0 game on an unearned eighth-inning run on May 25 to the Twins, and a 2-1 game on another unearned run on June 18.

On June 13, in a nightmare incident, one of José's pitches hit Paul Schaal and fractured his skull. Schaal was out for weeks, came back for just two more appearances in early August, but then only returned to major league play in 1969. Schaal performed well after his return, but the incident may have shaken Santiago, too. Jim Murray of the *Los Angeles Times* wrote of Santiago weeping at Schaal's hospital bed and wondered in print in a late 1971 column that Santiago was never the same pitcher afterward, writing "because his elbow—or something—was bothering him."

Dick Williams named Santiago one of his seven pitchers for the 1968 All-Star Game, but he developed tendonitis in his right elbow in early July and did not pitch in the game. He returned on July 18, but it was his last appearance of the season. He'd only given up one hit and no runs in two innings, but the injury was aggravated and he had to turn things over the Gary Bell. He missed the rest of the year.

It was one of the rare winters that José did not keep busy playing winter ball as well. Unfortunately, even time off over the winter wasn't sufficient and late in 1969 spring training, Santiago reinjured his elbow, tearing a ligament in his right elbow after throwing just two warm-up pitches. A few weeks later, on April 22, he had elbow surgery in Boston. Doctors said it was 50/50 whether he could ever pitch again, but if he could, it would probably not be until 1970.

In fact, the surgery and rehab went quite well, and he rejoined the Red Sox in August, less than four

Jose and Edna Santiago and son Alex, 3, welcome the pitcher's parents, Mr. and Mrs. Alejandro Santiago, to Boston before the first game of the 1967 World Series.

months later. In his first appearance since July 18, 1968, Santiago threw a scoreless eighth and final inning in relief on July 24. Five days later, he did the same: a scoreless ninth. Appearing from time to time, he got in 10 games, pitching just 7⅔ innings, but with a good 3.38 ERA.

Before spring training opened in 1970, he said that he could no longer effectively throw his money pitch—the slider. He worked at it during the exhibition season, but he wasn't ready for big league action and so started the season with Louisville in the International League. He pitched in 19 games for Louisville (7-4, 3-62 ERA).

He got the call to Boston at the end of May. His first appearance, though, was as a pinch-hitter in the May 29 game at Fenway Park against the White Sox. Chicago was winning 3-1, and the Red Sox had a man on first with one out. Santiago was put in to pinch-hit for Jim Lonborg and singled sharply to left field. Mike Andrews drew a walk to load the bases and Billy Conigliaro singled to drive in two, José scoring the tying run. Yaz walked, and Jerry Moses won it with a walk-off single. His first stint on the mound came on May 31, giving up three runs in two innings as one of six Red Sox pitchers mauled by Chicago batters, in a 22-13 slugfest. Apart from the pinch-hit cameo, José appeared in eight games for the 1970 Red Sox. He tallied 11⅓ innings, 0-0, with a 10.64 ERA; they were his last games in the major leagues.

Louisville beckoned, and Santiago gave another shot in 1971, throwing 128 innings and pitching well enough (7-6, 4.08 ERA) but those were his last years in American baseball. The Red Sox offered him a job as a coach in the organization, but José declined. He harbors good memories, though, telling Herb Crehan, "One thing I will always remember is that the Red Sox treated me with as much respect when I was a sore-armed pitcher as when I was an All-Star. Dick O'Connell, who was the general manager at the time, was wonderful to me. And the Yawkeys were very special people."

He was out of American baseball for the years 1972 through 1975, playing most winters on Puerto Rican teams. He told Crehan, "I still knew how to pitch, but I knew I wasn't at big league form. Some of my teammates would say, 'You could probably make a comeback,' but I knew better." In 1976, José pitched for Union Laguna in the Mexican League, appearing in 43 games, winning 13 against 6 losses, with a 3.35 ERA.

Since his final season in Mexico, José has resided fulltime in Puerto Rico. In 1980, he founded the Academia Beisbol Palillo Santiago, and the school served as many as 300 boys a year between ages 7 and 17. He had the school for 10 or 15 years, but as more kids chose to play video games than baseball, the number of students began to drop. José remains devoted to trying to foster youth baseball, however. For the past 25 years, he has helped Little League baseball, in which he strongly believes. For a good long time, he was president of Little League for the whole San Juan area. "Half of my time, I dedicated to the Little League program. All the programs are great, but Little League is the one that I really enjoy, because if you're crippled or any kind of problems that you have, you can play Little League. They'll let you play. Not the other leagues. So that's why I'm there. I love Little League so much. And I still help them out. As soon as I have time, I'll do anything for the Little League. And for the kids."

Santiago also managed the Puerto Rican team for some time, and was pitching coach as well. During the 1980s, he served as Press and Publications Officer

for the Sports and Recreation Department of the Government of Puerto Rico. In fact, after leaving major league baseball, José has been very energetic with an almost bewildering array of activity. Among other things he has been:

–Voice of the San Juan Senators for five years

–General Manager and Voice of the Santurce Crabbers for almost 10 years, named Narrator of the Year three times

–President of Little League baseball for 20 years

–Manager of the Puerto Rican national team

–Manager of a number of AA Amateur Baseball League teams, including Coamo, Juana Díaz, Río Piedras, Juncos, San Sebastian, and Río Grande.

–Pitching Coach for the Chicago Cubs Daytona Beach Class A team in 2000

–Voice of the Carolina Giants in the Puerto Rico Professional Baseball League team 2004-2006

As Crehan wrote this author, "José is to Winter Baseball in Puerto Rico what Johnny Pesky is to the Red Sox."

Today, José Santiago lives in Carolina, Puerto Rico with his wife Edna, whom he met while playing for Kansas City. They have been married for more than 45 years and raised four boys: Alex, Arnold, Albert, and Anthony. Three of the boys played baseball to one extent or another. Alex was offered a signing bonus by the Phillies, but he turned it down and runs a business working with computers. Arnold was drafted by the Cleveland Indians, but never had enough playing time to show what he might have been capable of achieving. A third son got into umpiring for a while, but left to raise horses and do other work.

Today, José keeps busy with his work broadcasting for Carolina. He also enjoys writing and reciting poems about love and family, perhaps reflecting the "City of Poets" where he was raised.

Lee Stange

by Les Masterson

	G	ERA	W	L	SV	GS	GF	CG	SHO	IP	H	R	ER	BB	SO	HR	BFP
1967 RED SOX	35	2.77	8	10	1	24	2	6	2	181.2	171	64	56	32	101	14	735

If the Detroit Tigers had only won their final game of the 1967 season, Lee Stange would have started the most important game in nearly 20 years for the Boston Red Sox. After the Red Sox beat the Minnesota Twins on the last day of the magical season, manager Dick Williams told Stange to take it easy in the clubhouse. If the Tigers beat the California Angels in the second game of a doubleheader, Stange would start the one-game playoff against the Tigers the following day.

The Tigers went on to lose to the Angels in the second game of the doubleheader, which gave the American League pennant to the Sox and sparked a champagne- and shaving cream-filled party in the Sox clubhouse. Without a chance to start a playoff, Stange figured he would still start a World Series game, but that didn't happen.

"I don't understand why I was good enough to start a playoff game, but not a World Series game," Stange said 40 years later.

The disappointment was nothing new to Lee Stange. In a time of tall, strapping hurlers like Bob Gibson and Denny McLain, Stange suffered from the unfortunate fact of being under six feet tall. His career was marked by managers and front office people telling him he was too small to start games.

He now thinks back to those days and believes that being a starter is easier than coming out of the bullpen. "I enjoyed short relief. I think the easiest job for a pitcher is starting pitcher," said Stange, adding that one reason is that starters know when they are going to pitch.

Albert Lee Stange was born to Albert and Dorothy Stange on Oct. 27, 1936, in Chicago. Young Lee grew up with two brothers and a sister in suburban Broadview, a small industrial community 13 miles west of Chicago smaller than 10,000 people. His father worked in the mailrooms for the *Chicago Daily News* and the *Chicago Sun-Times*.

Stange attended Proviso Township High School in Maywood.

At Proviso, he played three sports, including football and baseball with football legend Ray Nitschke, who was also a pitcher with control problems.

While Nitschke was listed at 6-foot-1 and 190 pounds in high school, Stange topped out at 5-foot-9. "It got to the point where everyone else grew and I didn't," said Stange.

Stange enjoyed an active sporting life in high school. Pitching for local coaching legend Doc Appleton, he led the 1953 Proviso Pirates to a state championship. The junior hurled a number of postseason masterpieces, including knocking off reigning state champ Morton. Finishing the year with a 7-1 record, Stange was one of five players from Proviso chosen on the *Chicago Tribune*'s Suburban League All-Star Team in 1953. As a senior, Stange beat Morton 8-1 in the state tournament, striking out 10 and surrendering eight hits. But the chance to repeat as state champs ended with a loss to York High School.

Stange won eight games in 1967, throwing 181 2/3 innings, and led the staff with a 2.77 ERA.

Professional scouts took notice of the Broadview pitcher. Washington Senators scout Ossie Bluege approached him about a contract, but Stange declined the offer, saying that he was headed to Drake University. But after a successful high school pitching career, Stange's college time was not nearly as glorious. The freshman quarterback hurt his knee in a football game, and later reinjured the knee in a scrimmage. When the basketball season started, Stange hoped to play guard for the college team, but he twisted his leg and needed knee surgery. He missed the baseball season. "The only thing I didn't play in college was baseball," said Stange.

Stange left Drake with the hope of joining the military, but was rejected because of his bad knee. There was only one other place to turn—pro baseball. He contacted Bluege, who sent him a $200-a-month contract with the Washington Senators. During his first year in professional baseball, Stange played for the Fort Walton Beach Jets in the Class D Alabama-Florida League, where he struggled to a 5-6 record with a 5.40 ERA.

Stange did enjoy some success the following year with Fort Walton Beach as he won 13 games. But the following year saw him languishing in the bullpen for Appleton in the Three-I League. The young pitcher contemplated quitting baseball as he approached the end of the season with an ERA of nearly 6.00.

He talked to his manager, Jack McKeon, who asked Stange to give it another shot and the pitcher was promoted to the Wilson Tobs in the Class B Carolina League for the 1960 season. Stange took his new league by storm. He finished 20-13 with a 3.59 ERA for the Tobs, who posted 73 wins. The young pitcher collected accolades that year, including being named the Topps Minor League Player of the Year for the Carolina League and being selected for the Carolina League All-Star Team.

"The Stinger" thought his 1960 season showed everyone that his height could no longer be used against him after he threw more than 250 innings and won 20 games. He went to the Florida Winter Instructional League, where the whole height issue returned and the Senators front office reaffirmed their view of him as a short reliever. "(The organization) always said I was too small to be a starting pitcher—even after I won 20 games," recalled Stange.

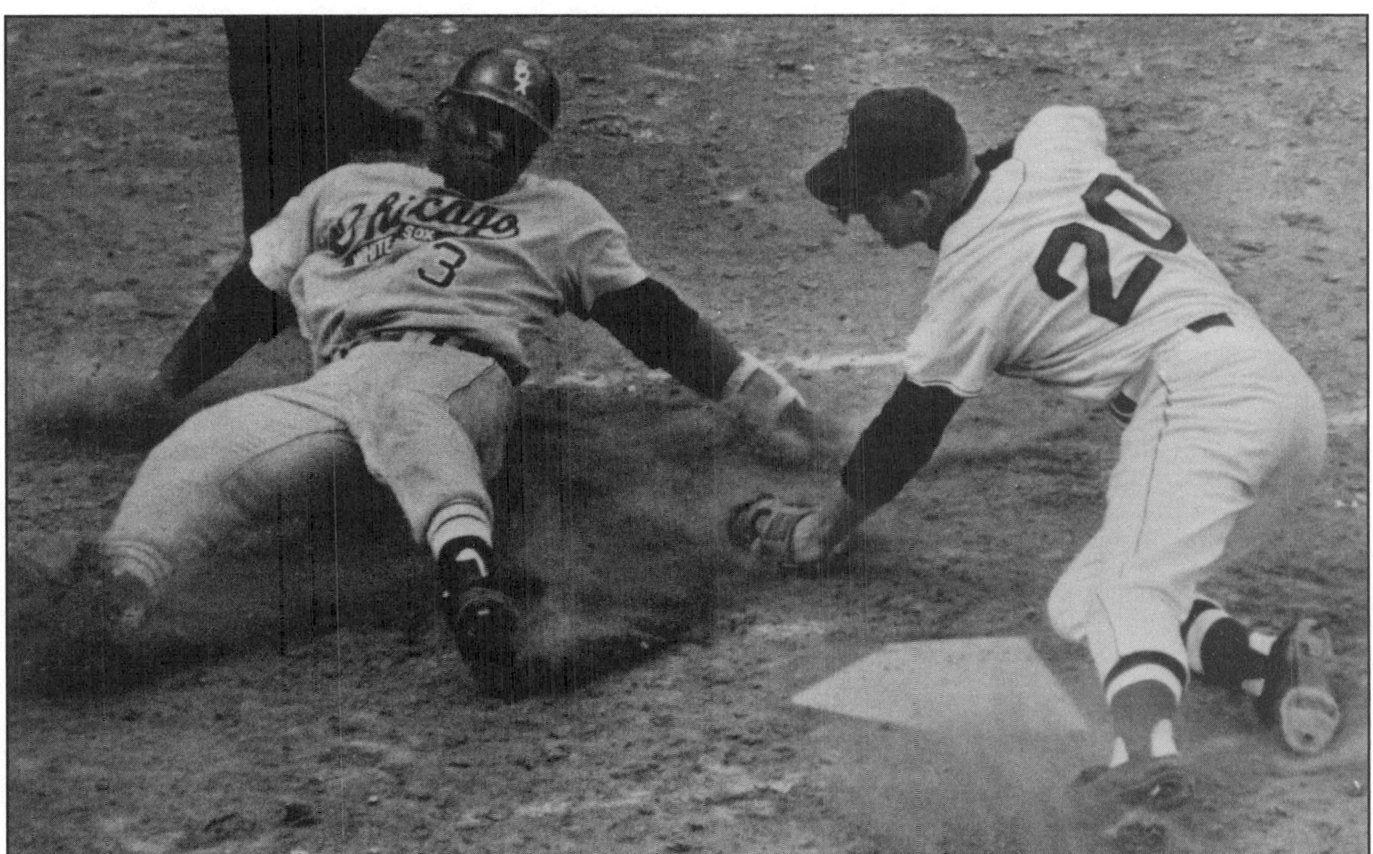

Lee Stange retires Walt "No Neck" Williams in a play at the plate, September 3, 1967.

In the November 30, 1960 *Sporting News*, Fred Lieb wrote how Stange was "possibly the most likely to succeed" in the instructional league's rookie crop by displaying a curve, slider, low breaking balls, "and lots of moxie."

Manager Del Wilber told *The Sporting News*, "Stange is one of the best boys here and I think he can help the parent club as a relief pitcher. While he was a starter last season in Wilson, where he pitched 251 innings, my instructions were to consider his development largely as a relief pitcher. He should be a good stopper. He has a lot of confidence, and runners on base don't bother him. He is likely to make quite a name for himself."

During the offseason, the Senators moved to Minneapolis-St. Paul and became the Minnesota Twins. Stange made the club out of spring training, as teams were allowed to carry 28 players. After two relief appearances, he spent the majority of the 1961 season with Syracuse (International League), where he finished 7-12, 3.78. Recalled by the club again in September, he won his first major league game on September 15, pitching two scoreless innings against Cleveland.

"It was a new team, but most of those guys played in Washington," Stange recalled about the Twins. "It wasn't really an expansion team. They had a nucleus of a pretty good team at that time."

In 1962, Stange spent the whole season with the big club—and impressed his manager. In his first six appearances over 13⅓ innings, Stange complied a 1.35 ERA. Manager Sam Mele gave him a start on May 5 against Detroit, which he won 7-2 on a seven-hitter. "This was the first time I've gone nine innings since September 1960 at Wilson of the Carolina League," Stange told the press after the game.

His starting career quickly ended in his next start when he gave up four runs in 1⅓ innings against Kansas City. Stange was sent back to the pen, and pitched well. He finished the season at 4-3 with a 4.45 ERA pitching for the upstart Twins, who finished second behind the Yankees.

During spring training of 1963, Stange set aside balls with seams for a day and picked up balls with three holes. He won *The Sporting News'* Major League Bowling Championship in Tampa, and Stange and bowling became synonymous for many in the baseball press. They photographed him on the pitcher's mound with a bowling ball and *The Sporting News* didn't let a mention pass without a line about his bowling expertise.

The Brunswick bowling company signed Stange to tour Minnesota, Iowa, and the Dakotas during the winter on exhibition tours. One year, Stange said, he was offered a sponsorship to go on the pro tour, but he declined.

Forty years after his brush with bowling fame, Stange said hitting the lanes in the winter helped his arm. "I think it kept my arm stronger," he said.

Stange once again found himself in the minors in 1963. This time, he pitched for the Dallas-Fort Worth Rangers of the Pacific Coast League. Pitching as a starter, Stange went 7-1 with a 2.05 ERA. He completed five games and allowed 53 hits in 66 innings. In one start, he held San Diego to three hits and struck out 15 in a 4-0 win. "All Stange needed was to gain confidence. I'd say he's found it," Dallas-Fort Worth manager Jack McKeon told *The Sporting News*.

After a little more than a month in the minors, Stange was recalled on June 15, and was in the majors for good. He enjoyed a strong second half, picking up 12 wins and collecting a 2.62 ERA for the year. After the season, Stange was honored by the Minneapolis Baseball Writers as the most improved player

The year 1964 saw its highs, lows, and changes for Stange. After a rough two months with the Twins in which he won only three games and compiled a 4.73 ERA, the team traded him to Cleveland with minor leaguer George Banks for Jim "Mudcat" Grant. Many Cleveland fans spoke out about the trading of fan favorite Grant.

Stange went from a team on the rise to a mediocre club that at the time was rumored to be leaving Ohio. "It was kind of hard going to Cleveland," he recalled. "It wasn't everyone's favorite place."

But Stange pitched better for the Indians (finishing 7-14, 4.41 between the two clubs) and even tied a major league record in one game. In the seventh inning of a 9-0 win over the Senators on September 2, 1964, he struck out four batters: Don Lock, Willie Kirkland, Don Zimmer, and John Kennedy.

The following season saw Stange back in the bullpen as Sam McDowell, Luis Tiant, Sonny Siebert, and Ralph Terry started in the rotation. Stange did occasionally start because of injuries. He had a fine season in the two roles, ending up 8-4, 3.34.

In early June 1966, Stange was traded along with Don McMahon for Dick Radatz, whose once promising career had taken a decided turn for the worse. For the second time in three years, Stange was involved in a trade that was panned by fans of his new team. Though Sox fans had turned their venom on Radatz, the team could have surely gotten more for him than Stange and

Dick's son Ricky Williams watches Lee Stange kill time in the clubhouse on April 11, 1967 as the Sox await postponement of the original seasonal opener.

McMahon, said the experts. But Tribe manager Birdie Tebbetts predicted big things for Stange in Boston.

His Red Sox career didn't start positively as he gave up five runs in three innings against the Yankees on June 3. But Stange found his groove during the second half of 1966, pitching seven complete game victories, including a two-hitter against the Yankees on September 23. After his 8-9 season, the Boston Baseball Writers gave Stange the Unsung Hero Award at their annual banquet.

Stange said the Sox players saw in 1966 that something special was happening. "I think everybody thought that after finishing '66 so good that we could be a pretty good team," he said.

The next season saw a new Red Sox skipper. Fiery Dick Williams took over leadership, and served as an adversary for Stange during the pennant-winning season. "I think Dick was a very good baseball man. He wasn't much fun to play for. He didn't have much of a personality," said Stange.

Though he didn't get along with the manager, Stange was used mostly as a starter in '67 and enjoyed some of his best stuff in his career. Stange remembers throwing the best game of his career on July 31 against the Twins. He threw 6⅔ innings of perfect baseball before allowing a single to Harmon Killebrew, and wound up tossing a three-hit shutout.

Though Stange won only eight games in 1967, he led the staff with a 2.77 ERA. After almost starting a playoff game against the Tigers, Stange was used once in relief in the World Series against the Cardinals, going two innings and giving up one unearned run in a 5-2 Cardinals' win in Game 3.

After a successful season as a starter, Stange was

back in the bullpen in 1968. Pitching alongside Sparky Lyle in short relief, he led the staff with 50 appearances and 12 saves. Stange came in fourth in *The Sporting News*' Fireman Award for the American League.

In the following season the flexible Stange was called on to start 15 times among his 41 appearances. He was 4-8, 4.48 as a starter, but 2-1, 2.34 out of the bullpen.

In the middle of the 1970 season, with Stange struggling with an ERA well over 5.00, the Chicago White Sox picked him off waivers from the Red Sox. Stange told the press after the waiver deal that he enjoyed his time in Beantown, adding, "I hope I can help Chicago. If not, this may be my last year, we'll have to wait and see." He didn't have to wait long. In his first start with the White Sox, Stange went 1⅓ innings and gave up seven hits.

Stange retired as a player after the 1970 season, and was named minor league pitching instructor by the Red Sox in 1971. The following year, he took over the major league pitching coach duties from Harvey Haddix. Stange became the 10th pitching coach in 13 years for the Sox. He told *The Sporting News*, "I'm thrilled and surprised with the appointment. I had no idea a chance to coach in the major leagues would come so quickly."

Stange lasted as pitching coach through the 1974 season when he was fired, and coached with the Twins the following year. Stange later coached for Oakland before he went back to Boston in 1980 under manager Ralph Houk. Houk was Stange's favorite manager. "He was just great to work for. He was a great old baseball man. I think everybody loved playing for him, working for him," said Stange.

During this second tenure with the Red Sox, Stange helped the progression of eventual big-league winners Dennis Eckersley, Bob Ojeda, John Tudor, Bruce Hurst, Roger Clemens, and Curt Schilling.

Talking to *The Sporting News* in 1984, Hurst praised Houk and Stange. "They stuck with me, showed their confidence in me and gave me the chance to prove myself," he said.

The Sox didn't show the same confidence in Stange. He was replaced by Bill Fischer as pitching coach after the 1984 season, and again became minor-league pitching instructor, a job he held for the next 10 years.

While working as a minor-league pitching instructor, Stange helped Ken Ryan, who stands out in Stange's mind as someone he helped get to the majors. At the time, Stange said, no manager wanted Ryan. The coach worked with Ryan in spring training at Winter Haven, Florida, and convinced him that the reliever's job was a better role for him though the tall hurler wanted to start. "I said, 'You sit with me and you throw, and don't ask me when you're starting. You're not starting,'" Stange recalled telling Ryan. Ryan found himself in the bullpen and wound up enjoying an eight-year career in the majors with the Sox and Phillies.

Looking back on his career, Stange said Gary Bell was a favorite teammate. The Stinger joked that he thought he was rid of Bell after Stange was traded from Cleveland, but Bell wound up with Boston, too. "Bell kept everybody loose. He's the same way today. He hasn't changed a bit in 40 years," said Stange.

Stange still sees some of his former teammates at fantasy camps and autograph shows. Though he has been out of major league baseball for more than two decades, he continues to help young pitchers as a coach with the Florida Tech Panthers in his current hometown of Melbourne, Florida.

He doesn't remember who coined his nickname, Stinger. "I remember being called Stinger a long time," said Stange. "I was called stinker a lot of times, too."

Looking back at the 1967 season, Stange views the year as a highlight of his career, not only because of the pennant-winning team, but the men he played alongside.

"I think we pretty much enjoyed it because we were winning and had a great bunch of guys. We got along well and hung out together all the time," said Stange.

Jerry Stephenson

by Bill Nowlin

	G	ERA	W	L	SV	GS	GF	CG	SHO	IP	H	R	ER	BB	SO	HR	BFP
1967 RED SOX	8	3.86	3	1	1	6	1	0	0	39.2	32	18	17	16	24	4	161

The careers of Jerry Stephenson and his father Joe encompass over 100 years of major league experience. Jerry broke into the big leagues in 1963 and has been involved with the game ever since. Joe broke in with the New York Giants during World War II and scouted for the Red Sox from 1948 until nearly the end of the century. There may never be another who scouts 50 years for the same ballclub.

Joe Stephenson was born in Detroit on June 30, 1921. He was a multi-sport athlete in high school, but liked baseball best. Joe was a right-handed batter who appeared in nine games for the Giants in 1943, debuting late in the season on September 19. He was 6-for-24, driving in just one run. The following year, Joe was with the Cubs and had only eight at-bats, with just one single. In 1945, he played for the American Association's Milwaukee Brewers and with the Pacific Coast League's Los Angeles Angels in 1946. Joe and his wife liked the area, so they moved to southern California.

Joe spent part of 1947 with the Waterloo White Hawks of the Three-I League, and was able to return to major league ball with Chicago's other team, the White Sox, accumulating five hits in 35 at-bats. The following year, 1948, he was still in the White Sox system and began with the Memphis Chickasaws of the Southern Association but was moved to Birmingham, a Boston Red Sox farm club. There, Joe broke his leg. He tried to come back in '49, but broke his leg again and that was it. The Red Sox liked him, though, and Joe turned to managing, serving as skipper of another Red Sox farm team , San José in the California League. In 1951, he got in some playing time with San José, too, driving in 40 runs. In the early 1950s, he turned to managing full-time but soon wound up scouting for nearly a half-century. Among the players he signed were Rick Burleson, Dwight Evans, Bill Lee, and Fred Lynn—every one of them on the 1975 Red Sox team—and Mike Andrews, Ken Brett, and Tony Horton—all of whom joined his son Jerry in spring training for the 1967 Red Sox.

There were inevitably players he missed out on. Joe Stephenson signed Ken Brett to a contract at age 17. The Brett brothers recall Ken's father telling Joe, "The one you really want is the skinny, barefooted one, George." At the time Ken signed, in 1966, George Brett was only 13 years old. When George's time came around five years later, Joe wanted the Red Sox to take him as their first pick, but Red Sox upper management declined and Kansas City grabbed him in the second round. Jerry said his father often told of a time he was at Anaheim Stadium when George Brett first made the big leagues: "During batting practice, I guess my dad was sitting in the stands and George Brett spent the whole batting practice screaming at my dad that he signed the wrong Brett." According to Peter Gammons, Joe actually wanted to sign Ken Brett as a center fielder but the Red Sox were desperate for better pitching—and over the years, Ken racked up 83 wins while appearing in 349 ballgames. (George did pretty well for himself, too.)

Joe Stephenson was on the Red Sox scouting staff right into the year 2001; Joe died on September 20, 2001.

Joe's son Jerry was born on October 6, 1943, just 17 days after his father's first major league ballgame. Jerry was also born in Detroit and grew to the same height as his father at 6'2". He was right-handed like his father, but batted left. As one might expect, the fact that his dad played professionally influenced Jerry as well. The seeds were planted early on, Jerry recalls, "I've got pictures of me like six months old laying in a crib with a small bat and ball in my hand. That was at six months, so I started kind of early."

Jerry's mother was very supportive of his interest in baseball, and he grew up in Hermosa Beach until he was in the seventh grade, at which point the family moved to Anaheim. Jerry is the oldest of six children. The second-oldest was his brother Tom, who signed with the Red Sox as well. He played a couple of years of pro ball in the organization—as a pitcher like Jerry—but never got out of lower level ball. He went into accounting and currently works in Reno as a CPA with one of the large gaming establishments there.

Little League had just starting in Hermosa Beach as Jerry was growing up and he played on what he thinks was the first Little League team they had. Of course, he played sandlot ball, too, just for fun, but he began one other experience soon after moving to Anaheim that he believes really made a difference. "My dad—for years—ran a Red Sox scouts team. A lot of clubs had the scouts run a team during the winter." It wasn't just a tryout

over two or three days; this was a regular team. "Guys who had played pro ball, you know. This was before instructional league and all that. Pros and college guys, top high school guys played every Saturday and Sunday. There was like five or six major league clubs had scouts teams, so I used to go out and shag fly balls and all that stuff during the winter when I was just a little kid. That helped me, because I started playing—my dad would put me in for an inning or two—when I was like 13 years old, playing against guys that played pro ball. There was a lot of guys that had played in the minor leagues. I was like an eighth grader. He'd put me in, he'd start me off when I was like 13 and in Little League. I was a catcher first, and then a pitcher. He let me... I can remember pitching the last inning or something like that. I always thought that really helped me."

Jerry was one of those unusual players who threw right, but batted left. Asked about it, he admits to being predominantly left-handed as a batter, but also credits his father for encouraging him to stick with it: "When I was a little kid, my dad made me a left-handed hitter.

Stephenson got some late-season work, with a 3-1 record. He is shown here warming up before his first appearance on August 17.

There are a lot of advantages to being a left-handed hitter, like the hole between first and second when there's a runner on. There's always more right-handed pitchers. It used to be that the right-field fences used to be shorter than the left-field fences in the old ballparks. Plus you're a step or two closer to first base. But I was a left-handed hitter from the time I was a little tiny kid."

As one might expect, Jerry excelled in high school baseball. He had a couple of advantages there, too. Not only did he play ball at Anaheim High School, but "Legion ball was very big. The Legion team in Anaheim was almost like a minor league club. Anaheim had one of the few fields at that time that had lights. We used to play night games. Other teams would come in who had never played night games. We used to kill them. Legion ball was very good. We traveled all over. It was like a minor league club. We used to play everybody, which was unusual at that time. I have old clippings where we used to draw eight or ten thousand people a game."

Joe Stephenson had a legitimate prospect for the Red Sox on his hands, but the prospect was his own son. He was in a bit of a tough situation. Near the end of Jerry's senior year at Anaheim High, about a month before graduation, Red Sox scouting director Neil Mahoney came to check out a workout on a local field in Anaheim. With him came Ted Williams, who'd just retired the previous September. This was in the days before the major league draft.

Mahoney and Ted were there to look over a number of prospects including Bob Bailey (who wound up with the highest bonus ever given at the time, signing with the Pirates), Andy Etchebarren (Orioles), and a kid named Roy Gleason who got about $100,000 from the Dodgers for signing. Joe ran the workout, and Jerry pitched batting practice to the various players. It would have been difficult for Joe to tout his son to the Red Sox, but quite a number of clubs including the Yankees and White Sox had offered Jerry a fair amount of money and Joe had to say something.

Joe told Mahoney about the offers, and as Jerry tells it, "I guess Neil Mahoney went back and told Mr. Yawkey. And Mr. Yawkey says, 'Well, it wouldn't look too good if the son of one of our scouts signs with the Yankees.' So the night I graduated from high school, I flew back to Boston and worked out back there for the manager, Pinky Higgins. I think Sal Maglie was the pitching coach. I worked out back there for a couple of days and I remember Neil Mahoney says, 'Well, if we give you the same money that the Yankees and the White Sox offered you, would you sign with the Red Sox?' Naturally, I said, 'Yes.' I ended up signing back there."

Jerry signed straight out of high school, on June 17, 1961, but he promised his mother and his father that he would get a college degree. That was part of the deal, in the family. "Of course, I wanted to sign so bad I would have told them anything," Jerry admits. He got his degree. It just took him a while. He went to Fullerton Junior College the first four winters he was in pro ball, and after Cal State Fullerton opened up, he enrolled there. It took him 14 winters, but he got his degree. "Guys used to ask my dad during the winter, after I'd been out playing seven or eight years, 'What's Jerry doing this winter?' He said, 'Well, he's still going back to school, going back to college.' They'd say, 'Well, gee, what's he going to be when he graduates?' He used to tell them, 'He's going to be about 33.' And he was accurate. I was 33 when I got my college degree."

Not only had Jerry signed just a couple of days after high school graduation, he was a young graduate, too. He turned 18 that October. He played Connie Mack ball the summer of '61, and that winter played again in his father's scout camp. In the spring of 1962, he made his way to spring training in Ocala, Florida, and played Class B ball under manager Eddie Popowski for Winston-Salem in the Carolina League. It was a good year. Jerry made the league all-star team, and posted a record of 11-5 with an ERA of 2.47. He struck out 152 men in 135 innings, while walking just 69.

There was a rule at the time for bonus players under which the major league team had to keep a "bonus baby" on the big league club for up to two full years or lose rights. The 1962 modification of the rule permitted Jerry to be assigned to the minors that year. In 1963, Jerry went to spring training with the Boston team and made the team, but he might have been better served with another full year or two of development in minor league ball. The 1963 year, he says, was "downhill all the way."[1] He got a start early on, in the fifth game of the season. Johnny Pesky was in his first year as manager for the Red Sox and Harry Dorish was his pitching coach. Jerry started the game at D.C. Stadium on April 14, but the first two batters singled and then he threw a wild pitch and walked the third batter. He worked his way out of the inning with just one run, but promptly got into trouble in the second inning as well with a walk and a single—before striking out the side. When the leadoff man tripled in the third, scored on a sacrifice fly, and then the next batter singled, Pesky had seen enough. Stephenson gave up five hits and two runs in 2⅓ innings. It was Hal Kolstad who bore the defeat, though, in a 7-6 loss to the Senators. It was Jerry's only major league appearance until 1965. He was with the team for a month, but was then sent down to Seattle to work under Mel Parnell. With the Rainiers, Stephenson was 2-11 with an ERA of 5.57. As he puts it, "I had a horrible year. I got sent down to Reading, from Seattle. I was working my way back down."

With Reading, things weren't a whole lot better. He was 2-9, though improved his ERA to 3.96. He improved his strikeouts-to-walks ratio, though, and the Red Sox were by no means ready to give up on the 19-year-old prospect.

In 1964, Stephenson was assigned to Seattle again. He pitched 92 innings, and was pitching very well (6-4, 1.57) when he hurt his elbow. He hurt the elbow pitching from a poorly-prepared mound in San Diego. Worse, Stephenson says that he never really received proper pitching instruction. Seattle manager Parnell told him that the Red Sox brass said to "just let you throw." Jerry needed more than that: "I suppose there is something to helping yourself, but I needed a lot of help, and I never did get it."[2]

In 1965, he made the big league team and stuck with them for the full year, but recalls, "I was like the last pitcher on the staff. I hung around all year." The polite way to put it might be that he was used sparingly; he spent a lot of time on the bench. It wasn't an inspirational season, just 52 innings and a record of 1-5 with a 6.23 ERA. He already had a bit of a reputation; Peter Golenbock says "he was wild, on and off the field. His nickname was 'Teens' because he loved *Teen* magazine. He loved the Beatles and wore turtleneck shirts. Once he peroxided his hair. It ended up with a green tint."[3] Today, Stephenson rebuts the hair story. "Oh, that's a story. That's not true. I was a little goofy, though. That was one of the stories that was made up. I was nuts. I was like 20, going on about like 10. I was just too young. I was that age pitching in the big leagues or in Triple A."

In 1966, Jerry opened the season with the Red Sox, got himself 11 starts, then came into four games out of the bullpen. He was 2-5 (5.83 ERA.) Sent down to Boston's Toronto triple-A club in '66, he failed to report and the papers ran stories that he was missing. Maybe he did do a little soul-searching: "I was supposed to drive from Boston to Toronto, but I detoured to southern California." Within a fairly short time, he turned up to play for Toronto but developed a pilonidal cyst and had to have it operated on. That was the end of his '66 season.

Jerry didn't really impress Dick Williams in spring training 1967. In a March 15 exhibition start, he walked the first three Yankees he faced, then gave up a couple

In a year where every game counted, Stephenson started six games from August 22 on, winning three and losing just one. Jerry is shown here with Warren Spahn.

of hits, and followed that with another walk. He started off 1967 playing for Eddie Kasko in Toronto, though not without a parting shot at Williams when he was sent down in early April. He called Williams "flaky" and added, "He thinks he's a drill instructor. It's going to be a long season."[4] Jerry pitched well in Toronto, winning eight games with a 2.91 ERA and with two shutouts to his credit. He was called up to Boston in mid-August and pitched well down the stretch, with a 3.86 ERA in 39⅔ innings of work. Stephenson—touted by the *Boston Globe*'s Clif Keane as "the kid with the golden arm"—had a couple of scoreless relief appearances and then got his first start against the Senators at Fenway Park on August 22. He threw 7⅔ innings, giving up six hits and just one run, and the Red Sox won the ballgame, 2-1. On August 26, at Comiskey, Jerry faced off against Joel Horlen and admitted, "I was nervous, but Dick told me to throw as hard as I could for as long as I could. 'We don't want a complete game, Jerry,' he told me. 'We want you to go out there and do the best you can for as long as you can. Don't pace yourself.'" Stephenson threw five innings of no-hit ball before tiring in the sixth, when he allowed a couple of runs on three hits, and the Red Sox took over first place, beating Chicago, 6-2. In a year where every game counted, Stephenson started six games from August 22 on, winning three and losing just one.

Stephenson's back to back wins on August 22 and 26 propelled the Red Sox into first place.

His experience in the World Series was disappointing. He threw two innings, the third and fourth innings of Game Four, giving up three doubles and two runs—though he'd entered a game which the Cardinals were already winning, 4-0, after José Santiago got hammered so badly he never closed out the first inning.

Despite the "drill instructor" comment, Jerry insists he really had no complaints about Dick Williams. "Dick was more than fair to me. He gave me a chance to pitch, and I didn't do the job for him. He just wanted you to do the job, and if you didn't do it, he'd let you know... Dick didn't go out of his way to be nice to anyone. He wanted to win and wanted you to do the job... I never hated the guy. I have no complaints."[5] Williams gave a number of young players a chance and collectively they came through.

1968? "I couldn't pitch. I had a terrible year. I don't know. I just couldn't do the job. By that time, I was an old man. Really! The Red Sox told me the next year that I was too old. I was 25. [laughs] I mean, I'd been around a long time, but I was all of 25. Now, at 25, you'd be considered a babe right out of the woods." Stephenson turned 25 that September. He had a 2-8 year (5.64 ERA.) And 1969 wasn't any better. The Red Sox released him just a week into the season, on April 17, but he signed on with the Seattle Pilots the very same day. Sal Maglie was the pitching coach, and he knew Jerry well. Jerry saw '69 as a "lost year... I basically sat around. They called me up to Seattle for a week, two weeks, and then they sent me back to Vancouver. Bob Lemon was the manager [at Vancouver.]" Jerry appeared in two games with Seattle—on June 29 and July 12, pitching 2⅔ innings and giving up three earned runs—then went back to the PCL.

The Pilots lasted only the one year, becoming the Milwaukee Brewers. Before spring training 1970, Jerry was traded in a Triple-A deal from the Brewers Pilots to the Los Angeles Dodgers organization. A fresh start with the Dodgers proved quite the tonic. Jerry played for Tommy Lasorda in Spokane in the Pacific Coast League and led the league in both ERA (2.82) and wins (with a record of 18-5). Stephenson was tied for the league's win totals with Dennis Bennett, pitching for Hawaii. Stephenson's work earned him another trip to the big leagues, and he appeared in three September games for L.A., but had a 9.45 ERA, giving up seven

earned runs in 6⅔ innings of work. These were his last three games in major league baseball.

In 1971, Stephenson played at Spokane again, for the full year. He was 9-13 with an ERA of 5.18, striking out 140 batters in 179 innings. The Dodgers moved their franchise from Spokane to Albuquerque and he had a better year there in 1972, with an ERA just of 4.14 and a 10-8 record. In 1973, he was made a coach with the Albuquerque Dukes but the team had so many injuries that he was pressed into duty and pitched some 57 innings. He won three and lost two, with an ERA of 3.95. In 1974, he was asked if he wanted to scout for the Dodgers, and he agreed, working under Al Campanis and Tommy Lasorda. "They picked the right time to tell me they didn't want to see me pitch anymore."

Jerry had done well at the plate. He hit for a better average than his father (.231 in 65 at-bats), though he never had an extra-base hit. ("If I'd had any power, I probably would have stayed a catcher.")

Stephenson worked as a scout with the Dodgers for more than 20 years, mostly as an advance scout, from 1974 to 1995. These were "the good years"—when the Dodgers were a winning organization. When the Dodgers let him go, he signed on with the Red Sox. "You always love the first organization you signed with," he says. "I always loved the Red Sox, so I inquired about coming back, and they hired me."

He now works as a major league scout, covering about 14 or 15 big league clubs. "I basically have the National League West and the American League West; I have part of the National League Central, too. That's my coverage. Mostly on the West Coast. I go to Houston—I don't have the Cubs—Pittsburgh, I go to St. Louis. I go to Arizona a lot, I go to San Diego a lot. L.A."

The heavy reliance of the current Red Sox on computers makes scouting different these days. "I advance scouted for the Dodgers for a long time. I couldn't advance scout anymore. It's gotten out of hand. It's very technical now. Computer-driven." Discerning talent, though, still relies on the human eye and Stephenson's talents remain valued by the Red Sox organization.

Jerry and his wife have two children, a daughter, Shannon, who was more into cheerleading than sports and graduated from Arizona State, and a son, Brian. Brian was a pitcher, a second-round pick for the Chicago Cubs in 1994. He played five years, getting as high as Double A, but had to undergo two elbow operations in the five years. He got a degree from UCLA and currently works as a scout for the Dodgers.

Stephenson has seven championship rings—two from the Red Sox—1967 and 2004—and five from the Dodgers. That leaves three spare digits: "I hope the Red Sox win three more. On March 1 each year, he starts working spring training, covering the teams that train in Arizona.

Notes:

1. Interview with Jerry Stephenson, January 30, 2006. All quotations otherwise unattributed to Jerry Stephenson come from this interview.
2. Golenbock. p. 331
3. *Ibidem.*
4. Miller, p. 14
5. Golenbock, p. 293

Gary Waslewski

by John Cizik

	G	ERA	W	L	SV	GS	GF	CG	SHO	IP	H	R	ER	BB	SO	HR	BFP
1967 RED SOX	12	3.21	2	2	0	8	1	0	0	42	34	18	15	20	20	3	177

Gary Lee Waslewski woke in his Peabody, Massachusetts, apartment on the morning of October 11, 1967, as the starting pitcher in Game Six of the World Series. "I was reading the papers, and one guy wrote 'Waslewski has as much chance of winning as Custer had of beating the Indians,'" Gary said. "It didn't bother me. I just went out and tried to do my job." His major league experience to that point consisted of 12 games, eight starts, a 2-2 record, and a 3.21 ERA. He had made his major league debut four months earlier. Hadn't won a game since July 2; hadn't started one since July 29. He had never pitched a major league complete game, and was declared eligible for the World Series only two days before Game One, when Darrell Brandon was placed on the injured list.

Gary Lee Waslewski was born on July 21, 1941, in Meriden, Connecticut, the first child of Michael Waslewski and the former Adelaide Lee. Dad was a master tool and die maker at a silversmith plant in Wallingford. Adelaide died in early 1970, a cancer victim at 51. The family heritage was pure Polish on Dad's side, and a mixture of German and Cherokee Indian on Mom's.

Gary's younger brother, Michael, was born in 1943. "We spent all of our time running around in the woods playing cowboys and Indians," Gary says. "And we played a lot of baseball in the open fields because there was nothing much else to do. There were only about seven kids within a few miles of each other, and we'd play in somebody's driveway, or in the cow fields across the street, and use cow flops for bases."

There was a big pond in the back yard, about 15 feet from the house. In the summer, it became Ebbets Field. "The Dodgers—that was my ball club!" Waslewski says. "I would stand out there and hit.... I had a board I used as a bat.... I would throw up rocks and try to whack them across the water, and if I hit it into the trees it was a home run. I'd be hitting left-handed like Duke Snider, maybe Gilliam if he was switch-hitting, and right-handed like Hodges and Campanella and the rest of them."

There was no Little League in Berlin, Connecticut, where they lived when Gary was younger, so childhood baseball consisted simply of those games in the cow fields and games of catch with his parents. "I would sometimes go out and have a catch with my mother," Gary recalls. "My father would come home from work at 6:00 at night and he'd catch for a while if I wanted to pitch, until it got to the point where I was throwing too hard and he couldn't handle me anymore." Finally, when Gary was about 13, organized ball came to town. Waslewski remembers always being a pitcher.

Berlin's Little League ended at age 15. Without some motherly intervention, Gary's career might have ended there. "My mother had grown up in Meriden," Waslewski says. "And she went down to some friends of hers, guys she had gone to school with, who were running the Meriden Intermediate League, and asked them to make an exception to let me play there." While playing in the Meriden league, Gary was also recruited by the semipro Meriden Knights of Columbus. He pitched a lot during this period, usually throwing one game of a doubleheader for the Knights on Sunday, one or two games with the Intermediate League during the week, and maybe an American Legion game on Friday.

In 1956, it was off to Berlin High. "I don't know what my record was altogether," says Gary, "I remember that [my junior year] it was 10-0." Berlin won the State Class C Championship that year. Waslewski attended the University of Connecticut on a partial scholarship. After his freshman year in 1960, it was back to playing ball for the Knights. "We played [a game] against a bunch of college all-stars that were barnstorming around," Waslewski recalls. "And there were a couple of good players on the team I was told were being scouted by some local scouts. I beat them 9-0, struck out 13, 14 guys, got four hits myself, and after the game [Pittsburgh Pirates scout] Milt Rosner, who was there to watch somebody else, came down and said, 'Gee, would you consider playing ball?' I probably wasn't going to go back [to UConn] because I just wasn't into the schooling and stuff." Bird-dog scout Rosner contacted his superiors, and Chick Whelan came down to sign Waslewski.

The right-hander was off to the Rookie Class D Appalachian League Kingsport Pirates, managed by James Gibbons. Of the 164 players in that rookie camp, only four survived the minor leagues. One other was familiar to Gary: Falls Village, Connecticut native Steve

Blass. "I had just seen him pitch against my brother at an All-Star game," Waslewski recalls. "He was playing for Housatonic High... and my brother was pitching for Wilcox Tech in the State tournament just before I left to go to the rookie camp. And he beat my brother 1-0."

With about a month to go in the 1960 season, Waslewski was 4-2 with a 2.86 ERA. He was called up to New Mexico to play for the Class D Hobbs Pirates. Gary went 0-1 with a 7.36 ERA as Hobbs made the Sophomore League playoffs. It was back to the desert in 1961. Al Kubski was the manager, and the Pirates went 77-48 to lead the league. Waslewski was 12-7 with a 4.10 ERA.

In 1962, Gary headed to North Carolina and the Class B Kinston Eagles. Teammate Steve Blass was an All-Star, and the team won the championship. Waslewski was 7-8, with a 3.76 ERA. 1963 saw Waslewski back in Kinston, where he went 1-1 with a 4.13 ERA before being called up to the Class A Reno Silver Sox of the California League. "At night they almost had to ban you from going downtown," Gary says of Reno. "Guys were going who were only getting paid $275-300 a month and they'd wipe you out in one night." The team went 71-69, finished fifth, and drew only 17,182 fans. Gary went 13-5 for the Silver Sox with a 3.83 ERA.

An incredulous "Gary Waslewski?" *echoed Williams' choice of the Game Six starter. With only two major league wins under his belt, and making his first start since July, Waslewski proved all doubters wrong.*

It was back to Kinston and manager Pete Peterson for the 1964 season—not a demotion; the Carolina League had become Class A. Kinston took first place again, 79-59; Waslewski was 12-1 with a stellar 1.64 ERA. He wasn't around for the postseason, promoted to the Double-A Asheville Tourists (Southern League) with around a month to go in the season. He went 5-5 for the Tourists, with an ERA of 3.84.

During the off-season, the Pirates left Waslewski unprotected, and he was taken in the minor league draft by the Red Sox. Waslewski did not make the Sox roster, and they had to offer him back to the Pirates. "Luckily, the Pirates said, 'We don't want him' or my career might have ended right there," Waslewski told author Jack Lautier.

The Sox sent Waslewski to manager Eddie Popowski and his Double-A Eastern League Pittsfield Red Sox to start 1965. Pittsfield beat out Earl Weaver's Elmira Pioneers to win the league by one game. Waslewski went 6-2 with a 2.45 ERA, but again was called up before season's end. Dick Williams was managing the Toronto Maple Leafs in the Triple-A International League and needed another starter. The Maple Leafs won their league championship, beating Columbus four games to one.

Waslewski won only five games for that Toronto team, but his biggest win came off the field. "I went to a party... [with] two stewardesses from Air Canada." One of his teammates went with a girl named Nancy. "[He] kind of ignored her, and the two girls I was with ignored me, so we were just kind of sitting there, started talking, and started going out!" Nancy was a big baseball fan, and often attended Leafs games with her brother. She became Mrs. Gary Waslewski in September 1966.

In 1966, Boston's faith in the lanky right-hander paid off. The Leafs were in a dogfight for the league lead. They ended up winning the IL championship, and the Pitcher of the Year honors went to 25-year-old Gary Waslewski. He went 18-11 to lead the league, with a 2.52 ERA. He threw 200 innings, gave up only 143 hits, walked 84, and struck out 165.

After the season, it was off to Caracas in the Venezuelan League, and a honeymoon for the Waslewskis. With winter ball, and the 200 innings for Toronto, by spring training in 1967 Gary had thrown

more innings than he was used to. "I ended up with tendonitis, inflammation in the shoulder." He had to stay behind with the Toronto club as spring training ended. Billy Rohr got off to a terrific start, but became less effective. After a two-week stint for Uncle Sam, Rohr was sent to Toronto, and Waslewski was called up.

Gary's first start came in the second game of the June 11 doubleheader against the Washington Senators. The first hitter he faced was Norwalk, Connecticut native Bobby Saverine. "He hit the ball to the best shortstop in the league, and he boots it!" Waslewski exclaimed. Rico Petrocelli's error was an inauspicious beginning. "I used to tell people when I talked on the circuit after [my career] that I started out in a slump and tailed off from there!" Two errors in the inning led to three unearned runs and a trip to the showers after three-plus innings.

Gary's second start was a big improvement. "For nine innings he shut out Chicago before he had to leave in the 10th with a muscle pull behind his left shoulder," Larry Claflin reported. "A crowd of 16,775 at Fenway gave the rookie a standing ovation when he left the field."

The muscle strain cost him a start, but he was back on the hill in Minnesota on June 27, facing Dean Chance. An RBI single by Reggie Smith in the seventh helped give Waslewski his first major league win. He won his next start against Kansas City as well, throwing a 2-1 three-hitter with "nothing but a high school curveball." In the sixth inning, he picked off American League stolen base leader Bert Campaneris with his tenth throw to first. "I showed Campy a different move on that tenth time," Waslewski told the Associated Press. A's manager Alvin Dark insisted it was a balk move, but Dick Williams felt differently. "It was a great move," the manager said. "He learned it in the Pittsburgh organization, before we drafted him. He bends his front knee and pivots on his back foot, all in one motion. It isn't a balk. Hoyt Wilhelm does it, but not as well." In 26⅓ innings, Waslewski had allowed only three earned runs, and was 2-0.

The 1967 Red Sox were not quite a 25-guys, 25-cabs ball club, but it was close. "Some of the old guys that had been there hung together, some of the younger guys hung together, and it wasn't really cohesive off the field," Waslewski says of his teammates. "During the game everybody would pull it together, but the main thing in our offense was Carl Yastrzemski. It was like—let's get on base so Yaz can knock us in. He was just incredible." The legendary Sal Maglie was the Sox pitching coach, but not a lot of help, according to Waslewski. "Yeah, Sal was useless. Jim Lonborg and I one day asked him about how to pitch to the Twins, and he told us how to pitch to the Dodgers! 'Well you know, Campy was kind of like Killebrew, and I would do this with Campy...' and he was telling us about throwing a slow curveball, and Lonborg and I were saying, 'We're just trying to get the curveball to break, never mind different speeds!' Sal was just... he was just there."

Gary had four more starts and a relief appearance in July, none worth writing home about. When his record fell to 2-2 after a start against the Twins on July 29, he was sent back to Toronto. After a September 3 start for the Maple Leafs, and Bill Landis' departure for military service, Boston brought him back. He made three relief appearances, pitching a total of eight innings as Boston held on to win the pennant. Waslewski assumed his season was over, as he was not on the Series eligibility roster, but two days before Game One in Boston, he replaced injured pitcher Darrell Brandon.

Game Three began badly for the Red Sox. Gary Bell started the afternoon affair at Busch Stadium and immediately gave up a Lou Brock triple and a Curt Flood single. In the second, Tim McCarver led off with a base hit, and Mike Shannon followed with a home run. Bell got out of the inning, but George Thomas batted for him in the third. Dick Williams called on his rookie to stop the bleeding. "I remember walking in from the bullpen," Waslewski says. "And I felt like the matador walking into the ring." The first batter he faced was the speedy Lou Brock, who struck out. "I remember saying to myself, if I screw up, everybody in the world is going to see it! You screw up, it's not just a local thing anymore!" Flood grounded out, Roger Maris flied to right, and the rookie had a perfect inning. He followed it with a perfect fourth, striking out Orlando Cepeda, and a perfect fifth, fanning Julian Javier. "He looked remarkably like Jim Lonborg," wrote one reporter. "I can't throw as hard as Lonborg," Waslewski told another scribe. "At least, I haven't been able to throw that hard lately. When I'm right I'm as fast as Jim, but not now."

The Red Sox lost Game Three, 5-2, but Waslewski impressed his manager. "I think it was after that game that Dick came and said something about starting the sixth game if we have a sixth game. And I said, 'OK.'" Williams hoped to save his ace, Jim Lonborg, for a seventh-game appearance against Bob Gibson. "I'm not even going to think about it until tomorrow," Waslewski told Dave Anderson of the *New York Times* the day before Game Six. He told the *Washington Post's* Bob Addie, "I've been observing from the bullpen, and

The rookie Waslewski was Dick Williams' surprise starter in Game Six of the 1967 World Series, and held the Cardinals to just two runs in 5⅓ innings of work before turning the game over to John Wyatt. Williams said after the game, "Waslewski did just what we wanted him to. He threw the hell out of the ball for five innings."

I've been talking to Lonborg and the other pitchers a lot about how to handle the Cardinals. I'll have Elston Howard back of the plate, and that's all I need." Williams talked with Dick Young about his young starter and his various ailments:

"He has had everything but the galloping dandruff," says Dick Williams. "He had rheumatic fever when he was a kid, and then his lung collapsed. I wouldn't be surprised if his eyesight started to go out on the mound tomorrow. He's developing into a hypochondriac, but he has a good arm, a great arm."

Fellow rookie Dick Hughes, Game Two loser, started for St. Louis. "Trailing three games to two," Leonard Koppett wrote in the *Times*, "the Boston Red Sox will rely on the least experienced pitcher ever to start a World Series game..." "So what?" said Dick Williams. The media scrutiny was intense. "The day of the game," Gary recalls, "somebody was up at the apartment in Peabody at about 6 o'clock in the morning. They wanted to come in, watch you shower... what are you eating? More reporters. I remember answering the same questions over and over and over and over again!"

Waslewski put on his No. 19 jersey and headed out to the Fenway mound. The Cardinals couldn't touch him in the first. Brock struck out, Flood grounded out, and Maris went down swinging. In the second, Gary got Cepeda, McCarver, and Shannon. Petrocelli's home run made it 1-0 Sox after two. Julian Javier doubled to lead off the Cardinals' third. Brock drove him in with a single and stole second. Flood drove in Brock with a hit; at the end of three, the Sox trailed 2-1. Boston took the lead with a record-breaking fourth inning, as three Sox (Yastrzemski, Smith, and Petrocelli) homered. The offensive explosion made it 4-2, Sox. Nelson Briles

replaced reliever Ron Willis to start the fifth inning and drilled Waslewski in the arm. The Sox didn't score; Waslewski was stranded on second.

Maris stepped into the box to start the sixth. He walked on four pitches. Cepeda flied out to right, and McCarver walked on four pitches. The tying runs were on base. John Wyatt came in and got out of the inning. St. Louis tied the game in the seventh, but Boston won to force a seventh game. "Waslewski did one heck of a job," Williams said. "He had no starting jobs for quite a while, but he did it today. He was marvelous. I told him that when I went out there to take him out. He had thrown his best for as long as he could. I wanted six innings out of him and he came pretty close." He told UPI, "I wish 'Waz' would have gotten the victory."

"I just ran out of gas," Gary told the same reporter. "I'm not especially proud of my performance. I'm glad we won, but I'd rather pitch nine innings. I was boiling inside, because I was so nervous."

Life was a little different after the 1967 World Series. "Everybody wants a piece of you," Waslewski remembers. "And it was an opportunity to make some money in the offseason, because we didn't make enough during the season! I was making $8,500 that first year, I think the minimum was $7,000. The Red Sox actually hired Gary Bell and I to go around and shake hands with the group sales guy who was trying to get all these companies to sign up and buy group tickets!" Larry Claflin reported in *The Sporting News* that "Red Sox execs are very pleased with the work Gary Waslewski is doing with season ticket customers and prospects. Waslewski, whose wife gave birth to their first child (a boy) recently, is working for the Bosox in the offseason."

1968 was a good spring for Waslewski. Darrell Johnson was his new pitching coach, and an unexpected

A number of men played winter baseball during the 1966-67 off-season. Jose Santiago and Gary Waslewski both saw duty in San Juan.

spot was open in the rotation because of Lonborg's offseason skiing accident. In his first 20 spring innings, Gary's ERA was 1.80. Williams penciled him in as the fourth starter after he ended the spring with a string of 18 shutout innings and a 1.13 ERA. Waslewski won his first game of the '68 season in Cleveland, 3-1, and had a big lead against the Tribe back in Boston during his second start. The Sox won, 9-2, as Gary pitched his first major league complete game. "And then I think I lost five in a row after that." Throw in one no-decision, and Waslewski actually lost seven in a row. "Darrell Johnson came to me one day," Waslewski says. "And he says, 'Waz, we're going to take you out of the rotation. We've got to get somebody in there who the team is scoring runs for.' And so they put somebody else in there to start." He stayed with the Sox all year, appearing mainly out of the bullpen, and wound up 4-7 with a decent 3.67 ERA. On June 15 at Cleveland, he picked up his first major league save, mopping up for Ray Culp with 3⅓ innings of scoreless relief in a 9-3 Boston win.

On December 3, 1968, Waslewski received a call from Red Sox Director of Player Personnel Haywood Sullivan. It was the year Kansas City and Seattle joined the American League. "He said, 'We had to make a trade to get a utility infielder, we have no backups for our infield. And we got Dick Schofield, who can play second, short, and third... and you were the only guy the Cardinals would accept." Gary would be heading west to join the team he pitched so well against in the 1967 World Series. "That was a shocker," he says of the trade. "That was like having your wife come up and say, 'I want a divorce.'" Once the initial shock wore off, the trade didn't seem so bad. Bob Gibson, Steve Carlton, and Nelson Briles anchored the Cardinals rotation. "They had also picked up Dave Giusti that spring from Houston," Gary recalls. "At the end of spring training they said the fifth starter was between [me] and Giusti." A one-on-one pitching matchup at the end of the spring would decide the job. "He beat me 1-0. I got a base hit off him, he didn't get any hits off me. So he got to be the fifth starter."

On April 14, Waslewski became the answer to a trivia question. At Parc Jarry in Montreal, he relieved Nelson Briles in the fourth inning with the Cards up 7-6. An inherited runner scored to tie the game. In the Expos' seventh, catcher John Bateman struck out, Coco Laboy doubled, and pitcher Dan McGinn drove him home, giving the Expos an 8-7 lead. The score held up, and Gary Waslewski became the first pitcher to lose a major league game played outside the United States.

By June 2, Gary had appeared in 12 games for St. Louis, with an 0-2 record and a 3.92 ERA. On June 3, he was traded to the Expos for veteran Jim "Mudcat" Grant. Waslewski was reunited with former manager Dick Williams, an Expos coach. After a string of 10 scoreless innings out of the pen, manager Gene Mauch tabbed him to start the second game of a twi-night doubleheader against the Phillies at Connie Mack Stadium. "I had a good sinker that day, the bottom was dropping out of it, and the only guy that got a hit was Ricardo 'Rick' Joseph. He hit a dribbler past me, and [shortstop] Bobby Wine just couldn't get to it. It was a 50-hopper, and it just got through." Deron Johnson hit into a double play to erase Joseph. Waslewski won the game, 5-0, a complete game shutout in which he faced the minimum 27 batters.

His next start was at Forbes Field against the Pirates. Gary led 1-0 with one out in the ninth. "Somebody hit a ground ball to Wine for an error"—it was first baseman Carl Taylor. He scored on a José Pagan single, ending Waslewski's scoreless inning streak at 25, an Expos record that would stand until 1975. He came out after the 10th inning, and the Expos fell, 2-1. Waslewski bounced between the rotation and the bullpen for the rest of the season, winding up 3-7 with the Expos, with a 3.29 ERA.

Gary began the 1970 season in the Expos bullpen, but moved to the rotation in late April. After four mediocre starts and an 0-2 record, he was placed on waivers. Advice from an old batterymate of Waslewski's persuaded the Yankees to pick him up—Elston Howard had returned to the Yankees as a coach. That Yankees team won 93 games, but finished second to Baltimore. Waslewski appeared in 26 games, with five starts. His ERA was again good at 3.11, and his record was 2-2. His last career start came on Sunday, July 5, against Washington at Yankee Stadium, and he didn't survive the first inning, giving up two walks, a hit batsman, and a Del Unser home run. His last career victory was in a relief outing against the Tigers at Yankee Stadium on August 7.

Waslewski got his final major league save on June 19, 1971, at Memorial Stadium in Baltimore, throwing a perfect 11th inning. As the season rolled into July, Waslewski was 0-1, with a 3.26 ERA. On July 6, he came into a game in Detroit, replacing Gary Jones with the Yankees trailing the Tigers 10-7 in the fifth inning. He was still in there to start the seventh. Willie Horton and Jim Northrup hit back-to-back singles, and Tiger second baseman Dick McAuliffe stepped to the plate. "I remember a ground ball hit to first," Gary remembers.

"So I had to get over to cover first base. [Felipe

Alou] threw it to [shortstop] Gene Michael at second for one out, and Gene... threw me one of those sinkers down... and I'm running to the bag. I hit the bag and turn to go get his throw, and it's going to short-hop me. I'm thinking, if I don't block this ball, it bounces right into the stands because the stands are close, and the guy on second scores. So if I can at least block the ball and keep it in play, we're going to have first and third and I can get the next guy and we'll be out of the inning. As I tried to turn to block it, something locked in my knee, and I heard POP!"

His season was over. "I qualified for the pension plan at Lenox Hill Hospital," Waslewski joked. "I got my four years in." The Yankees had him pitch some batting practice near the end of the season, but manager Houk didn't want him injuring the knee again in game play. The 1971 Yankees finished in fourth place at 82-80, 21 games behind the Orioles.

Gary started the 1972 season with the Yankees Triple-A club in Syracuse. He had no decisions with the Chiefs and a lofty 8.18 ERA when he was traded to the Oakland A's for former teammate Ron Klimkowski. In August, Waslewski was called up and reunited for a third time with Dick Williams, this time as an Oakland Athletic. His first appearance for the A's would be in—of all places—Boston on July 21. "The Boston writers said it looks like you have a different motion now," Gary told Ron Bergman of *The Sporting News*. "The only reason they say that is that I got someone out." His last major league appearance was in Oakland-Alameda County Coliseum in a September 28 game against the Minnesota Twins. The last batter he faced, Cesar Tovar, grounded to third.

In 1973, the A's moved their Triple-A team to Tucson, Arizona. Gary spent the entire season in the desert. "Not a good place for pitchers, because the air is very light," he says. Waslewski pitched well in relief for the Toros, helping them to the Eastern Division pennant under manager Sherm Lollar. They lost to Spokane in the PCL playoffs.

Near the end of spring training in 1974, Waslewski fell victim to A's owner Charlie Finley's penny-pinching ways. The word came down that Finley's wife had just served him with divorce papers, and he wanted everyone making more than $2,000 a month released. Gary asked Lollar if it was the end for him; his manager thought he could still pitch in the majors. But nothing materialized.

Back in Connecticut, Gary pitched in the Hartford Twilight League. He had obtained his securities and insurance licenses during his tenure in Boston, and he began to look for work. Career decisions were postponed when the Red Sox came calling. They signed Waslewski to a minor league contract to replace some injured prospects at Triple-A Pawtucket. He never made it back to the majors, winding up with no decisions and a 3.32 ERA. He knew the end had come.

Waslewski would go on to a career with The Hartford insurance company that lasted for 24 years. When he retired, Gary took up golf to keep the competitive juices flowing. "For the first couple of years, for the life of me I couldn't believe that people could shoot par," Waslewski jokes. As of 2005, he was a 13 handicap, and had many opportunities to play good courses. Gary plays 10 to 12 charity golf tournaments a year for Major League Baseball Alumni and other organizations. His son Daniel is a scratch golfer and director of food and beverage for the Tournament Players Club of Boston. Dan was a good hitter at Southington High School, went to UConn, but had to leave school because of mononucleosis and never went back. The Waslewskis' elder son, Gary, was a fine pitcher at Princeton, but his career was derailed when his car was struck by a drunk driver. Nothing was broken, but the baseball scouts lost interest. Gary is now an orthopedic surgeon in Arizona, specializing in sports medicine.

The starting pitcher in Game Six of the 1967 World Series remains a Red Sox fan to this day. "The organization was so good, and they bring us back every year for at least one or two games," Waslewski says. "They've got Autograph Alley...sit there for an hour or so, sign autographs for everybody, people take pictures. Most of the kids who come for autographs... they don't have a clue! But sometimes the parents will say, 'My Dad remembers you!' So that's nice." History has treated the former pitcher kindly. "It's what, 37 years since then, and I'll be out playing golf or something, and my name will come up," he told the *Hartford Courant*. "People come up to me and say, 'Aren't you the guy who pitched in the World Series?' They still remember."

John Wyatt

by Andrew Blume

	G	ERA	W	L	SV	GS	GF	CG	SHO	IP	H	R	ER	BB	SO	HR	BFP
1967 RED SOX	60	2.60	10	7	20	0	43	0	0	93.1	71	30	27	39	68	6	379

The 1967 Red Sox were much more potent at the plate than on the mound, though much of this can be explained by the hitter-friendly ballpark they called home. The Sox offense led the league in average (.255), slugging (.395), runs (722), hits (1,394), and home runs (158). The pitching staff finished eighth in the 10-team American League with a 3.36 ERA. The league average that year was 3.23, with the White Sox the front-runners, thanks to their impressive staff ERA of 2.45. Crucial to keeping the pitching afloat and the team in pennant contention were the starting of Jim Lonborg and the finishing of John Wyatt. Wyatt, acting as Boston's ace reliever in '67, appeared in 60 games during the pennant drive, finishing 43, saving 20, and finishing fourth on the staff with 10 wins.

Johnathon Thomas Wyatt Jr. was born on April 19, 1935, in Chicago. He graduated from Hutchinson High School in Buffalo, New York in 1953, though it certainly wasn't an easy life. When he was 16, he worked racking balls in a billiards parlor and became a pretty good player (on a four-hour layover in Atlanta on the way to his first spring training, he won $300). Soon after, he took on a much more demanding job, Wyatt told Will McDonough: "I worked in a steel mill from 11 at night until 7 in the morning. I'd go right from work to school. After school I practiced football and wouldn't get home until 6:30. Then I'd sleep four hours and my mother would wake me up to go to work in the steel mill again." He added, "I did most of my sleeping in school."

His professional baseball career began in the Negro Leagues, starting with the Indianapolis Clowns of the Negro American League from 1953 to 1955. The 1954 Clowns, managed by Hall of Famer Oscar Charleston in the final year of his career, won the Negro American League title. In 1954, Wyatt was signed as an amateur free agent by the St. Louis Cardinals, the franchise he would later face in the 1967 World Series. Offered a $1,000 bonus, he leapt to sign. "I never had seen that kind of money in one lump sum and I wasn't going to let it get away," he reminisced. In 1954, he compiled a 12-11 record with a 5.08 ERA in 156 innings for Hannibal of the Class D Mississippi-Ohio Valley League. In 1955, though, he spent the whole year playing again for the Clowns, having been released by the Cardinals.

In April, 1956, Wyatt was sent by the Indianapolis Clowns to the Milwaukee Braves, where he appeared in a pair of games for Jacksonville of the Class A South Atlantic (Sally) League. He was returned to Indianapolis in May and then compiled a 4-3, 4.14 record in 17 games for the unaffiliated El Paso club of the Class B Southwestern League. In July, he was sold by El Paso to the Kansas City Athletics organization and was 2-8, 8.84 for the A's Pocatello club of the Class C Pioneer League. Wyatt served in the military during the 1957 and 1958 seasons. In 1959, he was 1-6, 5.55 in 19 games for Albany in the Single-A Eastern League and 4-4, 3.41 in 74 innings for Sioux City of the Class B Three I League over 26 games.

The 1960 season was Wyatt's last full season in the minor leagues. He was 1-2, 5.21 in 38 innings for Dallas-Fort Worth of the Triple-A American Association, 4-6, 4.56 in 79 innings for Monterrey of the Mexican League, and 2-2, 3.66 in four games for Sioux City. He described his Mexican League experience in Bill Reynolds' *Lost Summer*: "It was bad down there. Bad baseball. Bad lights. Bad everything. It was as bad as when I was playing in the Negro Leagues, playing as much as three games a day. The ball had raised seams, and one day my finger blistered and began to bleed. When I told the manager I couldn't continue, he took a poke at me. Just as I pulled my fist back to let him have it, nine Mexican guys stood up. 'Cool it, man' they said. I cooled it."

In 1961, Wyatt earned his ticket to the show with Portsmouth of the Sally League. In 52 games, he struck out 91 and gave up only 87 hits in 101 innings, posting a 9-3 record and a 3.13 ERA. On Friday night, September 8, 1961, he made his major league debut for the Kansas City Athletics against the Minnesota Twins at KC's Municipal Stadium. He entered the game in the eighth inning to face Bob Allison and retired him on a foul pop to the catcher. After walking Joe Altobelli, he recorded his first strikeout, fanning Earl Battey. In the ninth, Zoilo Versalles earned the first hit allowed by Wyatt in his major league career. Wyatt wound up finishing the game, and earned what is now called a save, shutting out the Twins over two innings in a 6-4 win. Wyatt appeared in 7⅓ innings over five September games for Kansas City. Over the next six seasons, he

averaged more than 64 appearances a season.

Wyatt established himself as the workhorse of the A's bullpen. In 1962, he made the only nine starts of his major league career, establishing his career high in strikeouts with 106 in 125 innings. In 59 games, Wyatt was 10-7, with a 4.46 ERA and 11 saves. Ten victories were his one-season high, a number he matched in 1967. In 1963, he was 6-4 with a 3.13 ERA and a career-high 21 saves.

In 1964, Wyatt appeared in 81 games, a major league record at the time. Wyatt recorded a 9-8 record with a 3.59 ERA and 20 saves. He gave up only 111 hits in a career-high 128 innings. He pitched three innings or more in relief 10 times during that season. He was named for the only time in his career to the American League All-Star team. In a 7-4 loss to the National League, Wyatt came on in the fourth inning in relief of Dean Chance and had a less than stellar outing: Billy Williams and Ken Boyer homered, accounting for the two runs Wyatt allowed in his single inning.

In 1965, Wyatt was 2-6 with a 3.25 ERA and 18 saves in 88⅔ innings over 65 games. In 1966, Wyatt pitched poorly and lost the primary reliever role to Jack Aker (8-4, 1.99 ERA, 32 saves). Wyatt was 0-3 with a 5.32 ERA in nineteen games. Meanwhile, in Boston, ace reliever Dick Radatz had been equally disappointing, carrying an 0-2, 4.74 record in 16 games. On June 2, 1966, Radatz was traded by the Red Sox to the Cleveland Indians for Don McMahon and Lee Stange. The Sox followed up on June 13 with the acquisition of Wyatt, Rollie Sheldon, and José Tartabull from the A's for Jim Gosger, Ken Sanders, and Guido Grilli, securing additional help for the bullpen. McMahon and Wyatt split the important relief duties during the balance of the 1966 season with McMahon going 8-7 with a 2.65 ERA and nine saves in 49 games and Wyatt posting numbers of 3-4, 3.14 and eight saves in 42 games.

In 1967, Wyatt emerged as the ace reliever for the Red Sox (although he failed to endear himself to rookie skipper Dick Williams by hitting the hot-swinging Tony Conigliaro on the left arm with a fastball in batting practice during spring training), allowing the team the luxury of trading McMahon on June 2 to the White Sox along with minor leaguer Bob Snow in exchange for infielder Jerry Adair, who would become a clutch performer for the '67 AL champs. Wyatt helped stabilize the pitching staff in a year in which Jim Lonborg threw 273⅓ innings in 39 starts, winning 22. After Lonborg, there was a huge dropoff in starts, innings pitched, and wins. Lee Stange and Gary Bell were the only other starters with more than 20 starts (each had 24), though Bell had only been acquired on June 4. Stange was second on the staff in innings with 181⅔. After Lonborg, only three other Red Sox pitchers recorded 10 or more wins: Bell (12), José Santiago (12), and Wyatt (10). In contrast, the 1967 Cardinals had much more balance and stability in their starting rotation. Five Cards pitchers recorded 23 or more starts. Six pitched 152 or more innings. Five won 10 or more games. Wyatt's worth to the Sox was great in terms of filling a gap in the starting rotation.

The 5-foot-11½, 200-pound right-handed Wyatt appeared in 60 games in 1967, including 17 in August and 10 in September, compiling a record of 10-7 with a 2.60 ERA (1.45 on the road) in 93⅓ innings with 20 saves (10 at home, 10 on the road). He allowed only 71 hits and six home runs, striking out 68 and walking 39. He held opposing hitters to a .217 average (right-handed batters hit only .205). He pitched more than one inning in 33 of his appearances. Four times, he pitched three or more innings in relief, including 5⅔ innings against the A's on April 29 and four innings against the Yankees on August 30.

Wyatt opened the 1967 season by tossing 1⅔ scoreless innings in relief of starter (and winner) Jim Lonborg on Opening Day, April 12, in a 5-4 Red Sox victory over the White Sox before 8,324 fans at Fenway Park. He continued his hot early relief work, remaining unscored upon into his ninth appearance (16⅔ inings) before giving up an unearned run to the Tigers on May 12 after. During this stretch, he picked up his first win on April 24 with three innings of scoreless relief as the Red Sox rallied with a pair of runs in the seventh and three in the eighth of a 7-4 win in Washington over the Senators.

On April 29 at Fenway Park, he threw 5⅔ scoreless innings in a 15-inning 11-10 win over the A's, won on a José Tartabull single that scored Tony Conigliaro and George Scott. Wyatt's outing, according to Ken Coleman in *The Impossible Dream Remembered*, led K.C. manager Alvin Dark to complain about Wyatt's alleged Vaseline ball. Wyatt's out pitch was alleged to have been a Vaseline-assisted forkball. According to Glenn Stout and Richard A. Johnson in *Red Sox Century*, Wyatt had "think" written on four of the fingers of his glove. On the fifth finger was written "When in doubt—Use Forkball."

Bill Reynolds wrote in *Lost Summer* that the Vaseline charges originated, according to Wyatt, from ex-White Sox manager Al Lopez. Wyatt is reported to have said: "In a doubleheader they beat me in the first game and I saved the second. That's when Al Lopez

claimed I was doctoring the ball. 'How come you didn't say that in the first game?' I asked him. It's only when I win that anyone accuses me of anything illegal. The only time I ever threw a spitter was against Yaz. He hit it off the scoreboard. I never threw another spitter." Later in the season, the Yankees' Joe Pepitone is reported by Reynolds to have said (in the words of Reynolds) that "Wyatt has so much Vaseline on him that if he slid into second base he would keep right on going until he hit the outfield fence." Jim Prime and Bill Nowlin lend some credence to the Vaseline allegations in *More Tales From the Red Sox Dugout*: "Caught in a rundown between third and home, pitcher John Wyatt dropped several items from his Sox pitching jacket. The excess baggage included a tube of Vaseline, a pack of cigarettes, and his car keys. We're not sure what Sherlock Holmes would deduce from those clues, but possibly, Wyatt was up to no good."

Manager Dick Williams had no problem with Wyatt's "little tube of Vaseline," he and Bill Plaschke wrote in *No More Mr. Nice Guy*. "I never encouraged a guy to throw a spitball, probably because it's so hard to throw one right. But if he did throw it right, then I looked the other way. As long as he was getting batters out, he could pitch it out of his ass."

On May 7, Wyatt picked up his first save of the year in a 9-6 win in Minnesota over the Twins. On May 9, he earned his second win with a scoreless eighth inning in the second game of a doubleheader against the A's, the Red Sox scoring five times in the top of the ninth, including a Carl Yastrzemski bases-clearing double, to take a 5-2 win. On May 12, Wyatt was the victim of a bizarre play against the Tigers in Boston. He was drilled in the head by his catcher, Bob Tillman, who was attempting to throw out the stealing Al Kaline. Wyatt rebounded from the beaning, staying on the mound to finish the game, but the next day he probably wished he'd stayed in bed. He failed to protect a 5-4 lead against the Tigers, giving up six runs , the first earned runs of the year off him. Manager Williams was the subject of criticism for leaving Wyatt in to absorb the shelling. On May 16, Wyatt lost his second straight game, giving up four runs to the Orioles in two innings of work, including a three-run homer to Paul Blair.

From May 21 through August 1, Wyatt had another impressive stretch of relief pitching, going 3-2 with 13

John Wyatt threw four scoreless innings and earned the 2-1 victory over the Yankees on August 30 when Yaz hit a home run in the top of the 11th.

saves in 23 outings, allowing only five earned runs in 33 innings. On May 21, he picked up his third win, allowing no runs in two-thirds of an inning at Fenway. He was the beneficiary of four Sox runs in the bottom of the eighth. Carl Yastrzemski tripled home Dalton Jones and Reggie Smith and George Scott homered with Yastrzemski aboard, all the runs coming off Sonny Siebert for the 4-3 final score. On June 15, starter Gary Waslewski pitched nine scoreless innings against the White Sox. Ken Berry singled home Walt Williams in the top of the eleventh off Wyatt to break the scoring drought. Wyatt again benefited from a Sox rally as the "Cardiac Kids" got two on a Joe Foy single and a Conigliaro homer off John Buzhardt for the win, Wyatt's fourth of the year. He picked up win number five on July 29 at home in a 6-3 victory over the Twins. Wyatt pitched a pair of scoreless innings and the Sox again rallied with four in their half of the eighth as Jerry Adair and Dalton Jones each singled in a run and Foy doubled in two.

Wyatt was touched up for a pair of runs in both the seventh and eighth innings on August 2 in an 8-6 loss at home against the A's. He then embarked on yet another stellar stretch as he allowed no earned runs in his next eight appearances, from August 3 through August 20. On August 3, he saved Dave Morehead's first win of the year as the Sox beat the A's 5-3. On August 8, he picked up win number six with a scoreless inning against the A's in the second game of a doubleheader on the road. With two outs in the ninth, Yaz doubled off Bill Stafford. Conigliaro was intentionally walked. Foy also walked. Norm Siebern singled to left, scoring Yaz and Conigliaro, and Foy scored on an error by left fielder Jim Gosger.

On August 21, Wyatt allowed a two-run homer to Mike Epstein in two innings but picked up win number seven as Elston Howard snapped a tie in the ninth with a single to lead Boston over the Senators, 6-5. On August 24, Wyatt picked up his 17th save in shutting the door on the Senators in a 6-5 win after relieving Darrell Brandon with runners on first and third with one out in the ninth with Washington already having rallied for three runs in the inning. From August 27 through September 8, Wyatt again allowed no runs over a six-game stretch. August 27 was one of the more memorable games to Red Sox fans. Yaz had slugged homers 33 and 34 in the fifth and seventh innings and the Sox held a slim 4-3 lead in the ninth of the opener of a doubleheader in Chicago. Ken Berry led off in the bottom of the ninth with a double down the left field line. Sandy Alomar bunted Berry to third. With Duane Josephson coming up to pinch hit, Wyatt was called on to relieve starter Gary Bell. Wyatt threw a first-pitch fastball at knee level on the outside part of the plate. Josephson drove the ball to medium right field. José Tartabull made a one-handed catch with Berry tagging up at third. A high throw to the plate was caught by the jumping Elston Howard, who came down with his left foot, blocking Berry's foot to the side of the plate and applying a sweep tag to complete a thrilling Sox win.

On August 29, Wyatt threw 2⅔ scoreless innings from the seventh through the ninth in the 20-inning second game of a twin bill in New York won by the Yankees 4-3 on a Horace Clarke single that scored John Kennedy. Wyatt came back the next day, August 30, with a four-inning, two-hit, no-run effort in a 2-1 Red Sox victory in 11 innings for his eighth win. Al Downing was the hard-luck loser, pitching all 11 innings but surrendering the game-winning homer to Yastrzemski with two out in the 11th, Yaz' 35th dinger of the season.

On September 13, Wyatt earned win number nine, allowing one run over two innings of a 4-2 Red Sox win. In the Sox' eighth, Rico Petrocelli doubled in Foy and Ken Harrelson, and Reggie Smith singled home Petrocelli. On September 18, Wyatt gave up the go-ahead run to the Tigers on the road, a double by Jim Northrup scoring Al Kaline. The Sox responded with a game-tying homer by Yaz off Fred Lasher (his 40th) in the ninth and a Dalton Jones homer in the 10th off rookie Mike Marshall for the 6-5 win. On September 20, Wyatt earned win number 10 with 1⅔ innings of scoreless relief against the Indians in Cleveland. With two gone in the ninth, Yastrzemski singled to center off George Culver and Smith knocked in the 5-4 game-winner with a single to right.

On September 21, Wyatt threw a scoreless ninth to notch his 20th save in a 6-5 Red Sox win. On September 23, he came on in the eighth of a 5-5 tie with the Orioles. Frank Robinson singled, and Brooks Robinson homered for the 7-5 Orioles win, which dropped Wyatt to 10-7 for the season.

Wyatt had two appearances in the 1967 World Series against the Cardinals. In the Series opener on October 4 at Fenway Park, Wyatt relieved starter José Santiago, who had held St. Louis to single runs in the third and seventh and supplied the only Red Sox score with a third-inning homer off Bob Gibson. Wyatt set the Cards down in order in the eighth, striking out Julian Javier. In the ninth, he surrendered two walks but completed his second inning of scoreless, hitless relief in the 2-1 Red Sox loss.

Wyatt's second appearance in the Series, in Game Six on October 11 in Boston, was not as impressive as

his first but was far more meaningful in the end result. Starter Gary Waslewski had held the Cards to a pair of third-inning runs in 5⅓ innings on the hill. Rico Petrocelli homered in the second off Cardinals starter Dick Hughes. In the fourth, Yastrzemski led off with a homer. After Harrelson and Scott were retired, Smith and Petrocelli sent Hughes to the showers with solo homers for a 4-2 Red Sox lead (the three homers hit by the Red Sox in the inning set a World Series record that still stands). Wyatt entered the game with runners on first and second with one out in the sixth. He got Mike Shannon to pop to the shortstop and Javier to ground out to third to end the Cardinals' threat. However, in the seventh, Wyatt walked Bobby Tolan and surrendered a one-out game-tying homer to Lou Brock. He retired Curt Flood and Roger Maris to avoid any further damage. In the Red Sox' seventh, reliever Jack Lamabe retired Howard on a grounder to third. Jones, batting for Wyatt, singled to right. Foy doubled Jones home, going to third on the throw to the plate. Joe Hoerner succeeded Lamabe on the hill. Mike Andrews singled to left, scoring Foy. Yastrzemski singled Andrews to third. Larry Jaster entered the game in relief and pinch-hitter Adair got Andrews home with a fly to center. Scott singled to left and Smith singled Yastrzemski home to give the Red Sox an 8-4 lead, which would hold up as Gary Bell earned the save with two innings of scoreless relief. Wyatt picked up the win, the fourth African-American pitcher in history to record a World Series win.

Wyatt got off to a slow start in 1968, losing his ace reliever role to Lee Stange and Sparky Lyle. Lyle pitched in 49 games, finishing 29 and saving 11. Stange pitched in 50 games, finishing 30 and saving 12. Wyatt appeared in eight games from April 11 through May 16, giving up earned runs in his first four appearances. In posting a 1-2 record with a 4.22 ERA, he allowed nine hits and five earned runs in 10⅔ innings. On May 17, 1968, Wyatt was sold to the Yankees.

In the offseason before the 1968 season, Williams is reported by Peter Golenbock in *Red Sox Nation* to have made critical comments about Wyatt. Wyatt attempted to refute the comments in a letter to the *Boston Record American*. After the trade, Golenbock wrote, Wyatt said, "I been sold not because of my ability, but because of a personal thing. If that man [Williams] is your enemy, forget it." In seven games for New York, Wyatt was 0-2 with a 2.16 ERA. On June 15, he was again sold, this time to the Tigers. In 22 games for pennant-winning Detroit from June 19 through August 24, Wyatt was 1-0 with a 2.37 ERA and two saves in 30⅓ innings. He did not appear in the World Series for the champion Tigers.

On April 3, 1969, Wyatt was released by the Tigers and signed April 7 by the Oakland A's. He was 0-1 with a 5.40 ERA in four games for the A's, allowing five earned runs in 8.1 innings. He pitched his final game in the major leagues on May 1, 1969, in a 3-2 loss to the Angels in Anaheim. He threw a scoreless inning in relief of Jim Hunter, retiring Aurelio Rodriguez on a comebacker to conclude his career. He was released on May 27, 1969.

Wyatt finished his big league career with a 42-44 record, 103 saves, and a 3.47 ERA. During his playing career, he had begun work as a real estate developer in Kansas City, Missouri in the offseason. Wyatt's mother had owned some property in Buffalo and made a living off the rent, so John resolved to do the same. He saved $7,000 over his first seven years in pro ball and built a 12-unit apartment building on East 29th Street in Kansas City. "No one had ever built a new housing facility in Kansas City for Negroes," he told Will McDonough. "It was a long shot, but I'm a long shot player. ...You can't win if you never take the chance. ...The proudest day of my life came with the construction of that building. In one day, I sold three apartments and got a citation from the President [Lyndon B. Johnson]."

He moved to Omaha, Nebraska in 1987. On April 6, 1998, Wyatt died after a heart attack at his Omaha home at the age of 63. His survivors included his wife, Barbara, four children, three stepchildren, a brother, a sister, and 11 grandchildren.

Brief bios of coaches and players

from *1967 World Series American League Series Facts for Press/Radio/TV*

Dick Williams—One of the youngest managers in major leagues, Dick has experienced a most remarkable season, bringing the Red Sox from a ninth place finish in 1966 to the championship. And all this in one fantastic season.

Williams is described as a man who is not afraid to make an unorthodox move, or to pull the unusual, and his first year as a major league pilot has been liberally sprinkled with a daring type of play that has captured the imagination of the entire American League.

This should not be surprising, however, for Dick Williams cut a rather dashing figure himself during an active career that saw him break in with Brooklyn and eventually come into the American League as a member of the Baltimore Orioles and later move on to the Kansas City A's and the Red Sox.

He had two years of minor league managerial experience with Toronto in the International League where he finished second and third. He succeeded Billy Herman as manager of the Red Sox, coming here with a high recommendation of the Red Sox' brass. General Manager Dick O'Connell and Vice President for Player Personnel, Haywood Sullivan, were looking for a man with outstanding leadership qualities who could mould a team of youngsters into a cohesive unit. They felt they had one in Dick Williams and the results have more than borne this out. At 38, Dick Williams has shown outstanding leadership qualities and a canny facility for handling pitchers. The progress of such players as George Scott, Rico Petrocelli, Reggie Smith, and even Carl Yastrzemski is traceable to a large extent to the adroit management of young Mr. Williams. Dick is a native of St. Louis, but now resides in California. His performance in moving the Red Sox from ninth place to first put him in the middle of the contention for manager-of-the-year honors in the American League.

Bobby Doerr—One of the most popular players ever to appear in a Red Sox uniform, Bobby is enjoying his first season as a major league coach. Since his retirement as an active player, Bob has been a special instructor for the Red Sox organization. He was prevailed upon this season to return to the field where he started from 1937 to 1951. Bobby is ranked among the greatest second basemen the American League has ever had. He played on the last Red Sox pennant winner in 1946 and was known as the team captain of a team that included Ted Williams, Mike Higgins, Johnny Pesky, Rudy York, and Dom DiMaggio, among others.

Al Lakeman—Big Al has seen as many cities and towns during his baseball career as any player. His career as player-coach-manager took him into some 20 different cities and both major leagues. He is bullpen coach for the Red Sox and has been largely responsible for getting so many stellar performances from Dick Williams' staff. Al played first and pitched and caught during his lengthy career.

Sal Maglie—When great pitchers of the post-war era are mentioned, Sal Maglie's name is sure to come up. This grim-visaged pitching coach starred with the New Your Giants and later the Brooklyn Dodgers. He pitched a no-hitter, pitched in the All-Star Game, and pitched in two World Series with the Giants and one with Brooklyn. Few people remember that Sal Maglie pitched a tremendous World Series game the day that Don Larsen pitched his perfect game in the World Series for the New York Yankees. In the offseason, Sal conducts a business in Buffalo, NY.

Eddie Popowski—Little Eddie spent a lengthy playing career in the minor leagues and his appearance in a major league uniform occurred this year when he was named third base coach for the Red Sox. "Pop," a New Jersey native, played 11 years in the minors and managed another 11 in the minors. He once was a member of the famed House of David semi-pro team that was so popular in the 1930's.

Dick Williams

by Eric Aron

	G	W	L	WP
1967 RED SOX	162	92	70	.568

Dick Williams is regarded as one of baseball's premier managers and turnaround artists. He is only the second skipper in the sport's history to win pennants for three different teams—Boston, Oakland, and San Diego.[1] As a rookie manager in 1967, Williams led the Red Sox from ninth place to the World Series. Both personally and tactically, he took a no-nonsense, aggressive approach that electrified several teams he managed. His A's won back-to-back World Series, and he pushed the Padres to their first-ever postseason.

As a major league manager, he compiled a record of 1,571 wins and 1,451 losses over 21 seasons. His win total ranks him 17th on the all-time victory list. Williams also enjoyed a fine playing career. As a versatile utility man, he played with five teams over 13 seasons. After an appearance in the 1953 World Series with Brooklyn, he played three separate stints for Baltimore, playing for manager and key mentor Paul Richards.

Richard Hirschfeld Williams was born on May 7, 1929 in St. Louis, Missouri. He and his brother Ellery were raised in their grandfather's house during the Depression. Dick's father, Harvey, quit high school to join the Navy, then found jobs delivering fish, cleaning brewery vats, and collecting insurance debts. Dick has fond memories of attending Browns and Cardinals games at Sportsman's Park.

"I belonged to the Knothole Gang in St. Louis, and the seats were out in left field. So [Browns' left fielder] Chet Laabs and [Cards' left fielder] Joe Medwick were my favorites," he says.[2]

When the elder Williams found regular employment, the family moved to Pasadena, California. Dick graduated from Elliot Junior High School and Pasadena Junior College, lettering in seven sports and even winning a city title in handball. Baseball, however, was his first love. He was 6 feet tall, weighed 190 pounds and threw and batted right-handed.

In 1945, while playing a junior college football game, Dick suffered a leg injury. His father ran on the field to check on Dick, only to suffer a fatal heart attack. Dick blamed himself for his father's death and never forgot how he felt that day. Harvey Williams left a lifelong impression on his son. A stern man, he accepted nothing but excellence from his boys, even physically abusing them. Consequently, Dick never accepted losing and constantly had to prove to himself that he was not a failure. Despite it all, Dick loved his father. After her husband's death, Dick and Ellery's mother Kathryn found work at a plastics plant. She would later remarry.

While playing for Pasadena Junior College, Dick was spotted by Brooklyn Dodgers' scout Tom Downey, and signed his first baseball contract in 1947. After graduation, Dick reported to Class-C Santa Barbara in the California League. Appearing in 79 games, he hit .246 with four HR and 50 RBIs, playing outfield and third base.

In 1948, Dick attended his first spring training. Through repetition and systemization, the Dodgers drilled young players in elements of the game such as bunting, hitting the cutoff man, and breaking up double plays. Dick would later stress these details as a manager. He began the season in Santa Barbara, earning a promotion to Double-A Fort Worth of the Texas League after batting .335 with 16 HR and 90 RBIs. Again he played mainly the outfield, with a few games at third after he moved to Fort Worth.

Williams played again in Fort Worth in 1949, under the tutelage of another influential manager, Bobby Bragan, and was a Texas League All-Star, thanks to his 23 home runs, 114 RBIs and .310 average. Although Bragan bore a losing record in the major leagues, Williams credits him for all of Williams' own victories. Bragan taught Williams about discipline, winning at all costs, and not being afraid to demonstrate how much he hated losing.

Williams says, "Players give you 100 percent not because they want something, but because they hate something. Me, I gave a hundred percent, because I hated losing.... For the ones who treated losing and failure lightly, I figured I'd better give them something even better to hate. Me."[3]

Despite the great seasons, Williams was having a hard time getting promoted in the deep Dodgers organization. In 1950, Williams was back in Fort Worth, and in 144 games, he hit .300, with 11 home runs and 72 RBIs. After the 1950 season, he played winter ball in Havana, and faced a young pitcher by the name of Fidel Castro in batting practice. It was also in the winter of

1950 that Dick was drafted into the army to serve in Korea. After a three month tour of duty and with only two weeks left in basic training, Dick re-injured his knee during a camp baseball game. Missing all of 1951 spring training, he was expecting to play at Triple-A St. Paul, but the league, trying to maintain competitive balance, had a rule that returning servicemen had to go through waivers. Both the Pirates and Cardinals claimed him, so the Dodgers had to send Dick up to Brooklyn to keep him in the organization. He was the 26th man on the 25-man roster and not surprisingly, was first relegated to the bench. Dick worked hard to earn playing time, and his opportunity finally came midway through the season.

Williams made his major league debut with the Dodgers in the first game of a twin bill on June 10, 1951. Pinch-hitting for Gene Hermanski, he grounded out to the pitcher in his initial plate appearance. In the second game, he batted leadoff and started in left field, going 4-for-5 with three singles and a triple. With an outfield of Carl Furillo, Duke Snider, and Andy Pafko, there simply wasn't a lot of playing time for Dick. He appeared in only 23 games hitting .200 with one homer and five RBIs.

In the 1952 season, just as it appeared that Williams had won the Dodgers starting job in left field over Pafko, Dick was injured. It happened on August 25 in St. Louis in the second game of a doubleheader against the Cardinals. Williams suffered a three-way shoulder separation in the outfield while diving for a ball. Unable to play the rest of the season, he sat on the bench during the 1952 World Series against the Yankees, a series won by New York four games to three.

In 1953, he played for Brooklyn and Triple-A Montreal. In 30 games for Brooklyn he hit .218 with two home runs and five RBIs. The Dodgers won the National League pennant and once again played the Yankees in the World Series. In the 1953 World Series, Williams was used three times as a pinch-hitter. In Game Two, a 4-2 loss to the Yankees, Williams batted in the ninth inning, pinch-hitting for Preacher Roe against Eddie Lopat. He singled to left, but was stranded. He pinch-hit again in Game Five, striking out against Bob Kuzava. In the sixth and final game of the Series, Williams walked against Whitey Ford. The Yankees won the Fall Classic four games to two.

In 1954, he again spent time with the Dodgers but also played for Triple-A St. Paul. He spent the entire 1955 season back in Fort Worth, where he hit .317 and, in a season-ending doubleheader on September 5, he won the first contest with an inside-the-park grand slam, and in the nightcap, he played all nine positions, pitching a scoreless eighth.[4]

On June 25, 1956, while playing for Triple-A Montreal, Williams was sent on waivers to the Baltimore Orioles. In 1956, he hit 11 home runs with a .286 average for the O's, becoming the team's starting center fielder in the second half.

In 1957, he was a true utility man for the first time, playing left, center, right, first base, and third base for the Orioles in the first half before being dealt to the Indians for Jim Busby. He continued to play multiple positions for the Indians, as he did the rest of his career.

Just before the start of the 1958 season, Williams was traded back to the Orioles, with Gene Woodling and Bud Daley, in exchange for Larry Doby and Don Ferrarese. He went on to play 128 games all over the diamond, hitting .276.

After the 1958 season, he was dealt to the Kansas City Athletics for Chico Carrasquel. He had a fine year in KC, hitting 16 home runs, driving in 75, and batting .266 in 130 games. He had a similar season in 1960, 12/65/.288 in 127 games, playing multiple infield and outfield positions.

Once again, the Orioles felt compelled to call for his services. Early in the 1961 season, Williams was on his way back to Baltimore, traded with Dick Hall, for Chuck Essegian and Jerry Walker. He did poorly this time, hitting just .206 in 103 games. Back the next season, he managed to raise his average to .247, but with just one home run in 178 at-bats.

On October 12, 1962, Dick's contract was purchased by the Houston Colt .45s from the Orioles. He would never play a game for the organization, however, as two months later he was traded to the Boston Red Sox. The Red Sox acquired Williams in exchange for Carroll Hardy. Hardy is best remembered as the only player ever to pinch-hit for the "Splendid Splinter" Ted Williams.

Dick spent the final two years of his big league career as a utility player in Boston. The Red Sox teams of 1963 and 1964 hardly reminded Dick of "the Boys of Summer." He even claimed that Boston management did not expect the players to win. Moreover, he observed that players were treated differently depending on team status, aggravating natural resentments between highly competitive athletes.

"The place was a country club," Williams said. "Players showed up when they felt like it and took extra work only when it didn't interfere with a card game."[5]

During the winter of 1964, Williams was named manager of Boston's Triple-A affiliate in Toronto. He led the Maple Leafs to records of 81-64 in 1965 and 82-65 in 1966, winning Governors' Cup championships in

The diverse duties of Dick Williams.

Motivator

Teacher

Diplomat

both seasons. While in Toronto, Dick managed talent that would later come with him to the major league club. This included Billy Rohr, Mike Andrews, Joe Foy, Russ Gibson, and Reggie Smith. Foy was batting champion of the International League, hitting .302 and named the league's MVP in 1965. Smith led the International League in hitting the following season with a batting average of .320.

After the 1966 season, general manager Dick O'Connell promoted Williams to replace Boston manager Billy Herman. At 37, he was the youngest manager in the American League.

Williams inherited a club that had grown complacent. In 1965, the team finished ninth in the American League with a dreadful mark of 62-100. In 1966, they finished ninth again, 26 games behind the Baltimore Orioles, although they had played very well in the second half. The 1967 Red Sox were considered a young team with talent, but no one could have predicted that they would win the pennant. Signing a one-year contract, Dick felt that he had a lot to prove. Remembering his own years with the Red Sox, he understood the country club atmosphere and had a wealth of ideas about turning it around.

At spring training in Winter Haven, Florida, Williams made it perfectly clear that there would be only one person in charge—him—and he would bring many changes to management's processes and rules. He led off by stripping outfielder Carl Yastrzemski of his captaincy. All unmarried players were required to lodge at the team hotel. If players were late, they were fined. He stressed fundamentals, pitching, and defense. He was one of the first managers to use videotape to improve on adjustments.

Williams required his pitchers to play volleyball in the outfield to develop footwork skills while pushing their competitive instincts. Winning teams had to do only half of their post-workout sprints. When the great Ted Williams, incensed over the "boot camp" approach, walked out of spring training, the manager did not seem to mind.

In Las Vegas, Jimmy "the Greek" Snyder rated the Sox just a 100-to-1 shot at winning the pennant. Williams promised that "we will win more games than we lose." Opening day at Fenway Park drew only 8,324 fans. By contrast, on the last day of the regular season there was an attendance of 35,770. It would be one of the closest and most exciting pennant races ever. The Sox were an exceptionally young team; their average age was 23. Led by Yastrzemski, Jim Lonborg, Rico Petrocelli, Tony Conigliaro, and George Scott, they were surrounded by ex-Leafs including Foy, Smith, Russ Gibson, and Billy Rohr.

Throughout 1967, Williams was not afraid to exert his authority as the team's skipper. If someone played poorly, he was benched and even embarrassed in front of his teammates. Williams chastised first baseman George Scott for being overweight, comparing discussions with the Boomer to "talking to cement."[6] So many players were in the skipper's doghouse that it became a source of humor. One even said, "Listen, this thing is so full we're lucky we can field a team."[7]

On July 24, the team had rattled off a 10-game winning streak, including six on the road. Returning to Boston, the Red Sox were greeted wildly by thousands of fans. "I will never forget that night we landed at Logan Airport with that wild reception," Williams said later. "I felt the franchise was practically reborn."[8]

Despite the odds, the Sox kept on winning, even overcoming Tony Conigliaro's August 18 beaning, which sidelined the slugger for the remainder of the season. All season, it was a tight race. On October 1, the last day of the regular season, the Red Sox won the pennant by beating the Twins. In the 1967 World Series the Red Sox challenged the St. Louis Cardinals, armed with Orlando Cepeda, Lou Brock, and Bob Gibson. The Cardinals won the World Series in seven games. After the amazing season, Lonborg won the Cy Young Award, Yastrzemski, who won the Triple Crown, was voted the MVP, and Williams won the *Sporting News* Manager of the Year award.

For reestablishing the team as a winner, Williams received a three-year contract extension. In 1968, Boston's pitching staff was decimated by injuries to Jim Lonborg and José Santiago, and Tony Conigliaro missed the entire season. Despite injuries and poor performances, the team finished in fourth place at 86-76, 17 games behind pennant winner and World Series champ Detroit.

In 1969, the Red Sox improved their victory total by one. Williams, however, was fired with nine games remaining. His dismissal was attributed primarily to his acrimonious relationship with owner Tom Yawkey. Williams believed Yawkey was undermining his authority, pampering players after he had disciplined them. Media reports also claimed that Yawkey rated Williams a disrespectful and unrealistic 2 on a scale of 1 to 4. Finally, in a game on August 1, 1969, Williams benched Yaz and fined him $500 for not hustling. Williams did not give special advantages to his star players. Rather, he was tougher on them *because* they were stars.

Williams spent the 1970 season with the Montreal Expos as Gene Mauch's third base coach. That winter, he received an offer from Oakland owner Charlie Finley to manage the A's. Williams accepted, becoming the tenth Athletics manager in Finley's short reign. John McNamara had been fired after leading the A's to a second place record of 89-73. Finley fired McNamara, because he seemed unable to prevent internal bickering among his players. Backup catcher Dave Duncan remarked, "There's only one manager who manages this club—Charlie Finley...and we'll never win so long as he manages it."[9]

Right from the beginning, Williams knew he had talent on his team. There were outfielders Reggie Jackson and Joe Rudi, third baseman Sal Bando, shortstop Bert Campaneris, and pitchers Vida Blue, John "Blue Moon" Odom, Jim "Catfish" Hunter, and Rollie Fingers. Williams said that "...this club is head and shoulders above the Boston club I had in '67."[10]

Oakland finished the 1971 season 16 games ahead of the Kansas City Royals, winning 101 games. Williams once again won the Manager of the Year award. Hunter went 21-11 and Blue finished a remarkable 24-8, winning both the Cy Young and MVP awards. But the A's didn't make the World Series: They were swept in three games by Earl Weaver's Baltimore Orioles in the American League Championship Series.

The 1972 A's were infamous for their facial hair. It began when Reggie Jackson arrived at spring training sporting a mustache. When others decided to follow Reggie's lead, Finley seized another marketing opportunity, offering to pay anyone a $300 bonus if he would grow a mustache by Father's Day. The Mustache Gang was born. By now, Williams had changed as both a manager and a person, growing a mustache himself. Sal Bando said, "I think a lot of things are mislabeled on Dick, I mean he was a strong disciplinarian, in terms of fundamental baseball... but as far as a disciplinarian in terms of your curfew, your dress, your hair, Dick was very flexible there."[11]

The A's finished the season 93-62, winning the West by 5½ games over the Chicago White Sox. They won the League Championship Series by defeating the Detroit Tigers, three games to two.

In the 1972 World Series, the Oakland A's were matched up against the Big Red Machine, Sparky Anderson's Cincinnati Reds. With the hippie-like A's and clean-cut, conservative Reds, the Series was dubbed "the Bikers against the Boy Scouts."[12] Sparky and Williams had been friends since they were teammates in the Dodgers' organization. The A's led the Series two games to one, when in Game Four, Williams's aggressive managerial moves paid off. Trailing 2-1 in the bottom of the ninth, Williams used two pinch runners and three pinch hitters for a dramatic 3-2 comeback victory. The A's lost Games Five and Six, but rallied in Game Seven to win the Series.

In 1973, Oakland had three 20-game winners in Ken Holtzman, Vida Blue, and Catfish Hunter. The team won the American League West with a 94-68 record, then defeated Baltimore in the League Championship Series, three games to two. The World Series against the New York Mets, however, marked the beginning of the end of Williams's tenure in Oakland. In Game Two, with the score tied 6-6 in the 12th inning, Oakland second baseman Mike Andrews made two costly errors that allowed four runs to score. After the 10-7 loss, Andrews blamed himself for his mistakes. Remembering his own experience with the death of his father, Williams consoled Mike. Mental errors upset Williams, not physical ones.

After the game, Finley told Williams that Andrews should be placed on the disabled list with a shoulder injury. In reality, Finley was trying to add Manny Trillo to the postseason roster. Andrews was forced to sign a medical statement indicating that he was injured, and did not accompany the team to New York.

Prior to Game Three, Finley announced at a press conference that Andrews was officially unable to play. Sal Bando, the team captain, retaliated by asking all of his teammates to wear Andrews' number 17 on armbands to show their support. Finally, Commissioner Bowie Kuhn intervened, arguing that a player could be replaced on a postseason roster only after suffering a new injury. Kuhn said, "The handling of this matter by the Oakland club has had the unfortunate effect of embarrassing a player who has given many years of able service to professional baseball."[13]

In Game Four, Williams sent Andrews up as a pinch hitter to a standing ovation of 54,817 fans. For Williams, the Andrews incident was the last straw; he announced that he would resign immediately after the World Series. After the A's defeated the Mets, 5-2 in Game Seven, Finley announced that he would "not stand in [Williams's] way" should he decide not to return as manager.

It was no secret that Williams wanted to fill the managerial vacancy for the New York Yankees. Before baseball's winter meetings, Yankees general manager Gabe Paul asked Finley for permission to talk to Dick. Since Williams had one year remaining on his Oakland contract, Finley demanded player compensation.

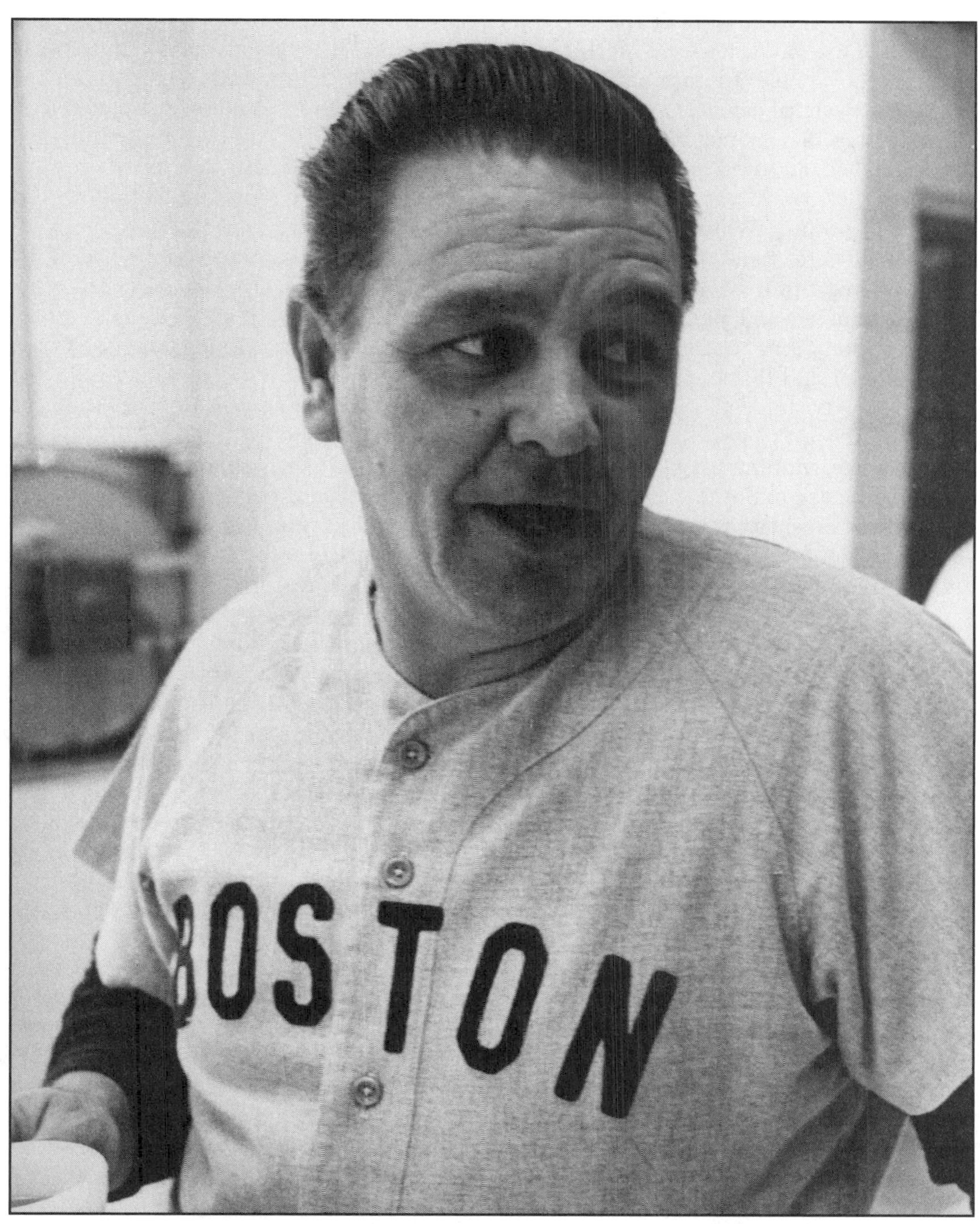

Dick Williams could look back on the 1967 season with satisfaction. He helped mold a promising young team into pennant-winners.

When protracted negotiations proved unsuccessful, American League president Joe Cronin intervened and determined that Finley was acting within his rights in retaining his manager. Eventually the Yankees hired Bill Virdon as their new manager.

Williams left baseball to work for John D. MacArthur, one of the richest men in America, but realized that he missed baseball. California Angels' general manager Harry Dalton persuaded Finley to allow his hiring of Williams as manager. Williams replaced Bobby Winkles on June 26. He took the job despite having been warned by former Detroit manager Mayo Smith against accepting it, saying, "I've scouted them and I know: They've got no talent in the major leagues and nothing in the minor leagues. Nothing... But enough about me. Good luck."[14]

Nine of the Angels' first 13 seasons resulted in losing records, and 1974 was no exception. Behind Nolan Ryan, Frank Tanana, and an aging Frank Robinson, Williams led the Angels to a record of 36-48 after replacing Winkles. Overall, the team finished dead last at 68-94, twenty-two games behind Oakland. The Angels fared no better in 1975, again finishing in last place at 72-89. The entire infield consisted of rookie or sophomore players: first baseman Bruce Bochte, second baseman Jerry Remy, shortstop Orlando Ramirez, and third baseman Dave Chalk.

Williams's frustration with the Angels was epitomized by a 1976 anecdote. While talking to the press in Chicago on June 30, he accidentally penciled Nolan in as the game's starting pitcher. Although it was not Ryan's turn in the rotation, league rules stipulated that the starting pitcher must face at least one batter. After Ryan retired Chicago's leadoff hitter, Chet Lemon, Williams yanked him. Unable to cope with the Angels' losing attitude, Williams was fired on July 24.

After three disappointing seasons in California, Williams got an offer to return to Montreal to manage the Expos. He worked his magic again and "in a span of three years, we won 95."[15] The 1977 Montreal Expos had nowhere to go but up. The previous season, they lost 107 games. Williams knew that a promising farm system generated the opportunity to build a winner. Montreal's young outfield consisted of Andre Dawson, Warren Cromartie, and Ellis Valentine. Playing at the corner infield positions were Larry Parrish at third base and Tony Perez at first. Chris Speier was the shortstop. And of course, there was the catcher nicknamed the Kid: future Hall of Famer Gary Carter.

The team finished in fifth place in 1977 at 75-87. In 1978 the Expos were one game better at 76-86, rising to fourth place in the National League East. In his autobiography, he recalled, "As we entered that 1979 season, [we] helped put together a team that would make people actually come to the park to watch baseball."[16]

The biggest pitching star in Montreal was Steve Rogers, who pitched his entire thirteen year career for the Expos. Montreal also had Ross Grimsley, who won 20 games in 1978, and added Bill Lee, who had broken in under Williams with the 1969 Red Sox. The team was in the divisional race until the final weekend of both 1979 and 1980. In 1979, the Expos finished at 95-65, two games behind Pittsburgh, and in 1980, they won 90 and lost 72, just one game behind Philadelphia. Attendance soared, and pennant fever arrived in Montreal.

The strike-shortened 1981 season was ultimately split into two halves. In the first half the Expos finished 30-25 for third place behind Philadelphia. In the second half the team was 14-12 when Williams was fired on September 8. Team president John McHale cited "lack of communication with players and poor clubhouse skills."[17] The team went on the win the "half-pennant," making the playoffs for the only time in franchise history.

Williams's next stop was San Diego. In their first thirteen seasons, the Padres finished over .500 only once, in 1978. Credit for building the Padres into a pennant contender belonged to Jack McKeon, general manager since 1980. In 1982, McKeon gave Williams a three-year contract as manager, asking him to turn a franchise into a winner. Wrote Williams in his autobiography, "At all my other managerial stops I'd molded winners out of players already present. Doing it the San Diego way was perhaps a more difficult feat, considering that there was a chance that guys wouldn't just hate me, but hate each other."[18]

McKeon drafted outfielders Kevin McReynolds and Tony Gwynn in 1981. He traded shortstop Ozzie Smith to the Cardinals for Garry Templeton in 1982. He signed the Dodgers' veteran first baseman Steve Garvey as a free agent in 1983. Additional trades netted Carmelo Martinez and Graig Nettles. McKeon also signed closer Rich Gossage and picked up Alan Wiggins in the Rule V draft.

Under Dick Williams, the Padres finished 81-81 in both 1982 and 1983. The Padres started the 1984 season poorly, losing seven consecutive games in May. But they moved into first place on June 9 and never looked back. They clinched the National League West on September 20.

On August 12, 1984, the Padres were involved in

one of the ugliest scenes in major league history. A brushback game in Atlanta resulted in two bench-clearing brawls, sixteen ejections, and five fan arrests. On the very first pitch of the game, Atlanta starter Pascual Perez plunked Padres second baseman Alan Wiggins in the ribs. For the rest of the game, the Padres tried to retaliate. By the time Perez was struck in the eighth inning, Dick had long been ejected from the game. For his role in the brawl, Williams was suspended for 10 games and fined $10,000, while Braves manager Joe Torre was suspended for three games.

The 1984 National League Championship Series against the Cubs provided the Padres with one of the greatest comebacks in playoff history. The Cubs featured Leon Durham, Ron Cey, Jody Davis, future Hall of Famers Ryne Sandberg and Dennis Eckersley, and ace starter Rick Sutcliffe. In Game One the Cubs blanked the Padres 13-0. After losing Game Two, the Padres faced elimination. Only the 1982 Milwaukee Brewers had rebounded from a two-game deficit to win a best-of-five series. In a scene similar to the '67 welcoming at Logan Airport, the Padres were greeted by thousands of fans upon arriving in San Diego.

Williams brought discipline to a Red Sox team that had for years been considered a bit of a country club. He was the enforcer, sometimes a non-nonsense prosecutor, judge, and jury all in one.

After winning Game Three by a score of 7-1, the Padres and Cubs were tied in the bottom of the ninth in Game Four when Garvey hit a dramatic walk-off home run to win 7-5. Game Five completed the comeback as the Padres, after trailing 3-0, won, 6-3. Meeting Williams's old foe Sparky Anderson again in the World Series, the Padres were clearly overmatched by a Detroit ball club that had won 104 games during the regular season. Behind Kirk Gibson, Alan Trammell, Lance Parrish, and Jack Morris, the Tigers demolished the Padres, four games to one.

In 1985, Williams led the Padres to an 83-79 record, twelve games behind the division champion Dodgers. However, constant struggles with management forced him to resign on the first day of spring training in 1986.

A few weeks into the season, Williams accepted an offer to manage the Seattle Mariners. Knowing that it was likely his last chance at managing, he wanted to prove that he could still turn around a bad team. He signed a three-year deal to pilot a club for whom 76 wins marked a record high. He took over a 9-20 team that finished at 67-95.

The Mariners featured an infield of Alvin Davis, Harold Reynolds, Spike Owen, and Jim Presley, with Bob Kearney behind the plate. In the outfield were Phil Bradley, Danny Tartabull, and John Moses. Pitchers included Mark Langston, Mike Moore, and Mike Morgan.

In 1987, Williams led Seattle to a then-record (for the Mariners) finish of 78-84, seven games behind division champion Minnesota. However, he resented management for a decision preventing him from replacing Billy Connors with a pitching coach who he felt would not coddle players or offer preferential treatment. Moreover, he lambasted Langston for asking to be removed early from games rather than "tough it out." Clearly, his hard-nosed management style had lost its effect. With the Mariners in sixth place at 23-33 on June 6, 1988, owner George Argyros let him go. Williams never managed again in the major leagues.

Williams became a skipper in the short-lived Senior Professional Baseball Association in Florida. Beginning play in November 1989, the eight-team league was made up of former professional ball players 35 and older. Williams managed the West Palm Beach Tropics, a team co-owned by John Henry, featuring stars Rollie Fingers and Dave Kingman.

In retrospect, a league consisting of aging stars seemed rather silly. As Williams remarked, "With

pitchers who could barely throw and runners who could barely run, [practice] games took nearly six hours."[19] But Williams enjoyed the spirit of the games as his Tropics led the league with a 52-20 record. They came within one game of winning the league championship, losing 12-4 to the St. Petersburg Pelicans. The league folded after its second season.

Dick Williams currently resides in the Las Vegas suburb of Henderson. He and his wife Norma, who have been married since 1954, have three children, Kathi, Marc, and Ricky, and five grandchildren. Rick was a Red Sox batboy in 1967 and later played college ball under coach Eddie Stanky at South Alabama. He is a coach and scout for the Devil Rays and previously was a pitching instructor with the Marlins and the Expos. He also played some minor league ball.

Dick Williams worked as a scout for the New York Yankees until 2002. Today, he broadcasts for both the University of Nevada-Las Vegas and the Las Vegas 51s of the Pacific Coast League. On November 9, 2006, in a ceremony in Boston, he was inducted into the Red Sox Hall of Fame along with two of his former players, George Scott and Jerry Remy.[20]

Notes:

1. The first was Bill McKechnie, who won pennants with the Pirates, Cardinals, and Reds.
2. Interview with Dick Williams by Jeff Angus, January 2006.
3. Williams, Dick and Bill Plaschke, *No More Mr. Nice Guy: A Life in Hardball*, (San Diego, CA: Harcourt Brace Jovanovich, 1990), p. 78.
4. *The Sporting News*, September 14, 1955, p. 42.
5. Williams, *op. cit.*, pp. 71-72.
6. Williams, *op. cit.*, p. 93.
7. McSweeny, Bill. *The Impossible Dream: The Story of the Miracle Boston Red Sox*. NY: Coward McCann, 1968, p. 186.
8. Stout, Glenn and Richard Johnson. *Red Sox Century*. Boston: Houghton Mifflin, 2004, p. 323.
9. Markusen, Bruce. *A Baseball Dynasty: Charlie Finley's Swingin' A's*, (Haworth, N.J.: St Johann Press, 2002), p. 1.
10. *Ibidem*, p. 6.
11. *Ibidem*, p. 117.
12. *Ibidem*, p. 171.
13. *Ibidem*, p. 248.
14. Williams, *op. cit.*, p. 183.
15. *Les Expos, Nos Amours*. Montreal: TV Labatt, 1989.
16. Williams, op. cit., p. 206.
17. *Ibidem*, p. 225.
18. *Ibidem*, p. 233.
19. Williams, *op. cit.*, p. 316.
20. *Red Sox Magazine*. 2006 spring training edition, p. 49.

Jeff Angus interviewed Williams and performed significant research and writing to contribute to Mr. Aron's essay.

The way it used to be

Dick Williams, Sox manager during 1967's Impossible Dream team season, couldn't rely on the Internet back then, following games via www.mlb.com. He reminisced a bit to the *Boston Globe's* Will McDonough about how he kept up with the competition during the home stretch. "The big break came from us in the middle of the last week. We had just lost two to Cleveland and it looked like we were finished. Chicago had the lead and looked like they were going to win it. They were playing Kansas City [in last place at the time] in a double-header. I was living in Peabody, so I went out in my car, with a six-pack of beer, and picked up both games [on the radio.] Kansas City beat them twice. That put us back into it."

Source:

5/26/2002 *Boston Globe*

Bobby Doerr

by Bill Nowlin

It was Ted Williams who dubbed Bobby Doerr "the silent captain of the Red Sox" and a more down-to-earth Hall of Famer might be hard to find. A career Red Sox player, Doerr's fame enjoyed a renaissance in 2003 with the publication of David Halberstam's book about him and his famous teammates.

Born in the city of Los Angeles on April 7, 1918, Robert Pershing Doerr was one of the four Sox from the West Coast who starred in the 1940s—Williams from San Diego, Doerr from Los Angeles, Dom DiMaggio from San Francisco, and Johnny Pesky from Portland, Oregon. Doerr was born to Harold and Frances Doerr. His father worked for the telephone company, rising to become a foreman in the cable department, a position he held through the Depression. The Doerrs had three children—Hal, the eldest by five years, Bobby, and a younger sister Dorothy, who was three years younger than Bobby. Doerr told interviewer Maury Brown, "If she'd have been a boy, she'd have been a professional. She was a good athlete."

Baseball came early. "We lived near a playground that had four baseball diamonds on it and when I got to be 11, 12 years old, I was always over at the ballpark practicing or playing or doing something pertaining to baseball. And when I wasn't doing that, I was bouncing a rubber ball off the steps of my front porch at home." Manchester Playground attracted a number of kids from the area, and a surprising number of them went on to play pro ball. Bobby's American Legion team, the Leonard Wood Post, fielded quite a team. The infield alone boasted George McDonald at first base (11 of his 18 seasons were with the PCL San Diego Padres), Bobby Doerr at second base (14 seasons with the Red Sox), Mickey Owen at shortstop (13 seasons in the major leagues), and Steve Mesner at third (six seasons in the National League). That was quite a group of 14-year-olds.

Bobby's older brother Hal played professionally as well, a catcher in the Pacific Coast League from 1932-1936. It was Doerr's father who helped bring about Owen's transition from shortstop to catcher in the winter of 1933. The team they put together for some wintertime ball didn't have a catcher so Harold Doerr urged Owen to give it a try. Mr. Doerr helped out in other ways, too. During these miserable economic times, the telephone company, rather than lay people off, reduced many people's hours to three days a week—which at least provided some income. "It was just Depression days," Bobby explained. "Sometimes he would buy some baseball shoes for some of the kids, or a glove. Things were tough. Kids couldn't afford to get it themselves, and he had a job... He tried to help when he could from time to time; some of those kids were even having a hard time having meals at home."

Wintertime play was important—unlike Legion ball, the games included people of all ages, including some players who had played minor league ball but wanted to pick up a little extra money playing semipro on the playgrounds. "So when I was 15 and 16, I got to play against pretty good professional ballplayers." That gave Bobby some valuable experience. It also got him noticed.

Doerr told author Cynthia Wilber that his fondest memory as a child was winning the 1932 American Legion state tournament on Catalina Island, winning a regional tournament in Ogden, Utah, then coming within a game in Omaha, Nebraska of playing for the national title in Manchester, New Hampshire.

Bobby played high school ball for two years at Fremont High, in 1933 and the first part of 1934, but he'd been working out some with the Hollywood Sheiks and they offered to sign both him and George McDonald.[1] Both were 16 at the time, and in high school. Bill Lane was the owner of the ballclub and Oscar Vitt was the Sheiks' manager. Hal was playing for the Portland Beavers at the time. The Sheiks offered an ironclad two-year contract guaranteeing they would not send Bobby out. Bobby's father let him sign, "but I had to promise that I'd go back to high school in the wintertime and get my high school diploma." He did. Bobby understands that more professional ballplayers came out of Fremont High than any other high school in the country.

Doerr played 67 games for Hollywood in 1934, batting .259, all but six of the 16-year-old's 52 hits being singles. In 1935, Bobby acknowledges he "had a pretty good year"—he hit for a .317 average and added some power, hitting 22 doubles, eight triples, and four home runs. He drove in 74 runs, playing a very full 172-game season.

Hitting instructor Bobby Doerr looks over Rico's swing.

That winter, the Red Sox purchased an option on the contracts of both Doerr and teammate George Myatt, paying a reported $75,000. Bill Lane moved the Hollywood team to San Diego early in 1936, where they were renamed the San Diego Padres. In July, Eddie Collins came to look over the pair while the Padres were playing in Portland, and took Doerr's contract but declined Myatt. Collins also noticed a young player named Ted Williams and shook hands on the right to purchase Williams at a later time. Doerr improved again in his third year in the Coast League, batting .342 with 37 doubles and 12 triples, though just two home runs. He led the league with 238 hits and scored an even 100 runs.

Doerr was 18 years old when he headed east for his first spring training with the Red Sox, traveling across the country to Sarasota, Florida, with Mel Almada. Doerr made the team in 1937, batting leadoff on Opening Day and going 3-for-5. He had won the starting job and held it until he was beaned by Washington's Ed Linke on April 26; the ball hit him over the left ear and bounded over to the Red Sox dugout. In Wilber's book, Doerr says, "It didn't knock me out, but I was out of the lineup for a few days and Eric McNair got back in. He was playing good ball, so I didn't play too much that first couple of months. The last month of the season I

got back in and I played pretty well for the rest of the year." Eric McNair played most of the games at second but by season's end, Bobby had accumulated 147 at-bats in 55 games.

Though he batted just .224, he took over second base full time beginning in 1938. The right-hand hitting Doerr (5' 11", 175 pounds) batted .289 in 1938, with 80 RBIs, playing in 145 games. He led the league in sacrifice hits with 22. Defensively, he helped turn a league-leading 118 double plays. Only once more did he hit less than .270—he batted .258 in 1947, driving in 95 runs.

Doerr explained to Wilber, "I never did work in the offseason, and I never did play winter ball or anything else. I think it was good for me to get away after a full season. In those days, I don't think anyone ever got too complacent. Even after I played ten years of ball, I still felt like I had to play well or somebody might take my place. They had plenty of players in the minor leagues who were good enough to come up and take your job, and I think that kept us going all of the time. I hustled and put that extra effort in all of the time."

In 1939, he upped his average to .318 and added some power, more than doubling his home run total with 12 round-trippers. Though his average slipped a bit in 1940 (to .291), he became a more productive hitter, driving in 105 runs, with 37 doubles, 10 triples, and 22 home runs. Again, he led the league in double plays, again turning 118 of them. His 401 putouts also led the AL.

Doerr was named to the first of nine American League All-Star teams in 1941; he played in eight games, starting five of them, and his three-run home run in the bottom of the second inning of the 1943 game, off Mort Cooper, was the difference in the 5-3 AL win.

Though his RBI total dropped to 93 in 1941, he bumped it back up to 102 the following year, the second of six seasons he drove in more than 100 runs. He led the league in fielding average, too. Come 1943, he played in every Red Sox game all year long (and the All-Star Game), and though his RBI total slipped to 75—a function of greatly weakened team offense—Doerr excelled on defense, leading the American League in putouts, assists, double plays, and fielding average.

Doerr anchored the second base slot for Boston through the 1951 season, missing just one year (and one crucial month) during World War II. The month was September 1944. When the war broke out, Bobby was exempt because he and his wife Monica had a young son, Don. He'd also been rejected for a perforated eardrum. As the war rolled on, the military needed more and more men and the pressures on seemingly-healthy athletes intensified. After the 1943 season, Doerr took a wintertime defense job in Los Angeles, working at a sheet metal machine shop run by the man who had managed his old American Legion team. When he left the defense job to play the 1944 season, he received his draft orders and was told to report at the beginning of September. By the time September came around, the Red Sox were in the thick of the pennant race, just four games out of first place—and both Doerr (.325 at the time, his .528 slugging average led the league) and Hughson (18-5, 2.26 ERA) had to leave. The team couldn't sustain those two losses and their hopes sputtered out.

Bobby's .325 average was second in the league, just two points behind the ultimate batting champion, Lou Boudreau, who hit .327. Doerr was named AL Player of the Year by *The Sporting News*.

Because of the war, Doerr missed the entire 1945 season. He had made his home in Oregon and so reported for induction in the United States Army in Portland. He was first assigned to Fort Lewis and a week later reported for infantry duty at Camp Roberts. After completing the months of training, word began to circulate within his outfit that they were being prepared to ship out to Ford Ord, and then overseas for the invasion of Japan. President Truman brought the whole thing to a halt by dropping two atomic bombs on Japan.

After the war, Staff Sergeant Doerr changed back into his Red Sox uniform and returned to the 1946 edition of the Red Sox. He drove in 116 runs, his highest total yet—thanks to the potent Boston batting order. Bobby once again led the league in four defensive categories, the same four as in 1943: putouts, assists, double plays, and fielding percentage.

The Red Sox waltzed to the World Series, but lost to the Cardinals in seven games. Doerr led the regulars in hitting, batting .409 with nine hits in 22 Series at-bats. Babe Ruth, asked who was the MVP of the American League, said, "Doerr, and not Ted Williams, is the No. 1 player on the team."

He averaged over 110 RBIs from 1946 through 1950, with a career-high 120 RBIs in the 1950 campaign. That last full season, he led the league a fourth time in putouts and a fourth time in fielding average. His .993 in 1948 remained the Red Sox record for second basemen until Mark Loretta topped it by one percentage point in 2006 at .994.

Doerr hit for the cycle twice (May 17, 1944 and May 13, 1947); he is the only Red Sox player to do it

more than once. In a June 8, 1950 game, he hit three homers and drove in eight runs. Despite the power demonstrated by his 223 career home runs, his fielding was at least as important. He was always exceptional on defense, more than once running off strings of over 300 chances without an error. He led the league 16 times in one defensive category or another and wound up his career with a lifetime .980 mark, making him the all-time major league leader at the time of his retirement.

On Aug 2, 1947, Doerr was given a night at Fenway. He received an estimated $22,500 worth of gifts including a car.

In early August 1951, in the midst of another excellent year, Bobby suffered a serious back problem. He'd hurt it a bit bending over for a slow-hit ground ball; he felt something give, but continued the game. Quite a while afterwards, he woke up one morning and found he could hardly get out of bed or put on his shoes. He got some treatment but missed nearly three weeks before returning to play. He got in only a few more games. The problem persisted, and he had to bow out after just one at-bat in the first game of the September 7 doubleheader. Fears that it was a ruptured disc proved not the case and surgery was ruled out, but Doerr was told to rest the remainder of the season.

At season's end, Doerr could look back on 1,247 RBIs, a career batting average of .288 and the aforementioned home run and fielding totals, and some 2,042 major league base hits.

Bobby had played most of his career for just two managers: Joe Cronin and Joe McCarthy. He felt Cronin was "firm, but he patted you on the back; he always encouraged you in different ways. That was when I was younger, and was a big help to me." McCarthy was a "much firmer disposition kind of guy" who was admittedly "a little more difficult to play for"—but Bobby recognized that he played some of his best seasons for McCarthy.[2]

He'd played 14 seasons in the majors and had a good career. Though only 33, he didn't want to risk more serious injury and decided to retire to his farm in Oregon. Over time, the back fused itself in some fashion and he found himself able to lift bales of hay and sacks of grain. He began raising cattle, fattening steers for resale, but there was almost no profit in it for the small herd of 100 or so that he could hold on his spread. When Bobby returned to Boston for a night to honor Joe Cronin in 1956, he was asked if he might like to manage in Boston's system. He declined, but did take a position that he describes as "kind of like a roving coach in the minor leagues" beginning in 1957. He is listed as a Red Sox scout for the years 1957-66. He did a lot of traveling, checking out Red Sox prospects in Minneapolis, San Francisco, Seattle, Winston-Salem, Corning, and other locations.

Doing this work for several years, Doerr came to know Dick Williams, particularly after Williams took over as manager of the Toronto farm club. "I got to know him pretty good when he was with Toronto. I have to say that seeing him operate in the minor leagues coaching and managing, and then three years at the Red Sox level, he was the best manager that I saw. Now Joe Cronin was very good. I loved Joe Cronin, to play for. But if I had to pick a manager to take a team that was potentially a winning team, Dick Williams someway was able to put something together, and I thought he was one of the best managers I saw."

After he was named Red Sox manager for the 1967 season, Dick Williams asked Bobby to serve as his first base coach. He served for the three seasons that Williams managed, 1967-1969. Doerr agrees that Williams "wasn't the most liked guy. He didn't tolerate easy mistakes. Some way or another, though, the players never got uptight playing for him. He kept a tight ship and to take that club in '67 and put it into a pennant winner, there were so many things he did that he was the best guy I saw." They did not have frequent coaches meetings. "He said what you're supposed to do and he let you do it. You worked with the batter. Nobody ever interfered with what I was supposed to do." Doerr's job was to work with the hitters, as well as coach first. He was familiar with most of the young hitters, having seen them while doing his work as a roving instructor. Eddie Popowski had the same store of experience, and both offered a stable, almost paternal influence to an exceptionally young ballclub. Dick Williams told interviewer Jeff Angus, "He helped me out quite a bit when I was in Toronto. In '67, he was a buffer between people, a soft-spoken guy who could help get the message across."

Second baseman Mike Andrews of the 1967 Sox told the *Boston Herald's* Steve Buckley, "Bobby Doerr was my mentor. When I was in the minors, I always seemed to improve when he came along. I had so much faith in him that if he told me I'd be a better hitter if I changed my shoelaces, I'd have done it."

After Williams was fired late in 1969, incoming manager Eddie Kasko brought in new staff for the 1970 campaign.

Several years later, Doerr was named coach for the Toronto Blue Jays, and served them for a number of years as the team's hitting coach. "I really didn't want

to go back into baseball," he says, "but they made it so nice for me. Pat Gillick was really good to work with. Peter Bavasi. I was there '77 through '81 and then I worked a couple of years in the minor leagues. More or less spring training, up to Medicine Hat with the rookie team. I didn't do much after '82, '83."

In 1986, Bobby Doerr and Ernie Lombardi were named to the Hall of Fame by the special veterans committee, and were inducted with Willie McCovey in August that year. On May 21, 1988, the Red Sox retired Bobby's uniform number, #1.

Bobby's son Don Doerr later played some college ball at the University of Washington and went into the Basin League in the middle 1960s, pitching for the Sturgis club against future major leaguers like Jim Lonborg and Jim Palmer. Bobby rated his curve ball of major league caliber, but says he "didn't have quite enough fast ball... didn't have quite enough to go far in professional ball."

In his later years, Doerr devoted his life to care for his wife Monica, wheelchair-bound for many of her later years due to multiple sclerosis. Mrs. Doerr suffered two strokes in 1999 and then a final one which brought about her passing in 2003.

Bob Doerr splits his time now between his two properties in Oregon, and has been able to enjoy more time with his son, now retired himself after a successful career as a manager with the accounting firm of Coopers and Lybrand, based in Eugene. Bob visits Boston two or three times a year now, such as for a reunion of the remaining 1946 Red Sox that kicked off the 2006 baseball season in Opening Day ceremonies.

Notes:

1. The Hollywood ballclub of the period was popularly known as the Sheiks, though one can find references to them as the Hollywood Stars. Dick Beverage, author of *The Hollywood Stars*, reports of Doerr's timeframe, "The players I've talked to from that era to a man referred to the club as the Sheiks. That was the most popular name. But they were sometimes called the Stars in the papers.
2. Doerr's remarks were made in an interview for the Oregon Stadium Campaign in 2002.

Albert Wesley Lakeman

by Bob Brady

The 1967 season marked the return of Al "Moose" Lakeman to the major league coaching ranks for a final three years with the Boston Red Sox. He coached for Boston throughout the Dick Williams years, from 1967-1969. It was his second stint with the Sox. Lakeman had also coached under manager Johnny Pesky in 1963 and 1964.

Al Lakeman was born on December 31, 1918 in Cincinnati, Ohio and raised in a large family of six boys and five girls. Lakeman achieved high school fame in football, swimming, and boxing but his first attempts to make the baseball squad were thwarted by his relatively small size. A late adolescent growth spurt that ultimately produced a 6-foot-2, 195-pound physique, allowed Lakeman to significantly improve his baseball skills.

As a young athlete, he was pulled in two directions: toward boxing and toward baseball. In the ring, he won a *Cincinnati Times-Star* tourney in 1936 and was runner-up for a Golden Gloves heavyweight title. The following year, Lakeman retained the newspaper's crown and became the area's American Legion champion as well.

Meanwhile, his performance on the sandlots of Cincinnati drew the attention of big league bird dogs. The pull of both sports reached a breaking point in 1938. Lakeman won the Ohio A.A.U. district boxing championship, qualifying for the national competition in Boston. In the meanwhile, baseball scout Ed Daly, a former minor league shortstop, recommended Lakeman to Cincinnati farm director Frank Lane.[1] The Reds appreciated the extra value of having a hometown prospect. Forced to choose between boxing and baseball, Lakeman chose the latter and became a professional at age 19.

Lakeman's first assignment was with the Union City Greyhounds in the Kitty League. In his first year as a right-handed hitting catcher, he caught 103 games and led the league at his position both in assists but also in errors, batting .275. During his sophomore season, his Erie Sailors (Middle Atlantic League) manager Jocko Munch, reflecting upon the hulking stature of his durable receiver, forever branded him "Moose." Lakeman had another solid season.

In 1940, Lakeman played with the Columbia (SC) Reds of the Sally League; it was the first time he hit above .300 (he posted a .314 mark). The other milestone of the year was his August 6 marriage to Margaret Merrill. Lakeman met his future wife during his South Carolina stay. She was a waitress at the lunch counter of the local Walgreen's where he and teammate Ray Lamanno would frequently stop by to eat and flirt. His wife's dislike of cold weather and homesickness led to Lakeman's relocation from Cincinnati to Spartanburg, South Carolina.[2] The following year, Lakeman headed north, promoted to Indianapolis in the American Association, where he batted .286 in more limited action.

The native son returned home a relatively short four years after his signing. He began the season with the parent Cincinnati Reds and pinch-hit uneventfully in the game on April 19. Two days later, he was optioned back to Syracuse, but on July 17, 1942, he rejoined the big league club.

Cincinnati had sold Ernie Lombardi to the Boston Braves over the winter, and had been trying to fill the void behind home plate. Making the major league club, Lakeman inherited the Schnozz's uniform number (4). However, his former minor league buddy and fellow Reds rookie Ray Lamanno had preceded him to the big league club and had already staked out the regular catching position. Moose replaced veteran backstop Rollie Hemsley, whose feeble hitting had led the Reds to jettison him in favor of the hometown recruit. Hemsley was given his unconditional release and Al Lakeman was a major leaguer.

The launch of Lakeman's big league career began with what would become a familiar pattern. His path was often blocked by entrenched incumbents, leaving him with second- or third-string roster duty. To a certain extent, though, Lakeman's active player experiences prepared him well for his post-playing responsibilities with the Red Sox.

When Ray Lamanno departed Redsland for military service, Ray Mueller arrived on the scene in 1943 and commenced an "Iron Man" stint by eventually catching 233 consecutive games. Rather than have him rust on the bench, Reds manager Bill McKechnie sent Lakeman down to the International League Syracuse Chiefs for the 1944 season to spend his time at a new position—first base. But it was the Reds' lack of backstop depth rather than his new first-sacker skills

that led to Lakeman's return to the majors in 1945.

Mueller's accomplishments as a catcher were insufficiently impressive to warrant exemption from Uncle Sam's call to military duty, and Lakeman was called upon to lead a 1945 catching triumvirate that included Al Unser and Johnny Riddle, both at the tail ends of relatively undistinguished years of big league service. Lakeman handled the bulk of the receiving duties, appearing in a career-high 76 games. This, his most notable season, finished with a flourish before the hometown fans at Crosley Field when he drove in the winning run in both games of a doubleheader against Brooklyn on September 9, followed just a week later by his September 16 single in the 11th-inning of a game to defeat the visiting Boston Braves.

That winter, Lakeman joined an entourage of ballplayers skippered by Brooklyn Dodgers coach Chuck Dressen that played exhibition games for servicemen in the Pacific Theater.

In 1946, both Mueller and Lamanno returned from the service and Lakeman was relegated to third-string work. Prompted by a lack of depth both at first base and behind the plate, the Phillies picked up Lakeman in the middle of the 1947 season. In turn, Cincinnati acquired Hugh Poland as a catching replacement and portside pitcher Ken Raffensberger. The latter went on to post double-figure victory totals for the Reds over the course of the next several years, ultimately rendering this deal a lopsided one in favor of the Rhinelanders. While backing up catcher Andy Seminick and first baseman Howie Schultz in the City of Brotherly Love, though, Lakeman was unable to hit his own weight, an anemic performance that he repeated the next year.

Lakeman's 1948 campaign was notable only to the extent that it marked his brief debut as a pitcher. Taking the mound during batting practice drills, Lakeman impressed teammates Dick Sisler, Del Ennis, and Harry Walker with his live fastball and sharp control.[3] His pre-game performances led manager Ben Chapman to provide opportunities for his backstop to gain game experience. On July 12, Lakeman took the hill for the Phillies at Cooperstown's Abner Doubleday Field for the annual Hall of Fame exhibition game. Facing the St. Louis Browns, he proceeded to yield 13 hits, including five home runs, over eight innings. Dismaying as this may have been, it did not discourage a regular-season trek to the mound eight days later in Pittsburgh, mopping up in a losing effort to record the final two Pirates outs in an 11-2 intrastate crushing. Abandoning the tools of ignorance to make his first and only big league pitching appearance, Lakeman found himself confronted by reminders of his usual craft. Bucs catcher Eddie Fitz Gerald stood at the plate and umpire Butch Henline, a former Phillies receiver, was calling balls and strikes. Fitz Gerald promptly hit Lakeman's first pitch over Forbes Field's left field wall for a three-run homer, putting the kibosh on any further thoughts of converting positions. He would only toe the pitching rubber a few more times, while managing in the minors. Lakeman's overall lackluster performance in 1948 resulted in a demotion. The Phils sold him to the American Association Milwaukee Brewers the following January.

His contract was purchased by the Boston Braves in April 1949 but Lakeman's first stay in the Hub resulted in only three game appearances. He never appeared on a major league baseball card while logging more substantial playing time both with Cincinnati and Philadelphia, but his abbreviated stop with the Braves resulted in his inclusion in the Eureka Sports Stamp Company's 1949 full-color stamp set of National League ballplayers. Lakeman knew that his days in Boston were numbered as he witnessed first-hand the emergence of 19-year-old rookie receiver Del Crandall, whom the veteran wisely described as "the best catching prospect I've ever seen."[4] Despite his brief stay with the Tribe, Lakeman made a lasting impression on the club's batboy, Charlie "The Greek" Chronopoulos. Over a half century later, the now retired former Tyngsborough, MA police chief recalls that Lakeman's tall, rugged appearance contrasted with a very pleasant personality and an ability to get along well with everyone.[5] Several years later, the bat boy and backstop would cross paths on the dusty minor league diamonds of the Pioneer League.

After another season in Milwaukee, Lakeman drifted over the next couple of years to the Pacific Coast League and then to the International League, eventually landing in 1953 in Buffalo with the Bisons. After his midseason acquisition from the IL Baltimore Orioles, Lakeman went on a hitting tear, collecting 10 hits in 16 trips to the plate, including a string of seven successive safeties. His uncharacteristic success with the bat continued throughout the season despite a six-week layoff to recuperate from a fractured right cheek bone. He finished with a career high .322 batting average. Behind the plate, Lakeman turned a rare feat in an August 14 game against Syracuse. On three occasions, he completed double plays by gunning down runners caught off second base after third strikes. However, his greater value to the team was in his ability to counsel young pitching prospects. With the Tigers' top farm club, he caught Frank Lary and Paul Foytack, soon to

become the mainstays of Detroit's starting rotation, and corrected flaws in their deliveries.

Lakeman's swan song occurred during the spring of 1954 when he appeared in five games for the Bengals before being sold to Buffalo on June 2. Before commencing his minor league managerial career, he returned to his home state of Ohio in 1955 for one last season on the active player roster with the Columbus Jets. In an unintentional tribute to his final fling, the club included his portrait in its commemorative team souvenir postcard set, Lakeman's only contemporary appearance in a minor league collectible offering.

Appearing in 239 major league contests over the course of his nine-year career, Lakeman batted .203, a number only slightly above his usual playing weight. In 646 career at-bats, he collected 131 hits, connected for home runs 15 times, and drove in 66. His one official trip to the mound in relief resulted in a lifetime ERA of 13.50. His fielding average of .981 reflected an 84%—16% split in playing time behind home plate and at first base.

Lakeman's minor league statistics were a bit more robust. Over the course of all or parts of 16 seasons

Coaching the Cardiac Kids. *In 1967, Al Lakeman worked with a very youthful Red Sox pitching staff.*

and some 1,177 games, he batted .262. Ninety-three of Lakeman's 985 hits were circuit clouts and he drove in 561 runs. As a playing manager in 1956-57, he pitched in four games, losing two while never claiming a victory.

In 1963, Lakeman re-entered major league ball. When Johnny Pesky was named Red Sox manager after the 1962 season, he chose to replace former skipper Mike "Pinky" Higgins' bullpen coach, Len Okrie, with a colleague from the Detroit Tigers' farm system. Pesky and Lakeman had worked together in several Detroit spring training camps while the two both toiled as managers in the Tigers chain. They were briefly teammates in early 1954 with the Tigers. Both ended their big league playing days that year, and both started their managerial careers in the Motor City club's bushes in 1956.

While Pesky was advancing in the ranks, ultimately earning a big league managerial shot in Boston, Lakeman perpetually drew assignments in the Class C and D low minors, with stops in the Alabama-Florida, Pioneer, New York-Pennsylvania, Carolina and Northern Leagues. Over the course of 881 games through seven seasons (1956-62), he recorded a .472 winning percentage.

At Idaho Falls in 1957, Lakeman extended a helping hand to his 1949 Boston Braves "teammate" Charlie Chronopoulos. The ex-bat boy had been signed as an outfielder-first baseman by the Tribe but met with limited success and was attempting a transition to the mound when he was let go by the Boise Braves. Having experienced the difficulties of trying to convert positions himself, Lakeman added his former chum to the Russets' roster and gave the lad an opportunity to attempt to hone his pitching skills. Chronopoulos still has vivid memories of that season and the admiration he and his mates had for their skipper. During a game in Salt Lake City, Chronopoulos caused a near-riot when he twice knocked down his opponent's slugging first baseman. As expected, a fight ensued and fans barraged the field with anything they could lay their hands on. Lakeman led the charge to come to the aid of his beleaguered pitcher. Notwithstanding his dominating presence and ring experience, Lakeman ultimately needed a police escort to safely remove his team from the ballpark.[6]

Despite his lowly position, Lakeman tutored such prospective major leaguers as catcher and future manager Bob "Buck" Rodgers, outfielders Gates Brown, Purnal Goldy and Mickey Stanley, infielder Jake Wood, and pitchers Mickey Lolich and Howie Koplitz. Leading the Montgomery Rebels in 1960, he mentored an eventual successor to his Williamsburg outpost, 1974-

76 Bosox bullpen coach Don Bryant.

Lakeman's initial coaching foray in Boston started in spring training 1963 but ended abruptly near the finish of the 1964 season, when general manager Higgins, with just two games left in the season, replaced Pesky with third base coach and Higgins crony Billy Herman—later a Hall of Famer based on his playing rather than managing prowess. Herman restored Okrie to his previous bullpen position until both were deposed in a shake-up that led to the appointment of Dick Williams as Red Sox skipper in 1967.

Prior to Williams' invitation to resume his former duties, Lakeman had gone back to the Tigers organization as a minor league manager and scout. He led the Rocky Mount Leafs of the Class-A Carolina League in 1965 and the Statesville Tigers of the Class-A Western Carolina League in 1966. Lakeman was credited with one notable signing: Tim Hosley, who eventually became a back-up big league catcher for parts of nine seasons, ironically mimicking his recruiter's playing experience. Upon rejoining the Red Sox, Lakeman and Okrie would flip-flop positions. Lakeman took over Okrie's big league job as well as his uniform number (34) and Okrie succeeded Lakeman as Statesville's pilot. Lakeman would remain a member of the coaching staff through the conclusion of Dick Williams' reign in Boston.

One of Lakeman's major projects while with the Sox was to work with catcher Bob Tillman on the latter's throwing and fielding mechanics. After home games, Lakeman would tote a screen out to second base and have the young backstop practice throwing to it.[7] Tillman improved enough under Lakeman's tireless direction to follow in his mentor's footsteps and perform in the majors for nine years. Lakeman generously shared his knowledge at both ends of the battery. Former Bosox southpaw pitching prospect and Gloucester native Bill MacLeod recalled that Lakeman helped him add a palm ball to his pitching repertoire.[8]

During the 1967 World Series, Lakeman worked with a sportswriter from the *Spartanburg Herald Journal* to provide a local's perspective of the unfolding Impossible Dream Fall Classic. The reporter conducted telephone interviews with the bullpen coach after games and prepared columns for the subsequent day's editions. For his contributions, Lakeman received the by-line on the newspaper's World Series insider reports.[9]

After departing the Red Sox, Lakeman reestablished his ties to the National Pastime by once again returning to the Tigers organization as a rookie ball manager with the Appalachian League Bristol Tigers in 1970. He filled the void left by Bill Lajoie, who was beginning his ascent in the Tigers front office and who eventually became a key member of Red Sox general manager Theo Epstein's World Series Championship brain trust. Lakeman later scouted for the 1972-73 American League Milwaukee Brewers to conclude a 36-year association with professional baseball.

Lakeman and his wife raised four children, equally divided between boys and girls. Over the years, as soon as the school year ended, the family would join Lakeman at the latest stop in his baseball odyssey. Their journeys took them across the country by car three times and to Cuba in 1953 where Lakeman was playing winter league ball.[10]

Outside of baseball, he worked for the Pickens Sheet Metal and Roofing Company in Spartanburg, South Carolina, using skills he acquired as a sheet metal worker during the off-seasons in Cincinnati, back in his early days with the Reds. Lakeman personally built the family home in Spartanburg and taught Sunday school at the local Baptist Church. His eldest son Charlie was named after Al's brother, a Bronze Star recipient killed in World War II. Lakeman would bequeath his 1967 Championship ring to Charlie, a high school baseball star who briefly pursued a professional career as a pitcher in the low minors.[11]

Lakeman unexpectedly passed away at age 57 on May 25, 1976 in Spartanburg, succumbing to a sudden heart attack. He was buried at Roselawn Memorial Gardens in Inman, South Carolina. A daughter, Margaret Ann Splawn, maintains a website devoted to her dad, replete with photographs taken during his career and accompanied by a heartfelt personal tribute.[12] One of her most cherished mementos is a ring that her father had made up for her with a diamond that had been removed from a bejeweled championship belt the he had been awarded during his boxing days.

Notes:

1. 1942 *National League Green Book*: 43.
2. Interviews with Margaret Ann Splawn (Al Lakeman's daughter) by Bob Brady, March-April, 2006.
3. *The Sporting News*, July 7, 1948: 13.
4. *The Sporting News*, July 6, 1949: 9.
5. Interview with Charles Chronopoulos by Bob Brady, January 18, 2006.
6. *Ibidem*.
7. *The Sporting News*, April 4, 1964: 31.
8. *The Sporting News*, August 21, 1965: 35.
9. Splawn interviews, *op. cit.*
10. *Ibidem*.
11. *Ibidem*.
12. For Margaret Ann Splawn's website tribute, *see* http://springerbiz.com/dad.

Sal Maglie

by Judith Testa

"He scares you to death. He's scowling and gnashing his teeth, and if you try to dig in on him, there goes your Adam's apple. He's gonna win if it kills you and him both."[1]

So the Cincinnati Reds' Danny Litwhiler described the unnerving experience of batting against Sal Maglie. Between 1950 and 1956 Maglie was among the most feared hurlers in baseball. A glowering, 6-foot-2-inch, 180-pound righthander whose game-day face bristled with thick black stubble, he looked capable of killing the opposing batters, and his pitching style confirmed the fears his appearance aroused. His high hard one came in so close to batters' heads that it seemed to shave their chins, gaining him the memorable nickname "Sal the Barber." Although best remembered for his on-field ferocity, Maglie didn't come by his reputation naturally. Off the field he was a gentle, courteous, good-natured man, and it took him a long time to learn his trade.

Salvatore Anthony Maglie was born on April 26, 1917 in Niagara Falls, New York, his parents' third and youngest child and only son. His father, Giuseppe Maglie, came from a prosperous family in Italy and had a high school education, but in America his lack of knowledge of English meant he could only hold jobs as a common laborer. Sal's mother, Maria Bleve, was from a peasant background, and never attended a day of school. But she was a woman of determined character, striking good looks, and unusual height—qualities her son inherited.[2] Sal's passion for baseball mystified and angered his parents, and as a child he had to sneak out of the house in order to play.[3] In his early years he was such a poor pitcher that his sandlot teams rarely let him take the mound. Since his high school did not have a baseball team, he went out for basketball, becoming one of the team's stars. Nearby Niagara University offered him a basketball scholarship, but he turned it down, maintaining a stubborn allegiance to baseball, and to pitching in particular.

In his early 20s Sal seemed destined for a life like that of his factory-worker friends. He held a job at Union Carbide, one of Niagara Falls' many chemical plants, and pitched for the company team, as well for local semi-pro teams. He had a tryout with the Rochester Red Wings of the International League in 1937, but after he had thrown only three pitches, whoever was in charge had seen enough. "Next!" he yelled.[4] The following year Sal joined the Niagara Cataracts, a local team that didn't even last one season. But there he caught the eye of Steve O'Neill, manager of the Buffalo Bisons. O'Neill saw some promise in the young pitcher and invited him to join his team. Sal spent almost three seasons with the Double-A Bisons, each worse than the previous one. In 1940 he asked to be sent down, so O'Neill placed Maglie with the Jamestown Falcons of the Class-D Pony League. In 1941 he moved up to the Elmira Pioneers of the Class-A Eastern League, and there Sal finally hit his stride, winning 20 games and achieving an excellent 2.67 ERA. The year 1941 was a busy one for Sal in his personal life as well, since he and his long-time girlfriend Kay Pileggi eloped in March. Their families hurried them into a proper Catholic church wedding two months later.

In 1942, shortly after the beginning of World War II, Maglie failed his pre-induction physical, due to a chronic sinus condition. With the manpower shortage in baseball, Sal's mediocre record was sufficient for the New York Giants to snap him up for their Jersey City farm team. He resigned after the 1942 season and returned to Niagara Falls, where he spent the next two years working in a defense plant. In the spring of 1945 Sal returned to the Jersey City Giants, where he compiled another losing record, but with the continuing lack of players due to the war, in August he was called up to the majors. Although in his two months with the New York Giants in 1945 the 28-year-old rookie compiled a modest 5-4 record, he tossed three shutouts, and believed he might join the Giants' regular rotation in 1946. But other events intervened.

At the end of the 1945 season Giants pitching coach Dolf Luque suggested that Maglie join the Cuban Winter League to pitch for Cienfuegos, the team Luque managed. The Cuban-born Luque had enjoyed a successful major league career as a right-hander with a reputation as a headhunter. Sal agreed to go to Cuba, and there began a tough, demanding apprenticeship with Luque that would transform him from a marginal wartime hurler into one of the top pitchers of his time.

As the 1946 season opened, major league clubhouses buzzed with the news that two wealthy Mexican brothers, Jorge and Bernardo Pasquel, were offering American players fabulous sums to jump their contracts and play in the Mexican League. Resentful at what he considered dismissive treatment by Giants manager Mel Ott during spring training, and already familiar with Mexican offers from contact with the Pasquels in Cuba, Maglie took the gamble. He left Organized Baseball and played for two seasons (1946 and 1947) in the Mexican League. Commissioner Happy Chandler banned all the "jumpers" from the majors for five years.

During Sal's two seasons with the Puebla Parrots, Dolf Luque was Sal's manager, and the flinty old Cuban molded the mild-mannered Maglie into a pitcher along his own lines. As he absorbed Luque's methods and pitched under varied and often extreme conditions, a very different Sal Maglie emerged—a grim, tough, ruthless competitor unfazed by weather, taunts, or pressure, a pitcher who could bend a curve like a pretzel, or send a batter sprawling with a fastball that grazed his chin.

After 1947 Maglie did not return to the crumbling Mexican League, but he was still banned from the majors. He then joined a barnstorming squad organized by fellow jumper Max Lanier, consisting of other Mexican League refugees, and the group traveled around by bus, taking on local semi-pro teams. The team failed to bring in enough money to cover expenses, and disbanded in August of 1948. Maglie had no choice but to return home. Back in Niagara Falls he

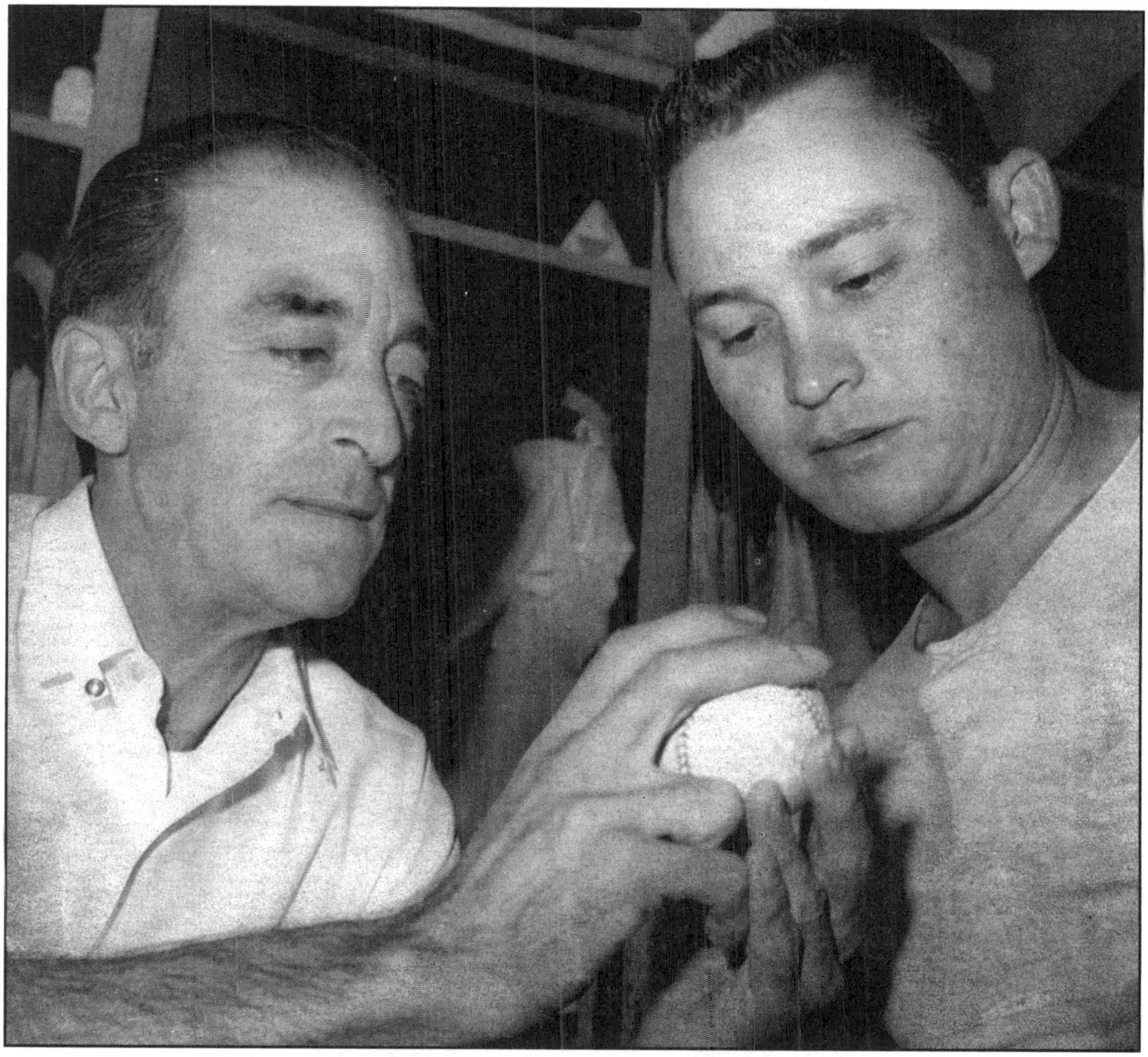

Maglie offers some friendly advice to World Series Game One starter José Santiago.

used money saved from his years in Mexico to purchase a home and a gas station, and tried to resign himself to life as a gas jockey. He was miserable. Invited to pitch in the Provincial League in Quebec, Maglie put in an outstanding season in Canada in 1949, leading the Drummondville Cubs to a championship.[5] During that season Maglie learned that Chandler had lifted the ban on the Mexican League jumpers, and he would be allowed to return to the New York Giants.

Maglie began his 1950 season with the Giants in the bullpen, working only sporadically, and in daily dread of being sent back to the minors or released. He flubbed his first few starts. But finally, in St. Louis on July 21, Sal pitched the contest that turned his career around. He threw an 11-inning complete game, defeating the Cardinals, 5-4. For the rest of the season Sal pitched brilliantly, finishing with an 18-4 record, and at one time hurling four straight shutouts and 45 consecutive scoreless innings. In 1951 Maglie enjoyed his most successful year, contributing 23 wins to the Giants' pennant drive. In the famous third playoff game against the Dodgers that the Giants won on Bobby Thomson's "home run heard 'round the world," Maglie labored eight innings, leaving for a pinch hitter with his team behind 4-1, so it was Larry Jansen—who threw only four pitches in the top of the ninth—who gained the win. In the Series against the Yankees, Maglie lost Game Four, allowing four runs in five innings as the Giants fell in six games.

Although Maglie enjoyed another successful season in 1952, he began experiencing back trouble that limited his effectiveness. In 1953 his back problems intensified, and he finished with an 8-9 record. Sal was 36, and many assumed he'd reached the end of the line. But he bounced back for a successful season in 1954, as the Giants won the World Championship, although he again failed to win his World Series start in Game One, allowing two runs in seven innings and coming away with no decision. In the top of the eighth, he allowed two base runners before being replaced by Don Liddle, who threw just one pitch to left-handed slugger Vic Wertz. The ensuing play—Wertz's blast to deep center field hauled in by Willie Mays—is among the most famous moments in baseball history, and almost certainly saved the Giants, and Maglie, from a loss. The Giants won the game in the 10th inning and the Series in a four-game sweep.

In 1955, although he had compiled a 9-5 record by the end of July, the Giants sold Maglie to the Cleveland Indians. There, Sal mostly warmed the bench, and even considered retirement, but a development in his personal life decided him against that. After almost 15 years of childless marriage, Sal and his wife had adopted a son, and the boy gave Maglie a new determination to continue his baseball career.

Early in the 1956 season the Indians sold Sal to his erstwhile arch-enemies, the Brooklyn Dodgers. In what may be the greatest "buy" in baseball history, the Dodgers' astute general manager Buzzie Bavasi outbargained the Tribe's Hank Greenberg and obtained Maglie for a mere *one hundred* dollars.[6] During his years with the Giants, Brooklyn had found Sal almost unbeatable, and on more than one occasion his pitching tactics had ignited nasty on-field brawls. Dodger fans, at first horrified that their team's nemesis had donned Dodger blue, soon warmed to Sal, as the aging hurler won key games that enabled the Dodgers to gain their final Brooklyn pennant. In one of those must-win late season contests Sal tossed a no-hitter; in another he won the game that clinched a tie for the pennant.

In the World Series against the Yankees Maglie enjoyed his only Series victory, besting Whitey Ford and the Bronx Bombers, 6-3, in Game One. But in Game Five his opponent was Don Larsen, who pitched the only perfect game in World Series history. Almost forgotten in the postgame frenzy was the fine game Sal Maglie pitched that day—in eight innings he allowed the Yankees only two runs on five hits. Asked afterwards if he had thought about his own no-hitter during Larsen's game, he answered, "I know just how he felt in the ninth inning and, in a vague way, I didn't want to see his no-hitter ruined. It would have been impossible, of course, but I wanted to see us win it without spoiling his performance."[7]

That famous game proved the final highlight of Maglie's major league career. During a listless 1957 season, as the aging Dodger squad played out its final Brooklyn season before the move to Los Angeles, Maglie was sent to the Yankees, making him the final player to wear the uniform of all three New York teams. At age 41 he pitched well for both teams that year, finishing with an 8-6 record, a 2.59 ERA, and a shutout for each team. Nonetheless, in 1958 the Yankees passed him on to the St. Louis Cardinals, where Maglie stumbled to a 3-7 record in his final major league season. When spring training ended in 1959, the Cards handed Sal his unconditional release. In an effort to give Maglie ten years in the majors and make him eligible for a pension, the Cards came up with a combination minor league coaching and scouting position for him for 1959, but Sal disliked the job, and did not renew his contact for the next year.

Instead, Maglie opened a new chapter in his baseball life on October 20, 1960, when he accepted the post of pitching coach for the Boston Red Sox. Sal's ferocious reputation preceded him to Beantown. Jerry Nason wrote in the *Boston Globe*: "Will some of Sal Maglie's desire rub off on the Red Sox pitching staff he will now coach?... Notorious for his knockdown pitch, this was merely an example of The Barber's cup of desire running over. He hates to lose."[8]

The Red Sox teams of the early 1960s were poor-playing squads, and Maglie's efforts to mold a winning pitching staff mostly went to waste. But not entirely. In 1961 righthander Bill Monbouquette set a new team record with 17 strikeouts in a single game, and he gave much of the credit for his achievement to Maglie. "I wasn't afraid to throw the ball inside and back you off the plate. If you didn't like it, it might be worse than backing you off," Monbo noted, sounding The Barber's intimidating note.[9] "Sal talked about stuff like 'move this guy off the plate, move his feet, move his legs,' and oh, he *did* preach: '*throw that ball inside!*' And he didn't mean pitch to get a strike on the inside corner. He meant you've got to set that hitter up with a pitch *way* inside!"[10]

In 1962, in an achievement almost unheard-of for a second division squad, two Boston pitchers tossed no-hitters: Bill Monbouquette and Earl Wilson. Both credited Maglie for the marked improvements in their pitching performances. In addition, Dick Radatz emerged as the team's ace reliever. As Sal watched the jumbo-size hurler work during spring training, he noticed that Radatz was not taking full advantage of his impressive bulk to get the maximum speed on his fastball. "He taught me how to use the lower part of my body," Radatz related. "He told me, 'you know, Dick, you're a big, tall guy, and you're strong, but you're not using your legs to drive off the mound, to get more velocity on your fastball.' That probably put four or five miles an hour more on my fastball. I think he was a fine pitching coach. What he taught me helped me for the rest of my career. Without that, I don't think I'd have been the pitcher I was."[11]

But coaching success is no guarantee of continued employment, as Maglie learned at the end of the 1962 season, when he fell victim to managerial changes. The new manager, former Sox star Johnny Pesky, wanted to name his own coaching staff, and Maglie was let go. The dismissal couldn't have come at a worse time. In early 1963 the Maglies adopted a second child. They'd scarcely settled down with their new son when a blow far worse than Sal's job loss fell on them: Kay Maglie, who had undergone cancer surgery in 1958, suffered a recurrence, and this time it was inoperable. For the next three years Sal remained at home with his ailing wife, supporting himself and his family through speaking engagements, the businesses in which he had invested in Niagara Falls, and his small pension. Although the Sox invited Maglie to rejoin their coaching staff in 1965, he couldn't, because he'd accepted a post with the New York State Athletic Commission. But the following year, with Boston's offer still open, the lure of baseball proved too strong, and he returned to the Red Sox for the 1966 season. In September of that year, the Boston front office announced the signing of Dick Williams as the team's manager for 1967.

Boston's season of "The Impossible Dream" proved a nightmare for Sal Maglie. In late February Kay Maglie died, leaving Sal a 49-year-old widower with two young children. From the start he did not get along with Dick Williams, who had wanted to hire his own pitching coach, but couldn't, because Maglie had signed a two-year contract in 1966. As one of the most exciting seasons in Red Sox history unfolded, Maglie's unhappiness deepened. He felt slighted and ignored by Williams. The one bright spot for him was the emergence of 25-year-old righthander Jim Lonborg as the ace of the staff. Like Monbouquette, Wilson, and Radatz, Lonborg credits much of his success to Maglie's coaching. "I needed to do something that would not allow hitters to stand in and wait for certain pitches," Lonborg recalled. "That's where he taught me the importance of the brushback pitch. He said you had to be able to throw very hard *inside*, and create intimidation, because the more you threw inside, the farther away the outside part of the plate looked to the batter."[12]

Despite whatever contribution Maglie made in 1967, the day after the Series ended, Dick Williams fired him. A couple of weeks later, a bitterly angry Maglie exploded to a sympathetic Boston reporter. "Dick Williams gave me the biggest disappointment I ever got in baseball," he declared, referring both to his firing and the way it was carried out. "Williams inked a three-year contract and then had me fired.... He should have done it like a man....Williams never even had the courage or decency to tell me himself that I was fired.... I've kept quiet long enough....I don't like being stepped on."[13] Bobby Doerr suggested that Maglie was too independent for Williams' taste. "Williams was a real organized type," Doerr recalled. "He wanted to know exactly when guys were going to pitch; he wanted a chart of all that. Sal never gave Williams the charts. Sal knew the stuff, but he had it in his head."[14]

Sal benefited from league expansion in the late '60s. In 1968 he was hired as a scout and pitching coach for the Seattle Pilots, set to begin play in 1969. Maglie spent 1968 coaching for the affiliated Newark (NY) Co-Pilots, and when the Seattle franchise began play in 1969, Maglie joined the team as its pitching coach. The Pilots lasted only that one season before declaring bankruptcy and being relocated to Milwaukee. Sal subsequently struggled to figure out what to do with the rest of a life that had been devoted almost entirely to baseball. His last baseball-related position was in 1970, when he served as general manager of the minor league Niagara Falls Pirates. He was a salesman for a wholesale liquor distributor, and later membership coordinator for the Niagara Falls Convention Bureau, before retiring in 1979, at age 62.

In 1971 Sal remarried, a satisfying union shadowed only by the severe emotional problems his older son had developed in the wake of Kay Maglie's death. Sal Jr. suffered a long downward spiral into depression, drugs, and alcohol, becoming a source of deep anguish for his adoptive father. Despite that worry, Sal enjoyed a few years of leisure, playing golf and socializing with friends, as well as attending card shows and old-timers games. His good health ended abruptly in 1982, when he suffered a brain aneurysm and nearly died. After making a remarkable recovery, Sal enjoyed several more good years. But then in March of 1985 Sal's troubled older son died. After that, Sal's physical and mental health declined rapidly, and he was placed in a nursing home in 1987, where he survived another five years. He died on December 28, 1992, at age 75.

The big New York newspapers that had reported on his games decades earlier all ran lengthy obituaries, but Bill Madden, writing in the *Daily News*, best summed up Maglie's career. He noted that Sal would never be elected to the Hall of Fame, unless "there's a Hall of Fame just for pitchers whom you wanted to have the ball in a game you had to win."[15]

Notes:

1. John Lardner, "Ned and the Barber," *Newsweek* (June 18, 1951): 39.
2. Information on Sal's early life comes from the author's interviews with Maglie family members, in particular his oldest nephew, Pat Grenga, and his niece Maria Grenga Rizzo.
3. Sal Maglie and Robert Boyle, "Baseball is a Tough Business," *Sports Illustrated* (April 15, 1968): 86.
4. Joe Overfield, "Giant Among Men," *BisonGram* (April-May, 1993): 36.
5. Bill Young, "Now Pitching for Drummondville: Sal Maglie," Dominionball. *Baseball Above the 49th*. Ed. Jane Finnan Dorward (Toronto: Society for American Baseball Research, 2005): 80-84.
6. Buzzie Bavasi, e-mail to the author, January 25, 2005.
7. *New York Herald Tribune*, October 9, 1956.

Eddie Popowski

by Wayne McElreavy

1967 RED SOX

"One of the greatest things the Red Sox ever did in all the years I've known them was when they brought Pop Popowski up here after 30 years in the minors working with young players and made him a coach. He's one of the greatest baseball men I've ever known in this game."—Ted Williams

"The reasons for my election are many. I can never forget, nor will I, the hundreds of hours of help and inspiration given me by so many people. Both in the minor leagues starting with Eddie Popowski...."—Carl Yastrzemski, 1989 Hall of Fame induction speech

Indeed, 30 years after his debut in organized baseball, Eddie Popowski finally made the major leagues in 1967—and the Red Sox won the pennant his very first year. Before the manager had even been selected, general manager Dick O'Connell hired Popowski as a coach for the 1967 season. A tough-talking but warm-hearted coach, Popowski had managed most of the players coming up in the Red Sox minor league system and was somewhat of a father figure to several.

Edward Joseph Popowski was born August 20, 1913, in Sayreville, New Jersey. His parents had immigrated from Poland and his father took a job at the brickyard in Sayreville. Eddie was one of five children—four boys and a girl. Eddie went to St. Stanislaus, the Polish Catholic school in town. He was known to play a little hooky from time to time so he could play more ball. There was sandlot ball, and he and his brothers played town ball for Holy Trinity church as well.

Universally called "Pop" in the Red Sox system, he was known as "Buddy" to his friends in Sayreville, his lifelong residence. Elston Howard attended a hometown banquet held in Pop's honor after the 1967 season and joked, "He may be small, but all the players look up to him. But I don't know where they get this name Buddy from. I've always known him as Ed."

Economics forced Popowski to leave school after the eighth grade. In 1931, he was working on an ice wagon for $18 a week and playing on the Sayreville town team when the House of David baseball team signed him. The 17-year-old was conspicuous not only for his size (only 5 feet 4½ inches and 145 pounds) but for his inability to grow the trademark long beard of the House of David players.

With the House of David touring team, Popowski played as many as 256 games in one season, often playing two or three games a day. By 1936 he was earning $175 a month as a player, with another $25 for participating in a vaudeville-style pepper game after the seventh inning of each game. His gimmicks would be put to use in his coaching days. In addition to juggling baseballs in the coaching box during a lopsided game, he would also field foul balls and return them to the pitcher with a behind-the-back toss that became known to generations of Sox players and fans as the Popowski Flip.

Red Sox scouts signed Popowski to a contract in 1936, but Popowski felt he owed it to the House of David to finish the season with them. His organized baseball debut would wait until 1937, when he reported to Hazleton, Pennsylvania, of the Class-A New York-Penn League. He led the league's second basemen in fielding average and batted a respectable .281 but with no home runs.

In those early years, he played in exhibition games against a number of greats of the game, including Babe Ruth, Satchel Paige, and Josh Gibson. He termed Paige "the best pitcher I ever faced." Ted Williams was the best hitter he saw.

Popowski remained with Hazleton in 1938, which was now part of the Eastern League. He again led in fielding, but his average dipped to .253 and again hit no round-trippers. The Hazleton franchise was shifted to Scranton, where Popowski labored in 1939-41 along with a short stint with Centreville of the Class-D Eastern Shore League. He didn't play enough games to qualify for fielding honors, while his batting dropped each year to .236, .212, and .176.

He missed the 1942 season due to a stint in the Army. Like a number of ballplayers, he played in the service as well, but unfortunately, Popowski broke his knee in Georgia, which led to his discharge from the Army.

Popowski was with Double-A Louisville in 1943, his only season above Class A. Again he led in fielding but batted only .225, effectively ending the 30-year-old's

The ultimate sign of respect—The Kid's tribute to Pop.

prospects of making the major leagues as a player.

"They had Bobby Doerr at second base," he said in a 1973 interview. "I knew I wasn't going to beat him out. But I enjoyed the game and I thought I might be able to manage." He'd had his first brief taste of managing at Centreville late in the 1941 season. After hurting his hand late in the year, he was headed home for the winter when farm director Herb Pennock suggested he take over the team. Pennock had just fired the manager. So Pop, just 28 years old, took over a team that included future star Mel Parnell and which traveled to road games in three packed automobiles.

He began a long career as a minor league manager in 1944 with Class-B Roanoke, though he continued to play through 1948. He was a regular from 1944 to 1946 and led his league in fielding each year, giving him the distinction of winning fielding titles in all six seasons he played as a regular. He also batted .321 in 1945, his only season above the .281 average of his debut season. His career minor-league mark as a hitter was .258 with just six home runs in 3,321 at-bats.

Eddie characterized his own play to the *Boston Globe*'s Bob Ryan thus: "I was a pretty good fielder, a hit-and-run guy, a push-bunt guy, and I could steal a base. I'd get my doubles and triples and hit my one home run a year. One year I got it when I hit a ball in the gap and George Stumpf and Augie Bergamo collided. While they were laying there, I ran around the bases."

Pop managed for a long list of teams—in sequence: Roanoke, Scranton, Lynn, Oneonta, Louisville (coach), Greensboro, Montgomery, Greensboro again, Albany, Allenton, Alpine, Minneapolis, Johnstown, Winston-Salem, Reading, and Pittsfield. His daughter Carole Garbowski remembers some of those days well: "We would have to take him to the ballpark if we were going to the game that day or night (and we almost always did). This was in the days when there was just one family car. He was always the first one to arrive and the last one to leave after a game. We would be falling asleep waiting for him to come out of the clubhouse."[1]

Popowski achieved a high level of success as a manager. In 20 years of managing in minor league ball, his teams won four pennants and finished in second place five times. Longtime associate and devoted friend Felix Maldonado recognized Popowski's many talents: "Pop is a great baseball man. His mind is always on baseball. Lots of people in this business don't know half of what Pop has forgotten... and he doesn't forget too much. He is like a policeman on the field, watching the kids, helping them to be successful in the game and in their lives."[2]

Eddie's wife, Mary, was Irish, from New Brunswick, New Jersey. "She loved and knew the game of baseball," says Carole. "They met in one of the parks there when he was playing ball. They were married for 46 years when she died in 1988. With Pop gone so much of the year she was the boss. She drove from New Jersey to Florida alone with us many times. Allied Van Lines packed us up just before the end of school every year and my mother drove us to our summer home. If the team was lucky enough to make the playoffs we started school in that city and then returned to Sayreville."

Never having managed higher than Class A in his first 14 seasons, Popowski was suddenly tabbed

Pop signals good days ahead.

as the manager of Triple-A Minneapolis in 1960 under unusual circumstances. After managing the Philadelphia Phillies' opening game in 1960, Eddie Sawyer announced that he no longer wanted the job and promptly resigned. On the eve of Minneapolis' opener, the team's manager Gene Mauch was hired to replace Sawyer in Philadelphia, while Popowski, only two days from his own opener for Alpine, was promoted to the helm of the top Red Sox farm club. It was in Minneapolis that Pop worked closely with Carl Yastrzemski to convert him from an infielder to an outfielder, which ultimately allowed Yaz to take over Boston's left field after the September 1960 retirement of Ted Williams.

After the season, he returned to manage in the lower minors until September 1966, when he was named a Red Sox coach for 1967. Manager Billy Herman had been fired near the end of the 1966 season. Coach Pete Runnels was named interim manager to finish the 1966 season but made it known he would not be in the picture in 1967 due to a private business commitment. Popowski was named to replace Runnels on the coaching staff, while the Sox searched for a manager.

Popowski would try anything to evoke the best from his pupils.

When Dick Williams was selected as the new skipper, he designated Popowski as second in command. Perhaps Popowski's most important contribution to the Impossible Dream Red Sox was his handling of players. He was more than just a coach or manager, but a confidant and adviser with whom many players talked over their personal, as well as their baseball, problems. Manager Dick Williams, who would gain a reputation as a non-communicator with his players, delegated Popowski to keep an eye on some of the younger players, particularly George Scott and Rico Petrocelli.

In a May 20, 2006, interview with biographer Ron Anderson, Scott said of Pop, "I've been around baseball a long time—in and out—and I never loved a lot of people in the game, but I loved the man so much. He was like a father to me. I used to talk to Pop about everything. You get my heart [when you talk about Popowski], because this guy here, if it wasn't for Pop I doubt if I would have played in the major leagues. Pop got me when I was a young kid in A ball, and he brought me to the Instructional League and he taught me how to play. He made me a good defensive player because he hit me about 200 ground balls a day. The year I won the Triple Crown—Pop was the manager up in Pittsfield. It would be impossible for me to put into words what he meant to me."

Rico was succinct: "Pop was good because he was understanding, but he would kick you in the butt."[4] Baseball is far from an easy profession, and at least one time in each of their careers, both Rico and Yaz contemplated quitting. In both cases, Popowski is credited with having talked them out of it.

"Dick wants me to handle some of these players, we've talked it all over," said Popowski in a spring training interview. "We'll have troubles. But, boy, it won't be because we didn't battle to find out what ails them. We won't perform any miracles, but there'll be nobody crying that we didn't handle them right."

When Jim Lonborg won the final game of the '67 season and the Sox clinched at least a playoff game, one of the first out of the dugout was Pop. "He wound up on the bottom of the pile and was scared to death because he couldn't breathe. If you watch a tape of that in slo-mo," says his daughter, "you can see him going under." He was quick, though; he only lost his cap and a few buttons.

Of course, he survived—but his suit almost didn't make it. As recounted in a commemorative book his family produced for Pop's 85th birthday: "'Thirty years,'" said coach Eddie Popowski. 'Thirty years in

Scott Gray retold a great story involving Popowski over radio station WTIC: Eddie was managing the Roanoke Red Sox farm team during the war. With troop movements it wasn't always easy to get a seat on the trains, which was how teams traveled, but his position and time spent on the trains left Pop well acquainted with many conductors and often, when he may have had to stand between cars or sit on his equipment bag, they found him a seat. On one such occasion a conductor entered a car in which Pop was sitting on his bag. "Eddie," he said, "you don't have to set here, I can find you a seat." The conductor took him through three or four cars toward the rear of the train until they came to a car occupied by patients from a regional asylum. Midway through was a vacant aisle seat, which the conductor turned over to Pop. About 20 minutes later, Pop looked up to see an attendant in hospital whites coming through the car taking a head count. "45, 46, 47," the attendant counted as he approached. He looked down at Pop as if he hadn't seen him the last time through and asked, "Who are you?" "I'm the manager of the Roanoke ballclub," Pop responded innocently. "Ay-yuh," said the attendant. "48, 49..."

the bush leagues I waited for this day.' Then they came and carried him like a maharajah and dumped him into the shower. 'My $25 suit,' Pop shrieked. 'You'll ruin my $25 suit!'"[4]

On the eve of the 1967 Series, Pop told Joseph O'Rourke of *The Home News*, a newspaper in his home town, "Thirty years and now, in my first year up there, a pennant. Our aim was about fifth place, first wasn't even a dream. Then we made a few deals and here we are."

When Williams was fired in 1969, Popowski was named interim manager for the final nine games of the season. He again was promised a coaching position before the new manager was hired. The other coaches were let go.

He remained on the coaching staff throughout the tenures of Eddie Kasko (1970-73) and Darrell Johnson (1974-75). He served again as interim manager for the final game of 1973, a win to finish his major league managerial record at 6-4.

Popowski was a minor league instructor at the beginning of 1976, but he was added to the coaching staff when third base coach Don Zimmer replaced Johnson as manager. He was not retained by Zimmer after the season.

He continued to work in the Red Sox system, serving as coordinator/manager/special instructor for the Red Sox in the Florida Instructional League from 1976 to 1989. From 1989 on, he was an infield instructor for the Red Sox in the Instructional League, and he was always a presence at spring training. In 1997, Field 1 at the Fort Myers spring training complex was named in his honor. One story he loved to tell, Carole Garbowski recounts, happened in spring training when Pop was in his 80s. "Pop used to drive Ted [Williams] around in the golf cart and one day a large group of people descended on Ted for autographs. Pop just sat in the cart with his arms folded, watching. A guy came over to him and said, 'Aren't you Eddie Popowski?' Well, my dad got all pumped up and said, 'Why, yes, I am.' The guy said, 'I thought you were dead, but you look good!'"[5]

Pop saw himself as fortunate to have spent a life in baseball. He told Bob Ryan, "I'm a lucky kid. I'm a grammar school graduate whose daddy and mommy let him do his thing. I've raised a family and they're all educated. I'm not rich, but the important thing is to be healthy, and I've got that. I'll keep doing this as long as they let me."

Eddie Popowski worked for the Red Sox right through spring training 2001—for the last 15 years or so reportedly without feeling the need for a signed contract. He was a Red Sox through and through until his death of lung cancer at his Sayreville home on December 4, 2001, ending 65 years of service with the organization. He was survived by two daughters, three sons, nine grandchildren, and three great-grandchildren. One son, Rickey, a standout at the Ted Williams Camp in Lakeville, Massachusetts, might have made it in pro ball; his life took him in other directions, but he played semipro softball and in 2003 was inducted into the New Jersey American Softball Hall of Fame. Son Terry played semipro softball with Rick, and daughter Sherry also played semipro softball for several years. Carole Garbowski's son Christopher played in seven father-son games at Fenway Park, and did well at high school ball. Terry's son Michael caught for Rutgers from 1998 to 2001.

Per his request, the family buried Eddie Popowski in his uniform. "The last thing we did," writes Carole, "was to put his cap on him. He always wore it and it had to be on the 'right' way." He is buried in Our Lady of Victories cemetery in Sayreville, the gravestone engraved with the Red Sox logo and the inscription "Coach."

Did Pop ever express disappointment that he himself never had a chance to play in the major leagues? "No, no," says his daughter. "He absolutely adored Mr. Yawkey and would do anything and go anywhere. One winter we went to Caracas, Venezuela, for winter baseball. He would do anything. He loved it. It made him so happy to teach anybody. He was always the teacher. That was his life."

Thanks to Ron Anderson, Jeff Angus, Carole Garbowski, and Debbie Matson. Carole Garbowski's grandchildren follow in a family tradition perhaps befitting a man who spent over 60 years working with the Boston Red Sox. She says that one of the first things they learn how to say is, "Boo Yankees!" The second is, "Yay, Red Sox!"

An appeal regarding the Popowski Flip: Pop's family would be very grateful if any reader of this book can turn up any film or video of Popowski performing his trademark flip. Please contact Rounder Books if you might be able to help.

Notes:

1. Letter from Carole Garbowski to Bill Nowlin, May 2006
2. "Happy 85 Pop," a booklet put together by Eddie Popowski's family to celebrate his 85th birthday
3. Ibidem
4. Ibidem
5. Letter from Carole Garbowski to Bill Nowlin, May 2006

With A Little Help from the Coaches

One aspect of the 1967 Red Sox often overlooked is the contribution of the coaching staff. From his hiring Williams made it clear that he would rely heavily on his coaches for the day-to-day administration of his overall managerial duties. Beyond the charter given them by Williams, the coaches also took on particular importance because of the personality of the manager. His no-nonsense, iron-willed, acerbic approach to managing—which would tolerate no wasted effort and which heavily emphasized fundamentals—created the need for a buffer zone between him and his players. This was recognized, consciously or otherwise, when the coaches were selected. Williams' selections constituted a masterful display of team psychology that would have made Freud proud. The buffers were to take some of the edge off of Williams' dictates, especially among the younger and more sensitive players. The two men who contributed the most to this effort were third base coach Eddie Popowski and first base coach (and hitting instructor) Bobby Doerr.

Popowski assumed the role of chief buffer. Pop came to the parent club after thirty years in the organization as player, scout, and manager. He managed most of the home-grown Red Sox in the minors, for example, George Scott and Reggie Smith just two years earlier in Double-A at Pittsfield. Pop did an outstanding job with the players and served as a pressure valve, a sounding board, and equal parts father confessor, psychiatrist, guidance counselor, and guru. He was especially helpful to Scott, Smith, and Rico Petrocelli. He knew these guys, knew how to get them off the floor when they were in the dumps—especially Scott, who would have been lost without Eddie.

Pop could also ride players when they needed it—for example, he got on Tony Horton for not practicing his fielding around first base—but he could do so without Williams' cutting edge. His guidance and temperament counterbalanced the manager's perfectly and provided a balanced chemistry that served the Sox well that year.

It's no doubt that Pop was highly responsible for the success of many players: Scott's .303 average and fielding; Smith's winning the Sox' rookie-of-the-year award; Petrocelli's being named the American League starting shortstop in the All-Star Game.

Doerr was the other major buffer. The Red Sox all-time great second baseman used his soft-spoken manner, incisive baseball smarts, and stable presence to great effect. He was very well liked by the players, knew all those who came up through the farm system (having worked for ten years as a special scout), and helped out a great deal with his hitting instructions.

From Ken Coleman and Dan Valenti, *The Impossible Dream Remembered* (Lexington MA: Stephen Greene, 1987). By permission.

Scouting the Opposition/Frank Malzone

by Bill Nowlin

"It was a great thing the club did in assigning Malzone to scout the Cardinals. He knows just what to look for, and for me it was just great. He tells me what I want to know—how a guy pitches in certain situations, where he likes to pitch."
—Carl Yastrzemski

Bob Gibson told reporters that he expected to do better against the Red Sox than against National League opponents simply because "the Red Sox don't know me as well." Yaz admitted as much before the Series began. "I don't know much about the Cardinals, except for a few exhibitions, but I do know they are a solid team," he told the *Boston Record American's* Larry Claflin, adding that Frank Malzone had been scouting St. Louis and the team was convening a meeting the day before the Series to discuss their players.

Malzone had played with the Red Sox for 11 years, then closed out his career with the California Angels in 1966. When Boston let him go after the 1965 season, Dick O'Connell told him to call after he finished his playing days. "We'll have something for you," O'Connell told their eight-time All-Star third baseman. Malzone wanted to stay in the game and when he came back to Boston after the '66 season, he called and spoke to Farm Director Neil Mahoney. Malzone worked all year, scouting around New England with area scout Jack Burns, learning the ropes. "He taught me a lot about scouting," Malzone said.

With the Red Sox still very much in the race, he spent most of September working as an advance scout following the Minnesota Twins. He was on his own. "They needed somebody to go in and watch Minnesota before we played them at the end of the year. I watched them for about 10 days. I was new to scouting and didn't really know what to expect when I came back. Next thing I know I'm going upstairs to a big meeting with all the wheels—Dick O'Connell, Haywood Sullivan, Dick Williams, Kasko.

"I was sitting at the big table and I just told them what I saw with that Minnesota ballclub, coming off being a player. It was a little different from what scouting is today. There was no computer involved. No numbers involved. It was just flat out: What can a guy do to hurt us? Basically, what it was—just some information that you'd spot, little things that can help you win a ballgame. A scout's not going to win a ballgame, but he can help win a ballgame. The players are going to win it.

"The way I approached it anyway, I just told them what I saw and the guys I wouldn't let beat us. There were a couple of guys on the ballclub that were struggling. The big thing was not let the big guy beat you—Harmon Killebrew. I just flat out said it: 'If I was coaching, I wouldn't let this guy beat me. He's done it before. He loves hitting in this ballpark. I wouldn't let him beat us. If you have to, I would just walk him and pitch to the next guy.'"

Jim Lonborg took in the advice. The crucial October 1 game was the first time in his career he had beaten the Twins. "I followed my game plan," he told Fred Ciampa of the *Boston Record American* after the game. "I kept the ball low, pitched around Killebrew and went to sliders and sinkers when things got rough."

While he was on the road, there were no phone conversations back to Fenway Park every night. Just the meeting upstairs before the series began, both the final games with the Twins and the World Series with the Cardinals. Malzone was perceptive and he made a good impression on ownership. "Everybody was there. Mr. Yawkey was there. For some unknown reason, he liked what I said. Later on, I heard when I said don't let Harmon Killebrew beat us, he liked that a lot. He told Dick O'Connell, 'He's doing advance work next year.'"

The Sox then sent Malzone to scout St. Louis, working as a team with area scout Don Lenhardt and Toronto manager Eddie Kasko, available now that his season was over. "They were covering the Cardinals and when I got through with Minnesota, I joined them. It was an assignment I had never done before. When you're by yourself, and you don't know what to expect... nobody had really said anything like 'This is what we want.' You weren't going to get that out of Dick Williams, anyway." It was better working with two other scouts, though. "You could kind of sit down at night and talk about what you saw. We got together in the room and Kasko did the written report."

The look Malzone had of Joe Hoerner helped Yaz. "Pretty good left-hand reliever but everything was sidearm. He had some kind of heart condition and he had trouble raising his arm. I saw he didn't throw

curveballs. All he did was throw two different speeds of his fastball. In and out, move it around, and that's all he'd do—but he'd get people out. His ball must move pretty good—you can't see it from the stands. He was their out guy and I followed him every time he came in, in relief. Never threw a breaking ball the whole time. The whole time. When I got back, I told Yastrzemski, he's not going to throw any breaking balls. Carl always wanted to know every bit of information he could get."

Hoerner came in to pitch to Yaz in the seventh inning of Game Two. The score was 2-0 and Lonborg had a no-hitter going through six innings. The Red Sox had two runners on base and nobody out. Not having to worry about the curveball gave Yaz an advantage. Bang! Three-run homer, which put the game out of sight, 5-0.

"I talked to Yaz to tell him all about the different pitchers. 'What do you think they're going to throw to me?' 'Two guys are not afraid to use their fastball against anybody. Take it from there.' 'You're sure about Joe?' 'Yeah, I'm sure about Joe. I have yet to see him throw a breaking ball.' 'Well... then I get hit.' I said, 'Yaz, come on. You can get out of the way anyway.' So he did hit a home run off him. He always appreciated what I did."

After Game Two, Yaz told reporters, "Frank told me exactly how Gibson and Hughes and Hoerner would pitch to me. Malzone could do this because he and I played together for five years and he knew my capabilities. Frank knows, too, how those guys pitch. On the basis of what he told me about the St. Louis pitchers, I have been able to guess with them all the way. That makes it a lot easier when you're facing a strange pitcher."

Scouting was, as always, an art—perhaps more so at the time than today. Just as the '67 Series was coming to a close, Orioles executive Frank Lane warned that asking players to follow scouting reports too closely could backfire. "Scouting reports should be used as a guide. Situations change, and batters often vary their styles during games. Catchers and pitchers should be allowed to think for themselves at times." Lane wondered if pitchers Gary Bell and José Santiago had tried to adhere too closely to scouting reports in Games Three and Four respectively. "Maybe they're trying to get things down too fine, and they're not pitching naturally." At the same time, veteran catcher Elston Howard revealed that he had been urging rookie right-handed reliever Gary Waslewski not to over-anticipate. "I'm trying to caution Gary not to think about the game. I told him not to worry himself about how he should pitch to Orlando Cepeda, or what he should throw to Lou Brock. I told him to just get the ball over the plate, and let me worry about what to throw. I'm not right all the time. I realize that. But I've been in nine of these things and Gary's just a rookie." [quotes from *Boston Record American*, October 11, 1967]

For the next 28 years, Frank worked in advance scouting for the Red Sox. He's seen a lot of changes, and wishes he'd had some of the tools players have today. Although Dick Williams just began to use video that spring for instructional purposes, it was not used anywhere near the way it is today, when some clubs are beginning to dispense with scouts in favor of video. "They've got videos. They've got everything else. I'd love to have had the videos they have today, when I'm playing. We had to keep it in our head. How'd this guy pitch the last time I faced him? Now all they have to do is walk into the other room and look it up. The pitchers can go out and have dinner and not worry about the next game. They can look at an out-take the next day, and they've got a guy in the room that picks it right up, the guy in the room there is good at it—Billy Broadbent [Red Sox Video/Advance Scouting Coordinator]—he's good at picking up the things, and he shows them, OK, two strikes and he tries to throw a fastball by him. Little things like that. Billy's good at it. Those are things I would like today if I were playing."

Interviews with Frank Malzone on October 4 and 15, 2006 by Bill Nowlin.

Architect of a Baseball Renaissance: Richard "Dick" O'Connell

by Kerry Keene

As an officer, O'Connell worked in Naval Intelligence, serving on the staffs of Admirals Chester Nimitz and Kelly Turner. Between 1943 and 1945, O'Connell was involved in the planning of all Pacific invasions, for which he was later awarded the Bronze Star.

While at Pearl Harbor in 1945, O'Connell met several members of the Red Sox family also stationed there, including Johnny Pesky, team publicist Ed Doherty, and radio broadcaster Jim Britt. Lt. Commander O'Connell was encouraged to drop by Fenway Park after his military discharge to inquire about the possibility of an opening for him in the organization. His official discharge came on January 2, 1946, and he subsequently did drop in at Fenway. Upon his visit to the Red Sox executive offices in early '46, he met Red Sox general manager Eddie Collins and minor league director George "Specs" Toporcer. The Red Sox were in the process of placing a minor league team in the New England League, and offered O'Connell the position of business manager. More than three decades later, O'Connell recalled for Boston sportswriter Kevin Dupont: "It was strictly by accident that I ended up in baseball. I walked into the Red Sox offices the same day they bought the Lynn team and I had a job." (*Boston Herald-American*, Feb.15, 1978)

He impressed the Red sox brass in his three-year stint in Lynn, and was promoted to the big club and an office at Fenway Park by 1949. O'Connell recalled for *Quincy Patriot-Ledger* writer Lin Raymond in June of 1969 that after Boston's affiliation with Lynn ended in 1949, he cleaned out his desk and went to Fenway to turn in reports and tie up loose ends. On his way out of the park, owner Tom Yawkey asked him where he was going. When O'Connell told him he was going home because his job was done, Yawkey replied "You stick around. Your job is just beginning. We don't let intelligent hustlers like you out of our organization."

He held various positions at Fenway over the following decade, including director of park operations, and actually played a role in the Jimmy Fund becoming a Red Sox charity after the Boston Braves moved away. Away from the park he had also become a well-respected college football referee by the late 1950s, but it was on September 27, 1960, the day before Ted Williams hit his historic final home run, that O'Connell received his first major promotion amongst the hierarchy of the Red Sox organization. On that day, Tom Yawkey fired general manager Bucky Harris, officially eliminating the position, and elevated O'Connell to the title of executive vice-president. He had become the first Boston-area man to occupy a top-level executive position with the team since owner John I. Taylor in the early twentieth century.

And though O'Connell was the team's top executive, aside from owner Yawkey, newly re-hired manager Mike Higgins still had the final say over player personnel decisions.

Upon the occasion of O'Connell's promotion, *Boston Globe* sportswriter Hy Hurwitz wrote of him, "[He is] a mild-mannered, frank, thorough person who is humble and honest." Virtually no one ever went on record to dispute this view.

After yet another miserable sub-.500 season in 1962, owner Yawkey decided to bring in the popular Johnny Pesky to take over as manager. Higgins was re-assigned to the front office as "executive vice-president in charge of baseball," with O'Connell's title re-defined as "executive V.P. in charge of business."

Pesky was gone by the end of '64, replaced by coach Billy Herman. A year later, the Red Sox were on their way to a 100-loss season and the team's poorest attendance in 32 years at 652,000. In one of the few memorable moments of the 1965 season, 23-year-old right-handed pitcher Dave Morehead threw a no-hitter versus Cleveland on September 16. Forty-five minutes after the conclusion of the game, the announcement came that Yawkey was firing Higgins as general manager. In the wake of the dismissal, there was much speculation in the press as to Higgins' successor, ranging from Sox manager Herman, to other well-known baseball men such as Eddie Stanky, Al Campanis, and Bing Devine. Ted Williams even made it known that if Yawkey wanted him for the job, he'd accept it.

But in the end, Yawkey realized that the right man for the job was right next to him. As the new general manager, O'Connell now had complete control over the makeup of the team, and was ready to put his indelible stamp on the Boston Red Sox. He told a friend at that

time, "I have a tremendous job ahead of me, and I can only hope I have the energy for it."

One of his first significant player acquisitions came a month later as he purchased pitcher José Santiago from the Kansas City Athletics. Santiago would become an important member of the Red Sox pitching staff over the following three seasons, as both starter and reliever. One significant executive hiring that occurred in November of 1965 was to bring in former Red Sox backup catcher Haywood Sullivan as director of player personnel.

O'Connell made what turned out to be a popular decision in relocating the Red Sox spring training home from Scottsdale, Arizona to Winter Haven, Florida beginning in 1966. The move was particularly pleasing to Boston-area sportswriters who had found it difficult to make deadlines from the Mountain time zone. But a more important contribution came with his philosophy of acquiring players that led to a noticeable change in the complexion of the team. In 1966, O'Connell was instrumental in promoting several black players to the majors that would help form the nucleus of the fabled 1967 team, including George Scott, Reggie Smith, and Joe Foy. The general manager was quoted as saying at that time, "I don't care what color a player is as long as he can play. If he is any good I want to sign him." O'Connell's son Kevin, who was 15 years old when his father took over as GM said in February of 2006, "I never saw racial bias in my father. He was only concerned whether or not the guy could do the job."

Is that a hint of a smile on Dick O'Connell's poker face? Most observers credit GM O'Connell, shown here with Carl Yastrzemski, as the architect of the dramatic turnaround for the franchise.

In June of 1966, the Red Sox added two more players of color who would contribute to the cause in '67 when they traded three fringe players to Kansas City for pitcher John Wyatt and outfielder José Tartabull. The young team was beginning to show flashes of potential by going 42-39 in the second half of the 1966 season, but by mid-September Boston was destined for a ninth-place finish in the American League. It was apparent to O'Connell that Billy Herman was not a part of the solution. While attending a team banquet in Boston at the end of the '66 season, the GM had the occasion to spend time with former Red Sox utility player Dick Williams, who had just managed Boston's top farm team in Toronto to the International League pennant. O'Connell liked what he heard, and spontaneously offered the 37-year-old Williams the Boston managerial job, which he accepted. The winds of change were about to blow strongly at Fenway Park.

O'Connell talked to the *Worcester Telegram's* Bill Ballou about hiring Dick Williams. "Williams was tough. That's why I hired him. That's what we needed. The Red Sox also had managers who kissed their players (behinds). I knew Williams would kick their (behinds)."

With the help of farm director Neil Mahoney, O'Connell started off 1967 by doing a tremendous service to the team's future by selecting high school catcher Carlton Fisk in the first round of that January's amateur draft. But there were several moves to come in the months ahead that put the Red Sox in a position to make their first World Series appearance in 21 years. On June 2, he traded relief pitcher Don McMahon to the White Sox for veteran infielder Jerry Adair. Two days later, he swapped bench players Tony Horton and Don Demeter to Cleveland for starting pitcher Gary Bell, who went 12-8 for the duration of the Red Sox season. One very important veteran presence O'Connell was able to add was catcher Elston Howard, acquired from the Yankees on August 3. Howard brought a wealth of World Series experience and was just what a young pitching staff needed. And one final stroke in the wake of the terrible injury to Tony Conigliaro was to virtually steal recently-declared free agent outfielder Ken Harrelson away from the Atlanta Braves, who had him all but signed.

While the pursuit of their first World Championship would ultimately fall one game short in October, O'Connell had overseen an incredible metamorphosis in the Fens. He had assembled a collection of mostly younger players, added more than just a dash of color and excitement, handed the reins over to a fiery, young, hungry, no-nonsense manager, and watched a team-record 1.7 million faithful fans march through the turnstiles.

To simply recall that he was named by *The Sporting News* as the Major League Executive of the Year for 1967 does not do justice to the impact Richard O'Connell had on a dying baseball franchise. Gone for good were the days like the game in September of 1965 when the Red Sox drew 465 fans to Fenway against the Angels. They were now poised to embark on an extended run as a power in the American League.

In just a few short years, O'Connell had catapulted himself among the most respected executives in the game. He had been appointed to several major league committees dealing with various issues in the game, and he had developed a reputation as a shrewd dealer and one cool customer. California Angels New England-area scout "Doc" Gautreau told writer Lin Raymond in June of 1969 of O'Connell "There's one guy I don't think will ever have ulcers. I don't think anything bothers him. If it does, he sure doesn't show it." Gautreau continued, "He's a wheeler-dealer, but he's a hard man to bargain with." From late 1967 through late '69, O'Connell engineered rather lopsided trades that brought Boston such quality starting pitchers as Ray Culp, Sonny Siebert, and Gary Peters. He also oversaw the drafting of such amateur stars as Cecil Cooper, Ben Oglivie, Bill Lee, Rick Burleson, and Jim Rice between June of 1968 and June of 1971.

In May of 1971, O'Connell took a chance on a 30-year-old pitcher who had been released by Minnesota after experiencing severe shoulder problems—Luis Tiant. He spent a month in the Braves system, and they released him as well. The gamble would pay enormous dividends as Tiant became the ace of the Boston staff for the majority of the 1970s. As the decade progressed, the GM continued to add players who would become key members of the team's future successes. The 1973 amateur draft yielded Fred Lynn and Butch Hobson, and a trade after the season with St. Louis added veteran National League hurler Rick Wise and outfielder Bernie Carbo. In January of 1974, the Red Sox selected pitcher Bob Stanley in the amateur draft.

Heading into his 10th season as Red Sox GM in 1975, O'Connell had assembled a team with few weaknesses. They were a terrific combination of home-grown talent such as Lynn, Rice, Burleson, Fisk, Cooper, and Dwight Evans along with shrewd additions to the pitching staff, including Reggie Cleveland, Dick Drago, Jim Willoughby, and, of course, Tiant and Wise. Acquiring second baseman Denny Doyle in

Dick Williams indicates he's signing a three-year contract with Dick O'Connell and Tom Yawkey on October 14, 1967. O'Connell commented, "We think he has done a tremendous job. Actually, it is superfluous for us to say that because everyone knows that."

mid-June also shored up the infield. They ended the three-year reign of Oakland as AL champs, but again, as had happened eight years prior, they fell one game short of the elusive World Championship. O'Connell, however, was once again recognized as the major league Executive of the Year.

The following season, 1976, O'Connell made significant moves at the trading deadline in mid-June in an attempt to catch the Yankees in the AL East. He took advantage of Athletics' owner Charles O. Finley's attempt to sell off star players for cash. O'Connell purchased ace reliever Rollie Fingers and outfielder/first baseman Joe Rudi for two million dollars. Before the pair could see action with the Red Sox, Commissioner Bowie Kuhn nullified the deal in the so-called "best interests of baseball." Three weeks later, the Red Sox franchise was dealt a tragic blow with the death of longtime owner Tom Yawkey. His will called for the team to be left to a trust, controlled in part by his widow Jean. Though O'Connell and Mr. Yawkey had always gotten along fine, the same could not be said of the general manager and Mrs. Yawkey. The two had barely spoken in some time, and Yawkey's departure marked the beginning of the end of O'Connell's time with the team.

But he continued making acquisitions in '76 that would be beneficial to the Red Sox' future. The team drafted 18-year-old Wade Boggs in the June amateur draft, and made the team's first major acquisition via the new free agency system with the signing of relief pitcher Bill Campbell.

The powerful Red Sox team that had been assembled for 1977 would lead the American League with an impressive 213 home runs, 29 more than the closest AL team. They also led the circuit in team slugging percentage by 21 points at .465, and their 97 wins was the most by a Red Sox team in 31 years, but it was only good enough for only a second-place tie with Baltimore. On September 29, with just three games left in the season, the trust owning the team announced that the new team owners would be the group headed by the trio of Mrs. Yawkey, Haywood Sullivan, and former team trainer Buddy LeRoux. Speculation began immediately that O'Connell would be fired as a result. Sullivan had been hired by O'Connell 12 years prior, and they had always had a good working relationship. The relationship deteriorated between the two because Mrs. Yawkey strongly disliked O'Connell while remaining very close with Sullivan.

Less than a month later, on the morning of October 24, O'Connell was handed a letter by an attorney representing the group informing him that he and two of his top aides were through, effective immediately. Sullivan was named the new general manager at that time. In the next day's *Boston Globe*, sportswriter Ray Fitzgerald referred to the act as "...a 20th century business execution." Boston sportswriter Ed Gillooly reported a month later that New York attorney Patrick Sullivan had revealed the details of O'Connell's very generous settlement package, which included $100,000 in severance pay and $50,000 a year for life. As the 1978 Red Sox spring training camp was about to begin a few months later in Florida, Kevin Dupont quoted O'Connell in a *Boston Herald-American* column on February 15: "I knew what was going to happen at this time last year. I didn't like the way the organization was being handled by certain executors and I told them so. I told them what they could do—in not-so-polite English."

Though he may not have endeared himself to the group taking over the team, it is hard to deny the progress the franchise had made on his watch. He assumed full control of a floundering team in 1965 that had averaged roughly 8,000 fans per game. Beginning in 1967, they would bring in well over a million fans each year, peaking at over two million fans by his final season of 1977. By that juncture, they were also receiving more local television and radio revenue than any other team in baseball.

At 63 years old, O'Connell was not yet ready to simply sit at home and collect his severance pay. He engaged in various private business ventures and later went to work for his old friend Red Auerbach as a consultant for the Boston Celtics. Several years later, in 1983, he was set to make his re-entry into major league baseball.

Red Sox co-owner Buddy LeRoux attempted a legal maneuver to assume controlling interest of the team, and was set to reinstate O'Connell as general manager. The action was extremely ill-timed, as it was announced at a press conference on June 5, 1983, the very night that the team was holding an event to honor Tony Conigliaro. The former star outfielder had been left incapacitated by a stroke in January of 1982.

LeRoux's attempted coup was eventually overruled in court, and O'Connell would not make his anticipated return.

More than a decade would pass before the Red Sox would announce the creation of the team's own Hall of Fame in 1995. Two years later, when the second class of inductees was named, Dick O'Connell was among them. He was formally inducted on September 8, 1997 at a ceremony that he was pleased to attend.

Five years later turned out to be a summer filled with sadness for the Red Sox franchise. In early July, the team's greatest all-time player, Ted Williams, passed away, followed a couple of weeks later by beloved team broadcaster Ned Martin. Roughly one month later, on August 18th, the team's greatest front office executive passed away from Alzheimer's disease at the age of 87.

"My Way"

by Dick WIlliams

The following article was written by Dick Williams prior to spring training, and published in the March 1967 Red Sox edition of American League Baseball News, the "official publication of the Boston Red Sox and American League" (Vol. 1, No. 2).

There will be little, if any, standing around for our squad in Winter Haven for the next six weeks. You can take my word for that.

We had well organized practice sessions in my Toronto camps, with a daily posted schedule. We'll do the same thing in Winter Haven, so that every player will always know what he is expected to do at all times.

We are also going to spend a great deal of time on simple, basic fundamentals of baseball. Looking back at the record for 1966, I'm disturbed at the number of one and two run games, which the Red Sox lost [in] the early part of the season.

To me that indicates two things...lack of proper conditioning and too many slipups in fundamental plays.

Trainer Buddy LeRoux and I have had long discussions about our conditioning program during the spring. We have arrived at a desired weight for each player when he leaves camp, and we're going to expect that every player meet that desired weight. Any player who fails will very likely not be coming back to Boston for the opening day.

I guess I'm sort of a bug on fundamentals. I know I made myself a more valuable player in the major leagues because I concentrated on the basic right way to play several positions. Too many times a club loses close games because some player overthrew the cutoff man, threw to the wrong base, failed to cover a base or back up a play. We're going to work very hard to make sure the Red Sox of 1967 are not guilty of these simple errors.

Here's a sample of an average daily schedule we'll follow before the first exhibition game:

10 A.M.—In Uniform on Field
10-10:15—Calisthenics
10:15-10:45—Warm Up, Pepper
10:45-11:25—Squad "A" Hits
11:25-12:05—Squad "B" Hits
12:05-12:25—Squad "A" Hits
12:25-12:45—Squad "B" Hits
12:45-Infield & Outfield work
12:45-Supervised Running, Pitchers
1:00-Supervised Running, Rest of squad

That's the basic schedule, around which such specialties as catchers working on pop-ups, pitchers working on fielding, covering first base and backing up plays, bunting drills, sliding drills, etc. are carried out. Pitching groups and hitting groups are listed each day, along with their particular supervisor for the day's activities.

I sincerely believe that we'll have the finest instructional staff in all of baseball in Winter Haven. Along with my own coaches, Eddie Popowski, Sal Maglie, Bobby Doerr, and Al Lakeman, we'll have Ted Williams on hitting, Dom DiMaggio to work with the outfielders, and Frank Malzone to help with the infielders before he has to report to the minor league camp in Ocala.

With all these men ready to help, there will be no excuse for anyone to be standing around. It will be a busy camp.

Spring Training 1967

by Bill Nowlin

Spring training 1967 was quite different from spring training 1966. We can remember 1966 as the year when Earl Wilson was turned away from the Cloud Nine bar in Winter Haven because of the color of his skin. He'd been playing pool with Dennis Bennett and Dave Morehead, and they crossed the street to get a beer at Cloud Nine where Wilson was denied service. All three left. Wilson was denied entry to another establishment as well. It made the front page of the *Boston Globe* in February, and Red Sox manager Billy Herman said, "Any place which is not suitable for one of our players is in turn unsuitable for all of our players." GM Dick O'Connell was embarrassed because he had just brought the Red Sox back to the Grapefruit League after six years of spring training in Scottsdale, Arizona. He'd been assured by Winter Haven that there would be no racial difficulties.

Some days later, Herman was asked about players drinking. A reporter asked him directly, "Are the Red Sox down here to train to play baseball—or are they down here to drink?" That wouldn't be a Boston reporter trying to stir up a little trouble, would it? Herman's response might not have set the tone the Red Sox wanted to convey, but was forthright and likely reflected one of the legacies of the Yawkey/Higgins years. "I don't care if a player of mine has a drink," said Herman, who'd been known to sock away a few himself from time to time. "There's nothing wrong with

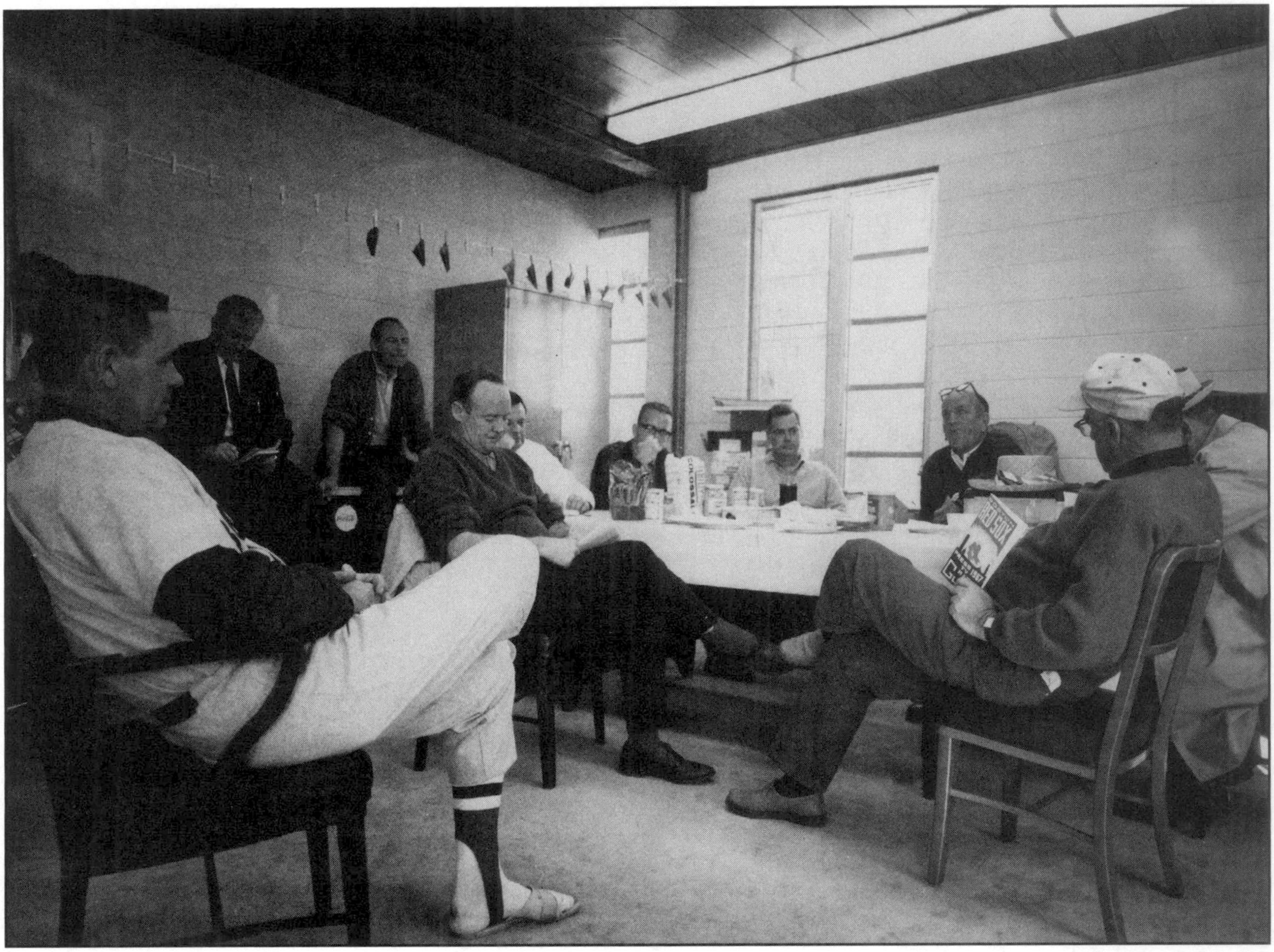

When manager Williams faced the press corps at Winter Haven, they had no idea what an amazing ride they were all about to take.

that," he added. So, he was asked, you don't have any objection to players drinking, either in spring training or during the regular season? "No, I haven't," he replied. "All I demand is that they get in shape—and keep in shape—to play baseball. If a player has a drink one night and plays ball well the next day, that's all right with me. It's all right, in moderation. In fact, if I meet one of my players in a bar, I'll buy him a drink." A short while later, Herman also volunteered, "There have been some pretty good ballplayers who have been drinkers." It would be understandable if some interpreted this as not exactly discouraging drink.

Another day, another quote. Herman later remarked, "I'll let the players decide themselves if they'll have a curfew this year." Herman, in the words of Bill Ballou, was "a member of baseball's old guard and a manager built for comfort, not speed."

After the '66 season was over, it didn't take long for O'Connell to make a move. Herman had already been relieved as manager on September 9, and Dick Williams was hired for 1967 on September 28, the very day after Boston's season ended. VP Haywood Sullivan made it evident there would be some changes made. On October 3, he said the only "Untouchables" were Elliot Ness and company on the old TV show of the same name; anyone might be traded. "There are men the ball club would like to keep," Sullivan said, "but if some outfit is in a frenzy to make a deal, then anyone can go." That wasn't exactly earth-shaking news; baseball executives had uttered similar words for years. What was startling, though, was the September 29 headline from Dick Williams' first day on the job: "Williams Strips Yaz of Red Sox Captaincy." It wasn't meant to demean the former Captain Carl but it was clearly intended to send a message. With him and his four coaches, he said, "There are five chiefs around, and no need for any more. I don't see any need of having another chief on the team."

Williams was asked if he realized he might need to be a bit of a baby-sitter on a team often accused of having a bit of a country club atmosphere. His no-nonsense reply: "There are some players who need a slap on the back, and others who need a slap somewhere else." He said he'd immediately tell a player if he was messing up, "but I will not have these team meetings unless it means cutting up money for first division spots." Williams had been given only a one-year contract and columnist Bud Collins said reporters had already begun a pool betting to see how long he'd last. "I consider this a challenge," Williams said. Collins picked up on that bit of understatement: "A challenge? This job is no more of a challenge than Premier Ky has in Saigon or Daniel had in that Babylonian zoo, or Eddie Fisher had with Liz Taylor." Veteran *Globe* scribe Harold Kaese's column bore the headline "Williams' Nerve Could Be Asset."

Kaese saw real improvement over the 1965 ballclub, and so did the 150,000 additional fans filling the seats at Fenway. In a September 19 column in the *Globe*, the morning after the last home game. Kaese noted that their 40-41 home record was a six-game improvement. There had been player turnover, and it had been for the better. The roster for the final game at Fenway in 1966 had only nine players who'd been with the team a year earlier. They'd kept Yaz and Rico and Tony C, of course, but added George Scott, Joe Foy, and Mike Ryan—bringing youth to some positions. The pitching was looking better as well.

The Sox lost five of their last eight games, though, and it was a fight for the finish—to see which team of four would end up in the cellar. Bud Collins discussed the reverse pennant race—the Dungeon Derby—he called it, in effect assigning a negative magic number for the rights to 10th place. Boston's season ended earlier than the other three teams. When Boston was all done, they would have to wait out the remaining games for Washington (one more), Kansas City (three more), and New York (four more games to play after the Red Sox were done.) No doubt it would be "sheer agony... torture" and they would have to "chain-smoke their way through Sunday helplessly as the other contenders decide their fate." As events transpired, even though the Yankees won four of their last five, it wasn't quite enough. They'd played three fewer games than the Red Sox, and while the Sox had lost one more game than New York, they'd won two more. That put them at a .444 winning percentage while New York was at .440, 26½ games out to Boston's 26. New York had earned sole possession of the cellar.

Dick Williams had played on the Red Sox team in 1963 and 1964; he wasn't that much older than many of the players and would now be managing some of his recent teammates. But he earned their respect. Bobby Doerr was named to Williams' coaching staff and admired the new manager. "There's something in Dick's voice, his way. When he says, 'Be at the park at 9 o'clock,' you know you'd better be there. He doesn't have to rant and rave. There's no falseness about him. Players soon sense falseness in a manager. Managing is like hitting—you either have it or you don't. Williams has it. There's no tension on his club [referring to Toronto], but he has the authority. The players respect him."

Postseason roster moves in October 1966 saw the

When there was a little time off during spring training, Darrell Brandon and Carl Yastrzemski joined in the Fishing Derby at Cypress Gardens.

Red Sox cut eight players including Lennie Green, Dick Stigman, and Billy Short. Eddie Kasko was cut but took over for Williams as manager in Toronto. Haywood Sullivan "admitted that hopes for a trade of major proportions were not good" (*Boston Globe*). Sullivan said, "Frankly, I don't think we're going to be trading much this winter. Most of the people now on our roster are young, and you don't want to trade for someone until you know for sure what he can do, or can't do." Promoted to the major league roster were: Billy Conigliaro, Russ Gibson, Ken Poulsen, and five pitchers: Gary Waslewski, Rob Snow, Mark Schaeffer, Dick Baney, and Billy Farmer.

In late November, Dick Williams said he was happy enough with the hand he'd been dealt: "You think it would be funny if a ninth place team stood pat, don't you? It could happen. I like my team." Williams went on to say that he would not tolerate any interference from above, but that he'd managed in the organization for two years already, "and I've had complete freedom." If there were interference? "The first time it happens, I'll pack my bags and go home."

In January, Williams laughed about his television activities—he'd appeared on "Hollywood Squares" and broke the bank. It came two years after he'd won more money than any male contestant on the show "You Don't Say." He was unhesitating when asked what would be his biggest problem: "Making them play as a team, as a unit," he told Will McDonough. "Our people have got to forget about individual statistics." After a couple of other comments, he added, "To be perfectly honest, I don't want any of the players to love me. I don't care if they all dislike me. We'll all get along great if they do just what I ask. If they don't, then I'll rip them good." A full month before pitchers and catchers were due to report, Williams didn't engage in any false platitudes about how everyone would have a chance to make the ballclub. He said he could pretty much name his starting position players—and then proceeded to do so: Foy at third, Rico at short, Mike Andrews at second, and a fight between Tony Horton and George Scott for first base. "I think the competition will be good for Scott," he added, likely tipping his hand a bit as to his motivation in setting up a contest at first. Yaz would play left field, Reggie Smith in center, and Conigliaro in right. The only other position up for grabs was catcher: Mike Ryan, Bob Tillman, and Russ Gibson were all in the mix. The pitchers would be Lonborg, José Santiago, Darrell Brandon, and Lee Stange, with John Wyatt and Don McMahon in the bullpen. That left a few spots open for pitchers on the team. Waslewski and Rohr he knew from Toronto, and Pete Magrini. Bennett, Morehead, Charton, and Stephenson would all have an equal shot.

In late January, O'Connell had said that Tom Yawkey wanted a "fiery manager." O'Connell denied Yawkey was selling the team. "He's never been more interested in his team." It appears Yawkey had found a fiery manager, or at least O'Connell had. At the Baseball Writers dinner on January 26, Harry Dalton (Orioles), Gabe Paul (Indians), Ralph Houk (Yankees), Joe Cronin (AL), and a number of Red Sox executives all talked about how much better the Boston club was going to be. The signs were there.

Not only had O'Connell found the man he wanted, but he began to introduce a number of innovations. One was what Will McDonough dubbed an "instant critic"—a videotape replay machine. The purchase was announced on February 7, a $3,000 Sony unit that would be used to record both pitchers and hitters so that coaches could sit with the players and evaluate what they were doing right or wrong. Such machines had been used in golf and pro football but, McDonough wrote, "To the Red Sox knowledge, no one has ever

attempted to use TV replay in baseball as a technical instructor." The regular photographer for the Red Sox, Jerry Buckley, had begun taking lessons in January as to how to operate the unit which was to be set up in Winter Haven. Player reaction was generally favorable (see sidebar).

Sullivan also shelled out a modest $175 to buy a batting machine constructed by Joe Torre's brother Frank. "It looks like a good machine," Sullivan said. "If they'd had something like this around when I was a player I might have batted .200 in the major leagues." (The self-effacing Sullivan may have mis-remembered his own stats; his career average was .226.)

One other new ingredient the Red Sox had was the Bosox Club. The fan booster club concept was brought to Boston by Ken Coleman, inspired by Cleveland's Wahoo Club. Dom DiMaggio became the first president of the Bosox Club when it formed in 1966 and it boasted about 200 members by Opening Day.

Some of the players were a little late returning their contracts, as Clif Keane noted on Valentine's Day. Six player contracts had arrived, but not Andrews, Demeter, Gibson, Horton, Jones, Petrocelli, Ryan, Smith, Stephenson, Thomas, Waslewski, or Yastrzemski. "Can you imagine having 12 holdouts on a ninth place team?" asked Keane. As to Stephenson in particular, Keane added, "He has exactly three big league wins posted in the five years he has been with the club. How a guy holds out under those conditions—well, as we said, Haywood has a very clever way of expressing himself, so he'll probably have Stevie under contract." Sullivan remarked, "I'm really not too worried. I don't mind too much getting their letters, and answering them. It's a little fun." By the 27th, only Horton was outside the fold.

A week before camp opened, the spotlight was being readied for Dick Williams. After Dick O'Connell had relieved manager Billy Herman of his duties in September, he'd said of Herman, "He ran a bad spring training." The Sox had finished last, with an 8-19 record but little of spring training had been reported to the Boston fan base because of the month-long newspaper strike that covered most of March 1966.

Williams elected not to let the players decide whether or not they felt like having a curfew. In a team meeting on the first day of camp, February 25, he told them that there would be a 12:30 a.m. curfew, and he told them they had to keep their weight down, too. Both the regimen and curfew would last through the season: "I'm not looking to get the men in shape and then have them dissipate the rest of the year." He installed a weight chart in front of the manager's dressing room. The weight issue would result in occasional benchings of players during the season, but should have come as no surprise. Williams had "started managing even before players arrived at Winter Haven" by sending letters to each player, telling each of them what weight he and trainer Buddy LeRoux had determined was

On the videotape machine:

"I wish we had it last year," said Tony C. "I had a terrible slump at the start of the season and I had 95,000 people telling me 95,000 things I was doing wrong. I started going to the plate thinking about all these things I was supposed to do instead of concentrating on hitting the ball. With this replay thing, there are a great many possibilities. First, it should be a tremendous technical help to a ball player if he could sit down and watch for himself what he is doing right or wrong, rather than depending on someone else's interpretation. I'd love them to tape a film of me when I'm hitting good and then file it somewhere. Then if I started going bad, I could take out the good reel, compare it with what I was doing wrong, and make the adjustment. In fact, if they could do it, I'd like to see them use it in the regular season."

In at least one case, though, it wasn't the use of video that achieved the desired result. Dick Williams talked with Ken Coleman and Dan Valenti about George Scott: "Scotty tried to pull a lot, and he'd take his eyes off the ball. With his power he didn't have to pull. He could hit the ball to the opposite field nine miles, and that's what we tried to impress on him.... We took shots of George chasing bad balls and pulling out. We told Scotty what he was doing, but he said he wasn't chasing balls. Once I remember taking him outside of the cage and showing him tapes of him in the case fishing for balls. You know what he said? He said, 'That's not me!'" What did work for Scott was a little financial incentive, and another adept move by the Red Sox GM. "Dick O'Connell gave him twenty dollars for every hit he got to the right of the shortstop. If he got a hit that he pulled, it cost George ten dollars, cash on the barrelhead. He made some pretty good money. He started going up the middle more and hitting to right center, and he was a better ballplayer."

their optimal weight and what weight they should be when they reported.[1] Williams was consistent. A month earlier, he'd said, "There's not going to be a Gestapo, by any means. Sure, I'll have a curfew. I had one at Toronto. But I think I checked once in two years. I don't think a manager has to be watching. He can tell by the way the players perform if they're getting the proper rest."

Perhaps not surprisingly, Dennis "The Menace" Bennett was the first player to break a rule. Two days later, he showed up 25 minutes late for a workout, bringing along roomie Bob Sadowski. Williams said, "I told the two men that the next time there might be some fine with it. And they missed a lot of sliding work Monday, so they'll do it today. After all, I wouldn't say they are sure of their jobs."

In March, Dick O'Connell mentioned that season ticket sales had increased 40% over the previous year, which isn't saying much but an indication that the new look of the club, the youth, and the manager (himself not all that old) were giving fans something to hope for—maybe that they'd win more than they'd lose.

Williams liked two of the young pitchers he'd had in Toronto. He said he didn't plan to keep Billy Rohr around the big league park when what he really needed was to get more innings. Mace Brown had worked with Rohr in instructional league. He said of Williams, "I know he doesn't intend to carry Rohr unless he is working regularly. But I say there is a chance he will work in a rotation. He's no Grove, but I sort of like him." Williams added, "He's far and away the best prospect we have in the organization. There may be some doubts about his strength. I'll have to watch for that. He's a skinny kid. But I like to think I have a big league pitcher in Rohr." Of Gary Waslewski, Mace Brown said, "He's the best of the new right-handers. He may need another pitch and his best bet is a curve." Williams said that Waslewski had a tendency to coast, and that he'd almost sent him down from Toronto in 1966, but he had really come around and pitched well the second half of the season. There was, he added, no one better at holding runners on base.

There were some of the usual communications issues—Sullivan said he'd not heard from Horton about his contract—but then learned that O'Connell had already called Horton and worked it out. "I wouldn't have called him," Haywood said. "He would have stayed in California if he didn't call me." Yaz said that O'Connell had promised him he would not be traded. "It's the first I've heard about it," said Sullivan.

As the exhibition season got underway, Williams felt he needed a little steadying influence in the infield so he turned to Petrocelli. "He's an intelligent ballplayer and I want him to have some authority out there... I told him I wanted him to take over in tight spots." It wasn't the same thing as naming him "captain" but the *Globe* used the word—albeit it in quotation marks—in its March 4 headline.

Several Red Sox veterans tutored the team. Doerr was a coach, of course, but Dom DiMaggio came to camp to work with center fielder Reggie Smith. George Smith tore a knee ligament while practicing rundown plays on March 5. Smith had been the starting second baseman in 1966, but now he'd been penciled in to back up Petrocelli at short. The injury looked to keep him out for eight weeks. As it happened, George never appeared in another major league game.

Pitching coach Sal Maglie's wife Kay had been seriously ill with cancer for quite some time. When she died, Sal went to Buffalo for the funeral, made arrangements for their two children, and returned to camp on the 5th. And Ted Williams came in to help with the hitters the next day.

On the same day, March 6, Dick Williams did something unusual: he put on umpire's gear and worked behind the plate for the first intrasquad game, all the

Lucky 7's–*Reggie Smith and Dominic DiMaggio. Dom gave Reggie a number of spring training suggestions on how to improve his centerfield play.*

better to judge both pitchers and batters. Williams worked the plate on a number of occasions. He also made use of the videotape equipment supplied by GM O'Connell.

Conigliaro was ready. He wanted to hit cleanup. "I want the pressure of batting fourth," he said, while Yaz was said to have told Dick Williams back on the second day of camp that he was no troublemaker. The two had played together on the Red Sox just a few years earlier. Williams had needled Yaz once, saying, "You run the bases just like Jackie Robinson, only you get caught." It was hard for Yaz to take it in stride, and he asked to see Williams. "I told him I had the reputation of not getting along with managers and I didn't want him to think I was that way," Yaz told Clif Keane.

Ray Fitzgerald wrote in the March 9 *Globe* that Sox management thought Lonborg could become a 20-game winner, and "So does Jim Lonborg. A year ago he didn't. ... In 1966... when he was good, he was very, very good, but when he was bad—Disaster City." Lonborg wanted to be in the regular rotation, and start every fourth day, and believed his control was much better. He had confidence in his ability to keep the ball low. Sal Maglie was working with him on a changeup but the main thing in Lonborg's favor was his self-confidence.

The first game of the exhibition season was at Payne Park in Sarasota on March 10. Conigliaro hit a home run, even though the White Sox won the game, 8-3. Dennis Bennett took the loss, giving up four runs in three innings pitched. Reggie Smith made two throwing errors. The following day, George Thomas' solo home run in the top of the ninth inning broke a tie game against Kansas City. Ted Williams proclaimed Reggie Smith the best prospect in years, including both Yaz and Tony C.

On March 12, Doerr said that one player he wouldn't trade was Tony Horton, saying that he was in a class with Harmon Killebrew. Maybe he wouldn't hit as many homers, but Doerr predicted he'd hit between 30 and 35. The trouble was, Horton was limited to first base, though, and Scott was the best fielder so it wasn't going to be easy to take the Boomer off the bag and stick him somewhere else.

On March 14, Conig hit a homer and two doubles, though the Red Sox lost to the White Sox, 5-4. Williams was "seething," according to Ken Coleman, when Tony Horton overran second base and was tagged out. It was another example of Williams treating an exhibition game as if it were the real thing.

Several pitching arms were of concern. Some were sore, others needed more work. This was spring training, after all. That's part of what it's all about. But Williams wasn't all that forgiving. When Jerry Stephenson walked the first three Yankees in the bottom of the first during a game at Fort Lauderdale, he told reporters that Jerry had better learn how to stay loose if he was going to pitch up north. Williams continued to ride George Scott. Asked if Scott was any better at laying off low pitches, Williams said, "Yes. He's improved slightly. At least now he waits until they come up to his shins."[2]

The next day, on the 16th, the *Globe* said "the only man who looked like a pitcher was Darrell Brandon" in a slugfest as the Red Sox beat the Mets coming from behind with a 10-run ninth inning—a game that both Yaz and Conig sat out. The Red Sox batters collected 23 hits and earned 13 walks. The final score was Red Sox 23, Mets 18.

Meanwhile, Williams was working with baserunners on speed. In a 7-5 loss to Cincinnati, he was pleased because they'd stolen four bases, with two of those coming on a double steal. "We've had speed on the club before," Williams said. "But have never used it. We've always waited for the wall. Now we're going to use our speed. The home runs will come anyhow."

Tony Conigliaro was hit by a John Wyatt batting practice pitch before the March 18 game and suffered a fractured shoulder blade. The Sox anxiously awaited word from X-rays taken back in Boston—was it a hairline fracture, in which case he'd just miss a couple of weeks, or was it a compound fracture which would probably cost him the season? Fortunately, this time, it was a minor injury to the scapula. It was, though, the fifth time that Conigliaro had suffered a broken bone when hit by a pitch. He clearly crowded the plate more than he probably should. Dennis Bennett had a good day, throwing five hitless innings against Detroit.

On the 19th, Dave Morehead was sent to Boston's Toronto farm club, along with Bob Sadowski, Jerry Moses, and Pete Magrini. The day's game ended oddly as Detroit's Dave Wickersham had the bases loaded and induced a bunt popup from Bob Tillman that sailed 15 feet into the air—and then he unaccountably stepped back and let the ball drop, allowing the Red Sox to complete a come-from-behind win in the ninth inning. "I don't know why," he said after the game. The game also featured some uncharacteristic play, aside from the nearly-botched squeeze that won the game: there was a double steal and a couple of hit-and-run plays with a baserunner on second. Rather than being pleased, Williams groused about the four Red Sox errors. As a team, the Red Sox were hitting well over .300.

The Sox were trying to see if they could get Tony Horton more playing time, and so asked George Scott

to play some in right field. Scott wasn't at all pleased, insisting that he was a first baseman, not a right fielder. The *Globe* sports page featured a headline in the March 23 paper: "Red Sox Willing to Trade Scott." The article said that José Santiago was trade bait, too. Both Santiago and Scott, plus Garry Roggenburk, were placed on waivers to see what interest might be generated. Will McDonough acknowledged that sometimes being listed on the waiver wire was just a way to "shake up a player." With Scott grumbling about battling Tony Horton for the first base slot, it may have just been a ploy. Weird things have happened with waiver wires. In late September the year before, just before being fired, McDonough wrote, "Billy Herman put the ENTIRE team on waivers." Only four were claimed by other clubs, and all four were withdrawn. Since he was the one sent packing, Herman never had the opportunity to follow up on the interest expressed in the four who'd been claimed.

The very day the "Red Sox Willing to Trade Scott" headline ran, Scott was indeed playing right field and ran back deep, slamming into the right field wall which was inconveniently made of cinder block. He suffered a concussion, and was expected to be out five or six days. McDonough commented: "Playing a foreign position—right field—Scott temporarily misjudged the ball. In his haste to adjust, he ran smack into the wall." He was knocked out for over a minute. Mike Andrews joked, "He moved the wall from 330 feet to 332."[3] X-rays of Scott's jaw and wrist proved negative, but he was kept in the hospital overnight for evaluation. Williams said that Scott would continue to play the outfield, but he would move him to the easier-to-judge-a-fly left field.

A week later, in the March 26 and 27 issues of the *Globe*, Harold Kaese penned a two-part series on Dick Williams. More important than questions about whether rookies Reggie Smith or Mike Andrews would produce as regulars was the question whether the Red Sox had a good manager in Dick Williams. He concluded, "The early returns are in and favorable." He had his players hitting, but also running, bunting, and thinking. The manager who called himself the "wrong Williams" (alluding to Ted) "is neither magnetic nor easy to warm up to. But he is aggressive, scrappy, cocky and terrier-tough... Williams belongs to the Society of the Under-Rated." He believes in hard work, condition, fundamentals, Kaese wrote, and he ran long drills, emphasizing that players work on the mistakes they made the day before. He had them playing what even before the DH rule came in was considered a little bit of "National League baseball," featuring "surprise and subtlety." Kaese approved. The "Williams trend is exciting," he wrote. "As never before under Yawkey's ownership, Williams has the Sox hit-and-running, bunt-and-running, hitting behind the runner, stealing and squeezing. The players have responded. Fancy Red Sox hitters giving themselves up by purposely hitting to right to advance a runner from second to third. Williams has restored the long-missing element of surprise to the attack."

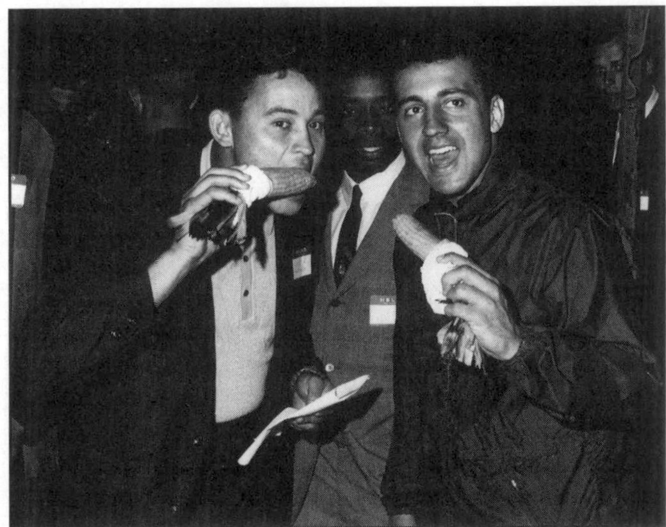

Spring Training Break—*José Santiago, José Tartabull, and Rico Petrocelli take a break in Winter Haven to enjoy delicious roast corn.*

Self-deprecatingly, Williams laughed about one aspect of his conditioning program: "Maybe all we'll end up with is the best volleyball team in Florida."

It was Kaese's column on March 27 that carried Williams' prediction: "I honestly believe we'll win more games than we lose." It was one he uttered on several occasions. "I think we can beat five teams anyhow, and if that puts us in the first division, I guess that's where we'll be." Kaese's piece was optimistic, but concluded, "Williams is quick, determined, intelligent, but how he eventually makes out as a big league manager and as a volunteer for that hornet's nest at Fenway Park probably will depend on how much iron he has in his makeup. I think he may have enough, but I'm not sure."

Mike Andrews developed a bit of a bad back, pulling some muscles and re-aggravating an injury he'd apparently suffered lifting weights in the offseason; Williams put Reggie Smith in to play some games at second base. Smith started the regular season at second. Williams was more worried about his pitching than anything. The staff had a 3.92 ERA in 1966, but improved to 3.36 in 1967.

Near the end of the month, on the 28th, Williams picked George Scott as his first baseman. The team was to embark on a trip to the Virgin Islands for a couple of games and Williams was ready to go with a set lineup that included Boomer. With Andrews still out, Reggie Smith would play second with José Tartabull and George Thomas platooning in center. It was looking like Mike Ryan had the edge as the first-string catcher.

Yaz was in the midst of his best spring season yet, and March 29 saw him excel, hitting two homers, driving in six runs, and making "three outstanding catches including the game-saver in the ninth inning." (Will McDonough) The Red Sox took that one from the Cardinals at St. Petersburg, 10-9.

The next day, Boston got some excellent pitching and beat the Orioles 1-0, Lee Stange and Hank Fischer combining to give up just three singles. Stange retired the last 13 batters he faced. Tony C was in his first game since fracturing his shoulder, and doubled in the game's lone run in the sixth. In the very same game, Yaz was hit on the hand by a Steve Barber fastball. Fortunately, X-rays were negative.

March 31 saw the Boston Red Sox playing baseball on St. Croix in the U.S. Virgin Islands, before some 4,100 islanders who watched the game played on a cricket pitch that had been converted to a baseball field for the occasion. The Sox lost to Mel Stottlemyre of the Yankees, 3-1, as Stottlemyre threw seven full innings, giving up just two hits while striking out seven. He was facing the lineup Dick Williams had determined would be his Opening Day lineup. Lonborg gave up two runs in his seven innings, and took the loss.

The next day, the two teams squared off again, this time on the island of St. Thomas, and this time the Red Sox won, 13-4, with Yaz (five RBIs), Rico, and Tartabull each hitting homers. Dennis Bennett was scheduled to start but was hit in the shin by a John Wyatt fastball and would have X-rays taken. That was the second pitch of the spring that Wyatt had unleashed that injured a teammate.

Playing second base didn't faze Reggie Smith. Filling in for five games, he played errorless ball and hit .360 during the stretch. The experience served him in good stead; he played the first six games of the regular season at second. On April 2, Reggie doubled and homered. George Scott, playing both first base and also third base, homered as well. Rohr and Galen Cisco each gave up one run and the Red Sox beat the Mets, 8-2. The Sox had started slowly in spring training, but now had won nine of their last 14 games. What was the difference between this Red Sox team and the one he'd played on in '63 and '64? "The difference is that this is a 'Team'," Williams said. "I'm not one for past history, but I know when I was around here before it was an individual thing. I feel that one thing that has been overlooked about us this spring is the way that the players are playing for one another rather than themselves individually."

Williams didn't hesitate to get on a player if he felt it was called for. When the Pirates beat Boston 3-1 at Ft. Myers, Boston's manager was livid. After Dennis Bennett had given up a triple that cost the Red Sox the lead, Williams gave him a "tongue-lashing" right on the mound. "I told him that it was a lousy pitch—and besides that, he should have been backing up third base on the play... My little boy could have handled that pitch." Bennett had to agree it was a pretty poor pitch. One mistake in a meaningless exhibition game and Williams exploded? It wasn't any big deal, was it? To Dick Williams, it was. Carl Yastrzemski, showing some team spirit, took some of the blame on himself for letting the ball get by him in the field.

The "other Williams"—Ted Williams—officially a VP at the time, kept a low profile in Winter Haven, but spoke out on at least one occasion. One day, he simply wasn't there and Harold Kaese murmured Ted had a "relatively insignificant status" in camp; he noted that Ted didn't hang around long. This Williams was back a few days later, though, criticizing Tony C on April 5 for bunting in a two-out situation with Yaz on first in a scoreless game. He popped up, but the point—Ted said—was "we want the big hit and Tony's capable of giving it to us. Instead he pops up to the pitcher. That's evidence of poor thinking. That's exactly how not to win games. Tony should know better." Ted's philosophy may have differed from that of the "wrong Williams," but in this situation he might have been right.

In the final roster cut of spring training, Jerry Stephenson, Gary Waslewski, and reserve infielder Al Lehrer were sent to Toronto. That put the Red Sox one man under what was then the 28-player limit. They could have held onto at least one of them, but felt it was better to get them more regular work in the minors.

Though he'd been quoted along the same lines in Harold Kaese's column a couple of weeks earlier, it was when he spoke to the press corps on April 7 that he made his famous prediction: "We'll win more games than we lose this year." McDonough wrote that, despite a strong spring season, most experts were picking the Sox for ninth place once again. After the final team meeting of the spring, Williams said he had told the players that they had given him 100% in spring training and if they

kept it up during the regular season, they wouldn't have any problems from him.

Ken Coleman later characterized spring training 1967 as "more of a boot camp than a spring training, especially when compared to his predecessors. [Williams] insisted that every player be on time, put in a hard day's work, not complain, and be there the next day for more. He wasn't interested in discussion or debate with his players. There was one chief in camp, and it was Williams. Dick and his coaches installed a precise schedule for workouts: each player knew where he had to be and what he had to be doing at all times. When nothing formal was scheduled, a player was expected to run or participate in volleyball games." Apparently, it worked. Coleman said, "Many grumbled, and a few made the mistake of doing it publicly; but no one actually challenged Williams. And so a funny thing happened on the way to the ball park—this unconnected bunch of young men developed into a spirited team whose fighting character reflected that of their manager."[4]

On April 9, the *Globe* published a story by Will McDonough evaluating each of the key Red Sox players. The story was accompanied by a chart showing how the *Globe* writers picked the race. Kaese, Clif Keane, and John Ahern picked Boston to finish sixth. McDonough and Ray Fitzgerald saw a seventh-place finish, and Roger Birtwell had them finishing eighth. Not one bought into the first-division optimism.

McDonough saw Yaz as in the best shape of his career, and noted that Tony C, hitting over .400 all spring could have the best season of his career, if he could "remain free from injury." George Scott was the best-fielding first baseman in the league and was hitting about .300 in the springtime. Williams worried he'd backslide during the season, and "assigned coach Eddie Popowski to keep after Scott constantly." With Andrews still unavailable, Reggie Smith was the second baseman. Though not as strong defensively, he would wield a good bat, as would Rico at short. Joe Foy was more of a worry, though he had potential: "Foy may be the best player on the team." Tartabull and Thomas would platoon in center; Tartabull was better all around but Thomas had the better arm. Mike Ryan still had first claim on the catcher's slot, the strongest defensively among the trio of Boston backstops, but Russ Gibson or Bob Tillman would get called on if his bat was too anemic. Lonborg was first on a pitching staff still not seen as particularly strong. At least the staff seemed to be healthy. Brandon, Rohr, and Bennett were in the initial rotation. Stange, Santiago, and Fischer weren't far behind the quartet, and could be called in as necessary.

On April 9, the Red Sox lost the final spring training game to the Tigers, 4-3 in the 10th inning, but the Sox nevertheless won more than they lost during Grapefruit League play, by one game: they had a 14-13 record. Tony Conigliaro led the team in hitting with a .405 spring average. Mike Andrews was second at .395, and Scott third at an even .333. Reggie Smith and José Tartabull both hit over .300. Yaz hit just .257 but tied for the team lead with Petrocelli (.247) with five home runs each. Yaz led the team with 15 RBIs. Williams thought the Red Sox had the best outfield in the American League. The Red Sox were ready.

Clif Keane's front page story on April 11 was headlined "Sox Open With Hope, High Praise." The temperature at Fenway Park that day was 35 degrees, with winds gusting to 40 mph. The game was postponed due to cold. The Yankees won their game in Washington, though, and took first place. The second attempt found temperatures had risen to 46 degrees and the gusts had moderated to just 20 mph. The game went on. Some 8,324 fans braved the conditions and saw Boston beat Chicago, 5-4. Feature columnist Diane White wrote a front page story in the *Globe*, which bore the headline "Red Sox Win, Optimism Runs Rampant." White cited a good omen: the "Lady in Red" was back. Though a dedicated fan of long tenure, Mrs. Carter S. Knight of Peabody had declined to come to Opening Day in 1965 or 1966 because she was "disgusted with their half-hearted performance." But she was giving the new-look team a chance: "I like Dick Williams' style of play. They really look better under the new leadership."

So they did.

Notes:

1. McKenna, Henry, "Skipper of the Sox," Official Souvenir Program of the 1967 World Series.
2. Coleman, Ken and Dan Valenti, *The Impossible Dream Remembered*, pp. 22.
3. *Ibidem*, p. 30
4. *Ibidem*, pp. 10, 11

All quotations taken from the *Boston Globe*, except as noted.

The '67 Broadcast Team, remembered

by Joe Castiglione

In 1967, the voices of the Red Sox were Ned Martin and Ken Coleman. Martin started broadcasting Red Sox baseball in 1961, working with Curt Gowdy and Art Gleason both on radio and TV—WHDH radio (850 on the AM dial) and WHDH-TV (Channel 5). Gleason's final year was 1964; Mel Parnell joined in as television analyst beginning in 1965. Gowdy and Martin handled radio duties by themselves that year, but it would be Curt's last year broadcasting for the Red Sox. In 1966, Ken Coleman came over from Cleveland to take Gowdy's place and broadcast through the 1989 season, except for the years 1975-1978.

The television crew from the year before—1966—included former Red Sox pitcher Mel Parnell, who worked from 1965-1969, when he was replaced by Johnny Pesky.

Joe Castiglione first began work on Red Sox radio in 1983, and worked many years with both Ken and Ned. He broadcast with Ken through 1989, and with Ned through 1992, though Joe was on radio and Ned on NESN for most of those years. Through 2005, Joe has taught broadcasting for 21 years at Northeastern University and nine years at Franklin Pierce College.

As a listener, Joe remembers hearing both Coleman and Martin in 1967, and as a colleague enjoyed hearing them reminisce many times about the 1967 Red Sox.

Joe Castiglione:

Ken and 1967: That was his favorite season by far... I think it was his favorite season in sports, despite all the great teams he had with the Cleveland Browns. He worked every game Jim Brown ever played in the NFL. But '67 was always his favorite year. '66 was his first year, and even though the Red Sox finished ninth just ahead of the Yankees, he sensed that in the second half of '66, there was development. Some of these guys started to blossom.

1967 was such a significant year, because the Red Sox took off. They had been so bad! As a kid growing up in Connecticut, I didn't even know any Red Sox fans. There were Yankee fans or Dodger fans or New York Giants fans. Or, later, Mets. The Red Sox were simply not a factor, because they had just been so bad.

Ned was also very, very fond of the 1967 team. He and Yaz were rookies the same year, 1961. He used to talk a lot about the way Yaz was in '67. He liked working with Ken; they were a great team and they were good friends. They both loved Sinatra; they were passionate about Sinatra. I used to get on them because I thought their musical taste—their musical knowledge—stopped about 1952.

1967 was The Year of the Yaz. They both had so many great calls there... the Tartabull play with Ken Berry was a favorite. I heard that myself. It was after my junior year at Colgate, and I was working at WDEW radio in Westfield, Massachusetts in the day, and in the evening in New Haven at WELI radio. I went back and forth. Our station in Westfield carried the Yankees; I don't know why. I was listening to Ken and Ned when Tartabull threw Berry out at the plate in the first game of a doubleheader *[for the final out of the game, giving the Red Sox a crucial 4-3 victory over the White Sox at Comiskey Park on August 27]*. I still don't see why Tartabull gets so much credit; Elston Howard made the play! I mean, he leaped and made a one-hand backhand stab with the catcher's mitt and came down and tagged him out. Elston Howard should have got the kudos.

Ken loved the Billy Rohr game, with the near no-hitter. And he loved to tell a story about Russ Gibson, who caught the Billy Rohr game. *[Rohr's major league debut on April 14 in Yankee Stadium. Rohr beat the Yankees on one hit, 3-0, and became part of Red Sox folklore.]* Gibson spent 10 years in the minors. Finally, he gets to the big leagues—and the first thing they do is take a bus trip to New York instead of flying. Another bus trip!

I know another one of Ken's favorites was when they were down 8-0 to the Angels. They rallied to tie it and then Jerry Adair won it with a home run. That was one of his favorite games. *[August 20, 1967, game two of a Sox doubleheader sweep—two days after the Conigliaro beaning.]*

People would tell Ken how they'd walk down Nantasket Beach and you could walk the whole beach and not miss a pitch, with all the people listening to radios all along the beach. That was a highlight.

I remember Ken telling me that in '67, some advertising guy, some agency guy, told me, "You sound so much better this year than you did last year." Ridiculous. He sounded better to the guy because they were winning. That's the way it works.

Working 1967 together, Ken and Ned had that bond that they shared constantly, with the '67 team. They were, all of them, so close. Bobby Doerr was a

The voices of the Red Sox: Ken Coleman, Mel Parnell, and Ned Martin.

close friend of Ken's. Eddie Popowski. The bonds just continued, when you think of the players. He later worked with Rico Petrocelli in radio in 1979. He always said George Scott was the best-fielding right-hand throwing first baseman that he'd ever seen.

They had so many reunions even after I joined them. One of the more memorable was my first year in '83, when they had that Coup LeRoux thing with the '67 team up in the old dining room. They were there at Fenway to raise money for Tony Conigliaro, and Buddy LeRoux tried to take over the club. They stayed so close—all of them—the team and Ken and Ned.

There was the Jimmy Fund connection, too. Ken became the chairman, and then Ken helped bring Mike Andrews into the Jimmy Fund. Mike eventually succeeded Ken as chairman. They had those bonds that were so strong.

He and Ned were both quite fond of Dick Williams, even though he could be difficult at times—he wasn't with them; he was great with them, but... I remember them telling some wild stories about being in a hotel room with some of the writers and Dick Williams, when the liquid started to flow.

Ken had a funny line. In '67, Ken was the highest-paid guy on the flight, on the team plane. In '86, I think—other than me—Ken was the lowest. Well, maybe the trainer, I don't know. That's how things have changed.

One of the true highlights for Ken, though, was when the Red Sox team voted a share to the Jimmy Fund that year. He didn't get any credit for it, but I'm sure he was influential.

Ken was especially close with Jim Lonborg. In fact, in later years, Jim hosted Ken on Thanksgiving and Christmas and holidays, after Ken's retirement. They were very, very close. Of course, that probably started in '66. He really had great relationships. He really loved to talk about Norm Siebern's triple into the triangle, as did Ned. *[August 16, Siebern pinch-hit for Wyatt and hit a bases-loaded triple in the bottom of the seventh inning, giving the Red Sox a 10-6 lead at the time, in a game that Boston won, 12-11.]*

I didn't know Mel Parnell as well. I remember him doing analysis, but I listened to more radio than I watched TV in those days. I was in western Mass and Connecticut, so we didn't see a whole lot of TV. I actually saw my first game in Fenway that season, though. I stood in the centerfield bleachers; they were just benches in those years. It was a late August game against Washington. I later looked up the box score on Retrosheet, and I do remember that Hank Allen won it with a double. It was late August, I think it was 3-2. That was my first game ever at Fenway. *[August 23. Batting for Mike Epstein, Allen pinch-hit a double leading off the top of the ninth, and came around to score the tie-breaking run in a 3-2 Washington win.]* I watched the World Series at Colgate. I was a senior at Colgate at that time.

I've gotten to know some of these guys at Fantasy Camp. Of course, I've gotten to know Mike because he's my boss at the Jimmy Fund. I know Lonnie well. He's such a class guy, and he's in the next town. My first year was Yaz's last year. José Santiago, he's one of the funniest guys at Fantasy Camp. Gary Bell, he's another great character. He and Radatz were the Kangaroo Court leaders at the Fantasy Camp, although Radatz was not on that team unfortunately. Bell was a factor. They just loved this club. It's unbelievable. They are such great guys, and they share a bond that exists forever.

I spent a lot of time off the air with Ned. The three of us would go out after every game for dinner on the road, so I was very close to Ned. In fact, Ned worked three years after Ken retired, so I was still with him. He was a great broadcaster, certainly a man of letters. He had great command of the language. He and Ken were

very similar in many ways, in terms of their style. Ned was very unassuming, and I don't think realized for a very long time how important he was to the fandom of New England. He didn't really have an ego.

We used to talk about a lot of things, mostly baseball, but we used to argue about things. I used to get on him about being a Republican. He'd tell me about World War II. He was a Marine. Iwo Jima. He was 18 when he joined. And he was very loyal to Duke, his alma mater where I think he went his freshman year, joined the Marines, and then I think he went back to Duke. He was bummed out about their football. He was much more a football fan than a basketball fan. Actually, he went to live right near Duke. He went to Clarksville, Virginia, which is about 45 minutes from Duke. We had a lot of good times with Ned on the road, a lot of fun discussion about different subjects. Baseball was always at the core. Many times it would revert to '67, because it was just a constant theme with Ken and Ned. They were such a part of it.

Ned was a really fun guy. We had a lot of good times. He more or less under-stated things, which was very effective, the way he did it. Hated TV. Much preferred radio, although he did the last 13 or 14 years on TV alone. No radio. But radio was his first love. I think he did much of the radio in '67, because they had the crossover. I don't know how many games were on TV that year. I would guess about 40 to start, and they might have added up to 50 or 60. There were still a lot of games that weren't televised. I'm sure they added as the season went on.

We used to go to the beach, the three of us, all the time in Anaheim—a beach that Dick Williams showed us, in fact—Laguna Beach. Otherwise known as the Hardbelly Beach. Beautiful scenery, both of the human and natural side. It was a beach Dick Williams told Ken and Ned about in '67. They went there right up until their retirement.

And I still go. Crescent Beach is the name of it. The restaurants and the beach. They wouldn't go to the Rock and Roll Hall of Fame, but we really had a lot of fun traveling in those days. We would be together almost every night to dissect the games on the road. In those days on the road, we had group dinners, usually with the broadcasters and Jack Rogers to take us all out on the road. Those things don't happen any more. Jack took us all out, always the best places in town, and of course picked up the tab. "Did you hear anything about tonight yet? Don't make any plans! What did Jack say?" He'd always come through.

We had great fun in those days, always great baseball discussions. I had a lot of fun with both Ken and Ned. I still keep in touch with their sons.

Ned and Ken set standards I emulated. They were never bigger than the game or the players....never tried to manage or general manager the club...and realized they were the eyes of the listener first and foremost....

When the Red sox finally won it all in 2004, I wanted to pay tribute to Ned and Ken. While I did not prescript my last out call, I did plan and did follow up by saying, "and to quote the late, great Ned Martin, 'there is pandemonium on the field.'" I also ended the broadcast that night, as I do now at the end of every season by following a tradition started by Ken in quoting from Bart Giamatti's *Green Fields of the Mind....* "it breaks your heart, it is designed to break your heart....."

Interview done by Bill Nowlin, December 23, 2005

Partners

by Ken Coleman

In 1967 I did play-by-play on both radio and TV as head of the three-man crew that included Ned Martin and Mel Parnell. It was more enjoyable doing both, rather than one or the other; and I think in that situation, a broadcaster has a tendency to do a little better job because of being less likely to fall into a rut. Doing radio and TV keeps you a little sharper, I think.

In '67 we broadcast all the games on radio and 56 games on TV. When we were doing a TV game, I would broadcast the first three innings on TV, the middle three on radio, and the last three on TV. Ned Martin would do just the opposite, 3-3-3 on radio-TV-radio.

My three associates in the broadcasting booth in 1967 were Ned Martin, Mel Parnell, and Al Walker.

Ned was the veteran. Ned broke in with the Red Sox along with Carl Yastrzemski in 1961 following five years of broadcasting minor league ball in Charleston, West Virginia. From 1961 to 1966, Ned was part of some terrible Boston teams. That's why 1967 was a very special time in his life. He loves the game, and he responded beautifully to the excitement of the Impossible Dream. The team was winning, there were big crowds, lots of drama. I know it meant a lot to Ned.

Ken Coleman.

In my opinion Ned is the consummate professional and one of the best broadcasters ever to have been associated with baseball. I have been blessed to work with Ned as a colleague and know him as a friend. He's intelligent, astute, well read, and wonderfully sensitive.

My other colleague in the booth that year was Mel Parnell. Mel handled color commentary on radio and TV and lent creative insight to our broadcasts. Mel was easy to work with and dependable. Also, the fact that he was—along with Babe Ruth—the premier left-handed pitcher in Red Sox history lent a unique perspective to our work in 1967.

The final member of the booth crew was Al Walker, our engineer. Al...started engineering Boston baseball in 1952 and continued until the early seventies. During the course of those years, Al probably saw more Red Sox games than anyone else alive. Al was a quiet, intense guy and one of the most conscientious workers I've ever met. He'd come to the park at 2 pm to check all the equipment and make sure everything was okay and set up right for a night game. I remember Al drumming his fingers on his console. That was a habit of his. And before each game, he would say, "Go get 'em, kids."

These three men gave us probably the strongest broadcasting team in all of baseball in 1967. Certainly that comes across on each relistening of *The Impossible Dream* record album we did following the '67 season. That record went on to become the greatest selling sports album in history and sold more than 100,000 copies.

From *The Impossible Dream Remembered* by Ken Coleman and Dan Valenti (Lexington MA: Stephen Greene Press, 1987).

Was it really "Impossible"?

by Mark Armour

In the past generation or so, we have learned a lot about how baseball players and teams are likely to evolve, although there are still enough surprises to warrant watching the games. I have often wondered whether more modern thinking would have better prepared us for some of the "surprise" player and team breakthroughs of the past. It seems likely, to state just one example, that there were plenty of signs that the 1969 New York Mets were a team on the rise, though obviously a 27-game improvement could not have been anticipated.

Growing up in New England, it was an article of faith that the 1967 Red Sox won the American League pennant with the help of divine intervention—that it was an "Impossible Dream." With the passage of time, this depiction has become less satisfying, if for no other reason than it gives short shrift to the people who actually built the team. Ken Coleman and Dan Valenti, in 1987's otherwise enjoyable *The Impossible Dream Remembered*, wrote: "The real miracle of 1967 is that it happened, not as the conscious effort applied to a preconceived plan, but in spite of just about everything." Notwithstanding this supposed lack of either effort or a plan, Dick O'Connell, the team's principal architect, was honored with the *Sporting News* Executive of the Year award.

Suffice it to say that no one saw it coming. Perusing several 1967 preseason publications, most of them envisioned the Red Sox finishing either ninth (as they had in 1966) or tenth in the ten-team American League. *Sports Illustrated* came the closest to expressing optimism, saying: "If [manager Dick Williams] can find some pitching, too, the 1967 Sox may revive baseball in Boston."

The Red Sox had been a sad outfit for several years. After a nice five year run in the late 1940s, fueled mainly by players signed and nurtured by the organization, the club wasted the last decade of Ted Williams' great career because they stopped developing talent. Joe Cronin became the team's general manager after the 1947 season, which is about the time that the well ran dry. The 1950s teams more or less treaded water, usually finishing third or fourth, but never sniffing a pennant race.

The Red Sox were also, of course, the last team to field an African-American player—second baseman Pumpsie Green in 1959—and it is tempting to blame their continued mediocrity on this organizational bigotry. Obviously, if the Red Sox had aggressively signed black players in the 1950s they might have won several pennants, but one could claim the same thing about every team in the league. The entire American League lagged pitifully behind the Nationals in this area, leading to a talent gap that was not eliminated until the 1980s. More to the point, the Red Sox weren't signing many good white players either.

The team finally cratered in 1960, Williams' coda, finishing seventh (of eight) at 65-89, their worst record in 28 years. The next six seasons were similarly dreary, with placements between sixth and ninth in the new ten-team league. The club was also unpopular, playing before crowds of eight or ten thousand people (although many other teams weren't drawing much better—only four AL teams reached a million in attendance in 1965, and only five in 1966). The Red Sox were playing in what was seen to be an old decaying ballpark, and their owner, Tom Yawkey, was trying desperately to hitch a ride on the new stadium bandwagon sweeping the nation.

Not only did the team play poorly, it was filled with "colorful" mediocrities. When Dick Williams finished his career with the Sox in 1963 and 1964, he complained about the lazy, careless attitudes of the veterans, whom he believed were rubbing off on the young guys. They were a lousy team loaded with funny stories—Dick Stuart pestering manager Johnny Pesky, Gene Conley getting drunk and trying to book a flight to Jerusalem—it was all great fun. The team's best player was a relief pitcher, Dick Radatz, who was called upon often enough that he was worn out after four great years. The team's general manager, Mike Higgins,

Was it destiny or by design? *L to R: Haywood Sullivan, Dick Williams, and Dick O'Connell—the new regime in place.*

Yaz worked exceptionally hard throughout the winter of 1966-67, and the conditioning paid off big-time.

was an old drinking buddy of Yawkey's, having been a player (twice) and manager (twice) for the team before taking over control of the organization in 1961.

A turning point in team history took place on September 16, 1965, the night that Dave Morehead no-hit the Indians at Fenway Park. Morehead did not have much of a career, perhaps partly because he was upstaged after the biggest game of his life. After the game, it was announced that Higgins had been mercifully cashiered and that Dick O'Connell would take his place atop the organization. O'Connell had joined the Red Sox in 1949 as assistant farm director, and climbed the ladder through hard work and competence—he was the first Red Sox GM who was not a personal friend of Yawkey. In the past six years he had been a team Vice President, quietly working with farm director Neal Mahoney to rebuild a long-neglected minor league organization. O'Connell was one of the most important people in the history of the franchise, arguably the best general manager the team has ever had.

Dick Williams, whom O'Connell hired to manage in 1967, is often credited with instituting the youth movement that propelled the team to contention. In fact, the philosophical shift started with O'Connell and manager Billy Herman in 1966. By the middle of that season, O'Connell had disposed of most of the old or middle aged players that he inherited—Bill Monboquette, Ed Bressoud, Lee Thomas, Felix Mantilla, Dick Radatz, Frank Malzone, and Earl Wilson, among them. Truth be told, the crop of players he got in return was not impressive, but O'Connell properly ascertained that he needed to start over.

When the dust settled, O'Connell had kept but three regular players from the 1965 team. Carl Yastrzemski was the lone success story in the team's repeated investments in "bonus babies" in the 1950s, signing in

1959, tearing up two minor leagues and taking over left field in 1961. He was seen as a disappointment to many who had wanted him to be the next Ted Williams, but he won the 1963 batting title, and led the league in on-base percentage and slugging percentage in 1965. Tony Conigliaro, an immensely popular swinger from nearby Revere, had burst on the scene with 24 homers in 111 games as a 19-year-old in 1964, following up with a home run title in 1965. Shortstop Rico Petrocelli was a 1965 rookie who had shown some promise on offense (18 home runs in 1966) and defense.

Now that he was at the wheel, O'Connell was ready to show off more of his system. Joe Foy, the 1965 third baseman for Toronto, was the MVP of the International League, winning the batting title and socking 14 home runs. George Scott, a third sacker for Pittsfield, was the MVP of the Eastern League, winning the league's Triple Crown. Two young third basemen—what to do? Herman moved Scott to first base a week into the season, and put both players in the lineup. Scott began the season on a tear, and actually started the All-Star Game, cooling off to hit .245 with 27 home runs. Foy was even better. His rate stats were impressive (.262/.364/.413), especially at a time when the league averages were .240/.304/.369. He improved substantially during the year, hitting .213 with four home runs in the first half, and .303 with 11 home runs thereafter. It was a great rookie year, and Foy looked to be a rising star.

With five positions now held by promising young players, two positions were manned by young players who did not develop—catcher Mike Ryan and second baseman George Smith—and a coterie of temps shared center field.

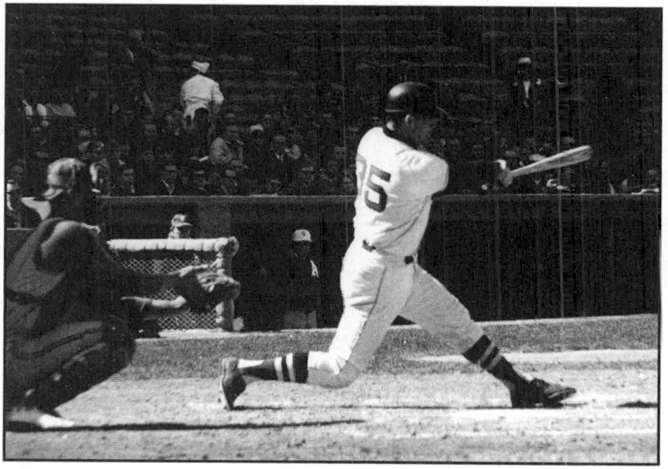

Notice all the empty early-season seats as Russ Gibson takes a cut.

The pitching staff was less promising. Monbouquette and Wilson had been the best two hurlers on the squad over the past several seasons, but both were gone. Monbouquette's effective days were behind him, but Wilson, supposedly traded for exposing the team's association with a segregated night club in spring training, would have been quite a help in 1967. The two pitchers who O'Connell kept were Morehead, who failed repeated trials over the next few years, and Jim Lonborg, a promising but erratic hard-throwing right-hander. By mid-year, Herman was using José Santiago (25), Lee Stange (29), Dennis Bennett (26) and Darrell Brandon (25) with Lonborg (24) in the rotation.

The 1966 Red Sox finished ninth at 72-90, which was one-half game better than the Yankees. Although the Orioles made short work of the pennant race, there was quite a four-team dogfight for the basement. The Red Sox seemed to have it well in hand most of year, reaching 29-51 on July 4 and holding 10th place into September, but, as usual, they were "overtaken" by the Yankees down the stretch. The Senators and Athletics, perennial losers in the 1960s, finished just off the pace.

In 1967 the team continued to mine the talent from its system. Dick Williams, who managed the Triple-A club in Toronto to consecutive championships in 1965 and 1966, was installed as the new Red Sox skipper. Williams brought the two best players from his Toronto team with him to Boston: switch-hitting center fielder Reggie Smith, who had won the batting title (.320) and hit 18 home runs; and second baseman Mike Andrews, who had hit .267 but with patience (89 walks) and power (14 home runs). As with Foy and Scott in 1966, Smith and Andrews walked right in and filled huge holes on the team.

To summarize, entering the 1967 season the Red Sox had good or promising young players at seven of the eight positions. Outfielders Yastrzemski (27) and Conigliaro (22) were established stars. Infielders Scott (23) and Foy (24) were two of the better young players in the league. Petrocelli (24) was making progress, and Smith (22) and Andrews (23) were prized rookies. Only at catcher, where Mike Ryan and Russ Gibson would share the load, was the solution less encouraging. Remarkably, all nine of these players came out of Neil Mahoney's farm system; all but Yastrzemski in just the last three years. The pitching staff began the season with the same young arms as the previous year, plus Billy Rohr, who had won 14 games for Williams in Toronto.

Most observers conceded the 1967 pennant to the

Within just a couple of years, GM O'Connell's Red Sox featured a good number of African American ballplayers. Here veteran catcher Elston Howard talks with a worn and weary Tom Yawkey.

Orioles. After romping through the AL in 1966, the O's had summarily swept the Dodgers in the World Series. The club had a few middle-aged stars—Frank Robinson (30), Brooks Robinson (29), and Luis Aparicio (32)—but they were showing no signs of slowing down. The rest of the starting lineup was in their early 20s, and Steve Barber, at 27, was the old man of a deep and talented pitching staff.

The rest of the league was fairly easy to sort out as well. The toughest challenge was likely to come from the Twins, who had won the pennant in 1965 and had as much front line talent as any team in the league. The Tigers and White Sox had been threatening for a few years, and would likely stay in contention through most of the summer. The Indians and the Angels had enough young talent to scramble for the fifth and sixth slots. The four clubs that had waged the classic battle for the cellar in 1966—New York, Washington, Kansas City and Boston—were generally picked to finish near the bottom of the league again.

The American League race generally worked out the way everyone had thought, except for two wrinkles: the Orioles, the overwhelming favorite, finished tied for sixth, and the Red Sox, a consensus also-ran, held off the three teams expected to challenge the Orioles, and played in the World Series. How in the world could such a thing have happened?

First of all, Baltimore was beset with a passel of misfortune. Boog Powell had a terrible season, Frank Robinson was injured much of the year, and the teams' two best pitchers, Dave McNally and Jim Palmer, got hurt, the latter derailing his great career for two full seasons. The Orioles outscored their opponents 654-592, totals that would typically yield a won-loss record of about 88-73, yet they finished 12 games worse, at 76-85. The 1967 season turned out to be a stumble in the road for the Orioles, who quickly retooled and became one of history's great teams by 1969.

With a surprising vacancy at the top, four teams spent much of the summer locked in a legendary pennant race, won by the Red Sox on the last day of the season. The other three contenders—Minnesota, Detroit and Chicago—came away from this great race feeling as if they had let it slip away, that a blown game or series here or there had cost them their chance at the flag. But let's face it: it was a great season and a great race, but these were not great teams. They were fine ballclubs with discernible weaknesses. The Red Sox' 92 wins were the fewest ever for an American League champion (before the league split into divisions).

The Red Sox vaulted from ninth to first place, it is true, but that fact overstates their improvement. The club's record increased by "only" 20 wins, from 72 to 92, which is impressive but not historically unusual. In 1967 alone, the St. Louis Cardinals, the NL champs, improved by 18 wins (83 to 101), and the Cubs by 28 (59 to 87). The 1965 Twins advanced by 23 wins (79 to 102), the 1969 Mets by 27 (73 to 100).

What makes the Red Sox leap look so dramatic is that they were playing in a highly compressed league. In 1966, the Yankees winning percentage of .440 was the "best" last place showing in American League history (again, before the league split in to divisions). The 10th-place Yankees were just 16.5 games behind

the 2nd-place Twins, whose winning percentage was .549. The only team that separated itself from this pack—the Orioles—collapsed in 1967, creating a unique confluence of events for the Red Sox.

Another thing largely missed from the Red Sox' escape from the cellar in September 1966: they stood at 29-51 on the Fourth of July, but finished 43-39, only one-half game worse than the Orioles. It was the pitching staff which fueled the improvement, as the team's ERA improved from 4.42 in the first half (easily the worst in the league) to 3.43 in the second half (basically the league average), playing in the worst pitcher's park in the league. Jim Lonborg (6-3, 2.91), Lee Stange (6-5, 2.53) and Darrell Brandon (7-6, 3.31) were all dramatically better at the end of the year.

Another way to look at the 1965-67 Red Sox is to divide each season into 81 game halves.

		W-L	Pct.
1965	**first half**	**31-50**	**.383**
1965	**second half**	**31-50**	**.383**
1966	**first half**	**30-51**	**.370**
1966	**second half**	**42-39**	**.519**
1967	**first half**	**42-39**	**.519**
1967	**second half**	**50-31**	**.617**

The Red Sox were remarkably consistently for a season and a half, before melding into a competitive squad in mid-1966. While it should not be ignored that this club was hopelessly out of the pennant race in the second half, an 81-game sample size is compelling evidence of genuine improvement. The 1967 team's promising start was really just a carryover from the previous year. Fueled by the emergence of a few of their young players and several key mid-season acquisitions, the team found another gear in July 1967, and completed their storybook campaign.

Should we have foreseen the 1967 Red Sox winning the pennant? No, of course not. A 20-win improvement is too much to expect, no matter the quality of the young talent. What's more, the collapse of the Orioles was a necessary component to the Red Sox dream season, and was similarly unlikely.

That being said, there were many reasons to be optimistic about the Red Sox. They showed real improvement in the latter half of the 1966 season. Their young core of position players was as promising as anyone's. They were playing in a historically compressed league, allowing for large gains in the standings with only a handful of additional wins. They had a new young manager who was committed to the youngsters. Considering all of this, no one should have been surprised by a 10-game improvement, to 80-85 wins.

Furthermore, everything did not go right for the 1967 Red Sox. Joe Foy, who had been one of the best young players in baseball in 1966, regressed a bit and spent a lot of time on the bench in the second half, as Williams became more enamored with Dalton Jones and Jerry Adair. Foy had on-base skills that were unappreciated in his time, and his career petered out while he was still a productive player. Tony Conigliaro, a 22-year-old veteran, was in the midst of perhaps his finest season when it was brutally terminated by a fastball to the left eye on August 18. Darrell Brandon had finished 1966 with a flourish and broke camp as the team's #2 starter, but finished 5-11, 4.17. Billy Rohr, the rookie who began the season as the #3 starter and just missed a no-hitter in his first major league game in Yankee Stadium, was back in the minor leagues by June.

Of course, several young players did break out with big years, including Petrocelli, Scott, Lonborg, and especially Yastrzemski. Yaz's season (.326/.418/.622) was the best by any player in the 1960s, and was likely responsible for a good chunk of the 20-game improvement. But the team had so many young players who had either shown ability in the major leagues or in the high minors that it only needed a few of them to break out.

O'Connell also made several astute pickups during the year. He landed Gary Bell from the Indians in June, and Bell became the team's second dependable starter (12-8, 3.16). The Sox also acquired Jerry Adair, Norm Siebern, and Elston Howard, all of whom played important roles. A few days after Conigliaro's beaning, Ken Harrelson fell into the team's lap after he was released by the Kansas City Athletics in a fit of pique by Charlie Finley.

The Red Sox' organizational improvement was sustained. Consider what happened next. In 1968 Conigliaro missed the entire season to his eye injury, Lonborg broke his leg, stalling his career for several years, and Scott suffered through a ridiculously ghastly season (.171/.236/.237). Despite all of this, the team finished 86-76, a drop of just six games, an accomplishment every bit as astonishing as their "Impossible Dream."

The combination of the big injuries and the emergence of the great Orioles teams kept the Red Sox away from pennant races for a few years, but Boston ran off 16 consecutive winning seasons, one of the

Lonborg, Waslewski, Bell, and Ryan watch the highlight film in December 1967 and reaffirm that the Impossible Dream really did occur.

longest streaks in baseball history. The talent from Dick O'Connell's farm system continued unabated, producing All-Stars Sparky Lyle, Carlton Fisk, Bill Lee, Cecil Cooper, Ben Oglivie, Dwight Evans, Jim Rice, Rick Burleson, and Fred Lynn by 1974. The homegrown team that emerged in the mid-1970s was better than the 1967 outfit.

Dick O'Connell would run the team until forced out by a new ownership regime in 1976. The organization he presided over enjoyed the most sustained success the team has had in the past 50 years. Although the team has enjoyed success again in the new century, the organization has never matched the crop of homegrown talent it produced in the O'Connell years.

The season was obviously not "Impossible," since it happened, but that makes it no less magical and heartwarming to have lived through.

Raise a glass.

Note: a version of this article originally appeared at www.baseball-prospectus.com.

The Cardiac Kids

by Harvey Soolman

The Boston Red Sox embarked on their 1967 season with a five-man rotation that had collectively won only 25 major league games in 1966 and with a starting lineup that averaged less than 24 years of age.

Baseball Digest declared the Red Sox might be "respectable if they got a little pitching." Most everyone else expected very little, and in Las Vegas oddsmakers booked them at up to 100-1 odds to win the pennant.

In a poll of writers, *The Sporting News* pegged the Bosox for a third consecutive ninth place finish, Til Ferdenzi in *Street & Smith's Yearbook* predicted likewise, *Baseball Yearbook* moved them up to seventh, but *Baseball Guidebook* saw the Sox dead last.

Locally, the *Boston Globe* had the club finishing sixth and openly conceded their generosity. And though the team's only two proven stars, Carl Yastrzemski and Tony Conigliaro, predicted a fifth-place first division finish, there was a generation of dwindling Red Sox fans growing up that was becoming all too accustomed to rooting for a second-division team.

Most pundits counted on the World Champion Baltimore Orioles to repeat atop the American League. Others picked the Minnesota Twins, winners of the 1965 AL flag, while some predicted it would be the Detroit Tigers making their move to take the pennant.

The Red Sox? Only Yastrzemski and Conigliaro among their starting position players had at least three seasons in the big leagues. Shortstop Rico Petrocelli had two full seasons under his belt; infielders Joe Foy and George Scott were coming off rather successful 1966 rookie seasons; catcher Mike Ryan had appeared in 150 major league games over parts of three seasons; and rookies Reggie Smith and Mike Andrews had each made but brief appearances at the end of the previous campaign.

The eight position starters combined for merely 14 full major league seasons and no starter other than Yaz or Tony had hit over .262 in the majors. Likewise, their projected starting pitchers (Jim Lonborg, Darrell Brandon, rookie Billy Rohr, and Dennis Bennett) brought a total of eight years major league experience along with a 65-73 cumulative record. The 1967 Boston Red Sox were, according to *Dell Sports* magazine's March 1967 issue, "a cast of juveniles unmatched in the majors."

Thirty-seven-year-old rookie manager Dick Williams vowed throughout spring camp that his team would win more than they would lose. While that seemed overly optimistic to some, that's just what the 1966 Red Sox had done over their final 83 games, compiling a 44-39 record but still managing only to climb out of an early summer cellar to finish ninth. And surprisingly, with fortunes on the rise, manager Billy Herman was released with 16 games left on the schedule.

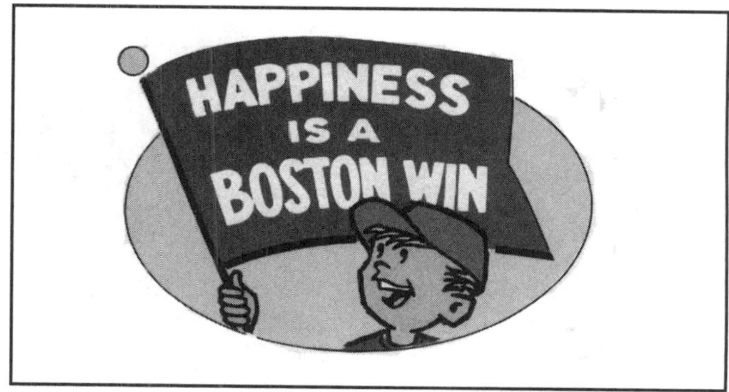

No Red Sox team had finished above .500 since 1958, the last time a Boston team finished in the first division.

When Lonborg and Wyatt combined on a July 9 shutout on the final game before the All-Star Break, the Red Sox record was 41-39. As Williams had predicted, they won more than they lost—at least to the season's midpoint—and were sitting unexpectedly in fifth place only six games off the lead. Not that playing .500 ball through the first half of the season had been boring. The Red Sox had made the American League stand up and take notice, and the excitement had begun to build, the losses often being as heart-stopping as many of the victories.

The standings at the All-Star break:

1. Chicago	47-33	
2. Detroit	45-35	-2
3. Minnesota	45-36	-2½
4. California	45-40	-4½
5. Boston	41-39	-6

Manager Williams said that for the first two months he wasn't managing a team, he was making a point. The Red Sox were playing exciting baseball, and they were playing as a team. No one was above a sacrifice bunt, and in one double switch Williams even removed Yastrzemski from the game.

The Red Sox returned to action following the break

and split a doubleheader at home against the Orioles. Stange won the first game with a save from Wyatt, and The Kids won despite getting only four hits. Petrocelli had a two-run single. Bell got lit up in the nightcap with eight hits and six runs in 4⅓, and Baltimore thumped their hosts, 10-0.

Despite being stomped on in that second game, Williams left his entire starting lineup in for two full games. Ryan caught all 18 innings.

On July 14, Lonborg won his 12th game and Yaz hit his 20th home run. The next afternoon, Waslewski walked the first two Orioles and went 2-0 on the next hitter, Paul Blair. Williams pulled the trigger right then and brought in José Santiago. Blair ripped a line drive to Foy's left. The Sox third baseman lunged, snared it, and turned a 5-4-3 triple play to get out of the inning. Santiago hurled six, and Bell came on in relief to finish with three scoreless frames, while Boston scored four in its half of the inning on four singles and an error. Foy (3-for-4) singled, tripled, and doubled in his first three trips to the plate.

Boston took the next two from the Tigers, and with four straight wins in the bag, the Sox took to the road, beating the Orioles twice in Baltimore, thanks to a couple of five-run frames.

Boston was now in third place, only 1½ games out. They had picked up 4½ games in the standings in just the eight games since the All-Star Break.

On to Cleveland for a four-game weekend set. Darrell Brandon threw a seven-hit complete game. Stange threw a stunning three-hit shutout on Saturday, facing only 30 batters.

The Sox took two on Sunday, with Conigliaro homering in each game, and Joe Foy hitting his second grand slam of the year. That summer's hit by Sonny and Cher seemed to say it all: "The Beat Goes On." Gary Bell beat his old mates a second time, 5-1, with a nifty five-hit complete game.

Ten wins in a row—the final six on the road. With the exception of Petrocelli starting in the first game of the streak, neither the starting lineup nor the batting order had changed. Ryan caught all 10 games, including his third twinbill of the season. The Red Sox had outscored their opposition 67-26 and 37-5 in the first three innings. The Sox had only trailed for three innings in the entire 10-game stretch—the first three innings, 1-0, of the 10th game.

Conigliaro had batted .424 with four home runs and 12 RBIs. Smith hit .395 with hits in nine games. Yastrzemski was .371 with five home runs and 11 RBIs. In one eight-game stretch, Foy sizzled at 15-for-33 (.455) with 10 RBIs. Lonborg won three games.

More importantly, Boston climbed from fifth place, six games back, to second place, just a half a game behind Chicago. California was two back, Detroit three, Minnesota three-and-a-half, and defending champion Baltimore, victimized four times in the Sox rampage, was in eighth place, 10½ out, and never again to be seen in the fray.

It was July 23. Boston was in a pennant race. And The Kids were coming home.

Their charter touched down at Boston's Logan Airport in the early morning hours of July 24, a Monday morning. The plane was greeted by an estimated 10,000 excited baseball fans—more fans than had been in the stands for nine of the club's first 15 home dates.

California won one, but lost the next two—Boston winning the rubber game after scoring three runs to tie it in the bottom of the ninth. Reggie Smith tripled and Adair spanked a grounder through the legs of Paul Schaal, who had come on defensively that half inning. And the ballgame was over.

The euphoria took a little beating after that. Minnesota came to town, five games out and in fifth place, and proceeded to take three of the first four games in a five-game set.

The Twins had now moved up a notch to fourth, four games out and two games behind second-place Boston, with one more game to play in Beantown. Stange came up huge and shut the Twins out on just

No hiding behind masks for the Cardiac Kids. L to R: Bob Tillman, Russ Gibson, and Mike Ryan.

Reggie Smith hit three homers, Yaz hit two, and both Petrocelli and Adair hit one, as the Red Sox took two from California. August 20, 1967.

three singles, 4-0. The right-hander walked none and dispensed with the powerful Twins in two hours and 15 minutes. The Red Sox had only four hits themselves, but one was Yastzremski's 26th round-tripper, a three-run job in the third. Stange himself knocked in the fourth run with a sacrifice fly.

When the Red Sox went back on the road, they were still clinging to second place, two games behind Chicago. They took with them a newly-acquired catcher, the Yankees veteran of several World Series, Elston Howard.

The trip took Boston into Minnesota, where the Twins took three straight and allowed the Sox but one run. Merritt threw a shutout, Boswell threw a three-hit complete game to defeat Stange, 3-1, and Chance capped off the miserable visit with a rain-shortened perfect game to get the better of Lonborg for the second time in 10 days. For the series, Boston got eight hits to go along with their solitary run. By the time the Red Sox left the Twin Cities, Cal Ermer's bunch had vaulted past them in the standings and into second place by a percentage point, 2½ games back.

It was a dismal 2-7 road trip and no thousands of fans waited for the club at Logan Airport. The Red Sox, by virtue of being swept by both Minnesota and California, returned home to face the Tigers on August 15 having sunk to fifth place:

1. Minnesota	63-50	
2. Chicago	61-50	-1
3. Detroit	62-52	-1½
4. California	62-54	-2½
5. Boston	60-53	-3

There were 49 games left, and the Sox would play 29 of them at home.

Smith and Scott jump-started the homestand with first-inning home runs. Dave Morehead spread out six hits and blanked Detroit, 4-0. In the second game of the set, Scott and Smith again homered in the first. The Boomer added his second two-runner in the third as Boston defeated Detroit's McLain for the third time that season. Brandon pitched seven innings of relief to finish the game and pick up the win.

Boston had cooled off, going just 10-14 since their 10-game winning streak. They were now 62-54 and in fourth place, but still in striking distance, 3½ behind Minnesota, whose starting pitching had allowed eight runs over seven straight wins—a streak that was ⅓ inning short of seven straight complete games and a streak that swept three-game sets from both Chicago and California. Minnesota was now at their high mark of the season to date: 65-50, a game-and-a-half up on Chicago.

California came to town on Friday night, August 18. The Red Sox won the ball game, 3-2. Gary Bell threw a complete game and limited the Angels to four hits—none for 6 ⅓ until Jimmie Hall's first of two home runs. Bell himself had a double and an RBI single. But this game would always be remembered as the game that a fastball from Jack Hamilton ran in on Tony Conigliaro and crushed his face, almost killing him and most certainly ruining his career and changing the course of his life.

Conigliaro was only 22 years old but already in his fourth full major league season. He hung in close to the plate and got hit by his share of pitches. In the second inning he had singled off Hamilton. Some joker threw a smoke bomb into the left field corner just before he came to bat in the fourth with two out and nobody on. After a brief delay, Tony stepped into the box to face Hamilton, who would hit only two batters over 150 innings for the Mets and Angels in 1967.

Conigliaro's good friend Petrocelli was the first to reach him as he lay face down in the dirt and in agony. Blood filled his nose and mouth and made breathing difficult. His left eye was already closing. It was a horrible sight not made any easier when they carried him from the field on a stretcher. Tartabull ran for Tony, and Petrocelli stepped up and hit a triple, scoring when Fregosi made an error on the play.

The Sox took the ball game and advanced to third place. A pall hung over the season, though. The initial hopes were that Conigliaro might return in September, reports by the following afternoon were beginning to say that he was probably lost for the season. Tony C had been the team's cleanup hitter for three months. Despite missing 22 of the club's 117 games for injury or military duty, he was among the league leaders with a .287 average, 20 home runs, and 67 runs batted in.

The on-field concern was Conigliaro's immediate replacement. On the bench, the Sox had Tartabull and Thomas. Jim Landis, a five-time Gold Glove winner (though one who hadn't hit over .250 since 1961), was released by the Tigers on the very day Tony was beaned; he was signed by the Sox on August 23.

August 18 became the launching pad for another Red Sox hot-streak. They proceeded to win seven in a row without their young slugger and nine out of ten. Whereas the 10-game winning streak in July

got folks' attention, propelled the Sox into serious contention, and attracted a mob scene at the airport, this less-celebrated skein carried them into first place as September arrived. And though Boston would still suffer their lumps to the finish line, after this winning streak they would never again be more than one game out of first place—42 games and 42 days—miraculously even though they would sink to third place on four different occasions.

By the time they left Boston, California was effectively out of the race. The Red Sox then took four out of five from Washington—all taut, one- or two-run ball games—and it was off to Chicago for a five-game set with the White Sox, who with a 7-3 run against non-contending teams, had moved back into first.

The standings as the square-off in Chicago began:

1. Chicago	69-54	
Boston	70-55	-.001
3. Minnesota	69-55	-½
Detroit	69-57	-1½

The second-place Red Sox came into Chicago trailing the White Sox by .001 and took three out of five. They nonetheless left town still trailing by .001 because Minnesota had taken three out of four in Cleveland and overtaken both Sox teams.

Nothing was coming easy at this point. In New York, the Red Sox won three of four, but then returned home and lost three out of four to the visiting White Sox.

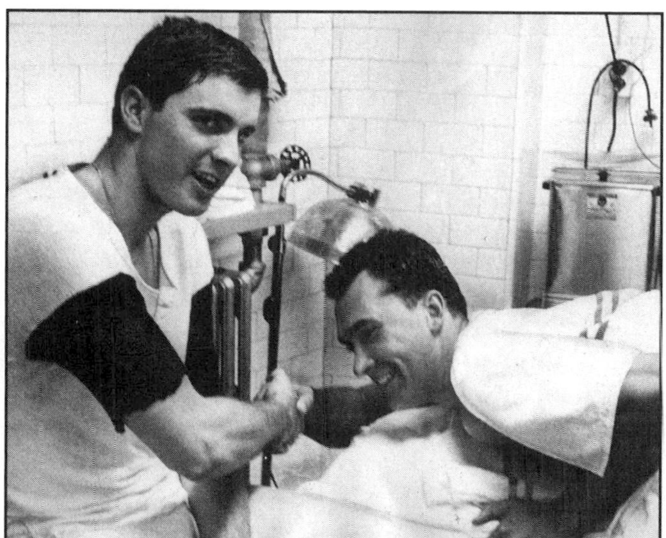

The June 15 game was a Cardiac Kids special as Gary Waslewski held the White Sox scoreless through nine. The game went into extra innings, 0-0. John Wyatt gave up a run in the top of the 11th, but Joe Foy hit a two-out single and Tony C (depicted here with Waslewski) hit a two-run homer.

By September 7, though, the standings were beyond belief:

1. Chicago	78-61	.561151
Minnesota	78-61	.561151
Boston	79-62	.560284
4. Detroit	79-62	.560284

Yes, .000867 separated the four teams.

Boston won three of four from New York at home, but lost ground—even dropping to third for two days, though only half a game out—as Minnesota took four of five in Baltimore.

Lonborg downed Kansas City at home for his 20th win, 3-1, on September 12. Boston swept the two-game set, 4-2, on the 13th while Minnesota won two of three in Washington, which left them tied for the top.

Chicago slipped to fourth, three games back, but then swept a three-game set from Minnesota back home. When the Red Sox lost at home to Baltimore on September 15, there was a three-way tie for first:

1. Boston	84-64	
Detroit	84-64	
Minnesota	84-64	
4. Chicago	83-66	-1½

But after Baltimore was through taking three in Boston, Chicago dispensed with Minnesota and Detroit was taking two of three from Washington there was a new leader on September 17:

1. Detroit	85-65	
2. Chicago	85-66	-½
3. Boston	84-66	-1
Minnesota	84-66	-1

With only 12 games left to play, Boston headed to Detroit for a two-game showdown. The Sox chased McLain in the third inning. Norm Cash hit two solo home runs, though, and Jim Northrup's double in the eighth gave Detroit a 5-4 advantage. Then with one out in the ninth, Yastrzemski (3-for-4, two RBIs) drilled one into the upper deck in right field to tie the game; and Dalton Jones, who hadn't started a game since September 7 (he was 4-for-5 with two RBIs), led off the 10th with a homer likewise to the upper deck for the 6-5 win and a tie for first place—well, a three-way tie for first since Kaat shut out Kansas City on six hits, 2-0, in 10 innings. And the White Sox lost a squeaker, 3-2, in

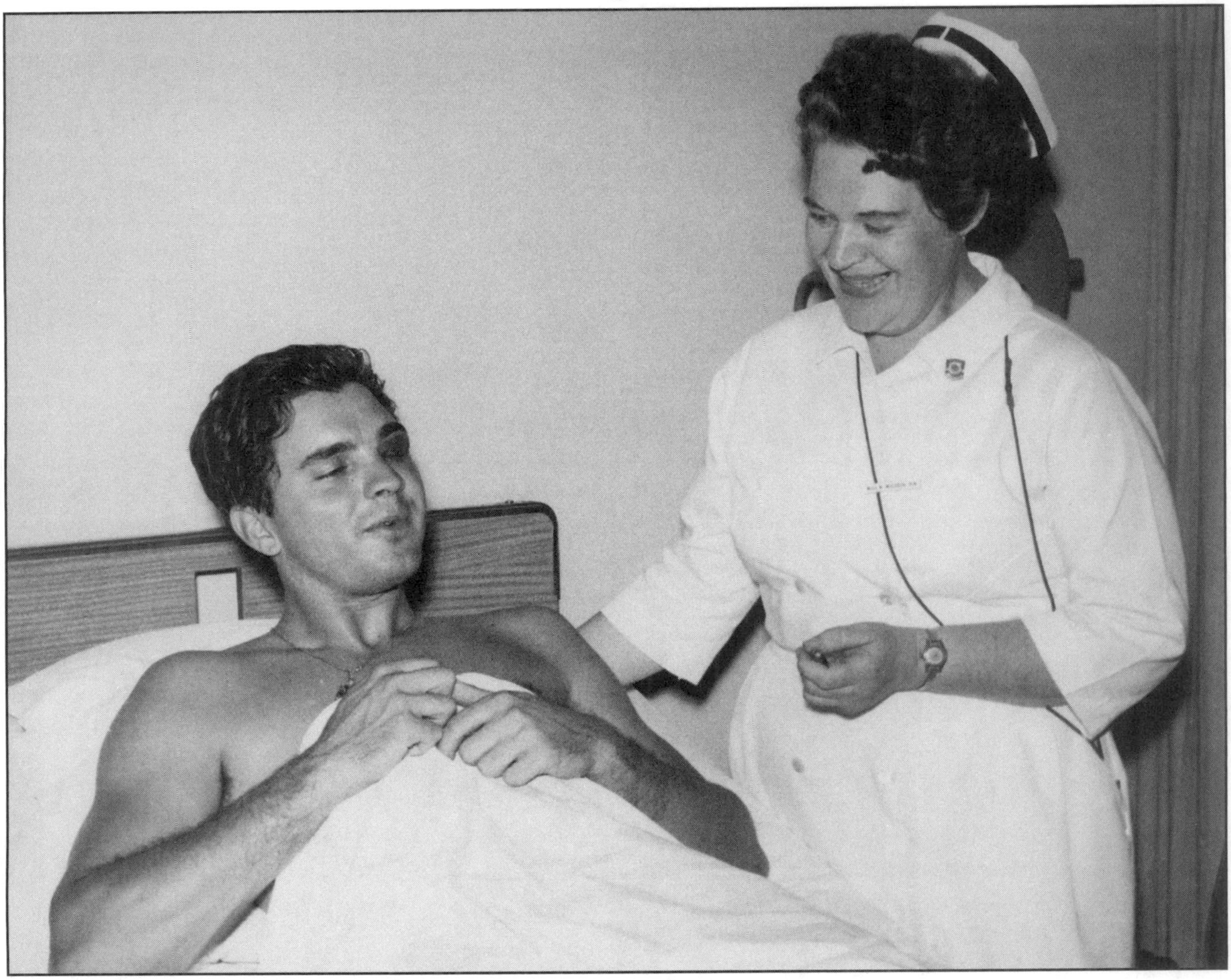

Tony Conigliaro recovering from his season-ending injury at Sancta Maria Hospital.

California to remain just a half-game out.

On September 19, Lolich fanned 13 Red Sox and held a 2-1 lead as he entered the ninth. Adair opened with a single. Tartabull ran for him. Yaz walked, and Scott singled to knot the score. Wilson came in for Lolich, and a wild pitch and Gibson sacrifice fly later, the Sox took a one-game lead on the Tigers—but not before two fine defensive plays by Yastrzemski and Smith in the ninth and Bill Landis coming on to strike out Eddie Mathews locked it up. The Twins beat Kansas City to keep pace with Boston, and Horlen shut out California to keep the White Sox a half-game off.

In Cleveland on September 20, the Red Sox were leading, 4-2, when Tony Horton and Max Alvis homered for the Tribe in the seventh to tie it. With two outs in the ninth, Yastrzemski (4-for-5, 41st HR) singled and moved up on a wild pitch; then was knocked in by Smith's single. Alvis singled with one out in the Indians' ninth, but a snappy Petrocelli-to-Andrews-to-Scott double play all around ended the game.

There were no changes in the standings. Chance won his 19th at home against the A's, Detroit crushed New York, 10-1, and Chicago beat California, 6-4.

On September 21, the St. Louis Cardinals announced that Bob Gibson would start the World Series. It was far from determined who he would face. Bell prevailed for a third time over Cleveland, 6-5, as the teams waited out an hour rain delay in the top of the ninth, and Merritt shut out Kansas City for Minnesota, 4-0, on two hits. The Red Sox and Twins were still deadlocked. Idle Chicago was one back and Detroit one-and-a-half.

On the next to the last weekend of the season,

Pennant Fever Hits Sox Wives. *Rico Petrocelli holds the newspaper showing the Red Sox in a virtual tie for first place. Looking on are Liz Brandon and son Darren, Marilyn Andrews and son Michael, and Elsie Petrocelli and son Michael.*

Boston played a twi-nighter on Friday, got trounced, 10-0, in the opener, and then with Foy (3 hits, two RBIs), Harrelson (3 hits, two RBIs) and Howard coming off the bench to start game two, Santiago hurled a complete game and won, 10-3. On the same night, Detroit took two in Washington on Wilson's major league-leading 22nd win and Lolich's four-hit shutout; Tony Horton led off the 13th with a home run to defeat Chicago, 2-1; and Minnesota grabbed possession of the top spot with an 8-2 win at home Friday afternoon over New York.

The next morning, the Twins were right back at it—a morning start so fans could also attend the University of Minnesota football game versus Utah. But New York rookie Tom Shopay connected for his first big league home run, a three-run shot, and Pepitone hit a two-run homer to snap Minnesota's five-game winning streak, 6-2. Horlen threw another shutout, his league-leading sixth, and defeated Cleveland, 8-0. Manager Mayo Smith, whose Tigers were inexplicably idle on a Saturday following two games on Friday, complained about scheduling doubleheaders this late in the season. He also said Wilson and Lolich would go on two days rest on Monday and Tuesday.

The Red Sox lost in Baltimore on Brooks

Robinson's two-run home run and dropped to third place, one-half game behind Minnesota and the familiar .001 behind Detroit.

On Sunday, the Red Sox final road game of the year, they pounded out a season-high 18 hits. Jones, who had gone 10-for-21 with 10 RBIs on the trip, went 4-for-6 and knocked in five. Adair and Scott also had four hits each. Boston had jumped out to a 7-0 lead, and manager Williams pulled Lonborg after six innings to rest him for the final week.

Boston had gone 6-2 on the trip. Chance won his 20th against the Yankees, 9-4, and gone the route despite being up, 9-2, after seven. Chicago defeated Cleveland, 3-1, on five solid innings of relief by Don McMahon; and Detroit coughed up a 4-2 lead in the ninth at Washington and lost, 5-4.

It was coming down to the wire. Boston had four games left. Williams was planning on going with a rotation of Bell-Lonborg-Bell-Lonborg. Jones was going to be at third base. Brandon tore a muscle on Sunday was lost for the season. Lyle was hurting, Bill Landis was in the military. Rohr and recent call-up 19-year-old Ken Brett were the team's only lefties.

The standings after Sunday, September 24:

1. Minnesota	90-67	
2. Boston	90-68	-½
3. Chicago	89-68	-1
3. Detroit	88-68	-1½

Chicago, though hardly in the driver's seat, would play their final five games against second division clubs, including two with Kansas City, who had won only once in their last 12 outings and were 5-19 for September and plummeting fast. Minnesota had three to play at home against California before coming to Boston for the final two, and Detroit had two in New York and four to play at home against the Angels.

On Monday, September 25, California belted around Merritt and the Twins for 15 hits and a 9-2 win. This dropped Minnesota into a first place tie with Boston. Downing beat Wilson and the Tigers in New York, 2-0, on four hits.

Boston, home for two with Cleveland and two with Minnesota, had their fortune in their own hands. Chicago was only a half-game out and tied in the loss column, but had the decidedly easier schedule.

On Tuesday, Fenway Park was, as Cleveland catcher Joe Azcue said, "like a church funeral all day [except for Yastrzemski's 43rd home run]." Tiant finally defeated Boston after three losses, and Bell finally lost to Cleveland after three victories. In New York, Lolich four-hit the Yankees, 1-0, on Mathews' sacrifice fly. And in Minnesota, Kaat won his seventh consecutive game of the month, 7-3, as Killebrew hit homers #42 and 43. The White Sox were rained out in Kansas City and would play a doubleheader on Wednesday.

Norma Williams, Dick, and son Marc read the July 24 Boston Herald's account of the welcome the Sox received at Logan Airport.

Wednesday wasn't much better for the Red Sox. Lonborg, on two days rest, lost to Sonny Siebert and the Indians, 6-0. *The Globe's* Kaese lamented, "The two games against the Indians were about as cheerful as weddings for which the bridegrooms failed to appear." The Sox left the bases loaded twice and managed only five hits.

However, Chance, also pitching on two days rest, lost to the Angels, 5-1. Detroit was idle, and the shock of the day was that the A's took two from Chicago, 5-2 and 4-0. Chicago went from the opportunity to leapfrog into first to now facing elimination and having to sweep the Senators in their three-game weekend series to have any chance (since either Boston or Minnesota would be winning at least once).

Later in the week, *Globe* columnist Jerry Nason would write, "Who would have wagered an embalmed sweat sock on last place Kansas City panicking pitchers like Joel Horlen and Gary Peters at both ends of a White Sox doubleheader?"

The *Boston Herald* ran a cartoon depicting the four teams backing toward the championship door. Yaz thought the Sox were, "gone, dead—not only dead but buried" after the second Cleveland loss. But the fact of the matter was that they only had to win both games at home against the Twins and hope that California could split four with Detroit. Their first of four got rained out on Thursday and they were scheduled to play two on Friday.

The standings through September 28:

1. Minnesota	91-69	
2. Detroit	89-69	-1
3. Boston	90-70	-1
3. Chicago	89-70	-1½

On Friday night, September 29, Chicago lost to Washington, 1-0, on an unearned run in the first inning, and the team which had led the league most of the summer was eliminated. With temperatures in the low 40s and drizzle, Detroit and California were postponed for a second straight night and would play two games on both Saturday and Sunday. At least a three-way tie was no longer possible. In a scheduling quirk, both Minnesota and Boston were idle Thursday and Friday. Boston was in third, one game out and .00079 behind second place Detroit.

Kaese wrote, "The turning point of the season probably will come in the ninth inning Sunday when a ground ball hits second base and some team has a collective faint on finding itself first and no games to play."

Dalton Jones was quoted: "A couple of months ago all of us were saying this thing will go right down to those last two games. Now that it's really happened it's even harder to believe." Yaz took batting practice on Friday and found the mood at Fenway much better than when he last left it on Wednesday.

Manager Williams announced he was going to start Santiago on Saturday (Lonborg thought he might get the call again with the team facing elimination) and would have Harrelson, Andrews and Gibson back in the lineup. The Twins would open up with Kaat, who had begun his 1967 campaign 1-7 but turned it around, winning 15 of his last 21 decisions and his last seven in a row. Kaat had a 14-6 lifetime record versus Boston and was 1-0 this year.

Minnesota scored one in the first on Oliva's single, but left the bases loaded when Carew lined out to third and Santiago got Ted Uhlaender to ground out to second on a 3-1 pitch. Kaat was on a roll, striking out four of the first nine Sox and looking sharp. But something popped in his left elbow as he fanned Santiago, and after throwing two balls to Andrews he was forced to leave the game. Perry came on to pitch.

Boston broke through for two in the fifth. Smith doubled leading off. Jones pinch hit for Gibson and hit a weak grounder to second, which took a bad hop for an infield hit. Santiago and Andrews struck out, but Adair dumped a single and the game was tied. Yastrzemski hit a ground ball wide of first. Killebrew couldn't reach it, but Carew did; and when he looked to throw to first Perry had not covered the bag. Yaz had an infield hit, and the Red Sox had the lead.

Minnesota came right back in the sixth and tied the game on Rich Reese's two-out pinch single. But for the second time they left the bases full against Santiago. Scott led off the bottom of the sixth and greeted Ron Kline, depositing his first pitch into the center field bleachers. In the seventh with one out, Andrews reached on a check-swing single to the mound. Adair hit one back to Kline, who threw to second—but Twins

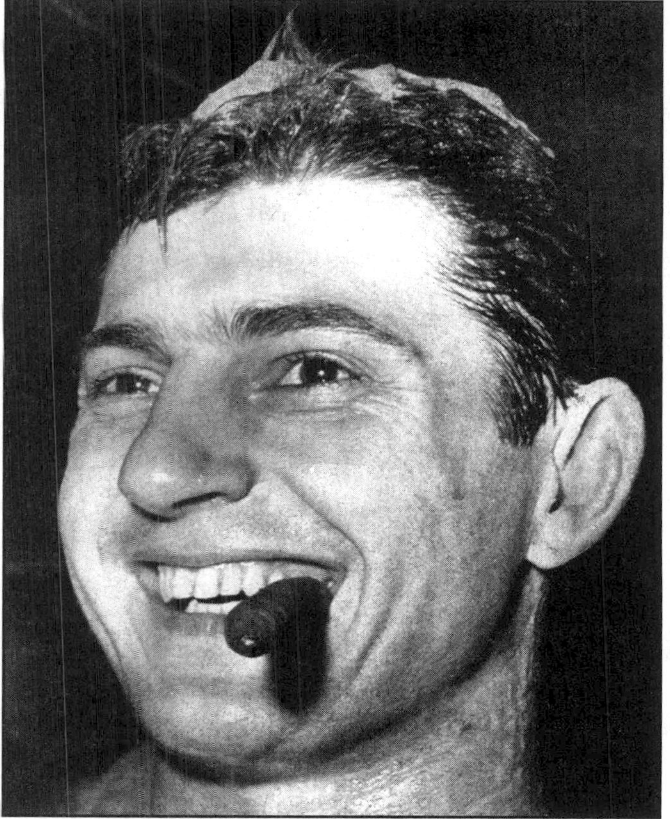

Carl Yastrzemski won the batting title, the RBI title, and tied for the league lead in home runs, but winning the pennant on the last day of the season saw Yaz with shaving cream in his hair and a cigar in his mouth.

shortstop Zoilo Versalles dropped the potential double play throw and both runners were safe. The lefty Merritt was brought in to face Yastrzemski, and Yaz crunched a high, 3-1 fastball and left it in the visitor's bullpen. Boston led, 6-2.

Killebrew hit a ninth-inning, two-run homer off Bell, but Boston had taken the weekend's first crucial game, 6-4. They were tied for first place. Well, not quite yet. In Detroit, Lolich shutout California in the first game, 5-0—the lefthander's third straight blanking. Temporarily, the Tigers at 90-69 were .001 up on both their rivals. Detroit led game two, 6-2, through seven innings with Wilson having gone five-plus. Jim Fregosi led off the Angels' eighth with a single. He would also finish it with a two-run single that capped off a six-run outburst against four Tiger pitchers. Detroit had let one get away, and now they were sitting in third place needing to sweep their Sunday doubleheader.

The season's largest crowd, 35,770, packed Fenway on the final Sunday. The two aces took the mound. Dean Chance, owner of the rain-shortened perfect game and a 4-1 season record against Boston, and Jim Lonborg, whose record was a discouraging 0-3 this year against the Twins and 0-6 lifetime.

In the first, Scott took the relay throw on Oliva's double and threw wide of the plate, allowing Killebrew to score. In the third, Killebrew singled to left, and as the ball got past Yastrzemski Cesar Tovar scored from first base. The Twins were up, 2-0.

The Boston sixth would be etched in Red Sox lore forever. Lonborg—consistent with other occasions was allowed to bat—dropped a bunt single down third base. Tovar had no play. Adair singled him to second. Jones stroked a single to left and loaded the bases off Chance. Yastrzemski ripped a single up the middle, and the game was tied.

Boston had first and third, nobody out, and then the Twins unraveled. Harrelson hit a high bouncer toward the second base bag. Versalles had no play at the plate but threw home just the same. Jones was safe, and Boston led. Worthington relieved Chance and threw a wild pitch advancing Yaz to third and the pinch runner Tartabull to second. Worthington then uncorked a second wild pitch and Yastrzemski scored. Smith banged a grounder off Killebrew's knee, and Tartabull scored. Boston left second and third but had taken a 5-2 lead.

Boston loaded the bases with nobody out in the seventh but came up empty. Yaz had his fourth hit of the game, a single off the lefty Roland. He went 7-for-8 in the two games with six runs batted in.

Dancing in the streets outside the ballpark after the young Red Sox team pulled off the Impossible Dream.

Minnesota got leadoff singles in both the eighth and ninth. Both runners were erased on groundballs to second, the runner tagged out and the relay made to first—in the eighth by Adair, who left after being spiked on the play, and in the ninth by Andrews. But in the eighth, Killebrew and Oliva followed with singles, and Allison also singled to left scoring Killebrew. Yastrzemski threw Allison out at second base, though, and that threat was stifled.

Rich Rollins pinch hit with Minnesota's last gasp in the ninth and lifted a lazy, soft liner to Petrocelli. And it was over. Well, again, not quite.

In a burst of emotion, the Fenway fans poured out onto the field. Lonborg was swept away on their shoulders down toward the right-field corner. With his shirt torn open it would be a full 10 minutes before he could reach the Sox clubhouse. It was as Sox announcer Ned Martin described, "pandemonium on the field!"

And it still wasn't over. Detroit held on and took the first game from California, 6-4. A Tiger win the second game would mean a two out of three playoff for the pennant. The Tigers took a 3-1 lead early in game two. Then the Angels struck back at McLain and the Tiger bullpen and took an 8-3 lead. While the Red Sox in their clubhouse listened to the game into the early evening, the Tigers put the first two men on in the ninth, trailing, 8-5. Shortstop McAuliffe, who had singled home a pair in the seventh, grounded into a season-ending 4-6-3 double play, and the Red Sox clubhouse went wild.

Now it was over. The 100-1 Boston Red Sox had won the American League pennant.

Bookies Blanch! Bosox 100-1 at Season's Start

If you had wanted to bet early on the Red Sox with the Del Mar Sports Book, based in Las Vegas, you'd have gotten 100-1 odds against them winning the pennant, according to a United Press International dispatch in February 1967. Del Mar picked the Orioles and the Pirates to prevail.

An Associated Press story in late March said that "Las Vegas bookmakers" were offering 100-1 on the Red Sox, and also picked Baltimore and Pittsburgh.

A week before the 1967 season opened, Las Vegas oddsmaker Jimmy (the Greek) Snyder offered 50-1 odds on Boston. He shared the sentiment picking the Orioles as favorites in the American League and the Pirates in the National League. He was willing to offer 8-1 odds against the Cardinals taking the National League flag. A UPI story did note, however, "There's still the formality of playing 162 games."

Number eight practically seemed to carry the team on his back for the crucial pennant stretch, getting 23 hits in his last 44 at-bats, driving in 16 runs in the process. In his final 13 at-bats, Yaz had 10 hits, and went 7-for-8 with six RBIs in the two-game finale for the pennant. He went on to hit .400 in the World Series, with three home runs and and five RBIs.

The Great Race

by Andy Andres

By all accounts, the 1967 pennant race was one of the greatest of all time. If it had not unfolded the way it did, and if instead someone wrote the tale, many would not believe it possible.

According to Glenn Stout and Richard Johnson in *Red Sox Century*, Jimmy "The Greek" Snyder laid 100-to-1 odds against the Red Sox winning the pennant.

On July 1, the White Sox enjoyed a comfortable five and one-half game lead over the second-place Tigers. Then on July 14, the Red Sox found themselves in fifth place, six games out of first, and only two games over .500. Then the Red Sox went on a 10-game winning streak to get into the race.

Fast forward to August 15, the Red Sox still found themselves in fifth place, but very much in contention—only three games back. That day the California Angels started a six-game losing streak—and then there were four.

Start of play August 15, 1967	G	W	L	T*	PCT	GB
Minnesota Twins	115	63	50	2	.558	-
Chicago White Sox	111	61	50	0	.550	1
Detroit Tigers	115	62	52	1	.544	1.5
California Angels	116	62	54	0	.534	2.5
Boston Red Sox	113	60	53	0	.531	3

Final Standings 1967	G	W	L	T	PCT	GB
Boston Red Sox	162	92	70	0	.568	-
Detroit Tigers	163	91	71	1	.562	1
Minnesota Twins	164	91	71	2	.562	1
Chicago White Sox	162	89	73	0	.549	3

Last 7 weeks in 1967					
Boston Red Sox	49	32	17	0	.653
Detroit Tigers	48	29	19	0	.630
Minnesota Twins	49	28	21	0	.571
Chicago White Sox	51	28	23	0	.560
Totals	197	117	80	0	.594

*Ties due to darkness were still recorded in 1967

From August 15 onward, the four teams in The Great Race played terrific baseball. Combined, they played at a .594 winning percentage (this translates into 96 wins for a 162-game season). Standings changed daily, sometimes hourly. Great performances and outstanding baseball were the norm.

One day, at the start of play on Thursday, September 7, all four teams were in a virtual tie for first place in the American League (ignoring the percentage point differences)!

Going into the last week of play, the Red Sox had only four games to play, the White Sox and Twins had five each, and the Tigers had six. Most thought the White Sox were best situated to win the pennant because in their last five games the Pale Hose were scheduled to play the last-place Kansas City Athletics twice and the eventual seventh-place Washington Senators three games.

Interestingly, at the start of play on Wednesday that final week, there was still the possibility of a four-way tie for first place—imagine the discussion regarding tiebreakers! All four teams could have ended up with either 91 wins or 92 wins. According to Jeff Miller, in his book *Down to the Wire*, in the spring of 1967, some engineers at Honeywell apparently decided to amuse themselves by calculating the odds of a four-way tie for first in either the National League or American League. Their calculations showed that the chances of a four-way tie were 30,315,229 to 1. As Miller mused, why the engineers chose to use the company's time this way remains unknown—baseball had never seen a tie involving more than two teams before 1967. It still has not.

Since the exact method used by the Honeywell engineers remains elusive, another quick, back of the envelope method of calculating the probability of a four-way tie was done to better understand how far-fetched it was. This method assumes balanced, independent schedules for teams, an assumption that is obviously not true in Major League Baseball. All 162 game team-seasons since 1961 were used to calculate the probability of winning 82 games (the minimum number of wins needed to achieve a four-way tie), 83 games, 84, etc., up to the maximum of 116 (2001 Seattle Mariners). Making the probability of winning these numbers of games in a season the basis of the calculation, the odds of four teams winning 82 games (and the odds of another team not winning more than 82 games) was calculated. This was repeated for 83 games, 84 games, 85 games, etc., up to the maximum. Using this simple method, the odds at the start of the season of any four-way tie happening are just a mere

89,585 to 1. In other words, given a league setup like the American League in 1967, expect it to happen every 45,000 years or so.

But that Wednesday (September 27) a gloomy cloud fell over the South Side—the White Sox lost a doubleheader to the lowly A's. Nevertheless, they still had a chance going into the final weekend because at the start of play on Friday all four teams were within a game and a half in the standings. The other three teams had a harder row to hoe—the Twins and Red Sox would play each other twice on the weekend and the Tigers had to play four against the fifth-place Angels. And things got worse for the Tigers because of rain on Friday, requiring them to play back-to-back doubleheaders on the final weekend.

The ending is well known, and celebrated in Red Sox Nation. The White Sox were eliminated that Friday, as they lost to the Senators. Detroit ended up splitting both doubleheaders with the Angels. Then the Red Sox, led by Carl Yastrzemski's heroics (Yaz went 7-for-8, hit a homer, scored two runs, and drove in six in those two games), swept the Twins to win The Great Race!

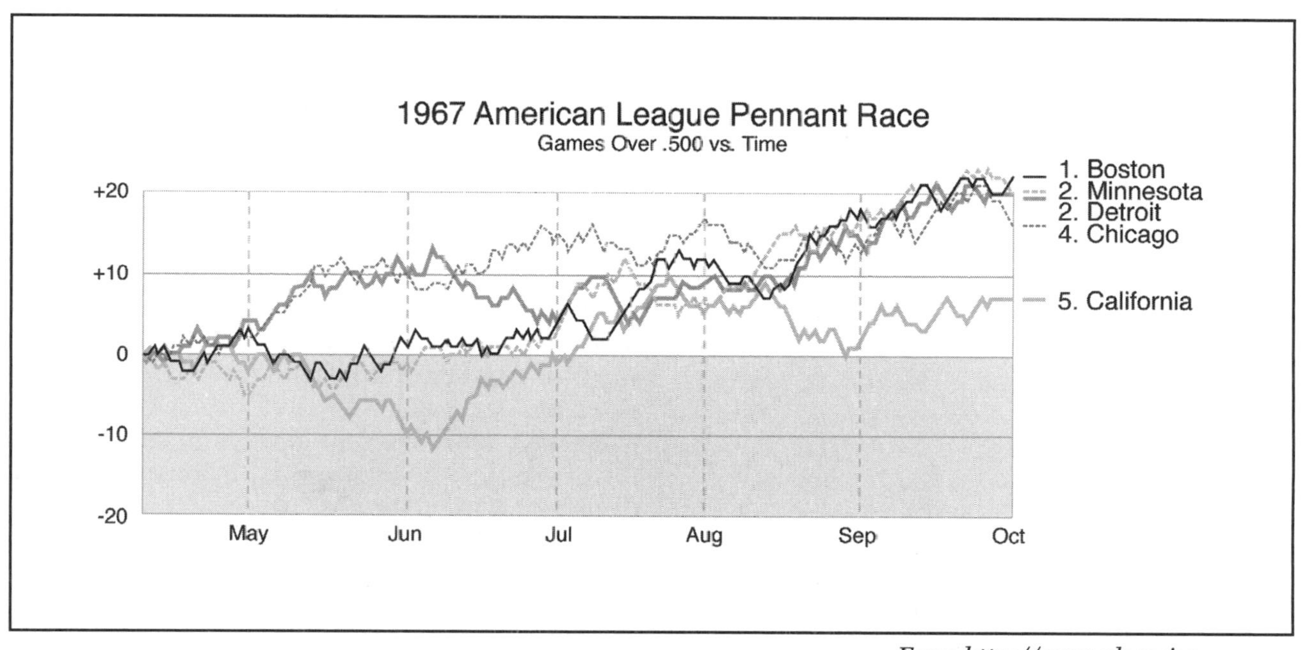

From http://www.alexreisner.com

Providence

by Father Gerry Beirne

Two or three weeks into September with all of New England absolutely agog over the rekindled, born-again Red Sox, a parishioner gave me a single ticket to the final game of the season on October 1, with the following caution: "They may be in first place or completely out of it by then. This ticket may be worth 50 cents or 50 dollars." I graciously accepted his kind ducat with an "I'll go either way" attitude.

On September 23, a week before that last date, Detroit, Chicago, Minnesota, and the Sox were all within one slim game of each other. Who would win the pennant? Who would fall short?

It seemed to be not a miracle, but an omen when Jim Kaat had to leave early during the game on Saturday the 30th and then Yaz blasted a glorious three-run wallop into the bullpen in the bottom of the seventh to keep the race alive. When that fateful Sunday came around, October 1, the Beirnemobile hiked up to the Hub, parked near downtown, and I took the "T" to Kenmore Square. Being alone, my trusty Sunday crossword puzzle was under the arm for "something to do with no one to talk to." Of course, the crowd was in a total frenzy. But I was quite determined to *not* get carried away in an emotional condition. Call it protection against the depression of possible defeat. After all, wasn't this Impossible Dream just too good to be true?

Hence, between pitches, I was filling in Across and Down with my usual ineptitude. The seat I'd been provided was a wonderful one just under the first base side of the screen behind home plate, about halfway up the grandstand. Dean Chance was immense on the mound for Minnesota. He would show his back to the batter in the windup and then zing the pellet untouched across the plate. The Twins scored single runs in the first and third; the Red Sox had none. But I was insulated from grief by the puzzle. Then it happened!

The Boston fifth opened with Lonborg beating out a bunt. Jerry Adair bled one up the middle that was fractions of an inch from the gloves of both Versalles and Carew. James Dalton Jones feigned a bunt and then slapped one past Tovar at third to "soak the sacks" for Captain Carl. By now, *all* of us were standing. It was a euphoric uproar. The silly crossword was under the seat, forgotten. And when Number Eight responded with a solid smash up the middle off the once-invincible Chance, even a man from Mars would have been caught up in the din.

Gentleman Jim Lonborg swaps chapeaus with His Eminence Richard Cardinal Cushing of Boston. Men of the cloth were frequent guest visitors at Fenway, and the Cardinal hosted over 2,000 sisters at Nuns Day 1967.

Still nobody out. Versalles threw Harrelson's grounder home, too late, 3-2; Worthington came in and two wild pitches later, the tally stood at 4-2, Boston. Scott fanned, but Reggie followed Rico's walk with a smash. Killebrew, playing first, showed why he would have been a wonderful DH. Harrelson's run made it 5-2.

Now to hang on for "only" four more innings, just one dozen Twins outs.

The rest was a blur until Rich Rollins popped up to Rico for the 27th putout of the game. The Little Team That Could—but which nobody ever expected would—had done it: won the American League pennant. There was a wait, but the word came in from Detroit that the Tigers had also lost, when Dick McAuliffe hit into just his second double play of the season. Strangers were hugging and kissing fellow fans. There were Red Sox fans all over the field. Terribly noticeable were three well-dressed men several rows in front who looked more than gloomy. Must have been Minnesota fans. Too bad! This was our year, finally. But how to celebrate? I knew no one and was not comfortable going into a bar, even in mufti. I wouldn't have fit in; it would have felt forced.

So I decided to walk back downtown to my 1962 Valiant and see what else might come to pass. A priest in vestments stood in front of a church on Newbury Street. So why not go in? Another adventure and nothing phony about it. Might be the perfect way to conclude the Fenway festivities. My attitude as I entered was remarkably similar as to the ballgame. I sat by myself in a back pew, not becoming involved, watching with a jaundiced eye these well-dressed (jacket and tie, or dress) young people smiling while warming up their guitars. Great Scott! A Folk Mass! I had heard of them but had never yet seen one. The Mass was undergoing change from Latin to English, a bit at a time, in those days, but Folk Mass was a new and radical concept.

At one point I heard myself say, "Why, they're smiling and enjoying themselves!" then quickly realized, "Well, isn't that a good way to be in church?" Just as at the Cathedral called Fenway Park, the Liturgy in this chapel caught me up. Enchanted and ensnared, my better feelings were brought out again. Euphoria. Peace. Contentment. Happiness. The homily was thoughtful and well delivered. The harmony of the entire day was irresistible. This Folk Mass was for me the perfect complement to a Red Sox pennant victory. What a wonderful twin bill! I wanted to be able to "bottle just a bit of those beautiful feelings" from that day, and take a dose or nip at future times as needed. But of course, memories have to do that. I had clearly chosen the better part in how to celebrate an Impossible Dream pennant victory. I sang all the way home in the car.

Father Gerald Beirne was born in Pawtucket, Rhode Island and has been a Red Sox fan at least since the 1946 season, though his first major league game was at Braves Field. In 1967, Father Beirne was a Roman Catholic priest at St. Martha's Parish in East Providence, Rhode Island. He had been a priest for five years, when he was provided the opportunity to attend the decisive final game of the 1967 season.

Front Page News Coverage of the Boston Red Sox 1966/1967

by Bill Nowlin

Every springtime, Red Sox fans hope for a pennant and the chance to win the World Series. It wasn't always this way. There were fallow periods in Red Sox history—the entire decade of the 1920s, for instance, and most of the 1930s. Another dead zone ran from 1951 to the middle '60s—there really was little hope during those years and, once Ted Williams retired at the end of the 1960 season, there was precious little reason for fans to come out to Fenway. Fewer and fewer did.

After the 1958 season through 1966, not a single Red Sox team even won half its games. The 1965 edition lost an even 100 games and the only thing good about the 72-90 ninth-place record posted in 1966 was that Boston finished a half-game ahead of the New York Yankees. Some consolation. It sounds comical today to read that new Red Sox manager Dick Williams had predicted in late March 1967, "I honestly believe we'll win more games than we lose." (*Boston Globe*, March 27, 1967) Though it hardly sounds like a pep talk from a fiery skipper to inspire the troops heading into battle, Williams was being much more assertive than it might appear. He had declared that the Red Sox would become a first-division team. And that would truly be something. Most critics doubted it would happen.

Had someone come out and predicted that the Red Sox would win the pennant, they would have been ridiculed. It wasn't just an impossible dream. It would have been a preposterous notion. No one predicted it. *Boston Globe* sportswriter Will McDonough was optimistic; he agreed with Williams that Boston could make the first division; he picked the Red Sox to finish fifth.

"Yaz in the Spotlight" *This mid-September 1967 photo includes Yaz surrounded by Frank Curtain of* A.P., *chief photographer Myer Ostroff of the* Record American, *Jerry Buckley of Red Sox, and Danny Goshtigian of the* Globe.

There were signs, though; it's just that most people didn't see them. The *Worcester Telegram & Gazette's* Bill Ballou writes that the Impossible Dream began on September 16, 1965 when the Red Sox finally fired Mike Higgins, replacing him as GM with Dick O'Connell. The Red Sox were a team of young, aggressive players filled with considerable confidence. In Dick Williams, they had a new, young, very aggressive, demanding, and driven manager, fresh from two years of working with many of the same players while managing Boston's Toronto farm club. And they had a fairly new general manager in O'Connell who had clearly been given a firmer hand in running the club—witness the hiring of Dick Williams.

Furthermore, the Red Sox had played fairly well in the second half of 1966—as had the Toronto club under Williams. On July 7, the Red Sox were 32-52 with just five games to play before the 1966 All-Star break; from that point on, they won 40 games and lost 38. For a team to hope to win more than it lost was by no means a ridiculous idea.

But the whole thing did seem to come more or less out of the blue. No one expected the team to have the success it had. It's been said that the 1967 season saved the franchise. Red Sox attendance had been trending downward for years. Tom Yawkey hinted more or less openly about moving the team. There was little sense of optimism. But since 1967, things have never been the same.

There really were indications of sorts. Attendance at 1966 home games climbed back up over 1,000,000—a 14.7% increase from 1965. A group of businessmen formed a booster club, the BoSox Club. Before the '67 season began, the Red Sox announced a 40% increase in the number of season tickets sold. At least some veteran fans were showing a little more faith in the team. Not that this was a lot of season ticket holders. A 40% increase meant that 2,000 more people signed up—but that was quite a lot in those days. Newspaper coverage conveyed some of the details, but the placement of stories in the papers didn't proclaim that there was any turnaround underway. Analysis of front page coverage of Boston's largest-circulation newspaper demonstrates the degree to which the Impossible Dream season of 1967 was an entirely unexpected phenomenon.

What a difference a year made. Winning is indeed what it's all about, and as soon as the Red Sox began to win, newspaper coverage began to blossom.

Consider this chart, comparing coverage of the Red Sox on the front pages of the *Boston Globe* in 1966 and 1967.

	Front Page Story or Photo		First Page/Sports Page Story or Photo		Above Masthead Story or Teaser	
	1966	1967	1966	1967	1966	1967
JAN	2	0	17	6	0	0
FEB	2	1	14	10	0	0
MAR	0	3	6	29	0	0
APR	2	5	33	46	0	0
MAY	1	1	54	42	0	0
JUN	2	3	58	52	0	0
JUL	2	6	48	70	0	1
AUG	0	13	40	72	0	14
SEP	3	20	50	58	0	14
OCT	1	42	6	42	0	0
NOV	0	1	2	14	0	0
DEC	0	4	1	12	0	0

What does the chart indicate? The only newspaper studied in detail was the *Boston Globe*, but its coverage was not atypical. At the time, the *Globe* published both a morning edition and the *Boston Evening Globe*. We only analyzed the morning *Globe*, but the coverage was not distinctly different in the evening editions. Even the subjects of front page Red Sox stories changed over the two-year period studied. Very few of 1966's front page stories had to do with baseball play. The two January stories were about Ted Williams and his election to the Hall of Fame. One February feature was a light story about how the Red Sox were wanting to appeal to housewives; the other dealt with Earl Wilson being barred from a Florida nightclub because of his race. There were no stories in March, largely reflecting a month-long newspaper strike that ran from March 7 to April 7. Given the pattern of coverage throughout the rest of the year, there likely would have been one or two front page features had there been no strike. There is no reason to believe that this gap in coverage compromises our ability to compare 1966 coverage with that in 1967.

The stories in April through June 1966 included the obligatory Opening Day story and one about possible plans for a new multi-sport stadium in Boston. The trade of Dick Radatz to the Indians for Lee Stange and Don McMahon made the front page on June 3. Both of July's page one stories reported the induction of Ted Williams into the Hall of Fame. The three September front pagers were: manager Billy Herman getting the axe, the Red Sox losing the last game of the season, and the Sox preparing to hire Dick Williams as the new manager. The *Globe* gave daily front page play to the 1966 World Series, but those weren't Red Sox stories—the Red Sox hadn't been to the Series since 1946. The one October story that was Red Sox-related announced the hiring of Bobby Doerr to coach in the upcoming 1967 campaign.

By year's end, the only front page news story in all of 1966 that truly touched on baseball action was the one on the final game loss. There were no tags to inside stories on the front page all year long, and no teasers above the masthead. *Boston Globe* coverage was perfunctory and uninspired, reflecting the team's 72-90 record which saw them finish in ninth place, just a half-game out of the cellar in what was then the one-division, 10-team American League.

Come 1967 and little was different for the first half of the year. For the first two months of 1967, there was even less front page ink than there had been in 1966. The only page one story that was even remotely Red Sox-related was one in February on the prospects for a new stadium that would house both the Patriots and Red Sox. Even looking at the first page of the sports section, there were only about half the number of Red Sox stories that there had been in 1966. In March, the front page offered two more stadium stories and one photograph showing three helicopters hovering over the playing field at Fenway Park to dry out freshly-plowed frozen earth in order to lay new sod and better prepare the field for Opening Day.

Comparing coverage on the first page of the sports section between the two years shows a more striking difference in March and April, but that is largely attributable to the city-wide newspaper strike in 1966. That there were more stories in the first half of 1966 both before and after these two affected months indicates somewhat less coverage on the first page of the sports section in 1967 than in 1966. There were more stories featured on page two, though, particularly during spring training. It would be difficult to argue that sports page coverage of the Red Sox had expanded in any way during the first half of 1967.

April 1967 saw a bump in the number of front page stories, and three of the five stories reflected play. The first three stories were all related to Opening Day: one in advance of the home opener, which was postponed due to the cold, the second one foreshadowing another attempt to get the game in, and the third one reflecting that the game had been played, a 5-4 win over the White Sox. When rookie Billy Rohr threw his near no-hitter against the Yankees on April 14, that rated front page coverage, as did the 18-inning loss to the Yanks two days later.

The only front page story in all of May came on the final day of the month, reporting the Memorial Day doubleheader sweep of the visiting California Angels, 5-4 and 6-1. The first game's win brought the Red Sox to .500 on the season (20-20) and the second game victory put them up by a game. The team was in fourth place, 5 ½ games out of first. June saw three front page stories, one more than June 1966. One was a feature on Dick Williams, the second was another stadium story not purely Red Sox-related, and the third was a June 22 front page photograph with caption of the five-minute brawl the broke out the night before at Yankee Stadium after Jim Lonborg hit Yankees pitcher Thad Tillotson, in evident retaliation for Tillotson's beaning of Joe Foy in the top of the same inning.

It was in July that *Globe* front page editors really began to feature the Red Sox, as fans began to contract a germ of excitement that would later build into true pennant fever. The July 3 paper featured Joe Foy's

eighth-inning homer that won a 2-1 game for the Red Sox at Kansas City's Municipal Stadium. Rookie Gary Waslewski threw three-hit baseball (John Wyatt got the last two outs) and went to 2-0, while the Red Sox were a full five games over .500 (39-34) and in second place, albeit tied with three other teams for second-place honors.

At the All-Star Break, the Sox were in sole possession of fifth place but still only six games behind the White Sox in the tightly-bunched standings. They began to climb and when they reached second place once more, on July 21, with their seventh win in a row, this rated a teaser above the masthead in the next morning's paper. It was the first one for at least the 18 months studied here, but the first of some 29 that would occur in the remaining 10 weeks of the regular season. Clearly, the morning *Globe* was beginning to take notice.

The big breakthrough in *Globe* front page treatment began two days later, when the July 24 paper featured two stories reporting the wild welcome accorded the road warrior Red Sox who had flown back from Cleveland with a 10-game winning streak in their pockets after sweeping a six-game trip to Baltimore and Cleveland. The team traveling party was surprised Sunday night to find a crowd variously reported as from 5,000 to 15,000 fans awaiting them on their landing at Logan Airport. There were more fans waiting for the returning Red Sox than had greeted The Beatles the year before. "Cheering Crowd Engulfs Players at Logan" read the *Globe* subhead. Everything had changed. The *Boston Record-American* banner headline on Tuesday morning blared, "Whole Town Ga-Ga Over Sox." It had been a long time since there had been anything out of Fenway that stirred the blood, but this was the real thing. This was a spontaneous outpouring. The newspaper reported the phenomenon; it had not stimulated it.

The *Los Angeles Times* took notice from across the country (the Angels were visiting Fenway) and columnist John Hall described the Red Sox resurgence that had captivated the Boston area. "Captivated may not be the word," he admitted. "Enslaved is more appropriate." It was hot in Boston, but fans flocked to Fenway to buy tickets, creating lines around the block. Another article headlined, "Vaccine Rushed to Hub Fans" invoked pennant fever for the first time" "Boston is in the throes of its worst epidemic in 18 years. The diagnosis for the malady is a rare one for this community. It is labeled pennant fever."

The morning after the Sox beat the Angels in the bottom of the 10th inning, 6-5, putting them just one game behind the league-leading White Sox, the July 28 *Globe* featured the headline that provided the line for the season: "The Impossible Dream?" with a subhead reading "'Cardiac Kids' At It Again." The Sox had come from behind with three runs in the bottom of the ninth on a two-run homer by Joe Foy into the left-field netting and a solo home run over everything off the bat of Tony Conigliaro. They won it in the 10th on a leadoff triple by Reggie Smith and a subsequent error by California third baseman Paul Schaal on a Jerry Adair grounder. Bedlam reigned in Beantown.

Liftoff had occurred. There was no looking back. The *Globe* published 31 morning papers in August and a full 13 of them featured the Red Sox on the front page in one shape or another. On the inside pages, the paper offered a "Meet the Red Sox" series of individual profiles on the ballplayers and a companion series of profiles of the wives and fiancees of the Bosox. Beginning on August 25, Carl Yastrzemski wrote an exclusive thrice-weekly column, which usually began on page one. Above the masthead, some 14 issues of the *Globe* featured a teaser directing readers to previous day's score or other Sox stories featured within. The first page of the sports section had already seen a jump to 70 stories in July, an average of more than two per day—not counting the stories continued from the front page.

September offered even more of the same, with the pennant race now pretty intense and in earnest. The 20 front page stories combined with an additional 14

"This has been a frustrating year for Boston writers," Williams said in late September. "They've had to write too many nice things about the Red Sox; and there've been few opportunities to knock."

teasers. There was a decline in first page stories in the sports section, but to some extent that reflected the increasing number of front page features that jumped to the front of the sports section. The column inches devoted to stories about the Sox expanded; the stories were longer, too.

October saw an explosion of Sox coverage as the *Globe* practically surrendered its front page to the Red Sox through the final couple of days of the regular season and the World Series itself. Given that the Series ended on October 12, it's easy to understand that the lion's share of the 42 front page stories fell in the first half of October. The October 1 Sunday paper included a 16-page supplement on the team and the season. The entire front page of the October 2 *Globe* was Red Sox. It was pretty much all Red Sox, all the time. News from the rest of the world could be found inside. Given the Red Sox dominance of the front page, there was no need for teasers and none were offered.

After the season played out on October 12 with the final 7-2 defeat at the hands of Bob Gibson and the Cardinals, the world soon righted itself and the front page quickly reverted to covering the news of the day. "The Slipper Wouldn't Fit" headlined a story on the end of the season for the "Cinderella Sox."

On October 21 and 22, some 50,000 protesters marched on Washington and surrounded the Pentagon demanding an end to the war in Vietnam. The antiwar movement had reached critical mass and both principled and countercultural struggles would dominate news coverage for the next several years. But in Boston and throughout New England, the Red Sox had re-established themselves on center stage in the psyche of sports fans in the six-state region and captured the fancy of a new legion of far-flung fans as well. One can see a tremendous interest in the Red Sox in both November and December compared with 1966. The front page story in November was about Tony Conigliaro's attempt at recovery. One of the four front pagers in December was Carl Yastrzemski promoting *Globe* Santa to help bring some Christmas joy to children in the Greater Boston area. The other three stories were all about Jim Lonborg's skiing accident just before Christmas.

The stories on the first sports page discussed Darrell Johnson taking over as pitching coach from Sal Maglie—the November 2 *Globe* actually had three separate stories on that, plus another on Yaz's salary. Yaz wrote another column in the November 15 paper. The 19th pronounced that the Red Sox "will trade almost anyone" to improve the team. November 30, the *Globe* reported that the Red Sox had acquired Ray Culp from the Cubs for Bill Schlesinger and $50,000. Jim Lonborg re-signing for $45,000 was big news in mid-December, as was the gathering of folks to watch the 1967 World Series film at Fenway Park. The next day the Red Sox traded Mike Ryan and cash for Dick Ellsworth and Gene Oliver. December 20 saw a story "Yaz Deserves Own Stadium." Of course, the end of the month had a number of stories on the Lonborg accident.

All in all, though, one sees a dramatic increase in coverage on the *Globe's* first sports page, too, from 1966 to 1967—sure signs that the interest in the Red Sox continued well after the Series was over.

Attendance in the years after Ted Williams dropped from the million-plus range to an average of 812,160 from 1961 through 1966. Some 1,727,832 came to Fenway in 1967, marking the first time Boston had led the American League in attendance since the 1915 season. Ticket sales increased another 200,000 in 1968, but there was a bit of an ebb until 1975, with an average for the years 1969 through 1974 of 1,648,168—in other words, double the average attendance in the years preceding 1967. The 1975 season cemented the relationship and sealed the deal. The franchise was never the same again.

"1967 not only turned on the fans, but I think it turned the whole Red Sox organization around. I think we became winners instead of losers. We expected to go out and win, instead of lose. The thinking changed. We became winners."

—Carl Yastrzemski to Ken Coleman, in *The Impossible Dream Remembered*

The BoSox Club

by Bill Nowlin

There is a lengthy tradition of Red Sox booster clubs, ranging from the Royal Rooters to the Winter League and the Red Sox Half Century Club—even a World War II era organization of bleacherites named "We the People Speak," which held a number of annual meetings. Then there are the BLOHARDS in New York—the Benevolent Loyal Order of Honorable and Ancient Red Sox Diehard Sufferers. The most venerable of all, though, is the BoSox Club, founded in early 1967.

Ken Coleman helped found the new club when he arrived from Cleveland. As Ken explained in a December 2001 interview, "I was a member of the Wahoo Club in Cleveland, an Indians booster club. When I came to Boston I spoke with Bill Crowley, the public relations director of the Red Sox and told him about the Wahoo Club and what they were doing. In 1966, the Red Sox weren't doing well at all. So we got a group of people together up in the old press room at Fenway and we put in a call to Gabe Paul and Al Rosen on a speaker phone." The two Indians execs explained how the Wahoo Club worked, and Coleman's group founded the BoSox Club. The club has grown over time and numbers over 850 members presently.

Dominic DiMaggio was voted the first president of the club, and the early meetings were usually held at Boston's Somerset Hotel. In later years, monthly luncheons were held during the season at Anthony's

BoSox Club members pose for a photograph before taking an August 27 trip to New York. The Red Sox took three of four at Yankee Stadium.

Pier Four, site of the very first luncheon. In the early 21st century, the venue shifted to the Newton Boston Marriott Hotel.

The club was organized early in 1967 at a meeting of some "50 prominent Boston businessmen" who met in the Fenway Park press room. Some 35 of those assembled became charter members. The original officers were, aside from President DiMaggio, Brad Jernegan as vice president and treasurer, Larry Polans as secretary, and Edward Hanify and Truman Casner as legal advisers. The other directors were Bernard Ballwin, Dean Boylan, Bob Cheyne, Tom Feenan, Jim Kelso, and Clarence March. The club's first luncheon was a Welcome Home to the Red Sox luncheon held on April 10, the day before the home opener. Some 260 members and their guests attended and heard Dick Williams introduce the entire Red Sox squad and outline his plans for the 1967 season.

The club's second meeting, at the Somerset on May 19, drew 120 members, who heard from Cleveland manager Joe Adcock and Sam McDowell, as well as Ken Coleman interviewing Dick Williams and George Scott. Luncheons were also scheduled for May 31, June 13, July 17, August 2, August 22, September 1, September 15, and September 29.

Coleman recalled the commitment that manager Dick Williams showed in the club's launch year: "The first year that we had them on a regular basis, Dick Williams never missed a meeting. He was at every one of them." At their first meeting in 1968, the Club gave Williams an admiral's chair for outstanding cooperation in community relations. Rico Petrocelli was given their first "Most Underrated Player" award.

On August 25, 2002, a plaque was placed on the exterior of Fenway Park honoring the 35th anniversary of the BoSox Club. The *Springfield Republican's* Garry Brown asked Dom DiMaggio whether it was good karma that the BoSox Club was organized the very year the Red Sox won their first pennant in 21 years. "I don't know. Maybe our club spurred them on," DiMaggio allowed.

The club kicked off 1968 by expanding the board, adding Eddie Pellagrini, Ted Lepcio, and Dick Casey. Ken Coleman was named an honorary member of the board. The club maintained its offices at Fenway Park. By the club's third annual organizational meeting, held January 10, 1969, it had grown so significantly that membership was cut off at 540 members.

Over the years, the BoSox Club has prospered, with an active schedule of players and team personnel both from the Red Sox and visiting ballclubs. The club has also been active in providing a number of scholarships, Family Day programs, road trips to Red Sox minor league affiliates and away games, and annual spring training gatherings.

The current membership includes die-hard Red Sox fans from all over New England (and beyond). It is the largest officially sponsored baseball booster club in the world.

The club's mission statement declares that it is "first and foremost an organization of the fans, by the fans and for the fans... formed to promote baseball at all levels and to assist the Boston Red Sox in community and charitable endeavors. Traditionally, the BoSox Club has raised funds both inside and outside its membership to support many worthy causes including the Red Sox Foundation, the Jimmy Fund and New England Little League organizations. The BoSox Club is also instrumental in proving seating for challenged fans at Fenway Park through the Challenger Program, and provides financial assistance to a select group of deserving athletes to attend the Mike Andrews Baseball Camp each summer." Members of the club volunteer in a number of ways around the ballpark, helping staff Autograph Alley and welcoming new visitors to Fenway during playoff seasons.

As 2006 club president Ed Keohane puts it, "The club is open to anyone who enjoys the thrill of the game, who is responsive to the charitable needs of the community, and enjoys the company of a group of people who can talk knowledgably about baseball. The club has a web site, www.bosoxclub.com where you can receive further information or apply for membership."

Jimmy Fund
In '67, Red Sox honored another dreamer: "Jimmy"

by Saul Wisnia

They were the youngest team in the major leagues, filled with guys who were under 25 and making considerably less than $20,000 a year. Yet when members of the 1967 Red Sox gathered in their clubhouse during the pennant race to discuss how to break up the bonus that would come their way with a World Series berth, they decided to vote a full share—about $5,500—to someone who hadn't had a single at-bat for the club all season:

A kid named Jimmy.

Even rookies on the Boston team were well aware of the team's relationship with its official charity—the Jimmy Fund of the Children's Cancer Research Foundation (CCRF), today the Dana-Farber Cancer Institute. The name "Jimmy" was a pseudonym given to one of the young patients to protect his privacy, and came to represent all youngsters with the disease.

Owner Tom Yawkey had banned advertising from Fenway Park around 1950, with the only exception being a Jimmy Fund billboard above the grandstand in right field. Yawkey had accepted responsibility for promoting the charity from Boston Braves owner Lou Perini (whose team had helped found it) after the Braves left town in 1953, and he took the role seriously. By '67 Yawkey was on the Board of Directors for the CCRF and making sure Red Sox broadcasters spread the word about its research and treatment efforts during each game.

"Those game announcements prompted fans to send in contributions and sponsor dances, pancake breakfasts, and hundreds of other fundraising efforts," says Mike Andrews, a rookie second baseman for the club in '67 and now chairman of the Jimmy Fund—which maintains its strong bond to the team. "Things just snowballed from there."

The Fenway billboard depicted a youngster returning to the Little League field after his treatment, but too many kids who developed cancer back in the 1960s never did so. Players were asked to do what they could to keep spirits high and generate fundraising dollars for the cause. They complied, meeting with young patients before games and attending events in the community when time allowed.

Nobody did more than the great Ted Williams, and when the Splendid Splinter retired, his left-field successor Carl Yastrzemski also became a leading Jimmy Fund spokesman. It was Yaz who suggested that the team honor all children fighting cancer with a portion of their championship winnings, and the vote was unanimous—"Jimmy" would get his cut.

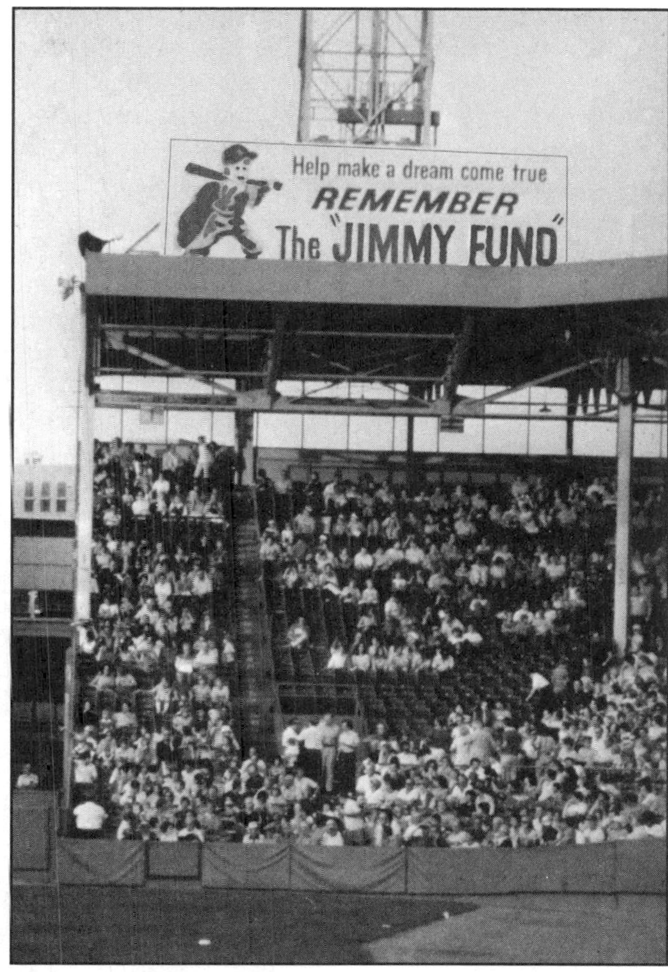

The Jimmy Fund billboard in Fenway's right field, for decades the only advertising sign permitted inside the ballpark.

To make a gift, choose "make a gift" online at www.jimmyfund.org, or call the Jimmy Fund toll-free at (800) 52-JIMMY (1-800-525-4669).

You can also contact the Jimmy Fund care of Dana-Farber Cancer Institute, 10 Brookline Place West, 6th floor, Brookline, MA 02445-7226, ATTN: Contribution Services.

When Defeat is Not a Loss

by Glenn Stout

It was, perhaps, the last time the Red Sox entered postseason play without either the burden or curse of history, perhaps the last time they played to beat only one team and not bring down an entire legacy. From the Boston perspective, when the Red Sox and Cardinals met in the 1967 World Series there was no expectation either of impending doom or certain victory. No one in the press hearkened back to the heartaches of 1948, or 1946, or any other year. If the 1967 regular season had taught the Red Sox and their fans anything, it was that the story of the 1967 Sox was the journey itself, the crazed elevator ride of emotions that—over the course of a single season—had introduced a new generation of fans to the Red Sox. On the precipice of the Series, all anyone knew was that, for better or worse, the Series marked the end of the ride. The only question that remained was, win or lose, whether or not anyone's heart could take it.

At the start of the Series, all logic pointed to a Cardinals victory. They were the experienced, veteran club of established stars like Orlando Cepeda, Lou Brock, and Curt Flood, a team that had steamrolled to the National League pennant by 10½ games despite being without ace Bob Gibson for seven weeks after he had stopped a Roberto Clemente line drive with his shin. He was healthy now and, with only 175 innings on his arm, fresh. Moreover, the Cardinals had weeks to rest and set up their pitching rotation.

The Red Sox, meanwhile, had ridden the elevator up and down at breakneck speed for weeks, going from

The Impossible Dream Team introduced as the World Series begins.

the lowest of lows, like the beaning of Conigliaro, to the highest of highs, like the José Tartabull game-saving throw a little over a week later that launched the Red Sox into first place. In the end, the elevator screeched to a halt and when the door suddenly opened the Red Sox tumbled out and found themselves alone on the top floor, American League champions. They were simultaneously exhilarated, exhausted, and ecstatic. So were their fans.

The logic that indicated a St. Louis victory appeared trumped by the accumulated magic and mojo that had been in evidence almost nightly over the past six months. The improbable and impossible had somehow won, and so—it seemed to almost everyone in Boston—would the Red Sox.

The Series opened in Boston and Game One featured Gibson opposite José Santiago. In the third inning, the Cardinals scored first after Brock singled, Flood spanked a double, and Maris knocked Brock home with a ground ball. That was predictable—elevator going down. But so was what came next. José Santiago, of all people, cracked a home run off Gibson and everyone piled back on the elevator going up.

That woke Gibson up, and he shut the Sox down from there. Brock scored another run in much the same fashion to give the Cardinals a 2-1 win.

The Sox turned to Lonborg in Game Two and Lonborg turned to superstition, wearing his lucky mismatched spikes, spending the night in a downtown hotel, and carrying a gold paper horseshoe in his back pocket that had been sent by a fan. He stopped Brock with a dose of reality in the first inning, knocking him to the ground, then let the magic happen.

He was perfect. Yaz cracked two home runs and the Sox opened up a 5-0 lead entering the eighth inning. The Cardinals hadn't even had a hit yet and the elevator threatened to go through the roof and disappear from sight. Four outs away from immortality, Julian Javier rapped a double to left to return Lonborg to mere legendary status. The Sox won 5-0 and the Series was tied.

Both teams withdrew to St. Louis for Game Three. The Cardinals brought the Red Sox back to earth with a tidy 5-2 win as they knocked out Gary Bell in the third and Nelson Briles went the distance to win. It was more of the same in Game Four. This time José Santiago was the victim. He never got out of the first inning as St. Louis exploded for four runs, three more than Gibson needed. This time he shut out the Red Sox on five hits to win 6-0.

Now all that stood between the Red Sox and 1968 was Jim Lonborg. That was plenty as the eventual Cy Young Award winner sent Boston hearts soaring with a three-hitter, setting a record for the fewest hits allowed in back-to-back Series starts, as Boston won 3-1.

When the Red Sox returned to Boston's Logan Airport, some 1,500 people, mostly teenage girls with huge crushes on Lonborg, broke through a plate glass door to surround the Sox as they got off the plane.

The Sox were riding high again and manager Dick Williams kept his finger on the top button. In Game Three, 26-year-old rookie Gary Waslewski had been impressive in relief. Williams had been putting his faith in kids all year long, and there was no reason to stop now. Hell, Lonborg was only 25. Williams skipped over his veterans and started the rookie.

Waslewski teetered and tottered and the stomachs of Boston fans did flip-flops with each pitch, but by the time he left the game in the sixth inning, the Red Sox led, 4-2. Red Sox hitters had finally woken up—Petrocelli homered in the second inning, then in the fourth, Yaz, Reggie Smith, and Petrocelli—again—all hit home runs. After Brock cracked a two-run home run in the seventh to tie the score, the Sox exploded for four more runs, Gary Bell slammed the door, Boston won 8-4, and the Series was tied at three games apiece.

When a reporter asked Dick Williams who would pitch Game Seven, the manager quipped, "Lonborg and Champagne." Those words filled the front page of the *Boston Herald American* the next morning. Confident Sox fans scrambled to the liquor store to stock up, expecting to pop the cork later that day. The elevator was going up again, and the sky was the limit.

But there was one big difference between the Red Sox and Cardinals, one irrefutable fact that no amount of magic or mojo could change. Lonborg, after pitching 275 regular season innings, entered Game Seven on only two days' rest. Bob Gibson, fresh to begin with, would pitch on his normal three days of rest.

From the start, the Cardinals sensed Lonborg didn't have it. He escaped the first inning on only nine pitches, but the Cardinals hit him hard. Meanwhile, after walking Joe Foy to start the game, Gibson pitched as if offended.

Lonborg and the Red Sox slowly came down to earth. Dal Maxvill, he of the .279 slugging percentage, tripled leading off the third to start the Cardinals rally, and in the fifth Gibson joined the party with a home run of his own. In the sixth inning, Lonborg hit bottom, and the Cardinals scored three more runs to make the score 7-1. A week earlier, Lonborg had been carried off the field by ecstatic Boston fans. This time, after striking out Flood to end the inning, he walked off the field in

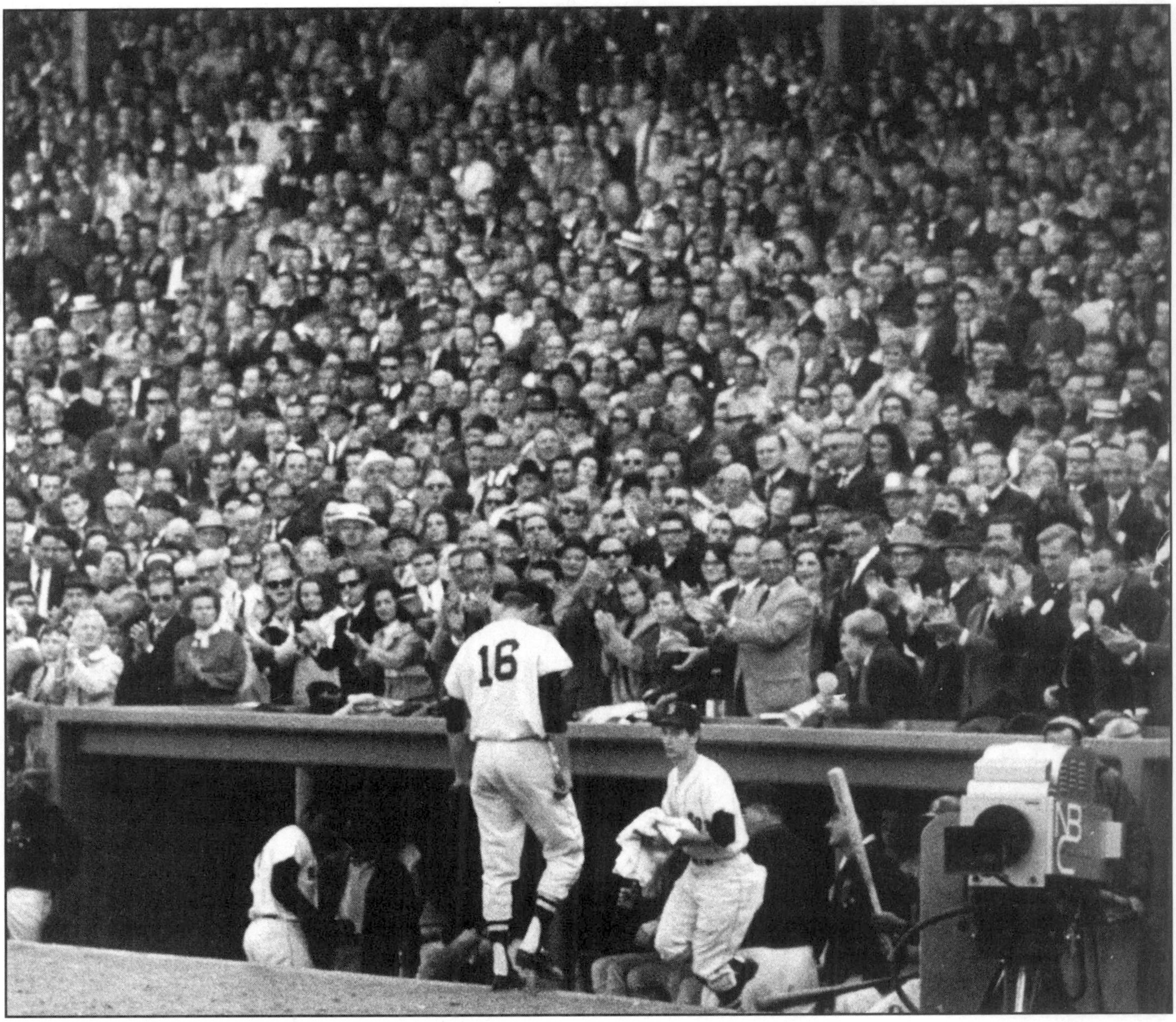

A dejected Jim Lonborg starts down the dugout steps, leaving Game Seven with the score St. Louis 7, Boston 1. The Sox ace had pitched on two days' rest. The standing ovation from the fans signaled that the Red Sox had won again the hearts of all New England. Many of the fans were in tears and so was Lonborg, who commented later on the ovation, "I heard it, but I didn't know how to respond, I was so disappointed."

tears as Boston fans stood and cheered, knowing the ride was over. Two innings later the Cardinals popped the cork, chanting, "Lonborg and champagne, hey!" as they celebrated their victory.

The Red Sox had been defeated, and the Impossible Dream was over, but somehow that defeat was not a loss. Over the course of a remarkable season the Red Sox had won something more important. After all the ups and downs, in the end, they had won their city back. A year or two before, Red Sox fans could have all shared an elevator with room to spare. Now, the door was bursting and the overflow was packing the stairwell. No one was ever going to get out of the car again until it ended with a world championship. Although they all knew there would surely be more ups and downs, Sox fans were in it for the long haul, convinced that a world championship was now somehow inevitable. They couldn't wait for 1968.

Now if only Jim Lonborg had not made plans to go skiing...

The Kind We Call Immortal

by Gordon Edes

This piece by Gordon Edes ran in the Boston Globe *the day after the Red Sox won the 2004 World Series. The 1967 team came so very, very close. We had to wait another 37 years but the 2004 edition finally won it all. A meditation about mortality, Edes's article reflects on how many of the Dreamers died so young—focusing on Ken Brett as the youngest of the '67 team, also gone too soon—and how we should cherish the 2004 team, because they, too, will remain immortal only in memory.*

They are young and strong and vibrant, their hair blowing in the wind, their smiles incandescent, their eyes awash with confidence in their own specialness.

We call them larger than life. We call them immortal.

It is no different now than it was in 1967, when another Red Sox team played the Cardinals in the World Series and captured the hearts of New England. Imagine life without Manny and Pedro, Johnny Damon and 'Tek, Schill and Big Papi. As unthinkable as imagining life without the Impossible Dreamers.

Elston Howard was the first from that '67 team to go, the proud catcher who integrated the Yankees before he came to the Sox, dead of a heart attack in 1980, at age 51.

Then it was Tony Conigliaro, at 37 suffering a heart attack that left us numb. That was in 1982. By 1990, at age 45, he died of a lung infection and kidney failure.

Joe Foy, the third baseman. Heart attack, gone at age 46 in 1989.

Jerry Adair, the supersub, dead of liver cancer at age 50 in 1987.

Johnny Wyatt, the former Negro League star who came out of the bullpen to win Game Six against the Cards, heart attack in 1998. He was 63.

Don McMahon, another relief pitcher, dropped dead of a heart attack while pitching batting practice as a Dodgers coach in 1987. He was 57.

Bob Tillman, the catcher, heart attack, 2000. Sixty-three years old.

There is at least one more name on that list.

"You have to be a Red Sox fan, if you hate the Yankees as much as I do," George Brett said yesterday afternoon. We remember George Brett for his Hall of Fame career with the Kansas City Royals, the pine tar incident, his run at becoming the first since Ted Williams to hit .400 (he finished at .390). But you may be surprised to know that Brett, who still works for the Royals, walked around Kansas City this summer wearing a Red Sox cap—"a red hat with a blue B"—reflecting a loyalty that began in 1966, when the Red Sox drafted his older brother, Ken, out of El Segundo (Calif.) High School, in the first round. A year later, Ken Brett was in the big leagues with the Sox, a late September call-up, and when Sparky Lyle went down with an injury, Brett was added to the World Series roster.

"I was 13, maybe 14 years old," George Brett was saying yesterday. "The next thing you know, your parents are saying, 'We're going to the World Series.' How great is that?

"I remember riding on the buses to the ballpark, sitting next to Yaz and Jim Lonborg, meeting all the guys on the club."

In 1967, at age 19, Ken Brett became the youngest pitcher to appear in a World Series game, a distinction he still holds. George Brett idolized him.

"I remember him coming home, driving a 1967 GTO—it was burgundy," Brett said. "He'd come home for Christmas, people were always around him.

"He was a great, great big brother. Those were tough shoes to fill. The Red Sox were the only team that wanted him as a pitcher. The other teams scouting him would have drafted him as a center fielder. He might have been a Hall of Famer, he was just such a natural. The ball jumped off his bat.

"Every year, the coach of our old high school team, who is still there, would have an alumni game to raise money for the school. Every year, my brother would

Ken and George Brett enjoy a moment at an event in 1977.

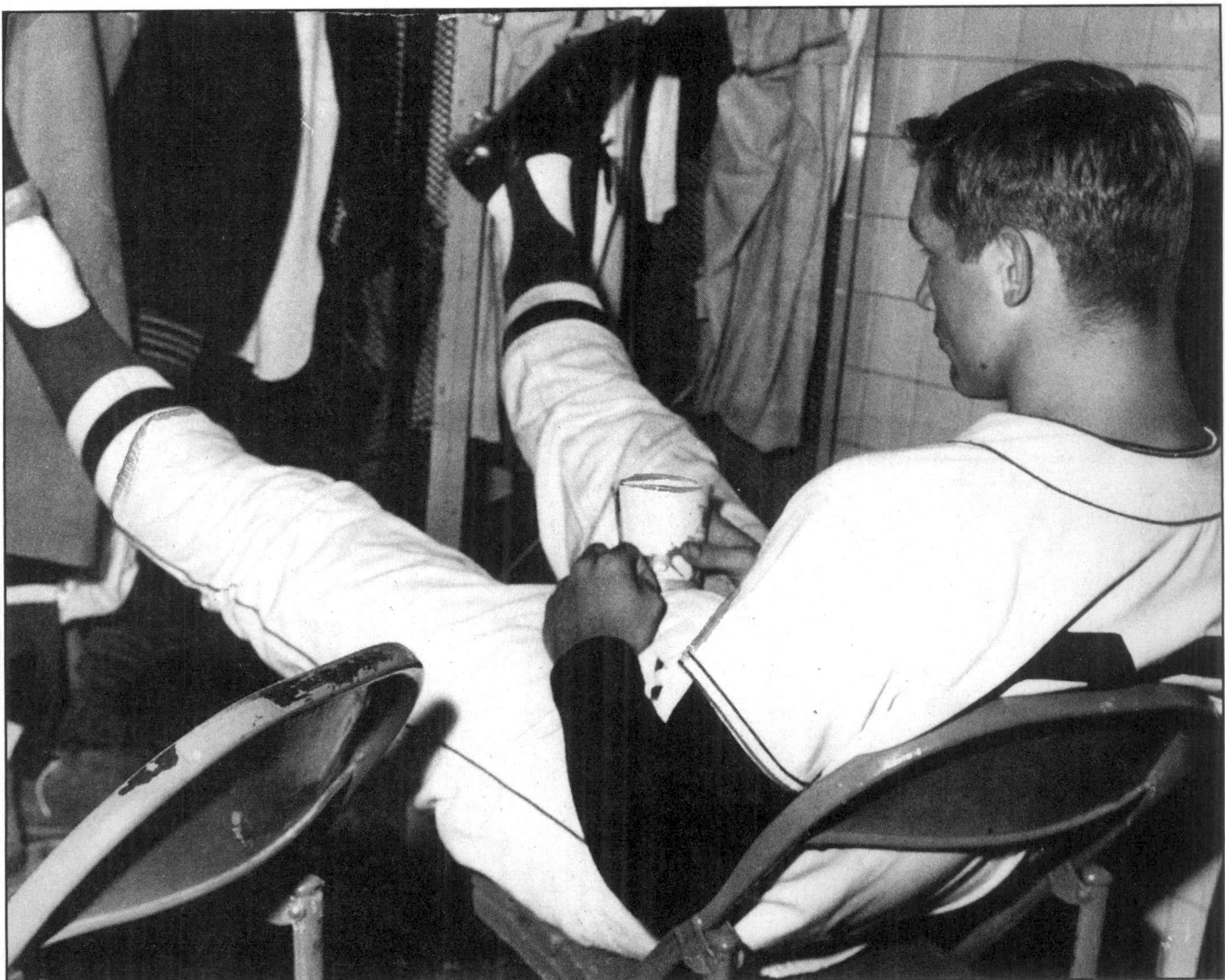

The final game. 19-year-old Ken Brett after Game Seven of the 1967 World Series ponders what might have been.

beat me in the home run-hitting contest. A lot of people said he was the best hitter in the family, and maybe he was."

But the following season, 1968, Brett hurt his elbow and never came close to fulfilling his promise with the Sox. In 1971, he was traded to the Milwaukee Brewers, and would play for another eight teams before his 14-year big-league career came to an end. He finished, in 1981, playing with his brother, George, by then a perennial All-Star. "It was a lot of fun," George Brett said, "playing together."

About five years ago, George Brett said, he received a phone call from Ken, who had gone into broadcasting. "My youngest boy, Robin, had surgery when he was 17 months old," George Brett said. "He had some internal bleeding in his brain, and we took him to a hospital in Arizona and they removed a blood clot from his brain. Kemer was aware of that, of course, and he called me and asked, `When Robin had seizures, what were the symptoms?'"

That was hard to say, George Brett responded. The toddler wasn't old enough to tell mom and dad that he was having headaches. "I don't know," George Brett told his brother. "Sometimes it seemed like he would just freeze in his tracks.

"Kemer said, `I think I'm having seizures, too. When I drive my car, I feel numbness in my toes and my fingers.' I said, `Well, maybe you're having circulatory problems or something, but go get it checked out.'"

Ken Brett went to the doctor, and they found

a tumor in his brain. He had surgery, underwent chemotherapy and radiation, and seemed to be OK for the next four years—until doctors found an even bigger tumor. This one was cancerous.

Last Nov. 18, Ken Brett died at home in Spokane, Wash. He was 55. George Brett was at his bedside. "I was the one who told his wife he had passed," George Brett said. "I had the unenviable task of calling his old teammates, Jerry Moses, Jim Lonborg, Mike Ryan. Somebody had to do it. They took it hard. The oldtime Red Sox really are like family.

"One of the last things he told me was he wanted to see his kids graduate from high school. He'd say, 'I had a good life.' He never felt sorry for himself." Next June, Sheridan Brett, Ken's daughter, and her twin brother Casey, are scheduled to graduate from high school. Sheridan, a volleyball player, is hopeful of attending Brown. Casey, who plays baseball, has designs on Cornell.

"My brother would be so proud," George Brett said.

Yesterday morning, George Brett, who was in town as part of a promotion for the mortgage company Ameriquest, had breakfast with a father and son from Maine. They had won World Series tickets in a contest in which first prize was to go with a legend. They went to last night's game with three Hall of Famers: Brett, former Cardinals shortstop Ozzie Smith, and former Dodgers manager Tom Lasorda.

"It was so weird," George Brett said. "The dad brought up my brother's name. It brought back great memories.

"The neatest thing, when I go back to Boston, is that everybody remembers my brother, even though he was there for a short time and never really lived up to the expectations or fanfare, but they still remember him, and they don't remember him as a failure but as a success."

Brett was rooting like crazy for the Sox, for these ballplayers young and vibrant and strong. The kind we call larger than life. The kind we call immortal. WORLD CHAMPIONS.

The Birth of Red Sox Nation

by Bill Nowlin

The 1967 Red Sox team surprised everyone by winning the pennant and taking the World Series to a seventh and final game. Before the season began, new manager Dick Williams predicted the team would "win more games than we lose." That in itself was a bold claim for a team that had one foot on the cellar floor the year before, finishing in ninth place, just half a game out of last place. Fans at Fenway were few and far between for most of the 1960s, with crowds often as not in four digits—and from time to time less than 1,000. Most observers of the game picked the '67 edition to improve to seventh place, maybe sixth. Come mid-summer '67, the team was puttering along quite well when suddenly they won 10 in a row and the returning heroes were improbably met at Logan Airport by a crowd estimated at up to 10,000—more than had greeted The Beatles when the Fab Four had last come to Boston.

This was a different era in baseball, with 10 teams in each league and no playoff other than the World Series. Virtually every player had to work a second job in the offseason to make ends meet, players roomed together on the road, and often shared apartments with teammates when in Boston. Kids who followed baseball knew the averages of their favorite players, but had no idea what the players were getting paid.

It was a year when a number of players captivated the imaginations of a fan base that grew and grew—players like Rico Petrocelli, who caught the popup that secured first place; Jim Lonborg, who barely made it off the field when he was engulfed by fans surging in celebration; Tony C, who had to follow from the sidelines with his vision permanently impaired, and Yaz, who won the Triple Crown, defined clutch down the stretch, and made every play in the field as well.

It was a magical season, a very special season for the Red Sox franchise, for the fans, and for baseball overall. If not for the '67 Sox, were would Boston baseball be today?

To win the pennant was truly an Impossible Dream, but a dream come true. Those who lived through it will never forget it. The experience formed a bond between the Boston Red Sox and a reborn fan base that has been tested—many times—but never broken. This truly was the birth of what's now termed Red Sox Nation.

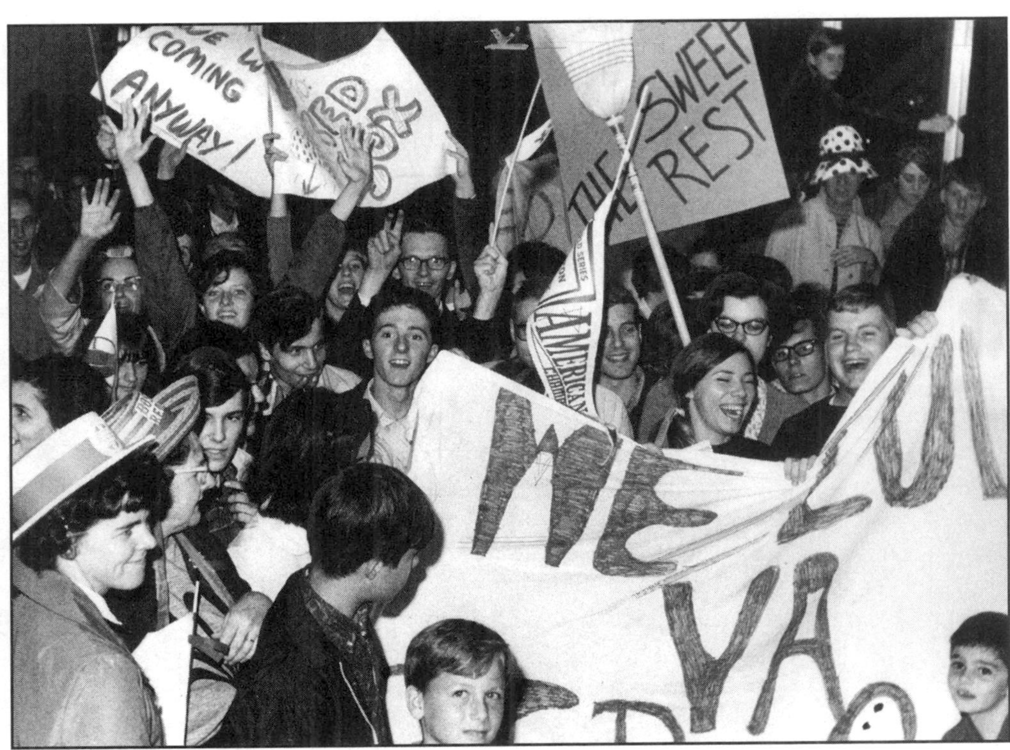

"Red Sox Nation" was truly born in 1967. Fans crush into Logan Airport awaiting home the Red Sox after Boston won World Series Game Five in St. Louis.

1967 Season Timeline

by Bill Nowlin

April

April 12—Some 8,324 hardy fans braved wintry temperatures to see the Red Sox outscore visiting Chicago in the season opener, 5-4. It was the smallest home crowd for an opener since 1953. Lonborg started and pitched six full innings, giving up just one run, before tiring in the seventh. Rico Petrocelli starred on offense, with a single and a homer giving him four RBIs on his first two swings of the season. One never would have guessed this of the Red Sox, but Joe Foy, George Scott, and José Tartabull all stole bases in the first six frames.

The Opening Day starting lineup:

Tartabull	CF
Foy	3B
Yastrzemski	LF
Conigliaro	RF
Scott	1B
Smith	2B
Petrocelli	SS
Ryan	C
Lonborg	P

April 13—Darrell Brandon started, giving up three runs over five innings. The Red Sox scored three times in the bottom of the sixth and added a run on Hank Fischer's suicide squeeze to take a 5-3 lead, but Fischer got squished in the top of the ninth thanks to three Red Sox errors and five unearned White Sox runs. 8-5, Chicago.

April 14—The Sox started rookie Billy Rohr at Yankee Stadium in his major league debut. Despite walking five Yankees, Rohr had a no-hitter going through 8⅔ innings. He'd been spared a hit in the sixth when a hard-hit ball struck him in the shin—but fortunately ricocheted right to Joe Foy who had time to throw to first to retire the batter. On a 3-2 count, Yankees catcher Elston Howard lined a single to right—and was booed by the Stadium crowd. In Toronto in 1966, Rohr previously had a two-strike, two-out, bottom of the ninth no-hitter get away from him. He won this game, 3-0, with Reggie Smith hitting a solo homer and Joe Foy hitting a two-run bomb.

April 15—Boston starter Dennis Bennett followed Rohr's one-hitter with a five-hitter, allowing the Yankees just one run but New York's Mel Stottlemyre shut out the Sox, not allowing a single Sox batter to reach third. 1-0, Yankees.

April 16—After two days without much offense, both teams racked up hits, Boston out-hitting the Yankees, 20-15. The score stood tied 6-6 after nine. The game itself ran nearly six hours. Both Yaz and Tony C had five hits apiece, but the Sox had 13 batters who left men stranded in scoring position. Four times, George Scott made outs with runners in scoring position. Joe Pepitone's third hit of the night drove in the winning run off Lee Stange in the bottom of the 18th. 7-6, Yankees. After the game, Dick Williams chewed out, and benched, George Scott, saying afterwards that "talking to him was like talking to cement."

April 17—No game scheduled.

April 18—After a 5-2 loss to Chicago, and just three Red Sox hits through the first eight innings, Williams told Joe Foy to join Scott on the bench and was thinking of sitting Tartabull, too. "For Dick Williams to consider it just another ball game may be impossible," wrote Harold Kaese, while warning the rookie manager not to press any more than his players should press.

April 19—The Patriot's Day doubleheader against Washington was rained out due to (check one or more): snow, cold, impending rain, wet grounds. The April 11 scheduled opener had been postponed due to cold weather.

April 20—No game scheduled.

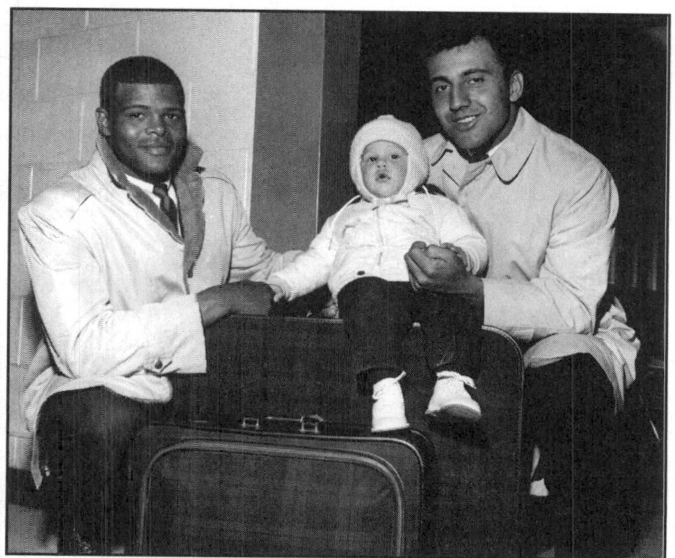

Mike Petrocelli (14 months) shakes hands with new second baseman Reggie Smith, while his proud father Rico looks on in this photograph taken when the Red Sox arrived at Boston's Logan Airport prior to Opening Day.

April 21—Billy Rohr faced the Yankees again, this time in Boston and this time against Stottlemyre, who'd started the season with two straight shutouts. Rohr doled out eight hits, but won the game 6-1 (the one run knocked in by Elston Howard in the top of the eighth). Dalton Jones had a two-run homer as Boston scored three times in the fifth and three times in the seventh.

April 22—YAZ, SCOTT PACE 5-4 SOX WIN. Back briefly from his benching, Scott did just what Williams told him: "get me a fly ball" and his sixth-inning pinch-hit appearance resulted in a sacrifice fly providing the fifth and final run for the Red Sox. Lonborg had given up four, but Don McMahon closed with three scoreless innings. Yaz hit his first homer in a 3-for-3 game, and stole a base, too.

April 23—SOX GO DOWN FIGHTING UMP. Home plate umpire Red Flaherty ejected both Yaz and Dick Williams (for Yaz, it was only his second major league ejection) in a game. Williams griped, "It's the first time I've ever been thrown out of a game before I cussed the umpire." He'd been yelling about a pitch to Elston Howard he thought should have struck him out. Granted a reprieve, Howard doubled home the two runs that proved to win the game, 7-5.

April 24—Frank Howard's three-run homer in Washington looked like it would give the Senators a win, but Mike Andrews slapped the ball right at first baseman Ken Harrelson on a bases-loaded hit-and-run play in the top of the eighth and all three runners scored on Harrelson's error.

Before the season began, Yaz told Eddie Popowski that he thought he might have a chance for the Triple Crown. No one's won one since Yaz in 1967.

April 25—FISCHER, 3 HOMERS RIP SENATORS, 9-3. Reggie Smith led off with a homer and the Sox scored five times in the first three innings. Tony Conigliaro hit his first home run of the year. AL President Joe Cronin sent Dick Williams a warning to watch his words; Williams had continued to chew out Flaherty and added that if Cronin hadn't left the game so early, he would have seen how bad Flaherty's umpiring was.

April 26—Game postponed due to rain.

April 27—No scheduled game.

April 28—LONBORG FANS 13 A's; SOX WIN 3-0. Another cold Friday night at Fenway, but Reggie Smith threw out a runner at third and drove in a run in the 3-0 shutout while Lonborg struck out 13 without issuing a walk.

April 29—SON WIN IN 15th ON TARTABULL'S HIT. Boston and New York both won, and shared first place as Baltimore lost. It was a long game tied 9-9 after nine, and it looked like it was over when Kansas City's Rick Monday homered off Don McMahon in the top of the 15th, but José Tartabull hit a bases-loaded single off his old teammate Jack Aker and drove in the tying and winning runs. Final: Boston 11, KC 10.

April 30—CATER'S HOMER NIPS SOX, 1-0. It was Bat Day and the Red Sox gave 18,000 bats out to kids, but the only player who used one to effect was Danny Cater, who hit Darrell Brandon's high fastball for a home run. From his South Carolina estate, Tom Yawkey said, "I like people who fight for what they believe, and I'm with Williams 100 percent."

May

May 1—Dennis Bennett shut out the Angels 4-0, three of those runs coming on his own home run, hit over Anaheim's right-field fence. The other came on George Scott's first homer of 1967.

May 2—The Angels turned the tables, beating Boston 3-2, as Jim McGlothlin set down the first 19 Red Sox he faced. Scott hit his second homer.

May 3—Jim Lonborg had faced California 10 times but never won. This time he had a no-hitter through six and a one-hitter going into the bottom of the ninth, with a slim 1-0 lead thanks to Mike Andrews' home run in the fifth. A bases-loaded wild pitch brought home the winning run two batters after the Angels had tied it. 2-1, Angels. It was the Sox' fifth loss by just one run.

May 4—No scheduled game., but Ken Coleman says that most of the team visited Disneyland before

flying to Minnesota, where they had been 3-24 over the previous three seasons.

May 5—GRANT STIFLES SOX OFFENSE, 5 TO 2. Mudcat Grant gave the Twins a win as Billy Rohr lasted just two-plus innings at Metropolitan Stadium.

May 6—CHANCE 5-HITTER TOPS SOX. Dean Chance had a shutout until the ninth inning, winning 4-2 in part thanks to two runs donated by Boston on a couple of errors. On top of that, Brandon "walked a guy who later scored and to me that's like an error on the pitcher's part," said the ever-blunt Dick Williams.

May 7—WYATT SAVES 9-6 SOX WIN IN NINTH. With one out and the bases loaded in the bottom of the ninth, Wyatt struck out Harmon Killebrew and got Bob Allison to pop up. Yaz had been benched before the game for not hitting (.276). The Red Sox overcame a four-run lead with Tony Horton's two-run pinch-hit double tying it up 5-5.

May 8—WILLIAMS BENCHES CONIG, REGGIE. On an off-day, a day after benching Yaz, word came out that two more starters would be sat down, too. The Red Sox were in fifth place, three games out of first.

May 9—SOX GAIN SPLIT ON 5-RUN 9th, 5-2. The one thing the headline omitted was that Carl Yastrzemski, coming off the one-game benching, hit a bases-clearing double to give the Red Sox the victory in the day's second game. Kansas City had won the first game, 4-3, after Don McMahon walked in the winning run in the bottom of the eighth.

May 10—Red Sox pitchers walked seven (McMahon

How many people came to Opening Day?

How many people came to Opening Day? It's a good question. We have to confess: we don't know.

It was likely either 8,234 or 8,324—or some other number—but the two cited are the ones that appear in print. The *Boston Globe* box score shows neither figure. Clif Keane's game account says there were 8,324, but Harold Kaese's column in the same paper says there were 8,234. The *Boston Herald* box score reports 8,324, but offered a summary of opening day stats from around the majors prepared by the Associated Press, and that says there were 8,234. The *Boston Record* box score shows 8,234, but Larry Claflin's game story cites the higher figure: 8,324.

Then there's the *Chicago Tribune*, which reports 8,324 in the game account, but 8,234 in the accompanying box score. The *New York Times* flips the figures, with the smaller one in their article and the larger one in their box score. The only newspaper we found that agreed with itself was the *Chicago Defender*, which reported 8,324 in both the UPI report and the box score.

One thing we can agree on: it was a very cold day, 46 degrees Fahrenheit at first pitch. The day before had been even worse, so bad that the game was postponed. That put a damper on turnout, and whatever the size of the crowd, it was the smallest for an opener since 1953. Larry Claflin noted a "sheet of ice on the roof" at Fenway, but said the field was in very good shape.

The *Globe's* Clif Keane criticized the presentation: "This had to be the dullest pre-game show ever. There were three half-frozen kids dancing around in their shorts in right field for a while, and four Marines hoisted the flag... But there was no band and the only fanfare came when Gov. Volpe threw out the first ball."

Perhaps Keane was in the men's room, or trying to keep warm at the press room bar, and missed the band. In her front-page feature story, his colleague Diane White wrote, "Before the game, the Northeastern University band was the main attraction, playing 'Spanish Flea' while three numb majorettes cavorted in the cold. One of the girls dropped her baton every fifth bar. A man in the right field stands said, 'It's got to be part of the act.' Universal optimism! There was enough for everybody. Gov. Volpe smilingly tossed out the first ball. Mayor Collins smiled approvingly. Johnny Mathis crooned the Star Spangled Banner. The magic moment arrived and the Season began." White was writing about the interest women were showing in the Sox. "The girls say the Sox are overburdened with sex appeal. Sighing tenderly, they mention Carl Yastrzemski, Bill Rohr, Jim Lonborg, George Scott, and Tony Conigliaro. Tony is everybody's favorite pin-up boy."

It was Eddie Popowski's major league debut, after decades of minor league work in the Red Sox system. Popowski was Boston's third base coach. Meanwhile public address announcer Sherm Feller was making his return to Fenway after a couple of years in New York and California "working on a book and some music."

One other change: the center field flagpole was no longer an obstacle on the field. The *Record's* John Gillooly explained: "It is no longer a problem to center fielders at Fenway. The C. F. wall has been extended beyond the flagpole. No longer will fielders have to go behind it and dig out hidden baseballs. No longer will it be used to provide shade on a hot day... Jimmy Piersall, for one, used to cool off behind the mast."

Waiting for the season to begin. Dick Williams on Opening Day.

walked four in a row in the eighth) and Red Sox fielders committed a couple of key errors, as Rohr couldn't get through the third and squandered a 3-0 Red Sox first inning, leaving with the game tied. The final score was KC 7, Boston 4.

May 11—There was no game scheduled, but the story of the day was that Tony Conigliaro had to report to Camp Drum, New York for training with the Army Reserve from May 19 to June 3. He could have taken the training in the late fall of 1966, but had gone on safari instead.

May 12—RED SOX HAND GAME TO TIGERS, 5-4. A very unusual incident earned a strange subhead: "Tillman Beans Wyatt." Throwing to second to try to stop Al Kaline from stealing, the catcher's throw hit Wyatt on the back of the head and "bounced all the way to the batter's circle between the plate and first base." Kaline took third. Wyatt finished the game. Balls hit off the gloves of Petrocelli and Andrews each accounted for a Detroit run; the Tigers scored three of their runs without benefit of a hit.

May 13—After losing to the first-place Tigers 10-8, the Red Sox were in eighth place, 11-14, 6½ games out of first, but tied for last with the Twins and Orioles. A six-run Detroit top of the ninth, all the runs scored off John Wyatt, overshadowed even the three runs that Boston came back with. They were the first earned runs off Wyatt in 1967.

May 14—SOX HIT 6 HOMERS, SWEEP TIGERS. The bats were needed, since the pitching wasn't very good, but Boston took two, 8-5 and 13-9, and leapt all the way from the American League cellar to third place (virtually tied with three other teams). Six Sox homers carried the day; Petrocelli hit two homers in the first game while Yaz hit one in each. Scott hit a bases-loaded triple and initiated a 3-2-3 double play. The 28 extra-base hits by both teams in the day's doubleheader was a new league record.

May 15—The game was postponed due to rain but another military summons arrived at Fenway: Billy Rohr had to report for a 14-day tour of reserve duty in the Army. Dick Williams wasn't that pleased with his

pitching, anyhow, and took Rohr out of the rotation.

May 16—Even though John Wyatt had started the season without giving up a run in his first eight appearances, he lost his second game in a row when Paul Blair hit his first home run of the year, a three-run blow in the top of the eighth. The Red Sox had been riding a 5-4 lead after Yaz broke a tie with a solo shot in the bottom of the seventh. Williams wasn't happy; he'd just called time, strode to the mound and told Wyatt to be careful on the first pitch to Blair. The first pitch was the one Blair hit out. Final score: Orioles 8, Red Sox 5.

May 17—10 HOMERS HIT AS O's RIP SOX, 12-8. Four seventh-inning homers gave the Orioles all the runs they needed, as Baltimore scored nine times to overcome a 6-3 Boston lead. Don Demeter took over for Conigliaro in right field, and hit his first home run of the year.

May 18—No scheduled game.

May 19—HORTON'S HIT IN 9th BEATS TRIBE, 3-2. Subhead: "Tartabull's Speed, Triple by Reggie Set the Stage." It was a pinch-hit, walk-off single to right by Tony Horton that lifted the Red Sox over Cleveland. "After I hit the ball into right field I almost forgot to run—that's how excited I was," Horton enthused afterwards.

Billy Rohr had a no-hitter going against the Yankees when Tom Tresh knocked what looked like a sure hit to lead off the bottom of the ninth. Those who saw the play said there was no way Yaz could ever be expected to catch the ball hit well over his head. Catch it, he did.

May 20—On the third pitch from Don McMahon, Chuck Hinton found one he liked and pounded out a two-run homer in the top of the 10th for a 5-3 Cleveland win. The Indians had led 3-0; Boston tied it with three in the seventh but all for naught.

May 21—RED SOX TURN BACK INDIANS TWICE. The Indians led 3-0 in the eighth inning of the first game, but a Yaz triple drove home two, and George Scott's home run brought home Yaz and himself for a 4-3 win. In the second game, Darrell Brandon pitched a good one for a 6-2 win, even hitting a double himself and scoring in the seventh inning thanks to a single by Yaz.

May 22—No scheduled game. At the close of the day, the Sox were in sixth place.

May 23—BENNETT, WYATT CHECK TIGERS, 5-2. Rico, Yaz Rip Homers. Yaz was batting an even .300 and leading the club with 27 RBIs. Petrocelli was second with 21. Yaz had eight homers to Rico's five. The team was back to playing .500 baseball (17-17).

May 24—JONES' HR, LONBORG NIP TIGERS, 1-0. "I have thrown better games, but I have never pitched a better game," said Lonborg. Dick Williams was even more enthused: "It was the greatest game I have even seen pitched in my life. I mean the way he pitched under fire." This was still May. There was no thought of any pennant race. Lonborg allowed four hits, walked four, and had to get out of a few jams. He had some fielding help from Scott at first base, but he bore down when he had to, striking out 11, and was nearly perfect in the clutch. The one run came on Dalton Jones' second-inning homer off Denny McLain.

May 25—The Tigers brought out former Red Sox pitcher Earl Wilson and gave him a 9-1 lead, as José Santiago had a rough day. Six Tiger runs scored in the bottom of the fifth. Final score: 9-3, Detroit. Conigliaro was doing cleanup work at Camp Drum—cleaning out GI cans in the mess hall.

May 26—DRABOWSKY CHILLS RED SOX RALLY, 4-3. Rohr, on leave, started for Boston and took the loss, giving up four runs in three-plus innings. McNally started for Baltimore and gave up three in the fifth until Moe Drabowsky came in and threw 4⅔ innings of one-hit relief. Scott struck out four times and earned himself a spot on the next day's bench.

May 27—ORIOLES TROUNCE FUMBLING SOX, 10-0. Five Red Sox errors more or less threw the

Yaz and George Scott both hit homers and Dave Morehead pitched a 4-0 shutout to tame the Tigers on August 15. Yaz, Tony C, Scott and Morehead, left to right, combined efforts to defeat the Tigers 4-0 on August 15. Yaz hit his 28th HR, Scott hit his 14th, and Tony made a spectacular tumbling fifth-inning catch with the bases loaded.

game away while Frank Robinson hit a pair of two-run homers. A poll of Red Sox players picked the Tigers and the Orioles to contend for the pennant. They'd been asked not to vote for their own team, but Yaz said he did anyway: "Why not? The Tigers, Orioles and White Sox are the top ones, but I'd put us up there, too. We're up there now, aren't we? Nobody's going to run away this season."

May 28—LONBORG, WYATT END O's SPELL, 4-3. Frank Robinson hit another homer but so did Petrocelli. Lonborg gave up two runs in the first but let only one runner reach as far as second from the third through the seventh. Wyatt pitched 1⅓ innings of hitless ball in relief. Reggie Smith was 3-for-5 and scored three runs.

May 29—No scheduled game.

May 30—SOX SWEEP 3rd TWIN BILL IN ROW. Taking two from the Angels, 5-4 and 6-1, the Red Sox stayed in the hunt. Mike Andrews hit two doubles in the first game and Dennis Bennett tried a new delivery and won the second game. "I found a sinker today for the first time in three years," he said. More than 32,000 fans came to Fenway, the largest crowd in five years. Tony Horton's pinch-hit double, batting for Mike Ryan,

drove in the winning run in the first game's eighth inning. It was his sixth hit in 13 pinch-hit at-bats.

May 31—YAZ HR's, SQUEEZE WIN FOR SOX, 3-2. Billy Rohr was due to start, but the Army called him at the last minute and Darrell Brandon filled in. He might have had a shutout but for an error by Rico. Yaz hit his ninth and tenth home runs—both solo homers leading off innings. The real excitement came when George Scott beat out an accidental dribbler down the third-base line, and moved up on a walk to Reggie Smith. Rico advanced both runners with a sacrifice and Joe Foy was walked intentionally. Mike Ryan was up, and he executed a perfect suicide squeeze back to the pitcher with the speedy Scott rumbling in from third base.

MONTH-END: As of the end of May, the Red Sox were in third place, 4½ games behind leader Detroit. The White Sox were just half a game out of first. The Red Sox had won more games than they'd lost, but not many more: 22-20.

June

June 1—Dean Chance ran his record to 9-2 for the Twins, shutting out the Sox, 4-0. Rohr, back from an overnight with the Army that had deprived him of the start the previous day, gave up three runs on four hits, two of them home runs.

June 2—LONBORG ALMOST NO-HITS TRIBE, 2-1. Gentleman Jim came within five outs of a no-hitter in Cleveland before Duke Sims hit a ground-rule double. Yaz's two-run homer provided all the Red Sox runs. Lonborg knew he had a no-no going after six, and admitted, "I was thinking it would be great if I could strike out those next nine hitters." He got the first three, in the seventh. "As long as we won, it's fabulous," Lonborg said. The Red Sox acquired Jerry Adair from the White Sox for Don McMahon and Rob Snow, and optioned Galen Cisco to Pittsfield since Tony Conigliaro had completed his Army Reserve stint.

June 3—SANTIAGO SAVES 6-2 BENNETT WIN. José retired all nine batters he faced, a perfect relief effort. George Scott showed signs of emerging from a slump, hitting his fourth home run of the season.

June 4—The Red Sox were shut out again, 3-0, on a five-hitter by Steve Hargan of the Indians. Yaz was robbed of a home run, and Rico hit a ball that just missed being fair for another. While visiting Cleveland, the Sox made a trade, giving the Indians Tony Horton and Don Demeter in exchange for pitcher Gary Bell.

June 5—No scheduled game.

June 6—Chicago overcame Boston's 3-0 lead and beat Darrell Brandon, 5-3. The day after Chicago manager Eddie Stanky called Yaz "an all-star from the neck down," Belmont (MA) high school hero Wilbur Wood came on in relief and on his second pitch got Yaz to hit into a game-ending double play. The Sox called up Gary Waslewski from Toronto.

June 7—Dick Williams managed to get himself ejected from a game that never happened. The two Sox teams squared off in Chicago for a scheduled twi-night doubleheader and Williams was ejected in the second inning. Within minutes, the games were called due to downpour.

June 8—BELL, YAZ GIVE SOX SPLIT, 2-5, 7-3. After dropping the first game, making it a three-game losing streak, Gary Bell started his first game for Boston, a complete game effort assisted by Yaz homer #12 to center field. The Red Sox won game two.

June 9—2 YAZ, 2 FOY HOME RUNS BEAT NATS. The Red Sox were in fourth place, but held their standing as Boston—back home now—topped Washington, 8-7. Lonborg gave up six runs in one of his weakest efforts of the year. Joe Foy had two solo homers; Yaz had three RBIs. Yaz also made two "outstanding catches."

June 10—Big Frank Howard hit two big homers, the second one hit so hard that "nobody on the Red Sox team dared to follow its course. Yastrzemski lowered his head once the ball was hit and never budged." Lee Stange's record ran to 0-4 with the 7-3 loss. The Red Sox remained in fourth place. Attendance had reached 320,670—already 79,264 ahead of 1966. Even if the press hadn't fully picked up on it yet, the fans were responding.

June 11—SOX RALLY TO WIN, 4-3; THEN BOW, 8-7. After spotting the Senators three runs in the doubleheader's first game, Boston got two in the sixth and one each in the next two frames to win it for Santiago, on in relief of Brandon. The game-winner came on a Conigliaro scorcher that hit opposing pitcher Dave Baldwin hard on the wrist. The Sox spotted the Senators three runs again in game two, but that was a bad idea. Even though the Red Sox rallied for three in the bottom of the ninth, they needed four to tie.

June 12—SOX BATTERY SHOCKS YANKEES, 3-1. Gary Bell threw a seven-hit complete game and Russ Gibson's first major league homer won the game.

June 13—A frustrated Dick Williams castigated Conigliaro for "dumb baserunning" when Tony tried to stretch a single into a double and was out by a mile. It cut short a rally the Red Sox needed. They fell short—as did Lonborg's pitching—as the Yankees beat Boston, 5-3.

June 14—STANGE WINS 6-1; STANKY OUSTED.

It was "one of the wildest nights in some time," wrote Will McDonough. Chicago had won the first game, 8-7, George Scott unfortunately striking out with the bases loaded and two outs in the bottom of the ninth after the Red Sox had already scored twice. Stanky came out at least a half-dozen times in the second game to argue calls before he was finally told to take a shower. He was showered with debris and later threatened to sue if he and his wife didn't receive better protection at the park.

June 15—TONY'S TWO-RUN HR LIFTS SOX. Now there's a way to re-ingratiate yourself with your skipper. Gary Waslewski pitched nine innings of shutout ball, but the Red Sox hadn't scored, either. In the top of the 11th, Chicago scored a run off John Wyatt. In the bottom of the 11th, after both Yaz and Scott made outs, Joe Foy singled and then (down 0-2, both swinging) Conig patiently waited out three close balls, then hit a two-run walk-off homer for the 2-1 triumph.

June 16—The Senators took two from the Red Sox, 1-0 and 4-3, overcoming a three-run Red Sox lead in the second game when Brandon wilted in the heat after throwing eight shutout innings. Bell and Santiago combined to pitch a strong five-hit first game, but Bob Priddy pitched even better.

June 17—LONBORG WINS 8th, HALTS NATS, 5-1. Tony C hit his sixth home run, Yaz doubled in a pair, and Lonborg got back on track with a complete game five-hit effort.

June 18—Even though Yaz hit a homer to tie the score in the top of the ninth, Washington wore down Red Sox relief for a run in the 10th, and the Sox lost, 3-2.

June 19—Game postponed due to rain, and Bill Landis was prevented from pitching his first major league start.

June 20—FOY SLAM, YAZ HR DEFEAT YANKS, 7-1. Gary Bell had a shutout going into the ninth inning, but was glad for the run support as Joe Foy hit a grand slam off Mel Stottlemyre in the top of the fifth. Early on the morning of the 19th, Foy had arrived home and found his parents' Bronx home on fire. He led his confused parents to safety. Bell had now won three games for the Red Sox, his only loss coming when the Sox were shut out, 1-0.

June 21—SOX WIN, 8-1, AMID WILD BRAWL. There was a story on the front sports page headlined "Red Sox Going to Milwaukee?" With no new stadium in Boston and poor attendance, the Wisconsin city fathers were making a pitch to Tom Yawkey. In New York, a melee broke out when Joe Foy was beaned in the top of the second inning and Jim Lonborg just happened to hit offending pitcher Thad Tillotson between the shoulder blades in the bottom of the second. "I'm out to protect my teammates," Lonborg said. Tony C hit a three-run homer and Yaz hit three singles.

June 22—Postponed due to rain. Landis had his first start postponed for the second time. Yaz declared that as long as Waslewski was in good shape, the Red Sox were "ready for a drive for the pennant in September."

June 23—FOY'S FOUR HITS SPARK RED SOX, 8-4. Petrocelli was hit on his left wrist and was expected to be out for a week. More bad news came when Jim Lonborg was ordered to report for his reserve duty in the Army from July 30 to August 13. Conig hit another homer and Lee Stange pitched decent ball, but the game story was Joe Foy getting four hits and scoring three times.

June 24—Steve Hargan beat the Red Sox again, 3-2, as the Indians spoiled Family Night at Fenway. The Red Sox sold Dennis Bennett to the Mets and optioned Billy Rohr to Toronto. They called up pitcher Al "Sparky" Lyle from the Toronto farm club.

June 25—Red Sox 8, Indians 3. Yaz hit #18 and

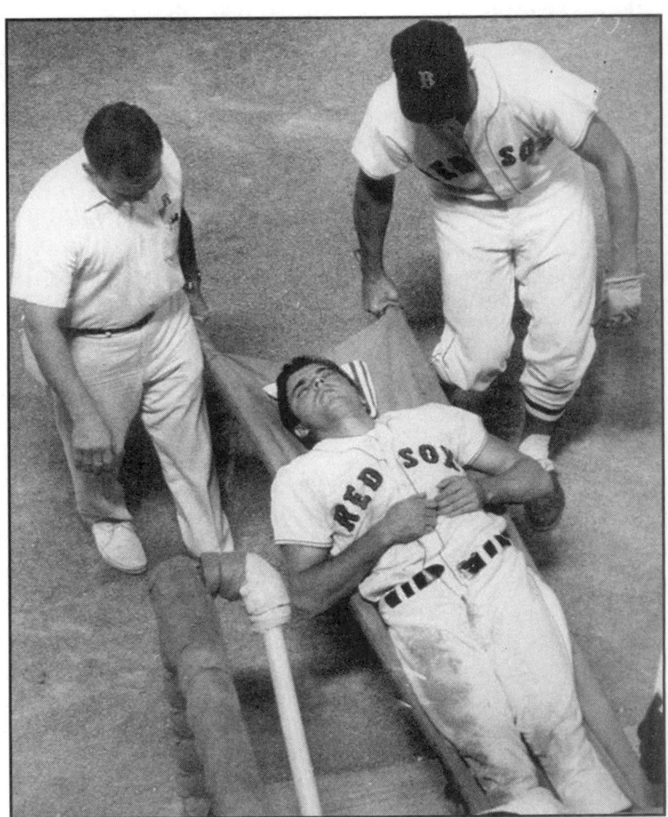

The season took on a somber tone on August 18 when Conig was hit in the head by a Jack Hamilton pitch.

both Bob Tillman and Joe Foy homered, too, as the Sox closed a homestand to head out on a two-week road trip. Tillman had only eight hits in 42 at-bats, but added three more. Gary Bell beat his former teammates and Cleveland's Luis Tiant bore the loss.

June 26—TWINS WIN, 2-1, TIE SOX FOR THIRD. This sort of headline wouldn't have been possible any time in the last few years. The Red Sox lost, but were still in third place. They were six games out of first. Yaz was out with the flu and missed his first (and last) of the year. Lonborg pitched well but with no run support.

June 27—RED SOX HOLD ON, EDGE TWINS, 3-2. Tony Conigliaro hit a two-run homer in the top of the first. Gary Waslewski pitched well and won his first major league game. The Sox finally defeated recent nemesis Dean Chance. Now the Army was after Dalton Jones, who had to report for two weeks beginning June 30. Petrocelli and Yastrzemski were both named starters for the 1967 All-Star Game.

June 28—SCOTT ERROR AIDS TWINS' 3-2 WIN. Another one run game, this one going to Minnesota when George Scott uncharacteristically made two errors, one of which cost Lee Stange a fine outing. Credit Dave Boswell for striking out 13 Red Sox.

June 29—No scheduled game.

June 30—SOX TRIP A'S, 5-3, ON CONIG BLAST. Gary Bell won his fifth game for the Red Sox, in large part thanks to Tony's 450-foot three-run homer in the sixth. Conig was named to the All-Star squad.

END OF JUNE, the Red Sox were three games over .500 with a 37-34 record, in third place, 5½ games behind the White Sox but just one game behind second-place Detroit.

July

July 1—LONBORG, CONIG PACE 10-2 SOX WIN. Tony C had three hits, one of them his 11th homer. Mike Ryan drove in three runs and helped Jim Lonborg win his 10th game. Lonborg was named as a pitcher for the A.L. All-Star team. Dick Williams, who had umpired in spring training intrasquad games, took up coaching third base for the Red Sox since Eddie Popowski had several days off for his daughter's wedding.

July 2—The Red Sox swept the third game of the series in Kansas City, with a 2-1 win as Gary Waslewski allowed just three hits in 8⅔ innings. Just before the eighth inning began, first base coach Bobby Doerr had mentioned that he thought Joe Foy was bailing out a bit. Foy adjusted his at-bat, and hit a home run to break a tie and ultimately win the game. "The nice thing about it is that someone different is making the big play each game," said Dick Williams. The Sox were in a three-team tie for second place with the Twins and the Tigers.

July 3—3 SOX HR's HELP STANGE TOP ANGELS. The Red Sox won their fourth game in a row as Lee Stange pitched well in Anaheim and Conig, Andrews, and Smith all homered for Boston. It was a 9-3 win.

July 4—The Red Sox rallied for two runs in the top of the ninth, but the Angels closed it out holding what was then a 4-3 lead. Gary Bell just hadn't had it, giving up the four runs in just 4⅔ innings. Sparky Lyle made his major league debut, allowing just one hit in the final two frames. The Red Sox were back in fourth place.

July 5—MINCHER HR IN 9th NIPS SOX, 4-3. The Angels took another one, dealing the Red Sox their 18th one-run loss of the season, when Don Mincher took Santiago deep with a two-run homer to win it. Petrocelli played short in the ninth, coming off his wrist injury. Both George Scott and Mike Ryan were ailing as well.

July 6—No scheduled game.

July 7—TIGERS SHADE RED SOX IN 11th, 5-4. The streak of one-run losses continued as the Sox honed their talent as "masters of the heartbreaking loss." The Red Sox scored three times in the top of the ninth to send the game into extra innings, but Bill Freehan doubled deep off John Wyatt scoring a runner from first base and the Tigers won it in the 11th. It was the 10th loss in a row for the Red Sox that had been decided by just one run.

July 8—The Red Sox lost their fourth game in a row, 2-0, as Denny McLain shut them down on four hits. The Red Sox dropped to fifth place just before the All-Star break.

July 9—LONBORG SAVES SPLIT, STOPS SOX SPIN. The Red Sox were pounded 10-4 in the first game, Detroit's Earl Wilson pitching way better than Gary Bell. Jim Lonborg came to the rescue in the nightcap with a 3-0 shutout as Reggie Smith and Carl Yastrzemski both homered. Wyatt saved it.

July 10—The Red Sox hosted their annual clambake at South Yarmouth as they enjoyed the first of three days off for the All-Star break.

July 11—Yaz was 3-for-4 in the All-Star Game but Tony C went 0-for-6. Petrocelli was 0-for-1. No Sox pitchers had to stress their arms. The National League won it, 2-1, in 15 innings.

July 12—FOY SEES SOX FLAG WINNER. Joe Foy made a bold prediction, but most of the team thought Minnesota would prevail. Even Dick Williams thought

the Twins were the team to beat. Williams had a morning workout at the ballpark and decried Darrell Brandon for pitching in a way he deemed "pussyfooting."

July 13—A dual-admission doubleheader drew 42,282 to Fenway Park. The Red Sox won the first game behind Lee Stange, 4-2, grabbing three unearned runs in the bottom of the first inning. They should have just conceded the second game; Dave McNally shut out the Sox, 10-0. Gary Bell was bombed again for the third time in a row. That was no one-run loss.

July 14—SOX FIND BATTING EYES, RIP O's, 11-5. As sometimes occurs, the bottled-up bats of the day before broke loose behind Jim Lonborg. Yaz and Tony C each homered in the barrage.

July 15—TRIPLE PLAY LIFTS SOX OVER O's, 5-1. Before the game, Russ Gibson was warming up Gary Waslewski and told Williams that the pitcher just didn't have it. Williams had him start nonetheless, and Waslewski couldn't seem to get a ball over the plate. He walked the first two Orioles, but on Gibson's advice Williams had reliever José Santiago ready and brought him in with the count 2-1 on Paul Blair. The embattled pitcher's best friend: Joe Foy one-handed a low liner, threw to Andrews at second to double off the runner. Andrews was knocked back in a collision with the oncoming runner from first, but held the ball and then threw over to Scott at first. Yaz drove in two runs with a sac fly in the first and a single in the second. The Sox optioned George Smith to San Francisco's Phoenix affiliate and acquired Norm Siebern from the Giants.

July 16—The annual father-son game was canceled due to wet grounds, but the regular contest was held and Boston beat Detroit, 9-5, as Yaz and Tony C each homered and Sparky Lyle held back the Bengals. The Red Sox climbed into third place.

July 17—The Red Sox were starting to draw some real crowds at home, averaging 23,887 over the six-game homestand. The fan base was awakening. The Sox slugged out seven runs, Yaz hitting another homer and driving in three while Lee Stange threw a complete game 7-1 win with such control that in seven of the innings, he threw nine or fewer pitches.

July 18—SOX TROUNCE O's, 6-2, FOR 5th IN ROW. They gained a game in the standings, now just 2½ games out of first. Lonborg pitched a complete game, allowing just five hits. Harold Kaese's column in the *Boston Globe* was headlined "Sox Not Cocky—Or Scared."

July 19—SOX WIN 6th IN ROW; 1½ OFF TOP. The headlines were looking better and better, and Kaese's column diagnosed pennant fever. Joe Foy was 3-for-5 while Mike Andrews hit a homer and drove in three runs. Both Bell and Santiago pitched well enough for a 6-4 win. The Red Sox were still in third place, though it was a very tight race. Even the fifth-place Tigers were just 3½ games behind Chicago.

July 20—The Sox had a 2-0 lead over Baltimore, but the game was called in the third inning and the Sox never got the chance to cash in.

July 21—SOX IN SECOND PLACE, WIN 7th IN ROW, 6-2. The Sox had gone to Cleveland and gotten a good game out of Darrell Brandon, whose record was now 4-7. Joe Foy drove in three on a home run in the second inning.

July 22—SOX WIN 8th STRAIGHT—HALF GAME OUT. Lee Stange threw a three-hit shutout, blanking the Indians. Former Cleveland MVP Al Rosen remarked, "Without that guy you Red Sox would be nothing." He was talking about Mike Andrews, who hit a leadoff home run. "He turns the double play, knows the game, and looks like he will hit some, too." Yaz homered, too. Lonborg was hit by an Indians line drive during pre-game batting practice, but was deemed OK. It was a 4-0 shutout.

July 23—5000 FANS MOB RETURNING SOX AFTER 9th, 10th STRAIGHT WINS. That was the front page headline of the *Boston Globe*, accompanied by a photo of a large crowd around a bus full of players and the subhead: "Cheering Crowd Engulfs Players at Logan." Many estimates had the crowd size as high as 10,000 fans. "Pennant Hopes Soar After Cleveland Sweep" read the headline of the second story on the paper's front page. Boston took two, with torrid Joe Foy hitting a grand slam to help Jim Lonborg win game one, 8-5, and Gary Bell pitching a complete game 5-1 win, Tony C homering and driving in two. The Red Sox hadn't won 10 in a row since May 1951.

July 24—No scheduled game.

July 25—"Cinderella dumped the Red Sox and stayed with the Angels," wrote Clif Keane leading off his game story that told of the 6-4 Angels win that derailed Red Sox hopes to extend their 10-game win streak. Don Mincher's ball went into Conig's glove, then popped out and California went on to score three first-inning runs. The Angels had been ahead 6-2 after four innings, and when the grounds crew pulled the tarp off the field following a 42-minute rain delay, they were booed. In a separate story, Harold Kaese suggested that after seven long years, the Sox were finally drawing fans again, finally recovering from the void left by the retirement of Ted Williams.

July 26—Bill Landis won his first big league

Chowing down to celebrate a late July win over the Angels at Fenway.

game, 9-6, thanks to a six-run Red Sox rally in the "lucky seventh" inning. Mike Andrews bunted in the tying run with a base-hit bunt toward third base, and Yaz drove in three with a double off the Wall in left-center. Outside Fenway, a few fans picketed, calling for a new stadium.

July 27—RED SOX CATCH UP IN 9th, WIN IN 10th. The five-run fifth put the Angels in good position to win the game, but Joe Foy hit a two-run homer in the bottom of the ninth to bring Boston within a run, and Tony Conigliaro hit one into the screen to tie it. In the 10th, Reggie Smith tripled into the right-field corner and scored two batters later when the Angels third baseman couldn't handle a "tricky bouncer" from Jerry Adair. "We cannot be beaten," crowed Conigliaro. Sparky Lyle got his first win. Red Sox attendance was 727,275 at this point, about 300,000 ahead of 1966 at the same point.

July 28—MINNESOTA TWINS BOMB RED SOX, 9-2. The front-page teaser above the *Globe's* masthead conveyed the bad news. Lonborg was on the mound for what was thought to be the last time before leaving for two weeks of Reserve duty and he got bombed for seven runs in 3⅔ innings before Dick Williams sent him on his way. Before the game, Ted Williams predicted the Red Sox would win the pennant.

July 29—RED SOX EXPLODE TO WIN OPENER, STUMBLE IN 2nd. The biggest Fenway crowd in over 10 years saw Yaz cut down two runners and four pinch-hitters execute successfully as the Red Sox rallied with four runs in the bottom of the eighth to take the first of two by a 6-3 score. The Twins outpowered Waslewski, Landis, and Osinski in the second game, 10-3.

July 30—The Sox lost, 7-5, with the tying runs on base with two outs and Carl Yastrzemski at the plate. Two Twins collided in the infield trying to catch Yaz's weak pop fly, but Rich Reese held on to snuff out the four-run rally that had energized fan hopes.

Dave Morehead had rehabbed his sore arm and the Sox brought him up from Toronto, sending Waslewski down.

July 31—STANGE PERFECT 6⅔ INNINGS; YAZ HOMER LEADS SOX, 4-0. It was Yaz's three-run homer in the third that provided the lead. Lee Stange threw a three-hitter, the first being a Killebrew single in the seventh. Yaz was hit in the elbow by a pitch, but he was able to play both games the following day.

The Red Sox finished the month with a record of 56-44, two games behind Chicago, in second place, two games ahead of third-place Detroit.

August

August 1—SOX REBOUND, 8-3, AFTER 4-3 LOSS. Dave Morehead, back for a second stint, gave up four runs in the third and Yaz's three-run homer in the sixth (his 27th HR) still left them one run short. Mike Ryan's three-run homer in the seventh inning of the second game, helped key the first of two four-run Red Sox rallies and helped give Jim Lonborg win #15. Lonborg was pitching on a day pass from his Army Reserve duties.

August 2—Boston had a 5-3 lead after three, but the A's scored twice in the seventh and twice in the eighth, John Wyatt tagged for all four runs. The Sox lost, 8-6, and lost the opportunity to pick up a game on Chicago.

August 3—The Red Sox acquired veteran catcher Elston Howard from the New York Yankees and optioned José Tartabull to Pittsfield. The Women's pages in the *Globe* immediately inserted a profile of Arlene Howard into their ongoing series on Red Sox wives which had begun on July 28 with Ernestine Smith. Mike Ryan's finger had been injured the night before. Howard didn't play in the game, but Dave Morehead earned his first win of the year as the Red Sox battled to overcome a three-run Kansas City first inning and won, 5-3. Harrelson (KC) and Andrews (BOS) hit homers.

August 4—Jim Merritt threw a 3-0 shutout for the Twins, Darrell Brandon taking the loss despite giving

up just one earned run. The Red Sox were 2½ games behind first-place Chicago.

August 5—SOX HELD TO THREE HITS; BOW, 2-1. Petrocelli's solo homer was one of just three hits off Minnesota's Dave Boswell, so Stange couldn't get a win out of his strong effort. The Red Sox were three games out of first and now just one game ahead of the Twins and the Tigers, and only two ahead of California.

August 6—Was it a perfect game or wasn't it? Dean Chance retired every Red Sox batter from the leadoff man in the first until the end of the game. The game lasted only five innings, though, before rain washed out the remainder. Jim Lonborg came up on the losing end of a 2-0 game which catapulted the Twins over the Red Sox into second place by one percentage point, .543 to .542.

August 7—No scheduled game.

August 8—SIEBERN'S HIT IN 9th OF 2d GAME GIVES SOX SPLIT. Though they rallied for a couple of runs in the top of the ninth on Tony C's 20th home run, the Sox fell short, losing the first game to KC, 5-3. They entered the final frame of the second game tied, 4-4, having battled back from a 4-0 deficit. Dick Williams used four pinch-hitters in the game, three of whom stayed in to play; Norm Siebern's pinch-hit single drove in two, a third run scoring on a throwing error on the play. Williams used seven pitchers in the game, 19 players in all, and it worked: Boston won, 7-5.

August 9—LONBORG WINS 16th, 5-1, SOX 1½ OUT. Lonborg arrived one hour before game time on an overnight pass from the Army—he never missed a turn in the rotation despite a two-week hitch. Jerry Adair drove in two, collecting three hits for the second game in a row. Yaz made another great catch.

August 10—There was no scheduled game for Boston, but the White Sox won theirs and held a two-game lead.

August 11—ANGELS DROP RED SOX INTO THIRD PLACE, 1-0. The Twins beat the White Sox. The top five teams in the American League were tightly bunched; California was only three games behind. Lee Stange's wild pitch allowed a runner to score from third base, totally spoiling his four-hitter. Red Sox bats only mustered three off Jim McGlothlin.

August 12—The Red Sox dropped to fourth place after dropping another game to the Angels, 2-1. Gary

The watermelon tastes even sweeter after the Sox sweep two from the Senators. August 22, 1967.

Bell pitched a fine game but without run support. George Scott was on the bench for the second straight game, in Dick Williams' doghouse for overeating. He was only four pounds overweight, but Williams was strict on weight control. A front-page story in the August 16 *Boston Evening Globe* told of the banana split Scott ate that helped him gain seven pounds on one off-date in Anaheim. One banana split?

August 13—RED SOX LOSE, 3-2, DROP TO FIFTH—TWINS TAKE LEAD. Lasting just four innings, Lonborg's record dropped to 16-6, though he pitched a complete game five-hit effort in Anaheim. The Red Sox batted .185 in the nine games on the road trip. Yaz slammed into the wall in the first inning, stayed in the game, but reported some vision problems after his last at-bat: "I didn't see a pitch. Everything was blurry."

August 14—No scheduled game.

August 15—The Sox came home for a 12-game homestand. Of the 49 remaining games, 29 would be at home. The teaser over the masthead the next morning read: MOREHEAD BLANKS TIGERS, 4-0, SMITH, SCOTT, YAZ HOMER. What more could you ask for? Conigliaro's one-handed catch saved the shutout. Boston optioned out Hank Fischer and Russ Gibson, bringing back Jerry Stephenson and José Tartabull. Conig would miss the next night's game because of National Guard duty.

August 16—SOX WIN, SCOTT 'POUNDS' 2 HOMERS. The slimmed-down Scott had now hit three homers in his first two games off the bench. Reggie threw out a runner at the plate, Dick Williams got himself ejected from another game, and Boston moved up to third place on the strength of an 8-3 win, beating the Tigers in large part thanks to a strong seven innings of three-hit shutout relief by Darrell Brandon.

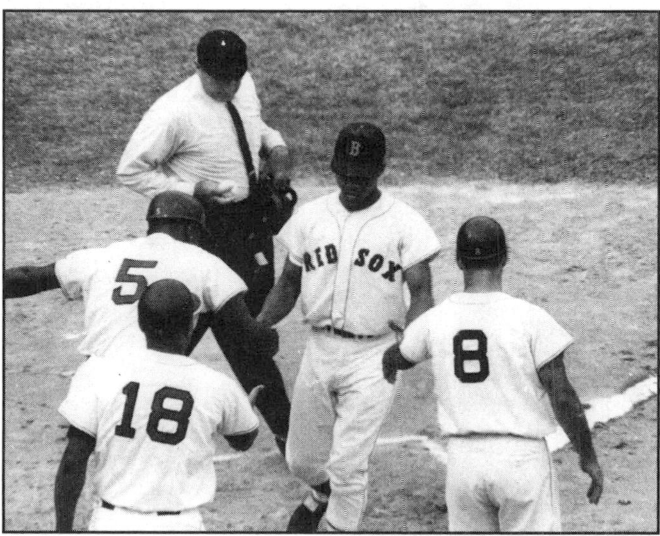

On August 20, 1967, Reggie became the first Boston player to hit home runs from both side of the plate in a single game. A third home run in the second game helped the Red Sox rally from an 8-0 deficit in the second game to sweep a doubleheader, 12-2 and 9-8.

August 17—The Tigers won it in 10 innings, 7-4, but the Red Sox had rallied with two to tie it in the bottom of the eighth and would have won it in regulation had Jerry Adair not been cut down at home plate on a throw from Al Kaline. Dick Williams didn't blame the umpires; it wasn't the only baserunning mistake of the game for the Red Sox.

August 18—BELL HURLS SOX TO 3-2 WIN; CONIGLIARO 'BEANED,' HURT. How badly Tony Conigliaro was hurt by Jack Hamilton's fastball was not known at first, though everyone knew it was bad. It was thought he could be out for three weeks. His cheek was fractured and he was out for the season, as it happened, and was never again the star he had been. That very day, Ted Williams had sent him a message that he was crowding the plate too much and could get hurt. And before the game, Dick Williams had complained to the umpires about Hamilton maybe loading up on pitches; back on the 12th, Mike Andrews had complained to the home plate umpire that Hamilton was throwing spitters. Gary Bell pitched a four-hit game; he had a no-hitter going at the time Tony was hit, and kept it going through six. Tartabull ran for Conigliaro and scored the first run of the game.

The Red Sox were in fourth place, three games behind.

August 19—SOX SALVAGE 12-11 SPREE. Yaz had four hits, including his 29th homer, and though Darrell Brandon was hit hard for five runs late in the game, Jerry Stephenson was able to shut it down with the final two outs. Siebern's pinch triple drove in three. Osinski got the win. Yaz said that he'd come to believe the airport reception by the fans hurt the team; they were no longer as loose as they'd been on the road trip, "Maybe it made us realize how close we were to winning this thing. The next week we all started to tighten up."

August 20—SMITH BANGS 3 HOMERS, SOX SWEEP. The Red Sox completed a four-game sweep of the visiting Angels, dominating them 12-2 in the first game and then overcoming an 8-0 deficit in the second. Two homers by Reggie, one by Rico, and one by Carl helped Lee Stange take game one, Reggie's five RBIs more than enough. In the second game, Morehead gave up six runs and Osinski two, and the Angels were up

8-0 after 3½. Reggie hit a solo shot in the bottom of the fourth, and Yaz hit his second HR of the day for three more runs in the fifth. Boston tied it with four more in the sixth, Dalton Jones driving in two. A sac fly and Jerry Adair's single tied the game. In the bottom of the eighth, Adair put the Sox ahead to stay with a solo home run to right. José Santiago let runners get on second and third in the top of the ninth, but Dick Williams stuck with him and he escaped unscathed. Boston was in third place, 1½ games behind the Twins.

August 21—The Sox won their fifth in a row with a 6-5 win over the Washington Senators when Elston Howard (.191 at the time before his final at-bat) singled in the winning run in the bottom of the ninth inning. The Twins and White Sox were tied for first place, but Boston was just one game behind.

August 22—SOX SWEEP, 2-1, 5-3, NOW .001 OFF. Just one percentage point (.562 to .561) separated the Sox from the White Sox atop the AL standings. Jerry Stephenson won the first game, letting up just one Washington run in 7⅔ innings, saved in part by a 4-2-3 double play in the top of the ninth with Wyatt on in relief. Gary Bell won the nightcap, thanks to a three-run bottom of the seventh. George Scott's two-RBI single was the clincher. Scott had to leave the first game after he helped hold back the Senators, lunging and sprawling over the first-base bag to get an out just before he was run over by Dick Nen.

August 23—RED SOX LOSE, 3-2, FALL GAME OFF PACE. Apparently, you can't win 'em all and Bob Priddy allowed only five hits. Sox doctor Tierney said "my thinking is definite" that Conigliaro would be back to play before the season was over. An exuberant fan named Duncan MacKenzie was able to shake hands with all three Sox outfielders and continued to elude Sox security long enough to greet three infielders before being apprehended. "I wish I'd had more time to talk to Scott," he said of the one infielder he didn't reach.

August 24—It was Nuns' Day at Fenway and the Red Sox fared well, 7-5, out-scoring the Senators on the strength of three home runs. Elston Howard's was a three-run homer, and Jerry Adair and Jim Landis each hit solo shots. Boston and Chicago were separated by .001, with the White Sox due in for a twi-night doubleheader.

August 25—RED SOX SPLIT, NOW THIRD;

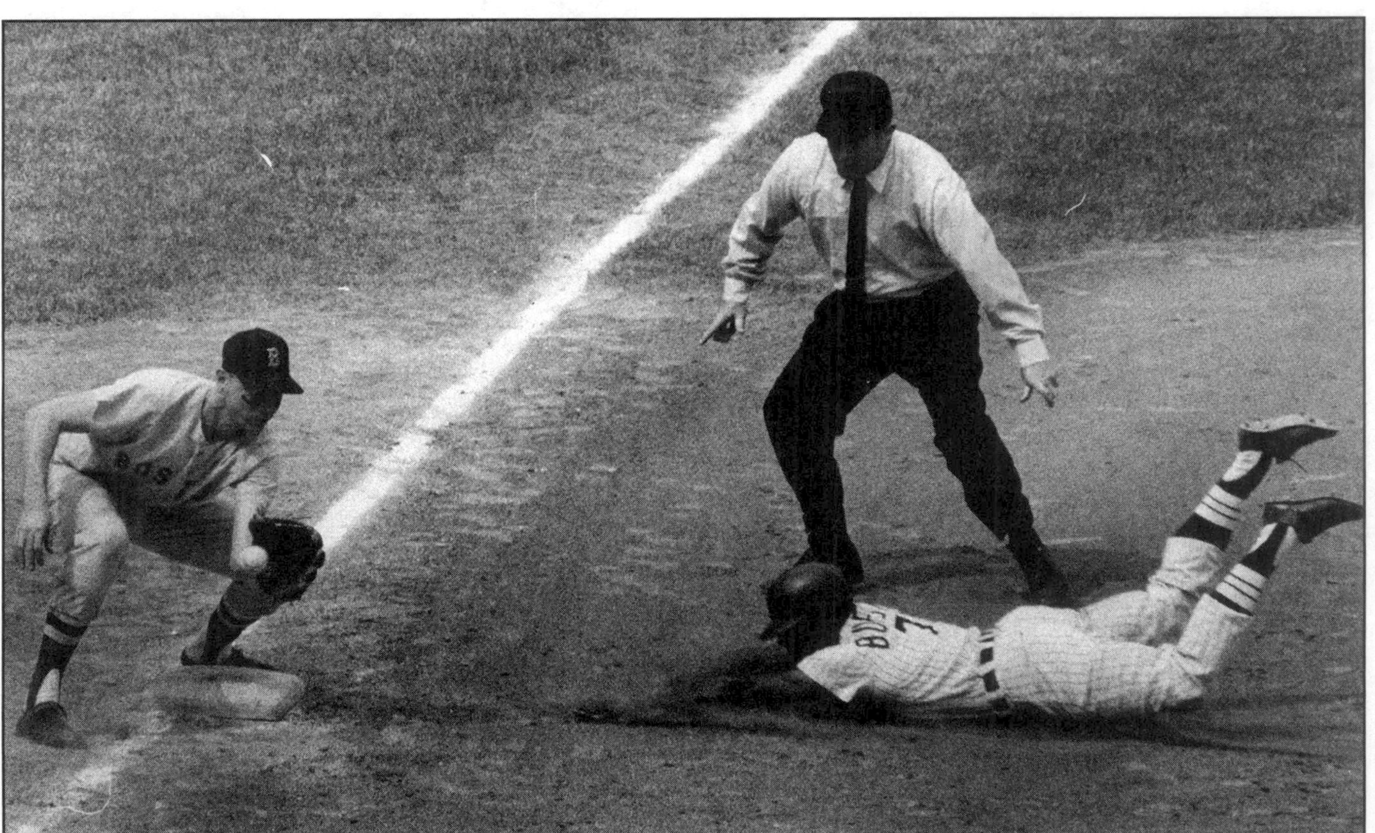

Third baseman Jerry Adair ready to tag out Don Buford on an attempted steal of third base, August 26 in Chicago.

Lonborg improves to 18-3 with a complete game, three-hitter over the Yankees in NY. Reggie Smith singled, stole second, and scored on Lonborg's seventh-inning single for the go-ahead run in the 2-1 win.

TWINS IN 1ST PLACE. Every time the Sox were poised to take first place, some setback (like losing a ballgame) held them back. In fact, the 7-1 win (Lonborg's 17th, a complete game win) over the White Sox in the first game put them in first for about three hours, but Chicago took the nightcap, 2-1, despite a fine effort by Stange. Minnesota's Dean Chance no-hit the Indians as Minnesota took two, so Boston was in third place in the tight, tight race. Ken Harrelson was released by Kansas City after calling out owner Charlie Finley; on August 28, he signed with the Red Sox.

The morning of the 25th saw the front-page debut of Carl Yastrzemski's exclusive new column in the *Boston Globe*.

August 26—SOX ON TOP—1ST LATE SEASON LEAD IN 18 YEARS. The Sox beat Chicago 6-2. Jerry Stephenson threw no-hit ball for the first five innings and got the win. Eddie Stanky, White Sox manager, took a shot at Dick Williams: "Except for the stupidity of the other manager, we would have lost three games," he said, criticizing Williams for letting Mike Andrews bunt when his team was down by a run in the 2-1 second game the day before. It's doubtful Dick cared.

August 27—Boston split two with the White Sox, winning 4-3, but losing a heartbreaker, 1-0, in 11 innings on four non-consecutive bases on balls. That Boston won the first game was thanks to Tartabull's throw from right field in the bottom of the ninth, and Elston Howard's one-handed grab of the sailing throw, blocking of the plate with his left foot, and sweeping tag of the sliding Ken Berry after Berry had been unable to touch the plate. The run would have tied the game. Instead, Tartabull's throw and Howard's ability to turn it into a double play ended the game. Moments later,

a Chicago fan ran on the field and threw a cup of beer into umpire Marty Springstead's face for calling Berry out. Santiago and Thomas were both hurt in the second game. Why Yaz was bunting in the 11th with a runner on first and no one out remains a mystery, but Darrell Brandon's four walks sank the Red Sox.

August 28—RED SOX SHUT OUT YANKEES, STILL .001 OFF TOP. Massachusetts Governor John Volpe joined a large number of Carl Yastrzemski fans from his Long Island home in honoring Yaz at Yankee Stadium. It was a 3-0 shutout for Dave Morehead and Sparky Lyle. Elston Howard drove in a run to beat his former teammates, Yaz hit a sac fly, and Reggie Smith hit a homer for the third run. A Yankees spokesman couldn't remember another time the visiting team had hosted a "Night" at Yankee Stadium. Ken Harrelson reported to the Red Sox, who had secured his services despite, Harrelson said, the rival White Sox having offered more money.

August 29—The Sox split a pair of one-run games with the Yankees at the Stadium, winning the first game, 2-1, Lonborg's 18th win, a three-hitter. Lonborg singled in the winning run in the seventh. They got good pitching in the second game, too, but so did the Yankees. Ken Harrelson hit a home run in his first Boston at-bat, but the two teams were tied 2-2 after nine. Both teams scored once in the 11th, and endured 20 innings of baseball. In the top of the 20th, the Sox loaded the bases but couldn't score. Darrell Brandon yielded a single to New York's John Kennedy and then hit Jim Bouton. José Santiago came on in relief, and Horace Clarke singled in the game-winner. Because the Twins lost their game, though, the exhausted Red Sox found themselves in first place.

August 30—Another extra-inning affair, but this one was mercifully shorter. Jerry Stephenson allowed just one run on four hits in the first seven innings and John Wyatt threw four scoreless innings in relief. Al Downing threw 10 innings of one-run ball and got the first two outs in the top of the 11th, but made a mistake throwing to Carl Yastrzemski, mired in an 0-for-18 slump. Yaz jumped on Downing's first pitch for a home run into the seats in right center. John Wyatt got the 2-1 win. The Red Sox were now 1½ games ahead of the Twins and Tigers, in first place.

August 31—The White Sox paid a visit to Fenway and took the first of four, 4-2, teeing off for three against Gary Bell in the eighth inning—enough to overcome the slim 2-1 lead that Boston had built despite not getting a hit for the first six innings. Winner for the White Sox was Don McMahon, who'd started the season with Boston before being swapped for Jerry Adair. McMahon came on in relief and got the first man he faced: Adair, then retired Yaz and Scott. He set down the Sox 1-2-3 in the ninth.

At month's end, the St. Louis Cardinals led the National League by a full 10 games over the second-place Cincinnati Reds. The Red Sox held a half-game lead over the Twins. The Tigers were one game out of first and the White Sox were just a game and a half out.

September

September 1—Ken Harrelson had a double, a triple, and a home run, drove in four runs, and helped José Santiago to a complete game 10-2 win. The Sox held onto their half-game lead. Harrelson admitted after the game that both he and Dick Williams agreed that had Hawk gotten up to bat once more and hit safely, he was

Yaz scores on Al Worthington's wild pitch with the fourth run of the five-run rally that toppled the Twins. Sixth inning, October 1, 1967.

Smith and Petrocelli each drove in runs in a three-run bottom of the eighth, and flank John Wyatt who won his ninth game, 4-2 over Kansas City. September 13, 1967.

going to hold up at first base no matter what.

September 2—After four nights in first place, the Sox dropped a notch, losing 4-1 to Chicago when the White Sox scored three runs off Lonborg in the first and Joel Horlen allowed just the one run in the bottom of the fourth. The Red Sox recalled Russ Gibson from Pittsfield and called up 18-year-old lefthander Ken Brett, too.

September 3—Tommy John shut out the Red Sox, 4-0, inducing 19 outs on ground balls, as Chicago took three of four at Fenway. Lee Stange gave up two runs in six innings. A light moment came in a letter from Dick Stuart in Japan. Dick Williams said Stuart noted that Yaz had a chance to lead the league in the three Triple Crown categories. Stuart remarked that he'd once led the league in errors, strikeouts, and best quotes to the press.

September 4—RED SOX SPLIT BUT KEEP PACE WITH TWINS. The Red Sox lost the first game, 5-2; Morehead wasn't at his best. They overcome a 4-2 deficit with four runs in the top of the sixth to take the second game, 6-4, the key play coming on Mike Ryan's bunt with two runners on board. The attempt to throw out Rico at third was off the mark, and Rico scored on the error. Adair pinch-hit for Stephenson and singled in the tying and winning runs.

September 5—YAZ' 2 HOME RUNS, BELL LEAD RED SOX, 8-2. Yaz singled, too, and drove in four, giving him a league-leading 102 RBIs. Yaz led in homers, too, with 38. Bell lost his shutout in the ninth, but threw a complete game win.

September 6—There was no game for the Red Sox but the Tigers swept two, the White Sox won a 13-inning game, and the Twins lost. This created a virtual deadlock atop the American League. None of the four teams were even a half-game behind the leaders. The Twins and White Sox were both 78-61 (.561) while the Red Sox and Tigers were both 79-62 (.560). Unfortunately, Tony Conigliaro's vision had taken a turn for the worse. It didn't look like the Red Sox were going to be able to get any late-season help from Tony C.

September 7—LONBORG WINS 19th, SOX STILL .001 OFF TOP. Boston beat the Yankees, 3-1, at Fenway behind another three-hitter from Gentleman Jim. Lonborg struck out 10 Yankees. On offense, he reached first base on a third-strike wild pitch from Mel Stottlemyre, and then stole second for his only career stolen base. Petrocelli homered and drove in two.

September 8—"Sure, I'd like to see the Red Sox win it," said Medford's own Bill Monbouquette. "But what the heck, I'm fighting for a job, too. I've got to look out for myself." So he did, pitching for the ninth-place Yankees and beating the Red Sox, 5-2. Lee Stange took the loss, and the Red Sox sank to third place.

September 9—Jerry Stephenson became ill, so Dave Morehead was the surprise starter. He held the Yankees to just one run. Yaz and Rico both homered, and Sparky Lyle pitched two perfect innings in relief. Red Sox 7, Yankees 1.

September 10—The Red Sox clinched one thing this day: the prediction Dick Williams had made in spring training came true as the Red Sox won game #82, trouncing the Yankees 9-1 at Fenway. "We'll win more than we'll lose," Williams had said. Win this one they did, Gary Bell allowing just four hits, while Mike Ryan tripled in three, Boomer doubled twice, driving in two, and Ken Harrelson homered to drive himself in.

September 11—No game scheduled.

September 12—SOX WIN, TIE FOR LEAD ON LONBORG'S TRIPLE. Lonborg was going for his 20th win, not pitching very well but rescued by four double plays. He was locked in a 1-1 tie with Catfish Hunter after giving up a solo homer to Bert Campaneris in the top of the eighth. Come the bottom of the inning, and Lonborg was due up with pinch-runner Tartabull on first and one out. Williams let him hit and Lonborg choked up on the bat to advance the runner. The .126-hitting Lonborg then straightened up and drove a triple to right-center field. After driving in the go-ahead run, Lonborg scored himself when Mike Andrews hit a sacrifice fly deep to center. The final score was 3-1.

September 13—The Sox, Twins, and Tigers all won, the Sox and Twins remaining tied for first place and Detroit just one game behind. Petro's three RBIs were enough for the 4-2 win over KC. Stange started but had to leave after seven when he felt something pop in his arm. John Wyatt got the win.

September 14—It was officially over; Tony C was done for the year. There was no game for the Red Sox.

September 15—Dave Morehead lacked control and the Orioles beat Boston, 6-2. The Twins lost, too, but Detroit won over Washington. A year before, the Red Sox were 27 games out of first place, with a record of 67-85. This year—this impossible year—they shared first place at mid-September. Jerry Adair had a groin pull, and Joe Foy came in to play third.

September 16—In the "anything-can-happen" pennant race, now the Tigers were in first place, and the Twins and Red Sox shared second. Both Boston and Minnesota had lost. Boog Powell hit his first homer in almost two months when John Wyatt "forgot to dip into the Vaseline" in relief of Lonborg, pulled while the game was still tied. Boston lost 4-1.

September 17—The Red Sox lost yet again, as the Orioles swept the three-game series at Fenway Park with a 5-2 win over Gary Bell. Williams announced that he was going to change things a bit for the incoming Tigers, playing Tartabull in place of Harrelson in right, and Gibson in place of Ryan behind the plate. He was going to play Dalton Jones at third. There were just 12 games left on the schedule. The Red Sox were one game out; four teams were in first place or within one game.

September 18—JONES' HR TIPS TIGERS IN 10TH; SOX SHARE THREE-WAY TOP TIE. Given a start at third base, Dalton Jones went 4-for-5, drove in two runs, put the Red Sox ahead with his homer in the top of the 10th, and saved the game defensively on the final play in the bottom of the 10th. Yaz hit a homer, drove in two, and had a 3-for-4 game, but Jones deservedly got all the headlines.

September 19—SOX SCORE 3 IN 9TH, SWEEP. It was just a two-game series against Detroit, but the Sox were quite glad to take both games. José Santiago was credited with the win in each game. George Scott singled in one run to tie, Yaz scored the winning run coming in from third on a wild pitch, and Russ Gibson

Boomer (2-for-4) offers Yaz (4-for-5, and his 41st home run) a smooch after the 5-4 win on September 20 against the Indians.

drove in an insurance run in the Red Sox ninth. 4-2, Boston. Now it was just the Twins and Sox on top.

September 20—SOX WIN AGAIN IN 9TH. On the day the Red Sox finally began to accept World Series ticket applications, it was the ninth inning again. Mike Andrews walked, but Jerry Adair bunted into a double play. Yaz, involved in his third ninth-inning rally in a row, singled to left-center field. George Scott looked at four pitches for a base on balls. Reggie Smith lined a drive to right, scoring Yaz. Wyatt kept the Indians from scoring for a 5-4 win in Cleveland. Ticket prices for the World Series ranged from a $2 bleacher seat to a high of $12 for box seats. The Red Sox reportedly received 100 times as many orders as there were tickets to be had.

September 21—The "usual nerve-shattering thriller" ended up with another one-run game and the Red Sox on top again, 6-5, over the Indians. This one was a matter of holding on, as the Sox had a 4-0 lead after 5½ but saw it erode to 6-4 in the seventh. Gary Bell got the win. Speaking in Buffalo, Jackie Robinson said that because Tom Yawkey was "probably one of the most bigoted guys in organized baseball...I'd like to see them lose." He predicted the Twins would win the pennant. The one-run decision proved to be the final one in a season where the Red Sox were 27-28 in one-run games.

September 22—Playing a doubleheader in Baltimore, the Red Sox were dumbfounded in the first game, losing 10-0. Stephenson started, and he and Rohr gave up the 10 runs between them. José Santiago started, and finished, the second game, winning 10-3 for his third win in a five-day stretch. Un-benching three men (Foy, Harrelson, and Howard) paid off in game two; the trio drove in five of Boston's 10 runs.

September 23—SOX LOSE, 7-5, DROP TO 3d BEHIND TWINS, TIGERS. The Sox came from down 4-0 long enough to take a 5-4 lead, but coughed it up in the seventh and eighth as Waslewski let the Orioles tie it and Wyatt let them score twice to win it. The Red Sox were indeed in third place, but just half a game out.

September 24—SOX RIP ORIOLES, 11-7, GAIN 2d. An 18-hit attack gave Jim Lonborg win #21, who left the game with a 7-0 lead. The score stood 7-3 after eight full innings. Fortunately the Red Sox scored four times in the top of the ninth, because the Orioles scored

It was pandemonium in the neighborhood after the Red Sox won their first pennant in 21 years.

four in the bottom of the ninth. The Red Sox made four errors, so only three of Brandon's six runs were earned, but a win's a win. Brandon had torn a back muscle, too, and was out for the rest of the year. There were only four games left to play, all at home.

September 25—The Red Sox had the day off but reached first place again, tied for the lead, when the Twins lost 9-2 to the California Angels.

September 26—SOX LOSE, SLIP TO 3d; 3 GAMES LEFT. That front-page headline seemed to spell doom. Cleveland had beaten Boston, 6-3, and the Twins had won over California. The White Sox were in second place. Boston found itself in third place with just three games to play. Well, they were still just one game out. Yaz had knocked in all three Red Sox runs with his 43rd homer. The Sox committed a couple of errors and played less than inspiring baseball, and neither Bell nor Santiago had been up to the task of beating Cleveland's Luis Tiant.

September 27—With just three games to play, feeling they had to win them all, the Red Sox lost once more. This time, they had Jim Lonborg on the mound and were facing the mediocre Indians again, but for the second day in a row Cleveland scored six runs while a trio of Tribe pitchers shut down the Sox bats. Fortunately, neither of the other contenders won: the Twins lost, 5-1, and the White Sox lost two games to the last-place Kansas City Athletics. The Tigers, who didn't play, went from fourth to second place.

September 28—No scheduled game.

September 29—Another scheduled day off, with the Red Sox all too aware that they might well have to win both of the final two games against the Twins to even tie for first. The White Sox committed two first-inning errors, letting in one run, and lost to Washington, 1-0, eliminating themselves from the race. The 1967 Twins, though, arrived at Fenway with an 11-5 season record against the Red Sox.

Red Sox front office executives display a tangible symbol of '67 success.

September 30—SOX WIN, KEEP PENNANT HOPES AGLOW. Hosting the Twins at Fenway, José Santiago had the game ball and, despite giving up a run in the top of the first, he kept the Sox in the game. It was 3-2 in Boston's favor after six innings when Yaz struck. Adair's double play ball was misplayed by Versalles at second base, giving Yaz an at-bat. He took advantage: his 44th home run landed in the Twins bullpen, giving the Red Sox some real breathing room. Even the two runs the Twins scored in the top of the ninth off Gary Bell in relief saw them fall short, 6-4. Both teams were tied for first place, with a deciding final game of the season set for October 1. And it was Jim Lonborg going for the Red Sox against Dean Chance of Minnesota. The Tigers had split a doubleheader and were ½ game out of what could have been a three-way tie.

October

October 1—RED SOX TAKE PENNANT AS HISTORIC SEASON ENDS. The team barely escaped the field as thousands of wild fans stormed out of the stands at Fenway, climbed the netting behind home plate, tore plates off the scoreboard, and ripped blades of grass from the infield. Jim Lonborg was pitching for the Red Sox; unfortunately, he had gone 0-3 against the Twins this year (and was 0-6 lifetime against them.) Dean Chance was on the mound for Minnesota; he was 4-1 against the Red Sox in 1967. The Sox were losing to 20-game winner Chance by a 2-0 score when 21-game winner Jim Lonborg beat out a bunt to start off the sixth inning. Adair singled through the middle. Dalton Jones faked a bunt, but singled to left. Bases loaded, and who was up next? Of course: Yaz. He singled to drive in two and tie the score. Versalles threw home on Harrelson's

bouncer, but he shouldn't have; his throw was high and the Red Sox took the lead. Out went Chance; in came Al Worthington in relief. Facing George Scott, he threw one wild pitch, and then another, giving the Sox another run. One more came in a few minutes later on Reggie Smith's drive off Killebrew's leg. The final was 5-3, Red Sox. The Twins were eliminated. The Red Sox had clinched at least a tie for first place, and a possible playoff against the Tigers.

The Tigers won their first game against the Angels in Anaheim. If they won the nightcap, too, they'd be tied with the Red Sox for first place. All New England followed the score from the Coast. California won it, 8-5, and the Red Sox had won the pennant for the first time since 1946, positioned for a re-match against the St. Louis Cardinals, who had finished 10½ games ahead of the second-place Giants.

Sources:

All quotations and headlines come from the *Boston Globe*, unless otherwise indicated..

Welcoming home the triumphant Red Sox in the summer of '67

One of the contributors to this book was there when the team came home from its road trip the night of July 22. The Sox had just won eight games in a row, and were just a half-game out of first place. Tom Harkins had just turned 22 in June.

"I had graduated from Notre Dame and was going to BU Law School at the time. I was sitting home watching the game in Cleveland. I remember them saying that the Red Sox would be coming into Logan Airport. I don't remember if I called Bob McGarr, or he called me. He lived in Wellesley and I lived in Needham, and we drove in, in his little beat-up old Ford. Parking wasn't like it is now. It was at night, nine or ten o'clock at night, and we just parked the car. We never went in the terminal. There were a lot of people just milling around. Very happy. There was nothing malicious. People were just very happy. It had been a while since the Red Sox had done so well.

"I can remember being a little out of character that night, at Logan Airport. I pulled out my Boston Braves pennant and went around yelling, 'Bring back the Braves!' Completely out of character, but everyone was having a good time. There were a few people who had signs. I didn't see a lot of older people. I didn't see a lot of kids up that late. Almost all guys, everyone maybe five years either way from me. I remember approaching the terminal. 'Are they going to come out here?' You know how word of mouth gets around. We saw the plane. It went to the general aviation area. It was a charter, I think. It had taxied over, but it was dark. The lighting was mixed.

"I guess they got on a bus. I talked to Russ Gibson about it recently and his memory was... they were apprehensive. There were all these thousands of people, spread out over a wide area. They approached the bus and I guess were rocking the bus; I don't remember that at all. Inside the bus, they were concerned.... Funny story, someone said, 'Let's throw out Conigliaro; they like him!' But he said he was concerned, because his wife and young child were waiting in the terminal for him. Interestingly enough, if I'd known him at that time, I could have given him a ride back to Needham.

"People were out on the tarmac, but not on the runway. The tarmac was a long wide area. I don't remember seeing any police. There were some chants occasionally, 'Let's go, Red Sox'—something like that, but it wasn't anything sustained. The only thing I compare it with was my senior year at Notre Dame the year before. They were national champions and they had a pep rally at the end of the season. Notre Dame pep rallies are crazy. I never felt that there was any danger. I never felt any reason to feel concerned about safety."

Harkins attended the anti-war Moratorium in Washington in late 1970, choosing not to wear his Coast Guard uniform at the time. In October 2004, as a lifelong Red Sox fan, he was exceptionally glad to take the train in to Boston and line up to watch the parade celebrating Boston's first world championship since 1918.

Thousands of fans overflowed Boston's Logan Airport, and the team bus (still empty in this photograph) had to try to make its way through the multitudes.

World Series Recap

by Dan Desrochers

St. Louis Cardinals and Boston Red Sox

The Red Sox were in the World Series for the first time since 1946, matched against the same team that beat them in seven games 21 years earlier.

The 1967 Cardinals clinched early, surprising most observers as Red Schoendienst led an up-and-coming team to the pennant in a bit of a breeze, finishing 10½ games ahead of the second-place Giants.

St. Louis won 101 regular season games while the Red Sox won their pennant with 92 victories, recording the then-lowest percentage (.568) for a first-place finisher in the American League.

The Redbirds boasted speed, power to all fields, and pitching against a Red Sox team strong on defense, guts, and determination, and deemed "clutch."

The Cards were stacked. St. Louis featured All-Star players like outfielder Lou Brock, catcher Tim McCarver, NL MVP first baseman Orlando Cepeda, 1964 World Series MVP pitcher Bob Gibson, as well as stellar outfielders Curt Flood and Roger Maris, and nifty infielder Julian Javier. The Cards were quick and aggressive with their hit-and-run style with base-stealing threats Brock and Flood.

Starting lineup match-ups clearly favored St. Louis, with only Boston's Carl Yastrzemski in left field and Rico Petrocelli at shortstop prevailing on paper.

St. Louis' pitching seemed equally dominating, with a strong bullpen and key starters like Gibson who won 13 games despite suffering a broken leg in July, rookie Dick Hughes with 16 wins, and Nelson Briles and Steve Carlton each recording 14 wins.

The seasoned Cards were given the edge in power and speed, and they hit higher than the Red Sox. Boston skipper Dick Williams had an unflinching retort: "Experience. Napoleon had experience. But he didn't always win."

The Red Sox led the American League in batting, homers, RBIs, runs scored, and in some priceless intangibles.

"Our scouts have been following all the American League contenders since the All-Star break," said Schoendienst, "and every time we got a report on Boston, the word 'clutch' was always underlined. The information we got always pointed that the Red Sox would not quit and would always fight back." [*Boston Globe*, October 3, 1967]

The Cards were 3-2 favorites, with bookmakers setting 6-5 odds for them to win Game One.

Despite battling to the final day, the Red Sox appeared relaxed and confident. Dick Williams, who had grown up in St. Louis and was looking forward to playing the Cardinals, posed the simple question: "After what we've been through, how can anything else be tougher?"

The *Boston Record American* trumpeted, "IT'S IN THE CARDS. WE'LL WIN IN SIX! The greatest underdogs of all baseball times, the Boston Red Sox, will take the World Series in six games, so predicted Carl Yastrzemski as he called the shots while working out at Boston's Fenway Park Tuesday."

Dick Williams felt that Boston's defense would be better than the Cards and also picked the Sox to win, repeating his spring training prediction: "We'll win more than we'll lose."

Managers Williams and Schoendienst initially planned to use just three starters: José Santiago, Jim

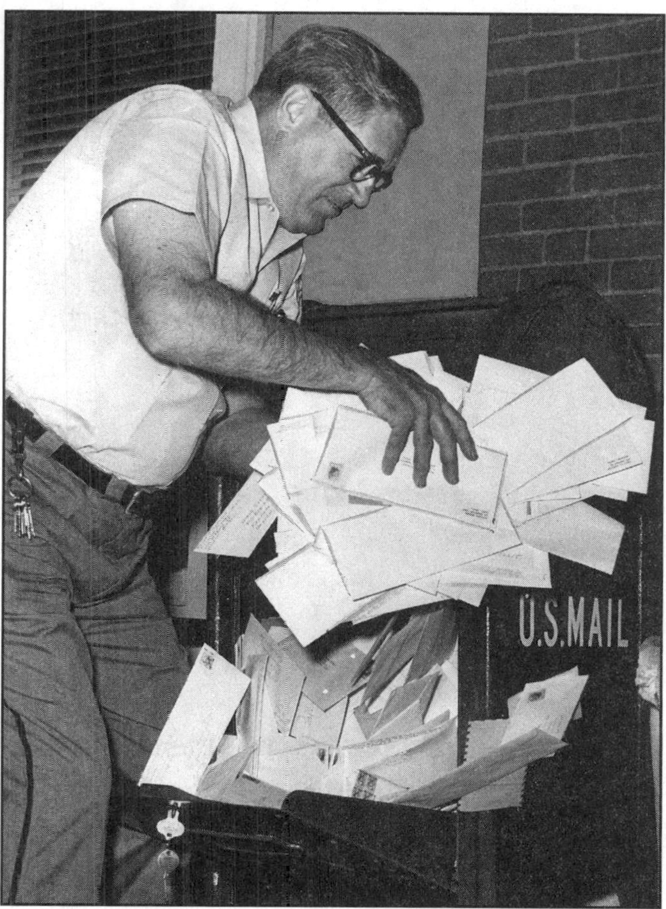

Full House—*The Post Office was deluged with about 135,000 ticket application requests to attend the 1967 World Series.*

Lonborg, and Gary Bell for the Sox; Bob Gibson, Dick Hughes, and Nelson Briles for the Cards. Forced to use star pitcher Jim Lonborg in the pennant-clincher just three days prior to Game One, Williams was unable to set up his ideal rotation—Lonborg facing Gibson in Games One, Three, and Seven. So 12-game winner José Santiago was slated to face the dominating Gibson in Game One.

For the Red Sox, after a grueling, energy-filled, ninth-place-to-first-place "Impossible Dream" season, reporter Harold Kaese's World Series sendoff line in the October 2 *Boston Globe* seemed fitting:

"And now for the great anti-climax—the World Series."

Game 1—Awed and Paralyzed

October 4, 1967 (Wed.) 1:00p.m. EST Fenway Park, Boston, MA

	1	2	3	4	5	6	7	8	9	R	H	E
St. Louis Cardinals	0	0	1	0	0	0	1	0	0	2	10	0
Boston Red Sox	0	0	1	0	0	0	0	0	0	1	6	0

Ecstatic and anxious Red Sox fans participated in round-the-clock vigils hoping to get World Series tickets while fans lacking tickets developed different strategies to follow the afternoon weekday games. Mill workers, cab drivers, and business people called in sick to work. And kids schemed to listen to pocket transistors at school.

Fenway Park appeared ready as the Red Sox grounds crew hastily repaired the venue following the fans' wild on-field pennant celebration.

Football at Fenway got a holiday as Billy Sullivan's American Football League Boston Patriots, who played their home games at Fenway Park, shifted their Saturday night home opener against the Chargers to a Sunday evening game in San Diego.

"The crowds bristled with anticipation built up over two decades in Boston and New England." [*Boston Record American*, October 5, 1967] Fans overflowed the streets around Fenway, some climbing 100 feet to mount billboards overlooking the park.

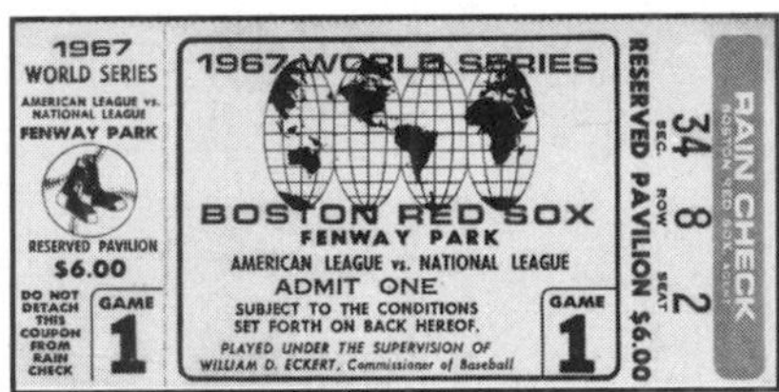

But while the near-perfect short-sleeve weather provided a warm setting, Bob Gibson, Lou Brock, and the Cardinals did not, chilling the Red Sox offense in Game One by a score of 2-1.

Fenway was the place to be in 1967, with celebrities such as Lee Remick, Dale Robertson, and Connie Francis (seen here with Harrelson and Gov. John A. Volpe), the ever-present Cardinal Cushing, Vice President Hubert H. Humphrey, former Ambassador Joseph Kennedy and his sons Edward and Bobby, Jacqueline Kennedy and son John Jr., and Freddy Parent, the Red Sox first shortstop and oldest living member of the 1903 World Champion Boston American team.

Red Sox defense kept the score close featuring exceptional plays by Carl Yastrzemski and two sparkling double plays started by third baseman Dalton Jones, while José Santiago's clutch pitching kept St. Louis to two runs, both on groundouts. Sox bats were cold and their only score came courtesy of their number nine hitter, pitcher José Santiago's solo home run.

After two scoreless innings, St. Louis' Brock opened the third with a single. Flood doubled him to third, and he scored the first run of the Series on a Roger Maris groundout to first.

In the bottom of the third, Santiago tied the score with his blast to left, barely clearing the wall before landing in the left-center-field net. It was Santiago's second home run of the year.

Gibson was dominant, striking out nine through the first five frames—he ended with 10 Ks. His execution was near perfect, with the exception of his 0-2 pitch to Santiago. Yastrzemski, who overshadowed the Twins in the pennant-clinching games, was shut out, hitless in four at-bats. Other than Santiago, only two Sox managed to reach second.

Yaz, however, showed dazzle in the field. He made a spectacular play in the fourth, with a rocket-like throw after Brock's two-out line single to left that nabbed

Fervent fans catch a glimpse of the action in sold-out Fenway from their perch on the other side of Lansdowne Street.

Cards second baseman Julian Javier at the plate.

In the fifth, Yaz made an incredible catch, leaping high into the air to snare a Flood liner over his head for the inning's first out. Columnist Red Smith described Flood's drive in the *Boston Globe*: "By the laws of God, Congress, and General William D. Eckert, [it should] have been his second straight double, if not a triple. Yaz fled to his right, leaped like a springbok with a hot foot, and flung up his gloved paw."

The score remained tied until the seventh when the Cards struck again. Brock opened the inning with a single—his fourth hit of the day—and the National League's leading base-swiper stole second base. He advanced to third on a groundout by Flood. Then, with a drawn-in infield, Maris, playing in his sixth World Series, hit a shot past second baseman Jerry Adair who made a spectacular stop and, unable to make the play at home, had to settle for getting Maris at first as the lead runner scored.

Gibson allowed just two singles in the final three innings. Brock starred in the Cardinals 2-1 win, walking once, getting four hits, scoring two runs, and stealing two bases.

Despite all the hype and drama, the Sox lost the first game, but with Jim Lonborg scheduled next, the Sox throng remained optimistic.

Years later, Yaz stated, "Someone messed up the pregame schedule and our batting practice was cut from 45 minutes to 20. We got only half the swings we should have received. I had about a third, and felt rusty. And we needed them after the emotional turmoil we had gone through for a solid month...I just didn"t feel ready. I don"t know how many of us did." [Carl Yastrzemski and Gerald Eskenazi, *Yaz, Baseball, The Wall, and Me*]

A frustrated Yastrzemski left the clubhouse shortly after the game and took extra batting practice, with third baseman Joy Foy serving up pitches.

Yaz remained confident, though, confirming his prediction that the Sox would win in six, hoping for a chance at redemption against Dick Hughes in Game Two.

Game 2—Simply Lonborg

October 5, 1967 (Thurs.) 1:00p.m. EST Fenway Park, Boston, MA

	1	2	3	4	5	6	7	8	9	R	H	E
St. Louis Cardinals	0	0	0	0	0	0	0	0	0	0	1	1
Boston Red Sox	0	0	0	1	0	1	3	0	x	5	9	0

The Cardinals lineup remained the same, going with the regulars that won them Game One.

Sox manager Dick Williams made both positional and tactical moves, replacing slumping Ken Harrelson with José Tartabull in right field, adding speed to the lineup. He moved George Scott—the only Boston batter to get two hits off Bob Gibson in Game One—to the cleanup spot, providing greater protection in back of Carl Yastrzemski.

Brock was a threat to "steal the World Series." Williams said, "We pitched him four different ways, and couldn"t get him out." [*Boston Record American*, October 5, 1967] Williams replaced catcher Russ Gibson with veteran Elston Howard, who caught for the Yankees in the 1964 World Series against these Cards. When asked about a different pitching plan for Brock, Williams responded saying, "There's a few things we"re going to do. But I"m not going to tell you beforehand." [*Boston Globe*, 10/5/1967]. To most fans the answer was clear and simple: Jim Lonborg.

The starting pitchers matched right-handers: Cy Young candidate Lonborg against St. Louis rookie Dick Hughes.

Lonborg buzzed the game's first pitch high and inside to leadoff batter Brock: "it bore straight and true for the right ear of Lou Brock," wrote Red Smith. Lonborg then disposed of Brock on his soft liner to short.

Statement made for Game Two, tone set for the Series.

The game was scoreless through three, with Lonborg pitching hitless ball, and with Hughes equally effective; Yastrzemski walked in the first, and Rico Petrocelli singled in the second.

Jerry Adair's brilliant play near second in the top of the fourth denied Brock's second attempt for a base hit.

Yaz led off the bottom of the fourth. Looking for a Hughes fastball on an 0 –1 count, Yaz sat back, got one, and drilled it into the right-field seats for a home run, staking the Sox to a 1-0 lead. He'd told Williams before the game, "I feel great, and I bet anything I"ll hit one out here today."

Petrocelli made a nice play behind second base on a smash by Cards shortstop Dal Maxvill, helping hold the

Yaz and Lonborg hold court after Jim's one-hit shutout in Game Two of the World Series. Yaz hit two homers and drove in four of Boston's five runs.

Cards hitless through six innings. In the bottom of the inning, he knocked in the second Sox run on a sacrifice fly, with George Scott scoring an unearned run.

In the seventh, Fenway's lights came on as clouds darkened. Rain began with Brock's at-bat in the seventh; he grounded again to Adair at second. Lonborg remained perfect, having retired his 19th consecutive batter.

Curt Flood followed. After fouling off two pitches on a full count, he walked on a pitch that just missed the strike zone, low and away, becoming the first St. Louis base runner of the day, ending Lonborg's attempt at history. Petrocelli ended the inning with a great play on Orlando Cepeda.

In the Sox half of the seventh, Tartabull walked, followed by Dalton Jones' hit past third baseman Mike Shannon. Schoendienst summoned southpaw Joe Hoerner to face the left-hand hitting Yastrzemski. On a 2-2 count, Yaz stroked a long three-run home run that soared into the bleachers beyond the Red Sox bullpen in right-center field.

In the eighth, Lonborg continued his quest for World Series glory, getting McCarver and Shannon on groundouts. With two outs, Cards second baseman Julian Javier—a .257 lifetime hitter coming off a career

Gary Bell and Elston Howard go over their game strategy in St. Louis, prior to the third game of the World Series.

year—stepped in. On the first pitch, Javier lined a high slider that Lonborg later described as the "only bad pitch I made all day" into the left-field corner for a double, spoiling Lonborg's no-hit bid. The crowd initially moaned, but quickly responded with an extended standing ovation. Lonborg's effort to reach baseball immortality by pitching a World Series no-hitter fell just four batters short.

With great defensive support in the game from Petrocelli and Adair, Lonborg finished off the Cardinals to preserve his historic one-hitter. Don Larsen, who pitched a perfect game in the 1956 World Series noted, "You can"t get much closer than that." [*Boston Record American*, October 6, 1967].

They"d held Brock hitless. Behind Lonborg's masterful one-hitter and Yastrzemski's two homers and four runs batted in, the "Beantown Bombers" tied the Series, winning by a score of 5-0.

Both teams left for St. Louis, each with one win, thanks in both cases to their dominant starting pitching and to their excellent left fielders.

Game 3—The Spirit of St. Louis

October 7, 1967 (Sat.) 1:00p.m. CST Busch Stadium, St. Louis, MO

	1	2	3	4	5	6	7	8	9	R	H	E
Boston Red Sox	0	0	0	0	0	1	1	0	0	2	7	1
St. Louis Cardinals	1	2	0	0	0	1	0	1	x	5	10	0

The lineups remained unchanged. Boston's hard-throwing Gary Bell faced curveballer Nelson Briles, who sparked the St. Louis staff after Gibson's broken leg. Briles finished the year winning nine straight decisions after August 1.

Bell was out to disprove his label as a mediocre pitcher. Briles aimed to set the stage and stop Boston. Both were in the limelight for the first time in their careers.

But the big news of the day concerned the Redbirds' hostility towards the Red Sox before their anticipated Game Three match-up against the rejuvenated Red Sox at Busch Stadium in St. Louis.

In the eyes of the Cardinals faithful, "Gentleman" Jim Lonborg he was no more.

"You bush so and so" [*Boston Globe*, October 6, 1967] were amongst the Cards version of mid-60's expletives directed to Lonborg from the normally cordial Midwesterners. Lonborg had admittedly unleashed a rising close-shave fastball under Lou Brock's chin in Game Two, which could have portended a donnybrook of a Series.

"Tell the Red Sox we can play it [the inside game], too," Curt Flood announced. "And we're not going to get Petrocelli or Adair or anybody like that. We"ll get Yastrzemski." [*Boston Globe*, October 6, 1967]. The Lonborg "duster" represented the line drawn in the sand.

Bell proved ineffective, lasting just two innings after giving up five hits and three runs, while Briles went on to pitch a complete game seven-hitter. There were few highlights for the Red Sox this day, but Gary Waslewski's effort would not go unrecognized. He looked sharp replacing Bell, mowing down the Cards

with three perfect innings.

Brock led off the bottom of the first with a triple, followed by Flood's run-scoring single. In the second, third baseman Mike Shannon blasted a two-run homer with Tim McCarver on board.

Brock's speed continued to raise havoc for the Red Sox. He led off the sixth with a drag bunt single. He proceeded to third base on a wild pick-off throw to first base and later scored on a Roger Maris single.

The Cards scored their final run in the eighth when Orlando Cepeda, who previously had gone hitless in 10 at-bats, doubled to score Maris.

Briles was stellar. Referred in the newspapers as "Choir Boy" for his interest in singing, the right-hander shut down the Red Sox through the fifth inning. In the sixth, Mike Andrews singled pinch-hitting for reliever Waslewski. Dalton Jones knocked in Andrews with his second hit of a three-hit day. The Sox managed only one more run, a seventh-inning solo home run by centerfielder Reggie Smith, whom Briles had agitated earlier with a brushback.

During this game, brushback episodes made it appear that retaliation was in order for the Lonborg/Brock Game Two duster. Trouble loomed from the onset. The bitterness that carried over resulted in outbreaks in three separate innings, while arguments loomed in between.

Briles drilled Carl Yastrzemski on the leg with his first pitch to him in the first inning with two outs and none on. Captain Carl glared at Briles. Dick Williams charged out, complaining to the home plate umpire. The umpire notified both managers that he would deal with any situation that arose.

Yaz subsequently went hitless, grounding out weakly to second in each of his next three at-bats. As the Cardinals established in Game One, if they could beat Yaz, their odds improved. The following day's *Boston Globe* headline echoed a similar theme, "YAZ GOES DOWN; SOX GO TUMBLIN' AFTER."

In the second inning Scott was called out on a close play and Williams again came out to argue.

Then an inside pitch upset rookie Reggie Smith who finger-pointed a challenge to Briles, with whom he had a previous run-in in minor league ball. Scott came running to help Smith, with the Cards' Cepeda also entering the scene.

Calmness appeared restored, until the top of the ninth with one out and Smith at bat. With what *Boston Globe* writer Harold Kaese described as "the most overt sign of belligerency," the short-tempered Smith lowered and dug his shoulder into catcher Tim McCarver's chest protector as he attempted to catch a high foul pop-up towards first base. McCarver doubled over. The home plate umpire immediately called Smith out for interference on the play as first baseman Cepeda came in and caught the fly. Jerry Adair then popped out to third base for the game's final out.

Pardon me! *Interference was called on Reggie Smith as he "brushed" Cards catcher Tim McCarver attempting to catch the ball.*

Afterwards, the Red Sox shared their thoughts about Briles. In the Red Sox locker room, Smith stated, "He's a big mouth, pop-off." Yastrzemski noted, "He tried to hit me."

Lonborg had admitted he'd brushed back Brock in Game Two. But when the soft-spoken, articulate Briles was questioned about hitting the Red Sox captain, he professed innocence: "I held the ball way too tight and it got away. The same thing happened with Reggie Smith. Why did Yaz say anything?" [*Boston Sunday Advertiser*, 10/8/67]

In a game highlighted more by bitterness and controversy than great play, the Cardinals defeated the Red Sox 5-2, taking a 2 –1 Series lead.

The Bushwhack was completed as "Choir Boy" avenged the "Gentleman."

"This thing is starting to get a little warm, isn't it?" observed Dick Williams. [*Boston Globe,* October 8, 1967]

Game 4—A One-Inning Game

October 8, 1967 (Sun.) 1:00p.m. CST Busch Stadium, St. Louis, MO

	1	2	3	4	5	6	7	8	9	R	H	E
Boston Red Sox	0	0	0	0	0	0	0	0	0	0	5	0
St. Louis Cardinals	4	0	2	0	0	0	0	0	x	6	9	0

"The St. Louis Cardinals are as bush as the name of the beer company that owns them," sniped Williams in his ghostwritten column, referring to the inside pitching of the St. Louis staff.

But, neither the bad blood between the teams nor the pre-game retort prompted any Red Sox retaliation. Quite the contrary, as Larry Claflin summed up in the *Boston Record American*, "The Red Sox, who roared like lions after Carl Yastrzemski got hit by a pitch Saturday, acted more like lambs Sunday...."

The inherent intimidation and overall excellence of Bob Gibson made the difference.

Poor José Santiago. The Red Sox right-hander was again pitted against the seemingly un-hittable Cards ace. Santiago failed to survive the first inning, giving up four runs on six hits.

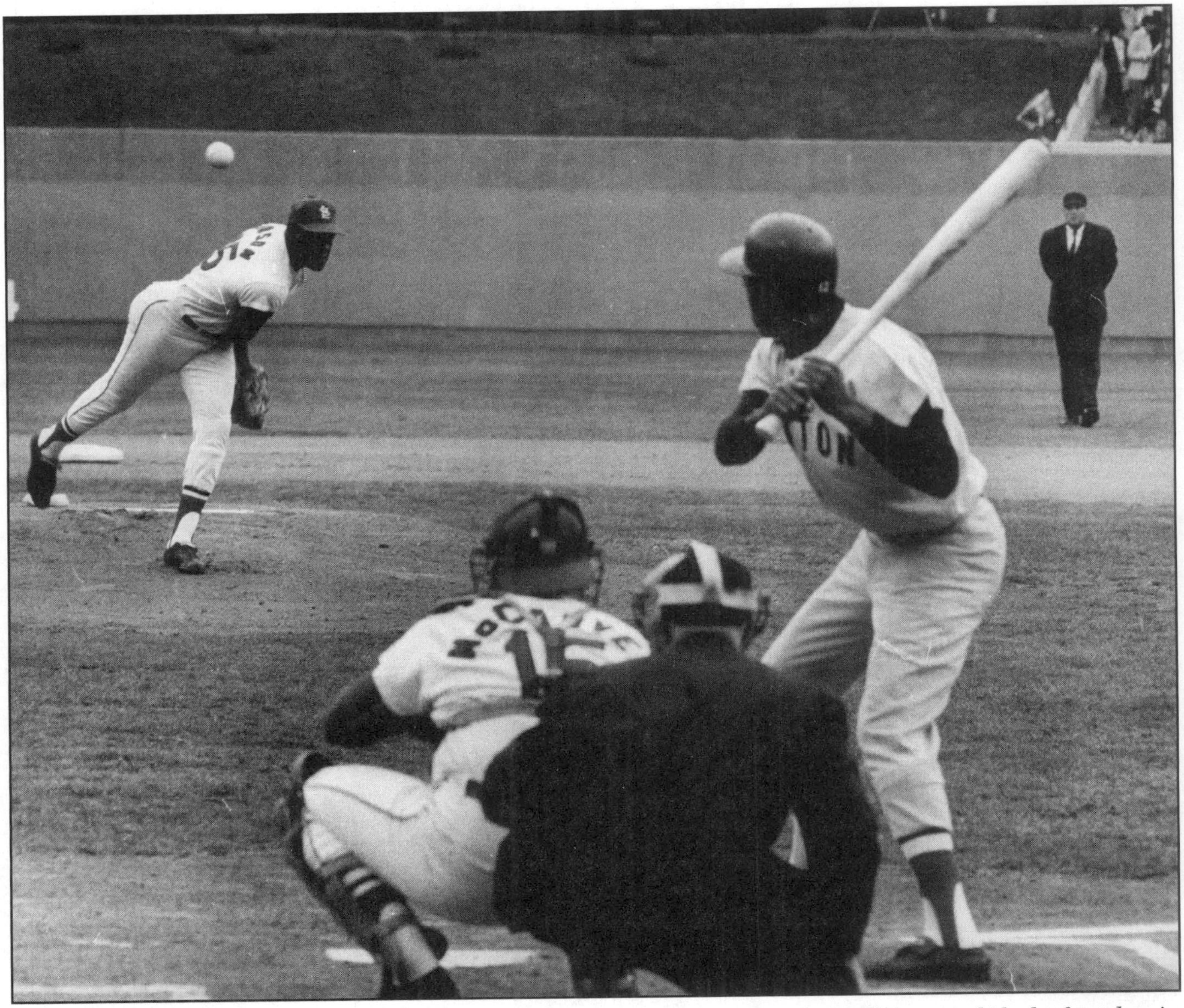

St. Louis starter Bob Gibson throws to Boston leadoff batter José Tartabull. Both Tartabull and Yastrzemski had 2-for-4 days in Game Five, but Gibson shut out the Red Sox, 6-0.

complete game 6-0 win.

"Gibson was simply too much for us. He overwhelmed our right handed hitters," wrote Williams. Boston reporters provided a different perspective. The *Boston Globe's* Ray Fitzgerald described the Red Sox effort that day as being "flatter than the leftover champagne from last week's victory celebration."

Down three games to one, the Sox appeared doomed.

Carl Yastrzemski provided some encouragement as he reminded all of the many Red Sox comeback efforts in this magical year, "We've had our backs against the wall before."

Dick Williams announced the Sox would go with their stopper in Game Five. The "darlings of destiny" desired to extend their miracle season, and those hopes lay in the right arm of Jim Lonborg.

Lou Brock led off the bottom of the first with an infield single. "Every time Lou gets on," said St. Louis shortstop Dal Maxvill, "things begin to happen" [*Boston Globe*, October 9, 1967]. After drawing two pick-off throws, Brock faked a steal on Santiago's pitch home, drawing Petrocelli towards the second-base bag. Curt Flood slapped a hit through the hole Petrocelli had vacated. Roger Maris, quietly having a great World Series, doubled to left field scoring both Brock and Flood. Tim McCarver followed with an RBI single. Julian Javier added a single, and Maxvill's base hit to left knocked in the fourth run. Gary Bell, who had lasted only two innings as the Game Three starter, replaced Santiago and retired Gibson to close out the first. The score after one inning, 4-0 Cards.

Flood continued to contribute sparkling defensive play in centerfield. And Gibson was Gibson—magnificent! It was an upward battle for the BoSox from the onset. With Gibson on his game, the four-run deficit proved insurmountable.

After Yaz singled in the first, Gibson recorded nine outs in a row before George Scott managed an uneventful single with two outs in the fourth. The husky right-hander spread five hits and one walk over nine innings, with the Sox reaching second base only once with Yaz's lead-off double in the ninth.

With Jerry Stephenson pitching for Boston, the Cards scored two more runs in the third inning. Orlando Cepeda led off with a double, and took third on a wild pitch. He scored on McCarver's sacrifice fly to center. Shannon drew a walk and scored on Javier's double.

After Santiago and Bell, Dick Williams resorted to a couple of forgotten pitchers in the pen and one rookie to finish the game. Stephenson had relieved Bell and given up the two runs in the third, but pitched well in the fourth. He was followed by Dave Morehead, who pitched three no-hit innings. Williams then brought in rookie southpaw Ken Brett—a roster replacement for injured pitcher Sparky Lyle—who pitched a hitless eighth.

Brett, a 19-year old whose only major league experience was a two-inning stint against the Cleveland Indians in late September, became the youngest pitcher in a World Series game.

Jerry Adair's ground out in the ninth sealed Gibson's

Game 5—Down, But Not Out

October 9, 1967 (Mon.) 1:00p.m. CST Busch Stadium, St. Louis, MO

	1	2	3	4	5	6	7	8	9	R	H	E
Boston Red Sox	0	0	1	0	0	0	0	0	2	3	6	1
St. Louis Cardinals	0	0	0	0	0	0	0	0	1	1	3	2

"It's as one-sided as a cat eating a canary," wrote Jim Murray in the *Los Angeles Times*.

The Cards had overpowered the Red Sox. They out-hit, out-ran, and, with the exception of Jim Lonborg, had out-pitched Boston's Cinderella boys. Hoping for a quick knockout punch to finish the Series, the Cards started hard-throwing 22-year-old lefthander Steve Carlton.

Murray suggested, "Maybe the Red Sox should just phone in the last game and save everyone a lot of trouble."

As bleak as things seemed, the overmatched Red Sox had no plans to abandon this year's miracle ride while in St. Louis. The never-say-die Bosox had successfully overcome similar odds before. As Harold Kaese noted in the *Boston Globe*, "[The Red Sox] had overcome more obstacles this season than Rin-Tin-Tin ever had in the original dog operas."

Dick Williams sought further wizardry, with yet further line-up changes.

Captain Carl Yastrzemski conveyed optimism: "If we win today we will win the Series. We can beat them twice in Boston."[*Boston Record American*, October 10, 1967]

With his team on the brink, Williams set the tone in his off-the-cuff pre-game speech in Boston's somber locker room. "It could end here today. But I don't think

Jim Lonborg takes batting practice during the World Series.

it will." [*Boston Globe*, October 10, 1967] A win created a similar scenario as when they beat the Twins and won the pennant. "We have been in tough spots before and we got out of them. We can do it again." [*Boston Record American*, October 9, 1967].

He proceeded to post a *Los Angeles Times* news clipping that stated: "The Red Sox are now the Dead Sox." He followed by shouting, "Let's show them that we're far from being dead." [*Boston Globe*, October 10, 1967]

Lou Brock led off the game with the Cards' hardest hit ball of the game—a tremendous drive that outfielder Hawk Harrelson, in his first appearance since Game One, grabbed going deep in right.

The Sox scored first with a run in the third. With one out, Joe Foy singled to left field. Mike Andrews reached first on a sacrifice bunt muffed by third baseman Mike Shannon. Harrelson drove Foy home with a single to left. Foy, the forgotten third baseman making his first World Series start, also sparked the Red Sox with two spectacular defensive plays, robbing Dal Maxvill of a potential double in the fifth and making a game-ending play off Orlando Cepeda in the ninth.

Both Lonborg and Carlton pitched effectively through the sixth inning. Future Hall of Fame player Carlton was lifted for a pinch hitter having allowed only one unearned run and three singles in six innings.

Lonborg continued to be spectacular. Through eight innings, he allowed only a couple of meaningless singles—Maxvill in the third and Roger Maris in the fourth.

For Lonborg, who had been nursing a cold, the eighth was his 17th consecutive scoreless inning in the World Series, having allowed only three hits. "I was better today than I was in Boston [when he pitched a one-hitter against the Cards]. My fastball was alive. I knew where it was going every pitch," reflected Lonborg after the game. [*Boston Globe*, October 10, 1967]

In the ninth inning, the Red Sox scored some needed insurance runs. George Scott led off the inning with a walk. He advanced to third on a double by Reggie Smith. Rico was then walked intentionally, loading the bases for

13-year veteran Elston Howard. Familiar with big game situations, Howard proceeded to slice a 150-foot "Texas League" single down the right-field line. The "dying quail," as Howard later described his hit, scored Scott and Smith and gave the BoSox a three-run cushion.

Lonborg got the first two Cards out in the bottom of the ninth as Lou Brock and Curt Flood both grounded out. Maris followed, hitting a home run on a low, inside change-up that just cleared the fence near the 330-foot sign in right field. But it was too little, too late. With Orlando Cepeda's ground out for the game's final out, the Boston "Dead" Sox "became the Boston Dread Sox once more." [John Gillooly, *Boston Record American*, October 10, 1967]

Behind Lonborg's stellar pitching and a supporting cast of new Series stars including Howard and three new players inserted into the line-up—Andrews, Foy, and Harrelson—the Red Sox beat the Cardinals, 3-1.

"Lonnie was beautiful," said a smiling Howard afterwards. "He did it all by himself. You don't have to talk to anyone else on this team. He was the story all by himself." [*Boston Globe*, October 10, 1967]

So once again it was the 25-year-old Jim Lonborg who rekindled the Red Sox hopes and righted their ship. They would return to Boston and get to play yet another game.

"The Red Sox got up at the eight count," reflected West Coast scribe Jim Murray, whose prior article denoted Boston as the "Dead Sox."

"The ninth place team just refuses to return to the cinder box. They like the glass slippers. They'll die in their own time. Don't rush them."

Game 6—Bucking the Odds

October 11, 1967 (Wed.) 1:00p.m. EST Fenway Park, Boston, MA

	1	2	3	4	5	6	7	8	9	R	H	E
St. Louis Cardinals	0	0	2	0	0	0	2	0	0	4	8	0
Boston Red Sox	0	1	0	3	0	0	4	0	x	8	12	1

For the "Cardiac Kids," there was no place like home. More than 1,500 screaming fans greeted their darling Red Sox at Logan Airport on their return flight from St. Louis. The following day, U.S. Marines were called in to control over 15,000 cheering fans who lined the streets in Peabody in a tribute honoring Dick Williams.

While the Cardinals were noble hosts in their impressive new Busch Stadium with its symmetrical field and sparkling, picture-perfect facilities, only Fenway Park could provide the fitting ambiance to finish this magical season.

"Obviously this is the place for a World Series to reach its climax," wrote the *Boston Globe*'s Bud Collins. "The Red Sox know they are America's team, even if the gods allow the Brewery Nine to win. Nothing that happens today or Thursday [a possible Game Seven] will change that. The Red Sox, having an affair with the Fate Sisters, saved baseball from boredom in 1967, and their Fenway should [serve as the venue for the final games] and be preserved as a historical shrine."

The announced starters pitted Cardinals rookie pitcher Dick Hughes against Red Sox rookie hurler Gary Waslewski.

Gary Waslewski?

Neither starters José Santiago nor Gary Bell had met Red Sox rookie manager Dick Williams' expectations. If a player did not perform, Williams simply used another. Change was in order, and Williams elected Waslewski, who had pitched well in relief in Game Three.

Waslewski would start this vital game with only two prior wins, and but 42 regular season innings pitched in major league ball. This would be his first start since July 29, nearly two and one-half months earlier.

Williams' choice in an elimination game came as a great surprise to those unfamiliar with his succeed-or-out approach. Even to those accustomed to his risk-taking efforts and his use of multiple players and lineups (89 different lineups in 162 regular season games), this would be Williams' biggest gamble.

For Waslewski, it would be the opportunity of a lifetime, a dream come true—and he established himself early, pitching a 1-2-3 first inning, striking out Lou Brock and Roger Maris in the process.

A four home run attack sparked the Red Sox to an 8-4 victory, tying the World Series at three games apiece. Rico Petrocelli led the home run binge with two solo homers, with Reggie Smith and Carl Yastrzemski each adding solo shots of their own.

The Red Sox started the scoring in the second inning with Petrocelli's first home run, a line drive shot to left field.

15,000 fans line the streets of Peabody for a mile-long parade to cheer on Dick Williams in his adopted city. "I didn't realize there were this many people in Peabody," Williams noted.

St. Louis took a 2-1 lead in the third. Julian Javier opened the inning with a double. With two outs, Brock singled to right field, scoring Javier. Brock stole second and scored on Flood's single to left.

The Red Sox unloaded their long-ball bats in the fourth, chasing starter Hughes. The Boston Bombers unleashed three home runs, starting with Yastrzemski who led off with a shot into the net above the left-field wall, his third home run of the Series. With two outs, Smith and Petrocelli hit back-to-back solo homers. Three home runs in one inning established a World Series record. Four home runs, four runs scored, all off Hughes. The BoSox led, 4- 2. "SHOTS HEARD 'ROUND THE WORLD" headlined the *Boston Record American* the next day.

Waslewski pitched hitless ball in the fourth and fifth innings, but tired in the sixth, walking two of the first three batters, and was replaced by John Wyatt. Wyatt got the next two batters, thwarting the Cardinals threat.

The Redbirds tied the score in the top of the seventh on St. Louis' first Fenway home run, a two-run bomb by Brock deep into the centerfield bleachers behind the Red Sox bullpen. Gary Bell called it a shot that could have "passed the spaceship *Discovery*." [Peter Golenbock, *Red Sox Nation: An Unexpurgated History Of The Red Sox*]

The Sox took the lead to stay in the bottom of the seventh. Pinch-hitter Dalton Jones started the rally with a one-out single to right field. Jones scored on Joe Foy's double, with Foy moving to third on the throw home. Mike Andrews singled through a drawn-in infield, scoring Foy. Yaz singled, and Andrews reached third base. Jerry Adair's sac fly brought in Andrews. Smith knocked in the final run with a ball that dropped between three Cards in short centerfield. The fourth Cardinals pitcher of the inning, Ray Washburn, retired Elston Howard for the final out.

Easy as one, two, three. Smith, Petrocelli, and Yastrzemski all homered in the bottom of the fourth to give the Red Sox a 4-2 lead in Game Six.

Overall, there were 11 pitchers used in the game, setting a new World Series record—eight used by St Louis and three by Boston.

Gary Bell pitched the final two frames for Boston, earning the only save of the Series. John Wyatt got credit for the win, though some challenged the official scorer's ruling; they felt the "W" should have gone to Waslewski.

Williams' faith in the freshman paid off. "Waslewski did just what we wanted him to do. He threw the hell out of the ball for five innings. He got tired, but that was expected. He hadn't pitched that long for a while." [*Boston Record American*, October 12, 1967]

Game Six was symbolic of this miracle season—bucking the odds, another player used, another risk assumed, but another victory for Dick Williams and the Destiny Darlings.

The stage was set for a dream match-up between two undefeated aces, Jim Lonborg (2-0) and Bob Gibson (2-0).

Clif Keane's title to his October 12, 1967 *Boston Globe* article seemed like a fitting lead to Game Seven: "NOW... 'CINDERELLA' TRIES ON THE SLIPPER!"

Game 7—There is No Encore

October 12, 1967 (Thurs.) 1:00p.m. EST Fenway Park, Boston, MA

	1	2	3	4	5	6	7	8	9	R	H	E
St. Louis Cardinals	0	0	2	0	2	3	0	0	0	7	10	1
Boston Red Sox	0	0	0	0	1	0	0	1	0	2	3	1

It all boiled down to one game.

The Boston unbelievables had once again come back from adversity, and in the process had defied all odds and logic.

Called the Darlings of Destiny by local and national scribes, the preseason 100-1 long-shot Red Sox had swept the Twins in the final weekend showdown and won the American League pennant. They came back from a 3-1 deficit in the World Series and forced a decisive Game Seven.

This spirited comeback prompted *Boston Globe's* Bud Collins to write, "...the Fenway Phoenixes [Red Sox] have risen from the ashes so many times that they must be on pulleys, like Peter Pan."

Dick Williams declared, "They can call it destiny,

luck, ability, or a combination of all three. Whatever it is, I hope it lasts one more day." [*New York Times*, October 12, 1967]

The stunned Cards were heavy favorites to win the Series after Game Four, but it was now a virtual toss-up. The bleak and suggestive headlines in the *St. Louis Globe-Democrat* provided little optimism—"Take Your Pick; Bosox Have Plenty of Heroes."

Momentum favored the Cinderella team, who had consistently transformed such intangibles into opportunities.

"My line-up is simple. Lonborg and champagne," smirked Williams referencing the title of his *Boston Record American* article. Possibly written by an overzealous ghostwriter, this comment enraged the Cards and would haunt the Red Sox.

The Cardinals hoped to stop Boston's miracle ride with ironman Bob Gibson. "It's time to stop talking about the breaks, and to start making our own breaks," Red Schoendienst told his team. [*Boston Globe*, October 12, 1967]

So the stars were aligned, the script perfected. Lonborg and the better-rested Gibson would duel in the epic World Series finale.

Both aces were fastball right-handers, both thrived in pressure games, and neither would hesitate to throw a brushback pitch or two.

Each had allowed only one run in 18 innings pitched. Lonborg gave up a miniscule four hits in his two games compared to the 11 allowed by Gibson.

Gibson would pitch on three days' rest, Lonborg with only two. Lonborg had twice pitched on two days' rest during the season, beating the Kansas City Athletics on 8/9 and losing to the Cleveland Indians on 9/27.

"I'd rather have Lonborg with two days' rest than anyone else in baseball," said Williams [*New York Times*, October 12, 1967]

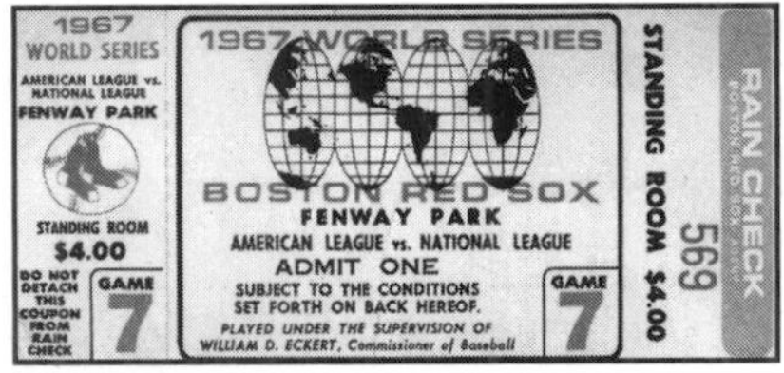

Lonborg retired the Redbirds on nine pitches in both the first inning and the second. Light-hitting shortstop Dal Maxvill's leadoff triple off the center-field fence in the third started Lonborg's demise. With two outs, Flood stroked a single to center scoring Maxvill.

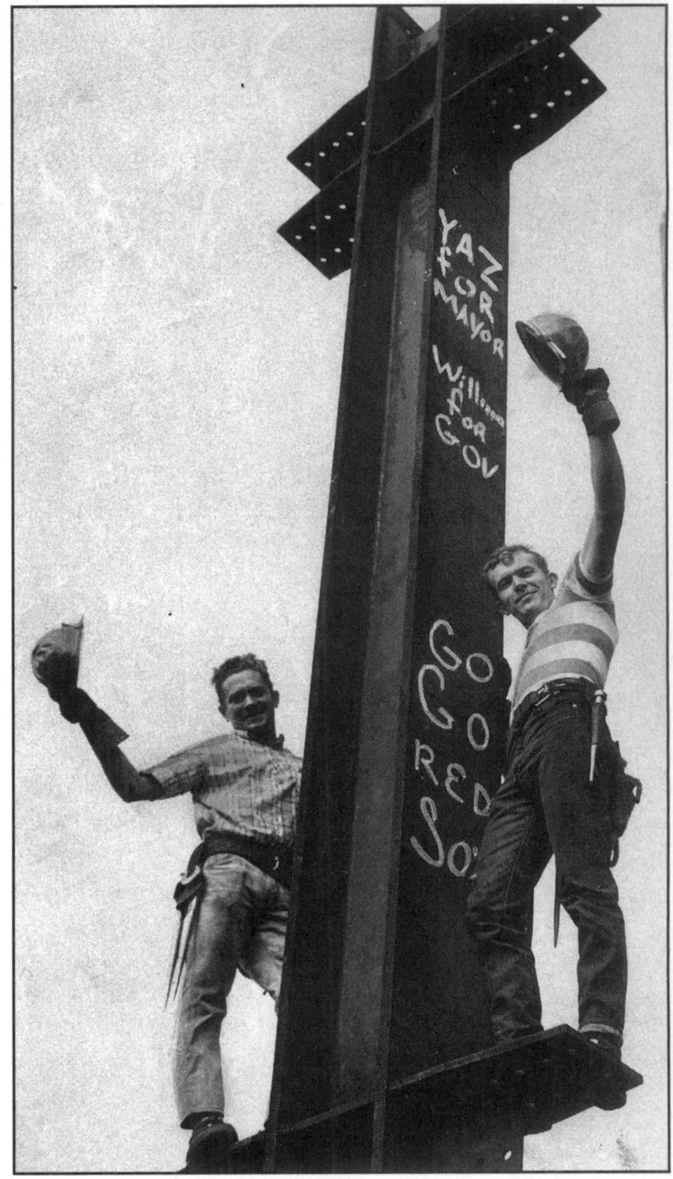

Hats off to the 1967 Red Sox!!! *Like countless other captivated fans during this season, steelworkers Mike Collins of Dedham and Colin Holfe of Quincy demonstrate their appreciation and enthusiasm for the darlings of destiny.*

Roger Maris followed with a single to right, and Flood reached third. On a wild pitch, Flood scored the Cards' second run, one more than Lonborg had allowed the prior 20 innings.

Gibson himself took a tiring Lonborg deep in the fifth with a home run to center. Lou Brock followed with a single to left, then stole both second and third, scoring on a Maris sacrifice fly to right field. Brock

ended the day with three stolen bases and seven overall, a new Series record.

Gibson simply dazzled the Red Sox. Though he walked leadoff hitter Joe Foy in the first inning, he pitched hitless ball through four innings, striking out seven. He gave up only one hit through seven innings—a triple to the center-field triangle by George Scott in the fifth; Scott scored on a Julian Javier error.

The sixth inning marked the end for Gentleman Jim Lonborg. Tim McCarver led off with a sinking line-drive double to right field. Shannon reached first on Foy's error. Javier followed with a three-run homer to center field to extend St. Louis' lead to 7-1. With Gibson on the mound, the end was near for Lonborg and the Beantown team.

Having labored through six innings, a weary and dejected Lonborg walked off the mound for the final time that season to a standing ovation. It was an unfortunate departure for the young teary-eyed fallen star who had provided the fans with a lifetime worth of thrills during the prior six months. "Jim's heart was there, but his arm wasn't," Carl Yastrzemski said.

Gibson threw a complete game three-hitter and was rightfully named Series MVP.

In the Redbirds clubhouse, many a Cardinal spun a variation on Dick Williams' pre-game quote, reminding all that the champagne belonged to them.

For the Red Sox and their fans, their fairy-tale year ended in an uncelebrated fashion in an anticlimactic extension of the regular season. The pennant drive and pennant fever had taken its toll.

To many, this Series would simply serve as a benchmarked endpoint to one of the most remarkable Red Sox seasons ever. The spirit and memories of the Impossible Dreamers would forever endure, while any tears shed in the World Series were quickly forgotten.

Williams Proved He Was No Dummy—and that Winning Can Be Fun! *This March 1967 promotional photograph almost invites viewers to write their own caption. In the end, it wasn't about words. It was about motivation and molding a lot of young talent together, and to have fun winning both ballgames and new legions of fans.*

This is really a love story.
An affair 'twixt a town and a team.
A town that had waited and waited,
for what seemed an Impossible Dream.

The story had its beginning under the Florida sun.
The oddsmakers looked them over and said, 100 to 1.
But the team had a sort of a new look, a new manager stepping in.
And he taught them a baseball lesson,
It's much more fun to win.

From *The Impossible Dream*, a tribute album narrated by
Red Sox announcer Ken Coleman

RED SOX 1967

Thomas A. Yawkey, President
Richard H. O'Connell, Executive Vice President and General Manager
Haywood C. Sullivan, Vice President, Director, Player Personnel
Theodore S. Williams, Vice President
Neil T. Mahoney, Director, Minor League System
Joseph LaCour, Secretary
Joseph T. Cummiskey, Treasurer
Thomas B. Dowd, Traveling Secretary
William C. Crowley, Director, Public Relations
Charles J. Toomey, Group Ticket Sales
Daniel R. Marcotte, Director of Stadium Operations
Dick Williams, Manager
Thomas M. Tierney, MD, Team Doctor
Edward "Buddy" LeRoux, Trainer
Donald J. Fitzpatrick, Equipment Manager

Boston Red Sox
24 Jersey Street
Boston, MA 02215

Area code: 617
Phone: Copley 7-2530
Teletype: 262-1291

Game Times

Day games (Mon.-Fr.) – 1:30 p.m.
Saturday and Sunday day games – 2:00 p.m.
Day doubleheaders– 1:00 p.m.
Night games – 7:30 p.m.
Twi-night – 5:00 p.m.

Admission prices:

Roof box – $3.75
Boxes – 3.00
Reserved Grandstand – 2.25
General Admission – 1.50
Bleachers – 1.00

RED SOX MINOR LEAGUE SYSTEM: 1967

Neil T. Mahoney, Farm Director
Edward F. Kenney, Executive Secretary

Clubs

AAA	Toronto (International League), manager Eddie Kasko
AA	Pittsfield (Eastern League), manager Billy Gardner
A	Winston-Salem (Carolina League), manager Bill Slack
A	Waterloo (Midwest League), manager Rac Slider
A	Greenville (Western Carolina League), manager Matt Sczesny

Boston Red Sox Scouts: 1967

LeFebvre, Wilfred "Lefty"	Seekonk, MA
Bolling, Milton J.	Mobile, AL
Boone, Raymond O.	San Diego, CA
Burns, Irving "Jack"	Waltham MA
DeLoof, Maurice	Detroit, MI
Digby, George	Boca Raton, FL
Doyle, Howard "Danny"	Stillwater, OK
Harrell, William	Troy, NY
Johnson, Earl	Seattle, WA
Koney, Charles	Chicago, IL
LeFebvre, Wilfred "Lefty"	Seekonk, MA
Lenhardt, Donald E.	St. Louis, MO
McCarey, C. J. "Socko"	Pitsburgh, PA
McCarren, William	Jersey City, NJ
Mazzone, Frank	Needham, MA
Nekola, F. J. "Bots"	New Hyde Park, L.I., NY
Philley, David	Paris, TX
Rice, Roderick B.	Norman, OK
Scott, Edward	Mobile, AL
Severeid, Henry	San Antonio, TX
Sheedy, Clayton	Groton, MA
Stephenson, Joseph	Anaheim, CA
Thomas, Alphonse	Dallastown, PA
Thomas, Larry Lee	Grove City, OH
Vazquez, Pedro	Santurce, PR
Wagner, Charles	Reading, PA
Wright, Glenn	Fresno, CA

CONTRIBUTORS

RON ANDERSON grew up in the Boston area and is a consummate Red Sox and baseball fan. Ron attributes his love for the game to his father who played ball in the Boston City Park League, and who got him started in a life of baseball. He was a contributing writer to the *'75:The Red Sox Team That Saved Baseball*, and he is currently working on a biography of former Red Sox standout George Scott. He is now retired and lives with his wife Gail, in Plymouth, Massachusetts.

ANDY ANDRES is a diehard Red Sox Fan who lives in Cambridge, MA with his wife, Kate, and their three children, Maddie, Aubree, and Griffin. When not spending time coaching and playing softball, he teaches biology at Boston University and Harvard College. He plays P/3B for The Jumbo's Peanut Surprise in various Tufts Softball Leagues, and has been schooled at Universities Brown, Harvard, and Tufts. He teaches what is likely the first ever college course in Baseball Analysis and Sabermetrics at Tufts University with David Tybor and Morgan Melchiorre.

JEFF ANGUS is a management consultant, author of the book *Management by Baseball: The Official Rules for Winning Management in Any Field*, and corporate speaker on the same subject. He would have had a perfect attendance record for five years of high school (don't ask) except he faked an illness to watch two games of the '67 Series. Angus is a member of SABR, a former baseball stringer for the AP and UPI, writes sabermetrics columns for the *Seattle Times* and management columns for *CIO Insight*.

MARK ARMOUR grew up in New England, and could correctly spell all of the ethnic names on this team by the age of seven. He now writes baseball from his home in Oregon. Mark is the co-author of *Paths to Glory*, the director of SABR's Baseball Biography Project, a contributor to many websites and SABR journals, and, most importantly, Maya and Drew's father.

JONATHAN ARNOLD finally returned to his family's New England roots as an 11-year-old, after his Dad finished up a world tour in the Air Force, and overcame a brief Cardinal romance to be a Red Sox fanatic ever since. Living in a Boston suburb, he's raising two daughters with his lifelong Sox-fanatic wife to be proud members of Red Sox Nation, while working as a software engineer.

ERIC ARON has been a SABR member since 2002. He holds a B.A. in history from Clark and a M.A. in history from Northeastern. He grew up in Westchester County as a Mets fan and still loves his visits to the Lemon Ice King of Corona after taking in a game at Shea.

FR. GERRY BEIRNE shares birthdays with Pie Traynor, Rabbit Maranville, and José Offerman (you can look it up). His earliest recollection of following the Red Sox goes back to attending games in 1946 with his Pawtucket fireman godfather who later lent him his "portable radio" to listen to the World Series (sigh). His most brilliant moment in Red Sox history is contained in this book. The author of *The New England Sports Trivia Quiz Book*, he is the pastor of St. Philip's Church in Greenville, RI where the Southern New England SABR meetings are held every Thanksgiving Saturday. He looks forward to retirement and another World Series victory, please!

CHARLIE BEVIS is the author of numerous articles on baseball history as well as two books, *Sunday Baseball: The Major Leagues' Struggle to Play Baseball on the Lord's Day, 1876-1934* (2003) and *Mickey Cochrane: The Life of a Baseball Hall of Fame Catcher* (1998). He was a 2003 recipient of the McFarland-SABR Baseball Research Award for his presentation "Evolution of the Sunday Doubleheader and Its Role in Elevating the Popularity of Baseball," made at the Cooperstown Symposium on Baseball and American Culture. He writes baseball from his home in Chelmsford, Massachusetts, where he lives with his wife Kathie, children Scott and Kelly, and dog Kasey.

RAY BIRCH lives in North Kingstown, RI. He is a retired middle school teacher where he co-taught a class on baseball to students. He has been a member of SABR since 2000. He wrote the article about Rick Burleson for *'75: The Red Sox Team That Saved Baseball*. Ray is a life-long Red Sox fan, who attended his first game at Fenway Park in 1961, just missing seeing the great Ted Williams play. He also was at the game at Fenway Park in July 1967 when the Red Sox turned a triple play against the Orioles.

ANDREW BLUME has long been obsessed with all things baseball and Red Sox. A SABR member since 2001 along with his dad Murray and a contributing author to *'75: The Red Sox Team That Saved Baseball*, he lives in Natick, Massachusetts with his wife Nancy, daughters Emily and Abigail, and feline Tigger. In his spare time, he practices law.

MAURICE BOUCHARD who lives in Shrewsbury, MA with his wife Kim, has been a baseball fan since Sandy Koufax struck out Bob Allison for the final out of the 1965 World Series. Bouchard, who grew up in upstate New York, was originally a Yankees fan but George Steinbrenner cured him of that. Since 1987, he has rooted for the Old Towne Team. He has two children, Ian and Gina, both of whom are inveterate Red Sox fans. Bouchard has been a member of SABR since 1999.

BOB BRADY grew up as a fan of the Boston Braves and Boston Red Sox and remains true to both to this day. In his free time, you can find him seated either in Section 26 at Fenway Park or working on the next newsletter for the Boston Braves Historical Association. His Impossible Dream came true at 11:40 EDT on October 27, 2004. Bob has been a SABR member since 1991.

JOE CASTIGLIONE has broadcast Red Sox radio since 1983. A member of SABR since 1984, Joe has taught broadcasting for 22 years at Northeastern University and for 10 years at Franklin Pierce College. He is author of the book *Broadcast Rites and Sites: I Saw It on the Radio with the Boston Red Sox*. Joe has worked in fundraising for the Jimmy Fund since 1990.

JOHN CIZIK grew up a Yankee fan in Wilton, Connecticut living next door to a Red Sox fan. Something must have rubbed off, because he married Jenny, a Sox fan, in 1990. A lawyer practicing in Waterbury, CT (hometown of Roger Connor, Jimmy Piersall, Dave Wallace, and Ron Diorio), he has always had an interest in doing research on and collecting memorabilia of Connecticut-born players.

HERB CREHAN is in his 12th season with *Red Sox Magazine*, the official program of the Boston Red Sox. A member of SABR since 1992, he is the author of *LIGHTNING IN A BOTTLE: The Sox of '67 and Red Sox Heroes of Yesteryear*, and a contributing writer to *Boston Red Sox*100 Years* The Official Retrospective*.

DAN DESROCHERS' ventures to Fenway Park began in 1967 as a 12-year-old who had a passionate desire to attend a Red Sox game. Unbeknownst to his parents, he schemed and plotted his "Impossible Dream" Maine-to-Boston venture that combined, bicycling, hiking, and bus and train rides to catch his first Red Sox game. He successfully completed the 200-mile trip and managed to get home before dark. He now lives in Rollinsford, New Hampshire though he still considers himself a Mainer—and he continues to organize trips to Red Sox games today without his mom's permission. He was in St. Louis when the Red Sox won it all in 2004.

ALEX EDELMAN lives in Brookline, MA, where he attends Maimonides School and obsesses over the Red Sox. He spends most of his spare time at Fenway Park, eating at his favorite restaurant Game On!, playing ice hockey for the Brookline Warriors, and leading an UrbanExploration expedition around abandoned sites in Boston. His essay, "Paradise Found," about the 2004 American League Championship Series was a recipient of the New England Sports Museum's Will McDonough Writing Award. Recently, Alex had a poem published in a poetry anthology and was honored with selection to the prestigious New England Young Writers Conference at Middlebury College, where he was taught by one of his favorite writers, Alexander Wolff of *Sports Illustrated*.

GORDON EDES' future as a sportswriter was cast in the fifth grade, when his essay on how he spent his summer vacation was on his first trip to Fenway, and watching Bill Monbouquette pitch. He's been writing about ballplayers ever since, for such papers as the *Chicago Tribune*, *L.A. Times*, *Atlanta Journal-Constitution*, the *National Sports Daily* and the *Sun-Sentinel* of South Florida. His first week at the *Boston Globe* was the week Roger Clemens left, and he was still here 10 years later, when Daisuke Matsuzaka arrived. He's a native of Lunenburg, Mass.

EDWIN FERNANDEZ CRUZ was born in the East Side of New York, but is not a Yankees fan. He grew up in San Juan, not too far from the old Sixto Escobar Stadium, home of the Santurce Crabbers in the PR Winter League. He was also a San Francisco Giants fan in the 50s and 60s. A banker in his other life, he is now a baseball historian and sportswriter, President of the Sportscasters Association in Puerto Rico and co-author of *Jonron*, a book on the Latin and Caribbean players in the Major Leagues. In October, 1967, while in a Softball Banking Tournament in Dominican Republic, he listened to the first World Series game, Gibson vs. Santiago. The Red Sox lost 2-1 and Santiago belted a solo shot against Gibson. He joined SABR in 1999 and is currently Chairman of SABR's Orlando Cepeda Chapter in Puerto Rico.

PETER GAMMONS' baseball writing career began in June, 1968, the day Robert Kennedy was shot. It was his first day as a summer intern, and for the late stocks edition of the *Boston Evening Globe* Gammons and fellow intern Bob Ryan co-authored a story on what baseball teams planned to do in the light of the assassination. Nearly 40 years later, Gammons is still covering baseball, from the *Globe* to *Sports Illustrated*, back to the *Globe*, back to *SI* and on to ESPN where he serves as a studio and game analyst. His books include *Beyond the Sixth Game*, he has thrice been honored as National Sportswriter of the year, in 2004, the National Baseball Hall of Fame honored him as the recipient of its prestigious J.G. Taylor Spink Award, and he still has a 45 RPM copy of Tony Conigliaro's single, "Why Don't They Understand?"

TOM HARKINS is a retired school librarian who lives in Needham, not too far from where Russ Gibson lived during the 1967 season. Tom has two vivid personal memories of the 1967 season: the uncontrolled frenzy at Logan Airport greeting the team, and the utter silence in Fenway after Tony C got hit.

JOANNE HULBERT (BR, TL) is co-chair of SABR's Music and Poetry Committee, resides in Mudville, a venerable, old neighborhood of Holliston, Massachusetts, a town rich in early baseball history. A distant cousin of William A. Hulbert, she accepts no responsibility, familial or otherwise, for the formation of the National League. And, contrary to the popular presumption, there can be joy in Mudville.

Worcester Native RICHARD JOHNSON has served as curator of The Sports Museum, located in Boston's TD BankNorth Garden, for the past 25 years. He has also authored, edited, or co-authored seventeen books including histories of the Red Sox, Yankees, Dodgers, Boston Braves and Bruins as well as upcoming volumes on the Cubs (w/ Glenn Stout) and Boston Celtics (w/son Robert Johnson). He has been a member of SABR since 1984 and served as a member of the Seymour medal committee in 2005.

MARK KANTER grew up in Bristol, PA where he became a life-long Philadelphia Phillies fan. He got the itch while watching the last few outs of Jim Bunning's perfect game on Father's Day in 1964. He has written several articles for SABR's *Baseball Research Journal* and was the editor for Boston's SABR 2002 Convention Publication. He has won a number of National SABR trivia contests since 1997. He and his wife, Lynne, who is also a great baseball fan, live in the idyllic seaside community of Portsmouth, RI.

KERRY KEENE is a longtime resident of Raynham, MA, along with his wife and two teenage children. A member of the Society of American Baseball Research since 1991, he has written several books on baseball, including *The Babe in Red Stockings* in 1997. A lifetime follower of the Boston Red Sox, he distinctly recalls thinking in October of 1967—"The Red Sox are actually going to be in the World Series???"

DAVID LAURILA is a lifelong Red Sox fan who grew up in Michigan's Upper Peninsula and now writes about baseball from his home in Cambridge, Massachusetts. A Red Sox season ticket holder, he runs the interview series on redsoxnation.net and is a frequent contributor to *Baseball America*. His new book, *Interviews from Red Sox Nation* (Maple Street Press), is available at bookstores and online at maplestreetpress.com.

LEN LEVIN had to make a potentially life-altering decision in the fall of 1967: whether or not to go on a long-planned honeymoon to Europe in the fall (planned, of course, when the notion of the 1967 Red Sox being in the World Series seemed but a pipe dream). Love of spouse won out over love of the Red Sox. He has been a SABR member since 1977, has been an officer of SABR twice, and currently is the custodian of the SABR Research Library. He is a former copy desk chief at the *Providence Journal* and now occasionally works as a copy editor at the *Patriot Ledger* in Quincy, MA.

DIANE MACLENNAN was a SABR member for one hour when she got the assignment to write for the 1967 Red Sox book. A Boston native who adores the Red Sox as well as every aspect of the game, her first memory of baseball was in 1967 when she heard Norm Crosby singing the "Carl Yastrzemski" song. She would often walk around with a small portable radio as a kid just to listen to the games. Baseball heroes include Dwight Evans, Dennis Eckersley, Jackie Robinson, and Branch Rickey. Diane has a Bachelor's Degree in Vocal Performance from Berklee College of Music, a Master's Degree in Arts Administrations from Boston University and is finishing up her Paralegal studies as Boston University. She lives in Somerville with her new husband Duane and has two wonderful daughters who also love baseball.

BARB MANTEGANI grew up in Manchester, NH, and became a Red Sox fan the summer her (much) older brother broke his leg playing Pony League ball and spent his days in a chaise lounge listening

to Red Sox games on the radio, with his adoring 5-year-old baby sister by his side. Barb departed New England for Virginia and a career in tax law in 1980 but has remained a member of Red Sox Nation, and watched the ball settle into Mientkiewicz's glove screaming into the phone with that same big brother who taught her how to love a team no matter what. Barb lives in McLean, VA with her husband, a Tigers fan. This is her first attempt at baseball research. It will not be her last.

R.R. MARSHALL has been a writer on the Boston sports scene for over a decade. His articles on the Red Sox, Patriots, and Boston College Eagles appear in both the print and electronic media year round. He also serves as a consultant to the Sports Museum of New England.

LES MASTERSON is a Malden, MA resident and editor of *The Arlington Advocate* newspaper in Arlington, MA. He has won numerous awards for his newspaper writing and editing from the New England Press Association and Massachusetts Press Association. He is also a rarity—a New York Mets fan who was born and raised in the shadows of Boston.

WAYNE MCELREAVY is a lifelong Red Sox fan who has contributed to numerous books and websites. He lives in Claremont, New Hampshire with children Ryan and Christine.

BILL NOWLIN was one of the first fans to the mound when Jim Lonborg induced the final out and the Red Sox won the 1967 pennant. He is national Vice President of SABR and the author of more than a dozen books on the Red Sox, the most recent being *Day by Day with the Boston Red Sox* (Rounder Books) and, with Cecilia Tan, *The 50 Greatest Red Sox Games* (John Wiley.) Bill is also co-founder of Rounder Records of Cambridge, Massachusetts. He's traveled to more than 100 countries, but says there's no place like Fenway Park.

ROYSE PARR is a native Oklahoman living in Tulsa who attended Oklahoma State University when Jerry Adair was a star athlete in baseball and basketball. While attending a Chicago Cub fantasy camp with Jimmy Piersall as his manager, he decided to retire as an attorney and spend more time doing baseball research and watching his grandchildren play baseball. He is the co-author of two books published by the Oklahoma Heritage Association: *Glory Days of Summer: The History of Baseball in Oklahoma* and *Allie Reynolds: Super Chief.*

MIKE RICHARD spent the "Summer of Love" falling in love that year with the Cardiac Kids, when he was eleven years old. In his basement family room he has a wall length mural of the Green Monster with the scoreboard reading exactly as it did when Rico Petrocelli caught Rich Rollins' pop-up to clinch the pennant. He is a high school guidance counselor at Gardner (MA) High School and also writes a weekly sports column for *The Gardner News*. He is currently co-authoring a book on *Baseball Markers, Monuments and Gravestones of New England*. He lives in Gardner with his wife Peggy and two college-aged children, Casey and Lindsey.

DOUG SKIPPER was born in Texas, grew up in Colorado, lived in Wyoming and North Dakota, and now resides in Apple Valley, Minnesota. He has worshiped the Red Sox from afar since his maternal grandfather escorted him and his two brothers to see their first major league game, on Thursday, August 3, 1967 at Fenway Park (a 5-3 win). A SABR member since 1982, he authored four biographies for *Deadball Stars of the American League*. Doug and his wife Kathy have two daughters, MacKenzie and Shannon. He is a marketing research, customer satisfaction and public opinion consultant, who reads and writes about baseball, and engages in father-daughter dancing.

HARVEY SOOLMAN was whimsically left "A Pennant" by his Brookline (MA) High School graduating Class Will & Testament in 1967. But by the time he was able to collect, after four years of razzing over Red Sox failures, the class had dispersed to colleges across the country. Deprived of his "last laugh" he nonetheless managed to survive to see more pennants and a World Series Championship and to play in an all-star game in Fenway Park at the age of 53. He manages Towne Club in the Boston Park League, still gets a hit or two against hurlers in their twenties and umpires in the Boston area. He tells all the younger guys the 1967 pennant race is still the biggest sports thrill.

In 1981 GLENN STOUT moved to Boston after college so he could live in a city with an old ballpark. Every Opening Day from 1982 through 1991 he recited baseball poetry underneath the Green Monster. He also pitched and played other positions in both the Worcester and Boston Men's Senior Baseball League. He is the author, editor, or co-author of more than sixty books, including *Red Sox Century* (with Richard Johnson), *Impossible Dreams: A Red Sox Collection*, and *Nine Months At Ground Zero: The Story of the Brotherhood of Workers Who Took on a Job Like No Other with Charles Vitchers and Robert Gray*. Series editor of *The Best American Sports Writing* since its inception, Stout writes a column for *Boston Baseball*. He now lives in Alburgh, Vermont.

CECILIA TAN is a freelance writer and editor living in Cambridge, MA. She co-edited both *The Fenway Project* and *'75: The Red Sox Team That Saved Baseball* with Bill Nowlin and has been active in the Boston chapter of SABR since 2001. She is the author of *The 50 Greatest Yankees Games* (Wiley, 2005) and co-author with Bill Nowlin of *The 50 Greatest Red Sox Games* (Wiley, 2006). She also writes baseball fiction and is a contributor to *Fenway Fiction*, edited by Adam Pachter. She writes about baseball online at the web magazine "Why I Like Baseball."

JUDITH TESTA grew up on Long Island, within driving distance of the Brooklyn Dodgers, New York Giants, and New York Yankees. She was a bred in the bone Dodger fan who harbored a secret fascination with Brooklyn's archenemy: Sal Maglie. When the Dodgers left Brooklyn she swore off baseball and later became an art historian. After retiring from a career as a scholar and university professor, she rediscovered her passion for baseball, began writing reviews of baseball books, and recently completed a biography of her childhood hero, entitled *Sal Maglie: Baseball's Demon Barber*, to be published in 2006 by the Northern Illinois University Press. She now lives in St. Charles, Illinois, and is an ardent Red Sox fan—whenever the Sox play the Damnyankees.

JOHN VORPERIAN spent his childhood summers at Fenway Park and Plum Island, MA. Those halcyon days led to an incurable Red Sox obsession. A SABR member since 2000 he hosts *Beyond the Game* on White Plains Cable TV. When not writing for johnnyvsports.fws1.com or teaching Sports Law at Concordia College (NY) John daydreams about flyfishing with Ted Williams, Tris Speaker, and The Babe.

DAVE WILLIAMS resides in Glastonbury, CT with his wife Julia and daughter Clara. Their unwavering support is something he cherishes more than they know. Dave has been a Territory Manager with Wilson Sporting Goods since 1998 and a SABR member since 2001. He contributed the Tim McCarver biography in the SABR book *'75: The Red Sox Team That Saved Baseball.*

SAUL WISNIA was born a Tony C homer from Fenway Park ten days before the Impossible Dream began there, and now works 100 yards from Yawkey Way as senior publications editor for Dana-Farber Cancer Institute. A former sports correspondent for the *Washington Post* and feature writer for the *Boston Herald*, he has written or co-authored several books on baseball and other subjects. His latest project (written with Dick Johnson), *From Yawkey to Milwaukee—Boston's Bloom and Demise as a Two-Team Baseball Town*, will be published by Rounder Books. A SABR-ite since 1992 and a founding member of the Boston Braves Historical Association, Wisnia lives in Newton with his children, Jason and Rachel, and more memorabilia than his wife, Michelle, knows about.

THANKS

This book on the 1967 Red Sox is a product of Boston SABR, a chapter of the Society for American Baseball Research. The original inspiration for our original book on the 1975 team came from chapter member David Southwick. The book that resulted from that work is *'75: The Red Sox Team that Saved Baseball.*

Over 60 SABR members contributed to the making of this book, but there are four we would like to single out for special thanks: Cecilia Tan, who prepared all the written material for publication, and ace readers Wayne McElreavy, Mark Armour, and Len Levin. Each one read every biography in the book and spared the authors numerous errors. Their work is an integral part of the success of the work contained in this volume.

We also want to offer special thanks to Debbie Matson of the Boston Red Sox for her assistance in helping us obtain the use of many of the photographs in this book. Most of the memorabilia and other photographs in the book come from the personal collection of '67 aficionado Dan Desrochers.

Very helpful as well was Jim Evangelou of Gallery of Champions. Visit their website at www.thoroughbredmemories.com.

The *Boston Herald* granted full access to their photo files and the use of all the many images in this book. We are particularly grateful to Alan Thibeault and Martha Reagan of the *Herald.*

From the Red Sox, we also wish to express appreciative thanks to Dick Bresciani, Tom Catlin, Henry Mahegan, and Dr. Charles Steinberg.

We are grateful for the contributions of many who helped bring this book together, including:

Marty Appel
Dan Ardell
Larry Auger
Leo Baubay
Dick Bresciani
Kathleen Cable
Tom Catlin
Charlie Chronopoulos
Ken Coleman
Clem Comly
Herb Crehan
Jon Daly
Dominic DiMaggio
Ron Dobbs
Jim Evangelou
Larry Fritsch
Christine Fry
Peter Gammons
Pam Ganley
Steve Gietschier
Bob Grim
Roland Hemond
Joseph Hetrick
Bill Hickman
Fred Ivor-Campbell
Richard A. Johnson
Steve Jurgensmeyer
Maxwell Kates
Seamus Kearney
Terry Kitchen
Glenn LeDoux
Jim Lonborg
Clay Luraschi, The Topps Company
Henry Mahegan
Ron Marshall
Debbie Matson
David McHugh
Larry Mishou
Tom Nahigian
Rod Nelson
Ray Nemec
Steve Netsky
Van Nightingale/ Los Angeles Times
Rod Oreste
David Paulson
Bob Payer
Dave Raglin
Marty Ray
Martha Reagan
Alex Reisner
Brad San Martin
Aaron Schmidt
Paul Shannon
David Smith
Dr. Charles Steinberg
Alan Thibeault
Neal Traven
Dan Valenti
Tom Werner
John Zajc

THANKS

We would also like to thank these 26 members of the 1967 Impossible Dream Team who took time to talk with our researchers and biographers:

Mike Andrews
Gary Bell
Dennis Bennett
Darrell Brandon
Galen Cisco
Don Demeter
Bobby Doerr
Russ Gibson
Ken Harrelson
Dalton Jones
Bill Landis
Jim Landis
Jim Lonborg
Dave Morehead
Dan Osinksi
Ken Poulsen
Bill Rohr
Mike Ryan
Jose Santiago
George Scott
Lee Stange
Jerry Stephenson
George Thomas
Gary Waslewski
Dick Williams
Carl Yastrzemski

And these family members:
Joyce Bachus (Jerry Adair)
Saundra Bellamy (Norm Siebern)
George Brett (Ken Brett)
Carole Garbowski (Eddie Popowski)
Pat Grenga (Sal Maglie)
Rosemary Lonborg (Jim Lonborg)
Kevin O'Connell (Dick O'Connell)
Maria Grenga Rizzo (Sal Maglie)
Kristin Smith (George Thomas)
Margaret Ann Splawn (Al Lakeman)
Dolores Tillman (Bob Tillman)

Authors of items in this tribute to the 1967 Red Sox are SABR members:

Ron Anderson
Andy Andres
Jeff Angus
Mark Armour
Jonathan Arnold
Eric Aron
Fr. Gerry Beirne
Charlie Bevis
Ray Birch
Andrew Blume
Maurice Bouchard
Bob Brady
Joe Castiglione
John Cizik
Herb Crehan
Dan Desrochers
Alex Edelman
Gordon Edes
Edwin Fernandez
Tom Harkins
Joanne Hulbert
Richard A. Johnson
Mark Kanter
Kerry Keene
David Laurila
Len Levin
Diane MacLennan
Barb Mantegani
Ron Marshall
Les Masterson
Wayne McElreavy
Bill Nowlin
Royse Parr
Mike Richard
Doug Skipper
Harvey Soolman
Glenn Stout
Cecilia Tan
Judith Testa
John Vorperian
Dave Williams
Saul Wisnia

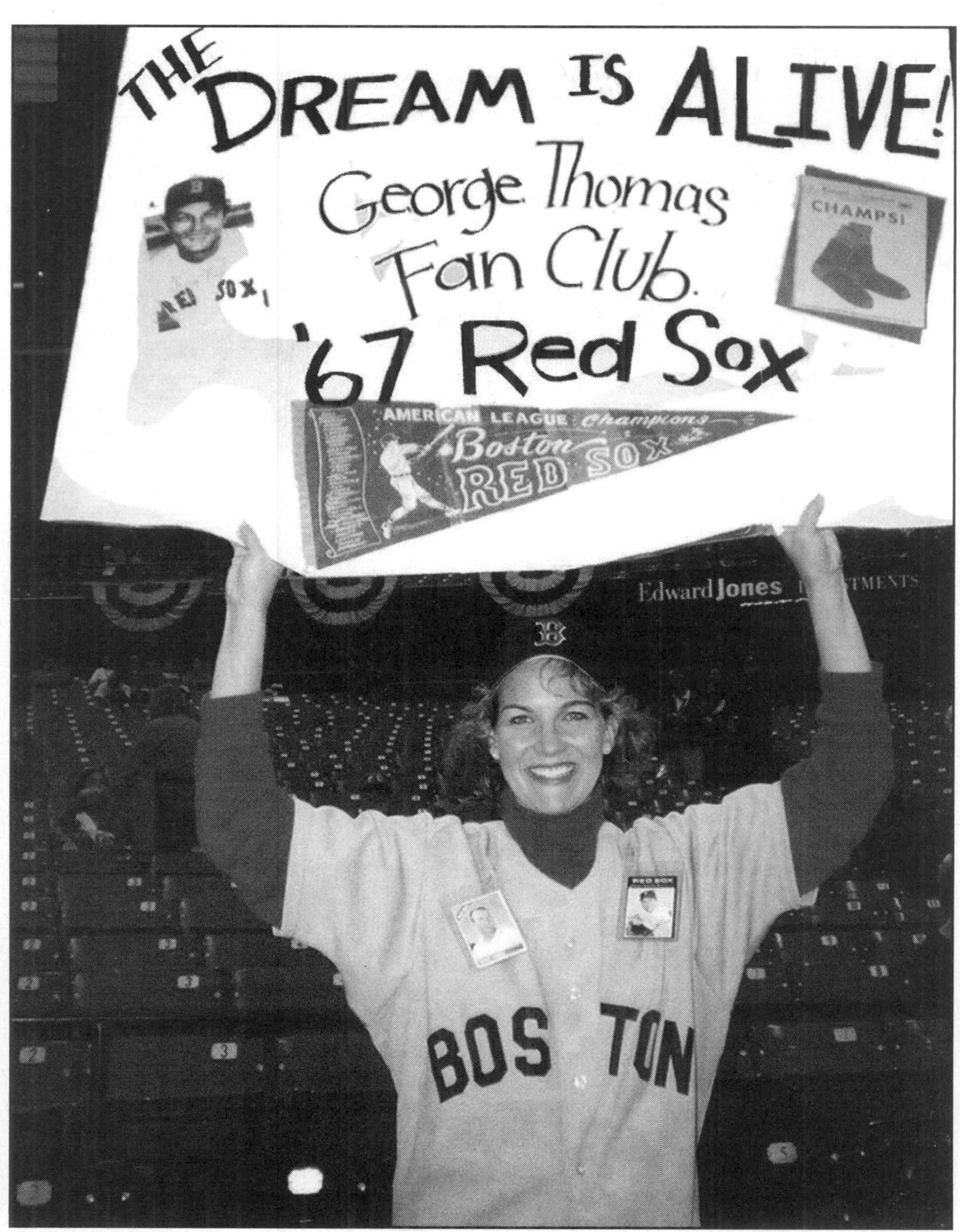

Kristin Thomas, George's daughter, was on the spot in St. Louis anticipating the night the Red Sox finally won it all in this October 2004 photograph taken pre-game by Dan Desrochers. The dream truly remains alive, and several generations of Red Sox fans have finally come to enjoy a World Championship.